D1519185

THE EU–NATO RELATIONSHIP

For Peter Macalister-Smith

The EU–NATO Relationship

A Legal and Political Perspective

MARTIN REICHARD
Austrian Mission to NATO (2005–2006)

ASHGATE

© Martin Reichard 2006

Published by
Ashgate Publishing Limited
Gower House
Croft Road
Aldershot
Hampshire GU11 3HR
England

Ashgate Publishing Company
Suite 420
101 Cherry Street
Burlington, VT 05401-4405
USA

Ashgate website: http://www.ashgate.com

British Library Cataloguing in Publication Data
Reichard, Martin
    The EU–NATO relationship : a legal and political
    perspective
    1. European Union 2. North Atlantic Treaty Organization
    3. National security - Europe 4. Europe - Foreign relations -
    1989- 5. Europe - Foreign relations - United States 6. United
    States - Foreign relations - Europe 7. United States -
    Foreign relations - 1989-
    I. Title
    341.7'2'094

Library of Congress Cataloging-in-Publication Data
    The EU–NATO relationship : a legal and political perspective / by Martin Reichard.
        p. cm.
    Includes bibliographical references and index.
    ISBN-13: 978-0-7546-4759-1
    ISBN-10: 07546 4759 5
1. European Union. 2. North Atlantic Treaty Organization. 3. Security,
International. 4. Europe--Economic integration. I. Title.

    JZ1570.A3 2006
    341.242'2--dc22

                                                 2006013331
    ISBN-13: 978-0-7546-4759-1
    ISBN-10: 0-7546-4759-5

Printed and bound in Great Britain by TJ International Ltd, Padstow, Cornwall.

Contents

Preface

This book was, for the greatest part, written during my time as a research assistant at the Max Planck Institute for Comparative Public Law and International Law in Heidelberg, Germany. Among the many people who have helped it on its way toward completion, the following must be counted in particular: Professor Hanspeter Neuhold, who has instilled me with crucial concepts, and to whose thinking on international security I owe a lot, as well as Professor August Reinisch, both from Vienna University. Their meticulous comments did much to improve the quality of presentation. My assigned research professor at the Max Planck Institute, Professor Ulrich Beyerlin, who gave me enough space to finish the main text on time, and much personal support. The great community of researchers at the Max Planck Institute, who – between many meetings, colloquia, mensa lunches and coffees – gave me many a valuable hint, a sense of common scientific spirit, and a mental home; in particular Pia Carazo, Leonie Guder, Holger Hestermeyer, András Jakab, Sebastian von Kielmansegg, Daniel Klein, Ludger Radermacher, Markus Rau, Dagmar Richter, Volker Röben, Christian Schaller, Gerd Schwendinger, Silja Vöneky and Kai Ziegler; also the friendly and professional library and other institute staff, in particular Petra Austen, Ursula Brummer, Wolfgang Schönig, Sara von Skerst, Petra Weiler and Jasmin Wendt, without whose continuous background labour none of this would have been possible. All my colleagues at the Austrian Foreign Ministry who, in the last stage, pushed me on towards the finishing line. Professor Torsten Stein from Saarbrücken, who also gave much support. Alison Kirk from Ashgate Publishing, for enduring many last-ditch changes amidst the jungle of the publishing process. But above all Peter Macalister-Smith, for his unswerving support and belief in this project, and to whom the book is dedicated.

Martin Reichard

List of Abbreviations

ACT	Allied Command Transformation
AFP	Agence France-Presse
AFSOUTH	NATO Allied Joint Force Command Naples
AJIL	American Journal of International Law
AnnIDI	Annuaire de l'Institut du Droit International
ANZUS	Australia-New Zealand-United States Treaty
AP	Associated Press
arg.	argumento (because of)
ARIEL	Austrian Review of International and European Law
Ariz. J. Int'l & Comp. L.	
	Arizona Journal of International and Comparative Law
ASEAN	Association of South East Asian Nations
ASIL	American Society of International Law
AU	African Union
Australian J. Int'l Aff.	
	Australian Journal of International Affairs
AVR	Archiv des Völkerrechts
AWACS	Airborne Warning and Control System (NATO)
B.C. Int'l & Comp. L. R.	
	Boston College International and Comparative Law Review
BFSP	British Foreign and State Papers
BBC	British Broadcasting Corporation
BiH	Bosnia and Herzegovina
BITS	Berlin Information-center for Transatlantic Security
BP	Berlin Plus agreement
Bull. E.C.	Bulletin of the European Communities
Bull. Quot.Europe	
	Bulletin Quotidien Europe
BVerfGE	Sammlung der Entscheidungen des Bundesverfassungsgerichts
BYIL	British Yearbook of International Law
C3I	Command & Control, Communications and Intelligence
Can.YIL	Canadian Yearbook of International Law
Case W. Res.J. Int'l L.	
	Case Western Reserve Journal of International Law
CDM	Capability Development Mechanism (EU)
CENTO	Central Treaty Organisation

CEPS	Centre for European Policy Studies
CER	Centre for European Reform
CFSP	Common Foreign and Security Policy
CFSP-HR	EU High Representative for the Common and Security Policy
CIG	Conférence Intergouvernamentale (EU) [= IGC]
CINCHAN	Commander-in-Chief Channel (NATO)
CIS	Commonwealth of Independent States
CJTF	Combined Joint Task Force(s) (NATO)
Cm.	British Command Paper
Cmd.	British Command Paper
CME	EU exercise
CMLR	Common Market Law Review
CMX	NATO exercise
Col. J. Eur. L.	Columbia Journal of European Law
Col. J. Transnat'l L.	
	Columbia Journal of Transnational Law
Cong. Rec.	US Congressional Record
Contr.	Contribution
CONV	European Convention Document
Coop. & Confl.	Cooperation & Conflict
COPS	Comité politique et de sécurité (= PSC)
COREPER	Committee of Permanent Representatives (EU)
Cornell Int'l L.J.	Cornell International Law Journal
CP [No.]	European Union (formerly Western European Union) Institute for Security Studies (Paris), Chaillot Paper
CP 47	M. Rutten (compil.), From St-Malo to Nice – European defence: core documents (2001), Chaillot Paper 47, Institute for Security Studies of WEU
CP 51	M. Rutten (compil.), From Nice to Laeken – European defence: core documents, Volume II (2002), Chaillot Paper 51, Institute for Security Studies European Union
CP 57	J.-Y. Haine (compil.), From Laeken to Copenhagen – European defence: core documents, Volume III (2003), Chaillot Paper 57, Institute for Security Studies European Union
CP 67	A. Missiroli (compil.), From Copenhagen to Brussels – European defence: core documents, Volume IV (2003), Chaillot Paper 67, Institute for Security Studies European Union
CP 75	EU security and defence – Core documents 2004, Volume V, Chaillot Paper 75, Institute for Security Studies European Union
CSP	Contemporary Security Policy
CY	Cyprus
DCI	Defence Capabilities Initiative (NATO)
Dec.	Decision

Denv.J.Int'l L. & Pol'y

	Denver Journal of International Law and Policy
DG	Directorate-General (European Commission)
Doc.	Document
DÖV	Die Öffentliche Verwaltung
DPA	Deutsche Presse Agentur
DRC	Democratic Republic of Congo
DSACEUR	Deputy Supreme Allied Commander Europe
EAPC	Euro-Atlantic Partnership Council
ECAP	European Capabilities Action Plan (EU)
ECJ	European Court of Justice
ECOWAS	Economic Community of West African States
ECR	European Court Reports (ECJ)
ECSC	European Coal and Steel Community
EDC	European Defence Community
EEC	European Economic Community
EEZ	Exclusive Economic Zone
EFAR	European Foreign Affairs Review
EFJ	European Federation of Journalists
EI	Europainstitut, Wirtschaftsuniversität Wien
EJIL	European Journal of International Law
ELR	European Law Review
EMU	European Monetary Union
ENA	Ecole Nationale d'Administration
EP	European Parliament
EPC	European Policy Centre
EPIL I	R. Bernhardt (ed.), Encyclopedia of Public International Law, Volume I (A – D) (1992)
EPIL II	R. Bernhardt (ed.), Encyclopedia of Public International Law, Volume II (E –I) (1995)
EPIL III	R. Bernhardt (ed.), Encyclopedia of Public International Law, Volume III (J – P) (1997)
EPIL IV	R. Bernhardt (ed.), Encyclopedia of Public International Law, Volume IV (Q – Z) (2000)
ERRF	EU Rapid Reaction Force
ESDI	European Security and Defence Identity
ESDP	European Security and Defence Policy
ESDU	European Security and Defence Union
ESR	ISIS European Security Review
ESS	European Security Strategy
et seq.	and following
EU	European Union
EUCI	EU Classified Information
EUFOR	EU Force in BiH

EU-ISS	Institute for Security Studies European Union
EUMC	EU Military Committee
EUMM	EU Monitoring Mission in Former Yugoslavia
EUMS	EU Military Staff
EUPM	EU Police Mission in BiH
EuZ	Zeitschrift für Europarecht (Zurich)
FDCH	US Federal Documents Clearing House
Fed. Law Gaz.	Austrian Federal Law Gazette
FM	Foreign Minister
Fordham Int'l L.J.	
	Fordham International Law Journal
GA	UN General Assembly
Ga. J. Int'l & Comp.L.	
	Georgia Journal of International and Comparative Law
GAERC	General Affairs and External Relations Council (EU)
GAOR	UN General Assembly Official Records
GDR	German Democratic Republic
GR	Greece
GSC	General Secretariat of the Council of the European Union
GYIL	German Yearbook of International Law
HHG	Helsinki Headline Goal (EU)
HJIL	Heidelberg Journal of International Law
Houston J. Int. L.	
	Houston Journal of International Law
HQ	Headquarters
ICC	International Criminal Court
ICJ	International Court of Justice
ICLQ	International and Comparative Law Quarterly
ICTY	International Criminal Tribunal for the former Yugoslavia
IFDT	Information für die Truppe (German Bundeswehr)
IFIR	Innsbruck Forum on International Relations
IFOR	Implementation Force (BiH)
IGC	Intergovernmental Conference (EU)
IISS	International Institute for Security Studies (London)
ILC	International Law Commission
ILM	International Legal Materials
ILO	International Labour Organization
ILR	International Law Reports
ILSA J Int'l & Comp. L.	
	ILSA (International Law Students Association) Journal of International and Comparative Law
Iran-USCTR	Iran-US Claims Tribunal Report
ISAF	International Security and Assistance Force (Afghanistan)

ISIS	International Security Information Service, Europe
J. Int'l Legal Stud.	
	Journal of International Legal Studies
J'l of Int. Crim. Just.	
	Journal of International Criminal Justice
JA	EU Joint Action
Jb.d.eur.Int.	Jahrbuch der europäischen Integration
JCMS	Journal of Common Market Studies
JCSL	Journal of Conflict and Security Law
JHA	Justice and Home Affairs (EU)
KFOR	NATO Kosovo Force
LJIL	Leiden Journal of International Law
LNTS	League of Nations Treaty Series
Macedonia	The former Yugoslav Republic of Macedonia (FYROM)
MBT	WEU Modified Brussels Treaty
MC	Military Committee
MEP	Member of the European Parliament
Mich.J.Int'l L.	Michigan Journal of International Law
MN	Margin Note
MoD	Minister/Ministry of Defence
MoU	Memorandum of Understanding
MS	Military Staff
N.Z.	New Zealand
NAC	North Atlantic Council
NACC	North Atlantic Cooperation Council
NAT	North Atlantic Treaty
NATO	North Atlantic Treaty Organisation
NATO-IS	NATO International Staff
NBA	Non-Binding Agreement
NGO	Non-Governmental Organisation
NILR	Netherlands International Law Review
NJIL	Nordic Journal of International Law
NJW	Neue Juristische Wochenschrift
NRF	NATO Response Force
NSO	National Security Office (NATO)
NYIL	Netherlands Yearbook of International Law
NZWR	Neue Zeitschrift für Wehrrecht
OAS	Organisation of American States
OBS	Observatory of European Foreign Policy (Barcelona)
OHQ	Operation HQ
OJ	Official Journal of the European Communities/ European Union
ÖJIP	Österreichisches Jahrbuch für Internationale Politik
OP [No.]	European Union (formerly Western European Union) Institute

	for Security Studies (Paris), Occasional Paper
OPLAN	Operation Plan
ORF	Österreichischer Rundfunk
OSCE	Organization for Security and Co-operation in Europe
ÖsterrZÖR	Österreichische Zeitschrift für öffentliches Recht
ÖZP	Österreichische Zeitschrift für Politikwissenschaft
PCC	Prague Capabilities Commitment (NATO)
PCIJ	Permanent Court of International Justice
PfP	NATO Partnership for Peace
PJHQ	Permanent Joint HQ
PM	Prime Minister
PPEWU	EU Policy Planning and Early Warning Unit
PSC	Political and Security Committee
PSI	Proliferation Security Initiative
PSQ	Political Science Quarterly
RDI	Rivista di diritto internazionale
REDI	Revista Española de Derecho Internacional
RELEX	External Relations (European Commission)
Rep.	Report
Res.	Resolution
Rev.T.Dr.Eur.	Revue trimestrielle de droit européen
RGDIP	Revue générale de droit international public
RMA	Revolution in Military Affairs
Rom.J.Int.Aff.	Romanian Journal of International Affairs
RTO	NATO Research and Technical Organisation
SACEUR	Supreme Allied Commander Europe (NATO)
SACLANT	Supreme Allied Commander Atlantic (NATO)
SEA	Single European Act
SEATO	South East Asian Treaty Organisation
SFOR	NATO Stabilisation Force (BiH)
SG	Secretary-General
SHAPE	Supreme Allied Headquarters Europe
SI	security of information
SIA	Security-of-Information Agreement
SIPRI	Stockholm International Peace Research Institute
SOFA	Status-of-Forces Agreement
St. Louis U. Publ. L. Rev.	
	St. Louis University Public Law Review
Stan.J. Int'l L.	Stanford Journal of International Law
STANAVFORMED	
	NATO Standing Naval Force Mediterranean
Suffolk Transnat. L. Rev.	
	Suffolk Transnational Law Review
SWP	Stiftung Wissenschaft und Politik (Berlin)

TEC	Treaty establishing the European Community
TEU	Treaty on European Union
TEU(AT)	Treaty on European Union (Amsterdam version)
TEU(MT)	Treaty on European Union (Maastricht version)
TEU(NT)	Treaty on European Union (Nice version)
TK	Turkey
U.C. Davis J. Int'l L. & Pol'y	
	University of California Davis Journal of International Law and Policy
U.Miami Int.Comp.L.Rev.	
	University of Miami International and Comparative Law Review
U.Pitt.L.Rev.	University of Pittsburgh Law Review
US	United States
UEN	Europe of Nations Group (European Parliament)
UK	United Kingdom of Great Britain and Northern Ireland
UN	United Nations
UNC	Charter of the United Nations
UNCIO	Documents of the United Nations Conference on International Organisation
UNPROFOR	United Nations Protection Force (BiH)
UNOSOM	United Nations Operation in Somalia
UNSC	UN Security Council
UNTS	United Nations Treaty Series
UNTSO	United Nations Truce Supervision Organization
USMC	US Marine Corps
USSR	Union of Soviet Socialist Republics
Valp. U. L. Rev.	Valparaiso University Law Review
VCLT	Vienna Convention on the Law of Treaties
VCLTIO	Vienna Convention on the Law of Treaties between States and International Organizations or between International Organizations
VDST	Verein Deutscher Studenten
w.f.r.	with further references
WEU	Western European Union
WG	Working Group
WMD	Weapons of Mass Destruction
WTO	World Trade Organisation
YBEL	Yearbook of European Law
YBILC	Yearbook of the International Law Commission
ZEI	Zentrum für Europäische Integrationsforschung
ZEuS	Zeitschrift für europarechtliche Studien

Introduction

THE EU–NATO RELATIONSHIP AS A POLITICAL TOPIC

This is a book about the EU–NATO relationship. This relationship is relatively new, as each of the two organisations for a long time occupied a very different area of activity, so the possible interface between them was virtually nil. Today, in contrast, the EU and NATO seem to develop new areas of cooperation and harmonisation of their respective activities with amazing speed, the most widely documented example of which was the 2002 Berlin Plus agreement on the borrowing of assets by the EU from NATO for its crisis management operations in the Balkans. But there are many others. Indeed, it seems increasingly hard today to fathom them all in their entirety and to see them together in a coherent framework. From the entire range of this EU–NATO interface currently existing, this book will attempt to describe the most important areas, without claiming to cover them all. Cooperation on terrorism, the Western Balkans, military capabilities, civil emergency response and so on could all be treated as separate areas of EU–NATO cooperation, but this will not be done here. From the EU side, the policy which covers most if not all of the EU–NATO interface is ESDP.[1] Therefore, the term 'ESDP–NATO relationship' could equally be employed.

The relationship between NATO and the European Union evolved gradually though the 1990s, to an already mature state today. Yet, it seems bound for further changes in the future. During the Cold War, circumstances which shaped the socio-political division of the roles of the EU and NATO, as found enshrined in the organisations' statutes and practice, had remained constant for close to forty years. With the Berlin Wall gone, new and different forces began to unravel and underlying interests began to shift. After the threat of Soviet invasion had disappeared, old definitions of security centring mainly on territorial defence gave way to a broader view reflecting different, and more complex and diverse, security problems, taking

---

1   Single exceptions are e.g. EU–NATO co-operation in the field of anti-terrorism (which touches many 3rd pillar aspects of the EU) and in space-related activities (as the EU's Galileo programme falls within the purview of the EU Commission's DG Transport).

also account of the human dimension.² In search of answers to these problems, crisis management (including peacekeeping) became significantly more important.³

Both NATO and the EU were equally challenged for new roles after the end of the Cold War. In NATO's case this was evident as, its main *raison d'être*, the Soviet threat, had disappeared.⁴ Also, after German reunification, there was no more perceived need to 'contain' that country.⁵ For the EU as well, its respective evolution, politics and agenda were shaped before Maastricht by the logic of the Cold War.⁶

The old status quo between NATO and the European Community essentially consisted in an institutional division of labour between the two organisations: NATO for European security in the military sense, and the European Community, as a 'civilian institution'⁷ for economic prosperity.⁸ This combination – in which America's protecting role over Western Europe was inherent – is widely credited with restoring the continent from its ashes after the Second World War economically with remarkable speed, and has led to an era of unprecedented peace in this region of

---

2   T. Marauhn, *Building a European Security and Defence Identity* (1996), pp. 65–6; A.G. Harryvan and J. van der Harst, *A Threat of Rivalry? Dutch Views on European Security Today*, in: M. Dumoulin, *La communauté européenne de défense, leçons pour demain?* (2000), p. 401 at pp. 402–6; K.E. Eliassen, *Introduction*, in: *Id.* (ed.), *Foreign and Security Policy in the European Union* (1998), p. 1 at p. 2; S. Stavridis, *'Militarising' the EU: the Concept of Civilian Power Europe Revisited*, 36 The International Spectator 4 (2001), pp. 45–6; J. Medcalf, *Going Global? The North Atlantic Treaty Organisation and the Extra-European Challenge*, Ph.D. Dissertation, University of Bath, 2002 (unpublished; on file with the author), pp. 76–101; M.M. Gallagher, *Declaring Victory and Getting out [of Europe]: Why the North Atlantic Treaty Organization Should Disband*, 25 Houston J. Int. L. (2003), pp. 358–9. The European Convention's Working Group VIII (Defence) duly summarised this new development in its Final Report (16 Dec. 2002, CONV 461/02, at para. 6): 'The concept of security is very broad, by nature indivisible, and one that goes beyond the purely military aspects covering not only the security of States but also the security of citizens.'

3   T. Marauhn, *ibid.*, p. 131.

4   A. Deighton, *The European Security and Defence Policy*, 40 JCMS (2002), p. 719 at p. 724.

5   N.M. Abbasi, *Security Issues between the US and EU within NATO*, 20 Strategic Studies 4 (2000), pp. 83–4.

6   J. Verbeke, *A new security concept for a new Europe*, 51 Studia diplomatica (1998), p. 125 at p. 130.

7   A. Deighton, *The European Security and Defence Policy*, 40 JCMS (2002), p. 719 at p. 720.

8   H. Ojanen, *Theories at a loss? EU–NATO fusion and the 'low-politicisation' of security and defence in European integration*, Finnish Institute of International Affairs, Working Paper 35 (2002), p. 4; H. Larsen, *Concepts of Security in the European Union After the Cold War*, 54 Australian J. Int'l Aff. (2000), p. 337; W. Bradford, *The Western European Union, Yugoslavia, and the (dis)integration of the EU, the new sick man of Europe*, 24 B.C. Int'l & Comp. L. R. (2000), p. 13 at 75.

the world.[9] But even under this clear division of labour, each of the two organisations recognised that their main function, clearly defined as it was, also had implications into the other's. NATO profited from European economic integration because 'economic cooperation was a means to strengthen political and ideological cohesion with a view to ... the establishment and maintenance of a defence capability'.[10] The European Coal and Steel Treaty of 1951, although a purely economic project, was born out of the underlying security rationale to forestall another war in Europe and, in this way, also turned out an 'excellent security instrument'.[11] As long as the massive common threat existed, this division of labour was without alternative.[12]

In many ways, it also laid the tracks for a fully integrated Europe, heading today for confederation or maybe even federation. At the start of the 1990s the idea that the EU should itself take responsibility for the security of the European continent was too uncomfortable to old strategic and popular habits bred in the decades of the Cold War.[13] It was only the St-Malo process driven jointly by France and the UK after the latter's turn-about on European defence in 1998[14] which 'let the genie out of the bottle' and created the real possibility of a European defence capacity autonomous of the Atlantic alliance.[15] By that time, public opinion was also slowly swinging in favour of a common European defence policy.[16]

But this new development also created a new problem: from the moment the new European Community began – with Maastricht – to assume in addition to its primary economic role[17] a political role as the European *Union* (with its Common Foreign and Security Policy), gradually taking on responsibility for security in Europe and its

---

9   J. Solana, *The Washington Summit: A New NATO for the Next Century*, 34 The International Spectator 2 (1999), pp. 37–8; G. Robertson, *Die NATO und die EU: Partner oder Rivalen?*, in: W. Hoyer / G.F. Kaldrack (eds.), *Europäische Sicherheits- und Verteidigungspolitik* (2002), p. 181; M. Muschwig, *European Security and Defense Policy: European vs. Unites States: Crisis of Transatlantic Relations: Nato and the Future European Security and Defense Identity (ESDI)*, 13 Miami Int'l & Comp.L.Rev. (2002), p. 13 at 17.

10   M. Weller, *The European Union within the 'European Security Architecture'*, in: M. Koskenniemi, *International Law Aspects of the European Union* (1998), p. 57 at p. 69.

11   D. Smith, *Europe's peacebuilding hour? – Past failures, future challenges*, 55 Journal of International Affairs (Columbia University) (2002), p. 441 at p. 449.

12   G. Robertson, *Die NATO und die EU: Partner oder Rivalen?*, in: W. Hoyer / G.F. Kaldrack (eds.), *ESVP* (2002), p. 182.

13   J. Howorth, *European integration and defence: the ultimate challenge* (2000), CP 43, p. 4.

14   For a fuller account of these developments, see below Chapter 2 (ESDP Today).

15   *Ibid.*

16   See e.g. the opinion poll, taken in January and February 1996, cited in WEU Assembly Doc. 1523, *The armed forces, European defence and informing the public in WEU member countries*, Report by Mr. Benvenuti (Rapp.), 13 May 1996, para. 19.

17   J. Verbeke, *A new security concept* (1998), p. 130.

near neighbours,[18] it crossed the original Rubicon of the Rome Treaties[19] and ventured into ground traditionally covered by NATO.[20] NATO's one-time security monopoly ceased to exist,[21] and the possibility was opened for institutional competition.[22] But the entry of the EU into the security sphere did not just represent an additional animal in the jungle of international security institutions. It was also a phenomenon of the new emphasis in international security on crisis management[23] (in contrast, the EU could have provided nothing to Art. 5-type territorial defence in the 1990s).

Furthermore, the EU increasingly purported to be a peace zone, a kind of 'pluralistic security community',[24] also to prospective new members.

> The EU represents a security model based on the democratic peace theory, according to which integration transforms the security environment among the members into a pluralistic community where the issue of security has been transcended.[25]

This differed from NATO's attraction of the mutual benefits of military security. After the EU added a specific defence dimension to the CFSP after 1998, this development became more evident. Today 'the hitherto dominant civilian power discourse, which has shaped EU policies, is in the process of being replaced by an understanding of military means as a natural part of the Union's foreign policy instruments'.[26]

NATO, for its part, also underwent fundamental changes in order to adapt to the new environment after the Cold War. This included internal changes, changes related to its new non-Article 5 activities and a new geographical orientation: 'out of area', lastly also out of Europe.[27] It also tried to give more weight in international crisis management to European Allies within its 'European pillar', using its CJTF

---

18   J. Howorth, *Discourse, Ideas, and Epistemic Communities in European Security and Defence Policy*, 27 West European Politics (2004), p. 211 at p. 215.

19   A. Deighton, borrowing from feminist theory, has described this process of the EU's emancipation as 'breaking through a glass ceiling' which previously had reserved all military instruments to NATO. A. Deighton, *The Military Security Pool: Towards a New Security Regime for Europe?*, 35 The International Spectator 4 (2000), p. 41 at 42.

20   The new security and defence provisions of the Maastricht Treaty were hotly debated at the time, not least in national parliaments of EU member States. For an overview, see only WEU Assembly Doc. 1333, *Parliamentary debates on security policy under the Maastricht Treaty*, Report by Mr. Nuñez (Rapp.), 30 Oct. 1992.

21   T. Marauhn, *Building ESDI* (1996), p. 109.

22   A. Deighton, *The European Security and Defence Policy*, 40 JCMS (2002), p. 719 at p. 723.

23   See generally S. Stavridis, *'Militarising' the EU* (2001), pp. 43–50.

24   The term was coined by K. Deutsch in 1957. *Cf.* below Chapter 3 (NATO Today),.

25   K. Möttölä, *Collective and co-operative security arrangements in Europe*, in: M. Koskenniemi, *International Law Aspects of the European Union* (1998), p. 87 at p. 89.

26   H. Larsen, *Concepts of Security* (2000), p. 337.

27   See generally J. Medcalf, *NATO and the Extra-European Challenge* (2002).

concept created in 1994 and completed with the 1996 'Berlin Accords'.[28] NATO's development after the 1990s has been called a '*de facto* shift from collective defence to collective security [in an untechnical sense[29]]'.[30]

Looking at the two separate developments of the EU and NATO together, one could certainly say that, 'from two opposite directions, the organisations' tasks and fields of competences started to converge and overlap'.[31] The role specialisation of the Cold War has disappeared and both the EU and NATO now aspire to military security functions.[32]

At the national level, the most powerful member of NATO, the United States (and especially its Congress) does not have the same interest in an overstretched military presence in Europe today as in the Cold War, or even in the first years thereafter. The 'burden-sharing' problem, which remained alive in Congress debates even at the height of the Cold War, has returned with renewed vigour, and this is recognised in Europe.[33] The US has been looking for a new role in Europe too. The answer – however it turns out – will have to strike a new balance between NATO and the EU in European security. This assumes that the EU will rise to meet that challenge, and that NATO will allow this to happen.

For the greater part of the 1990s, especially in the historical window of opportunity of 1989–1993,[34] issues and interests concerning these new problems were still in flux on both sides of the Atlantic.[35] Put somewhat ironically,

> All sorts of theories were abroad, most of them interesting, many of them totally unrealistic. Statesmen and political leaders had great difficulty keeping up with the pace of events, let alone attempting to devise for them some sense of direction. Nobody had a blueprint for anything.[36]

Many of these voices simply argued for a continuation of the Cold-War status quo:[37] the EU should stick to what it was good at, namely economic integration and

---

28   An excellent overview of NATO's internal transformation in the mid-1990s is given by P. Cornish, *Partnership in Crisis – the US, Europe and the Fall and Rise of NATO* (1997).

29   See below: On terminology in international security, p. 9.

30   J. Howorth, *The ultimate challenge* (2000), p. 12.

31   H. Ojanen, *Theories at a loss? EU–NATO fusion* (2002), p. 13.

32   A. Deighton, *The Military Security Pool* (2000), p. 41 at 51.

33   Peter Mandelson (a close advisor of Tony Blair), put it thus: 'Should US taxpayers and US troops always have to resolve any problems that exist on Europe's doorstep?' (*Washington Post*, 5 Sept. 1999, Letters to the Editor, p. B06)

34   N.M. Abbasi, *Evolving a Common European defence: Challenges to the EU*, 21 Strategic Studies 2 (2001), p. 77 at p. 78.

35   WEU Assembly Doc. 1439, *A European security policy*, Report by Mr. Soell (Rapp.), 10 Nov. 1994, para. 108.

36   J. Howorth, *The ultimate challenge* (2000), p. 20.

37   This was so even after the new security and defence dimension of the EU had been fully recognised. See e.g. G. Bonvicini et al., *Security Links in the Making*, in: G. Bonvicini,

projection of 'civil' power.[38] However, the unflattering picture painted by political thinkers of the EU as an economic giant, political dwarf and a military pygmy was itself a testimony that the situation was increasingly perceived as unsatisfactory.[39] Many stirring opinions held that the EU should assume a role as an international actor able to face up to the United States and Japan on the world political and economic stage. The Maastricht Treaty and its successors were seen as an important vehicle in this regard.[40] Eventually, the need for the triangular NATO–WEU–EU relationship (in which the WEU acted as a bridge between the EU and NATO) to be replaced with a direct EU–NATO relationship became obvious.[41]

Towards the end of the decade, the confusion described above had largely ebbed. Previously loose positions gave way to more formal statements and declarations by both the Atlantic Alliance and by the EU. Lastly, specific arrangements were concluded between the two parties, fixing consensus in individual areas. Today, the time seems appropriate to put the question to what extent all these arrangements may also constitute legally binding instruments in their own right.

A constant feature of the EU–NATO relationship which complicates its analysis is that the membership of the two organisations largely overlaps. For the legal analysis, this problem is somewhat mitigated by the existence of a separate category of international legal personality of international organisations independent from their member States.[42] But viewed politically, the member States still retain their own policy priorities, and some readily use either organisation only as a forum to advance them, sometimes even showing different kinds of behaviour depending on whether they are sitting in the EU or in NATO. In order to avoid confusing inter-*state* with inter-*organisational* politics, the two organisations will be treated as entities entirely

---

et al. (eds.), *A renewed partnership for Europe – tackling European security challenges by EU–NATO interaction* (1996), p. 307 at p. 318.

38   A. Treacher, *From Civilian Power to Military Actor; The EU's Resistable Transformation*, 9 EFAR (2004), p. 49 at p. 58; A. Moravcsik, in: G. Lindstrom / B. Schmitt (eds.), *One year on: lessons from Iraq*, EU Institute for Security Studies, CP 68 (2004), p. 185 at 189–192.

39   R. Seidelmann, *Das ESVP-Projekt und die EU-Krisenreaktionskräfte*, 25 Integration (2002), p. 111 at 115; C.-R. Ancuţa, *EU CFSP and the Transatlantic Relationship*, Rom.J.Int. Aff. Vol. IX, 2–3 (2003), p. 152 at 170.

40   WEU Assembly Doc. 1333 (1992), para. 233.

41   WEU Assembly Doc. 1564, *Maastricht II: the WEU Assembly's proposals for European cooperation on security and defence – reply to the annual report of the Council*, Report by Mr. Antretter and Mrs. Squarcialupi (Rapps.), 9 May 1997, para. 109; G. Lenzi, *The WEU between NATO and EU*, 51 Studia Diplomatica (1998), p. 167 at p. 171; S. Bartelt, *Der rechtliche Rahmen für die neue operative Kapazität der Europäischen Union* (2003), pp. 135–6.

42   *Cf.* On the concept of treaty-making power of international organisations (liked to their international legal personality), see below Chapter 4 (EU–NATO Institutional Aspects).

separate from their member States throughout this book. It is to certain degree a concession to fiction but, for the purpose of this analysis, a necessary one.

CONCEPTS AND METHODS

Legal scholarship, and even more so the political sciences of international relations and European Studies, have already treated extensively the evolution of ESDP, as well as NATO's development through the nineties, including after September 11 and its fight against terrorism. The same is true for the EU's Common Foreign and Security Policy (CFSP), a development which emerged in 1992 from the EC's European Political Cooperation (EPC) existing already since 1986. Much has also been written about the Western European Union (WEU), the old triangular relationship which used to link the EU and NATO over the WEU bridge in the 1990s;[43] and about joint NATO–WEU and joint EU–WEU activities, as well as the respective relationships with the activities of the OSCE. As EU–NATO relations have today been replaced with a direct relationship, the WEU (today an empty shell) as an object of study will be left out in this book as far as possible.[44] The activities of NATO and the EU have also, to some extent, been subject to *comparative* analysis of their respective activities, structures and functions regarding European security. But a comparison is much wider than an analysis of a *relationship*, which is only the nexus between two entities in the stricter sense. Although some comparative elements will necessarily feature in it, this book will in principle be limited to the latter. This book is indebted to all this vast literature on European security studies, and builds on it. However, to achieve a better focus, it will only address the newest developments, that is EU–NATO relations, always mindful of their greater historical context.

Much writing has also in recent years appeared on the 'transatlantic relationship' which, even if limited to security issues, seems to belie any cogent definition so far. From a methodological point of view, the EU–NATO relationship is only a subset of transatlantic relations,[45] sometimes heavily influenced by it (as in the debate on decoupling Europe's security from the United States), sometimes hardly at all (as in the case of the Iraq war).

NATO's anti-terrorism agenda is mostly military in nature, and therefore also affects some security aspects of the EU. For this reason, it will be treated to some extent in this book. Contrastingly, the EU's responses to September 11 are not military,

---

43 E.g. T. Jürgens, *Die Gemeinsame Außen- und Sicherheitspolitik* (1994), p. 367; M. Warnken, *Der Handlungsrahmen der Europäischen Union im Bereich der Sicherheits- und Verteidigungspolitik* (2002), p. 126; R.A. Wessel, *The EU as a Black Widow: Devouring the WEU to Give Birth to a European Security and Defence Policy*, in: V. Kronenberger (ed.), *The European Union and the international legal order* (2001), pp. 405–434.

44 Concerning some policy areas which developed very incrementally, however (such as the last Chapter on the Security of Information) this will not be possible.

45 See Chapter 1 (Transatlantic Relations).

as they are taken mostly in the third pillar. ESDP has so far not been employed in the fight against terrorism, although this could change in the future.[46]

The book will further only deal with *military* aspects of crisis management, leaving out the whole field of activities known as 'civilian crisis management' (for example police missions). Naturally, these missions are today very important aspects of conflict prevention, especially of intra-state conflicts. Also, the EU's activities in this field are rooted in its comprehensive and broad view of international security and its responses, most of them non-military. However, NATO does not engage in crisis management of the civil kind, and there is consequently no interface with the EU. Hence civil crisis management does not constitute, strictly speaking, an aspect of the EU–NATO relationship.

The 'EU–NATO relationship' or 'EU–NATO relations' are often referred to in passing both in official documents or in literature, or even under own sub-headings covering individual aspects, namely single stretches of the EU–NATO interface, but no attempt has yet been made to look at the relationship as a whole. It is this gap which this book attempts, to help close.

The objective of this book is to analyse the most important aspects of the EU–NATO relationship. As has been said above, some single areas are left out. The desired result is rather to paint a coherent general picture of where this relationship stands today, and where it might be heading.

Methodology

The object of inquiry will be approached from a political science and an international law angle. The order of this sequence is based on the premise that, at least in the EU–NATO relationship, political reality preceded any legal regulation. The main reason for this interdisciplinary approach is that a limitation of the inquiry to any one of those two fields alone would create a very incomplete picture. The central point for this author is his object of inquiry: the EU–NATO relationship. Whatever tool of social or legal science helps to further its understanding will be considered. This is not to say (to stay with the metaphor) that the tools of the science will be broken into their atoms – that the proven standards of the traditional methods of inquiry of international law will be watered down and confused in any way with political arguments. The tools of legal inquiry will stay what they are, otherwise they would become useless.

The tool-kit will be a mixed one, and the relationship between the two sciences will be a complementary one, rather than exclusive.[47] In many of the chapters, the political background as described will serve no more than to prepare the factual

---

46   Art. I-42; *Cf.* M. Reichard, *The Madrid Terrorist Attacks – a midwife for EU mutual defence?*, 7 ZEuS 2 (2004), pp. 313–334; M. Sossai, *The anti-terrorism dimension of ESDP*, in: N. White / M. Trybus (eds.), *European Security Law* (forthcoming).

47   On this approach see e.g. F. von Martens, *Völkerrecht – Das Internationale Recht der Civilisierten Nationen* (1883), p. 153; H. Neuhold, *Internationale Konflikte – erlaubte und unerlaubte Mittel ihrer Austragung* (1977), p. 14.

evidence for testing the legal problem. The choice for such an approach springs from the recognition that the very object of study, the EU–NATO relationship, in most cases does not perceive itself in legal terms. This is evident even to a casual observer of statements and documents produced by the EU and NATO. Naturally, it should not be forgotten that it is always more attractive for an actor to phrase a statement in the way which has the greatest political effect yet formally commits him the least. This does not per se preclude legal analysis of his statement. But it does mean that the essence of that statement, politics, should be well understood also by the legal scholar. Otherwise, his analysis runs the risk of becoming somewhat meaningless in practice, even if scholarly sound. For example, when analysing the legal nature of an EU–NATO joint 'Declaration' of December 2002, the text of which is unclear and the *travaux préparatoires* and follow-up documents of which are classified, then the rules of interpretation of international law also allow, as a last resort, looking to the possible intentions of the parties at the time. In such a case, which is not uncommon in the EU–NATO relationship, knowledge of the political background becomes more than a fancy dress for a legal argument. Rather, it becomes decisive.

On terminology in international security

Both scholarship and practice in international security make extensive use of terms such as collective security, collective (self-)defence, peacekeeping and peacemaking. However, these terms are not used uniformly.[48] As this book will use each of them extensively, a brief clarification of their content seems in order.

Collective security   Collective security describes a universal or regional system of States in which any threat or breach of the peace by any member of the system, that is, from *within* its ranks, is met jointly by all others (including by military means).[49] The origins of collective security date from the Concert of Europe in the nineteenth century.[50] Certain political conditions can be identified which must be fulfilled for a system of collective security to work. Firstly, from a military point of view, there must be sufficient deterrence for any aggressor. This may consist of a standing peacekeeping or intervention force,[51] but equally, if not more important, is the political consensus of the main powers within the system. Secondly, it is important that there be clearly defined criteria on what constitutes an act of aggression, an

---

48   On this problem in general, see only H. Neuhold, *Terminological Ambiguity in the Field of International Security: Legal and Political Aspects*, Festschrift für Jost Delbrück (2005).

49   R.C.R. Siekmann, *National Contingents in United Nations Peace-Keeping Forces* (1991), p. 1; J. Delbrück, *Collective Security*, in: EPIL I (1992), p. 646 at 647; H. McCoubrey / J. Morris, *Regional Peacekeeping in the Post-Cold War Era* (2000), pp. 3 and 5.

50   J. Delbrück, *ibid.*, p. 646.

51   *Ibid.*, p. 648.

agreed procedure to determine such a case, and a central authority to establish it.[52] In addition, in an ideal system of collective security, a principle of anonymity must ensure that said criteria and legal requirements apply equally to all members, despite existing traditional ties of friendship and cultural proximity between some of them.[53] This criterion has proved impossible to achieve in practice. In this regard at least, the UN system of collective security departs from the ideal case (because of the in-built veto-power preference for five of its members), but it has proved more workable than its predecessor, the League of Nations.

Collective (self-)defence   Collective defence or collective self-defence describes a situation where a State or group of States come to the rescue of another State which is attacked by an outside party, be it on the basis of an international treaty obligation or spontaneously without prior specific preparation. The law and particular conditions and features of collective self-defence are described in detail in Chapter 6.

Although both collective security and collective self-defence may lastly serve the preservation of peace, they stem from a different situation of interests. Some would go as far as saying that 'self-defence and collective security represent antagonistic strains of thought on international relations'.[54] Despite their present-day harmonisation into one legal and political system in the UN Charter, they still stand in a certain theoretical tension to each other.

Peacekeeping   The system collective security originally envisaged by the UN Charter (Arts 42 and 43) was never realised in practice, owing to the great-power stalemate of the Cold War. Partly to fill this gap, the UN engaged in limited military operations,[55] mostly of an observing and interpositioning character,[56] from the UNTSO in 1948 and the 1956 Suez crisis onwards.[57] These 'peacekeeping operations' usually involved troops of smaller and non-aligned States. They were based on consent of all of the parties, and their troops had to exercise strict neutrality and could only use force in their own self-defence.[58] As there was no express legal basis for such

---

52   *Ibid.*

53   H. Neuhold, *Collective Security After 'Operation Allied Force'*, 4 Max Planck UNYB (2000), p. 73 at 76; H. McCoubrey / J. Morris, *Regional Peacekeeping in the Post-Cold War Era* (2000), pp. 3–4.

54   N. Krisch, *Selbstverteidigung und kollektive Sicherheit* (2001) (English Summary), p. 405.

55   R. Higgins, in: *UN Peacekeeping: An Early Reckoning of the Second Generation*, 89 ASIL Proceedings 1995, p. 275.

56   T.M. Menk, *Gewalt für den Frieden – Die Idee der kollektiven Sicherheit und die Pathognomie des Krieges im 20. Jahrhundert* (1992), pp. 197–202.

57   R.C.R. Siekmann, *National Contingents in United Nations Peace-Keeping Forces* (1991), pp. 3–9; J. Hillen, *Blue Helmets – The Strategy of UN Military Operations* (2nd ed., 2000), Ch. 4, p. 77.

58   D.W. Bowett, *United Nations Forces: A Legal Study of United Nations Practice* (1964), p. 200; M. Schaefer, *Die Funktionsfähigkeit des Sicherheitsmechanismus der Vereinten*

operations in the UN Charter, scholarship and practice came to call them 'Chapter VI ½' operations,[59] their legal basis in the UN Charter lying somewhere between Chapter VI (Pacific Settlement of Disputes) and Chapter VII (Action with Respect to Threats to the Peace, Breaches of the Peace, and Acts of Aggression).[60] This legal basis can be argued using the concepts of implied powers and *argumentum a maiore ad minus*, and is furthermore reinforced by customary international law.

The peacekeeping formula on the whole worked well to rein in or prevent from breaking out again many conflicts after 1945. The new security environment after 1990, however, and especially the experience of UNPROFOR in the Balkans, called for new approaches to maintaining the peace in conflict areas. Thus the concept of 'second generation' and even 'third generation' peacekeeping entered the international security debate.[61] This step-by-step adaptation of peacekeeping doctrine to new kinds of conflicts saw a departure from the strict principles of consent, neutrality and passive observation which had characterised the 'first generation' of peacekeeping during the Cold War.[62] The main UN documents through which this development from the early 1990s to this day can be traced are:

- An Agenda for Peace (1992)[63]
- Supplement to an Agenda for Peace (1995)[64]
- Report of the Panel on United Nations Peace Operations (2000) ('Brahimi Report')[65]
- Report of the Secretary-General's High-Level Panel on Threats, Challenges and Change (2004).[66]

Nationen (1981), pp. 402–421.

59   The term was first used by UN Secretary General D. Hammersköld, UN Department of Peacekeeping Operations, United Nations peacekeeping in the service of peace – An evolving technique, http://www.un.org/Depts/dpko/dpko/intro/1.htm (visited 12/03/05).

60   M. Herdegen, *Völkerrecht* (2nd ed. 2002), p. 280.

61   E.g. H.-G. Ehrhart / K. Klingenburg, *UN-Friedenssicherung 1985–1995* (1996), pp. 25–34; M. Kiani, *The Changing Dimensions of UN Peacekeeping*, 24 Strategic Studies 1 (2004), p. 177 at 181–194; H. Neuhold, *Terminological Ambiguity* (2005).

62   The concept of 'generations' is sometimes seen as misleading, as the new forms of peacekeeping have evolved and exist today in parallel. *Cf.* E.A. Schmidl, *Im Dienste des Friedens – Die österreichische Teilnahme an Friedensoperationen seit 1960* (2001), pp. 10–11.

63   An Agenda for Peace – Preventive diplomacy, peacemaking and peace-keeping, Report of the Secretary-General, UN-Doc. A/47/277 – S/24111, 17 June 1992.

64   Supplement to an Agenda for Peace: Position Paper of the Secretary-General on the Occasion of the Fiftieth Birthday of the United Nations, UN-Doc. A/50/60- S/1995/1, 3 Jan. 1995.

65   Report of the Panel on Peace Operations, UN-Doc. A/55/305-S/2000/809, 21 Aug. 2000.

66   A more secure world: Our shared responsibility – Report of the Secretary-General's High-level Panel on Threats, Challenges and Change, UN-Doc. A/59/565, 2 Dec. 2004.

A thorough analysis of the content of the above documents would exceed the limits of this book. However, a brief description of the main characteristics of the second and third generation of peacekeeping is given here:

'Second-generation' peacekeeping has been used to describe operations of a more complex and demanding character, using force not only in cases of self-defence. In addition, they involve active humanitarian and even quasi-political duties which may even go as far as building rudimentary institutions in situations of anarchy where these do not exist anymore.[67] The UNOSOM missions in Somalia from 1992 to 1995 would be an example. Because this implies basic functions of civil administration over a certain theatre of operations, this kind of peacekeeping was sometimes compared to a 'trusteeship' model.[68] This form of peacekeeping surfaced as a response to the phenomenon of 'failed states', but also to the chaotic and bloody conflict reigning in Bosnia from 1991 to 1995. As a result, peacekeeping missions also started to become more robust, as neutrality and consent of the parties were no more absolutes.

'Third-generation' peacekeeping is also known today by the term 'peace enforcement'. It still requires the consent of the affected host State. Examples were later operations in Bosnia, Kosovo and East Timor.[69] The need for robust peacekeeping became more acute throughout the 1990s. One notable element in the doctrinal change (for example in UNPROFOR's later mandate) was a broadening of the interpretation of self-defence to cover also 'defence of the mission'.[70] These operations were militarily better equipped to force a peace upon the conflicting parties,[71] and were usually provided with a Chapter VII mandate from the UN Security Council. In contrast, NATO's 'humanitarian intervention' Operation Allied Force in Kosovo was not.[72]

In the early 1990s it was still imagined that the line dividing peacekeeping from peace enforcement could indeed be a flexible one ('tactical flexibility').[73] However,

---

67   M. Doyle, in: *UN Peacekeeping: An Early Reckoning of the Second Generation*, 89 ASIL Proceedings 1995, p. 275.; J. Hillen, *Blue Helmets – The Strategy of UN Military Operations* (2nd ed., 2000), pp. 140–1; H.-G. Ehrhart / K. Klingenburg, *UN-Friedenssicherung 1985–1995* (1996), p. 34; E.A. Schmidl, *Im Dienste des Friedens* (2001), pp. 10–11; H. Neuhold, *Terminological Ambiguity* (2005).

68   E.g. F.-E. Hufnagel, *UN-Friedensoperationen der zweiten Generation – Vom Puffer zur Neuen Treuhand* (1996); P. Picone, *Il peace-keeping nel mondo attuale; tra militarizzazione e amministrazione fiduciaria*, 79 RDI (1996), p. 5.

69   H. Neuhold, *Terminological Ambiguity* (2005).

70   Brahimi Report, para. 49; *cf.* E. Greco, *UN-NATO Interaction: Lessons from the Yugoslav Experience*, 32 The International Spectator 3/4 (1997), p. 121 at 123–4.

71   J. Wouters / F. Naert, *How Effective is the European Security Architecture? Lessons from Bosnia and Kosovo*, 50 ICLQ (2001), p. 540 at 542.

72   *Cf.* only D. Rezac, *Militärische Intervention als Problem des Völkerrechts* (2002).

73   J. Mackinlay / J. Chopra, *Second Generation Multinational Operations*, in: P. F. Diehl (ed.), *The Politics of Global Governance: international organizations in an interdependent world* (1997), p. 175 at 186.

the bitter experiences of the UN in the Balkans quickly led to the recognition that they were very different, 'not adjacent points on a continuum', and should be kept separate.[74] The Brahimi Report in 2000 still cited the principles of classical first-generation peacekeeping as the main cornerstones of peacekeeping doctrine,[75] even if it recognised that particularly in internal conflicts impartiality 'can amount to a policy of appeasement'.[76] But the UN High-Level Panel Report in 2004 acknowledged that, while peacekeeping operations might differ in their function, their legal and factual capacity to respond with force if necessary should never be in doubt. More recent peacekeeping operations are now regularly equipped with a Chapter VII mandate.[77]

Peacemaking The term 'peacemaking' is used very differently by different organisations dealing with international security today. The main difference is between the UN's usage on the one hand, and the EU's on the other.[78] It is possible that this difference in terminology has its origins in the different background (military/political) of some of the actors involved.[79]

The EU equates peacemaking with 'peace enforcement',[80] as part of its third Petersberg task (Art. 17, para. 2 TEU), originally formulated in the WEU's 1992 Petersberg Declaration.[81] This meaning of the term used in the TEU,[82] if not already clear from the text of the third 'Petersberg task' ('tasks of combat forces in crisis management, including peacemaking'), clearly elucidates from the drafting history of the provision,[83] as well as from a comparison of the English text with other versions (French: *rétablissement de la paix*; German: *friedensschaffende Maßnahmen*). The TEU for the first ever enshrines the meaning of peacemaking in a legally binding

---

74 Supplement to an Agenda for Peace (1995), paras. 35 and 36; G. Venturoni, *NATO and the Challenges of European Security*, 34 The International Spectator 2 (1999), p. 43 at 46; N. D. White, *Commentary on the Report of the Panel on United Nations Peace Operations (The Brahimi Report)*, 6 JCSL 1 (2001), p. 127 at 130.

75 Brahimi Report, para. 48.

76 *Ibid.*, para. 50.

77 High-Level Panel Report, paras. 211–3.

78 J. Wouters / F. Naert, *How Effective is the European Security Architecture? Lessons from Bosnia and Kosovo*, 50 ICLQ (2001), p. 540 at 542–3; H. Neuhold, *Terminological Ambiguity* (2005).

79 D.A. Leurdijk, *The United Nations and NATO in Former Yugoslavia, 1991–1996 – Limits to Diplomacy and Force* (1996), p. 8.

80 E.A. Schmidl, *Im Dienste des Friedens* (2001), p. 12; M. Warnken, *Der Handlungsrahmen der Europäischen Union im Bereich der Sicherheits- und Verteidigungspolitik* (2002), p. 114.

81 Western European Union Council of Ministers, Petersberg Declaration, Bonn, 19 June 1992, II. para. 4.

82 *Cf.* on the interpretation of treaties Arts 31–33 VCLT.

83 Apparently, 'peacemaking' was chosen over the term 'peace enforcement' by the WEU in 1992 at the behest of the hesitant German government. *Cf.* W. F. van Eekelen, *Debating European Security 1948–1998* (1998), p. 127, cited in: H. Neuhold, *Terminological Ambiguity* (2005), n. 32.

treaty.[84] Another question, apart from the meaning of the text, is whether the EU in fact has the political will to go into robust peace enforcement.[85] This question would, however, exceed the limits of this book.

The UN, on the other hand, defined peacemaking in its Agenda for Peace (1992) as 'action to bring hostile parties to agreement, essentially through such peaceful means as those foreseen in Chapter VI of the Charter of the United Nations'.[86] The UN has continued to use it in this sense.[87] NATO gives peacemaking a similar meaning as the UN, describing peacemaking as 'good offices, mediation, conciliation and such actions as diplomatic pressures, isolation or sanctions'.[88]

For the purpose of this book, 'peacemaking' will be used in the UN/NATO meaning, that is, including crisis management by peaceful means, whereas 'peace enforcement' will be used to denote crisis management including also military means, up to the 'third generation' of peacekeeping.

On the use of legal arguments

A recurring crux for any legal research into the EU–NATO relationship is that legal rights and obligations in the context of this relationship – apart from the few provisions in the founding treaties – are seldom expressed in a clear form. Even when treating the North Atlantic Treaty (NAT) and the Treaty on European Union (TEU), one is faced with two treaties which were drafted about 50 years apart and in a very different context. Comparative analysis of these treaties must thus take careful heed of this circumstance and make sure to properly interpret a provision dating from a different day and age in light of its legal content today. Moreover, most of the other documents, such as NATO's Strategic Concepts, could readily be described as non-binding 'soft law'. As concerns the practice and the public statements of the actors

---

84   M. Warnken, *Der Handlungsrahmen der EU* (2002), p. 172.

85   J. Herbst, *Peacekeeping by the European Union*, in: A. Bodnar et al. (eds.), *The Emerging Constitutional Law of the European Union – German and Polish Perspectives* (2003), p. 413 at 422.

86   Agenda for Peace, para. 20.

87   UN Department for Peacekeeping Operations, Glossary of UN Peacekeeping Terms, http://www.un.org/depts/dpko/glossary/p.htm (visited 13/03/05).

88   Bi-MNC Directive MC-327/1, 'NATO Doctrine for Peace Support Operations', Brussels, 16 October 1998, cited in: K. Schmidseder, *Internationale Interventionen und Crisis Response Operations – Charakteristika, Bedingungen und Konsequenzen für das Internationale und Nationale Krisenmanagement* (2003), p. 35. This 1998 NATO Directive has since, however, been superseded by a new version MC 327/2 on 29 Aug. 2001, which completely eschews any narrower definition of different crisis response operations and opts for a broadest-possible range of Alliance activity, from support of civil agencies to military operations on the scale of a full war, instead. The latter document is classified. *Cf.* G. Velitchkova, *NATO-OSCE Interaction in Pecekeeping: Experience and Prospects in Southeast Europe*, NATO/EAPC Research Fellowship paper (2002), pp. 17–18, http://www. nato.int/acad/fellow/99-01/Velitchkova.pdf (visited 13/03/05).

(which may become legally relevant, for example to establish custom or estoppel under international law, or to interpret a written commitment), these are in their wide majority phrased in ambiguous terms, avoiding precision as to their legal content. Lack of clarity rather seems to be the norm. The inquiry as to the legal content of the multifarious statements made and practice shown over time, including the task of separating the wheat of legally relevant actions from the chaff of irrelevant ones, must therefore be all the more meticulous. An excellent example of how this can be done is given by F.R. Kirgis in his article in the AJIL in the 1970s on the duty to consult as a matter of binding custom within NATO.[89]

OVERVIEW OF THE CHAPTERS

Chapter 1 deals with transatlantic security relations at the turn of the century. The subject of this book – the EU–NATO relationship – is best understood and introduced from this wider angle, taking account also of international developments external to the two organisations.

During forty years of the Cold War, NATO ruled supreme as a security institution in Western Europe. After the demise of its former adversary, the Warsaw Pact, this supremacy, which was also conceptual, remained for a number of years. US security interests in Europe, although not on the level of the Cold War, remained strong, also by reason of the Balkan Wars. America, in short, was still a 'European power'. However, the automatic glue of a strong common political interest and security outlook, on both sides of the Atlantic did not exist anymore. The difference was increasingly being felt, but only fully came to the fore after September 11. This tragedy elicited very different strategic responses in the US and in Europe. The US embarked on a major overhaul of its global strategy, emphasising projection of armed force to counter asymmetric threats to its national security. European responses to the new threat of international terrorism were not as dramatic and of a non-military nature.

The United States is presently enjoying global military hegemony never known before, its means allowing it to engage when and where it chooses, without recourse to any allies. American global security in the longer term is founded not only on its unchallenged nuclear muscle, but also on its high-tech armaments advantage over any other military power in the world. This position is underpinned by its analogous economic strength and the willingness of the American taxpayer to keep defence spending at present levels. Both are not likely to change in the near future. What is changing, though, is America's relative position in the world. The European economy has risen as the continent integrated, and – in the future – so may Asia, especially China. This is not without defence implications. At present, however, the geopolitical position of individual European countries remains much more limited than the US. Only Britain and France today have any capacity for independent force

---

89   F.R. Kirgis Jr., *NATO Consultations as a Component of National Decision-Making*, 73 AJIL (1979), pp. 372–406.

projection; and even this is declining. This is because military technology is today gradually diffusing to a multitude of actors, many of them sub-state actors, in target areas. As a consequence, it is becoming increasingly costly also for developed States to maintain the technological edge to guard against high numbers of casualties when intervening in these areas. European countries are increasingly recognising that to make their values and their interests in the world heard, they have to, literally, join forces. Having said this, even for the EU, any independent military capacity is still a vision at best. And even if it materialises, it will be limited to the near abroad.

At present, some of the values and views about the global system are no longer shared by the US and Europe the way that they used to be before 1990 while many common ones remain. Important fields of divergence are use of force, multilateral institutions, the current unipolar structure of the global system, and the role of sovereignty in a globalising world. For the foreseeable time, however, the US and Europe will remain strategic partners by default, if only for a mutual lack of alternatives. The political crisis over Iraq has shown, by negative example, the value of transatlantic consensus on security issues of global importance. A new 'transatlantic compact' reflecting such a future consensus – whatever form it eventually takes – would therefore seem advisable.

Taking together these concurring trends a general shift becomes apparent for the transatlantic relationship regarding security on the European continent: it is a shift towards the EU, and towards a more even balance in the transatlantic relationship as a whole. This shift impacts back on the more particular EU–NATO relationship, so intimately enmeshed with the former.

The European Union and NATO today continuously fulfil a great number of functions in the international relations of their member States (and sometimes of other States), for which they are provided with vast bureaucracies (numbering tens of thousands in the case of the EU). Before entering into the relationship between those two organisations, a general description of each is warranted. This description will be limited by two criteria.

Firstly, it will be limited to describing precisely those functions of the EU and NATO which are relevant to their *relationship*, that is, only those which are affected by the EU–NATO interface. For the EU, this will leave out the greater part of its entire activities; only some parts of its second pillar concern interaction with NATO. Even the separate description, however, will already have to account for the fact that the EU and NATO have sometimes been shaped by each other.

Secondly, the emphasis will be on an up-to-date picture, dispensing with much of the organisations' earlier history which is by now already well documented for both NATO and the EU's ESDP. As a result, this chapter should provide the reader with a sound starting base for analysing the EU–NATO relationship.

These two chapters will give a description of the status and most important fields of activity of NATO and the EU.

In Chapter 2, an overview of the evolution of the EU's Common Security and Defence Policy (ESDP) will be given. Most of these facts are widely known and have been extensively commented on already; therefore I will try to focus on the most recent developments in ESDP. A description of the current status of the EU cannot ignore the fact that, in its crisis management and peacekeeping activities, the EU already relates to NATO in a substantial way.

Chapter 3 will continue with a brief description of NATO's role during and immediately after the Cold War. Of particular interest is the political question as to why the Alliance survived the collapse of its major adversary and *raison d'être*, the Soviet Union, defying most assumptions of political science. A greater emphasis will, however, be placed on newer developments in NATO after September 11, its reinvigorated role in fighting international terrorism, and its increasingly global role.

Since December 2003, there are basically four options of how a crisis management operation in Europe (and possibly beyond) may be executed, three of which have been tried already in practice:

- NATO can plan and conduct the operation entirely on its own, using its vast array of military and planning resources and infrastructure which it has built over the decades of the Cold War (but which has already been substantially adapted for its new non-Article 5 missions). This was the format for SFOR in Bosnia until December 2004 and continues to be so for KFOR in Kosovo today.
- The EU can conduct an operation, using NATO planning facilities and other assets, under the Berlin Plus agreement of 2002. The current EU military peacekeeping operation in Bosnia from December 2004 (Operation *Althea*) is run under this agreement.
- The EU can stage an operation independently of NATO support, using multinationalised national headquarters of a member State (acting as 'Framework Nation'). This option was born out of necessity, as the EU does not as yet have sufficient military and planning and headquarters facilities of its own. The EU's peacekeeping operation to restore order in the town of Bunia in the province of Ituri in the DRC in June 2003 (Operation *Artemis*) was carried out under this format, with France as the 'Framework Nation'.
- The EU can conduct an independent military crisis management operation, using an EU headquarters to be established in the future. Even under options 3 and 4, however, consultation with NATO is normally very close and on-going through all stages of an operation, for which institutional links between the EU and NATO have been specifically established (for example an EU planning cell at SHAPE, and NATO liaison officers at the EUMC taking part in meetings of the EU's military bodies). The Berlin Plus agreement, which regulates operations under option 2, will be treated in a separate chapter at the end of the book, due to the complexity of the subject matter.

Having described the political parameters of EU–NATO relations, stock is taken in Chapter 4 of the institutional framework in which the two organisations presently cooperate with one another.

For a long time, contacts between EU and NATO officials were only informal, as if the two organisations (particularly the EU) wanted to keep a certain safe distance from each other (though they were located in the same city of Brussels). The problem did not arise as long as the WEU was there to serve as a bridge between the two. However, starting with regular lunches of the two Secretaries-General, contacts between the respective officials became more and more common. Today, there are formal arrangements in place on the frequency of meetings for different levels. The institutional framework for EU–NATO cooperation is constantly being added to and expanded at the time of writing. Chapter 4 lays out the most important of these arrangements. Paramount among them is the *EU–NATO exchange of letters of 24 January 2001* establishing a brief *meetings schedule*, the legal nature of which will also be addressed in detail.

A central problem of the EU–NATO relationship, dealt with in Chapter 5, is the question of 'NATO primacy'. The concerns, long held by the United States about European defence, boil down to Madeleine Albright's famous conditions for the building of autonomous European military capacities, the '*Three Ds*': no duplication of existing NATO structures within ESDP, no discrimination against non-EU/NATO members, and no de-coupling of the EU from NATO structures. In addition, officials of some non-EU Allies, particularly the United States, have repeatedly claimed a general 'right of first refusal' of NATO vis-à-vis the EU, to choose first where and when the Alliance wants to become engaged in solving an international conflict, before the EU gets to consider the option of conducting a mission on its own. Those officials have based this right on the phrase dating from the St-Malo Summit 'where the Alliance as a whole is not engaged'. The claim can be extended to various levels: primarily, of course, it concerns the basic choice whether NATO as such conducts an operation or not. But, according to an opinion more widely expressed, even after the EU has decided to launch an operation of its own, NATO claims a say in the exact form such an operation will take, that is, with the use of its assets, or not, and whether it will happen under a national or a future EU-based headquarters, with an obvious preference for the former options.

Chapter 5 presents a legal case, departing from the 'conflict clauses' in favour of NATO found in the founding treaties (Art. 17 of the TEU and Art. 8 of the NAT), and evaluates the relevant opinions expressed over time by EU and NATO officials in public statements. The final answer whether such a 'NATO primacy' indeed exists in legal terms, however, has to await assessment of the evidence of the peacekeeping practice in Chapter 7.

In the area of collective self-defence, NATO has held an unchallenged monopoly in Western Europe since the late forties. The collective defence clause of Article 5 of the NAT, was, however, not played out in practice until the terrorist attacks of 11 September, 2001. NATO's collective defence function also played a role in the run-up to the 2003 Iraq war, when Turkey asked for NATO's protection under Article 4, which was, after initial internal squabbles, granted. The EU has, since mid-2004, included a similar collective defence clause in the European Constitution which has not entered into force at the time of writing. The political and legal importance of this new EU collective defence clause, however, may already be assessed in detail, including the relationship it would have to the already existing Art. V of the WEU's Modified Brussels Treaty. The most pertinent question, however, concerns how the EU's new mutual defence clause would relate to NATO's Article 5. The answer to this question differs among EU and NATO member States, as not all of them are members in both organisations.

Military crisis management is the most visible area of EU–NATO cooperation today. The EU Rapid Reaction Force (ERRF) agreed at the Helsinki Summit in 1999 – which has started to operate – is the most tangible form ESDP has so far taken. NATO has also, at its Summit in November 2002 in Prague, proposed its own Rapid Response Force (NRF), which is to be used against world-wide asymmetric threats. Those two contingents will draw partly on the same troops. What will be their relationship? Which has primacy in case of conflict, and how is this expressed (if it is) in legal terms? Does NATO's general 'right of first refusal', to the extent it is found to exist, impact on this particular question? Is there already a right or duty of consultation before operation planning, and at what stage of planning does it materialise? Is a division of labour (geographic, high end/low end) between them slowly emerging?

Chapter 7 will briefly describe the present status of the ERRF and the NRF, and compare the two, to assess how they relate to one another, also in legal terms.

As the possibility of a conventional attack by a State on Europe has greatly receded, international security is mainly concerned with crisis management in geographically limited trouble spots at the periphery of Europe. Peace enforcement (to end the wars in Bosnia, and later in Kosovo) has been exclusively done by NATO. In post-conflict peacekeeping and peace building, however, the Atlantic Alliance has drawn on the expertise of other regional organisations, such as the OSCE. As the EU gets ready for serious peacekeeping, NATO has already – in two cases at the time of writing – handed over an entire mission to the Union. Some of NATO's and the EU's past and existing peacekeeping operations are laid out, and the possibilities of whether this is a pattern which may be continued in the future is considered. The gradual receding of NATO from peacekeeping in the European theatre – in favour of the EU – is the prime example of the shifting balance in European security between NATO and the EU. Only brief descriptions of the missions are given, as such accounts already exist in plenty. This chapter shall draw together the evidence of the previously described EU and NATO peacekeeping operations in the light of the problem of NATO primacy, particularly with regard to a possible NATO right of first refusal.

Two legal problems regarding the EU–NATO relationship, even though they concern only narrow and technical spots of cooperation, nevertheless merit treatment in separate chapters, because of their complexity.

Chapter 8 analyses the EU's borrowing of NATO's military assets under the Berlin Plus agreement. Given present European shortcomings on capabilities, any sizeable military operation by the EU is still dependent on provision of NATO strategic assets such as airlift, C^4I and planning facilities. In December 2002, NATO committed itself to providing some of these assets to the EU, under the Berlin Plus agreement.

After presenting the contents, this chapter will start with the history and background to the agreement. The main part concerns its legal nature. First, the decisive question of whether the agreement is legally binding on the parties as an international treaty will be dealt with. This will be answered in the negative, leading to its determination as a legally non-binding agreement. Alternatively, other possible sources of legally binding force – external to the agreement as such, such as estoppel and regional customary international law – will be tested. Lastly, other relevant questions such as its position under European law will be briefly addressed. As a result of the analysis, the author concludes that the BP per se is not binding on the two organisations, but that legal circumstances surrounding it, taken in their entirety, may well make its contents so – to a limited extent – even in absence of an international treaty.

A final area of cooperation which should help to round up and deepen the picture of the EU–NATO relationship is the technical matter of joint handling of classified documents, that is the security of information. The history of international agreements on the security of exchanged classified documents goes back to the 1950s. They are considered a sine qua non for the release of classified documents (of which frequent use is made in military cooperation). The first such arrangements in Western Europe were concluded between NATO member States. Beginning in the 1990s, NATO concluded, first with the WEU, then twice with the EU, separate agreements on the security of information passing from its well-guarded precincts to these organisations. Chapter 9 will examine the provisions of NATO's and the EU's security policies, as well as the current legal status of classified information exchanged between the EU and NATO, governed by the EU–NATO Agreement on the Security of Information of March 2003.

Far from describing dry bureaucratic procedure, this area of EU–NATO cooperation serves as an excellent reminder that the values underpinning the two organisations are, for all official assertions to the contrary, sometimes not identical: freedom of information holds a different place in the overall EU system than in NATO. Nevertheless, in building ESDP, the EU has had to come to terms with a significant part of NATO's internal culture of military secrecy.

In conclusion of the theory and evidence on the EU–NATO relationship presented in the book, I argue that the legal and political relationship between the EU and NATO that is now emerging is characterised by a greater degree of balance in the sharing of security tasks in Europe than has previously been the case. Under the old consensus, NATO did all, or virtually all, of the security work (depending on how broadly one defines 'security'). Today, the European Union does – and is expected to do – a more substantial part in its 'near abroad', certainly covering the range of the new Petersberg tasks. The same shift will also happen in collective defence as stated in Art. 5 of the North Atlantic Charter which has traditionally remained exclusively in NATO's hands, if the European Constitution enters into force.

Chapter 1

The Wider Picture: Transatlantic Relations and the EU–NATO Relationship

The Alliance embodies the transatlantic link by which the security of North America is permanently tied to the security of Europe.... The fundamental guiding principle by which the Alliance works is that of ... the indivisibility of security for all of its members.[1]

No matter how many solemn reaffirmations emerge from the endless parade of NATO summits, the high-water mark of transatlantic security cooperation is past.... a powerful set of domestic and international forces is pulling the transatlantic alliance apart. The process may be delayed by adroit statesmanship and bureaucratic inertia, but a gradual parting of the ways is virtually inevitable.[2]

THE IMPORTANCE OF TRANSATLANTIC RELATIONS FOR THE EU–NATO RELATIONSHIP

The link between the transatlantic relationship and the EU–NATO relationship is close, but not too close. Fundamental developments which take place in the grand transatlantic arena may not always and immediately affect the cloister of EU–NATO cooperation down to its technical details.[3] Often, parallel debates take place,[4] as in the case of EU and NATO enlargements. For the central message of this book, however, namely that the balance of European security is shifting from NATO to the EU, the link is very direct. This development cannot be explained without recognising that, in the wider arena of transatlantic relations, a similar tectonic shift is taking place. Already before the Cold War, the economic interests of the United

---

1   The Alliance's Strategic Concept, Approved by the Heads of State and Government participating in the meeting of the North Atlantic Council in Washington D.C. on 23 and 24 April 1999, paras. 7 and 8.

2   S.M. Walt, *The Ties That Fray*, The National Interest (1998/1999, Winter edition), pp. 13, at para. 2.

3   '... developments in ESDP in autumn 2001 continued along the traditional lines laid down the previous year. as if the attacks of 11 September had changed everything – except ESDP.', N. Gnesotto, Introduction, in: CP 51, p. vii.

4   A. Deighton, *The Military Security Pool* (2000), p. 41 at 52.

States became more and more focused on emerging Asian markets. The rise of China as an international actor adds a security dimension to this American reorientation. Europe, as the centre of the East-West conflict, and later, during the 1990s, primarily for reason of the Balkan Wars in Bosnia and Kosovo, enjoyed prime security attention from Washington. After 2000, however, Europe is 'whole and free', and also at peace. Today, America's current security concerns are with rogue states,[5] international terrorism and weapons of mass destruction. At a time when Baghdad counts most, places like Berlin and Belfast have lost importance in Washington. Naturally, the transatlantic relationship is still and will likely remain, the strongest economic, political and cultural inter-state community on the globe. Some of the existing ties may fray,[6] but on the whole the ship is still sailing. Our interest here, however, is with a tendency rather than with absolutes: what happens in transatlantic relations impacts on the EU–NATO relationship in the long term. The most visible example for this functional connection between those two arenas was the hand-over of SFOR from NATO to the EU at the end of 2004 (subsequently renamed EUFOR):[7] the hand-over was in the obvious interest of the United States and NATO in order to free up military resources needed in Afghanistan and Iraq. Because of the fundamental transatlantic rift over Iraq in 2002 and 2003, however, the United States put all negotiations on the planned transfer of the mission on ice for about a year. When the transatlantic climate slowly improved again towards the end of 2003, one of the first implications was that suddenly preparations of the EU and NATO for the EUFOR transfer began to pick up speed. The delay – as long as it lasted – was in no way connected to the planned mission as such, but rather to the transatlantic Iraq dispute. This case of the Bosnia mission also exemplifies nicely that the connection between the large transatlantic and the small EU–NATO plane reaches only so far: the mission of the EU in Bosnia was only delayed for some time – its eventual hand-over was never really doubted by policy-makers.[8]

A great raft of books and articles on the transatlantic relationship has been published over the years[9] The object of this chapter is not to repeat them, but simply to introduce the EU–NATO relationship from a wider angle. This should later make it easier to engage in its particular issues in subsequent chapters, without forgetting the larger context.

---

5   On the concept of rogue states in international law, *cf.* e.g. P. Minnerop, *Paria-Staaten im Völkerrecht?* (2004).

6   S.M. Walt, *The Ties That Fray* (1998/1999).

7   On this mission and the NATO–EU hand-over in detail see below Chapter 7.

8   B. Ruge, *Europäische Sicherheits- und Verteidigungspolitik*, speech at the Max Planck Institute for Comparative Public Law and International Law, Heidelberg, 20 Sept. 2003.

9   See only G. Lindstrom (ed.), *Shift or Rift – Assessing US–EU relations after Iraq*, EU-ISS (2003); M. Muschwig, *ESDP: Crisis of Transatlantic Relations (ESDI)*, 13 Miami Int'l & Comp.L.Rev. (2002); J. Zielonka, *Transatlantic Relations beyond the CFSP*, 35 The International Spectator 4 (2000), pp. 27–40.

EU–NATO RELATIONS: PART OF THE TRANSATLANTIC RELATIONSHIP

From a theoretical viewpoint, the transatlantic relationship forms the greater context for a more narrow relationship – that between NATO and the EU.[10] The two, in other words, are not identical. The EU–NATO relationship proper only covers a small part of transatlantic relations,[11] although a very important one. The link between the two, however, is obvious: The United States, at the cost of thousands of American lives (and dollars),[12] has brought peace and prosperity, and in time unity, to Europe as whole. In this way, the transatlantic relationship also acted as a stabiliser and silent nurturer of European political and economic integration.[13] Richard Holbrooke's description in 1995 of 'America, a European Power'[14] is seen by many as the transatlantic relationship in a nutshell.[15] Others would go as far as reading into such a description a systematic subordination of the EU to the United States.[16] Today, NATO is still today regarded as the core[17] and the most important expression[18] of the transatlantic relationship which should remain its primary forum[19].

---

10   *Cf.* also J.-Y. Haine, *ESDP and NATO*, in: N. Gnesotto (ed.), *EU Security and Defence Policy – The first five years* (2004), EU-ISS, p. 131 at 132.

11   *Cf.* F. Heisbourg, *US–European relations: from lapsed alliance to new partnership?*, 41 International Politics (2004), p. 123.

12   'Many Americans feel, with some justification, that, during the two world wars, their participation and that of their forefathers who rest in European cemeteries have earned them a permanent voice in European affairs' (D.M. Bark, *The American-European Relationship: Reflections on Half a Century*, in: *Id.* (ed.), *Reflections on Europe* (1997), p. 4, reprinted in: W. Bradford, *The WEU ... the new sick man of Europe*, 24 B.C. Int'l & Comp. L. R. (2000), p. 13 at 79).

13   S. Walt (1998/99); *cf.* R. Kagan, *Power and Weakness*, Policy Review No. 113 (June and July 2002).

14   R. Holbrooke, *America, A European Power*, 74 Foreign Affairs, (March/April 1995), pp. 38–51.

15   J. Medcalf, *NATO and the Extra-European Challenge* (2002), p. 1.

16   W. Pfaff, *Holding the Line – the trans-Atlantic dispute simmers*, International Herald Tribune, 26 June 2003, p. 8 (Opinion).

17   N. Gnesotto, *Preface*, in: G. Lindstrom/ B. Schmitt (eds.), *One year on: lessons from Iraq* (2004), CP 68, p. 7 at 33; M. Muschwig (2002), p. 13 at 37.

18   A Secure Europe in a Better World – European Security Strategy, Council Doc. 15895/03, 8 Dec. 2003, p. 10; *cf.* J. Onyszkiewicz, in: G. Lindstrom / B. Schmitt (eds.), *One year on: lessons from Iraq* (2004), p. 95 at 99. *Cf.* European Council, Brussels, 12 Dec. 2003, Presidency Conclusions, Annex: European Council declaration on transatlantic relations: 'The EU–NATO relationship is *an* important expression of the transatlantic relationship' (emphasis added), CP 67, p. 297 at 298. The centrality of NATO becomes even clearer by this comparison.

19   *Renewing the Atlantic Partnership*, Report of an Independent Task Force sponsored by the Council on Foreign Relations under C.A. Kupchan (project director) and H.A. Kissinger and L.A. Summers (co-chairs), 2004, p. 24; J. Onyszkiewicz, in: G. Lindstrom / B. Schmitt (eds.), *One year on: lessons from Iraq* (2004), p. 95 at 100.

Before entering into the heart of the matter, some clarification of terms is useful. By 'transatlantic relationship' we understand the sum of relations and cooperation in a wide field of areas (economic, political, cultural, scientific and also military) between Europe and North America. Commonly, this is more simply (and perhaps unjustly) understood as the interface between the EU and the United States.

Such a simplification, that is leaving out the remaining countries would seem justifiable on the European side of the equation for most political analyses, for two reasons. First, most of the remaining countries concerned, even those who do not aspire to EU membership (that is, Norway, Iceland and Switzerland) usually align themselves with the greatest part of the policies the EU holds towards the United States (in such areas where a common positions exists, for example international environmental cooperation, world trade, cooperation in criminal matters and so on). In the military sphere, the core of State sovereignty, the alignment of these countries with the EU is less close, as for example the case of Norway shows.[20] Candidate countries to the EU (for example Bulgaria, Romania and Croatia) are more closely aligned to the EU here. Second, after the enlargement of the EU in 2004, the Union indeed does represent the vast majority of peoples and States in Europe.

The equation of Canada with the foreign policy of the United States seems, by comparison, a graver omission on the part of common parlance regarding the transatlantic relationship, and this has been pointed out increasingly.[21] It seems odd in this regard especially for Europeans to ignore that Canadian views on a number of issues, such as on the Kyoto Protocol, are almost identical to their own, and very different from those held by the United States.[22]

As a qualification of the picture of a transatlantic relationship, it is also sometimes pointed out that the most virulent arguments about transatlantic relations are not traded *across* the Atlantic but *within* EU member States, concerning the different approaches of the member States with the United States.[23] the tendency in the EU to disagree on relations to the US is likely to increase with the accession of ten new Central and Eastern European countries, many of whom are on average much more 'Atlanticist' than the old EU members.[24] However, it is submitted that, from the point

---

20   H.E. Sjursen, *Coping – or not Coping – with Change: Norway in European Security*, 5 EFAR (2000), pp. 539–559.

21   E.g. by H. Neuhold, *Transatlantic Turbulences: Rift or Ripples?*, 8 EFAR (2003), p. 457 at 467.

22   *Ibid.*

23   T.C. Salmon / A.J.K. Shepherd, *Towards a European Army – A Military Power in the Making?* (2003), p. 174; N. Gnesotto, in: G. Lindstrom (ed.), *Shift or Rift* (2003), p. 7 at 21; P.H. Gordon, in: G. Lindstrom / B. Schmitt (eds.), *One year on: lessons from Iraq* (2004), CP 68, p. 161 at 164.

24   C. Kovacs, *US–European Relations from the Twentieth to the Twenty-First Century*, 8 EFAR (2003), p. 435 at 454. US Secretary of State Donald Rumsfeld's division between 'Old' and 'New' Europe, made during an NBC interview on 22 January 2003 (NBC Nightly News 6:30 PM ET), is to be vehemently rejected as a useful distinction in this regard. It was made at the height of the transatlantic dispute over the use of force against Iraq, and clearly

of view of theoretical definition, these debates should not be called 'transatlantic', because the *actors* involved in them are Europeans only, notwithstanding that the main *object* of these debates is the United States and its relationship with Europe.

As a further topical limitation, this book is only concerned with security aspects of the transatlantic relationship. It mostly leaves out economic, cultural, and other aspects, and treats political aspects only insofar as they relate directly to military security issues. Furthermore, the book accepts the simplification described above. The object of inquiry, then, is the US–EU security relationship.

Both limitations are grounded in considerations of conceptual economy: in order to describe the transatlantic context for the EU–NATO relationship, no more is needed. Adding cultural aspects (such as perceptions of each other) or economics (such as trade disputes in the WTO), or specifically a Canadian, Norwegian or Bulgarian dimension, however enriching for the overall picture (and probably each worth an investigation of its own), would not significantly alter the core point of this book: that the balance within the EU–NATO relationship, as well as within the overall transatlantic relationship, is shifting towards Europe. Therefore, when we talk of 'transatlantic relations' in the following parts of this chapter, what we will mean is US–EU security relations.

FROM THE COLD WAR TO THE 1990S, AND BEYOND

Transatlantic relations during the Cold War

> [T]he glue behind the Deutschian security community ... required the galvanizing existence of a massive external threat. It is unlikely that the threat of global terrorism or the challenge of global injustice can play such a role.[25]

In the Cold War, a division of labour existed between NATO and the European community, relegating the former to military tasks, and the latter to economic integration.[26] This division of labour worked fine because, from the point of view of the realist school of international relations,[27] it reflected the basic interests of all the actors involved. The United States' strategic doctrine saw control of the opposite shores of the Atlantic as an indispensable requirement to its national security. The Western Europeans, for their part, needed the military help from the United States

---

constituted a political ploy according to the old Roman proverb of *divide et impera* (divide and rule). N. Serra, in: G. Lindstrom / B. Schmitt (eds.), *One year on: lessons from Iraq,* CP 68 (2004), p. 113 at 116 has aptly described it as a strategy of 'pre-emptive division'.

25   J. Howorth, *ESDP and NATO – Wedlock or Deadlock?*, 38 Coop. & Confl. 3 (2003), p. 235 at 238.

26   See above at p. 3.

27   Main representatives are: H. Morgenthau, *Politics among nations* (1993, brief ed., rev. by K.W. Thompson) (realist); K. Waltz, *Theory of international politics* (1979) (neo-realist); J.J. Mearsheimer, *Conventional deterrence* (1983) (neo-realist).

for their sheer survival.[28] Moreover, raw American political and military power seemed more acceptable to them when bridled by the institutional confines of NATO.[29] Whenever outward security circumstances improved, and dependence on the Alliance was not perceived as strongly anymore by an ally, that State sometimes adjusted the level of its commitment to the Alliance, as exemplified when France withdrew unilaterally from the NATO integrated command in 1966.[30] Some neutral States, such as Austria, Finland, Sweden and Switzerland, who were formally not members of the Alliance, nevertheless also in fact benefited from its existence as net security consumers, or 'free riders'. But the Alliance was more than a mere collusion of self-interested States otherwise indifferent about one another. It was a community of values,[31] or, to borrow from G.J. Ikenberry, an 'Atlantic political order',[32] shared among the élites of its member States who all had vivid memories of the Second World War and the American role in it, and who shared a commitment to the fundamental principles of liberty, democracy, economic growth and human rights.[33] When the Cold War ended, the situation was one of a United States which had, even if initially with reluctance, fully grown into its role as leader of the West, 'prioritizing and dealing with issues on a global scale, while always maintaining the greater part of its strength for Europe: ever the Central Front'.[34] Western Europeans, under the protection of the 'benevolent hegemon', had achieved a prosperity and life style comparable to that of the US.[35]

For all this neat separation of tasks between NATO and the EC, however, the very existence of two organisations with largely overlapping membership did create a certain underlying 'structural tension'.[36] Although mostly stifled by the existence of a major external threat, this tension became apparent whenever the interests across the Atlantic were in fact not the same, as for example with regard to oil embargoes and trade disputes. As a consequence, new discussions arose, even at the height of

---

28   W. Link, *Die NATO im Geflecht internationaler Organisationen*, Aus Politik und Zeitgeschichte (1999), B 11, p. 9 at 10.

29   G.I. Ikenberry, *Strengthening the Atlantic Political Order*, 35 The International Spectator 3 (2000), p. 57 at pp. 59 and 66.

30   'Nothing can cause an alliance to continue as it stands when the conditions in which it was created have changed.', F. de Gaulle, quoted in: E. Stein / D. Carreau, *Law and Peaceful Change in a Subsystem: 'Withdrawal' of France from the North Atlantic Treaty Organization*, 62 AJIL (1968), p. 577.

31   W. Hopkinson, *New Relationships*, The World Today, July 2003, p. 16.

32   G.I. Ikenberry, *Atlantic Political Order* (2000). Ikenberry argues that the roots of this Atlantic political order preceded the Cold War itself. *Cf.* also *Renewing the Atlantic Partnership* (2004), p. 4.

33   Preamble and Art. 2 of the NAT.

34   C. Kovacs, *US–European Relations*, 8 EFAR (2003), p. 444.

35   *Ibid.*, p. 445.

36   W. Link *Die NATO im Geflecht internationaler Organisationen*, Aus Politik und Zeitgeschichte (1999) B 11, p. 9 at 11.

the Cold War, regarding a European voice in security and defence.[37] All this led to the resuscitation of the WEU at the Rome Conference in 1984.[38]

The 1990s

During the Cold War, European defence had been synonymous with Atlantic defence.[39] With the end of the Cold War, however, the old 'central conflict' which has served as the main orientation pole for international relations,[40] was gone, leaving everybody, so to speak, with an old useless compass. The rationale for the role specialisation of NATO and the EU towards each other disappeared overnight.[41]

S.M. Walt concluded already in 1999 that '[a]lthough they retain certain common interests and will continue to cooperate on some issues, consensus will be neither as significant nor as automatic as it was in the past.'[42] International relations theory describes such a development as one going from 'entrapment' (that is, accepting institutional constraints and obligations) to 'abandonment' (that is, choosing to face possible future threats alone). For both the EU and the US, abandonment is now probably considered a price worth paying for greater freedom of action, as the risks previously associated with this freedom have been greatly reduced, whereas the political risks arising from entrapment are born more and more unwillingly, especially by the US.[43]

The possibility that NATO should therefore become the victim of its own success should not come as a surprise, and was to a certain extent even expected by the founding fathers of the Alliance.[44]

The new post-Cold War era brought the increasing realisation in European capitals that their global interests did not always coincide with those of the United States, a fact which early writers had pointed out since the 1980s;[45] International

---

37   See e.g. H. Bull, *Civilian Power Europe; A Contradiction in Terms?*, in: L. Tsoukalis (ed.), *The European Community – past, present and future* (1983), p. 149 at pp. 152, 162 and 164.

38   WEU Council of Ministers, Declaration, Rome, 24 Oct, 1984, http://www.weu.int/documents/841024en.pdf (visited 16/07/2004). W. Bradford, *The WEU ... the new sick man of Europe* (2000), p. 13 at 75.

39   J.-Y. Haine, in: N. Gnesotto (ed.), *ESDP – The first five years* (2004), EU-ISS, p. 131.

40   J. Fischer, *Europa und die Zukunft der transatlantischen Beziehungen*, Speech at Princeton University, 19 Nov. 2003, http://www.auswaertiges-amt.de/www/de/dausgabe_archiv? archiv_id=5116 (visited 11/12/03).

41   A. Deighton, *The Military Security Pool* (2000), p. 41 at 51.

42   S. Walt, *The Ties That Fray* (1998/1999), under: 'The Dorian Gray Alliance'.

43   O. Theiler, *Die NATO im Umbruch* (2003), pp. 281 and 299. Theiler, although writing in German, also employs the English terms 'Entrapment' and 'Abandonment'.

44   *Cf.* G.I. Ikenberry, *Atlantic Political Order* (2000), p. 64.

45   *Cf.* H. Bull, *Civilian Power Europe* (1983), p. 149 at 152.

trade was the most obvious of these areas.[46] But soon also transatlantic security became an issue. The realisation that different policy priorities were increasingly straining transatlantic relations was evident,[47] even before September 11, with regard for example to different perceptions held between some major EU members and Washington over the threat posed by weapons of mass destruction held by 'states of concern'.[48] The Israel–Palestine conflict also often provokes transatlantic discord.[49] The list could be extended much longer.[50] R. Asmus et al. noticed already in 1996

> a growing divergence between US and European security priorities and apparently differing perceptions on the two sides of the Atlantic regarding vital national interests.... There is thus a disconnect between current NATO missions and top US concerns regarding serious threats to perceived American vital interests: proliferation, the Persian Gulf, and Northeast Asia.[51]

Transatlantic relations post September 11

After the defining moment for American foreign and security policy that was September 11, the problem of international terrorism became the matter of utmost interest to the US,[52] in contrast to Europe, where the basic stance to that phenomenon remained roughly the same: European countries understand terrorism more as a phenomenon with its origins in global and regional political and social problems (a 'root causes' approach).

But the different policy interests between the US and Europe do not only concern this or that particular issue in international security. They also reflect a growing difference in strategic-geographic focus. For the United States, Europe has ceased to be of central strategic concern, as no conflict of a medium to major scale involving US troops is to be expected there for the foreseeable time. On the other hand, United

---

46   S. Blockmans, *A New Crisis Manager at the Horizon – The Case of the European Union*, 13 LJIL (2000), p. 255 at 259; *Hands across the water*, European Voice (online edition), Vol. 7, No. 9, 1 March 2001.

47   I.H. Daalder / J.M. Lindsay, *American foreign policy and transatlantic relations in the age of global politics*, in: G. Lindstrom (ed.), *Shift or Rift* (2003), p. 91 at 99.

48   S. Duke, *CESDP: Nice's overtrumped success?*, 6 EFAR (2001), p. 155 at 173.

49   C. Grant, in: G. Lindstrom / B. Schmitt (eds.), *One year on: lessons from Iraq,* CP 68 (2004), p. 61 at 68; *Renewing the Atlantic Partnership* (2004), p. 23. This topic would be worth an entire book. For some closer analysis, see P. Clawson, *US and European priorities in the Middle East*, in: G. Lindstrom (ed.), *Shift or Rift* (2003), pp. 127–146; M. Ortega, *The Achilles heel of transatlantic relations*, in: *ibid.*, pp. 147–168.

50   For a good summary of the issues that have divided Europe and the United States since the end of the Cold War, see J. Hulsman, in: G. Lindstrom / B. Schmitt (eds.), *One year on: lessons from Iraq,* CP 68 (2004), p. 169 at 174.

51   R.D. Asmus/R.D. Blackwill / F.S. Larrabee, *Can NATO Survive?*, 19 The Washington Quarterly 2 (1996), p. 79 at 88.

52   Z. Lachowski, *The military dimension of the European Union*, SIPRI Yearbook 2002, p. 151 at 166.

States trade with Asia is today more than one and a half times larger than that with Europe,[53] a fact which over time also helps to relocate American foreign policy interests. 'The priority on transatlantic relations that characterised American foreign policy ... no longer exists.'[54] Europe is at peace, and will increasingly be able to look after itself also in security affairs.[55] Dangers to the US national interest, as September 11 has brought home, today rather arise from far-flung places, the names of which the average US citizen sometimes even finds hard to pronounce, before they are found to have produced terrorists who kill a great number of American lives. It is Afghanistan, Iraq, North Korea and the Middle East (to name just the most important ones) where the next danger to American security is expected to arise from. It is those areas where the country is now focusing its vast resources – diplomatic, economic, and above all military. The interests of the US, having shifted away from Europe to other parts of the world,[56] therefore, will continue to be sketched in global terms.[57]

The EU, by contrast, has traditionally centred most of its attention on its own economic integration.[58] The Union is currently only tentatively marking its first steps

53   S. Walt, *The Ties That Fray* (1998/1999), at: 'Weakening Economics Ties'. For an overview of trade figures, see e.g. WTO International Trade Statistics 2004, Trade by subject, United States, http://www.wto.org/english/res_e/statis_e/its2004_e/section3_e/iii16. xls (visited 14/03/05).

54   S. Hoffmann, *The crisis in transatlantic relations*, in: G. Lindstrom (ed.), *Shift or Rift* (2003), p. 13; *cf.* N. Gnesotto, *EU, US: visions of the world, visions of the other*, in: *ibid.*, p. 7 at 33; in unmistakable terms, D.C. Gompert, *What does America want of Europe?*, in: *ibid.*, p. 43 at 45, 'Actually, thinking about Europe is something Americans rarely do.'

55   'It was one thing for the US to commit to, and spend heavily on, European defense to combat an evil empire whose forces were in the center of Europe; it is another to commit to allaying European uncertainties ... [O]ur presence creates an incentive for the Europeans to do less.... [T]he forces and money that we allocate to Europe might hurt our ability to deal with challenges elsewhere' (H.S. Rowen, *The Uncertain Future of the Atlantic Alliance*, in: M. Bark (ed.), *Reflections on Europe* (1997), p. 125 at 137, reprinted in: W. Bradford, *The WEU ... the new sick man of Europe* (2000), p. 13 at 79).

56   H. Neuhold, *Transatlantic Turbulences: Rift or Ripples?*, 8 EFAR (2003), p. 457 at 468; Z. Lachowski, *The military dimension of the European Union* (2002), p. 166; C. Kupchan, *The Rise of Europe, America's Changing Internationalism, and the End of U.S. Primacy*, 118 PSQ (2003), p. 205 at 226.

57   S. Duke, *CESDP: Nice's overtrumped success?*, 6 EFAR (2001), 171; N.M. Abbasi, *Security Issues between the US and EU within NATO* (2000), p. 87; S. Walt, *The Ties That Fray* (1998/1999), at: 'Domestic Changes'; A. Pradetto, *Funktionen militärischer Konfliktregelung durch die NATO bei der Neuordnung Europas*, in: H. Timmermann / A. Pradetto (eds.), *Die NATO auf dem Weg ins 21. Jahrhundert* (2002), p. 191 at 202.

58   It could be argued that the simultaneous efforts at the creation and deepening integration of the Union from Maastricht onwards diverted attention of European policy-makers from the necessity to build a viable EU security policy for the post-Cold War world (*cf.* W. Bradford, *The WEU ... the new sick man of Europe* (2000), p. 13 at 37), leaving it to watch helpless and incapacitated as the crisis in ex-Yugoslavia erupted in 1992. The tragedy was that, after the Dayton accords of 1995, the Union did not learn from this mistake at the

as an international security actor. Its radius of activity is directly dependent on its own very limited autonomous military capacity. It will for some time be restricted to its near abroad,[59] that is, its unstable periphery in South-East Europe and single zones to its East (perhaps Moldova, Georgia) and in the Mediterranean. In the long term, however, the EU also probably has ambitions, including in the security sphere, of a global scope, autonomous, 'neither an adversary nor a vassal to American power',[60] something that former German foreign minister Joschka Fischer has called Europe's 'strategic dimension'.[61]

There are varying views as to whether the EU is today such a global actor[62] or not.[63] It probably depends on the subject matter.[64] In international environmental negotiations[65] or judged by voting patters in the UN General Assembly,[66] EU foreign policy coordination seems to be running well for some time now. However, in the Iraq crisis, it was a disaster.[67] But even most of those European and other views which do not see such a role for the Union at present would deem it as a positive future development.[68] Adoption of the draft European Constitution was generally seen as a crucial step in this direction.[69]

A unitary Europe, also more militarily capable, could in time become a more effective partner of the United States,[70] and would also be more easy to deal with for

---

IGC in 1996 (*ibid.*, p. 56). Two years later, it found itself again facing a similarly frustrating situation in Kosovo.

59   N.M. Abbasi, *Security Issues between the US and EU within NATO* (2000), p. 87. This emphasis on European security by European States at the expense of other parts of the world was also evident within NATO throughout the 1990s (A. Pradetto, in: H. Timmermann / A. Pradetto (eds.) (2002), p. 202).

60   N. Gnesotto, *Vrai et faux débats transatlantiques*, Le Figaro, 19 May 2003, available at http://www.iss-eu.org/new/anaysis/analy055.html (visited 25/05/03) (author's own translation).

61   Quoted in: J. Vinocur, *Fischer's shifting vision of Europe's grand future*, International Herald Tribune, 13 April 2004, p. 2.

62   J. Onyszkiewicz, in: G. Lindstrom / B. Schmitt (eds.), *One year on: lessons from Iraq* (2004), p. 95 at 98.

63   P. Hassner, in: *ibid.*, p. 79 at 81; A. Lejins, in: *ibid.*, p. 87 at 90; J. Hulsman, in: *ibid.*, p. 169 at 172.

64   For a discussion in light of the new draft European Constitution, see M. Cremona, *The Union as a Global Actor: Roles, Models and Identity*, 41 CMLR (2004), pp. 553–573.

65   *Cf.* U. Beyerlin / M. Reichard, *German Participation in United Nations Environmental Activities: From Stockholm to Johannesburg*, 46 GYIL (2003), pp. 123–170.

66   P. Luif, *EU Cohesion in the UN General Assembly*, OP 49 (2003).

67   There is broad agreement of views on this point. See below at fn. 168.

68   P. Hassner, in: G. Lindstrom / B. Schmitt (eds.), *One year on: lessons from Iraq* (2004), p. 79 at 82; A. Lejins, in: *ibid.*, p. 87 at 91; A. Moravcsik, in: *ibid.*, p. 185 at 189, who, however, advocates a global role for the EU only as a 'civil power'.

69   A. Leijins, in: *ibid.*, p. 87 at 91; J. Hulsman, in: *ibid.*, p. 169 at 173.

70   *Renewing the Atlantic Partnership* (2004), p. 15; R. Asmus, in: G. Lindstrom / B. Schmitt (eds.), *One year on: lessons from Iraq* (2004), p. 131 at 134; *Cf.* D.C. Gompert, *What*

the US than numerous national capitals. Such a scenario, while imaginable, is still too far in the future to make any meaningful predictions as to how it would impact on the transatlantic relationship.

A QUESTION OF DIFFERENT VALUES?

> US and European approaches to security differ fundamentally. The USA defines security primarily in military terms.... If need be, it will also resort to pre-emptive self-defence.... Furthermore, it attaches rather little importance to international organizations [and] is reluctant to be bound by international treaties. These principles are regarded as inherent in the American approach to foreign affairs.... By contrast, European states tend to adopt a multilateral approach in their external relations. They are guided by a comprehensive concept of security, which also emphasizes the economic and ecological dimensions of international problems. European nations tend to be reluctant to resort to military force and rely more on political and economic means.[71]

R. Kagan has drawn a famous caricature of these US–European value differences, and explains them with the different military capabilities of the US and the EU.[72] US–EU differences may sometimes be exaggerated, but they are widely supported by opinion polls among the elites and mass populations on both sides of the Atlantic.[73] The EU is presenting its 'model' as an 'alternative approach to security'.[74] The two different 'value systems' could increasingly face a situation of competition. This situation cuts across a number of areas: the most important and widely recognised ones are the use of force in the international system and the basic approach to multilateral institutions. But there are others, such as views on whether the world should be centred on a single pole of power or be multipolar, or on the importance of sovereignty in international affairs. The list could be made longer.[75] We will briefly

---

does America want of Europe?, in: G. Lindstrom (ed.), *Shift or Rift* (2003), p. 68: 'fundamental US interests are not served by a Europe divided'.

71   H. Neuhold, *Transatlantic Turbulences: Rift or Ripples?*, 8 EFAR (2003), p. 458–9.

72   R. Kagan, *Power and Weakness* (2002); *cf.* D.C. Gompert, *What does America want of Europe?*, in: G. Lindstrom (ed.), *Shift or Rift?* (2003), p. 57. The reverse causality, i.e. that Europeans spend less on defence *because* they have different perceptions, concepts and values, is, however, even more plausible. *Cf.* A. Missiroli, *Mind the Gaps – across the Atlantic and the Union*, in: G. Lindstrom (ed.), *Shift or Rift* (2003), p. 77 at 78; H. Neuhold, *Transatlantic Turbulences: Rift or Ripples?*, 8 EFAR (2003), p. 459.

73   H. Müller, *Das transatlantische Risiko – Deutungen des amerikanisch-europäischen Weltordnungskonflikts*, Aus Politik und Zeitgeschichte (2004), B 3–4, p. 7 at 17; A.J.K. Bailes, *EU and US Strategic Concepts: A Mirror for Partnership and Difference?*, 39 The International Spectator 1 (2004), p. 19 at 25.

74   J. Howorth, *The ultimate challenge* (2000), p. 91.

75   E.g. the advent, with the first George W. Bush I Administration, of a distinguished moral element in American foreign policy (see e.g. J. Plender, *The New Moralism Confronts an Old Reality*, Financial Times, 13 June 2003, p. 19); S. Hoffmann, *The crisis in transatlantic*

present each of these contrast areas, and close with a look at efforts to find common ground between the existing gaps. The question of European or EU values in this context could be much enlarged upon.[76] For this part, however, it will be sufficient to demonstrate where the main areas of friction with US values exist.

The use of force

> To forestall or prevent such hostile acts by our adversaries, the United States will, if necessary, act pre-emptively.[77]

This passage in the US National Security Strategy amounts to an explicit affirmation by the US Administration of the United States' right to take action before the actual threat actually materialises.[78] It is interpreted as saying, even by American commentators, 'that it is up to the United States to decide what is right and to use its unprecedented power to achieve its goals.'[79] Contrasted with the old emphasis (which existed since 1947) on deterrence as a central element in strategic policy, this represents a considerable shift.[80] Apart from being a statement of policy, if not law,[81] it shows an important point about current American perception of international threats. Even R. Kagan points out that, while retaining Enlightenment's legacy about the perfectibility of man and the world, Americans believe in the necessity of power in a world that remains far from perfection.[82] More than that, however, they 'are quicker to acknowledge the existence of threats, even to perceive them where others may not see any'.[83] Military pre-emption is sometimes coupled to a strategy of 'political pre-emption in the form of democracy building'.[84] This mainstream

---

relations, in: G. Lindstrom (ed.), *Shift or Rift* (2003), p. 13 at 20; I.H. Daalder / J.M. Lindsay, *American foreign policy and transatlantic relations*, in: *ibid.* (2003), p. 91 at 101) or anti-Americanism in Europe, would be other points of analysis. For reasons of space, these topics, also important for the values aspect of the transatlantic relationship, cannot be treated in this book.

76   This 'EU value model' is also inherent in the European Security Strategy.

77   The National Security Strategy of the United States of America, Sept. 2002, http://www.whitehouse.gov/nsc/nss.pdf (visited 28/03/2004), p. 15.

78   Assembly of the WEU, *The United States national security strategy and its consequences for European defence* (Report by Rapp. Mr. Gubert), WEU Assembly Doc. A/1824, 13 May 2003, p. 12, para. 38.

79   P.H. Gordon, *Bridging the Atlantic Divide* (2003), p. 80.

80   S. Hoffmann, *The crisis in transatlantic relations*, in: G. Lindstrom (ed.), *Shift or Rift* (2003), p. 13 at 15.

81   On the implications of the US National Security Strategy under international law, see in detail C. Kratochvil, *Die Sicherheitsstrategie der Bush-Administration vom 17.9.2002 aus strategischer und völkerrechtlicher Sicht*. Ph.D. thesis, University of Vienna (2005).

82   R. Kagan, *Power and Weakness* (2002).

83   *Ibid.*

84   R.D. Asmus, *Rebuilding the Atlantic Alliance*, Foreign Affairs (Sept./Oct. 2003), p. 20.

approach to the use of force in international relations (at least in the George W. Bush Administrations) does not, however, go without vociferous criticism among the American establishment.[85] J. Nye, in particular, finds the emphasis on military solutions, ignoring 'soft power', too one-dimensional for the complex nature of challenges facing America.[86]

European States, while they went along with the operation fighting Al-Qaida in Afghanistan, did not share this 'forward defence' concept. Rather, because of their wider view of international problems, they did not see terrorist organisations as the central problem in international relations.[87] Their threat perception is also different in recognising an 'enemy within' and thereby blurring external and internal security challenges, feeding into the European style of neutralising enemies by absorbing them, all very alien to the clearly defined concept of frontiers in traditional US security thinking.[88] The differences between US and EU thinking on the international use of force[89] became more visible in 2003 after the European Security Strategy was introduced.[90] That European view of terrorism as essentially a phenomenon of deeper-rooted social and political origins was not even shaken by the terrorist attack on the Madrid city trains on 11 March 2004 or London on 7 July 2005.

The ideas presented by R. Kagan,[91] R. Cooper[92] and W. Ettmayer[93] (with different conclusions) of the basic difference between European and American views being one between a post-modern (Europe) and a modern, Hobbesian world (the United States) go a long way towards explaining the origins of these differences. They do not, however, offer any clear way forward.

---

85   See only S. Hoffmann, *US–European relations: past and future*, 79 International Affairs (2003), p. 1029 at 1035.

86   J.S. Nye, Jr., *The paradox of American* power (2002); *Id.*, *U.S. Power and Strategy after Iraq*, Foreign Affairs (July/Aug. 2003), p. 60.

87   S. Hoffmann, *US–European relations: past and future* (2003), p. 1032.

88   A.J.K. Bailes, *EU and US Strategic Concepts* (2004), p. 25.

89   See e.g. H. Neuhold, *Law and Force in International Relations – European and American Positions*, 64 HJIL (2004), pp. 263–279.

90   Comparisons of the two strategy documents already abound at the time of writing. For some good examples, see e.g. J.-Y. Haine, *Idealism and Power: The New EU Security Strategy*, Current History (March 2004), pp. 107–112; S. Duke, *The European Security Strategy in a Comparative Framework: Does it Make for Secure Alliances in a Better World?*, 9 EFAR (2004), pp. 459–481.

91   R. Kagan, *Power and Weakness* (2002).

92   R. Cooper, *The breaking of nations – order and chaos in the twenty-first century* (2003).

93   W. Ettmayer, *Eine geteilte Welt – Machtpolitik und Wohlfahrtsdenken in den Internationalen Beziehungen des 21. Jahrhunderts* (2003).

Multilateral institutions

> Legitimacy must reside in the policy and derive from the ends and means of the
> intervention, not from some external organisation or international court of law.[94]

This sentence, although from an independent US academic publication, does not differ
much from the current US official foreign policy approach concerning multilateral
institutions. On the contrary, it is submitted that it interprets this policy in clearer
terms than most official sources. Multilateral institutions, and particularly the United
Nations, play no significant role in the US National Security Strategy.[95] A prominent
US scholar of international law, M. Glennon, links the legitimacy of the UN Security
Council to its relevance to US interests.[96] Thus for the United States, international
institutions, also NATO, are essentially functional to its national interests,[97] resulting
in a form of 'selective multilateralism'.[98] This contrasts sharply with the European
approach in which multilateralism is an absolute.[99]

Unipolarity vs. multipolarity

US official foreign policy[100] and much of the country's scholarship[101] today takes a
central place in the world for granted, although the need to 'cooperate' with other
'main centers of global power' is recognised.[102] Hubert Védrine, then French Foreign

---

94   R.N. Haas, *Intervention* (1999), p. 151.

95   *Cf.* WEU Assembly Doc. A/1824 (2003), p. 8, para. 20.

96   M. Glennon, *The UN's Irrelevant Relevance*, Frankfurter Allgemeine Zeitung
online, 2 July 2003.

97   E.g. 'Yes, the United Nations is a tool' (J. Chace, *Is NATO Obsolete?*, in: K.W.
Thompson (ed.), *NATO and the Changing World Order* (1996), p. 61 at 75).

98   Z. Bereschi, *The Dilemma of the Future of Transatlantic Relations: Multilateralism
or Unilateralism?*, Rom. J. Int. Aff. 2–3 (2003), p. 177 at 188.

99   P. Struck, *Perspectives of a Renewed Transatlantic Partnership*, NATO's Nations
3 (2003), p. 33 at 38 (speaking about Germany's views); E. Barbé / A.G. Bondía, *La Política
Europea de Seguridad y Defensa en el Escenario Internacional Actual*, Arbor No. 678 (2002),
p. 357 at 372; *cf.* H. Neuhold, *Law and Force in International Relations – European and
American Positions*, 64 HJIL (2004), p. 263 at 266–7.

100   *Cf.* US National Security Strategy (2002), Introduction: 'Today, the United States
enjoys a position of unparalleled military strength and great economic and political influence',
and at p. 30: 'The United States must and will maintain the capability to defeat any attempt
by an enemy ... to impose its will on the United States'. This hegemonic strand in American
foreign policy emerged soon after the end of the Cold War. *Cf.* P.E. Tyler, *U.S. Strategy Plan
calls for ensuring no rivals develop*, New York Times, 8 March 1992, p. 1.

101   'If America is to use its hyper power over the next quarter-century to build a better
world, it will need help' (T.A. Chafos, *The European Union's Rapid Reaction Force and
the North Atlantic Treaty Organization Response Force: A Rational Division of Labor for
European Security* (2003), p. 69).

102   US National Security Strategy (2002), Part VIII.

Minister, in 1999 coined the term of the United States as a *hyper-puissance*, against which France and other 'great powers' should act as a counter-weight.[103] Originally espoused only by France, this view now also finds support to varying degrees in Germany, Sweden, the Netherlands and in the European Commission.[104] Such a development, which S. Huntington warned of in that same year,[105] would seem to find support in other States like Russia or China[106] but it is rejected in the United States, sometimes fiercely,[107] sometimes in more qualifying terms.[108]

The (relative) importance of sovereignty

Europeans, with their 50 years' tradition of integration, have become used to the idea of transferring State sovereignty to an international organisation or to a treaty body like the International Criminal Court. In the prevailing American foreign policy view, by contrast, such a transfer is viewed with suspicion, as an unnecessary curtailing of international freedom of action[109] and indeed as a loss of democracy.[110] This view seems to stem particularly from the US Senate, whose advice and consent is needed for the ratification of international treaties concluded by the US.[111]

Despite differences, much common ground

In the fierce transatlantic rift over Iraq in 2003 (see on this below) the 'traditional common transatlantic value base' was often invoked as an anchor whenever political interests were visibly not shared anymore by some of the major players. This cultural value base does exist. It is founded in common historical-cultural roots stretching from the Greek–Judeo–Christian tradition, over Humanism, the Renaissance and

---

103   *To Paris, U.S. Looks Like a 'Hyperpower'*, International Herald Tribune, 5 Feb. 1999, p. 5; T.G. Ash, *The Peril of Too Much Power*, New York Times, 9 April 2002, p. 25: 'America has too much power for anyone's own good, including its own.' Such an act of political counter-weighing is called 'balancing' in international relations theory.

104   R. de Wijk, in: G. Lindstrom / B. Schmitt (eds.), *One year on: lessons from Iraq,* CP 68 (2004), p. 41 at 45.

105   S.P. Huntington, *The Lonely Superpower*, Foreign Affairs (March-April 1999), pp. 35–49.

106   H. Neuhold, *Transatlantic Turbulences: Rifts or Ripples* 8 EFAR (2003), pp. 465–6.

107   According to then U.S. National Security Advisor Condoleezza Rice, multipolarity is 'a necessary evil ... a theory of rivalry [diverting] us from the great tasks before us', *Condoleezza Rice delivers remarks*, FDCH Political Transcripts, 26 June 2003.

108   *Renewing the Atlantic Partnership* (2004), p. 12.

109   P.H. Gordon, *Bridging the Atlantic Divide*, Foreign Affairs (Jan./Feb. 2003), p. 70 at 74.

110   Z. Bereschi, *The Dilemma of the Future of Transatlantic Relations* (2003), p. 180.

111   H. Neuhold, *Law and Force in International Relations – European and American Positions*, 64 HJIL (2004), pp. 263 at 266.

Enlightenment.[112] Democracy and individual freedoms are key to conceptions of state and society on either side of the Atlantic, also regarding internal legitimacy of these States towards their own citizens. This core value base remains largely intact today.[113] Moreover, not only do the two continents share a very large volume of trade, and are thus very interdependent, but economically their dependence on energy resources leads them to favour an international system that enables trade.[114] Most practitioners and commentators seem to agree that the value differences between Europe and America are not so much in the ends but in the means, or 'tactics'.[115] The majority of their interests,[116] and also of their values[117] such as preserving freedom and security for their citizens, maintaining an open democracy and human rights, can be shown to be the same, and would therefore still seem to make them partners by default.

ARE THE EU AND THE US STILL DEFAULT PARTNERS?

At least three main reasons may be noted why the United States and Europe have more to gain as allies than as neutrals or adversaries,[118] why they will continue to strongly depend on one another for the foreseeable time, and indeed, why they are condemned to doing so.[119]

Firstly, there is a negative reason: looking for suitable partners in an increasingly unpredictable world, the United States and the EU have hardly anywhere else to turn to. What are the alternatives? For the United States, the obvious alternative would be Asia with its generally fast-growing markets (apart from downturns such as in 1997) and populations. But, although US trade with Asia is more now than with Europe (and overall investment may soon be too), US relations with that continent are still today primarily bilateral. Asian countries, despite efforts by regional organisations such as ASEAN, are still very diverse and far from presenting a common front, that is, a uniform partner for the United States. To this is added the strategic dimension. The United States has strategic and military commitments (and thus interests) in many

---

112   H. Neuhold, *Transatlantic Turbulences: Rifts or Ripples* 8 EFAR (2003), p. 460.

113   I.H. Daalder / J.M. Lindsay, *American foreign policy and transatlantic relations in the age of global politics*, in: G. Lindstrom (ed.), *Shift or Rift* (2003), p. 91 at 100.

114   N. Neuwahl, *The Atlantic Alliance: For Better or Wars...*, 8 EFAR (2003), p. 427 at 429.

115   E.g. P.H. Gordon, *Bridging the Atlantic Divide* (2003), pp. 74–75; J. Dempsey, *Strategy Document – EU foreign ministers agree WMD policy*, Financial Times, 17 June 2003, p. 3; *Renewing the Atlantic Partnership* (2004), p. 7.

116   D.C. Gompert, *What does America want of Europe?*, in: G. Lindstrom (ed.), *Shift or Rift?* (2003), p. 62.

117   J. Fischer, *Europa und die Zukunft der transatlantischen Beziehungen* (speech, 2003).

118   *Renewing the Atlantic Partnership* (2004), p. 28.

119   R. Asmus, in: G. Lindstrom / B. Schmitt (eds.), *One year on: lessons from Iraq* (2004), p. 131 at 136.

Asian countries. Asian countries differ on the desirability of this state of affairs; not all of them are entirely positive (because it strengthens their respective opponents in the region). China, which would be large enough by population to present a global strategic partner for the United States by itself, is a very different country from the United States, in cultural and political terms. Given these alternatives it is better for the United States 'to have differences and difficulties with countries that have similar values and traditions than with those who have a different world view altogether'.[120]

For Europe, the obvious alternative would be Russia. Good relations with Russia, aimed at stabilising the country, are in the EU's evident interest. Since Putin's second term as Russian President, a reasonable degree of stability has already arrived in that country, after the Yeltsin era in the 1990s in which the country was shaken by the upheavals of transition. But this new stability has clearly come at the price of stifling Russia's democracy in the bud. This fact throws a deep chasm between European and Russian values which would make impossible any long-standing and deep strategic partnership. In addition, most of Europe is today already very dependent on Russian energy resources such as oil, and (even more so) natural gas. Any partnership of Europe with Russia would over time only enhance these dependencies. This may be what Russia wants, but it runs counter to Europe's tried and trusted policy of diversifying its global supply of vital resources. Besides, the new EU member States (10 of 25) would certainly oppose any move of the EU in the direction of such a strong EU–Russia partnership. Thus, for rather more than security reasons, the United States and Europe are still each other's best and most reliable option.[121]

Secondly, there is a positive reason internal to the European theatre itself. NATO is still the most important expression of the transatlantic relationship.[122] In a nutshell, it could be put like this: 'The EU needs NATO because, for the foreseeable future, it will remain militarily impotent without it. The US needs NATO to legitimize its ongoing presence and influence in Europe'.[123] EU dependence on US military assets for its own operational capacity (especially for projection of any sizeable military force abroad) could remain a fact for at least the next ten years. Whether the 'logic of autonomy' will lead to an 'indigenous' EU military at some point in the future, is still uncertain.[124] The US, through NATO, underpins the readiness of many European States to engage in security and defence cooperation and integration at the EU level.

---

120   A. Lejins, in: *ibid.*, p. 87 at p. 92.

121   *Cf.* S. Sloan, *A Perspective on the Future of the Transatlantic Bargain*, Presentation to the NATO Parliamentary Assembly, Ottawa, 4 Oct. 2001, http://www.atlanticcommunity. org/NPAtext.html (visited 29/05/03).

122   See above at fn. 18.

123   J. Howorth, *ESDP and NATO - Wedlock or Deadlock?*, 38 Coop. & Confl. 3 (2003), p. 236.

124   *Ibid.*, p. 252.

Partly as a side-effect of this, NATO also serves as a significant 'transmission belt' for US influence in Europe.[125]

Thirdly, economics: The US and the EU combine 60 per cent of world GDP and 40 per cent of world trade. Sixty per cent of all foreign direct investment in the US originates from Europe, and 70 per cent of Europe's investment abroad is in the United States.[126] Indeed, economic cooperation is sometimes described as the remaining 'healthy body' of US–EU relations which might help to repair the transatlantic relationship as a whole.[127]

Each of these three reasons (to which more could be added) would be sufficient in itself to justify the continuation of the transatlantic relationship. Together, they make it an imperative.

SOME LESSONS FROM THE IRAQ CRISIS

The danger for the transatlantic relationship, including NATO, from the dispute over the use of force against Iraq in late 2002 and spring 2003 was profound and possibly long-term.[128] The last time such a division among the major Western powers had been seen was a generation ago,[129] in 1956 over the Suez crisis.[130] It also surprised most actors and analysts that so much of the transatlantic solidarity and common identity which had been displayed after September 11 seemed to dissipate over a matter of months.[131] The events which led to the Iraq war have been well chronicled and will doubtless be extensively analysed for a long time.[132] What interests here

---

125   A. Pradetto, *Funktionen militärischer Konfliktregelung durch die NATO* (2002), pp. 206–7.

126   G. Burghardt, *It's make or break time – summit of ambitions for EU-US relations* (interview), European Voice, 19–25 June 2003, p. 15.

127   *Ibid.*

128   This assessment holds sway among the multitude of authors who have commented on this dispute, as, for example, the survey by G. Lindstrom / B. Schmitt (eds.), *One year on: lessons from Iraq*, CP 68 (2004) showed. E.g. N. Gnesotto, in: *ibid.*, p. 51 at 57; P.H. Gordon, in: *ibid.*, p. 161 at 165; D.C. Gompert, *What does America want of Europe?*, in: G. Lindstrom (ed.), *Shift or Rift* (2003), p. 43.

129   *Renewing the Atlantic Partnership* (2004), p. 1.

130   M. Dassu, in: G. Lindstrom / B. Schmitt (eds.), *One year on: lessons from Iraq*, CP 68 (2004), p. 29 at 36; A. Vasconcelos, in: *ibid.*, p. 121 at 125; C. McArdle Kelleher, in: *ibid.*, p. 177 at 180–1; P. Hassner, in: *ibid.*, p. 79 at 82.

131   R. de Wijk, in: G. Lindstrom / B. Schmitt (eds.), *One year on: lessons from Iraq,* CP 68 (2004), p. 41 at 45.

132   'There is undoubtedly a great book to be written on the crack-up of transatlantic relations over Iraq', R. Asmus, in: *ibid.*, p. 131 at 136. For a collection of the most important public statements in chronological order, see only CP 67, Part II.

are some of the origins of this dispute, its impact on transatlantic relations, and the lessons that have so far been drawn from it.[133]

After the tragedy of September 11, Europe reacted with spontaneous and intense expressions of solidarity with the American nation ('We are all Americans now'). About 18 months later, nothing of this general solidarity reaching across the Atlantic could be felt anymore.[134] Why? 'The attacks of that day', reads a survey by the Council on Foreign Relations of spring 2004 'produced the most sweeping reorientation of US grand strategy in over half a century.'[135] The country embarked on a complete overhaul of its strategic priorities, embracing the pre-emptive 'Bush doctrine' against presumed terrorist targets and a new brand of systematic unilateralism, underpinned by moralistic tones, sidelining (although not completely forgetting) more balanced considerations on possible root causes of terrorism such as poverty.[136] The new view, widely and firmly held in the Bush Administration, cast the world as an essentially dangerous place, primarily because of the spread of weapons of mass destruction, the rise of international terrorism, and rogue states.[137] Furthermore, from the point of view of international law, the United States henceforth considered itself in a permanent state of self-defence, hence in a kind of permanent exceptional status vis-à-vis international law.[138] The result was a general new theory of relativity regarding international law as far as the US was concerned.[139] 'Europeans no longer recognised the America they had previously known'.[140] Americans, for their part, were equally surprised by what they saw as European apathy to clear and present danger.[141] Perhaps they had mistaken European solidarity in the wake of September 11 for a European self-interest, grounded in similar fear of the global threat. But, in general, Europeans did not feel threatened by proliferation of weapons of mass destruction and international terrorism the same way the average US citizen did.

---

133   This part is mainly based on Lindstrom / Schmitt, *One year on* (2004), and on Lindstrom (ed.), *Shift or Rift – Assessing US–EU relations after Iraq*, EU-ISS (2003). The various views by a multitude of European and American authors collected in those two works are regarded as sufficiently representative for the purpose of the overview below.

134   R. de Wijk, in: G. Lindstrom / B. Schmitt (eds.), *One year on: lessons from Iraq,* CP 68 (2004), p. 41 at 45.

135   *Renewing the Atlantic Partnership* (2004), p. 2.

136   E.g. 'Of course, poverty did not cause 9/11', D.C. Gompert, *What does America want of Europe?*, in: G. Lindstrom (ed.), *Shift or Rift* (2003), p. 70.

137   *Cf. ibid.*, p. 50.

138   N. Gnesotto, *Visions of the other*, in: G. Lindstrom (ed.), *Shift or Rift* (2003), p. 7 at 26.

139   N. Gnesotto, *ibid.*, p. 27. *Cf.* also N. Krisch, *Amerikanische Hegemonie und liberale Revolution im Völkerrecht*, 43 Der Staat (2004), pp. 267–297.

140   N. Gnesotto, *ibid.*, p. 37.

141   D.C. Gompert, *What does America want of Europe?*, in: G. Lindstrom (ed.), *Shift or Rift* (2003), p. 56.

As a consequence of this 'perception gap',[142] The European strategic adjustment after September 11 was much less dramatic.[143] While feeling pity with the victims of New York and Washington, they did not experience the scope of trauma that the US nation as whole underwent.[144] Looking to the United States, the majority of Europeans 'failed to appreciate the intensity of America's outrage and the nature and seriousness of its declaration of war against terrorism'.[145] The gap in global policy outlook widened further when the most visible symbol of European solidarity with the US after September 11, the invocation of Art. 5 of the NAT, was in practice set aside by the Bush Administration in its campaign against Al-Qaida and the Taliban in Afghanistan.[146] The European reaction was disappointment,[147] complaints of unilateralism, and in some cases fear that the principle of 'indivisible security' was being put at risk.[148] This enhanced impressions, already dating from before September 11,[149] that European leaders simply did not get a hearing in Washington anymore. In sum, overall transatlantic relations can be said to have been already somewhat sore even before the Iraq crisis erupted in 2002.

The events of the political crisis and the legal arguments traded have been well described in other places.[150] What were the lessons to be drawn, after the smoke cleared?

The view prevails today that the Iraq crisis was only a *symptom* of deeper structural political differences between the United States and Europe which had

---

142   J. de Hoop Scheffer, cited in: W. Hoge, *NATO Chief criticizes terror 'gap'*, International Herald Tribune (online edition), 12 Nov. 2004.

143   I.H. Daalder / J.M. Lindsay, *American foreign policy and transatlantic relations in the age of global politics*, in: G. Lindstrom (ed.), *Shift or Rift* (2003), p. 91 at 99.

144   W. Drozdiak, in: G. Lindstrom / B. Schmitt (eds.), *One year on: lessons from Iraq*, CP 68 (2004), p. 153 at 157. D. de Villepin's speech at the Royal Institute of International Affairs on 27 March 2003 ('We understand the immense trauma that this country has suffered', *Law, force and justice*, http://www.iiss.org/showdocument.php?docID=114 (visited 27/06/04), p. 3) rang rather hollow with American ears. *Cf.* A. Cowell, *Kind words from France (so to speak)*, International Herald Tribune, 28 March 2003, p. 1.

145   C. Kovacs, *US–European Relations*, 8 EFAR (2003), p. 449. Kovacs continues that 'Had they done so, the crisis in transatlantic relations over the Iraqi Campaign would probably not have occurred.'

146   See on the political importance of this invocation and legal questions concerning Art. 5 NAT see below Chapter 6 (Collective Self-Defence).

147   The story of an unnamed European general who sat at SHAPE beside his phone in October 2001, waiting for a call which never came, has become legend. *Cf.* Col. R. Ostermeyer (German Bundeswehr, Joint Hq. Centre, Heidelberg), *Die NATO in Afghanistan und die europäische Verteidigungspolitik*, speech at VDST Heidelberg, 8 June 2004.

148   *Renewing the Atlantic Partnership* (2004), p. 3.

149   J. Hulsman, in: G. Lindstrom / B. Schmitt (eds.), *One year on: lessons from Iraq*, CP 68 (2004), p. 169 at 174.

150   See e.g. H. Neuhold, *Law and Force in International Relations – European and American Positions*, 64 HJIL (2004), p. 263 at 274–9.

slowly grown since the end of the Cold War, but had been largely ignored.[151] According to this line of reasoning, the fall-out was something waiting to happen.[152] In this sense, the Iraq crisis is also seen as a healthy 'catharsis',[153] that is, a starting point for re-balancing the transatlantic relationship to reflect more accurately the realities of power, interests and values today.[154] The Western powers had weathered many a storm during the course of the Cold War, such as Suez, the French part withdrawal from NATO, and the Yom Kippur War,[155] but the glue of a common massive threat had always held them together in the end. It was this framework, an agreed-upon danger, that was missing in the Iraq crisis.[156] It was the first time since the end of the Cold War that Western powers came to disagree on the solution to an international security problem in such stark and vociferous terms. In more philosophical concepts, the dispute has also been cast as the relationship between ethics and law,[157] by differences in legal culture,[158] or over the nature of a future international order.[159] The rift between Europe and America was also reflected by the respective public opinions, leading to estrangement of those publics from each other.[160] While European populations were by a large majority against the war, the American population was more evenly split.

Running in parallel, however, there were also more encouraging developments. Trade and investment between the two continents – a powerful common interest – hardly ebbed during the crisis,[161] and transatlantic cooperation in global trade matters immediately after the Iraq war, such as at the WTO negotiations in Cancún,[162] was not affected. In peacekeeping in Afghanistan, cooperation between French, German, British and US troops continued unaffected throughout. The same is true

---

151   E.g. *Ibid.*, p. 2; D.C. Gompert, *What does America want of Europe?*, in: G. Lindstrom (ed.), *Shift or Rift* (2003), p. 45.

152   *Ibid.*, p. 49.

153   *Ibid.*, p. 45.

154   A different view is taken by G. Gustenau, in: G. Lindstrom / B. Schmitt (eds.), *One year on: lessons from Iraq,* CP 68 (2004), p. 71 at 75–6, who argues that the 1990s saw a uniquely close US–European relationship which was only brought back to 'normal status' by the Iraq war.

155   *Renewing the Atlantic Partnership* (2004), p. 8.

156   *Ibid.*, pp. 8–9.

157   N. Gnesotto, *Visions of the other* (2003), p. 7 at 30–33.

158   H. Hestermeyer, *Die völkerrechtliche Beurteilung des Irakkrieges im Lichte transatlantischer Rechtskulturunterschiede*, 64 HJIL (2004), pp. 315–341.

159   N. Serra, in: G. Lindstrom / B. Schmitt (eds.), *One year on: lessons from Iraq,* CP 68 (2004), p. 113 at 117–8; P.H. Gordon, *ibid.*, p. 161 at 165.

160   E. Brimmer, *ibid.*, p. 139 at 143; M. Winter, *Bürger für Abnabelung Europas von USA*, Frankfurter Rundschau, 18 March 2004. Even those public opinion polls can, however, be interpreted differently, leading to a narrowing of the said differences. *Cf.* N. Serra, in: G. Lindstrom / B. Schmitt (eds.), *One year on: lessons from Iraq,* CP 68 (2004), p. 113 at 118.

161   *Renewing the Atlantic Partnership* (2004), p. 16.

162   C. Grant, in: G. Lindstrom / B. Schmitt (eds.), *One year on: lessons from Iraq,* CP 68 (2004), p. 61 at 67.

for the Balkans, where the United States is now increasingly ceding responsibility to the EU. About half a year after the Iraq war, the gap slowly began to diminish.[163] The catharsis was beginning to show effect in mutual efforts of healing between governments who recognised clearly that the fall-out in 2003 had gone too far.[164] From the American side, this was increasingly the case as realisation of the lack of a 'league' between Osama bin Laden and Saddam Hussein began to gain broader ground,[165] no weapons of mass destruction were found in post-Saddam Iraq, and as peace-building efforts in the country seemed to go from bad to worse during 2004. As a result, some of the basic divisive issues across the Atlantic began to be addressed more seriously by both sides.

Another, internal, healing process was also soon underway within the EU. This had direct implications for ESDP, as shown in the agreement of the 'Big Three' on the question of European Military Headquarters in December 2003.[166] In the medium term, strategic-military cooperation under ESDP seems to have been accelerated by the Iraq dispute,[167] despite the eclipse of the CFSP during the crisis.[168] This also brings the EU a few steps closer to becoming a global actor,[169] a goal which finds increasing support in public opinion after the Iraq crisis.[170] It is an interesting continuation of the fast improvements which European security policy saw as a result of the frustrations over European incapacity in the Balkan Wars.[171]

What will last, however, is first, the essential lack of trust between Europeans and Americans,[172] which will probably take a new generation of leaders on both sides to repair. 'The problem is that each of the partners now doubts the sincerity of the other'.[173] Second, the differences in respective policy priorities which existed before

---

163   *Ibid.*, p. 66.

164   W. Drozdiak, in: *ibid.*, p. 153 at 156.

165   See e.g. *Renewing the Atlantic Partnership* (2004), Additional View by S.M. Walt, p. 30. *Cf.* U.S. Senate Select Ctte. on Intelligence, *Report on the U.S. Intelligence Community's Prewar Intelligence Assessments on Iraq*, 7 July 2004, http://intelligence.senate. gov/iraqreport2.pdf (visited 16/07/2004); J. Cirincione et al., *WMD in Iraq: Evidence and Implications*, Carnegie Endowment for International Peace (2004), http://www.ceip.org/files/ pdf/Iraq3FullText.pdf (visited 16/07/2004).

166   P. Hassner, in: G. Lindstrom / B. Schmitt (eds.), *One year on: lessons from Iraq* (2004), p. 79 at 82. On this development, see below Chapter 2 (ESDP today).

167   R. de Wijk, in: *ibid.*, p. 41 at 47; E. Brimmer, *ibid.*, p. 139 at 142.

168   There is broad agreement that in the Iraq crisis, CFSP and the EU's role as a global actor failed completely. See, e.g. *ibid.*, on this point the converging views by e.g. C. Bertram, p. 13 at 16; C. Bildt, p. 21 at 23; M. Dassu, p. 29 at 34; N. Gnesotto, p. 51 at 55; C. Grant, p. 61 at 65; G. Gustenau, p. 71 at 74; in more relative terms also P.H. Gordon, p. 161 at 164.

169   J. Sedivy, in: *ibid.*, p. 103 at 107.

170   A. Vasconcelos, in: *ibid.*, p. 121 at 124.

171   J. Dobbins, in: *ibid.*, p. 147 at 149. On this point, see below Chapter 2.

172   C. Grant, in: *ibid.*, p. 61 at 69; E. Brimmer, in: *ibid.*, p. 139 at 143; P. Hassner, in: *ibid.*, p. 79 at 83.

173   C. Kovacs, *US–European Relations*, 8 EFAR (2003), pp. 450–1.

the war have increased.[174] Third, despite the widespread impression that Europe is the United States' most 'natural partner' for security cooperation,[175] Europe is in fact unlikely to be a reliable strategic partner for US global engagements, not only because its limited capacity to project military force fast, but also because of its lack of desire for such engagements.[176]

TOWARDS A NEW TRANSATLANTIC BALANCE

As the United States prepares to decamp from the continent, the two sides of the Atlantic are heading toward a new division of labor. Europe will increasingly assume responsibility for its own security, while America focuses its attention and resources on other parts of the world.... The traditional trans-Atlantic link, predicated upon the notion of the indivisibility of American and European security, will be no more.[177]

It is not necessary to assume such drastic conclusions for the transatlantic relationship, but the basic facts from which C. Kupchan draws them are real. The 1990s have certainly seen a growing reluctance by the United States to stay involved in European affairs on the level of the Cold War, and also a US preference for increased European involvement in situations which affect Europe more than the United States,[178] such as policing the Balkans.[179] But as the transatlantic relationship cannot be separated from the larger international system of which it is a part,[180] such a shift within Europe is also expected to lead to a somewhat more equally distributed power between the two sides of the Atlantic,[181] if and when the EU further integrates and finally assumes in full its anticipated role as a global actor.[182] How would the daily rules of the game be different from today in such a re-balanced transatlantic relationship? Europe would retain friendly relations with the United States, but it would be more dependent on its own interests, resulting in the option to 'agree to

---

174   *Cf.* C. Bildt, in: G. Lindstrom / B. Schmitt (eds.), *One year on: lessons from Iraq,* CP 68 (2004), p. 21 at 24.

175   See above: Are the EU and the US still default partners?, at p. 36.

176   *Cf.* J. Dobbins, in: G. Lindstrom / B. Schmitt (eds.), *One year on: lessons from Iraq,* CP 68 (2004), p. 147 at 150–1.

177   C. Kupchan, *The Rise of Europe, America's Changing Internationalism, and the End of U.S. Primacy,* 118 PSQ (2003), p. 205 at 226. For Kupchan's extended argument, see *id., The End of the American Era: U.S. Foreign Policy and the Geopolitics of the Twenty-first Century* (2002).

178   Z. Lachowski, *The military dimension of the European Union* (2002), p. 152.

179   D.C. Gompert, *What does America want of Europe?*, in: G. Lindstrom (ed.), *Shift or Rift* (2003), p. 68.

180   *Renewing the Atlantic Partnership* (2004), p. 17.

181   C. Kupchan, *The Rise of Europe* (2003), p. 210.

182   *Cf.* A. Lejins, in: G. Lindstrom / B. Schmitt (eds.), *One year on: lessons from Iraq,* CP 68 (2004), p. 87 at 91.

disagree' on occasion.[183] On this basis the US would also increase the possibility for finding support in Europe for some of its global policies.[184] The downside (if indeed it is one) for the United States would be the end of a European docile ally.[185] Judging from the Iraq experience, this development is arguably already well underway. The jury is still out on the eventual form transatlantic relations will take, once they have been settled to the new global power landscape. The only thing that seems certain is that they will not remain the same.

> Relations between Europe and the United States have reached a turning point. Either it comes to an end or it will be renewed.[186]

As I.H. Daalder and J.M. Lindsay epitomise, the option of a transatlantic 'divorce' is still a possibility. There are basically two scenarios for such a divorce, a hard and a soft one. Under the hard scenario, Europe and the United States will simply drift further and further apart.[187] The United States would revert even more to unilateralism, which in turn might lead Europeans to a 'continental fortress mentality', or simply passivity in face of threats beyond their region, until the point when its external interests become directly affected.[188] However, Americans point out that 'if Europe defines its identity in terms of countering US power, the world is likely to return to a balance-of-power system reminiscent of the era prior to World War I – with the same disastrous consequences'.[189] *The Economist*, pondering on this sentence in spring 2004, wrote that 'the idea that Europe and America might actually come into armed conflict still seems absurd. But the notion that Europeans and Americans may increasingly be rivals rather than partners seems less implausible than it once did'.[190] However dark this scenario, abandonment by US security protection would at least have the effect of pushing the EU – thus devoid of other security options – to fully and institutionally developing its own defence structures.[191] The divorce may not be complete. A softer, and more likely divorce would result in a Europe employing 'critical involvement' with the United States, able and willing to say 'no' in certain

---

183   F. Heisbourg, *US–European relations* (2004), p. 119 at 123.

184   *Ibid.*; W. Drozdiak, *The North Atlantic Drift*, 84 Foreign Affairs (Jan./Feb. 2005), pp. 88–98.

185   B.S. Posen, *ESDP and the Structure of World Power*, 39 The International Spectator 1 (2004), p. 5 at 17; Kupchan, *The Rise of Europe* (2003), p. 212.

186   I.H. Daalder / J.M. Lindsay, *American foreign policy and transatlantic relations in the age of global politics*, in: G. Lindstrom (ed.), *Shift or Rift* (2003), p. 91 at 103.

187   R. de Wijk, *The Reform of ESDP and EU–NATO Cooperation*, 39 The International Spectator 1 (2004), p. 71 at 81; *cf.* G. Schöllgen, *Das Ende der transatlantischen Epoche*, Frankfurter Allgemeine Zeitung, 27 Aug. 2003, p. 6.

188   A.D. Botticelli, *The premier of the North Atlantic Treaty's Article V: Is Article V Still a Deterrent?*, 26 Suffolk Transnat. L. Rev. (2002), p. 51 at 77.

189   *Renewing the Atlantic Partnership* (2004), p. 15.

190   *We told you so*, The Economist, 15 May 2004, p. 30. This prediction is the one promoted by R. Kagan, *Power and Weakness* (2002).

191   W. Bradford, *The WEU ... the new sick man of Europe* (2000), p. 13 at 80.

circumstances (as described above) without splitting completely apart.[192] Its field of competition with the United States would be soft power, by presenting itself to other societies and regions as a 'kinder and gentler' alternative, as an example of human progress.[193]

There are, on the other hand, enough voices who dismiss altogether the notion of transatlantic divorce (whether in its hard or soft version),[194] and who tend to concentrate on rebuilding the old transatlantic relationship in full, albeit under new premises, reflecting the new power realities and interests of both sides. A bottom-up approach is regarded as instrumental for this building effort. It would start, bit by bit, from those areas where US–EU cooperation is currently working best,[195] such as the Balkans,[196] and would leave other more contentious areas, such as the future of Iraq, aside for the moment.[197] One of those obvious well-working 'raisins in the cake' is the peace operation in Afghanistan.[198] A similar approach is suggested by a Council on Foreign Relations study in 2004, stating 'that Europeans and Americans [should] acknowledge what unites them and reaffirm their commitment to a common purpose'.[199] This 'common purpose' understanding may also, as US voices are often heard arguing, involve an understanding of a hard/soft power division of labour between Europe and the United States, on the basis of complementarity.[200] Nevertheless, the EU will also not be able to do without some 'hard' capacity,[201] for example for peacekeeping.[202] A new formal transatlantic 'compact', 'partnership',[203]

192   A. Vasconcelos, in: G. Lindstrom / B. Schmitt (eds.), *One year on: lessons from Iraq,* CP 68 (2004), p. 121 at 126.

193   D.C. Gompert, *What does America want of Europe?*, in: G. Lindstrom (ed.), *Shift or Rift* (2003), p. 68.

194   P.H. Gordon, *Bridging the Atlantic Divide* (2003), p. 79, however, warns of it as a 'self-fulfilling prophecy'.

195   A. Vasconcelos, in: G. Lindstrom / B. Schmitt (eds.), *One year on: lessons from Iraq,* CP 68 (2004), p. 121 at 125.

196   D. Serwer, *The Balkans: from American to European leadership*, in: G. Lindstrom (ed.), *Shift or Rift* (2003), p. 169 at 183; D. Triantaphyllou, *The interplay between the EU and the United States in the Balkans*, in: G. Lindstrom (ed.), *Shift or Rift* (2003), p. 191.

197   M. Dassu, in: G. Lindstrom / B. Schmitt (eds.), *One year on: lessons from Iraq,* CP 68 (2004), p. 29 at 36.

198   *Ibid.*; H. Müller, *Das transatlantische Risiko – Deutungen des amerikanisch-europäischen Weltordnungs-konflikts*, Aus Politik und Zeitgeschichte (2004), B 3–4, p. 7 at 17.

199   *Renewing the Atlantic Partnership* (2004), p. 5.

200   *Ibid.*, p. 11; W. Drozdiak, *The North Atlantic Drift*, 84 Foreign Affairs (Jan./Feb. 2005), pp. 88–98.

201   N. Neuwahl, *The Atlantic Alliance: For Better or Wars...*, 8 EFAR (2003), p. 432.

202   H. Neuhold, *Transatlantic Turbulences: Rifts or Ripples* 8 EFAR (2003), p. 462.

203   R. Asmus, in: G. Lindstrom / B. Schmitt (eds.), *One year on: lessons from Iraq,* CP 68 (2004), p. 131 at 135.

'bargain',[204] or possibly a 'New Atlantic Charter'[205] is seen by some as essential for harnessing the political will to reshape and then maintain the new transatlantic relationship in absence of the clear and present common threat that ensured a constant focusing of leaders' minds on the need for such a partnership in the past.[206] The results of the US–EU summit on 20 June 2005 look like an encouraging step, in particular the US–EU Declaration on Enhancing Cooperation in the Field of Non Proliferation and the Fight Against Terrorism;[207] even though a more important draft US–EU declaration, setting out cooperation in the field of crisis response and conflict prevention,[208] was eventually not finalised. US–EU summits could further be provided with a permanent secretariat, entrusted with preparation of the meetings and with the monitoring of the decisions made.[209] Even the idea of this compact taking the form of a legally binding international instrument is occasionally mooted.[210]

Whichever form it eventually takes, certain conditions must be met for such a new transatlantic compact to succeed. First, it must be based on the real interests of Europe and America today, which must be stated clearly by the two sides, free from past perceptions[211] and without the usual mutual flattery about 'common traditions and values'. It will take the EU some time for internal adaptation before it can state its interests unambiguously, especially until the ten new members' views have been properly identified and accommodated into the EU whole.[212] This includes their views regarding NATO.

Second, some agreement on the role of multilateral institutions must occur. This may be the most difficult part. However, there is the hope that the Iraq quagmire has increasingly taught the United States the limits of geopolitical world power.[213] As a result may come greater US acceptance of the utility of such multilateral institutions and the legitimacy they confer (if used according to their terms), and hence also

---

204   J. Sedivy, in: *ibid.*, p. 103 at 108.

205   *Renewing the Atlantic Partnership* (2004), p. 14.

206   *Ibid.*, p. 27.

207   EU–US Summit, Washington, 20 June 2005 – Joint Declarations, Council Doc. 10359/05, 22 June 2005.

208   *Cf.* A. Beatty, *EU-US plot a joint strategy to tackle failed states and conflicts*, European Voice, Vol. 11, No. 23, 16 June 2005, p. 2.

209   F. Heisbourg, *US-European relations* (2004), p. 123.

210   R. Ginsberg, *Together apart: ESDP, CFSP, and a New Transatlantic Security Compact*, in: A. Maurer / K.-O. Lang / E. Whitlock (eds.), *New Stimulus or Integration Backlash? EU Enlargement and Transatlantic Relations* (2004), SWP Berlin, p. 36 at 37. A. Lejins, in: G. Lindstrom / B. Schmitt (eds.), *One year on: lessons from Iraq*, CP 68 (2004), p. 87 at 91 also employs the term 'contract' to describe this notion of a necessary new transatlantic compact.

211   D.C. Gompert, *What does America want of Europe?*, in: G. Lindstrom (ed.), *Shift or Rift* (2003), pp. 57–8.

212   *Cf.* H. Neuhold, *Transatlantic Turbulences: Rifts or Ripples* (2003), p. 462; C. Kovacs, *US-European Relations*, 8 EFAR (2003), p. 454.

213   G. Gustenau, in: G. Lindstrom / B. Schmitt (eds.), *One year on: lessons from Iraq,* CP 68 (2004), p. 71 at 76.

the value a partnership with Europe as a whole would have in the long term for the Iraq operation theatre.[214] For Europeans, the Iraq war has also had a certain waking up effect from their 'Kantian paradise'. European enthusiastic multilateralism, as demonstrated above, is grounded in the EU's own huge success in international integration, but the EU has realised that its experience 'is not an automatic precedent for every part of the world'.[215] Hence, 'robust intervention' is embraced in its new Security Strategy.[216]

Third, European leaders must resist the temptation to cater to ever-present anti-American voter segments (which does not exclude admitting differences where they exist), and concentrate on the grander transatlantic project. The United States, for their part, must overcome its growing ambivalence about their gains from European integration[217] (wanting burden-sharing but refusing to share influence), which is sometimes manifested as fear,[218] and results in a preference to exploit divisions between European capitals.[219] You cannot both eat a pie and keep it, as an American saying goes.[220] The recent foundation of a European Union Caucus in the US House of Representatives shows that American lawmakers have begun to grasp the necessity for the US to deal with the EU as a whole entity.[221] US global pre-eminence will not last forever, and once it starts to decline, a future transatlantic compact, struck from a position of strength and in wise anticipation of this development, will be an invaluable asset to the US.[222]

---

214   J. Dobbins, in: *ibid.*, p. 147 at 149.

215   *Renewing the Atlantic Partnership* (2004), p. 20.

216   A Secure European in a Better World – European Security Strategy, Council Doc. 15895/03, 8 Dec. 2003, III., p. 12.

217   D.C. Gompert, *What does America want of Europe?*, in: G. Lindstrom (ed.), *Shift or Rift* (2003), pp. 60–1; S. Hoffmann, *The crisis in transatlantic relations*, in: G. Lindstrom (ed.), *Shift or Rift* (2003), p. 13 at 18; *Renewing the Atlantic Partnership* (2004), p. 16; *cf.* H. Neuhold, *Transatlantic Turbulences: Rifts or Ripples* (2003), p. 461.

218   *Cf.* W. Pfaff, *Seeing mortal danger in a superpower Europe*, International Herald Tribune, 3 July 2003.

219   P. Cornish, *Partnership in Crisis* (1997), p. 110; *Cf.* S. Hoffmann, *The crisis in transatlantic relations*, in: G. Lindstrom (ed.), *Shift or Rift* (2003), p. 13 at 19.

220   *Cf. Amerikanisches Paradox*, Süddeutsche Zeitung, 18 Oct. 2003, p. 4.

221   US Mission to the European Union, *Lawmakers Introduce Congressional European Union Caucus*, Press Release, 4 May 2005.

222   This forms the central argument in C. Kupchan, *The End of the American Era* (2002). See also P.H. Gordon, *Bridging the Atlantic Divide* (2003), p. 81. This basic recognition, despite official statements from the US Administration, seems to have reached even US military circles not long thereafter. *Cf.* T.A. Chafos, *The European Union's Rapid Reaction Force ...* (2003), p. 4: 'As the U.S. sets out to enforce a world order underlying the 2002 *National Security Strategy*, it will need partners around the world.' *Cf.* also R.N. Haas, *The Opportunity: America's Moment to Alter History's Course* (2005).

Chapter 2

ESDP Today

Despite the relative novelty of security and defence in the EU, volumes have already been written on the various aspects of ESDP by political scientists,[1] and increasingly also by legal scholars,[2] not even counting scientific articles. After a brief history of the origins of ESDP this part will focus on the legal base and the most recent developments of ESDP under the Treaty Establishing a Constitution for Europe (CIG 87/04).

DEFINITION OF ESDP: NOT 'ESDI'

It is important to distinguish the EU's European Security and Defence *Policy* (ESDP) from NATO's European Security and Defence *Identity* (ESDI).[3] ESDI is an older NATO concept, an attempt made in the early 1990s to shift responsibility and influence *within* the Alliance to the European allies.[4] It was an innovation introduced

---

1   E.g. T. Marauhn, *Building ESDI* (1996); M. Meimeth (ed.), *Die Europäische Union auf dem Weg zu einer Gemeinsamen Sicherheits- und Verteidigungspolitik* (1997); W. Hoyer / G.F. Kaldrack (eds.), *ESVP* (2002); T.C. Salmon / A.J.K. Shepherd, *Toward a European Army – A Military Power in the Making?* (2003). See in addition the publications by the EU-ISS on http://www.iss-eu.org/ (visited 11/08/2004).

2   E.g. M. Warnken, *Der Handlungsrahmen der EU* (2002); K. Gerteiser, *Die Sicherheits- und Verteidigungspolitik der Europäischen Union* (2002); U. Schürr, *Der Aufbau einer europäischen Sicherheits- und Verteidigungsidentität im Beziehungsgeflecht von EU, WEU, OSZE und NATO* (2003); S. Bartelt, *Der rechtliche Rahmen für die neue operative Kapazität der Europäischen Union* (2003); K. Blanck, *Die europäische Sicherheits- und Verteidigungspolitik im Rahmen der europäischen Sicherheitsarchitektur* (2005); S. von Kielmansegg, *Die Verteidigungspolitik der Europäischen Union – eine rechtliche Analyse* (2005); N. White / M. Trybus (eds.), *European Security Law* (forthcoming); M. Trybus, *European Community Law and Defence Integration* (2005).

3   J. Howorth, *The ultimate challenge* (2000), p. 5; M. Kremer / U. Schmalz, *Nach Nizza – Perspektiven der Gemeinsamen Europäischen Sicherheits- und Verteidigungspolitik*, 24 Integration (2001), p. 167 at 169; A.D. Rotfeld, *Europe: an emerging power*, SIPRI Yearbook 2001, p. 196; J. Medcalf, *NATO and the Extra-European Challenge* (2002), p. 7, n. 21; T.C. Salmon / A.J.K. Shepherd, *Toward a European Army* (2003), p. 172.

4   WEU Assembly Doc. 1564 (1997), para. 3; J. Solana, *The Washington Summit: A New NATO for the Next Century*, 34 The International Spectator 2 (1999), p. 37 at 41.

by the Summit in Brussels in January 1994[5] to adapt to the new post-Cold War realities in Europe. Part of ESDI consisted in resuscitating the WEU to serve as NATO's 'European pillar', using, inter alia, the concept of Combined Joint Task Forces (CJTF), which would allow different levels of participation by allies (and later also by the Partners for Peace) in European-led operations. ESDI reached its high point at the Alliance's Berlin Summit in June 1996. NATO circles and the more Atlanticist voices confusingly used the term ESDI to describe also ESDP after its birth for some time.[6] This is understandable as the political process of ESDP really grew out of ESDI.[7] Even today one sometimes finds them described as essentially the same thing[8] or as 'Siamese twins'[9]. However, the fundamental difference between the two is that ESDP is fully an EU project (even though, in many areas, factual cooperation with NATO remains essential), while ESDI is (or was) always part of NATO.[10]

THE POLITICAL ORIGINS OF ESDP

External origins: the Balkan wars

Today there is wide agreement among most commentators of ESDP that the wars in former Yugoslavia in the 1990s were the political cause for the creation of the CFSP and ESDP.[11] At first, events on the Balkans threw the project of a common foreign and security policy into a deep crisis.[12] In the long term, they generated the realisation that the Union needed to have some means of harnessing political consensus, diplomacy and military means to stop atrocious wars in its close proximity from

---

5   Ministerial Meeting of the North Atlantic Council/ North Atlantic Cooperation Council, NATO Headquarters, Brussels, 10–11 Jan. 1994, Declaration of the Heads of State and Government, NATO Press Communiqué M-1(94)3.

6   *Cf.* S. Duke, *CESDP: Nice's overtrumped success?*, 6 EFAR (2001), p. 174.

7   J. Howorth, *The ultimate challenge* (2000), p. 23; *cf.* M. Vasiu, *The role of the European Security and Defense Identity in the new security environment*, 6 Rom.J.Int.Aff. 3/4 (2000), p. 125 at 143.

8   See C. von Buttlar, *The European Union's Security and Defence Policy – A Regional Effort within the Atlantic Alliance*, in: A. Bodnar et al. (eds.), *The Emerging Constitutional Law of the European Union* (2003), p. 387 at 388.

9   N.M. Abbasi, *Evolving a Common European defence* (2001), p. 84.

10   J. Howorth, *The ultimate challenge* (2000), p. 26.

11   *Cf.* only J. Solana, speech at the Annual Conference of the EU-ISS, Paris, 10 Sept. 2004, Council Doc. S0232/04: 'The EU has a special responsibility for the Balkans. In a sense, the CFSP and ESDP were born in the region'.

12   In the words of R. Cooper: 'The escape from power politics has brought great benefits to Europe. Unfortunately it has also brought illusions. Some of these were visible in the early days of the Balkans conflict, when some in Europe seemed to believe that peace and justice could be achieved by simply asking people to be reasonable' (*Id.*, *The breaking of nations* (2003), p. 160).

repeating themselves.[13] The European Community (later the European Union) failed to recognise the early signs of the coming violent break-up of Yugoslavia, and then, once the civil wars raged in Croatia and Bosnia, it failed to bring enough pressure to bear on the various actors to end the conflict. 'Europe's hour', prodigiously proclaimed in 1990 by Belgian foreign minister Jacques Poos[14] in effect went past.

This foreign policy failure in the Balkans, however, was not the EU's alone. The UN community as a whole was faced with a new type of intra-state conflict, for which its traditional peacekeeping model, elaborated and tested in many cases since the first Suez observer mission in 1956, knew no solution. The 'sub-contracting' model, a loose framework of cooperation between the UN and regional security organisations, envisioned in UN Secretary-General's Agenda for Peace in 1992,[15] did not manage to address the fundamental gap between expectations and available resources and political will to engage in dangerous international peace missions. As a recent study succinctly put it, 'it was impossible to keep a peace that did not exist or impose one without becoming involved in the conflict'.[16] This recognition was more or less soberly admitted by the UN's Agenda for Peace Supplement in 1995.[17] A new 'second generation', and later a 'third generation' model of peacekeeping emerged.[18] According to these new peacekeeping doctrines, strictly neutral observation was not enough to stop the parties from continuing hostilities and subjecting civilian populations to unspeakable atrocities in the process. 'Robust peacekeeping' gradually entered the security thinking not only on the East River in New York, but also in Brussels. The starting point of the European regional security effort was made by the Petersberg Declaration of the WEU of 1992 which (in formal

---

13   E.g. P.J. Teunissen, *Strengthening the defence dimension of the EU: An evaluation of Concepts, Recent Initiatives and Developments*, 4 EFAR (1999), p. 327 at 336; M. Kremer / U. Schmalz, *Nach Nizza – Perspektiven der GESVP* (2001), p. 167; A. Pradetto, *Funktionen militärischer Konfliktregelung durch die NATO bei der Neuordnung Europas*, in H. Timmermann / A. Pradetto (eds.), *Die NATO auf dem Weg ins 21. Jahrhundert* (2002), p. 191 at 203; G. Robertson, *Die NATO und die EU*, in: W. Hoyer / G.F. Kaldrack (eds.), *ESVP* (2002), p. 182; A. Treacher, *From Civilian to Military Actor: The EU's Resistable Transformation*, 9 EFAR (2004), p. 49 at 50.

14   A long hour, *The Economist*, 22 July 1995, p. 48.

15   An Agenda for Peace – Preventive diplomacy, peacemaking and peace-keeping, Report of the Secretary-General, UN-Doc. A/47/277 – S/24111, 17 June 1992.

16   EU-ISS, *European Defence, proposal for a White Paper* (2004), p. 39.

17   Supplement to an Agenda for Peace: Position Paper of the Secretary-General on the Occasion of the Fiftieth Birthday of the United Nations, UN-Doc. A/50/60- S/1995/1, 3 Jan. 1995; *cf.* M. Kiani, *The Changing Dimensions of UN Peacekeeping*, 24 Strategic Studies 1 (2004), p. 177 at 193.

18   On these terms in detail, see Introduction – On terminology in international security.

terminology sometimes different from the UN's[19]) admitted the need also for 'tasks of combat forces in crisis management, including peacemaking'.[20]

Bosnia

At the outbreak of the wars in former Yugoslavia, there were a number of potential international organisations with some security function in Europe: NATO, the EC, the OSCE, the WEU, and of course the UN. Until summer of 1995, however, none of them managed, in the end, to prevent the hostilities on the ground. The hybrid 'framework of interlocking security institutions'[21] soon came to be mocked by the term 'interblocking' institutions. Certainly an 'institutional vacuum' existed in the Balkans from 1991–1995, measured not by the number of available institutions, but by its incapacity to stop the war. It was also a conceptual vacuum which was only filled in 1995, albeit reluctantly, by NATO.[22] The Alliance was not constrained by the strictly-defined peacekeeping limits which had prevented the UN from developing a credible deterrence on the ground.[23] NATO's military action was backed by active American diplomacy, both of which brought the Bosnian war to an effective end.

One of the first institutions to devise a plan for 'robust' intervention in Bosnia was the WEU at the request of the European Council in September 1991. The WEU examined several military options, the most far-reaching of which included a division made up of 20 000 troops of WEU member States which would be able to implement an expanded peacekeeping option.[24] This, and also the more limited versions of the proposal, however, failed to find political consensus among the main

---

19   For the difference in terminology between the EU and the United Nations, see *ibid.*

20   Western European Union Council of Ministers, Petersberg Declaration, Bonn, 19 June 1992, II. para. 4.

21   M. Wörner, *A Vigorous Alliance - A Motor for Peaceful Change in Europe*, NATO Review (online edition), No. 6, Vol. 40. (Dec. 1992); *cf.* U. Nerlich, *The relationship between a European common defence and NATO, the OSCE and the United Nations*, in: L. Martin / J. Roper (eds.), *Towards a common defence policy* (1995), p. 69 at 96.

22   D.A. Leurdijk, *The United Nations and NATO in Former Yugoslavia, 1991-1996 – Limits to Diplomacy and Force* (1996), pp. 17–9; J. Wouters / F. Naert, *How effective is the European Security Architecture? Lessons from Bosnia and Kosovo*, 50 ICLQ (2001), p. 540 at pp. 551, 572; A. Pradetto, *Funktionen militärischer Konfliktregelung durch die NATO bei der Neuordnung Europas*, in H. Timmermann / A. Pradetto (eds.), *Die NATO auf dem Weg ins 21. Jahrhundert* (2002), p. 191 at 194.

23   See above Introduction – On terminology in international security; *cf.* E. Greco, *UN-NATO Interaction: Lessons from the Yugoslav Experience*, 32 The International Spectator 3/4 (1997), p. 121 at 124–6.

24   W. Bradford, *The WEU ... the new sick man of Europe* (2000), p. 31–2. The figure of 20 000 is debated today. *Cf.* H. Beuve-Mery / P. Grasset, *La défense européenne: rapports transatlantiques*, 57 Défense nationale 11 (2000), p. 17 at 31 [15 000]; S. Biscop, *Able and Willing? Assessing the EU's Capacity for Military Action*, 9 EFAR (2004), p. 509 at 511 [30 000].

actors of the EU. In theory a sufficient collective military capacity to decisively intervene to prevent the impending genocide would have existed.[25] The United States, at this early stage, did not want to become involved in a conflict that was then deemed an entirely European affair which involved no strategic American interests.[26] Moreover, there were budgetary concerns limiting the US freedom of action.[27] Diplomatic efforts such as the Carrington-Cutiliero partition plan of 1992[28] and later the Vance-Owen plan[29] followed but, in the absence of a credible threat to use force from Western European countries (or from anyone else), were easily rejected by the fighting parties.[30] The EU's Common Foreign and Security Policy (CFSP) created by the Maastricht Treaty of 1992, went as far as recognising the need for a common security approach for exactly this kind of scenario. This was done mainly at the insistence of France, for the reason of the perceived gap in relative military capacity with the United States, which had already been starkly felt by the French military in the Gulf War of 1991.[31] But the need for European defence integration in face of the European 'embarrassment' in the Balkans was found also in the Dutch Queen's Speech in 1993.[32] The statement of purpose in Art. J.4 of the TEU to provide for a future European defence could not, however, overcome the political mindset of mainstream European statesmanship at the time which was still mostly occupied with digesting the end of the Cold War:[33] Large projects such as German reunification, the completion of the common market and the creation of the European Monetary Union (EMU),[34] problems such as the general lack of orientation as to the new European security architecture, coupled with the EC institutional requirement of unanimity for decisions with defence implications, all made it difficult to find fast and effective responses to the Yugoslav crisis which developed so fast at Europe's doorstep.

---

25   *Ibid.* The proposition that European militaries would have been fully capable of intervening at such a grand scale in Yugoslavia, however, is not unproblematic. Most of them were still primarily geared for Cold War-era scenarios of territorial defence. *Cf.* EU-ISS, *White Paper* (2004), p. 40.

26   EU-ISS, *White Paper* (2004), p. 40.

27   J. Howorth, *The ultimate challenge* (2000), p. 21.

28   *Ibid.*, p. 35.

29   *Ibid.*, p. 43.

30   *Cf.* E. Yesson, *NATO, EU and Russia: Reforming Europe's Security Institutions*, 6 EFAR (2001), p. 197 at 213.

31   J. Howorth, *The ultimate challenge* (2000), p. 18; WEU Assembly Doc. 1333, *Parliamentary debates on security policy under the Maastricht Treaty*, Report by Mr. Nuñez (Rapp.), 30 Oct. 1992, para. 51.

32   Cited in: A.G. Harryvan / J. van der Harst, *A Threat of Rivalry? Dutch Views on European Security Today*, in: M. Dumoulin, *La Communauté européenne de défense, leçons pour demain?* (2000), p. 401 at p. 411.

33   *Cf.* J. Herbst, *Peacekeeping by the European Union*, in: A. Bodnar et al. (eds.), *The Emerging Constitutional Law of the European Union – German and Polish Perspectives* (2003), p. 413.

34   T.A. Chafos, *The European Union's Rapid Reaction Force ...* (2003), p. 31.

The Dayton peace accords[35] were concluded after NATO's air strikes against the Bosnian Serbs in late August of 1995, and after the simultaneous successful Croatian Krajina offensive that same summer (Croatian forces had been armed and trained by the Americans for years previously). Among the hard lessons drawn by Europe from this event were:

1. that civil war situations outside the territories of EU member States could affect major European security interests, due to proximity, a mass exodus of refugees, genocide or even an escalation into the EU security zone;[36]
2. that, owing to the impotence of EU 'civil power' in the face of such a hard security challenge,[37] solutions to security problems of the scale of the war in Bosnia and Croatia depended largely on the United States' will to get involved;
3. that this dependency could be against the interest of major European countries.

The interplay between political and military objectives in Bosnia had become evident, for example, to British and French commanders of UNPROFOR who feared retaliation of the Serbs against their peacekeeping troops in response to the American air strikes in 1994 and 1995.[38] For similar reasons of the vulnerable position of their peacekeepers, European States had opposed in unison the idea of lifting the arms embargo against Bosnia. In the United States, in contrast, the idea of giving Bosnians the 'just chance to defend themselves' gained significant popularity, even though the Clinton Administration did support the embargo until the end of the war. Devoid of its own autonomous military options, however, Europe more or less had had to accept the solutions delivered by the United States to end the conflict. British military circles in particular, evaluating their operational experiences in UNPROFOR with their French counterparts, began to think about other options,[39] in contrast to the traditional unconditional Atlanticist orientation of the British government,

---

35   General Framework Agreement for Peace in Bosnia and Herzegovina (Dayton, 21 Nov. 1995), 35 ILM 75 (1996).

36   K. Kaiser, *Challenges and contingencies for European defence policy*, in: L. Martin / J. Roper (eds.) *Towards a common defence policy*, WEU-ISS (1995), p. 29 at 34. It will be remembered that in the short war of secession of Slovenia in 1991, Yugoslav fighter planes briefly penetrated into the airspace of Austria, then already an EU accession candidate.

37   A. Treacher, *From Civilian to Military Actor: The EU's Resistable Transformation*, 9 EFAR (2004), p. 49 at 57.

38   *Cf.* D.A. Leurdijk, *The United Nations and NATO in Former Yugoslavia* (1996), p. 7; K. Shake, *Constructive Duplication* (2002), p. 25.

39   *Cf.* N.M. Abbasi, *Evolving a Common European Defence* (2001), p. 77 at 81; A. Treacher, *From Civilian to Military Actor: The EU's Resistable Transformation*, 9 EFAR (2004), p. 49 at 57.

rejecting so far any European-only solution.[40] The Union's institutional response to the dilemma of its military incapacity was to provide itself with a 'security arm' through the WEU with its Petersberg tasks, in the Amsterdam Treaty of 1996. This did not add one soldier or transport plane to future European peacekeeping efforts, but it did insert, for the first time, into the process of EU integration an official mandate to develop a peacekeeping capability, if necessary of the robust kind (peace enforcement, called 'peacemaking'). In addition, the WEU had, since the Alliance's Berlin Summit of June 1996, also the possibility to draw on some NATO resources, resulting in the first connection of the EU with NATO.

When civil strife erupted in Albania in 1997, the EU played no role in the eventual intervention; 'Operation Alba', led by Italy, helped to stabilise the situation there. This disappointed many because, at that time, the Union already had some limited crisis management means at its disposal.[41] Use of the WEU was vetoed by Britain and Germany.[42]

Kosovo

The Kosovo war in 1999 confirmed Europe's military shortcomings (despite warnings to heed the lessons from years of failure in Bosnia[43]) and brought home again the disadvantageous political position of having to accept faits accomplis in peace solutions which were dictated by the American foreign policy priorities. The Clinton Administration categorically ruled out the option of committing troops for a ground campaign to drive out the Serbs from Kosovo and stop the massacre and exodus of the ethnic Albanians. Without the US, the option of staging a military ground campaign with European troops alone seemed too risky to military planners. Therefore, the intervention was executed from safe air distance alone. In air warfare, American military supremacy, thanks to technology advances unmatched by European militaries in the 1990s, was even more pronounced. European warplanes could only contribute a small fraction to the campaign.[44] In airlift (that is, the capacity to transport an army

---

40   Towards the end of the British Major government in 1996, however, even the Conservative leadership, traditionally with a staunch Atlanticist orientation, became convinced that some type of 'European solution' had to be found. *Cf.* J. Howorth, *The ultimate challenge* (2000), p. 22.

41   WEU Assembly Doc. 1564, *Draft Recommendation on Maastricht II: the WEU Assembly's proposals for European cooperation on security and defence – reply to the annual report of the Council*, Report by Mr. Antretter and Mrs. Squarcialupi (Rapps.), 9 May 1997, preamb. para. (ii).

42   C. Grant, *Can Britain lead in Europe?* (1998), p. 45. Unfortunately, Grant does not elaborate on the political reasons of Britain and Germany for doing so.

43   D. Scherff, *Die Fähigkeit der Europäischen Union zum aktiven Krisenmanagement: Lehren aus den Vermittlungsbemühungen 1991/92 während des jugoslawischen Bürgerkriegs und der derzeitige Konflikt im Kosovo*, 47 Südosteuropa (1998), p. 298 at 333; F. Heisbourg, *L'Europe de la défense dans l'Alliance atlantique*, 64 Politique étrangère (1999), p. 219 at 231.

44   Nearly 80 percent of the intelligence and high-risk combat sorties were conducted by the United States. For a detailed discussion, see J.E. Peters et al., *European Contributions*

at will to faraway places) the situation was similar.[45] The campaign was intended to make Milosevic back down fast, but it took much longer than had been hoped by NATO allies, while pictures of the suffering Kosovar refugees were reaching European and US living rooms night by night. For some European countries, such as Britain, which had emphasised the humanitarian rationale and urgency for the operation from the start, this situation was politically hard to bear. Relations among the NATO member States suffered strains accordingly. At the end of 1999, from a Washington point of view, the Alliance had lost value. Indirectly, this led to a shift in the debate on European defence: initiatives to this debate would in the future firstly come from the EU.[46]

In the peace stabilisation and implementation operations in both Bosnia (IFOR/ SFOR) and Kosovo (KFOR), however, European troops took the largest share. Foreign aid for national reconstruction was also predominantly European (both from member States and the Union). The sobering lesson drawn in Europe was that, while the United States with its highly mobile and technologically able forces was the only country with the means to solve a humanitarian crisis by force, the post-conflict 'cleaning up' fell to Europe more or less by default. Post-conflict rebuilding of a society is crucial for long-term peace. Europeans, most interested in such a peace due to their proximity to the region, did not resent peace-building, even if, compared to US air strikes, it was less heroic (in the eyes of the world press) and thanked (by the local Balkan populations). It did mean, however, missing the opportunity of having a say in the first phase: if and how to intervene militarily. The problem European leaders had with such a division of labour was that they would be left having to rebuild a country while having had little say on the initial intervention. In the discussions before Operation Allied Force, the link of this European deficiency in decision-shaping to the European argument in the intervention question was clear. It related to the post-conflict consequences: the ruling out a ground campaign exacerbated the humanitarian catastrophe and the number of refugees. Presumably, an early and massive intervention in early spring 1999 (or in late 1998) could have prevented the worst of the atrocities committed by the Serb forces in Kosovo. The need for Europe to start doing more on its own, particularly in its own 'back yard',[47] was thus starting to be voiced with increased vehemence after Operation Allied

---

to Operation Allied Force – Implications for Transatlantic Cooperation, MR-1391-AF, RAND Corp. (2001), pp. 18. *Cf.* T.A. Chafos, *The European Union's Rapid Reaction Force ...* (2003), p. 34; N.M. Abbasi, *Security Issues between the US and EU within NATO* (2000), p. 83 at p. 98.

45   J.P.H. Cazeau, *European security and defense policy under the gun*, 10 U.Miami Int.Comp.L.Rev. (2002), p. 51 at 58.

46   J.-Y. Haine, *ESDP and NATO*, in: N. Gnesotto (ed.), *EU Security and Defence Policy – The first five years* (2004), EU-ISS, p. 131 at 136.

47   The call for European action to prevent crises overseas, however, had already been evinced throughout the 1990s with reference to Somalia or Rwanda. See e.g. WEU Assembly Doc. 1439, *A European security policy*, Report by Mr. Soell (Rapp.), 10 Nov. 1994, para. 4.

Force.[48] Underlying these voices was the realisation that the United States would not be eager to intervene in every regional European conflict with its own forces,[49] indeed, that this would be less and less likely given the gradual reorientation of US strategic interests away from Europe.[50] US Deputy Secretary of State Strobe Talbott observed in the autumn of 1999 that Europeans were 'determined never again to feel quite so dominated by the US as they were during Kosovo'.[51] As a result, even while the air bombings in Serbia were still taking place, the European Council in Cologne decided to create new EU military bodies.[52] As J.A.C. Lewis argued, 'Many believe that Kosovo has done more for the cause of a European defense identity in the past six months than the previous six years of deliberation'.[53]

In terms of European foreign policy, however, the Kosovo experience was not catastrophic. The crucial mediating role played for example by M. Ahtisaari in the spring of 1999 was a success for the CFSP.[54] This stood in contrast to the situation during the Bosnian war, where three major European powers had pursued their

---

48   British-Italian Summit, London, 19–20 July 1999, Joint Declaration Launching European Defence Capabilities Initiative, CP 47, p. 46, para. 1; *Cf.* S. Blockmans, *A New Crisis Manager at the Horizon – The Case of the European Union*, 13 LJIL (2000), p. 255; C. Grant, *European defence post-Kosovo?*, CER (1999); A. Moens, *Developing a European intervention force*, 55 International Journal (1999/2000), p. 247 at 248.

49   J. Herbst, *Peacekeeping by the European Union* (2003), p. 415; B.R. Posen, *ESDP and the Structure of World Power*, 39 The International Spectator 1 (2004), p. 5 at 14; F. Heisbourg, *US-European relations* (2004), p. 119 at 121. The fruits of such considerations became evident as soon as the EU took over its first peacekeeping mission in Macedonia in spring 2003, *cf.* T.C. Salmon / A.J.K. Shepherd, *Toward a European Army* (2003), p. 78.

50   *Cf.* F.S. Larrabee, *ESDP and NATO: Assuring Complementarity*, 39 The International Spectator 1 (2004), p. 51 at 53. Warnings against such a development were voiced in the US Congress as early as 2000, *cf.* 106th Cong., 2nd Sess., 146 Cong. Rec. S 4037 at S 4079 (Sen. J. Biden): 'If the U.S. Congress were to compel the President of the United States to unilaterally withdraw all U.S. combat troops from the NATO force in Kosovo, you can rest assured that the Europeans would get the message that the ESDP is the wave of the future, not NATO. I can hear the grumbling all over Western Europe: "The French are right. We'd better have our own army, because we can't count on the U.S. in NATO any more."'

51   Speech at the Royal Institute for International Affairs, London, 7 Oct. 1999, see Financial Times, 8 Oct. 1999, p. 8.

52   On these institutions more in detail, see below, under 'The Legal Base'. *Cf.* A.M. Rizzo, *Towards a European Defence Policy*, 36 The International Spectator 3 (2001), pp. 47–48.

53   J.A.C. Lewis, *EU Military Maneuvering*, 32 Jane's Defence Weekly 23 (1999), p. 27; C. Deubner had already stated in 1991, that the crisis in Yugoslavia 'had done more for the development of the EC than the latter had helped Yugoslavia' (translation by the author, cited in: G. Koslowski, *Die NATO und der Krieg in Bosnien-Herzegowina – Deutschland, Frankreich und die USA im internationalen Krisenmanagement* (1995), p. 146); *cf.* A. Treacher, *The EU's Resistable Transformation* (2004), p. 49 at 63.

54   *Cf.* U. Schmalz, *Aufbruch zu neuer Handlungsfähigkeit: Die Gemeinsame Außen-, Sicherheits- und Verteidigungspolitik unter deutscher Ratspräsidentschaft*, 22 Integration (1999), p. 191 at 192.

own path in the Contact Group, in the absence of common action by the Union.[55] A fundamental lesson in diplomatic crisis management, evident since the outbreak of hostilities in 1992 in Croatia and Bosnia, was the value of prevention.

Political disunity in the EU, along with initial hesitance to use force abroad in a misplaced emphasis on economic and cooperative instruments,[56] was likewise perceived as a central failure preventing decisive action in the Balkan wars. As recently as 2000, US academics doubted that the EU would ever live up to this challenge.[57]

The recognition that some military muscle was an essential ingredient to prevent humanitarian catastrophes was already starting to show effects in some efforts such as the Franco-British St-Malo Declaration of Dec. 1998.[58] But the birth-hour of ESDP came too late to have an effect on the Kosovo crisis.[59]

By 2001, however, the EU was in a different position. ESDP was now more developed, it had the first institutional structures, most notably the High Representative, who, appointed in 1999, creatively used the office to some success. Early-warning capacity was also much improved, with the Early Warning Unit since 1999 and the Union's first military structures in place since the beginning of 2001.[60] The collective will of member States not to repeat the mistake of letting a crisis escalate because of European disagreements was also much stronger. A certain strategic culture already prevailed.

Under these improved conditions the EU soon faced two more potential crises: the inter-ethnic tension in Macedonia and the looming break-up of rump Yugoslavia into its Serbian and Montenegrin parts.

Lessons learnt: Macedonia and Serbia-Montenegro

In Macedonia, the growing tension between the Slav and Albanian population parts was recognised early enough by the EU to force the parties to the conference table, eventually producing the Ohrid Framework Agreement of summer 2001,[61] which to

---

55   H. van den Broek, *Why Europe Needs a Common Foreign and Security Policy*, 1 EFAR (1996), p. 1 at 3.

56   W. Bradford, *The WEU ... the new sick man of Europe* (2000), p. 46 attributes this anti-militarist strand in European foreign policy, harmful to the Balkans crisis, to the EU's four neutral member States.

57   W. Bradford, *The WEU ... the new sick man of Europe* (2000), p. 15.

58   See below, at p. 66.

59   *Cf. EU cavalry arrives too late for Kosovo,* European Voice (online edition), Vol. 5, No. 9, 4 March 1999.

60   On the institutions of ESDP for early warning, see below, the Legal Base.

61   Ohrid Framework Agreement, 13 Aug. 2001, http://www.coe.int/T/E/Legal_affairs/ Legal_co-operation/Police_and_internal_security/Police_cooperation/OHRID%20Agreeme nt%2013august2001.asp (visited 11/08/2004). *Cf.*, D.L. Ludlow, *Preventive Peacemaking in Macedonia: An Assessment of U.N. Good Offices Diplomacy*, Brigham Young University Law Review (2003), p. 761 at 786–8.

this day serves as the main framework of reference for reconciliation in that country. Observers attribute this success partly to the fact that 'the European Union has absorbed and attempted to apply the lessons of the crises in Bosnia-Herzegovina and Kosovo in its approach [there]'.[62]

Again, in 2002, EU diplomacy prevented break-up of rump Yugoslavia, by giving it a new constitution[63] and renaming it Serbia-Montenegro.

Those two last cases are examples of successful preventive intervention by the EU at the right time, nipping a possible later conflict in the bud. They were helped by a powerful carrot: the long-term perspective of eventual EU membership for all countries involved. But the stick proved as influential: the EU's voice was heeded more, because it was also silently backed up by some military might (and the political will to use it if necessary). It seems, therefore, that the EU has indeed drawn its lesson from the Balkan wars. By 2001, it was difficult to detect even a nuance of difference between Berlin, London and Paris on Balkans policy, in contrast to the summer of 1991.[64] The military part of the lesson was manifestly the Union's new defence dimension: ESDP.

Internal reasons: the logic of European integration

Functionalist theory about the European Community has long claimed that integration in one sector (for example freedom of goods) over time also leads to integration in other areas (for example competition, environment), because it creates a certain degree of systemic distortion and inconsistency in those areas not yet integrated. This 'integrationist pull' is often described as the 'spill-over effect'. Functionalist spill-over refers to a long-term development, and is in tune with what political scientists describe as the gradualist approach (that is, in small, separate unconnected steps) as opposed to an evolutive approach to European integration (that is, developing from a core, following a pre-determined DNA-style 'logic'): sometimes process counts over results because, in the long term, process *leads* to results. From a legal perspective, the small steps that lead towards further integration in any policy are not only found in primary Community law, that is, in formal treaty amendments. Secondary legislation, regulations and directives, as well as other non-binding instruments or legislation limited in scope, all in execution of 'mandates' derived from primary EU law, are the prime playing field for this process. The traditionally integration-friendly role played by the Commission and the European Court of Justice (each in their own different way) furthermore enhances this development.

---

62   D. Smith, *Europe's Peacebuilding Hour? Past Failures, Future Challenges*, 55 Journal of International Affairs, Columbia University (2002), p. 441 at 445.

63   *Cf.* A. Jakáb, *The Constitutional Charter of 'Serbia and Montenegro'* (English summary), 63 HJIL (2003), pp. 814–5.

64   J. Howorth, *European Defence and the Changing Politics of the EU*, 39 JCMS (2001), p. 765 at 787.

Functionalist logic does not confine itself to the supranational first pillar of the European Communities. The intergovernmental second and third pillars are likewise affected, although their intergovernmentalism has acted as a break in this regard, as they are largely exempt from Commission and ECJ integrationist influence. Nevertheless, it has been argued since Maastricht that the Union could not remain a fully integrated body economically without also assuming some political weight on the world stage:[65] further political integration was in a way dictated,[66] natural and indispensable[67]. Further, no integrated EU foreign policy towards third States could be credible without a defence component. Enter the argument to include the WEU's Art. V mutual defence commitment into the EU system, which was forwarded by some in the debates leading up to the 1996 IGC as a 'logical conclusion'.[68] Even though this did not happen, a sound case has repeatedly been made for tightening the relationship between defence and integration.[69] The creation of ESDP after the Amsterdam Treaty in 1997 was thus a logical next step to the CFSP,[70] also in tune with popular expectations by many Europeans.[71]

A next argument for developing ESDP is its great integrative potential[72] as a catalyst[73] for the EU as a whole. After the completion of EMU, the EU's internal need for new dynamism may indeed be great.[74] The process of European integration may in its entirety have reached the point where adding a military capacity can help it work more comprehensively.[75] Bradford even argues that 'continued failure to craft

---

65   WEU Assembly Doc. 1333, *Parliamentary debates on security policy under the Maastricht Treaty*, Report by Mr. Nuñez (Rapp.), 30 Oct. 1992, para. 136 (debates in the Spanish parliament).

66   *Cf.* A. Pliakos, *The Common European Policy of Security and Defense: Some Considerations Relating to its Constitutional Identity*, 6 Col. J.Eur. L. (Fall 2000), p. 275 at 281.

67   C. von Buttlar, *The European Union's Security and Defence Policy – A Regional Effort within the Atlantic Alliance*, in: A. Bodnar et al. (eds.), *The Emerging Constitutional Law of the European Union* (2003), p. 387.

68   WEU Assembly Doc. 1564 (1997), para. 112.

69   A. Menon, *Defence Policy and Integration in Western Europe*, 17 CSP (1996), p. 264 at 281; *cf.* N. Winn, *Towards a Common European Security and Defence Policy? The Debate on NATO, the European Army and Transatlantic Security*, 8 Geopolitics 2 (2003), p. 47 at 51.

70   R. de Wijk, *The Reform of ESDP and EU–NATO Cooperation*, 39 The International Spectator 1 (2004), p. 71 at 72.

71   F.S. Larrabee, *ESDP and NATO: Assuring Complementarity* (2004), p. 51 at 53.

72   H. Ojanen, *Theories at a loss? EU–NATO fusion* (2002), p. 7.

73   J. Howorth, *European Defence and the Changing Politics of the EU*, 39 JCMS (2001), p. 765 at 787.

74   H. Ojanen, *Theories at a loss? EU–NATO fusion* (2002), p. 13.

75   G. Robertson, cited in: V. Epping, *Rechtliche Rahmenbedingungen der Gemeinsamen Außen- und Sicherheitspolitik der EU*, 44 NZWR 3 (2002), p. 90 at 107. *Cf.* K.A. Eliassen (*Introduction: The New European Foreign and Security Policy Agenda*, in: *Id.* (ed.), *Foreign and Security Policy in the European Union* (1998), p. 1) who argued that 'the EU "is only as strong as its weakest link" which, at present, is to be found in the second pillar'.

a European defense identity and to meld it to effective European security institutions will ... ultimately ... threaten the project of European integration'.[76] Even within the second pillar, the long-term relationship between the CFSP and ESDP goes both ways: ESDP was born out of the CFSP, but there is also increasingly a feedback effect: activity in defence matters creates new common European interests on the world scene.[77] For instance, already in the mid-1990s discussions about European defence began to have a direct bearing on prospects for more autonomy on the world stage, particularly in relations with the United States.[78] More recently, it has been seen that the bulk of agreements of the EU with third parties under the second pillar (Art. 24 TEU) have in fact been concluded on ESDP matters.[79]

Independently of these theoretical considerations, defence integration may happen also 'from the simple reality that the politics of security and crisis management demand rapidity and efficiency of decision-making'.[80]

The logic of integration does not stop here. Voices are being raised today who call for turning defence into a supranational policy area, that is, ceding substantial parts of the inner core of sovereignty from member States to the Union, alone able to coordinate and pool military resources without leading to their inefficient allocation and 'redundant planning'.[81] The European Armaments, Research and Military Capabilities Agency is a first step in this direction.[82] Already today, several of the European Commission's competencies have defence implications, such as the consolidation of the defence industry, military research, and the part-financing of peacekeeping operations.[83]

Even though there is some support for departing from the current strict intergovernmental base of ESDP, particularly among German scholars and

---

76   W. Bradford, *The WEU ... the new sick man of Europe* (2000), p. 13.

77   A.M. Rizzo, *Towards a European Defence Policy*, 36 The International Spectator 3 (2001), p. 47 at 49.

78   M. d'Oléon / M. Jopp, *The way ahead for European defence integration*, in: L. Martin/J. Roper (eds.) *Towards a common defence policy*, WEU-ISS (1995), p. 99 at 100.

79   On these agreements in detail, see below Chapter 4 (EU–NATO Institutional Aspects).

80   J. Howorth, *European Defence and the Changing Politics of the EU*, 39 JCMS (2001), p. 765 at 769.

81   E.g. H. Ojanen, *Theories at a loss? EU–NATO fusion* (2002), pp. 8–12; H. Borchert, *The Future of Europe's Security and Defense Policy (ESDP) and the Limits of Intergovernmentalism*, in: A. Weidemann / A. Simon (eds.), *The Future of ESDP, A Conference Report 'The (not so) Common European Security and Defence Policy'* (2003), p. 55 at 60; T.A. Chafos, *The European Union's Rapid Reaction Force ...* (2003), p. 68.

82   Council Joint Action 2004/551/CFSP on the establishment of the European Defence Agency, 12 July 2004, OJ L 245/17 of 17/07/04; *cf.* Art. III-311, Treaty establishing a Constitution for Europe, 6 Aug. 2004, CIG 87/04.

83   H. Boguslawska, *Le lien transatlantique* (2003), NATO-EAPC Fellowship papers 2001–2003, http://www.nato.int/acad/fellow/01-03/boguslowska.pdf (visited 11/08/2004), p. 55.

practitioners,[84] opposition to any such move comes from the most influential camps in the EU: the British have traditionally pointed out that in defence, intergovernmentalism is what works best.[85] Even French military circles are loath to give up the last anchor of the security of the nation to an international body 'the failure of which cannot be ruled out' (sic).[86] In addition, supranationalisation of the second pillar finds enemies among those who adhere to the lofty goal of Europe as a civilian, rather than military, power.[87]

Not far from the thought of a supranational European defence policy is that of forming a true sovereign political union, starting with the CFSP.[88] Defence is at the heart of state sovereignty,[89] for 'it is beyond any doubt that the ultimate expression of a nation-state's sovereignty lies in its power of wartime and peacetime leagues and alliances. Implicating the life and death of the citizens, this power justly symbolizes a great historical force'.[90] R. Cooper writes that 'foreign policy is about war and peace, and countries that only do peace are missing half of the story – perhaps the more important part'.[91] The 'country' he is referring to is, incidentally, the EU. Transferring this concept of sovereignty to the European level – at the risk of over-simplifying – the meaning of 'an ever closer union among the peoples of Europe' (Art. 1 TEU)

---

84   E.g. M. Kremer / U. Schmalz, *Nach Nizza – Perspektiven der GESVP* (2001), p. 167 at 173; R. Seidelmann, *Das ESVP-Projekt und die EU-Krisenreaktionskräfte: Konstruktionsdefizite und politische Perspektiven*, 25 Integration 2 (2002), p. 111 at 116.

85   Mr. Heathcoat-Amory, Secretary of State for the Foreign Office, *The next step for the Western European Union: a British view*, The World Today, July 1994, p. 133 at 135.

86   'A realistic stance should require us not to slip the prey for the shadow, admitting that a failure of the EU still cannot be ruled out; it should therefore remain part of our present planning. The EU as it stands is not yet solid enough for us to start relying on new defence mechanisms to the detriment of our existing national defence.' S. Vinçon et al., *Défense: quels projets après 2002?*, 57 Défense nationale 6 (2001), p. 82 at 97 [translation by the author].

87   H. Maull, cited in: S. Stavridis, *'Militarising' the EU: the Concept of Civilian Power Europe Revisited*, 34 The International Spectator 4 (2001), p. 43 at 49.

88   S. Blockmans, *A New Crisis Manager at the Horizon* (2000), p. 255.

89   Mr. Bérégovoy, statement at the forty-fifth session of the Institut des hautes études de défense nationale, reprinted in: WEU Assembly Doc. 1333, *Parliamentary debates on security policy under the Maastricht Treaty*, Report by Mr. Nuñez (Rapp.), 30 Oct. 1992, para. 62 (debates in the French National Assembly); *Cf.* D. Krüger (*Die EVG – Ein Vorbild für eine zukünftige Europaarmee?*, in: W. Hoyer / G.F. Kaldrack (eds.), *ESVP* (2002), p. 43 at 57) who emphasises possible historical parallels to the European Defence Community project of the 1950s in this regard. *Cf.* the remarks of the Belgian foreign minister on 10 Dec. 1951, cited in: J. Trempont, *La communauté Européenne de Défense*, 1 ICLQ (1952), p. 519 at 532.

90   A. Pliakos, *The CESDP*, 6 Col. J.Eur. L. (Fall 2000), p. 275 at 281.

91   R. Cooper, *The breaking of nations* (2003), p. 162.

becomes clearer.[92] Security policy relates to the finality of European integration.[93] Hence the description of defence as the EU's 'ultimate challenge'.[94] In one of the many conferences held on ESDP during 2003, in Heidelberg (Germany), the final discussion produced a universal consensus that this development is eventually linked to full statehood, and that ESDP holds the potential to give the Union the decisive push in that direction.[95]

THE LEGAL BASE[96]

ESDP is based on Art. 17 TEU: the CFSP comprises 'all questions relating to the security of the Union, including the progressive framing of a common defence policy, which might lead to a common defence'.[97] There are no further definitions of 'security' or 'defence' in the TEU, but para. 2 of Art. 17 circumscribes activity meant by the 'common defence policy': 'humanitarian and rescue tasks, peacekeeping tasks and tasks of combat forces in crisis management' (the so-called 'Petersberg tasks'[98]). The term 'common defence' clearly means something different: this is collective

---

92   On this wording, see e.g. P. Kirchhof, *Die rechtliche Struktur der Europäischen Union als Staatenverbund*, in: A. von Bogdandy (ed.), *Europäisches Verfassungsrecht* (2003), p. 893.

93   U. Schmalz, *Aufbruch zu neuer Handlungsfähigkeit* (1999), p. 191 at 201; *cf.* A. Peters, *European Democracy after the 2003 Convention*, 41 CMLR (2004), p. 37 at 83, who calls defence a 'question of constitutional importance' for the EU.

94   J. Howorth, *The ultimate challenge* (2000), p. 97.

95   M. Reichard, *Conference Report – 'The (not so) Common European Foreign and Security Policy'– Max Planck Institute for Comparative Public Law and International Law – Heidelberg, Germany, 19–20 September 2003*, 5 German Law Journal 2 (2004), p. 177 at 183; Max Planck Institute for Comparative Public Law and International Law, Heidelberg, Tätigkeitsbericht 2003 (A. van Aaken, ed.), p. 141. *Cf.* R.A. Wessel (*Revisiting the International Legal Status of the EU*, 5 EFAR (2000), p. 507 at 523 n. 58) who notes that the common constitutive criteria of a State are, in theory, all assembled for the EU. In this sense also K. Gerteiser, *Die Sicherheits- und Verteidigungspolitik der Europäischen Union* (2002), p. 261–2; T. Tilikainen, 6 EFAR (2001), p. 223 at 228; *contra* A. Deighton, *The European Security and Defence Policy*, 40 JCMS (2002), p. 719 at p. 728.

96   The structure of this part is partly based on B. Martenczuk, *The Legal Bases of ESDP*, in: A. Weidemann / A. Simon (eds.), *The Future of ESDP* (2003), pp. 29–32.

97   This formulation was only arrived at after bitter negotiation (EU-ISS, *European Defence, proposal for a White Paper* (2004), p. 38). There were successively futile attempts to rephrase this possibility to a more concrete goal, e.g. before the 1997 IGC, 'in the perspective of a common defence' (WEU Assembly Doc. 1564 (1997), Draft Recommendation, p. 62). Instead, all the Amsterdam Treaty changed was to drop the qualification 'in time' in Art. J.4 (now Art. 17) TEU. On this change, see e.g. H. Neuhold, *The Provisions of the Amsterdam Treaty on the CFSP: Cosmetic Operation or Genuine Progress?*, in: G. Hafner et al. (eds.), Liber Amicorum for Professor I. Seidl-Hohenveldern, in honour of his 80th birthday (1998), pp. 495.

98   See WEU Petersberg Declaration, 1992, fn. 20.

self-defence in meaning of Art. 51 UN Charter. In the TEU, it is a possibility even further in the future and more uncertain than the common defence policy. Whether a future 'common defence' also contains the possibility of an integrated European army (along the lines of the EDC in the 1950s) is an interesting question,[99] but outside the scope of this book.

Art. 17 thus contains a mandate for the Council (the central decision-making organ in the CFSP) to gradually develop a defence policy. As any such move has defence implications, the Council (and any body under it) can only proceed by unanimity (Art. 23 TEU).

INSTITUTIONS[100]

At present, the Council has created three sub-bodies for the Union's common defence policy, ranked roughly in hierarchical order:[101]

1. The Political and Security Committee[102] (PSC/COPS, Art. 25 TEU) monitors, examines, supervises, and also reports to the Council, which may delegate decision-making power to it for the duration of a crisis management operation regarding its political control and strategic direction. It has a central role to play in the definition and follow-up to the EU's response to a crisis. It also manages regular consultation with third parties (such as NATO) on all defence-related issues. It is composed of senior national representatives at ambassadorial level.
2. The EU Military Committee[103] (EUMC) provides the PSC with military advice, worked-out planning options and recommendations. This includes, for example, Concepts of Operations and Operation Plans. It is composed of the national Chiefs of Defence, represented by their military representatives,

---

99   *Cf.* H. Neuhold, *Terminological Ambiguity* (2005), p. 1 at 4 w.f.r.

100   A good broad overview over the institutions of ESDP can be found, e.g. in T.C. Salmon / A.J.K. Shepherd, *Toward a European Army* (2003), pp. 87–112.

101   The structure of these three bodies was in part modelled on that in NATO and the WEU, without, however, repeating the separation between the civil and military branches. This mirrored the experience already gained by some EU member States under the regime of the WEU in its regular institutionalised contacts with NATO (*cf.* M. Warnken, *Der Handlungsrahmen der EU* (2002), pp. 133–5, with further references). See, e.g., the German Presidency Paper, Bonn, 29 Feb. 1999, Information Reflection at WEU on Europe's Security and Defence, CP 47, p. 14 at 15: 'What would be the permanent body equivalent to the WEU Council?'. F. Dehousse / B. Galer, *De Saint-Malo à Feira: Les Enjeux de la Renaissance du Projet de Défense Européenne*, 52 Studia diplomatica (1999), p. 1 at pp. 41–44; *cf.* E. Yesson, *Reforming Europe's Security Institutions* (2001), p. 197 at 206, n. 25.

102   Established by Council Decision of 22 January 2001 setting up the Political and Security Committee (2001/78/CFSP), OJ EC L 27/1 of 30/1/2001.

103   Established by Council Decision of 22 January 2001 setting up the Military Committee (2001/79/CFSP), OJ EC L 27/4 of 30/1/2001.

chaired by a four-star general acting in international capacity. The EUMC is the highest military body of the EU.

3. The EU Military Staff[104] (EUMS) is composed of military personnel (currently about 130[105]) seconded by the member States to the GSC. It develops detailed military and strategic analysis such as planning and situation assessment, and has a capability for early warning. The EUMS is a GSC department directly attached to the SG/CFSP-HR.

In addition to these three new bodies, the ESDP has since the Nice Treaty taken over all functions from the WEU not covering the mutual defence commitment in Art. V of the Modified Brussels Treaty (MBT) of 1954. Among these institutions are, most prominently, the WEU's Institute for Security Studies in Paris[106] and the Satellite Centre in Torrejón (Spain).[107]

The role of the SG/CFSP-HR is described in broad terms in Arts 18, para. 3 and 26 TEU: to assist in formulating, preparing and implementing policy decisions by the Council. In practice, the first incumbent Javier Solana has taken a very active role, assisted by a growing number of staff in his General Secretariat.

The element with the highest political profile in the CFSP-HR's staff is the Policy Planning and Early Warning Unit[108] (PPEWU), composed of personnel seconded from member States, the GSC and the Commission. Its main tasks, reporting to the SG/CFSP-HR, are early warning, assessment and policy formulation (such as, for example, the European Security Strategy of 2003[109]). There is some institutional overlap of this civil body with its military counterpart, the EUMS.[110]

---

104   Established by Council Decision of 22 January 2001 setting up the Military Staff (2001/80/CFSP), OJ EC L 27/7 of 30/1/2001.

105   B. Ruge, *Europäische Sicherheits- und Verteidigungspolitik*, in: A. Weidemann / A. Simon (eds.), *The Future of ESDP* (2003), p. 33 at 36.

106   Newly created as the EU Institute for Security Studies. See Council Action establishing a European Union Institute for Security Studies of 20 July 2001, OJ L 200/1 of 25.7.2001.

107   Newly created as EU Satellite Centre. Council Joint Action establishing a European Union Satellite Centre of 20 July 2001, OJ L 200/5 of 25.7.2001.

108   Created by the IGC in 1996, it had been widely suggested before by e.g. Commissioner H. van den Broek, *Why Europe Needs a Common Foreign and Security Policy*, 1 EFAR (1996), p. 1 at 4) and jointly by France and Germany (Letter to the Irish Presidency of 9 December 1996, cited in: WEU Assembly Doc. 1564 (1997), para. 19). Treaty of Amsterdam amending the Treaty on European Union, the Treaties establishing the European Communities and certain related acts – Declarations adopted by the Conference – Declaration on the establishment of a policy planning and early warning unit, OJ 340, 10.11.1997, p. 0132.

109   A Secure European in a Better World - European Security Strategy, Council Doc. 15895/03, 8 Dec. 2003.

110   T.C. Salmon / A.J.K. Shepherd, *Toward a European Army* (2003), p. 95.

MILITARY CAPABILITIES

The Council has, in conjunction with regular impulses from the European Council, worked on developing military capabilities to be put at the disposal of the Union. Prime among them are the Helsinki Headline Goal of 1999[111] (60 000 troops, at 60-days notice, sustainable in operation for a year), and the ensuing apparatus which resembles NATO's 'force generation'. This included identifying the main capability gaps to be filled in order to arrive at a European intervention force with all the means at its disposal to react quickly to a crisis. The Capabilities Development Mechanism (CDM) has produced a European Capabilities Action Plan (ECAP). This process in particular was aided by external expertise from NATO.[112] Europe's defence industry, which has close links to the first pillar, has a direct bearing on capabilities, and is thus addressed as a matter under ESDP. Despite member States' continuing prerogative concerning national defence industries contained in Art. 296,[113] the EU has recently begun to tackle the issue, by creating a European Armaments, Research and Military Capabilities Agency to coordinate procurement and create economies of scale, particularly in R&D.[114] Although this last area formally pertains to industry policy, and thus to the first pillar, it clearly has a strong importance also for building ESDP.

'VARIABLE GEOMETRY' OF MEMBERSHIP

Not all member States have the same status in ESDP. On the other hand cooperation is formally open even to third States, resulting in a 'variable geometry'.[115] Most EU members are also NATO members, but some, such as the neutral and non-allied countries, are not. Third countries participating in EU peacekeeping are also classed differently according to whether they are NATO members. Their status of participation also depends on whether the operation draws on NATO resources or not.[116]

---

111   For details on the Headline Goal, see below Chapter 7 (Military Crisis Management).

112   E.g. in the EU–NATO task group on capabilities.

113   On the problem of the consolidation of the European defence industry and Art. 296 TEC, see only: M. Trybus, *The EC treaty as an instrument of European defence integration*, 39 CMLR (2002), pp. 1347.

114   See above p. 60.

115   The term which was originally used to describe the varying forms of membership and association in the WEU. *Cf.* F. Dehousse / B. Galer, *De Saint-Malo à Feira* (1999), p. 1 at 33.

116   The question of participation is regulated under the EU–NATO Berlin Plus agreement of 2002, referring to EU Nice Presidency Conclusions of Dec. 2000. See below Chapter 8 (Berlin Plus Agreement).

OVERVIEW OF THE MAIN DEVELOPMENTS OF ESDP

In the latter half of 1998, Britain under Tony Blair announced an about-face in its position on European security[117] which had up until then consisted in arguing against any institutional reform of Europe's security architecture which could weaken NATO and put at risk the continued American military commitment to Europe.[118] In December of that year, France and Britain decided at a bilateral meeting in St-Malo that the EU should in the future acquire

> the capacity for *autonomous* action, backed up by credible military forces, the means to decide to use them, and a readiness to do so, in order to respond to international crises.[119]

It should be able to take decisions on military actions where 'the Alliance as a whole' was not engaged.[120] The US supported this initiative from the start,[121] but warned against decoupling from NATO, duplication and discrimination against non-EU NATO members.[122]

At the European Council in Cologne in June 1999, the EU as a whole repeated the goal enunciated at the bilateral meeting of St-Malo,[123] and thus formally introduced

---

117   Informal European summit, Pörtschach, 24–25 October 1998, Press Conferences by British Prime Minister Tony Blair (Extracts), CP 47, pp. 1–3. The complex various political factors to this British policy change – including peacekeeping experiences in the Balkans (see above, p. 54) and the indirect effect of not participating in the European Monetary Union (EMU) – are well documented. See e.g. S. Taylor, *Kosovo crisis likely to boost case for EU defence policy overhaul*, European Voice (online edition), Vol. 4, No. 7, 15 Oct. 1999; S. Biscop, *The UK's Change of Course: a New Chance for the ESDI*, 4 EFAR (1999), pp. 253; A. Moens, *Developing a European intervention force*, 55 International Journal (1999/2000), p. 247 at 257–9; A. Deighton, *The European Security and Defence Policy*, 40 JCMS (2002); U. Schürr, *Der Aufbau einer ESVI* (2003), p. 225; S. Rynning, *Why not NATO? Military Planning in the European Union*, The Journal of Strategic Studies, Vol. 26, No.1 (March 2003), pp. 60–1; J. Howorth, *Discourse in ESDP*, 27 West European Politics 2 (2004), p. 211 at 220–3. On the EMU factor in particular, see P.J. Teunissen, *Strengthening the defence dimension of the EU: An evaluation of Concepts, Recent Initiatives and Developments*, 4 EFAR (1999), p. 327 at 328–9; M. Vasiu, *The role of the ESDI*, 6 Rom.J.Int.Aff. 3/4 (2000), p. 125 at 143; B.R. Posen, *ESDP and the Structure of World Power*, 39 The International Spectator 1 (2004), p. 5 at 12–13.

118   See e.g.: *Polygamy and the Illusion of Union*, Le Monde, article in The Guardian, 4 Aug. 1994, p. 15.

119   British-French summit, St-Malo, 3–4 Dec. 1998 (= CP 47, p. 8) [emphasis added].

120   *Ibid.*

121   M. Warnken, *Der Handlungsrahmen der EU* (2002), p. 191.

122   M.K. Albright, *The Right Balance Will Secure NATO's Future*, Financial Times, 7 December 1998, p. 22.

123   European Council, Cologne, 3–4 June, 1999, Declaration of the European Council on Strengthening the Common European Policy on Security and Defence, para. 1, CP 47, p. 41.

it into the EU framework. The Cologne Summit is thus sometimes referred as the birth hour of ESDP.[124]

At the European Council in Helsinki, the EU decided to give the policy goal of international crisis management more substance by deciding on the creation of a 'Headline Goal Task Force' of 50 000–60 000 troops, deployable within 60 days and sustainable for at least one year, by 2003.[125] It created the three new ESDP bodies (PSC, EUMC, EUMS) which were created, first on an interim basis.[126] This new goal of the EU was without prejudice to the traditional collective defence functions of NATO and WEU.[127]

At Santa Marta de Feira, on 19–20 June 2000, the European Council further elaborated the concepts and particular objectives for creating an independent EU crisis management capacity, particularly capability goals for the Headline Goal.[128]

A first Capabilities Commitment Conference on 20–21 November 2000 produced a 'Force Catalogue', broken down in individual national capability goals, a total of 100 000 persons, approximately 400 aircraft, and some 100 vessels.[129] Problems were identified with regard to strategic capabilities providing availability, deployability, sustainability and interoperability of those forces. As these military means could in the medium term only come from external sources, relations with NATO (for example the compatibility with the Alliance's Defence Capability Initiative (DCI)) took a particularly prominent part in that meeting.

At the European Summit of Nice in December 2000, the EU formalised the three interim bodies created at the Helsinki Summit.[130] The Nice Treaty amending the TEU

---

124   B. Ruge, *Europäische Sicherheits- und Verteidigungspolitik*, in: A. Weidemann / A. Simon (eds.), *The Future of ESDP* (2003), p. 33 at 34. British and French commentators, for obvious reasons, mostly refer to the St-Malo Summit as the 'birth hour' of ESDP (*cf.* G. Robertson, *Die NATO und die EU: Partner oder Rivalen?* (2002), p. 184; but see also J.-Y. Haine, *ESDP and NATO*, in: N. Gnesotto (ed.), *EU Security and Defence Policy – The first five years* (2004), EU-ISS, p. 131 at 134).

125   European Council, Helsinki, 10–11 December 1999, CP 47, pp. 82, Presidency Conclusions, II. Common European Policy on Security and Defence, para. 28 (= *ibid.*).

126   See above at: Institutions. They were accordingly called the interim Political and Security Committee (iPSC), the interim Military Committee (iEUMC) and the interim Military Staff (iEUMS), until they became permanent in January 2001. Annex IV, Presidency Reports to the Helsinki European Council on 'Strengthening the Common European Policy on Security and Defence' and on 'Non-Military Crisis Management of the European Union', CP 47, p. 87.

127   *Ibid.* p. 83.

128   European Council, Santa Marta da Feira, 19–20 June 2000, Annex I: Presidency Report on Strengthening the Common European Security and Defence Policy, II.A., B., CP 47, p. 122–4.

129   Capabilities Commitment Conference, Brussels, 20–21 Nov. 2000, Declaration, CP 47, p. 158 at 160.

130   European Council, Nice, 7–9 Dec. 2000, Presidency Conclusions, IV. Common European Security and Defence Policy, Annex VI, II., CP 47, p. 171 and Annexes III-V to Annex VI (CP 47, pp. 191–9).

also introduced the possibility of enhanced cooperation for the CFSP, that is, not necessarily including all member States (Arts 27a–27e), but not for matters having military or defence implications (Art. 27b).[131] Thus, coalitions of the willing for peacekeeping operations were ruled out. Nevertheless, in 2003, two such operations involving only some member States did in fact take place.

As it stood, the Nice Summit document also staked the outer limits for the EU's defence ambitions. It stated that the St-Malo–Helsinki process did not involve the establishment of a European army,[132] and also reiterated the key role NATO continued to play in the collective defence of its members.[133]

At its Laeken Summit on 14–15 December 2001, the EU announced that progress on the build-up of its crisis management capabilities had reached the point where it was 'capable of conducting some crisis-management operations'.[134]

With the conclusion of the EU–NATO Berlin Plus agreement with NATO at the Copenhagen European Council in December 2002 on the borrowing of strategic military assets,[135] the way was opened for the first EU crisis management operations in 2003.

A PARTICULAR TASK OF ESDP: THE INTERNATIONAL FIGHT AGAINST TERRORISM

In the wake of the terrorist attacks of September 11, the EU began to envision ESDP as one tool among others, such as police and judicial cooperation, to combat international terrorism. This connection was first made in the EU's official reaction to the attacks, on 14 September 2001,[136] and the Spanish Presidency in 2002

---

131   Such closer cooperation may, however, be effected outside the EU framework under the WEU or NATO, as long as it does not run counter to CFSP (Art. 17, para. 4 TEU). *Cf.* Answer given by Mr Patten on behalf of the Commission to a Written Question (E-1116/01), OJ C 318/208 of 13.11.2001; *cf.* below Chapter 5 (NATO Primacy).

132   *Ibid.*, Annex VI, Presidency Report on the European Security and Defence Policy, Introduction, CP 47, p. 168, and Annex I to Annex VI, para. 1, CP 47, p. 176.

133   *Ibid.*, Annex VI, Presidency Report on the European Security and Defence Policy, Introduction, CP 47, p. 169.

134   European Council, Laeken, 14–15 Dec. 2001, Presidency Conclusions, I., para. 6, CP 51, p. 110.

135   On the details of this agreement, see below Chapter 8 (Berlin Plus Agreement).

136   Joint Declaration by the Heads of State and Government of the EU, the President of the European Parliament, the President of the European Commission and the HR-CFSP, Brussels, 14 September 2001, CP 51, p. 147: 'These tragic events oblige us to take urgent decisions on how the European Union should respond to these challenges ... We shall make the European Security and Defence Policy operational as soon as possible'.

made it one of its priorities.[137] The idea gained ground during 2002.[138] It carried notions of fighting international terrorism which differed from the American blend, emphasising, inter alia, also the social, economic and political 'root causes' of the phenomenon.[139]

The Seville European Council on 21–22 June 2004 officially stated the comprehensive approach to EU anti-terrorist measures, including contributions by ESDP, that is, by military means.[140] Debates in the European Convention in autumn 2002 acknowledged that the original EDSP (including the definition of the Petersberg tasks, dating from 1992) which had been created in response to challenges and threats of the 1990s, had been 'overtaken' by September 11.[141] After the terrorist attacks in Madrid on 11 March 2004, the 'Solidarity clause' produced by the Convention, and contained in Art. I-42 of the draft European Constitution, gained a new importance as it was made immediately applicable with the 'Declaration on Solidarity against Terrorism' of 25 March 2004.[142] The terrorism dimension of ESDP is today fast becoming a permanent field of EU policy.[143]

CHANGES IN THE EUROPEAN CONSTITUTION

Introduction

At the European Council in Laeken, on 14–15 Dec. 2001,[144] the EU decided to convene a broad forum to elaborate a new treaty framework which would enable

---

137   Presentation of the EU Spanish Presidency's Objectives for ESDP, speech by F. Trillo (Spanish MoD), Madrid, 10 Jan. 2002, CP 57, p. 14.

138   *Cf.* J. Solana, *CFSP: The State of the Union*, speech at the Annual Conference of the EU Institute for Security Studies, Paris, 1 July 2002, IV., CP 57, p. 108; Franco-German Defence and Security Summit, Schwerin Statement, 39 July 2002, at III., CP 57, p. 116.

139   European Parliament report, Strasbourg, Adoption of the Report on 'The Progress achieved in the implementation of the CFSP', 26 Sept. 2002, Preambular para. F, last bullet, CP 57, p. 119.

140   European Council, Seville, 21–22 June 2002, Presidency Conclusions, Annex V, Draft Declaration of the European Council on the contribution of CFSP, including ESDP, in the fight against terrorism, CP 57, p. 272.

141   Barnier Report (Final Report of Working Group VIII on Defence), paras. 46 and 47, CP 57, p. 257.

142   Annexed to the 'Declaration on Combating Terrorism', 25 March 2004, Brussels European Council 25/26 Council Doc. 7906/04. On this aspect of the ESDP's anti-terrorism dimension, see M. Reichard, *The Madrid terrorist attacks*, 7 ZEuS 2 (2004), pp. 313–334; M. Sossai, *The anti-terrorism dimension of ESDP*, in: N. White/M. Trybus (eds.), *European Security Law* (forthcoming).

143   See e.g. the EU Plan of Action on Combating Terrorism, 11 June 2004, Council Doc. 10010/3/04 REV 3, at 3.7. and 3.8.

144   European Council, Laeken, 14–15 Dec. 2001, Presidency Conclusions, Annex I, III., CP 51, pp. 117–9.

it to continue operating efficiently at 25 members, and to face also the new challenges of the twenty-first century. The 'European Convention' [hereinafter: the Convention], composed of 102 representatives from EU institutions and the governments and parliaments of its member States and accession candidate States, began its deliberations in September 2002. In July 2003, it delivered its first draft Treaty establishing a Constitution for Europe [hereinafter: the Constitution].[145] The European Council of December 2003 did not arrive at consensus on all provisions, particularly with regard to the most contentious issue of the double majority. Despite the December 2003 text being described by the Italian Presidency as a '"negotiating acquis" not open to further discussion',[146] many provisions, including on ESDP, were in fact still changed in the first half of 2004 before adoption. The rough text of the Treaty was finally adopted at the European Council of 17–18 June, 2004,[147] and is awaiting ratification by the member States at the time of writing.[148]

It would be an interesting task to trace the negotiating history of the draft European Constitution of all the provisions on ESDP.[149] But this would reach beyond this book. Instead, this part shall concentrate on the changes made in comparison to the TEU. The history of the relevant new provisions will only be treated where this is absolutely necessary to understand their context.[150] Some emphasis will, however, be placed on the new 'battle group' concept, as it is deemed to be a more important innovation. Collective self-defence will be treated in full in a subsequent chapter.[151]

General provisions (Art. I-41, paras. 1 and 2)

In the system of the Constitution, ESDP is set more strictly apart from the CFSP than in the TEU. Nevertheless, ESDP is still an 'integral part' of the CFSP.[152] The operational capacity of the Union shall be provided by the member States. The tasks for which this capacity will be used are described in very general terms only: 'peace-keeping, conflict prevention and strengthening international security in accordance with the principles of the United Nations Charter'.[153] They are spelled out in greater

---

145   2003/C OJ 169/1 of 18 July 2003.

146   Conference of the representatives of the governments of the member states, Brussels, 13 Dec. 2003, Declaration of the President, CP 67, p. 454.

147   CIG 86/04 of 25 June 2004.

148   On the question of the European Constitution after the negative referenda in France and the Netherlands, see below at p. 80.

149   Mainly Arts I-41, 43 and III-309 to 312 (CIG 87/04), with annexes and protocols.

150   For reasons of brevity, the negotiating materials below are rendered by document number and date only (e.g. CONV 779/03, 4 June 2003), leaving out the title. All European Convention documents are readily accessible at http://www.european-convention.org/ (visited 11/08/2004).

151   See below Chapter 6 (Collective Self-Defence).

152   Art. I-41, para. 1.

153   Art. I-41, para. 1.

detail as part of the Petersberg tasks (see below). The UN Charter features more prominently regarding use of force than was the case in the TEU.[154]

A significant change is in the wording of Art. I-41, para. 2. While the goal of framing a common defence policy 'progressively' remains,[155] a common defence 'will' now be formed 'when' the European Council so decides. In contrast, in the TEU it 'may' be formed 'should the European Council so decide'.[156]

In addition, a short Protocol No. 24 on Art. I-41, para. 2 states that 'bearing in mind the need to implement fully the provisions of Article I-41(2) ... The Union shall draw up, together with the Western European Union, arrangements for enhanced cooperation between them'.[157] Art. 41, para. 2 refers both to EU crisis management (common defence policy) and to a possible future mutual defence (common defence). Protocol No. 24 does not specify which of the two it addresses – crisis management or mutual defence. Its language harks back to EU-WEU crisis management cooperation arrangements implementing the Treaty of Amsterdam.[158] However, with the Nice Treaty the EU already took over of all the WEU's crisis management functions, and the WEU Council has not met since November 2000.[159] The only function left to the WEU today is collective self-defence under Art. V MBT. Hence, only this second area is open for any WEU-EU cooperation. The Protocol could relate to some kind of planned inclusion of the WEU's Art. V into the Union framework. Bearing in mind the programmatic character and spirit of Art. I-41, para. 2, such a reading would be very much in line with the need stated in the Protocol's preamble to 'fully implement' the provisions of that Article, implicitly also an EU mutual defence should it come to pass. If this is the result, then it does not elucidate from the text what the relation Protocol No. 24 has to the general mutual defence clause in Art. I-41, para. 7. Nor would there be any need for it after the entry into force of the European Constitution,

---

154   Art. 11 TEU only states this principle (in much the same wording) at the beginning of its Title V (CFSP). In the deliberations of the European Convention, there were also suggestions to mention 'observance of international law' in addition (*Cf.* CONV 779/03, 4 June 2003, p. 18).

155   This is interesting because major advances in this activity have been made since the Nice Treaty, most importantly the first EU peacekeeping missions have taken place in 2003. In contrast to this reality, the unchanged wording seems to suggest that there has been no progress.

156   These changes were very disputed in the Convention, see e.g. CONV 779/03, 4 June 2003, p. 18. On the implications of changes in the wording more in detail, see M. Reichard, *The Madrid terrorist attacks*, 7 ZEuS 2 (2004), p. 313 at pp. 318–9.

157   Protocol No. 24 on Article I-41(2) of the Constitution, CIG 87/04 ADD 1, 6 Aug. 2004.

158   Treaty of Amsterdam, Protocol on Article 17 (ex Article J.7) of the Treaty on European Union, OJ C 340 of 10/11/1997, pp. 355; Council Decision of 10 May 1999 concerning the arrangements for enhanced cooperation between the European Union and the Western European Union (1999/404/CFSP), OJ L 153/1 of 19/6/1999. These provisions were partly based on WEU-EU arrangements dating already from 1994.

159   *Cf.* WEU Ministerial Council, Marseille, 13 Nov. 2000, Marseille Declaration, CP 47, p. 147.

as the EU mutual defence clause in Art. I-41, para. 7 would have the legal effect of derogating the Art. V WEU Treaty.[160] It has indeed been speculated that the Protocol was included in the European Constitution by accident.[161]

New Petersberg Tasks (Art. III-309)

Following the recommendations of the 'Barnier Report' (Convention WG VIII) of 16 December 2002,[162] the Petersberg tasks have been updated to include, beside the three tasks currently listed in Art. 17 TEU[163]

- joint disarmament operations
- military advice and assistance tasks
- conflict prevention tasks
- post-conflict stabilisation.

The European Constitution does not contain any further definition of these terms, in particular with regard to important questions such as whether consent of the target State or authorisation of the UNSC is required. The European Security Strategy of December 2003 and the Battle Groups concept of 2004, as relevant EU practice, would seem to answer both in the negative. However, both of the above elements are still deemed desirable by the EU.

All of the (now, seven) Petersberg tasks may also be used to combat international terrorism 'including by supporting third countries in combating terrorism in their territories'.[164] In other words, the new Petersberg tasks include operations along the whole spectrum of intensity, short of collective self-defence.[165] Art. III-309, para. 2 provides for the procedure of implementation of the new Petersberg tasks.

---

160   See below Chapter 6 (Collective Self-Defence).

161   K. Blanck, *Flexible Integration in the Common Foreign and Security Policy*, EI Working Paper No. 61 (2004), p. 35.

162   Barnier Report (Final Report of Working Group VIII on Defence), para. 51, CP 57, p. 258.

163   Art. 17, para. 2 TEU lists 'humanitarian and rescue tasks, peacekeeping tasks and tasks of combat forces in crisis management, including peacemaking'.

164   In an earlier draft anti-terrorist measures were also included as a separate Petersberg task (CONV 685/03, p. 43).

165   S. Biscop, *Able and Willing? Assessing the EU's Capacity for Military Action*, 9 EFAR (2004), p. 509.

Enhanced cooperation in ESDP

'Task groups' (Arts I-41, para. 5; III-310)

The general principles for enhanced cooperation under ESDP are described very briefly, based on the regime under the TEU (Arts 27a-e). Such cooperation by groups of member States must serve the Union's values and interests as a whole. However, the competence of the participating States to manage these tasks is left to them alone,[166] with only a regular reporting duty to the Council.[167]

New 'battle group' concept (Arts I-41, para. 6; III-312)

History   The idea that, beyond the Helsinki Headline Goal formulated in 1999, the humanitarian crises that the Union wanted to be able to respond to effectively would also require smaller rapid response elements with very high readiness, able to take on the 'high end' of the Petersberg task spectrum (for example interventions on the scale of NATO's Operation Allied Force in Kosovo) was already contained in the Convention's 'Barnier Report'.[168] Historically, the concept of such 'battle groups' was not new.[169] It was already part of the ancient Pleven Plan and the EDC project in the early 1950s[170] and was also employed in the field in NATO's SFOR mission in Bosnia.[171] It had also for a long time been evident that not all member States would be militarily willing or able to participate in a project calling for a high degree of integration among elite units of the armed forces. Thus, the idea of applying certain military 'convergence criteria' along the lines of the European Monetary Union (EMU), resulting in some sort of a 'defence Euro-zone', has been much discussed since the founding days of ESDP,[172] despite warnings of old that in

---

166   Art. III-310, para. 1.

167   Art. III-310, para. 2.

168   Barnier Report (Final Report of Working Group VIII on Defence), para. 10, CP 57, p. 251.

169   A battle group is defined as 'the smallest self-sufficient military-operational formation that can be deployed and sustained in a theatre of operations'. The concept is based upon standard NATO doctrine. G. Quille, *'Battle groups' to strengthen EU military crisis management?*, ESR No. 22 (April 2003).

170   J. Trempont, *La communauté Européenne de Défense*, 1 ICLQ (1952), p. 519 at 521.

171   C. Schwegmann, *EU-Friedensmissionen auf dem Balkan – eine Alternative zur NATO?*, Studien und Berichte zur Sicherheitspolitik 5/2002, Austrian Federal Ministry for Defence, p. 12, http://www.bmlv.gv.at/pdf_pool/publikationen/09_euf_01_schweg.pdf (visited 12/08/2004).

172   See e.g. P.J. Teunissen, *Strengthening the defence dimension of the EU* (1999), p. 328–9; G. Gustenau, *Die Europäische Gemeinsame Außen- und Sicherheitspolitik – eine Herausforderung für die 'Post-Neutralen'? – Eine Einschätzung aus österreichischer Sicht*, in: *Id.*, *Sicherheitspolitischer Dialog Österreich-Slowenien* (2000), p. 15 at 20; M. Jopp,

defence integration 'flexibility' could lead to an undermining of trust between its members.[173] A Franco-British plan published at the bilateral summit in Le Touquet on 4 February 2003 spoke of the need to have initial deployment bridgehead air and sea forces able to deploy within 5 to 10 days.[174] This seemed to resound well in the Brussels community.[175] The 'Mini-Summit' of April 2003 likewise made a fleeting reference to the need for 'a European rapid reaction capability'.[176] In November 2003, Britain and France proposed a more detailed concept.[177] The new 'battle groups' drew direct lessons from the latest autonomous EU peacekeeping operation in the DRC, *Artemis*.[178] The EU should create a pool of highly-trained units of 1500 troops of 'battle-group sized forces'. These peacekeeping 'crack units' (undoubtedly designed for third-generation peacekeeping) should be compatible with the NATO Response Force,[179] and work closely with the United Nations, for whose longer-lasting missions they should help prepare the ground. They were conceived for failed or failing states. In terms of geography, only Africa was explicitly mentioned. By December 2003, the European Council had officially signed up to the idea.[180]

On 10 February 2004 Britain and France came out with further details. There should be 'battle groups' specialised for different terrains, that is, for combat in

---

Gemeinsame Europäische Sicherheits- und Verteidigungspolitik, Jahrbuch der europäischen Integration 1999/2000 (2000), p. 243 at 249; A.M. Rizzo, *Towards a European Defence Policy*, 36 The International Spectator 3 (2001), p. 47 at 55; H. Ojanen, *Theories at a loss? EU–NATO fusion* (2002), p. 11; J. Shaw, *Flexibility in a 'reorganized' and 'simplified' treaty*, 40 CMLR (2003), p. 279 at 294; *cf.* F. Heisbourg, *L'Europe de la défense dans l'Alliance atlantique*, 64 Politique étrangère (1999), p. 219 at 226.

173   J. Wright, *Trusting Flexible friends: the dangers of flexibility in NATO and the Western European Union / European Union*, 20 CSP 1 (1999), p. 111 at 125–6.

174   Franco-British summit, Le Touquet, 4 February 2003, Declaration on Strengthening European Cooperation in Security and Defence, 3) (c), CP 67, p. 36 at 39. *Cf.* J. Howorth, *ESDP and NATO – Wedlock or Deadlock?*, 38 Coop. & Confl. 3 (2003), pp. 249–250.

175   See only Written question E-0334/03 by Cristiana Muscardini (UEN) to the Council, 12.02.2003, reprinted in: Council Doc. 7881/03, p. 2.

176   European defence meeting – 'Tervuren', Meeting of the Heads of State and Government of Germany, France, Luxembourg and Belgium on European Defence, Brussels, 29 April 2003, para. 1, CP 67, p. 76 at 78. It would seem overstated, however, to claim that the 'battle group' concept arose from that Summit (*cf.* T. Risse, *Auf dem Weg zu einer gemeinsamen Außenpolitik? Der Verfassungsvertrag und die europäische Außen- und Sicherheitspolitik*, 26 Integration 4 (2003), p. 564 at 572).

177   Franco-British Declaration – Strengthening European Cooperation in Security and Defence, 24 November 2003, CP 67, p. 280.

178   D. Cronin, *EU's peacekeeping ambitions set to move up a gear by 2007*, European Voice, 18 Nov. 2004, p. 6. On Operation *Artemis* in detail, see below Chapter 7 (Military Crisis Management).

179   See below Chapter 7 (Military Crisis Management).

180   European Council, Brussels, 12 Dec. 2003, ESDP Presidency Report, para. 7, CP 67, p. 299 at 301; *cf.* already: GAERC, Brussels, 8–9 Dec. 2003, Conclusions, European Security and Defence Policy, EU military rapid response, CP 67, p. 289.

jungle, desert, urban and mountain operations.[181] The initiative was open to other countries, but they had to show a high degree of interoperability, in which military effectiveness would be an the overriding criterion. Germany announced the next day that it would join the French-British initiative.[182] Smaller countries, especially the neutrals, were less enthusiastic.[183] Even in Germany, opposition politicians had misgivings about suspected post-colonial motives by the two first proponents.[184] It was furthermore not clear immediately whether these new 'battle groups' would be counted as part of the participating countries' contributions to the Headline Goal or not.[185] In April 2004 further details emerged about the plan by the three countries, then presented to the plenary of EU defence ministers: there should be six or seven 'battle groups', ready for action at 15-days notice, they should be able to stay in the field for 30 days, and should be ready for deployment by 2007.[186] The 'battle groups' concept was incorporated into the new Headline Goal 2010.[187] A Military Capabilities Commitment Conference in Brussels on 22 November 2004 brought the number of battle groups up to 13, excluding additional niche capabilities.[188] Initial operating capability will likely be achieved by 2006.[189]

Participation in the 'battle groups' by core ESDP countries such as the United Kingdom was never in doubt.[190] In July 2004, it appeared that Italy would also join in the project.[191] During the autumn of 2004, more and more smaller EU States such

---

181 *Cf.* H. Mahony, *UK and France take new defence step*, EUObserver, 10 Feb. 2004; J. Dempsey, *UK and France join forces on combat units defence initiative*, Financial Times, 10 Feb. 2004, p. 5; News in brief, ISIS NATO Notes, Vol. 6, No. 1, Feb. 2004.

182 H. Mahony, *Germany joins Anglo-French defence plan*, EUObserver, 11 Feb. 2004; N.K. Pries / M. Winter, *Berlin für EU-Elitetruppen*, Frankfurter Rundschau, 11 Feb. 2004, p. 6.

183 E. Tuomioja (FM Finland), *Europe needs to work as a whole on defence*, Financial Times, 28 October 2003, p. 23; *Id.* / L. Freivalds (FM Sweden), *We want a stronger EU security policy*, Dagens Nyheter, 11 November 2003, English translation in: CP 67, p. 429; *Kerneuropa: Wien warnt vor EU-Direktorium*, Die Presse (online edition), 12 Feb. 2004.

184 T. Kröter, *Wirren um Schnelle Truppe*, Frankfurter Rundschau, 20 Feb. 2000, p. 4.

185 *Ibid.*

186 A. Beatty, *Defence ministers meet in Brussels*, EUObserver, 5 April 2004; *Id.*, *EU to have 'battle groups' by 2007*, EUObserver, 5 April 2004; *Cf.* Déclaration du Conseil franco-allemand de Défense et de Sécurité, Paris 13 May 2004, http://www.defense.gouv. fr/actualites/discours_divers/2004 /a140504/140504.htm (visited 14/05/2004).

187 European Council, Brussels, 14 June 2004, Presidency Report on ESDP, Annex I, Council Doc. 10547/04.

188 Draft Council Conclusions on ESDP, 22 Nov. 2004, Annex A to Annex II, p. 22, Council Doc. 14887/2/04 REV 2.

189 European Council, Brussels, 16–17 June 2005, Presidency Conclusions, para. 79, Council Doc. 10255/05

190 *Cf.* A. Beatty, *UK to create Africa battle group*, EUObserver, 8 Oct. 2004.

191 UK-Italy Summit, 13 July 2004, Joint Statement, 10 Downing Street Press Releases, http://www.number-10.gov.uk/output/Page6102.asp (visited 17/07/2004).

as Sweden and Finland announced they would join,[192] even Norway,[193] a non-EU country which had hitherto stayed deliberately away from any European defence cooperation outside NATO.[194] In some countries such as Austria and Norway, participation in the 'battle groups' raised serious constitutional questions.[195] In Ireland, such constitutional barriers were not immediately overcome, and as a result the country did not participate initially in the 'battle groups' concept.[196]

Provisions of the European Constitution   The battle group concept would in legal terms be covered by Arts I-41, para. 6, III-312 and the 'Protocol on permanent structured cooperation' annexed to the Constitution.[197] Member States can establish closer cooperation on a permanent basis to realise the 'most demanding missions'. Art. 41, para. 6 cites two conditions: that the member States concerned have military capabilities fulfilling 'higher criteria' (described in the Protocol), and that they 'have made more binding commitments to one another in this area'. It is not clear what this second condition exactly means, particularly 'this area'. Probably (*arg.* 'this') it refers to the first condition, that is, member States must have committed themselves jointly to maintain or improve their military capabilities. The prime forum for such capability commitments will likely be the new European Defence Agency.[198] Probably the Agency is not named explicitly in Part I of the Constitution in order to maintain the highest possible degree of flexibility for further developments. The 'battle groups' envisioned by the article 'shall not affect' the Petersberg tasks, which would seem to indicate that their troops would *not* count towards member States' contributions to the Headline Goal.[199]

Art. III-312 contains the procedure for establishing and joining an initiative under Art. I-41, para. 6. This procedure is to some extent based on the old Arts 27a-e TEU. The Council decides on the establishment, but only participating States may vote (with qualified majority).[200] When a participating member State no longer fulfils the

---

192   L. Kirk, *Sweden and Finland announce joint EU battle group*, EUObserver, 5 Oct. 2004.

193   A. Beatty, *Norway interested in EU defence role*, EUObserver, 21 Sept. 2004; K.K. Devold (Norwegian MoD), *Vital for Norway to be part of Europe's military future*, European Voice, 4 Nov. 2004, p. 8.

194   *Cf.* H.E. Sjursen, *Coping – or not Coping – with Change: Norway in European Security*, 5 EFAR (2000), pp. 539–559.

195   L. Kirk, *Norwegian participation in EU battle groups disputed*, EUObserver, 19 Nov. 2004; S. Wittich, *EU-Battle-Groups: Selbstverteidigung oder UN-Mandat*, Die Presse (online edition), 29 Nov. 2004.

196   H. Mahony, *Ireland may not take part in EU battlegroups*, EUObserver, 10 Jan. 2005.

197   CIG 87/04 ADD 1, 6 Aug. 2004, Protocol No. 23 [hereinafter: Protocol].

198   Protocol, Art. 1 (a).

199   *Cf.* above fn. 185.

200   Art. III-312, para. 4, *in fine*. This sentence was rephrased several times during the drafting stage, to make the point unmistakable (*Cf.* CONV 685/03, 23 April 2003, pp. 45–6 (old draft Art. 20, para. 2); CONV 727/03, 27 May 2003, p. 66 (old draft Art. III-208, para.

first condition of 'higher criteria', its participation may be suspended by the same procedure (the member State in question not taking part in the vote).[201] There is likewise a possibility for unilateral withdrawal from the initiative.[202]

The Protocol describes in more detail the 'higher criteria' regarding military capabilities which member States are expected to meet: taking part in European defence equipment programmes (such as for example the Eurofighter, or the A-400M transport aeroplane) and in the activity of the European Defence Agency.[203] The 'battle groups', which should be ready by 2007, should be ready to take on any of the Petersberg tasks within 5–30 days,[204] staying self-sustained in the field for 30 days, and possible to be extended (presumably through rotation) up to at least 120 days. Participating member States undertake to maintain high investment in defence equipment, integrate their defence structures and procurement, and improve the interoperability and flexibility of their forces.[205] These capability enhancement measures are 'without prejudice to undertakings in this regard within NATO'.[206] This refers to NATO's Prague Capabilities Commitment (PCC).[207] In theory, the objective legal meaning of this wording would point to completely separate (and therefore duplicated) resources and structures. However, looking at the general principles of EU–NATO cooperation at the time of the adoption of this text, one of which is to avoid 'unnecessary duplication',[208] this can safely be interpreted to mean simply compatibility.[209] Member States' performance on the 'higher criteria' is assessed regularly by the European Defence Agency whose reports may also be taken as a basis for decisions under Art. III-312 (including the suspension of participation by a member State which no longer fulfils the criteria).[210] This gives the Agency a powerful background role in advising which member States will be the 'ins' and 'outs' of the 'battle groups'. Already at the end of 2003 it became clear that a majority of member States would probably join the Protocol.[211]

---

2)). *Cf.* M. Jopp, *GASP und ESVP im Verfassungsvertrag – eine neue Angebotsvielfalt mit Chancen und Mängeln*, 26 Integration 4 (2003), p. 550 at pp. 552–3.

201   Art. III-312, para. 4.

202   Art. III-312, para. 6.

203   Protocol, Art. 1 (a).

204   Note the extension of this time limit from the ambitious first proposal at the UK-French Le Touquet Summit (see p. 73).

205   Protocol, Art. 2 (a)-(c).

206   Protocol, Art. 2 (d).

207   See below Chapter 3 (NATO Today).

208   See below Chapter 5 (NATO Primacy).

209   On the problem of practical compatibility between national forces assigned both to EU and NATO special forces, see below Chapter 7 (Military Crisis Management).

210   Protocol, Art. 3.

211   C. Grant, *EU defence takes a step forward*, CER briefing note, Dec. 2003.

The battle group concept was further developed in the first half of 2004 as a matter of urgency for the Irish Presidency.[212] A first 'draft military Battle Group concept' was presented to the EUMC by the EUMS in early March 2004.[213]

On the whole, the 'higher criteria' of the Protocol are deemed stringent.[214] Only the future will tell whether they will be as stringently applied. The EMU precedent is not too encouraging in this respect. However, realisation of the battle group concept, and thus overcoming the old prohibition for enhanced cooperation in defence in the EU, is deemed crucial in order to prevent a 'defence avant-garde' of single member States proceeding with defence integration of their own outside the EU framework.[215]

Although not directly related, the European Constitution's provisions on permanent structured cooperation are also sometimes seen as paving the way for a future European military headquarters.[216]

Collective self-defence (Art. I-41, para. 7)

The Constitution contains a classical mutual defence clause with explicit reference to Article 51 of the United Nations Charter, qualified by an exception for 'the security and defence policy of certain Member States'. It is interesting to look at the negotiating history of this important provision. Initially, the draft of 18 July 2003,[217] had conceived this clause as enhanced cooperation, that is, as an 'opt-in' model, and had mentioned the possibility of employing military means explicitly, although the wording had also allowed other means (*arg.* 'military *or* other').[218] Both these characteristics are gone in the final version of CIG 87/04. Mutual defence is a primary obligation in the Constitution[219] (not requiring additional forms of cooperation), but its language is weaker. A proposal in December 2003 by the four

---

212   Council Conclusions on ESDP, 14 May 2004, Council Doc. 9385/04, para. 15.

213   Progress report on the Battle Group Concept, 9 June 2004, Council Doc. 10282/04, para. 3.

214   J.-Y. Haine, *A new impetus for ESDP?*, EU-ISS Bulletin No.11 (July 2004).

215   *Cf.* F. Riccardi, *A Look Behind the News*, Bull. Quot. Europe No. 8652, 25 Feb. 2004.

216   See below, p. 79. Interview with Eurocorps commander J.-L. Py in *L'Eurocorps, un exemple de défense commune à suivre*, Dernières Nouvelles d'Alsace, 4 May 2005, p. 2.

217   Art. I-40(7), Draft Treaty establishing a Constitution for Europe, 2003/C OJ 169/1 of 18 July 2003.

218   Emphasis added. *Cf.* in contrast Art. V of the WEU's Modified Brussels Treaty (1954) 'military *and* other aid' according to which additional aid does not replace the military obligation per se.

219   Therefore, the entire implementing provisions relating to the procedure of the previous enhanced cooperation for mutual defence (old Art. III-214) became redundant in the final Constitution, and were deleted.

neutral and non-aligned member States to further weaken the language of the mutual assistance obligation had not been accepted by the IGC.[220]

The caveat for 'certain Member States' concerns in the main those member States already covered by the old 'Irish formula' of Art. 17, para. 1, second sentence TEU, that is, the neutral and non-allied countries. As mentioned already above, the relationship of Art. I-40, para. 7 to the Protocol on Art. I-40, para. 2 is not clear. Mutual self-defence in the EU context will be fully analysed in detail in a later Chapter.[221]

Afterword: The fate of the European Constitution's ESDP provisions after the negative referenda in France and the Netherlands

The negative ratification referenda in France and the Netherlands on 29 May and 2 June 2005 respectively threw the ratification process for the European Constitution into crisis. As a result, the European Council on 17 June 2005 called for a period of reflection on the European Constitution among the member States until 2006.[222] Even before those dates, however, European policy-makers and analysts began to think about a 'Plan B' which would save some parts of the European Constitution in case ratification of the whole should fail.[223] Such considerations mostly concentrated on those parts of the Constitution which could be implemented without the legal requirement of ratification. The ESDP provisions described above were surprisingly mentioned seldom in this regard.[224] Hence, a brief summary of possibilities for the post-Constitution implementation of these provisions seems useful here.

On a political basis, the Solidarity Clause of Art. I-43 was already implemented by the European Council's Declaration on 25 March 2004.[225] The same has already

---

220   Letter from Erkki Tuomioja (FM Finland), Brian Cowen (FM Ireland), Benita Ferrero-Waldner (FM Austria) and Laila Freivalds (FM Sweden) to F. Frattini (EU Council President) – IGC 2003 – European Security and Defence Policy, CIG 62/03, 5 Dec. 2003 (CP 67, p. 437).

221   See below Chapter 6 (Collective Self-Defence).

222   European Council, 16 and 17 June 2005, Declaration by the heads of State or Government of the Member States of the European Union on the ratification of the treaty establishing a Constitution for Europe, 17 June 2005, http://www.eu2005.lu/en/actualites/ conseil/2005/06/17conseur-decl /index.html (visited 18/06/05).

223   C. Grant, *There is life beyond a European Constitution,* Financial Times (online edition), 23 May 2005; S. Kurpas, *What Could be Saved from the European Constitution if Ratification Fails?,* CEPS Policy Brief 70/May 2005.

224   E.g. A. Bouilhet, *Le «plan B» de Bruxelles si le non gagnait,* Le Figaro (online edition), 18 April 2005; comments by Commission President J. Barroso, cited in: B. Baumann / A. Föderl-Schmid, *London reagiert kühl auf Schröder/Chirac-Initiative,* Der Standard, 6 June 2005, p. 3.

225   For details see M. Reichard, *The Madrid terrorist Attacks – a midwife for EU mutual defence?,* 7 ZEuS 2 (2004), pp. 313–334,

happened as a matter of secondary EU law for the European Defence Agency,[226] the new Headline Goal 2010[227] and the Battle Groups.[228] It will also likely be the case for the Emergency Response measures the EU will eventually set in place as a follow-up to the Tsunami earthquake in December 2004.[229] Further, extension of the Petersberg tasks to cover also the new tasks in Art. III-309 could be done for each individual crisis management operation through a Joint Action by the Council. However, legal implementation of paras. 6 and 7 of Art. I-41 (that is, permanent structured cooperation and collective self-defence) is impossible without formal ratification. This may not be so serious in practice, as the substance of both these provisions is already very far developed on a political basis. In case of para. 6 (permanent structured cooperation), this consists in the gradual development of the Battle Groups. Permanent structured cooperation is a fairly recent development in the EU system, with little pre-existing texts or 'path dependency'. Hence, there is much room for innovation and it is unlikely that the Battle Groups will stall as a result of the negative referenda.[230] In case of para. 7 (collective self-defence), this notion already exists to a high degree among EU member States, albeit on a political, not a legal, basis.[231] For NATO, the EU in any case 'regardless of the fate of its draft constitution, will continue to be a major international actor'.[232]

THE ISSUE OF INDEPENDENT EUROPEAN MILITARY HEADQUARTERS

The issue of whether the EU should have any military planning centre separate and independent from NATO, and at which level, was the main source of contention in EU–NATO relations in 2003, after the Berlin Plus issue had been resolved in December 2002.[233] It was not formally part of the discussions in the European Convention or the 2004 IGC, and thus not included anywhere in the Constitution. But it was clear to all actors that, once such an EU planning centre – no matter how small – would be in existence, this would set in train an irreversible process of the EU developing its own military options, and interests.[234] Hence, politically, the

---

226   See above fn. 82.

227   See below at p. 229.

228   See above fn. 186.

229   *Cf.* Earthquake and tsunamis in the Indian Ocean – follow-up to European Union Action Plan, Council Doc. 8961/1/05 REV 1, 20 May 2005.

230   I am indebted to Sebastian Kurpas (CEPS) for this insight.

231   For details see below Chapter 6 (Collective Self-Defence).

232   J. de Hoop Scheffer, *A Changing Alliance in a Changing World*, speech in Bratislava, 30 June 2005, http://www.nato.int/docu/speech/2005/s050630a.htm (visited 01/07/05).

233   See below Chapter 8 (Berlin Plus Agreement).

234   'People will regard this as a Trojan Horse. You start with 30 and end up with 300. It is a bridgehead to something much bigger.' (Unnamed NATO diplomat, cited in: J. Dempsey / G. Parker, *Hopes rise for deal on new EU framework*, Financial Times, 1 Dec. 2003, p. 1).

issue quickly became a kind of proxy war about the general question of EU military autonomy versus NATO.[235] The debate was sparked off by the Mini-Summit of the 'Gang of Four' in April 2003, and was finally resolved in the EU document titled 'European Defence: NATO/EU Consultation, Planning and Operations' of December 2003.[236] To understand this very concisely worded 2-page document, it is instructive to look into the debate between April and December in some more detail before proceeding with its textual analysis.

Origins

Discussions about European facilities for military planning independent from NATO did not arise suddenly in 2003. They had already been part of the debates on the right role for the WEU in European security throughout the 1990s.[237] These debates had not made much headway in face of the prevailing view that ESDP did 'not require turning the EU into a defence institution with military experts and structures'.[238] France, not being part of NATO's integrated planning and therefore always supportive of European military independence, had traditionally supported them.[239] By 2002, the argument that autonomous European military peacekeeping forces would sometimes perhaps need 'ad hoc multinational headquarters' began to surface.[240] The EU, in any case, already since 2001 had its EUMS with a very limited planning capacity. The idea of a *permanent* European HQ seems to have been raised first by Belgian PM Guy Verhofstadt in July 2002.[241]

Part of the rationale for the idea of an EU military HQ fermented during the two years of the 'Turkish deadlock' over the Berlin Plus agreement,[242] which led European leaders to think of an independent European option, in case the expected

---

235   *Cf. UE: Le projet britannique torpille l'idée de Paris et Berlin d'état-major européen; Londres veut cantonner la défense européenne dans l'Otan*, Le Figaro, 3 Sept. 2003.

236   European Defence: NATO/EU Consultation, Planning and Operations, Council Press Release, 15 Dec. 2003.

237   *Cf.* J. Roper, *Defining a common defence policy and common defence*, in: L. Martin / J. Roper (eds.) *Towards a common defence policy*, WEU-ISS (1995), p. 7 at 9 (n.3); M. d'Oléon / M. Jopp, *The way ahead for European defence cooperation*, in: *ibid.*, p. 99 at 106.

238   K. Möttölä, *Collective and co-operative security arrangements in Europe*, in: M. Koskenniemi, *International Law Aspects of the European Union* (1998), p. 87 at p. 89.

239   J. Howorth, *The ultimate challenge* (2000), p. 61; Abbasi, *Evolving a Common European defence* (2001), p. 99; F.S. Larrabee, *ESDP and NATO: Assuring Complementarity* (2004), p. 59.

240   E.g. K. Shake, *Constructive Duplication* (2002), p. 26.

241   Letter from Guy Verhofstadt, PM of Belgium, to Tony Blair and Jacques Chirac, Brussels, 18 July 2002, CP 57, p. 113.

242   See below Chapter 8 (Berlin Plus agreement).

agreement over using NATO's military assets should eventually fail.[243] Once born, however, the idea persisted and survived beyond the successful conclusion of the Berlin Plus agreement at the end of 2002.

'Mini-Summit' of April 2003

On 29 April 2003, Belgian PM Guy Verhofstadt convened a small 'Mini-Summit' in Brussels with the Heads of State and Government of France, Germany and Luxembourg. The resulting Declaration[244] stated the need for closer cooperation in defence, called a 'European Security and Defence Union' (ESDU).[245] Furthermore, for EU-led operations without recourse to NATO assets and capabilities, the EU needed to be provided with some independent planning capability. They therefore proposed to the other member States 'the creation of a nucleus collective capability for planning and conducting operations for the European Union',[246] and resolved to put in place 'not later than 2004, a multinational deployable force headquarters for joint operations, building on existing deployable headquarters'.[247] This new headquarters should be placed at the Brussels suburb of Tervuren.

It was argued later by the architects of the St-Malo Declaration of 1998[248] that this was in essence a goal already stated at St-Malo: that the EU should be able to act, whether using NATO assets or in its own 'outside the NATO framework'.[249] The proponents defended the initiative's exclusive character, arguing that various European projects, later successful, had started in this way.[250]

Criticism was levelled at the Mini-Summit from the United Kingdom and other European countries as well as the United States because of the Summit's bad timing at the height of the contentious debate of the Iraq campaign. Three of the four countries

---

243   S. Duke, *CESDP: Nice's Overtrumped Success?*, 6 EFAR 2 (2001), p. 155 at 174; A. Missiroli, *Sicherheitspolitische Kooperation zwischen Europäischer Union und Nato: Der türkische Verdruss über die Europäische Sicherheits- und Verteidigungspolitik*, 24 Integration 4 (2001), p. 340 at 352; H. Boguslawska, *Le lien transatlantique* (2003), p. 27; N. Winn, *Towards a CESDP?* (2003), p. 56.

244   European defence meeting – 'Tervuren', Meeting of the Heads of State and Government of Germany, France, Luxembourg and Belgium on European Defence, Brussels, 29 April 2003, para. 1, CP 67, p. 76.

245   *Ibid.*, Introduction. The concept of an ESDU had appeared first in the Franco-German summit celebrating the 40th anniversary of the Elysée Treaty. See Joint Declaration by C. Chirac and G. Schröder, 22 Jan. 2003, CP 67, p. 16, at para. 9; Declaration by the Franco-German Defence and Security Council, Paris 22 Jan. 2003, CP 67, p. 22, at II.

246   *Ibid.*, para. 6.

247   *Ibid.*, para. 7.

248   G. Errera, *Time to be serious about European defence*, Financial Times, 31 Oct. 2003, p. 19.

249   British-French summit, St-Malo, 3–4 Dec. 1998, para. 3, CP 47, p. 9.

250   C. Winneker, *Defence Summit in the firing line*, European Voice (online edition), Vol. 9, No. 16.

of the 'Mini-Summit' had been the ones who had blocked NATO's Art. 4 assistance to Turkey only in February, and the initiative was suspiciously regarded as a further effort to undermine the Alliance.[251] In the case of Germany, this was particularly serious for the United States. Secretary of State Colin Powell reacted by saying that what was needed was not more headquarters, but more capabilities.[252] Apart from this, however, the American reaction was still astoundingly quiet.

Towards a full compromise in December 2003

The United Kingdom recognised the necessity of some initiative to take the steam out of the proposal of the 'Gang of Four'. At the end of August, it published a non-paper titled 'Food for Thought' in which it proposed the creation of 'an EU planning cell at SHAPE', that is, an EU body, but situated within NATO confines,[253] for all kinds of EU operations, NATO-supported or otherwise. The idea of a permanent headquarters solely for autonomous EU operations was decisively rejected.[254] The paper was purposefully leaked to the press,[255] to have a maximum effect on the next informal meeting of EU foreign ministers in Riva del Garda (Italy) on 5 September. Despite being located at NATO, the EU cell proposed would be 'more' (in terms of European autonomy) than the Berlin Plus agreement provided[256] because planning would be conducted by EU personnel at SHAPE themselves, not by NATO personnel for the EU. The idea was, it seemed, not in principle rejected even in NATO military circles.[257] For Tony Blair, this first-time concession to an EU planning facility was a huge step, risking fierce criticism from the Conservative opposition at home.

Towards the end of September the views of the 'Big Three', Britain, France and Germany,[258] were starting to converge on European defence. The result of this first compromise was an internal document approved by Blair, Chirac and Schröder

---

251   P. Conradi, *France accused of building Trojan horse to break up NATO*, Sunday Times, 7 Sept. 2003.

252   R.J. McCartney, *4 European Leaders Form Pact to Boost Defense Cooperation; Foes of Iraq War Seek to Operate Independently of U.S.*, Washington Post, 30 April 2003, p. A17.

253   Reprinted in: Informal meeting of EU defence ministers, Rome, 29 Aug. 2003, British Non-Paper 'Food for Thought', at b), CP 67, p. 205.

254   *Ibid.*, p. 206, at c).

255   R. Bennet, *Blair sabotages French plan for EU army*, The Times, 25 Aug. 2003.

256   *Cf.* G. Lebel, *Défense en Europe*, 60 Défense nationale 2 (2004), p. 175 at 179.

257   *NATO chief backs EU's military autonomy*, World News Connection, 10 Sept. 2003.

258   Analysts of European defence had long argued that, to take the project of an independent European defence forward, discussions would first start between these three major powers. See U. Nerlich, *The relationship between a European common defence and NATO, the OSCE and the United Nations*, in: L. Martin / J. Roper (eds.) *Towards a common defence policy*, WEU-ISS (1995), p. 69 at 77; U. Schmalz, *Aufbruch zu neuer Handlungsfähigkeit* (1999), p. 197; M. Kremer / U. Schmalz, *Nach Nizza – Perspektiven der GESVP* (2001), p.

in a trilateral summit in Berlin on 20 September which read that the EU 'should be endowed with a joint capacity to plan and conduct operations without recourse to NATO resources and capabilities'.[259] It was mooted that this capacity should comprise about 40 to 50 military officers.[260] The project was to be explicitly open to other countries, not necessarily all EU members.

Belgium, which had before 20 September still insisted on building the EU planning headquarters in Tervuren,[261] now fell into line,[262] and the plan was endorsed by the Italian Presidency in early October in an own 'compromise proposal'.[263] Some two weeks later, the European Parliament likewise issued a resolution in support.[264]

The reaction of the United States and NATO to this emerging consensus within the EU on defence for a long time did not go beyond remarking occasionally that Belgian 'chocolate-makers' were best ignored.[265] However, during the summer, US ambassador to NATO N. Burns had vociferously warned Europeans 'not to go it alone' on defence, an area where NATO was 'the only show in town'.[266] After Britain's concession over the EU planning cell in August, however, the US diplomatic campaign against plans for a more independent European military capability began to mount. The United States called an extraordinary meeting of the NAC on 20 October and, during reportedly heated discussions, apparently called the EU's plans the 'most significant threat to NATO's future'.[267] The European allies took the point, and went to great length to reassure the US that all their initiatives were complementary to NATO.[268] To further soothe the waves, Germany a few days later firmly held that

172; J. Howorth, *European defence and the changing politics of the EU*, 39 JCMS (2001), p. 772. *Cf.* already H. Bull, *Civilian Power Europe* (1983), p. 149 at 164.

259   B. Benoit / B. Hall / W. Proissl, *Blair backs EU plans for joint defence project*, Financial Times, 22 Sept. 2003, p. 1.

260   *Blair sagt ja zur EU-Armee*, Der Spiegel online, 20 Sept. 2003.

261   *Belgium stands firm over EU military HQ plans*, AFP, 2 Sept. 2003; C. S. Smith, *Europeans Plan Own Military Command Post*, New York Times, 3 Sept. 2003, p. 10.

262   *Verhofstadt removes obstacles to EU defence*, De Standaard (online edition), 27 Sept. 2003, [in Dutch], English translation in: *Belgian daily upbeat on prospects for EU defence accord*, BBC Worldwide Monitoring, 29 Sept. 2003.

263   B. Evans-Pritchard, *Italy tables new defence proposal*, EUObserver, 3 Oct. 2003.

264   European Parliament Resolution on the Annual Report from the Council to the European Parliament on the Main Aspects and Basic Choices for CFSP, including the Financial Implications for the General Budget of the European Union, Strasbourg, 23 Oct. 2003, para. 34, CP 67, p. 235 at 242.

265   E.g. U.S. State Department spokesman R. Boucher, cited in: A. Kamen, *Not So 'New' After All*, Washington Post, 5 Sept. 2003, p. A19.

266   E.g. at the joint NAC-PSC meeting on 15 July 2003. *Cf.* M. Winter, *Von weißen Elefanten und bitteren Pillen*, Frankfurter Rundschau, 2 Sept. 2003, p. 3.

267   Cited in: *US presses Europe over defence plans*, AFP, 20 Oct. 2003. *Cf.* M. Winter, *Zählappel beim Botschafter*, Frankfurter Rundschau, 22 Oct. 2003, p. 6.

268   T. Fuller / B. Knowlton, *Europeans try to reassure U.S. on NATO*, International Herald Tribune, 22 Oct. 2003, p. 7.

the planned EU planning cell should be attached to NATO.[269] Britain underlined its refusal to accept any EU planning unit outside the NATO headquarters.[270] By mid-November the general European consensus, summarised by the CFSP-HR Javier Solana, was that the planned EU cell should not in any quantitative way duplicate the vast planning resources already available at SHAPE (partly available also to the EU, under the Berlin Plus agreement), but should be restricted to a small number of persons, and should facilitate EU–NATO cooperation in general.[271] US President G.W. Bush himself felt reassured by Tony Blair that none of the EU's incipient defence plans would undermine NATO.[272] By the end of 2003 US opposition to most of the plans enunciated by the Mini-Summit in April would effectively cease;[273] it still occasionally called them 'hypothetical'.[274]

Drawing a preliminary balance over the debate on 17 November 2003, the Council acknowledged that

> various proposals have been made in recent months in order to address the need to improve the EU's capacity for planning and conducting military operations. These should be examined further, in a framework of compatibility with NATO and aiming at avoiding unnecessary duplication.[275]

The consensus was already so far advanced among the EU 15 that on the same day a Status-of-Forces agreement (EU SOFA) could be concluded, concerning national military personnel to be made available to the future EU headquarters and crisis management operations.[276]

The IGC Summit on 29 November 2003 in Naples delivered the final breakthrough between the 'Big Three'. Britain dropped its resistance to an EU planning cell situated at the EUMS, that is, outside NATO. Its limited operational capacity would

---

269   J. Vinocur, *Germany moves to allay U.S. fears on EU defence*, International Herald Tribune, 28 Oct. 2003, p. 3.

270   *Britain renews its opposition to EU defence headquarters*, AFP, 5 Nov. 2003.

271   *Solana für europäischen Führungsstab*, Frankfurter Allgemeine Zeitung, 13 Nov. 2003, p. 7.

272   C. Adams, *Blair faces hangover when the party ends and his guest is gone*, Financial Times, 17 Nov. 2003, p. 3.

273   R. de Wijk, *The Reform of ESDP and EU–NATO Cooperation*, 39 The International Spectator 1 (2004), p. 71 at 79.

274   M. Gherghisan, *Rumsfeld: EU defence plans still hypothetical*, EUObserver, 2 Dec. 2003.

275   GAERC, Brussels, 17 Nov. 2003, Conclusions, para. 9 (CP 67, p. 256 at 257).

276   Agreement between the Member States of the European Union concerning the status of military and civilian staff seconded to the institutions of the European Union, of the headquarters and forces which may be made available to the European Union in the context of the preparation and execution of the tasks referred to in Article 17(2) of the Treaty on European Union, including exercises, and of the military and civilian staff of the Member States put at the disposal of the European Union to act in this context (EU SOFA), 17 Nov. 2003, OJ C 321/6 of 31.12.2003.

only, however, start operating as a 'last resort' measure,[277] and NATO-supported missions (organised over an EU cell at SHAPE) would have a clear preference. The compromise was enshrined in the document 'European defence: NATO/EU Consultation, Planning and Operations'.[278] This document will be analysed in detail in the next part. The compromise at Naples was realised as a grander package deal – the price to be paid for the British concession lay in a different place, namely in the negotiations at the IGC:

- a weakening of the obligation on mutual defence in the draft European Constitution (old Art. I-40, para. 7[279]) and a strengthening of the reference to existing NATO obligations;[280]
- the fulfilling of two British demands concerning the 'battle groups' provision (old Art. I-40, para. 6):
  - unanimity in decisions to establish such enhanced cooperation[281] and
  - no minimum number requirement for the member States which wanted to participate.[282]

Reactions to this deal from NATO quarters were expectedly cool,[283] but the US government, apparently informed beforehand by the British, went along.[284]

At the European Council in Brussels on 12 December 2003, the compromise document was tabled by Germany, France and Britain and adopted without changes.[285] The European Council further called for speedy implementation of the document, in particular the establishment of the EU cell at SHAPE and the EU civil/military planning cell at the EUMS.[286] An informal meeting of EU defence ministers on 5–6 April 2004 decided that the EU civil/military planning cell should be up and running

---

277   C. Gourlay / J. Kleymeyer, *Defence deal at the IGC*, ISIS European Security Review, No. 20 (Dec. 2003), p. 3.

278   The paper was not officially published, but is reprinted in CP 67, pp. 283–4.

279   Draft Treaty Establishing a Constitution for Europe, 18 July 2003, OJ C 169/1-105.

280   L. Zecchini, *Paris, Londres et Berlin sont parvenus a un compromis sur la défense européenne*, Le Monde, 29 Nov. 2003, p. 6.

281   *Cf.* C. Grant, *Europe can sell its defence plan to Washington*, Financial Times, 2 Dec. 2003, p. 23. Art. III-213, in contrast, in fact now provides for qualified majority for such decisions, see at p. 75.

282   Such a minimum requirement is still found in Art. 40a TEU, para. 2, and was part of the Italian 'compromise proposal' in October 2004. *Cf.* L. Zecchini, fn. 280.

283   J. Dempsey, *Nato split over separate military planning unit*, Financial Times, 1 Dec. 2003, p. 6

284   *Id.*, *Rumsfeld emollient over EU military planning move*, Financial Times, 2 Dec. 2003, p. 10.

285   It was published by the Council as a Press Release from 15 Dec. 2003, with no further document specification.

286   European Council, Brussels, 12 Dec. 2003, Presidency Conclusions, V. B., para. 89, CP67, p. 296.

in the latter half of 2004,[287] a goal which was confirmed by the European Council on 17–18 June 2004,[288] but not achieved in time. The High Representative issued a report on preparations in this regard on 15 June 2004.[289] The Council decided on a more detailed outline for the civil/military cell on 10 November 2004.[290] A proposal for modalities concerning the EU cell at SHAPE and the NATO Liaison Team at the EUMS were shortly thereafter sent in a letter from the High Representative to the NATO SG.[291] With the endorsement of an enlarged NATO/EU Consultation document of December 2004 by the European Council on 17 December 2004, the way was opened for the cell to start its work and prepare the establishment of an EU operations centre by June 2006.[292]

THE DOCUMENT 'EUROPEAN DEFENCE: NATO/EU CONSULTATION, PLANNING AND OPERATIONS' (DECEMBER 2003) – FOUR OPTIONS FOR PEACEKEEPING IN EUROPEAN SECURITY

Text of the document

The document 'European defence: NATO/EU Consultation, Planning and Operations' of December 2003 establishes a systematic hierarchy of options for conducting peace operations between NATO and the EU. The four options described in the document are:

- **Option 1:** A NATO-led campaign, using also contributions from European allies, but with no independent element from the EU (for example Operation Allied Force);
- **Option 2:** An EU-led operation under political control and strategic direction of the EU's PSC, using NATO planning facilities and other military hardware and intelligence,[293] under the existing Berlin Plus agreement of 2002 (for example Operation *Concordia* in Macedonia in 2003, or Operation *Althea* in Bosnia from December 2004);

---

287   ISIS NATO Notes, Vol. 6, No. 4 (April 2004), *News in brief*, p. 1.

288   European Council, Brussels, 17–18 June 2004, Presidency Conclusions, VI. Annex (European defence: NATO/EU Consultation, Planning and Operations), Council Doc. 10679/04, p. 20.

289   Council Doc. 10596/04, 15 June 2004 (classified). It is mooted that it contains preparations for a separate agreement to enter into force towards the end of 2004. *Cf.* F. Terpan, *La dimension politique de la sécurité européenne au premier semestre 2004*, 60 Défense nationale 8/9 (2004), p. 97 at 106.

290   European defence: NATO/EU Consultation, Planning and Operations, Council Doc. 13990/04 (classified), 10 November 2004, Annex I.

291   *Cf.* Draft ESDP Presidency Report, 13 Dec. 2004, Council Doc. 15547/04, para. 27.

292   European Council, Brussels, 16–17 June 2005, Presidency Conclusions, para. 82, Council Doc. 10255/05.

293   For the distinction between those military assets, see below Chapter 8 (Berlin Plus Agreement).

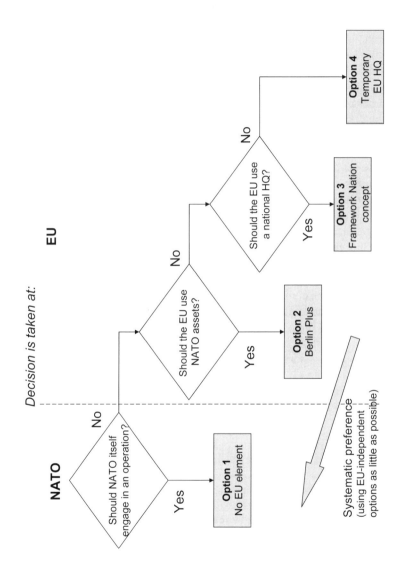

Figure 2.1   Decision tree

- **Option 3:** An autonomous EU-led operation without support of NATO assets, planned, organised and conducted through the multinationalised national military headquarters of one member State acting as 'Framework Nation' (for example like Operation *Artemis* in the DRC);
- **Option 4:** Like option 3, but planned, organised and conducted through the future EU civil/military planning cell at the EUMS, temporarily augmented by additional staff from the EUMS and the member States for the duration of the operation.

These four options are not equal alternatives.[294] Rather, they are to be used in descending order of preference. The procedure is as follows: discussions on which option to use shall start at NATO, being the 'natural choice for an operation involving the European and American allies'. EU/NATO consultation must obviously be very tight at this early stage, in order to avoid faits accomplis by either side,[295] according to the procedure set down in the Nice Presidency Conclusions.[296] In a case 'where NATO as a whole is not engaged'[297] the EU may proceed to options 2, 3 or 4. NATO reads that phrase as a right of first refusal,[298] but such a reading is not necessarily compelling. Once option 1 is excluded, the EU must decide whether it wants to conduct its operation on its own or with NATO facilities. It is not entirely free in this choice, and must in the first instance consider using NATO facilities,[299] 'taking into account the Alliance's role, capacities, and involvement in the region in question'.[300] In most cases, it will in fact need those NATO facilities in any case, except for the least-demanding missions, until its military capabilities improve in the future. Should the EU, after due consideration, nevertheless decide on an autonomous operation, the first choice would be option 3, that is, an operation using national headquarters under the 'Framework Nation' concept. Only 'in certain circumstances',[301] that is, exceptionally and as a last resort, may the EU civil/military planning cell at the EUMS, under option 4, be activated and temporarily upgraded to serve as headquarters for an operation, without being a standing HQ.[302] The procedure can be conceived as a decision tree (see Figure 2.1 above).

294   *Cf.* K. Pries, *Pragmatische Angelsachsen*, Frankfurter Rundschau, 6 April 2004, p. 5.
295   F.S. Larrabee, *ESDP and NATO: Assuring Complementarity* (2004), p. 61.
296   See below Chapter 8 (Berlin Plus Agreement).
297   NATO/EU Consultation document, para. 3.
298   NATO Press Release (2003)154, 11 Dec. 2003. *Cf.* F. Faria, *Crisis management in sub-Saharan Africa – The role of the European Union*, EU-ISS Occasional Paper No. 51 (2004), p. 49. ('where NATO has no interest').
299   B. Evans-Pritchard, *Deal struck on EU defence*, EUObserver, 12 Dec. 2003.
300   NATO/EU Consultation document, para. 3.
301   *Ibid.*, para. 6.
302   *Ibid.*, para. 7.

NATO's reaction

NATO's own interpretation of the EU's NATO/EU consultation document – as made public in its Press Release containing the NATO-SG's comments of 11 December 2003[303] – conformed, on most of the points, with the letter and spirit of that text. It restated NATO's position as the 'natural choice' for operations involving European and North American allies. It confirmed that 'there will be no duplication of NATO's standing operational planning capabilities' and that 'there would be no permanent EU operational staff'. In addition, it elaborated, somewhat more than the NATO/EU Consultation document itself, on the requirement for 'transparency' between NATO and the EU.

However, in two crucial points NATO's interpretation did deviate from the wording of the EU's document. Firstly, it said that the 'EU arrangements for civil-military coordination' (meaning option 3 and 4) were 'firmly within the context of Berlin Plus'. The EU's document, contrastingly, says that only option 2 'will be conducted through the "Berlin Plus" arrangements'.[304] However, NATO-SG Robertson's comments could still be reconciled with the language of the EU's document if one understands 'within the context' to mean 'in conformity with' or 'not prejudice'.

Secondly, the phrase 'where NATO as a whole *is* not engaged'[305] in the EU's document was adapted in NATO's Press Release to 'where NATO as a whole *has decided* not to be engaged'.[306] While the EU's formulation – in an exercise of constructive ambiguity – leaves open the crucial question whether NATO *has* a right of first refusal to any future operation before the EU can consider engaging in it, NATO's formulation is crystal clear in the affirmative. The lacuna between those two formulations cannot be healed by even the most creative interpretation. The conclusion must be that NATO, while being in agreement with most of the points in the EU's 'NATO/EU Consultation document', still insisted on a right of first refusal versus the EU concerning crisis management operations. The question of NATO's right of first refusal will be analysed in detail in a later chapter.[307]

Legal nature

Concerning the legal nature of the document, despite its title, it is certainly *not* any agreement between the NATO and the EU (like the 2002 Berlin Plus agreement or the 2003 Security-of-Information agreement). Despite its immediate reaction to it on 11 December 2003, NATO was not in any formal way involved in its drafting or adoption. Rather, the NATO/EU Consultation Document has the character of a

---

303 See above at fn. 298.
304 NATO/EU Consultation document, para. 3.
305 NATO/EU Consultation document, para. 3 (emphasis added).
306 NATO Press Release (2003)154, 11 Dec. 2003.
307 See below Chapter 5 (NATO Primacy).

declaration of the EU member States, much like the Presidency Conclusions of the European Council (in fact it was issued together with them in December 2003). Hence, it is not legally binding under international law. However, its provisions are arguably sufficiently precise to be deemed self-executing, even though much remains to be defined in subsequent implementation.[308]

Context

The options for peacekeeping operations between the EU and NATO contained in the NATO/EU Consultation document were not invented on the spot in the winter of 2003. They had largely already been identified in 2000,[309] and were part of the decision-making procedure agreed between NATO and the EU in the Berlin Plus agreement.[310] The distinction between NATO-supported and EU-only missions was thus known from 1999 onwards.[311] The old CJTF model for NATO-WEU cooperation had also been based on a very similar model.[312] The only true innovation made by the NATO/EU Consultation document was option 4. Politically, the widened spectrum of options reflected a strategic rationale. For the Europeans, it was the dissatisfaction with dependence on US military assets, the implications of which had been manifest in the Balkan Wars.[313] For the Americans and NATO, it was the diminishing strategic interest for the European theatre in relation to other trouble spots in the world, coupled with military overstretch. However, the NATO/EU Consultation Document was the first time any of the last three options had been defined as precisely. It is therefore worth examining in detail.

Analysis of the document

Option 1: NATO-only campaign   In terms of formal procedure, there is little new to be said about option 1. It runs entirely under NATO's military administration, using

---

308   Many of these implementation documents are, however, classified due to their military content.

309   E.g. J. Howorth, *The ultimate challenge* (2000), p. 60; C. Schwegmann, *EU-Friedensmissionen* (2002), pp. 25–29.

310   C. Wernicke, *Amerikas Argwohn,* Süddeutsche Zeitung, 23 Oct. 2003, p. 9. *Cf.* the detailed Nice arrangements being part of Berlin Plus, below Chapter 8 (Berlin Plus agreement).

311   See e.g. already the informal meeting of EU foreign ministers, Eltville, 13–14 March 1999, German proposal, para. 4, CP 47, p. 17 at 18. *Cf.* C. von Buttlar, *ESDP – A Regional Effort within the Atlantic Alliance,* in: A. Bodnar et al. (eds.), *The Emerging Constitutional Law of the European Union* (2003), p. 405.

312   M. Warnken, *Der Handlungsrahmen der EU* (2002), p. 123.

313   B.R. Posen, *ESDP and the Structure of World Power*, 39 The International Spectator 1 (2004), p. 5 at 15.

the CJTF concept,[314] the procedural rules of which are all contained in classified NATO documents.

The formula 'where NATO [or the Alliance] as a whole is not engaged' certainly refers to a case where NATO is already active in peacekeeping on the ground,[315] for example in Kosovo or Afghanistan. But, as seen in NATO's reaction on 11 December 2003, and also in US government sources, this phrase is often interpreted to imply an automatic NATO 'right of first refusal' in cases where a future operation is being considered, but neither the EU nor NATO have yet in fact engaged in it. Such a right would, through the unanimity principle prevailing at NATO, also give the US a direct veto over the general direction of EU peacekeeping. Questions of any 'right' apart, the US also has a strong political incentive to insist on a NATO mission rather than leave it to the Europeans, even if the mission did not directly serve its security interests: 'to keep it out of the EU's hands and avoid the loss of prestige associated with an EU success'.[316]

NATO-only decision-making procedures have been shown to be very effective in many operations in the past. Throughout the 1990s, they were the only option available in Europe. Two such NATO operations are still ongoing, in Kosovo (KFOR) and Afghanistan (ISAF). Others may soon follow, in Iraq or in Israel/Palestine. However, as has been shown in Kosovo,[317] US primacy in military-technical matters, and hence long-term policy formulation, is ingrained under this format. For this reason, it is today regarded as unsatisfactory by many European countries.

Option 2: Berlin Plus   EU-led operations supported by NATO assets are covered by the Berlin Plus agreement since 2002.[318] In order to facilitate cooperation between the administrations of the two organisations under this framework, a small EU cell is established at SHAPE, and NATO liaison arrangements are equally made at the EUMS.[319]

The principle that an EU-led mission should, if at all possible, be conducted in close consultation with relevant NATO bodies and using NATO assets, historically stems from the fact that, as recently as 2000, an independent EU mission was in practice not imaginable. There was thus little distinction made between a case when the EU would simply need NATO's assets, and a case where it would in addition be obliged to do so.[320] American specialists on European security like P.H. Gordon

---

314   See below Chapter 3 (NATO Today).

315   P.H. Gordon, *Their Own Army? Making European Defense Work*, Foreign Affairs (July/Aug. 2000), p. 12 at 16.

316   B.R. Posen, *ESDP and the Structure of World Power*, 39 The International Spectator 1 (2004), p. 5 at 16.

317   See above.

318   See below, Chapter 8 (Berlin Plus Agreement).

319   NATO/EU Consultation document, para. 4.

320   See e.g. J. Solana, *The Development of a Common European Security and Defence Policy – The Integration Project of the Next Decade*, speech, 17 Dec. 1999, reprinted in:

certainly insisted on the 'NATO-first' principle.[321] Most of the EU's peacekeeping operations in fact cannot do today without assistance from NATO (primarily US) force multipliers.[322] Once such an operation using NATO assets is under way, close and transparent consultation with NATO bodies and non-EU contributors is essential, and runs according to the procedure described in the Nice Presidency Conclusions,[323] being part of the Berlin Plus agreement. At the same time, despite the 'assured access'[324] of that agreement, this same cooperation severely limits the EU's capacity to plan and act autonomously according to its own interests, remaining in a permanent and systemic dependence on the NAC, and thus on non-EU NATO members.[325]

The first practical application of option 2 came with the EU's first-ever military peacekeeping mission *Concordia* in Macedonia.[326]

The evaluation process after the completion of this mission revealed that on the whole, the Berlin Plus arrangements worked well in *Concordia*, despite some minor complaints from the United States (about the sharing of information) and France (about the factual position of NATO's AFSOUTH command in Naples in the EU command structure).[327] Option 2 was also tested in November 2003 in a joint NATO-EU exercise called CME/CMX 03 which involved a fictional scenario

---

A.A. Levasseur / R.F. Scott, *The Law of the European Union: A New Constitutional Order – Materials and Cases* (2001), p. 1028 at 1030.

321   P.H. Gordon, *Their Own Army? Making European Defense Work*, Foreign Affairs (July/Aug. 2000), p. 12; *cf.* J. Howorth, *The ultimate challenge* (2000), p. 65.

322   Yesson (2001), p. 213; A. Monaco, *Who takes care of European Security? EU and NATO: Competition or Cooperation?*, in: A. Weidemann / A. Simon (eds.), *The Future of ESDP* (2003), p. 40 at 45; F. Terpan, *Premier semestre 2004*, 60 Défense nationale 8/9 (2004), p. 99 at 105.

323   European Council, Nice, 7–9 Dec. 2000, Presidency Conclusions, Annex VII to Annex VI: Standing Arrangements for Consultation and Cooperation between the EU and NATO, at III.B., CP 47, p. 206. The details of procedure for cooperation with non-EU European allies is spelled out in the 'Ankara document', negotiated in 2001, which found its way into the Presidency Conclusions of the European Council, Brussels, 24–5 Oct. 2002, Annex III, CP 57, pp. 136–140. For the Berlin Plus agreement in detail, see below Chapter 8 (Berlin Plus agreement).

324   This does not mean 'assured' in the legal sense, see below Chapter 8 (Berlin Plus Agreement).

325   M. Álvarez Verdugo, *La relación de Consulta y Cooperación entre la Unión Europea y la Otan*, REDI No. 12. Year 6 (May-Aug. 2002), p. 471 at 481; E. Barbé / A.G. Bondía, *La Política Europea de Seguridad y Defensa en el Escenario Internacional Actual*, Arbor No. 678 (2002), p. 357 at 372; T.C. Salmon / A.J.K. Shepherd, *Toward a European Army* (2003), p. 127.

326   For details on this mission, see below Chapter 7 (Military Crisis Management).

327   A. Monaco, *Operation Concordia and Berlin Plus: NATO and the EU take stock*, ISIS NATO Notes, Vol. 5, No. 8 (2003), p. 9 at 10.

(Operation *Atlantia*).[328] This exercise went beyond the cooperation in Concordia, because the full decision-making process previous to the launching of a mission was tested. The exercise was deemed successful, providing a good test of the Berlin Plus agreement.[329] At present, the EU's most sizeable operation *Althea* in Bosnia also runs under Option 2 mode, that is, with Berlin Plus support.

Option 3: Framework Nation Concept   The textual provision on option 3 in the NATO/EU Consultation document is very brief: 'national HQs, which can be multi-nationalised for the purpose of conducting an EU-led operation'.[330] This refers to the EU's 'Framework Nation Concept' under which one member State's national military headquarters serves as multinational headquarters, added to by military officers from all the other member States participating in the operation.[331]

This is then called the EU operational headquarters (EU OHQ). In practice, the framework nation will be the State with the highest interest in the operation, and with the most troops involved. Not all the member States have headquarters suited for this purpose. The most capable are the UK's Permanent Joint Headquarters (PJHQ) at Northwood and France's Permanent Joint Headquarters at Creil.[332] These two countries already have some limited experience in overseas military interventions in Africa. Such headquarters must be able to accommodate officers from other troop-contributing States. Practical implementation of the Framework Nation Concept is not without problems. Planning should be conducted jointly, but would in fact probably have to rely on the long-time plans of the framework nation. In addition, ad-hoc incorporation of foreign officers may cause delays in planning at precisely the moment when swift and efficient action is needed.[333]

---

328   D. Manca, *Operation Atlantia: A Fictional Test for Berlin Plus*, ESR No. 20 (Dec. 2003), pp. 9–11. The EU had been planning for such exercises (involving scenarios using NATO assets, and without such recourse), since at least three years previously (*Cf.* European Council Göteborg, 15–16 June 2001, Presidency Conclusions, Annex IV to the ANNEX: Exercise Policy of the European Union, III., para. 16 (CP 51, p. 55)).

329   European Council, Brussels, 14 June 2004, Presidency Report on ESDP, para. 20, Council Doc. 10547/04.

330   NATO/EU Consultation document, para. 4.

331   The 'EU Framework Nation Concept' is not listed on the Council Documents Register, and therefore is probably classified. Its existence may, however, be inferred from a reference in Council JA 2003/423/CFSP of 5 June 2003, OJ L 143/50 of 11/6/2003, Preambular para. 5.

332   T.C. Salmon / A.J.K. Shepherd, *Toward a European Army* (2003), p. 127. Germany and Italy have also established joint operations headquarters in recent years (*ibid.*).

333   *Ibid*, p. 128.

The Framework Nation Concept was initially developed under the auspices of the WEU in 1996.[334] The EU subsequently adapted it for its purposes as it began to envisage operations without recourse to NATO assets.[335]

The first practical application was Operation *Artemis* in the DRC in July–September 2003.[336] France acted as framework nation, since the EU still lacked a deployable headquarters and other command and control facilities.[337] On the lessons-learned side, France as framework nation is reported to have been dissatisfied particularly by the slow reimbursement of financial costs for the operation.

In May 2004 an EU military crisis management exercise (CME 04) took place to test the ESDP institutional structures relating to the Framework Nation Concept. The EU OHQ was co-located at UK's Northwood headquarters.[338] Another exercise involving multinationalised national headquarters took place in October 2004.[339]

Option 4: EU military headquarters at the EUMS The new EU headquarters, being the innovation of the NATO/EU Consultation document, takes a prominent place in its provisions. The wording is very careful, almost hesitant to the point of unclarity.[340] 'In certain circumstances', the Council may decide (presumably unanimously[341]) to 'draw on the collective capacity of the EUMS'.[342] Two material conditions must be fulfilled for this to be possible: a 'joint civil/military response' must be required, and no national HQ must be identified.[343] The first condition would apply to most potential peacekeeping scenarios at the planning stage. Only high-end missions such as Operation Allied Force were purely military. The EU is yet far from conducting anything on that scale alone. The second condition could mean that no member State

---

334   WEU Council of Ministers, Paris Declaration, 13 May 1996, para. 22, http://www.weu.int/documents/970513en.pdf (visited 11/08/2004). The concept is also mentioned e.g. in the Report submitted on behalf of the Defence Ctte. by Mr. De Decker (Rapp.), *The organisation of operational links between NATO, WEU and EU*, WEU Assembly Doc. 1624, 9 Nov. 1998, para. 133.

335   See e.g. Anglo-French summit, London, 25 Nov. 1999, Joint Declaration on European Defence, para. 5, CP 47, p. 77; Meeting of European Union defence ministers, Sintra, 28 Feb. 2000, Military Bodies in the European Union and the Planning and Conduct of EU-led Military Operations, para. 19 (CP 47, p. 94 at 99).

336   For details on this mission, see below Chapter 7 (Military Crisis Management).

337   R. de Wijk, *The Reform of ESDP and EU–NATO Cooperation*, 39 The International Spectator 1 (2004), p. 71 at 73.

338   European Council, Brussels, 14 June 2004, Presidency Report on ESDP, para. 21, Council Doc. 10547/04.

339   L. Zecchini, *Cinq jours de guerre virtuelle à vingt-cinq participants européens*, Le Monde, 20 Oct. 2004, p. 6.

340   This is understandable in light of the political compromise character of the document, after more than half a year of heated debate between the major European players.

341   Art. 23, paras. 1 and 2 TEU. *Cf.* C. Grant, *EU defence takes a step forward*, CER briefing note, Dec. 2003, p. 3.

342   NATO/EU Consultation document, para. 7.

343   *Ibid.*

wants to be the framework nation for option 3. Theoretically, it could also cover cases where more than one member State has indicated an interest, to avoid political competition.[344]

The next paragraph already speaks of '*the* civilian/military cell'[345] in the EUMS, and proceeds to describe its functions, procedure and staffing details, adding immediately that 'this would not be a standing HQ'. As any clause on *how* this body should be established is manifestly lacking, it seems reasonable to read this into the formulation 'to draw upon the collective capacity of the EUMS' in the previous paragraph. In other words, the Council decides unanimously to set up the EU planning cell in the EUMS, once the two above mentioned conditions have been fulfilled.

In its last paragraph, the NATO/EU Consultation document contains a mandate for further development of option 4: 'further developments of the scope or nature of this capacity could be examined. It would require further decision by the Council'.[346] This reads similar to the mandate in Art. 17, para. 1 TEU for a future 'common defence'. 'Further development' arguably refers to turning the temporary EU planning cell into a real permanent headquarters by a further unanimous Council decision.[347] As an old French proverb goes: *Rien ne reste comme le provisoire.*

The EU civilian/military cell is independent from the EUMS with its own designated Operation Commander. Augmentation personnel will be made available, mostly 'double hatted' from the EUMS. National personnel from member States can also be provided.[348]

Option 4 seems to have been entirely negotiated and developed by intense negotiation between the member States between April and December 2003.[349] Further details were worked out during 2004.[350] The concept is still in elaboration at the time of writing.

Even though the NATO/EU Consultation document contains an in-built systematic preference for using more 'NATO-friendly' options wherever possible, it is clear from the political context that option 4 (complete EU operation) represents the most recent innovation, while option 1 (complete NATO operation) is historically the oldest. Developments over time thus seem to point towards more EU independence. This means that for all the systematic preference for NATO operations in theory, the very existence of options 2, 3 and 4 will make such operations more likely in future

---

344   T.C. Salmon / A.J.K. Shepherd, *Toward a European Army* (2003), p. 128, cite this contingency as one which may arise under option 3.

345   Emphasis added.

346   NATO/EU Consultation document, para. 7.

347   C. Grant, *Europe can sell its defence plan to Washington*, Financial Times, 2 Dec. 2003, p. 23.

348   A respective Status-of-Forces agreement for military personnel of EU member States was already concluded on 17 November 2003. See above fn. 276.

349   See above at p. 82.

350   *Cf.* Draft ESDP Presidency Report, 13 Dec. 2004, Council Doc. 15547/04, para. 26.

practice than option 1. This is another implicit signal that the balance in European crisis management is shifting from NATO to the EU.[351]

---

351   See the Conclusion.

Chapter 3

NATO Today

NATO has proved a popular topic in both the political sciences[1] and in international legal studies[2] (particularly attempts to subsume it under the regime of a regional arrangement under Chapter VIII of the UN Charter[3]) since its inception. This book cannot aspire to do justice to the vast body of writing on NATO of the last 60 years. Instead, the idea is to give a short overview over the legal framework as it stands today as well as over NATO's current functions, particularly where they are relevant to the EU–NATO relationship. Recent developments are given a priority.[4] The internal dimension of NATO (that is, civilian and military institutions and structures) will largely be left out.[5]

---

1   For example H.L. Ismay, *NATO – the first five years* (1954); S. Sloan, *NATO's Future – Towards a new Transatlantic Bargain* (1987); F.H. Heller / J. R Gillingham (eds.), *NATO: The founding of the Atlantic Alliance and the Integration of Europe* (1992); K.W. Thompson (ed.), *NATO and the Changing World Order* (1996); P. Cornish, *Partnership in Crisis – the US, Europe and the Fall and Rise of NATO* (1997); S. Kay, *NATO and the Future of European Security* (1998); M. Brenner (ed.), *NATO and Collective Security* (1998); D.G. Haglund (ed.), *New NATO, New Century – Canada, the United States, and the Future of the Atlantic Alliance* (2000); H. Timmermann / A. Pradetto (eds.), *Die NATO auf dem Weg ins 21. Jahrhundert* (2002); O. Theiler, *Die NATO im Umbruch* (2003). For a good bibliography on NATO until 1993, see for example P. Williams (comp.), *North Atlantic Treaty Organization* (1994). Interesting papers can also be found on: NATO Research Fellowships 1994–2003, http://www.nato.int/acad/fellow/ (visited 11/08/2004).
2   K. Ipsen, *Rechtsgrundlagen und Institutionalisierung der Atlantisch-Westeuropäischen Verteidigung* (1967); U. Schürr, *Der Aufbau einer ESVI* (2003); G. Warg, *Von Verteidigung zu kollektiver Sicherheit – Der Nato-Vertrag auf Rädern* (2004).
3   I. Pernice, *Die Sicherung des Weltfriedens durch Regionale Organisationen und die Vereinten Nationen* (1972); C. Walter, *Vereinte Nationen und Regionalorganisationen* (1996); D. Geyrhalter, *Friedenssicherung durch Regionalorganisationen ohne Beschluß des Sicherheitsrates* (2002).
4   This is also the way NATO presents itself today, as will become clear from a quick look at the content page of the NATO Handbook (2001).
5   For a detailed description of NATO's institutional structure, see only the NATO Handbook (2001). *Cf.* also for example D.L. Band, *The Military Committee of the North Atlantic Alliance* (1991).

THE NORTH ATLANTIC TREATY

The North Atlantic Treaty[6] (NAT), concluded on 4 April 1949 between Western European countries, the United States and Canada, is the founding charter of NATO. It was conceived as a mutual defence pact against the clear and present threat to Western Europe from the Soviet Union, a threat which also affected the security interests of the United States and Canada. In addition, as its preamble and Art. 2 make clear, it gave expression to and meant to foster a 'Western community of values' based on the principles of democracy, liberty and the rule of law. In 1949 and throughout the Cold War, this value community was perceived as a strong socio-cultural underpinning of the mutual defence commitment of the NAT.

Despite being arguably the most important document in European security in the latter half of the twentieth century, the NAT is quite brief, stipulating only the main obligations of the parties, and dispensing with procedural provisions for the largest part. This brevity is certainly an expression of NATO's legal culture.[7] As the NAT itself does not contain detailed provisions, a major part of NATO's intra-organisational law has evolved through 'subsequent conduct' of its parties.[8]

The preamble as well as Art. 1 NAT contain a commitment for jointly furthering international peace and security consistent with the purposes of the United Nations.

The central mutual defence commitment to the Alliance is provided in Arts. 3 to 5. Art. 3 provides for joint preparation to resist an armed attack against a State party. The Alliance's highly integrated defence structure is legally based on this article.[9] Art. 4 contains a consultation duty in case of a threat to the territorial integrity, political independence or security of any State party. This consultation duty was initially conceived as a preceding stage to the collective self-defence in Art. 5.[10] Since the end of the Cold War, however, it has been reinterpreted successively to cover also NATO's new peacekeeping functions outside the territories of its member States.[11] Art. 5 is the central provision of NATO. It is a mutual defence clause based on the 'one for all, all for one' principle. The exact legal obligation, however, does not commit every member State to military assistance to an attacked fellow party,

---

6   34 UNTS 243.

7   *Cf.* E. Stein / D. Carreau, *Law and Peaceful Change in a Subsystem: 'Withdrawal' of France from the North Atlantic Treaty Organization'*, 62 AJIL (1968), p. 577 at 606, who wrote of 'the propensity on the part of member states to gloss over the basic issues concerning the legal nature of the Organization because of their potentially divisive impact'.

8   J.S. Ignarski, *North Atlantic Treaty Organization* EPIL III, p. 650–1.

9   *Cf.* H.L. Ismay, *NATO – the first five years* (1954), pp. 13–14.

10   On the exact scope of the duty to consult under Art. 4 NAT, and the 'NATO spirit' of informal consultation, see only F.R. Kirgis Jr., *NATO Consultations as a Component of National Decision-Making*, 73 AJIL (1979), pp. 372–406; K. Ipsen, *Rechtsgrundlagen* (1967), pp. 100–101; S. Kay, *NATO and the Future of European Security* (1998), pp. 24, 32 and 36–9.

11   See below, p. 105.

but Art. 5 rather leaves the choice of means at the discretion of the aiding party.[12] Art. 6 further limits the geographical scope of application of Art. 5.

Art. 7 contains a conflict clause in favour of the UN Charter, in keeping with Art. 103 UN Charter. Subject only to this qualification,[13] Art. 8 obliges States parties to avoid other international engagements which could come in conflict with the NAT. In light of the precise language employed throughout the NAT, 'engagements' covers not only international treaties but also other, that is, non-binding or factual commitments. It thus represents a very far-reaching conflict clause in favour of the NAT.[14]

Art. 9 is the only institutional provision in the NAT. It establishes the North Atlantic Council (NAC) as the highest organ of the Alliance. The NAC takes decisions by consensus, that is, unanimity.[15] Establishment of a defence committee and other 'such subsidiary bodies as may be necessary' is also provided. Utilising this flexible mandate of intra-organisational competence, a large infrastructure grouped into civil and military bodies[16] has been set up since 1949 and regularly adjusted, under the authority of the Council,[17] for running NATO's day-to-day business and harmonising national defence plans.[18] Joint cooperation bodies with third parties have also been

---

12   This feature of Art. 5 has its historical roots in the need to placate the hesitant position of the US Senate, in order to make it possible to approve and ratify the North Atlantic Treaty in conformity with the US Constitution. For details, see Chapter 6 (Collective Self-Defence).

13   The subordination of Art. 8 to Art. 7 NAT is clear from their systematic position. In addition, it flows directly from Art. 103 UN Charter, to which all NATO member States are also parties.

14   See below Chapter 5 (NATO Primacy).

15   NATO Handbook (2001), p. 149; J.S. Ignarski, *North Atlantic Treaty Organization*, in EPIL III, p. 648. The unanimity principle is only expressly provided in Art. 10 NAT (accessions by new members), but has been applied in practice to all NAC decisions since. *Cf.* T. Gazzini, *NATO's Role in the Collective Security System*, 8 JCSL 2 (2003), p. 231 at 243.

16   The highest civil bodies are the Defence Planning Committee, the Nuclear Planning Group and the Committee on the Challenges of Modern Society. The NATO International Staff is organised into five divisions: political; defence planning and policy; defence support; infrastructure, logistics and council operations; scientific affairs. The most important military bodies before the transformation in 2002–3 were the Military Committee, the Military Staff, the Military Agency for Standardisation, and the regional commands, the Supreme Allied Commander Europe (SACEUR), the Supreme Allied Commander Atlantic (SACLANT), the Allied Commander in Chief Channel (CINCHAN), and the Canada–US Regional Planning Group; for a more detailed list *cf.* NATO Handbook 2001, NATO Office of Information and Press, Ch. 10–12.

17   J.S. Ignarski, *North Atlantic Treaty Organization* EPIL III, p. 648; *cf.* K. Ipsen, *Rechtsgrundlagen* (1967), 93–190.

18   However, in doing so, NATO does not exercise supranational functions (that is, piercing the State level and reaching down to the individual citizens, like the European Community) and leaves full sovereignty to its members. See I. Kinder, *Institucionalna*

created.[19] Some of these NAC decisions are published in Final Communiqués of the various Ministerial Summits.[20] All these organs only derive indirect powers under the NAT.

According to Art. 10 NAT, a European State which is in 'a position to further the principles of this Treaty to contribute to the security of the North Atlantic area' may be invited by the parties to accede to NATO. This invitation takes the form of a unanimous decision by the NAC. The material requirements stated in Art. 10 were elaborated in the 'Study on NATO Enlargement in 1995'.[21] The study contains accession criteria similar to the EU's Copenhagen criteria of 1993,[22] adapted to a NATO context. Before being invited, candidates must:

- have a functioning democratic, political system based on a market economy;
- treat minorities according to the relevant OSCE standards;

---

struktura i pravni položaj Sjevernoatlantske organizacije, 19 Zabornik Pravnog Fakulteta Sveucilista u Rijeci (1998), p. 282 (Summary in English); K. Ipsen, *ibid.*, p. 99.

19   For example North Atlantic Co-operation Council (inauguration announced in the NATO Ministerial Communiqué from 20 Dec. 1991, http://www.nato.int/docu/comm/49-95/c911220a.htm (visited 28/07/04)); NACC Ad Hoc Group on Cooperation in Peacekeeping (established by the Ministerial Meeting of the NAC, 10–11 June 1993, http://www.nato.int/docu/comm/49-95/c930611b.htm (visited 28/07/04)); Partnership for Peace Programme (launched by the Ministerial Meeting of the NAC/NACC, 10–11 Jan. 1994, http://www.nato.int/docu/comm/49-95/c940110a.htm); Euro-Atlantic Partnership Council (launched by the Ministerial Meeting of the NAC, 29 May 1997, NATO Press Release M-NAC-1(97)65; NATO-Ukraine Commission (set up by the Charter on a Distinctive Partnership between the North Atlantic Organization and Ukraine, 9 July 1997, http://www.nato.int/docu/basictxt/ukrchrt.htm (visited 28/08/03), para. 12); NATO-Russia Permanent Joint Council (set up by the NATO-Russia Founding Act, 27 May 1997, 36 ILM 1006).

20   Final Communiqués of Sessions of the NAC, for example 17 Sept. 1949 (setting up the Defence Ctte., the Military Ctte., the Military Standing Group, and five Regional Planning Groups); 18 Nov. 1949 (establishing a Defence Financial and Economic Ctte.); 16–18 Sept. 1950 (setting up a centralised command); 15–16 Dec. 1966 (Defence Ministers meeting as Defence Planning Ctte.); 20–25 Feb. 1952 (appointing a Secretary-General heading a unified international secretariat, and the NAC in permanent session in Paris); 15–16 Dec. 1966 (establishing a Nuclear Defence Affairs Ctte. and a Nuclear Planning Group); 5–6 Dec. 1978 (MoU for the setting up of an AWACS programme, at para. 16); 25–26 June 1980 (establishing a 'Science for Stability' programme); 11 Dec. 1992 (Transformation of Alliance force and command structures). All Ministerial Summit Final Communiqués are available at http://www.nato.int/docu/comm.htm. For the latest reorganisation of defence planning structures, see NATO Issues, 12 June 2003, *New NATO Command Structure*, http://www.nato.int/issues/military_structure_command/index-e.htm (visited 16/06/03); NATO's Nations and Partners for Peace 2/2003, pp. 22–25; *cf.* J. Howorth, *ESDP and NATO – Wedlock or Deadlock?*, 38 Coop. & Confl. 3 (2003), pp. 243–4; Hunter (2004), p. 49.

21   Study on NATO Enlargement, http://www.nato.int/docu/basictxt/enl-9501.htm (visited 04/04/2004).

22   *Cf.* European Council, Copenhagen, 21–22 June 1993, Presidency Conclusions, para. I.13., fifth and sixth para., Bull. E.C., 6-1993, p. 13.

- solve outstanding disputes with neighbours over for example territorial or ethnic issues, and make a general commitment to the peaceful settlement of disputes;
- have the ability and willingness to make a military contribution to the Alliance and to achieve interoperability with other members' forces;
- be committed to democratic civil–military relations and institutional structures (that is, control of the national military forces through democratic institutions).

Prior to an invitation, candidates participate in the Membership Action Plan,[23] a regular reporting and feedback mechanism with NATO bodies, which should help them meet these criteria. Practical experience in force planning gained by the candidate countries under the framework of the Partnership for Peace often renders many synergies in this respect, depending on the level of involvement of a candidate country, for example in NATO-led peacekeeping operations. But participation in the MAP is not a guarantee of future membership. Once they are invited, accession talks begin on all aspects of future membership (defence resources, political, financial, legal, protection of NATO-classified information, intelligence cooperation). Accession protocols (which are formal amendments to the NAT) are then signed and ratified by all NATO members. Accession is lastly effected by the deposition of the candidate countries' ratifications with the US government.

THE NAT AFTER THE STRATEGIC CONCEPTS OF THE 1990S AND THE PRAGUE SUMMIT 2002

After the fundamental changes in the European security landscape in 1989, NATO began to look for a new role, beyond collective self-defence. This new role was found in crisis management outside the territories of its members. Accordingly, the provisions of the NAT were reinterpreted and given new meaning by the parties, to adapt the Alliance to this new role. This happened in three main stages, by the Strategic Concepts of Rome (1991)[24] and Washington (1999),[25] and lastly by the Prague Declaration (2002).[26] The prevailing opinion today seems to view NATO's

---

23   NATO Membership Action Plan, http://www.nato.int/issues/map/index.html (visited 11/08/2004).

24   The Alliance's Strategic Concept, Agreed by the Heads of State and Government participating in the meeting of the North Atlantic Council in Rome on 7–8 November 1991, reprinted in: NATO Handbook, (October 1995), p. 235 [hereinafter NATO Strategic Concept 1991].

25   The Alliance's Strategic Concept, Approved by the Heads of State and Government participating in the meeting of the North Atlantic Council in Washington D.C. on 23–24 April 1999, (CP 47, p. 24) [hereinafter NATO Strategic Concept 1999].

26   NATO Prague Summit Declaration by Heads of State and Government, 21 November 2002, para. 3–4, NATO Press Release (2000) 127, 21 Nov. 2002, (= 42 ILM 244) [hereinafter

Strategic Concepts as political in nature, lacking the validity of legally binding documents,[27] even though the crisis management functions contained therein clearly go beyond the original scope of the NAT.[28] The position that decisions by the NAC expanding the activity of the Alliance in general do not constitute formal amendments to the NAT has also been taken for example by the German Federal Constitutional Court in 1994[29] and again in 2001.[30]

On the basis of the NAT and the three additional documents above, the Alliance has three main tasks today: maintenance of international peace and security, out-of-area operations serving the security of the member States, and collective self-defence.[31]

Maintenance of international peace and security

The legal bases in the NAT are preambular para. 4 ('preservation of peace and security') and Art. 1.

During the Cold War, this function, although always a broader goal of the Alliance in principle, played no role due to the overwhelming preponderance of mutual defence. In the first Strategic Concept of 1991, however, it held a prominent place for the first time,[32] as allies could be 'called upon to contribute to global stability and peace by providing forces for United Nations missions'.[33] The 1999 Strategic Concept, incorporating NATO's peacekeeping experience in Bosnia since 1995, cited expressly Art. 7 NAT and spoke of engaging 'actively in crisis management, including crisis response operations'.[34] All of NATO's conflict prevention and crisis management activities should be 'consistent with international law',[35] a formulation which, however, evaded directly addressing the question of a Security Council mandate. In the 2002 Prague Declaration, references to the peace preservation

---

NATO Prague Declaration 2002].

27   For example T. Gazzini, *NATO's Role in the Collective Security System*, 8 JCSL 2 (2003), p. 244–5.

28   U. Schürr, *Der Aufbau einer ESVI* (2003), p. 107.

29   'AWACS' judgement, 90 BVerfGE (1994), pp. 286. English translation in 106 ILR (1997), pp. 319.

30   104 BVerfGE (2001), pp. 151, English summary on http://www.bverfg.de/entscheidungen/frames/es20011122_2bve000699en (visited 06/04/2004) [German Federal Constitutional Court, 2001]; *cf.* M. Rau, *NATO's Strategic Concept and the German Federal Government's Authority in the Sphere of Foreign Affairs: The Decision of the German Federal Constitutional Court of 22 November 2001*, 44 GYIL (2001), pp. 545.

31   The NATO Strategic Concept 1991, para. 21 at IV. listed additionally the preservation of the strategic balance in Europe, a function which, however, still essentially reflected Cold War strategy.

32   NATO Strategic Concept 1991, para. 21.

33   *Ibid.*, para. 42.

34   NATO Strategic Concept 1999, para. 10.

35   *Ibid.*, para. 31.

function, the United Nations or international law are largely missing. However, as the 1999 Strategic Concept has not been formally overruled by this Declaration, the former's relevant provisions still stand to this day.

Out-of-area operations serving the security of the member States

In practice, this category of NATO activity is often hard to separate from measures taken in support of international peace and security. The difference lies in the interest in which the two respective functions of the Alliance are rooted, and in their legal base. International peace and security is by definition a general, global interest. Action taken in pursuit of this interest is legally based on the UN Charter (to which the NAT directly refers in its Preamble). In contrast, the security of NATO member States, more narrowly defined, does not necessarily extend to every case when international peace and security in the world is threatened. For example, the conflict raging in the Great Lakes Region, and particularly in the DRC, since the end of the Rwandan civil war in 1994 certainly qualifies as a 'threat to international peace and security' in the sense of Art. 39 of the UN Charter (and has even been called the first African World War). However, for all of its atrocity, it does not affect the security of NATO member States.

The legal base for acting in the more narrow interest of the NATO member States is therefore different. It is to be found in the NAT itself, and includes the general prerequisite of acting in conformity with the purposes and principles of the UN.

The legal base for out-of-area operations not related to collective self-defence ('non-Article 5 operations') is today mostly seen in Art. 4 NAT.[36] Originally, this article contained nothing more than a consultation duty in case of an armed threat to one party's territorial integrity, political independence or security, prior to invoking the mutual defence clause of Art. 5. However, a 'threat to security', and hence to the common security of the member States, may well arise from outside the territories of the member States. Regional conflicts at the periphery of Europe always carry a certain danger of spill-over, affecting the territory of the member States, particularly through the often ensuing mass exodus of refugees.[37] In the same vein, studies on regional organisations of collective security under Chapter VIII of the UN Charter going beyond the concept of the 'internal threat'-directed nature typical for such

---

36 See for example German Federal Constitutional Court, 2001; M. Rau, *NATO's Strategic Concept*, 44 GYIL (2001), p. 561 and 564; Resolution of the US Senate, Committee on Foreign Relations, 6 March 1998, at Sec. 3 (1) (A) (ii), reprinted in: M. Nash, *Contemporary Practice of the United States relating to international law*, 92 AJIL (1998), p. 491 at 499; S. Kay, *NATO and the Future of European Security* (1998), p. 68.

37 Considering this broad dimension of security threats, T.A. Chafos, *The European Union's Rapid Reaction Force ...* (2003), p. 37, in line with more recent statements by Western policy-makers (for example German Defence Minister Struck 'Germany's security interests of today are defended at the Hindukush.') even sees NATO's peacekeeping mission in Afghanistan (IFOR) as covered by Art. 4 NAT.

organisations (*Binnenrichtung*) point also to an external dimension of regional collective security (*Sicherheit im Außenbereich*).[38] NATO itself, however, has never considered itself a regional organisation under Chapter VIII of the UN Charter.

These considerations are supported by the texts of NATO's Strategic Concepts. The 1991 Strategic Concept cited Art. 4 in direct connection with coordination of the allies' efforts 'including their responses to such risks'.[39] This went beyond the mere 'consultation' provided in Art. 4. Describing those risks, it cited the new security environment in Europe after the Cold War, characterised by many ethnic rivalries and territorial disputes. These simmering dangers could 'lead to crises inimical to European stability and even to armed conflicts, which could involve outside powers or spill over into NATO countries, having a direct effect on the security of the Alliance'.[40] The perception of possible threats to the Alliance remained unchanged in the 1999 Strategic Concept.[41]

Another strand of legal opinion derives the legal base for 'non-Article 5 operations' by using the *implied powers* concept.[42] Yet others concede that there may indeed not be any sound legal base for them in the NAT.[43] However, it should be noted that neither is there any provision expressly forbidding the parties to engage in such actions.[44] The question of the legality of NATO's out-of-area operations under the 1999 Strategic Concept remains controversial in legal scholarship until today, and a full answer, which would have to take into account also practice by NATO member States, would go beyond the scope of this book.

Collective self-defence

The 'new promising era' in Europe[45] at the beginning of the 1990s led NATO to de-emphasise mutual defence as the previous core of its activities in words as much as in deeds. The 1991 Strategic Concept, while still focusing on mutual defence, did not want NATO to be seen as anyone's adversary anymore.[46] 'Forward defence', a

---

38   For example C. Walter, *Vereinte Nationen und Regionalorganisationen* (1996), p. 81.

39   NATO Strategic Concept 1991, para. 13.

40   *Ibid.*, para. 10.

41   NATO Strategic Concept 1999, para. 20.

42   For example G. Nolte, *Die 'neuen Aufgaben' von NATO und WEU: Völker- und verfassungsrechtliche Fragen*, 54 HJIL (1994), p. 95 at 109–110.

43   U. Schürr, *Der Aufbau einer ESVI* (2003), p. 107; G. Warg, *Der Nato-Vertrag* auf Rädern (2004), p. 170–1 and 254.

44   T. Gazzini, *NATO Coercive Military Activities in the Yugoslav Crisis (1992–1999)*, 12 EJIL 3 (2001), p. 391 at 413–4.

45   Declaration on a transformed North Atlantic Alliance issued by the Heads of State and Government participating in the meeting of the North Atlantic Council, London, 6 July 1990 ('The London Declaration'), para. 1, http://www.nato.int/docu/basictxt/b900706a.htm (visited 11/08/2004).

46   NATO Strategic Concept 1991, para. 36.

concept under which more than 300 000 American troops had been stationed in West Germany, seemed a thing of the past.[47] Overall troop sizes of the Allies, including the nuclear arsenal, were greatly reduced.[48] Eight years later, in the 1999 Strategic Concept, the 'indivisibility of security of Europe and North America' was still stressed,[49] and while NATO should retain the military capability to accomplish the 'full range' of its missions, it was stated that 'the overall size of the Allies' forces will be kept at the lowest levels consistent with the requirements of collective defence'.[50] Art. 5, while of course still formally part of the NAT, and in particular being the cherished object of desire of the new NATO candidates in Eastern Europe, seemed to have silently receded into the background of Alliance day-to-day activities.

But then came the terrorist attacks of 11 September 2001. They changed the world, and with it, also NATO. Art. 5 NAT was injected with new life after its first-ever invocation in October 2001.[51] At its 2002 Prague Summit, NATO embarked on a transformation to direct its resources to the fight against international terrorism. The last remaining inherent barriers to out-of-area activity were swept away by this transformation.[52] The Prague document indicates (although not expressly) that NATO's fight against terrorism is in the main based on the Art. 5.[53] Four measures flowed from this transformation:[54]

1. the decision to create a NATO Response Force (NRF), a high-readiness intervention force able to intervene wherever needed at the request of the NAC;
2. a complete overhaul of NATO's existing command structure, including the creation of an Allied Command Transformation (ACT) in the United States;
3. a new Prague Capabilities Commitment (PCC) relating to development of new military capabilities for modern warfare;
4. a new military concept for the defence against terrorism.

The mutual defence provided in Art. 5 is thus given a completely new face and applied in a way hardly imagined by its drafters. However, NATO officials stress that this is in keeping with the original flexible approach and wording of the NAT in light of uncertain future developments.

The importance of Art. 5 after September 11 will be the object of closer analysis in a subsequent chapter.[55]

---

47   *Ibid.*, para. 40.
48   *Ibid.*, para. 46.
49   NATO Strategic Concept 1999, paras. 7 and 27.
50   *Ibid.*, para. 52, at a.
51   On these events in detail, see below Chapter 6 (Collective Self-Defence).
52   J. Medcalf, *NATO and the Extra-European Challenge* (2002), p. 230.
53   NATO Prague Declaration 2002, paras. 3 and 4.
54   *Ibid.*, para. 4.
55   See below Chapter 5 (NATO Primacy).

GROWING COOPERATION WITH OTHER INSTITUTIONS

In addition to the three 'fundamental tasks' above, NATO's new documents reflect its increasing degree of cooperation with other international institutions. Such cooperation had been minimal prior to 1989, and did not happen in any systematic way. Internal efficiency of Alliance procedures, including secrecy, was given absolute precedence. The 1991 Strategic Concept admitted that dialogue and cooperation within all of Europe (meaning other institutions) could help diffuse crises, and that for example the CSCE, the EC, the WEU and the UN 'may also have an important role to play'.[56] NATO subsequently entered into formal and practical relations with the WEU, the 'Eurocorps'[57] and the United Nations.[58] In 1999, the European Security and Defence Identity (ESDI) as the European pillar of the Alliance was already fully part of NATO's procedures. It was recognised that ESDI would require 'close cooperation' with the WEU and, eventually, the EU.[59] At Prague in 2002, less than one month before the conclusion of the Berlin Plus agreement,[60] NATO–EU cooperation was already a given, and NATO and the EU were seen to 'share common strategic interests'.[61]

POLITICAL EVOLUTION OF THE ALLIANCE

NATO's history from its founding days can be classified into at least three phases.[62] The first and longest one lasted from 1949 until the end of the Cold War. It was characterised by stability. The 1990s brought substantial re-definition of the Alliance's core functions, the most fundamental of which was 'going out of area', and an according adaptation of internal procedures. Having adapted more or less successfully to the post-Cold War peacekeeping world, NATO had to reinvent itself for a second time after the Prague Summit of 2002, in reaction to the new challenges after September 11.

---

56   NATO Strategic Concept 1991, para. 34.

57   The 'Eurocorps' is an independent multinational military peacekeeping contingent founded in 1992, today containing troops from Belgium, France, Germany, Luxembourg and Spain. The Headquarters is located in Strasbourg. http://www.eurocorps.org/ (visited 14/03/05).

58   J.S. Ignarski, *North Atlantic Treaty Organization* EPIL III, pp. 654–5.

59   NATO Strategic Concept 1999, para. 30.

60   See below, Chapter 8 (Berlin Plus Agreement).

61   NATO Prague Declaration 2002, para. 11.

62   The following conceptual framework is based on J. Medcalf, *NATO and the Extra-European Challenge* (2002), p. 264.

Phase 1: The Cold War

Politically, NATO was a direct product of the Cold-War confrontation between the United States and the Soviet Union. By 1949, the war-time troop levels of Western European powers, as well as those of US troops based in Europe, had been greatly reduced, in contrast to the situation across the new 'Iron Curtain' in the Eastern bloc, where the standing divisions of the Red Army sometimes outnumbered those in Western Europe by a factor of 20.[63] This military imbalance was perceived as a direct menace by Western leaders, given the experience of Soviet foreign policy in Czechoslovakia in 1948 and particularly during the Berlin blockade of 1948/49. Strong Communist parties, especially in France and Italy, further augmented the general impression of a threat from outside and within. However, initially NATO only consisted of a small secretariat in Paris which exercised coordination mostly at the diplomatic level. The huge military-technical apparatus, integrated command structure, joint force planning and standardisation[64] which the Alliance has today were only added later, as the Cold War confrontation reached its height in the 1950s during the Korean War.[65] The Cold War confrontation was defined also in terms of culture, and this had a strong defining influence on the identity of NATO as well: the Alliance was conceived as a manifestation of an underlying 'community of values'.[66] Despite this rhetoric, pragmatic (that is, geo-strategic) reasons often outweighed such values. Thus Portugal, then under the Salazar dictatorship, also became a NATO founding member.[67] NATO's degree of institutionalisation and also its value dimension went beyond what had been seen in any military coalition or alliance before. The French departure from the integrated military command after General de Gaulle's decision in 1966 did not fundamentally disturb NATO's main defence function.[68]

Phase 2: The 1990s – out of area or out of business

With the onset of more relaxed relations with the East, a broader concept of security was quickly accepted by NATO. It committed the Alliance to building a political

---

63   S. Kay, *NATO and the Future of European Security* (1998), p. 35; *cf.* M. Ball, *NATO and the European Union Movement* (1957), pp. 73–5.

64   The last element, standardisation, was never fully realised until today.

65   Thus, it is often said that 'Korea put the 'O' in NATO'. S. Kay, *NATO and the Future of European Security* (1998), pp. 35; K. Ipsen, *Rechtsgrundlagen* (1967), p. 135.

66   S. Kay, *NATO and the Future of European Security* (1998), pp. 24 and 26.

67   *Ibid.*, pp. 28–9.

68   On the legal effects of the French withdrawal in 1966, see E. Stein and D. Carreau, *Law and Peaceful Change in a Subsystem: 'Withdrawal' of France from the North Atlantic Treaty Organization'*, 62 AJIL (1968), pp. 577–639.

dialogue with its former adversaries, in order to foster stability on its borders.[69] 'The political dimension of security was back on NATO's agenda'.[70] Daunting though this new political challenge was, it could not compensate for the sudden loss of NATO's core *raison d'être*: the Soviet threat. As a result, many political commentators at the beginning of the 1990s predicted that NATO would cease to exist as a matter of natural consequence. This has evidently not happened. The reasons are worth examining somewhat more in detail.

How did NATO survive the end of the Cold War? – different explanations by international relations theory

Realism   Neo-realist theory in international relations claims that alliances are born out of a perception of a common threat.[71] Conversely, once the common threat is gone, any alliance tends to disintegrate sooner or later.[72] This was also the prediction made for NATO at the beginning of the 1990s,[73] and some commentators still expect this to happen in the long term.[74] Defying most realist predictions, NATO has persisted,[75] and, rather than simply lingering on, it moved to the core of the new European security architecture.[76] Despite being only an 'institutional shell' after the disappearance of its main rationale, the Gulf War in 1991 already showed that the vast military apparatus which the Alliance had built during 40 years had many unexpected uses in the post-Cold War environment.[77] The institutional shell was seen

69   NATO Strategic Concept 1991, paras. 24 and 31. *Cf.* H. Gärtner, *Security Concepts*, 8 Rom. J. Int'l Aff. (2002), p. 40.

70   J.S. Ignarski, *North Atlantic Treaty Organization* EPIL III, p. 653.

71   S.M. Walt, *The Origins of Alliances* (1987), pp. 32–3; P. Cornish, *Partnership in Crisis* (1997), p. 10; H. Gärtner, *Security Concepts*, 8 Rom. J. Int'l Aff. (2002), pp. 19–31 (with many further references); J. Medcalf, *NATO and the Extra-European Challenge* (2002), pp. 17–21.

72   J.S. Duffield, *Why NATO persists*, in: in: K.W. Thompson (ed.), *NATO and the Changing World Order* (1996), p. 99 at 100; P. Cornish, *Partnership in Crisis* (1997), p. 12; S.M. Walt, *The Ties That Fray* (1998/1999); Y. Dinstein, *War, Aggression and Self-Defence* (2001), p. 223.

73   'NATO's *days* aren't numbered, but its *years* are.' (K. Waltz, *The emerging structure of international politics*, 18 International Security 2 (1993), p. 75). *Cf.* R.B. McCalla, *NATO's persistence after the Cold War,* 50 International Organization (1996), p. 445 at 469–470. Realist arguments were also used during the Bosnian War, in order to explain the absence of NATO activity there until 1995 with the fact that essential interests of the member States were not affected. *Cf.* G. Koslowski, *Die NATO und der Krieg in Bosnien-Herzegowina* (1995), p. 150.

74   M.M. Gallagher, *Declaring Victory* (2003), p. 358–360.

75   P. Schmidt, *Zum Verhältnis von GASP; NATO und WEU*, 25 ÖZP 4 (1996), p. 404.

76   S. Kay, *NATO and the Future of European Security* (1998), p. 60.

77   *Ibid.*

as useful to maintain as long as future security developments were uncertain.[78] It was easier and less expensive to adapt NATO to new challenges than to set up a new institution.[79] The survival of NATO as an institution, however, cannot be explained by realist arguments of state interest alone.[80]

Idealism and institutionalism Idealism holds that when States form alliances, even military ones, they are driven not only considerations of power and security, but also by 'softer' cultural preferences and values.[81] As NATO's founders took care to stress, the Alliance was founded on a pre-existing cultural affinity of the nations of its member States.[82] 'The West' in the Cold War could even be said to have constituted what K. Deutsch has called a 'security community', that is, a group of States so integrated by common practices and expectations over time that, although political differences may exist, war between them has become impossible.[83] An alliance built upon such an ideological base might be better able to function combating instability, even after the disappearance of its major threat.[84]

In addition, institutions, once constructed and running, actively promote cooperation among their members.[85] This approach, called (neo-)institutionalism, can be summarised by two words: institutions matter.[86] According to this theory which qualifies realist assumptions, NATO's institutional structures remaining from the Cold War mitigated the centrifugal effects after the disappearance of the major common interest.[87] NATO had some time to adapt to the new security environment, by adopting new functions useful to its members.[88]

Internalism A third explanation, closely linked to institutionalism, may be advanced for the survival of NATO. Complex bureaucracies are composed of individuals and interest groups who 'must be expected to have an interest in their incomes and careers,

---

78   *Ibid.*, p. 6.

79   R.B. McCalla, *NATO's persistence after the Cold War* (1996), pp. 462–3.

80   *Ibid.*, p. 446.

81   P. Cornish, *Partnership in Crisis* (1997), p. 16;

82   W. Lang, *Sind WEU und NATO noch Allianzen?*, 13 ÖJIP (1996), p. 1 at 7; G.J. Ikenberry, *Atlantic Political Order* (2000), pp. 60–63; J. Medcalf, *NATO and the Extra-European Challenge* (2002), p. 22.

83   For this concept, see in detail: K. Deutsch, *Political community and the North Atlantic area* (1957), p. 5.

84   P. Cornish, *Partnership in Crisis* (1997), p. 18.

85   S. Kay, *NATO and the Future of European Security* (1998), p. 9; H. Gärtner, *Security Concepts*, 8 Rom. J. Int'l Aff. (2002), pp. 31–32.

86   D.G. Haglund, *Must NATO fail? Theories, myths, and policy dilemmas*, International Journal (1995), pp. 651 at 662–663; C. A. Wallander, *Institutional Assets and Adaptability: NATO After the Cold War*, 54 International Organization 4 (2000), p. 705; J. Medcalf, *NATO and the Extra-European Challenge* (2002), p. 22.

87   R.B. McCalla, *NATO's persistence after the Cold War* (1996), p. 470.

88   O. Theiler, *Die NATO im Umbruch* (2003), pp. 300–302.

and therefore in the survival of the organisation in which they are employed'.[89] This organisational 'survival instinct' may manifest itself in bureaucratic inertia, but it can also provide an organisation with a 'life' of its own, and hence with a creative potential for inventing new tasks for the organisation once old ones are accomplished.[90] The pool of NATO supporters embodying its survival instinct is not restricted to its present staff. Rather, the accumulative effect of generations of former NATO staff who have moved on to other positions has a significant influence.[91] A recent example for this is Javier Solana, who became the EU's High Representative after finishing his term as NATO SG,[92] and went on to shape the EU's defence policy in a distinctive NATO-friendly way.

Taking together the considerations above, it should be possible to assemble enough reasons for NATO's survival through the 1990s. However, the continuation of this survival demands careful nurturing and constant reassertion of the case for continuing the organisation. Not anymore an 'alliance of necessity', NATO can thus only expect to survive as an 'alliance of choice'.[93]

Once the allies took the decision to enlarge to the East, this process instilled new life into the organisation as a whole. However, '[i]ronically, the new members, which have given NATO a degree of a sense of mission, do not seek to join a 'new NATO' but rather the 'old NATO' of collective defense.'[94] NATO needs to find some usefulness beyond enlargement,[95] that is, a new central task relevant to all of its members. The various responses found to this challenge throughout the 1990s, were more ad hoc than by grand design,[96] even if they were, for a time, successful, as the sudden need for effective crisis management in Europe could only be filled by NATO.

From collective self-defence to 'out of area' peacekeeping

In the Cold War the NAT had restricted the allies' activity to their national territories. After its end, however, the conclusion was soon reached that 'NATO must go out of area or it will go out of business'.[97] Some allies, such as France, initially opposed this new direction for NATO for political reasons, fearing that the central defence

---

89   P. Cornish, *Partnership in Crisis* (1997), p. 22; *cf.* J. Medcalf, *NATO and the Extra-European Challenge* (2002), p. 23.

90   R.B. McCalla, *NATO's persistence after the Cold War* (1996), p. 458.

91   *Ibid.*, p. 457; J. Medcalf, *NATO and the Extra-European Challenge* (2002), p. 23.

92   On the personal 'Solana effect' on the EU–NATO relationship, see below Chapter 4 (EU–NATO Institutional Aspects).

93   P. Cornish, *Partnership in Crisis* (1997), p. 24.

94   S. Kay, *NATO and the Future of European Security* (1998), p. 145.

95   *Ibid.*, p. 121.

96   *Ibid.*, p. 11.

97   R.A. Asmus / R.L. Kugler / F.S. Larrabee, *Building a New NATO*, 72 Foreign Affairs (Sept./Oct. 1993), p. 28 at 31.

function could be weakened by such an additional role.[98] Others, such as Germany, had to overcome constitutional barriers to sending national troops abroad on missions other than territorial or collective defence.[99] By most accounts, however, NATO's new out-of-area role in the Balkans seems to have been vital for its survival in the post-Cold War world,[100] holding it together in face of diverging interests of its member States.[101]

Without ever changing its legal treaty base, NATO in effect transformed itself from a mutual defence pact into a regional peacekeeping organisation.[102]

CJTF concept – a compromise formula[103]

In the mid-1990s, there were different opinions among the main allies as to which form NATO should take, in particular with regard to its 'European pillar'. The US was concerned about burden-sharing, while wary of any European initiatives at defence cooperation, such as the budding 'Eurocorps'.[104] The United Kingdom had a strong preference for NATO-only solutions, but recognised that the United States and Canada would not be involved in every single minor European crisis. This eventually brought it to accept a role for the WEU in crisis management within NATO structures. France, suspicious of American influence, was traditionally seeking for more independence, also in European security, but shied away from German avantgardist proposals for a full European army. It came to move closer to Alliance structures in 1996. Germany tried to balance between the Europeanist and the Atlanticist agenda.

In June 1996, these different paths converged to a compromise of sorts which became epitomised by a single formula: the Common Joint Task Forces (CJTF) concept, which was introduced at NATO's Brussels Summit on 10-11 January 1994[105] and completed in June 1996 with the so-called 'Berlin Accords'[106].

---

98   S. Kay, *NATO and the Future of European Security* (1998), p. 60.

99   *Cf.* the 1994 'AWACS judgement' of the German Federal Constitutional Court, 90 BVerfGE (1994), fn. 30 above.

100   For example J. Medcalf, *NATO and the Extra-European Challenge* (2002), p. 102.

101   S. Kay, *NATO and the Future of European Security* (1998), p. 155.

102   I.H. Daalder, *NATO, the UN, and the Use of force*, 5 International Peacekeeping 1/2 (1999), p. 26 at 27; F. Heisbourg (2004), p. 122. *Cf.* above Introduction.

103   This section is in part based on P. Cornish, *Partnership in Crisis* (1997), pp. 31–80.

104   See above at fn. 58.

105   Ministerial Meeting of the North Atlantic Council /North Atlantic Cooperation Council, NATO Headquarters, Brussels, 10–11 January 1994, Declaration of the Heads of State and Government, para. 1 (NATO Press Communiqué M-1(94)3).

106   Ministerial Meeting of the North Atlantic Council, Berlin, 3 June 1996, Final Communiqué, para. 6 (NATO Press Communiqué M-NAC-1(96)63).

A Combined Joint Task Force (CJTF) is a multinational, multi-service deployable task force generated and tailored primarily, but not exclusively, for military operations not involving the defence of Alliance territory, such as humanitarian relief and peacekeeping.[107]

The concept was already known in military doctrine and practice, but had so far only been used in limited, temporary missions, not as an institutionalised modus operandi for peacekeeping.[108] Such a force could, in a flexible way, contain NATO, and also non-NATO forces of different classes, as needed for a particular crisis, while always drawing on the mechanisms and structures provided by the Alliance as a whole. A CJTF headquarters could be detached from the regular permanent NATO command and deployed into a conflict area.[109] The concept worked on the basis of the 'coalitions of the willing' principle,[110] for missions along the whole range of NATO's tasks, that is, Art. 5 and non-Art. 5 missions. The military structures used throughout would be one and the same, avoiding duplication of resources.[111] The concept was first applied successfully in peacekeeping on the ground in IFOR/SFOR in Bosnia and had become the standard mechanism for NATO peacekeeping by June 1996.[112]

Politically, the CJTF concept bridged the need for a greater role of the European allies in managing their own security affairs independently, without participation of the United States, that is, through the WEU, while still staying within a NATO framework.[113] As a result NATO's central position in the European security architecture was preserved.[114] In the mid-1990s, the CJTF was seen as 'key to understanding the character and potential of the new NATO'.[115]

However, the flexibility of the CJTF concept did break with NATO's past: the first-time introduction of 'coalitions of the willing' as a standing concept compromised the basic principle of the 'indivisibility of security' of Europe and North America (the 'Three Musketeers' concept). On the practical side of piecing together a coalition to intervene quickly in a crisis, the concept was certainly most useful. In the long term, however, it could be expected to erode the deeper sense of solidarity

---

107   *The Combined Joint Task Forces Concept*, in: The Reader's Guide to the NATO Summit in Washington, 23–25 April 1999, p. 67, NATO Office of Information and Press; *cf.* NATO Handbook 2001, pp. 253–5.

108   P. Cornish, *Partnership in Crisis* (1997), p. 64; S. Kay, *NATO and the Future of European Security* (1998), p. 138.

109   *Ibid.*

110   S. Kay, *NATO and the Future of European Security* (1998), p. 132.

111   This was meant by the formula of 'separate but not separable military capabilities' (NATO Ministerial Meeting, Berlin, 3 June 1996, Final Communiqué, para. 6).

112   P. Cornish, *Partnership in Crisis* (1997), p. 65; S. Kay, *NATO and the Future of European Security* (1998), p. 136.

113   In ESDP terminology, all operations using the CJTF concept, would thus be 'option 1'-type missions (*Cf.* NATO/EU Consultation document (2003)).

114   P. Cornish, *Partnership in Crisis* (1997), p. 66–7; S. Kay, *NATO and the Future of European Security* (1998), p. 134.

115   P. Cornish, *ibid.*, p. 78.

within the Alliance.[116] Another problem was that a potential case of European allies conducting a peacekeeping mission on their own raised, in theory, the possibility of such a mission escalating into an international conflict which would involve Art. 5, thus drawing all other allies into a conflict they had specifically chosen not to engage in.[117] Lastly, the CJTF concept could do nothing to solve the military imbalance in the transatlantic relationship,[118] made even wider by the recent advances made by the United States in military technology in the 1990s.[119]

Phase 3: Further afield after September 11

Effects of September 11: enter the war against terrorism

The answer to many of the above problems was provided for NATO by the terrorist attacks of 11 September 2001 on New York and Washington. Collective self-defence, the traditional task of the Alliance for which it was created, moved centre stage again, or so it seemed. Before September 11, fighting terrorism, if ever it was mentioned,[120] had never been considered a main task of the Alliance. Immediately after this date, however, it became central,[121] and the Alliance enacted eight measures in support of the United States. Among them, it deployed its AWACS airplanes to the US East Coast (Operation Eagle Assist), freeing up resources of the US Air Force to be used elsewhere in the country's war against terrorism.[122]

NATO's presence in the Mediterranean to guard against terrorist attacks on commercial shipping (Operation Active Endeavour) manifests that the reaction to September 11 continues to this day. The operation was extended to cover the whole

---

116   *Cf. Ibid.*, pp. 78 and 114. The same problem still exists today with flexibility in institutional solutions in ESDP. See above Chapter 2 (ESDP Today).

117   S. Kay, *NATO and the Future of European Security* (1998), p. 134.

118   *Ibid.*, p. 149.

119   The 'Revolution in Military Affairs' (RMA). NATO tried to address this problem throughout the 1990s, but without much success. *Cf.* A. Deighton, *The Military Security Pool* (2000), pp. 46–7.

120   For example U. Nerlich, *The relationship between a European common defence and NATO, the OSCE and the United Nations*, in: Martin / Roper (1995), p. 87; NATO Strategic Concept 1999, para. 24. With hindsight, J. Medcalf, *NATO and the Extra-European Challenge* (2002), p. 235 calls this reference in the 1999 Strategic Concept 'far-sighted'.

121   'Defence against terrorism was already one of the new tasks highlighted in our 1999 Strategic Concept. Now it's front and centre – a main focus of our activities.' G. Robertson, speech at the American Enterprise Institute's New Atlantic Initiative, Washington, D.C. 20 June 2002, reprinted in: J. Medcalf, *NATO and the Extra-European Challenge* (2002), p. 234.

122   On the response to September 11 under Art. in detail, see below Chapter 6 (Collective Self-Defence).

Mediterranean after the Madrid terrorist attacks of 11 March 2004[123] (previously it had covered only the eastern half). NATO claims that it has, inter alia, reduced the cost of maritime insurance in the Mediterranean by 20 per cent.[124] Other similar initiatives, for example against the transport of WMD material along the lines of the US Proliferation Security Initiative (PSI), are not ruled out.[125]

However, for all the enthusiasm surrounding the 'revival' of Art. 5, there are many signs that using it to combat terrorism was a rather untypical case of self-defence[126] owed to a unique set of circumstances.[127] Its invocation in response to September 11 has even on occasion been called 'a mistake' [sic].[128] Indeed, for the main campaign against the Taliban in autumn of 2001, the US did not need NATO resources at all, and it chose not to employ them, because it wanted to avoid repeating the Kosovo experience of waging a 'war by committee'.[129] When a useful role for NATO in Afghanistan was eventually found, it was in peacekeeping, after the hardest part of the fighting had been done by US forces. This, however, is precisely *not* an Art. 5 task.[130] The idea promoted by the United States and the United Kingdom that NATO should have the ability to intervene in cases of Art. 5 anywhere on the globe[131] cannot detract from the fact that, apart from some very restricted tasks, NATO was not used under Art. 5 in Afghanistan, nor anywhere else, in response to the terrorist attacks of September 11.

Prague Summit 2002

At its Prague Summit on 21–22 November 2002, NATO decided on four measures to combat international terrorism.[132]

Of these, the NATO Response Force (NRF)[133] will be addressed in detail in a later chapter.[134] The only thing of interest here is that the NRF is conceived completely

---

123   Declaration on Terrorism, issued at the Meeting of the North Atlantic Council in Foreign Ministers Session, Brussels, 2 April 2004, NATO Press Release (2004)057.

124   G. Robertson, Speech at the BMVG-FAZ Forum, Berlin, 24 June 2003, http://www.bmvg.de/sicherheit/print/030624_bmvg_faz_rede_robertson.php (visited 26/06/03).

125   NATO Istanbul Summit Communiqué issued by the Heads of State and Government participating in the meeting of the North Atlantic Council, Istanbul, 28 June 2004, NATO Press Release (2004)096, paras. 10 and 15.

126   *Cf.* F.A. Biggio, *Neutralizing the threat: Reconsidering Existing Doctrines in the Emerging War on Terrorism*, 34 Case W. Res. J. Int'l L. (Fall 2002), p. 1 at 23, who, writing in 2002 (!), expected Art. 5 to be used only to address terrorism within NATO territory.

127   J. Medcalf, *NATO and the Extra-European Challenge* (2002), p. 253.

128   A. Deighton, *The European Security and Defence Policy*, 40 JCMS (2002), p. 731.

129   H. Neuhold, *Transatlantic Turbulences: Rift or Ripples?*, 8 EFAR (2003), p. 457 at 464.

130   *Cf.* J. Medcalf, *NATO and the Extra-European Challenge* (2002), p. 247, citing an unnamed UK official.

131   *Ibid.*, pp. 241–2.

132   See p. 104.

133   NATO Prague Declaration 2002, para. 4 a.

134   See below Chapter 7 (Military Crisis Management).

as a global force, not constrained to conflicts in Europe.[135] In many ways, this was a natural development, given that Europe was increasingly at peace in 2002, and that the US lacked an essential interest in being involved there militarily, preferring increasingly to leave it to the Europeans themselves.[136] Apparently, NATO's force goals have also been increasingly directed toward expeditionary warfare since at least 1999.[137]

The Prague Capabilities Commitment (PCC),[138] a continuation of the earlier Defence Capabilities Initiative (DCI),[139] is a vast topic which falls outside the scope of this book.

Lastly, the new military concept for defence against terrorism[140] does not seem to have been formally developed since Prague, although a very broad 'definition' of NATO's military activities against international terrorism was given in the Declaration on Terrorism of 2 April 2004:

> Defence against terrorism may include activities by NATO's military forces ... to help deter, defend, disrupt and protect against terrorist attacks, or threat of attacks, directed from abroad, against populations, territory, infrastructure and forces of any member states, including by acting against these terrorists and those who harbour them. Any operations undertaken in the defence against terrorism will have a sound legal basis and fully conform with the relevant provisions of the United Nations Charter and all relevant international norms and standards.[141]

The second sentence is remarkable compared with the Prague Declaration itself which hardly contains such references to the United Nations and international law. This return to multilateralism is likely to be a result of the search for renewed political common ground among the allies in the aftermath of the fierce disputes waged over the Iraq war in 2003.

The streamlining and reorganisation of NATO's command arrangements[142] addressed a need which was identified long before 2002.[143]

---

135 *Cf.*, however, already the NATO Strategic Concept 1999, para. 52 which spoke of the need for the Alliance's military forces to conduct military operations (of all classes) 'distant from their home stations, including beyond the Allies' territory' which may be read implicitly to mean that they would also have to go outside Europe.

136 'The Europeans can take care of Europe, and the Americans take care of the world,' F. Heisbourg (summarising US National Security Advisor C. Rice's vision), *NATO Can Manage Current Strains on Missile Shield*, International Herald Tribune, 13 Jan. 2001, p. 6.

137 B.R. Posen, *ESDP and the Structure of World Power*, 39 The International Spectator 1 (2004), p., p. 10.

138 NATO Prague Declaration 2002, para. 4 c.

139 See NATO Summit, 25 April 1999, NATO Press Release NAC-S(99)69.

140 NATO Prague Declaration 2002, para. 4 d.

141 Declaration on Terrorism, issued a the Meeting of the North Atlantic Council in Foreign Ministers Session, Brussels, 2 April 2004, NATO Press Release (2004)057.

142 NATO Prague Declaration 2002, para. 4 b.

143 *Cf.* S. Kay, *NATO and the Future of European Security* (1998), p. 147.

Further afield: NATO goes outside Europe

Apart from the very large operation in Kosovo, smaller elements left in the EU's peacekeeping mission *Althea* in Bosnia after its hand-over,[144] and the occasional AWACS protection for international sporting events such as the Greek Olympics in September 2004,[145] NATO's activities on the ground are all outside Europe today. In Afghanistan, the Alliance continues to conduct a demanding peacekeeping operation with many different elements, including some contingents of the NRF.[146] ISAF remains '*the* Alliance's key priority' today.[147] In post-war Iraq, it has supported the Polish occupation sector,[148] and started to train Iraqi security forces after its Istanbul Summit 2004.[149] Even an engagement in the Middle East is occasionally discussed in public.[150] Viewed from the historical perspective of the Cold War, when out-of-area was out of the question, to the 1990s when it became an imperative but constrained to Europe, to post-September 11, when the Alliance mostly operated outside of Europe,[151] this is a remarkable transformation. Indeed, there are reasons to assume that meeting this 'extra-European challenge' will be key to on NATO's long-term vitality.[152]

OUTLOOK

At least two unsolved problems can be identified with NATO's new functions, as defined and developed after the 2002 Prague Summit.

Firstly, it remains unclear how NATO intends to implement collective self-defence in the future, for example whether 'pre-emptive strikes' (according to the

---

144   See below, Chapter 7 (Military Crisis Management).

145   For example *NATO Commences Patrol of the Skies for Olympic Games*, NATO Joint Force Command Naples Press Release {24}, 10 Aug. 2004.

146   J. de Hoop Scheffer, Joint Press Point with J. Solana after the NAC-PSC meeting, 26 July 2004, http://www.nato.int/docu/speech/2004/s040726a.htm (visited 11/08/2004).

147   Ministerial Meeting of the North Atlantic Council, 9 Dec. 2004, Final Communiqué, NATO Press Release (2004)170, para. 2 [emphasis added].

148   *NATO Council makes decision on Polish request*, NATO update (online edition), 21 May 2003;. see also: NATO Ministerial Meeting, Madrid, 3 June 2003, NATO Press Release (2003)056, para. 5; *NATO steht Polen im Irak bei*, Süddeutsche Zeitung, 22 May 2003.

149   Statement on Iraq Issued by the Heads of State and Government participating in the meeting of the North Atlantic Council, Istanbul, 28 June 2004, para. 6, NATO Press Release (2004)098.

150   A. Monaco, *Who takes care of European Security? EU and NATO: Competition or Cooperation?*, in: A. Weidemann / A. Simon (eds.), *The Future of ESDP* (2003), p. 40 at 41; T.L. Friedman, *Expand NATO to Iraq, Egypt and Isreal*, New York Times, 27 Oct. 2003, p. 6.

151   *Cf.* J. Medcalf, *NATO and the Extra-European Challenge* (2002), p. 228; R. Freckmann, *Die NATO im 21. Jahrhundert*, IFIR Themenschwerpunkt, No. 01/2005, p. 2.

152   J. Medcalf, *ibid.*, pp. 249–250.

'Bush doctrine' enunciated in the US National Security Strategy of 2002[153]) should be covered by it or not.[154] Constructive ambiguity may sometimes not help in this regard, but, in absence of a common threat, may rather erode the continuing logic behind the commitment.

Secondly, there are still great differences in the allies' security orientation and hence their interest in some basic uses and functions of the Alliance,[155] for example regarding the US-sponsored concept that the 'mission defines the coalition' which would in effect reduce NATO to a toolbox, or a mere facilitator of coalitions.[156]

The long-term effect of September 11 was to bring NATO on the world stage and out of Europe. However, most European allies' main interests (and those of other EU member States) are today in managing security crises in their near abroad. NATO, after adoption of its global role, looks more and more unsuitable for such a regionally restricted role. A new framework exists today in which US security priorities do not have to be considered to the same degree: ESDP. The slowly shifting balance in European security from NATO to the EU thus seems to be helped by NATO's new global reorientation.

---

153   The US National Security Strategy employs the term 'pre-emptive' in the sense that is usually associated with 'preventive' use of force, that is, not in response to an imminent threat, but in order to disrupt potential preparation for a possible future attack at its roots. On the US National Security Strategy, see above Chapter 1 (Transatlantic Relations).

154   *Ibid.*, (2002), p. 256.

155   M. Clarke / P. Cornish, *The European defence project and the Prague summit*, 78 International Affairs 4 (2002), p. 777 at 788; J. Medcalf, *NATO and the Extra-European Challenge* (2002), p. 253.

156   J. Howorth, *ESDP and NATO – Wedlock or Deadlock?*, 38 Coop. & Confl. 3 (2003), p. 244; R. Cooper, *the breaking of nations* (2003), p. 166.

Chapter 4

Institutional Framework for EU–NATO Cooperation[1]

HISTORICAL ORIGINS

In the mid-1990s, an 'EU–NATO relationship' did not exist, despite the two organisations being located in the same city of Brussels.[2] The EU and the WEU had started harmonising their work in 1993,[3] and relations between WEU and NATO on administrative[4] and operational[5] levels were well established by 1996.[6] The WEU was thus the institutional 'bridge' between the EU and NATO. The legal base for this 'bridge' function from 1996 was the WEU's declaration, attached as a Declaration to the Amsterdam Treaty,[7] according to which the EU could draw on the planning resources of the WEU.[8] NATO's Berlin Accords of 1996 contained only one fleeting reference to the EU.[9] The Union was still largely left out of discussions on the

---

1   Parts of this chapter appeared already in a shortened version in: M. Reichard, *Some Legal Issues Concerning the EU–NATO Berlin Plus Agreement*, 73 NJIL (2004), pp. 37–67.

2   'As if they were living on a different planet.' G. Robertson (citing an unnamed former US ambassador to NATO), in: W. Hoyer / G.F. Kaldrack (eds.), *ESVP* (2002), p. 181; *Cf.* P. H. Gordon, *Their Own Army? Making European Defense Work*, Foreign Affairs (July/ Aug. 2000)pp. 16–7; A. Deighton, *The Military Security Pool* (2000), p. 51; A.D. Rotfeld, *Europe: an emerging power* (2001), p. 196.

3   Relations between the Union and WEU, 22 Nov. 1993, Annex IV of Chapter IV of the document on the implementation of the Maastricht Treaty, WEU Assembly Doc. 1412, 8 April 1994. *Cf.* Some first EU-WEU coordination, however, already took place in January 1991 (W. Bradford, *The WEU ... the new sick man of Europe* (2000), p. 23).

4   *Cf.* P. Cornish, *Partnership in Crisis* (1997), p. 101.

5   In their joint *Operation Sharp Guard*, the WEU and NATO operated under a single chain of command. NATO/WEU Operation Sharp Guard, IFOR Final Factsheet, 2 Oct. 1996, http://www.nato.int/ifor/general/shrp-grd.htm (visited 21/12/04). *Cf.* E. Greco (1997), p. 128.

6   *Cf.* also Council Decision of 10 May 1999 concerning the arrangements for enhanced cooperation between the European Union and the Western European Union (1999/404/CFSP), OJ L 153/1 of 19/6/1999.

7   Treaty of Amsterdam amending the Treaty on European Union, the Treaties establishing the European Communities and certain related acts - Declarations adopted by the Conference – 3. Declaration relating to Western European Union, OJ C 340, of 10 Nov. 1997, p. 0125.

8   *Cf.* F. Dehousse / B. Galer, *De Saint-Malo à Feira* (1999), p. 32.

9   P. Cornish, *Partnership in Crisis* (1997), p. 99.

European security architecture.[10] However, the 1996 WEU Declaration already raised the future possibility of an EU–NATO relationship.[11] The question gained relevance as the EU had also taken over the WEU's Petersberg tasks at the same time, thus gaining a competence in military crisis management.[12] As long as the EU had conceived itself purely as a civilian actor, points of contact with NATO were few,[13] even if separating its tasks from NATO's military role raised theoretical difficulties.[14] In the event, military means were now fast becoming a natural part of the Union's foreign policy instruments.[15] Gradually it became recognised that some form of direct EU–NATO cooperation would be impossible to avoid in the long term.[16] In practice, contacts between the two organisations were at best sporadic even in the second half of the 1990s.[17]

FIRST INFORMAL CONTACTS

Informal meetings seem to have been held with some regularity between NATO-SG J. Solana and the Commission President J. Santer and RELEX Commissioner H. van den Broek as early as 1997.[18] These informal contacts reached a new level when Solana became the EU's High Representative for the Common and Security Policy. He was replaced by G. Robertson, formerly British Defence Secretary and one of

---

10   *Ibid.*, p. 126, n. 20.

11   F. Dehousse / B. Galer, *De Saint-Malo à Feira* (1999), p. 32; A. Moens, *Developing a European intervention force*, Int. Jour. (1999), p. 268. *Cf.* Speaking notes of the Rt. Hon. G. Robertson MP, Secretary of State for Defence, for the Informal Conference of Defence Ministers of the EU, Vienna, 3–4 Nov. 1998, reprinted in: 4 EFAR (1999), p. 121 at p. 122: 'Mechanisms already exist. Important work has been carried out in the WEU. ... But these procedures are complicated. ... Can the procedures be streamlined? Can we create simpler connections?'.

12   K. Möttölä, *Collective and co-operative security arrangements* (1998), p. 96; F. Pagani, *A New Gear in the CFSP Machinery: Integration of the Petersberg Tasks in the Treaty on European Union*, 9 EJIL (1998), pp. 737–749.

13   *Cf.* G. Bonvicini et al., *Security links in the making* (1996), p. 319.

14   'How do we establish this sequence between the European Union going in to deal with the causes of tension while, if things do not stop, NATO will have to intervene until, once they have stopped, the European Union goes back in again? ... How do we connect these different roles, without necessarily expecting that the European Union slips into the shoes of NATO and goes into things military?'. (G. Lenzi, *The WEU between NATO and EU*, 51 Studia Diplomatica (1998), p. 172).

15   H. Larsen, *Concepts of Security* (2000), p. 354.

16   E.g. U. Schmalz, *Aufbruch zu neuer Handlungsfähigkeit* (1999), p. 196; A. Pliakos, *The CESDP* (2000), p. 283; J. Howorth, *Discourse in ESDP*, 27 West European Politics 2 (2004), p. 218.

17   See e.g. NATO Press Release (98)149, 7 Dec. 1998, *Austrian Minister of Foreign Affairs in his capacity as President of EU Council Meets with NATO Secretary General*.

18   W. Link, *Die NATO im Geflecht internationaler Organisationen* (1999), p. 18, n. 26.

the architects of the St-Malo agreement.[19] With Solana, Europe had finally got its famous 'number to call in Europe' (H. Kissinger). Immediately after his appointment, Robertson announced he would work with Solana, which implied a direct EU–NATO contact.[20] Solana, who had only recently been the NATO-SG himself, had already participated in the discussions of the NAC.[21] The two met regularly for lunch. This contact, started so informally,[22] may have been a cultural transfer carried over from NATO's common practice of informal consultation[23] which Solana and Robertson, already familiarised from NATO, simply continued in a new framework. As a side-effect, the two established for the first time some kind of informal EU–NATO institutional connection. This phenomenon would be described in political science as 'internalism'.[24] The Solana–Robertson connection soon began to show its effects. Both regularly reported on these meetings to their respective Councils.[25] The 1999 Helsinki European Council already made reference to it: 'Initially, relations will be developed on an informal basis, through contacts between the SG/HR for the CFSP and the Secretary General of NATO.'[26] By summer of 2000, these contacts bore first fruit in the interim arrangement on Security of Information between the Council's General Secretariat and NATO.[27] By that time there was wide agreement that EU–NATO institutional cooperation need to be deepened and intensified beyond the informal level.[28]

---

19   *Cf.* G. Robertson, in: W. Hoyer / G.F. Kaldrack (eds.), *ESVP* (2002), p. 183.

20   Speech by Lord Robertson, NATO Secretary-General, Annual Session of the NATO Parliamentary Assembly, Amsterdam, 15 Nov. 1999, CP 47, pp. 60 at 63.

21   Ministerial Meeting of the North Atlantic Council held at NATO Headquarters, Brussels, 15 Dec. 1999, Final Communiqué, NATO Press Release M-NAC2(99)166, para. 21.

22   H. Beuve-Méry / P. Grasset, *La défense européenne: rapports transatlantiques*, 56 Défense nationale 11 (2000), p. 20.

23   See above, Chapter 3 (NATO Today). The most famous 'institution' of the informal NATO consultation culture was probably the 'Tuesday's ambassadors' lunch' which took place before the weekly Wednesday meeting at the NAC. It seems to have been abolished after the last enlargement in May 2004. *Cf. Nato: game over,* The Observer, 18 Feb. 2004, p. 12.

24   See above, Chapter 3 (NATO Today).

25   H. Boguslawska, *Le lien transatlantique et le développement de l'identité européenne de sécurité et de défense* (2003), p. 21.

26   European Council, Helsinki, 10–11 Dec. 1999, Presidency Conclusions, II. Annex 1 to Annex IV, CP 47, p. 88.

27   *Cf.* N.M. Abbasi, *Evolving a Common European defence* (2001), p. 88. On this agreement and the circumstances of its conclusion in detail, see below Chapter 9 (Security of Information).

28   M. d'Alema, *A New NATO for a New Europe*, 34 The International Spectator 2 (1999), pp. 31–32; M. Vasiu, *The role of the ESDI*, 6 Rom.J.Int.Aff. 3/4 (2000), p. 132; P.H. Gordon, *Their Own Army? Making European Defense Work.* Foreign Affairs (July/Aug. 2000), pp. 16–7; A.D. Rotfeld, *Europe: an emerging power* (2001), p. 206.

TOWARDS PERMANENT INSTITUTIONALISATION

Permanent institutionalisation began to be envisaged by Javier Solana[29] and US ambassador A. Vershbow[30] from the end of 1999.[31] The EU's Helsinki Summit in December 1999 had stated that all EU member States would participate in decisions and deliberations of the Council relating to EU–NATO relations on an equal footing.[32] The US had only recently clearly come out in favour of ESDP,[33] overcoming earlier ambiguities.[34] Some hesitancy to establishing direct institutional EU–NATO relations on the part of some EU member States also existed[35] notably by France. In spring 2000, France's reservations were rooted in its policy goal to establish the future EU–NATO relationship on an equal footing.[36] The institutional base for ESDP was only just beginning to be built. Involving NATO at this early stage was seen as detrimental to the independence of the new ESDP institutions.

> The fear in Paris, shared to some extent by other capitals, was that the monolithic strength of NATO would steamroller the infant CESDP into adopting structures, procedures and policies which would be unduly influenced by Washington and would therefore be likely simply to replicate NATO practice.[37]

---

29   See e.g. Speech by J. Solana, EU High Representative, 17 Dec. 1999, *The Development of a Common European Security and Defence Policy – The Integration Project of the Next Decade*, reprinted in: Levasseur/Scott, *The Law of the European Union: Materials and Cases* (2001), p. 1028: 'we have agreed on the need for sound and transparent procedures for consultation and cooperation with non-EU countries, and with NATO ...'.

30   Remarks by A. Vershbow, US ambassador to NATO, 17 Dec. 1999, *The Next Steps on European Security and Defence: A US View*, reprinted in: *ibid.*, p. 1020 at 1023: 'we are going to see early movement forward [on] the NATO-EU institutional relationship'.

31   Within NATO, preparations for institutional co-operation with the EU had commenced already in that year. *Cf.* O. Theiler, *Die NATO im Umbruch* (2003), p. 275.

32   European Council, Helsinki, 10–11 December 1999, Presidency Conclusions, II. Common European Policy on Security and Defence, Annex 1 to Annex IV (Decision-making), CP 47, p. 82 at 86. *Cf.* M. Jopp, *GESVP*, Jb.d.eur.Int. 1999/2000 (2000), p. 244.

33   Speech by US Deputy Secretary of State S. Talbott at the NAC, 15 Dec. 1999, reprinted in: J. Howorth, *The ultimate challenge* (2000), p. 64: 'There should be no confusion about America's position on the need for a stronger Europe. We are not against it, we are not ambivalent, we are not anxious; we are for it.'

34   *Ibid.*, speech at the Royal Institute of International Affairs, London, 7 Oct. 1999, *America's Stake in a Strong Europe*, CP 47, p. 54 at 56: 'We would not want to see an ESDI that comes into being first within NATO but then grows out of NATO and finally grows away from NATO, since that would lead to an ESDI that initially duplicates NATO but that could eventually compete with NATO'.

35   A. Vershbow, fn. 30 above.

36   J. Howorth, *European defence and the changing politics of the EU*, 39 JCMS (2001), p. 772.

37   J. Howorth, *The ultimate challenge* (2000), p. 56. In the field of Security of Information this prediction turned out to be true. See below, Chapter 9 (Security of Information). *Cf.* further B. Kohler-Koch, *Die GASP im kommenden Jahrzehnt – Gewappnet für Krisen?*:

Therefore, France favoured a continuation of the existing informal structures for the time being.[38] By May 2000, however, France took the plunge and proposed creating a set of joint EU–NATO committees which should tackle the most difficult issues surrounding ESDP.[39]

At its next Summit in Feira, on 19–20 June 2000, the European Council proposed that four ad hoc joint working groups should be installed with NATO to address the various aspects of the EU–NATO relationship: security issues, capabilities goals, modalities enabling EU access to NATO assets, and permanent consultation mechanisms for non-EU European NATO members.[40] Chief among these aspects were military capabilities, where NATO expertise in time proved very beneficial to the build-up process of the ERRF.[41]

In a much-celebrated event, the new interim Political and Security Committee (iPSC) met the NAC at ambassador level on 19 Sept. 2000.[42] Such a meeting, although long expected from many sides,[43] still lacked any formal base. Towards the end of the year, NATO began to press harder for institutional links between NATO and the EU.[44] In an exchange of letters between NATO and the Swedish EU Presidency of 24 January 2001, it was finally agreed that NATO and the EU should meet at least three times per half-year at PSC-NAC ambassadorial level, and at least once at ministerial level.[45]

Under this new formal arrangement, the first EU–NATO ministerial meeting was held on 30 May 2001, followed on 12 June 2001 by the first formal PSC-NAC

---

in: R. Hierzinger (ed.), *Europäische Leitbilder* (2001), p. 155 at 164; R. Seidelmann, *EU-Krisenreaktionskräfte*, 25 Integration 2 (2002), p. 120.

38   S. Taylor, *Solana attacked over NATO role in EU defence policy*, European Voice (online edition), Vol. 6, No. 8, 24 Feb. 2000.

39   *Ibid.*, *France softens stance on NATO's involvement in EU defence policy*, European Voice (online edition), Vol. 6, No. 17, 27 April 2000.

40   European Council, Santa Marta da Feira, 19–20 June 2000, Annex I: Presidency Report on Strengthening the Common European Security and Defence Policy, II.D., CP 47, p. 125. See also the Principles and arrangements for setting up the four working groups, Council Doc. 10025/1/00 REV 1, 5 July 2000.

41   See below, Chapter 7 (Military Crisis Management).

42   Intervention by Dr Javier Solana, High Representative for CFSP, COPSi/NAC first joint meeting, 19 Sept. 2000, CP 47, pp. 140; *cf.* A.D. Rotfeld, *Europe: an emerging power* (2001), p. 196; H. Boguslawska, *Le lien transatlantique* (2003), p. 21.

43   E.g. P. J. Teunissen, *Strengthening the defence dimension of the EU*, 4 EFAR (1999), p. 331: 'What seems most likely in the longer run is the establishment of an EU–NATO Council for defence tasks'. W. Link, *Die NATO im Geflecht internationaler Organisationen* (1999), p. 11, points out an interesting historical parallel of a similar institutional link in the provisions of the Treaty on a European Defence Community (EDC) planned in the 1950s. *Cf.* J. Trempont, *La communauté Européenne de Défense*, 1 ICLQ (1952), p. 530.

44   Speech by NATO-SG G. Robertson, *Turkey and a European Security and Defence Identity*, Istanbul, 23 Nov. 2000, http://www.nato.int/docu/speech/2000/s001123a.htm (visited 16/03/04).

45   For details on this exchange of letters, see at p. 128.

meeting.[46] EU–NATO cooperation at lower levels (between the respective Military Committees and Military Staffs) had taken place already since the EU's Nice Summit[47] without any formal base. Planning activity by the EU's new military bodies does not seem to have conflicted with NATO's work.[48] Moreover, a harmonious collusion of respective activities in the EU and NATO seems to be assured by the fact that the military representatives of most EU member States in both organisations are the same persons.[49]

SOME ISSUES AND PROBLEMS

The importance of the PSC-NAC format

Since EU–NATO meetings on a ministerial level do not occur very often, PSC-NAC became the key meeting format in all important areas of cooperation between NATO and the EU. One example is the Berlin Plus agreement,[50] where it was tested for the first time in operational practice in the EU's peacekeeping mission Operation *Concordia* in 2003.[51] Under Berlin Plus, the primary channel for communication between NATO and the EU in regard to monitoring of the use of NATO's common assets and capabilities is from the PSC to the NAC. PSC-NAC meetings are also central for the procedural side of the principle 'where NATO as a whole is not engaged',[52] that is, between options 1 and 2 under the NATO/EU Consultation document decision tree.[53] Today, after more than four years of regular EU–NATO institutional cooperation, routine PSC-NAC meetings have already led to an atmosphere of high trust between the two organisations.[54]

---

46   T.C. Salmon / A.J.K. Shepherd, *Toward a European Army* (2003), p. 175.

47   *Cf.* S. Duke, *CESDP: Nice's overtrumped success?*, 6 EFAR (2001), p. 160.

48   K. Shake, *Constructive Duplication* (2002), p. 26.

49   K. Kastner, *Quelle culture de sécurité et de défense pour l'Union européenne?*, ENA thesis, Promotion Romain Gary «2003–2005» (2005) (on file with the author), p. 53.

50   The Berlin Plus agreement incorporates the procedural provisions on consultation and co-operation between NATO and the EU in times of crisis, as spelt out in detail in the Nice Presidency Conclusions. See below Chapter 8 (Berlin Plus Agreement), and *cf.* M. Álvarez Verdugo, *La relación de Consulta y Cooperación entre la Unión Europea y la Otan*, REDI No. 12. Year 6 (May-Aug. 2002), p. 482.

51   H. Vincze, *Beyond symbolism: the EU's first military operation seen in its context* (2003), p. 5. http://www.weltpolitik.net/texte/policy/concordia/beyond_symbolism.pdf (visited 15/08/2004).

52   C. von Buttlar, *ESDP – A Regional Effort within the Atlantic Alliance*, in: A. Bodnar et al. (eds.), *The Emerging Constitutional Law of the European Union* (2003), p. 411.

53   See above p. 89.

54   G. Robertson, *Time to Deliver*, The World Today, June 2003, p. 11 at 12.

Are decisions taken in the PSC binding on member States in the NAC?

It has been argued that the PSC can issue 'directives' to ensure coherence of policy of the member States which also bind those EU States acting in the NAC.[55] This claim merits some examination. The PSC's functions, as laid down in Art. 25 TEU, do not contain any such competence. The only EU bodies competent to do this would be the European Council or the Council, as part of the CFSP (Arts 12–16 TEU).[56] The PSC answers to the Council on all questions. The most it is entitled to do on its own initiative is to deliver respective opinions to the Council.

The binding force of PSC decisions for the member States in the NAC could, however, arise from general international law. It has long been mooted that by voting for (or at least not objecting to) resolutions in certain international bodies such as the UN General Assembly, States can become bound through Estoppel,[57] or through the principle of *venire contra factum proprium*.[58] From a pragmatic perspective, it is hard to conceive a case where a decision of the PSC relating to the mere control of a running EU peacekeeping operation could come into conflict with anything the NAC could wish to decide. This author has not been able to find any evidence, practical or otherwise, to contradict this factual state of affairs.

A second question would be whether an opinion issued by the PSC could bind those member States who voted for it, and are also represented in the NAC, not to act against it in this forum. Following the objective meaning of the term, however, an opinion does not have the same quality as a resolution: it is a mere assessment of a given situation.[59] A resolution, by contrast, expresses the definite wish of an international body to see a certain situation maintained or changed. This is something

---

55   C. Schwegmann, *EU-Friedensmissionen* (2002), p. 6.

56   The European Council can issue 'general guidelines' and 'common strategies' (Arts 12–13 TEU), and the Council can take 'joint actions' (Art. 14 TEU) and 'common positions' (Art. 15 TEU).

57   E.g. R. Higgins, *The Development of International Law by the Political Organs of the United Nations*, 59 ASIL Proceedings (1965), p. 166 at 122; *Certain Expenses of the United Nations*, sep. op. G. Fitzmaurice (ICJ Rep. 1962, p. 198 at 210) and sep. op. P. Spender (*ibid.*, p. 182 at 190–1); J.P. Müller, *Vertrauensschutz im Völkerrecht* (1971), pp. 249. For the same principle concerning State behaviour at international conferences, Müller, *ibid.*, pp. 244–5; M. Mendelson, *Book Reviews*, 10 EJIL (1999), p. 477 at 478. For Estoppel effects of decisions by the NAC, see T. Gazzini (2003), p. 244. For the concept of Estoppel in general, see below Chapter 8 (Berlin Plus Agreement).

58   E.g. G. Hafner, *Certain Issues of the Work of the Sixth Committee at the Fifty-Sixth General Assembly*, 97 AJIL (2003), p. 147 at 156, regarding the Scope of the Convention on the Safety of UN and Associated Personnel. *Venire contra factum proprium* is often regarded as the civil law counterpart to the better-known principle of estoppel in international law. Both are grounded in the broader notion of good faith. *Cf.* J. Klabbers, *The Concept of Treaty in International Law* (1996), p. 94; W. Fiedler, *Unilateral Acts in International Law*, EPIL IV, p. 1018 at 1021.

59   As such, it is also 'less' in quality than a declaration which typically determines that a certain situation exists. Such a declaration, although without legal consequence by itself,

the PSC cannot do. Therefore, its members cannot become estopped or contradict their former deeds in any way legally constraining them in the future.

'PERMANENT ARRANGEMENTS FOR CONSULTATION AND COOPERATION' BETWEEN THE EU AND NATO OUTSIDE TIMES OF CRISIS (EXCHANGE OF LETTERS, 24 JANUARY 2001) – AN INTERNATIONAL TREATY?

In the European Council Summit Conclusions of Nice, 7–9 December 2000, the matter of formalised contacts between NATO and the EU was first tackled in earnest.[60] The Conclusions identified three different levels at which formal meetings should take place (PSC-NAC, MC level and subsidiary bodies), in addition to 'regular contacts' between the SGs, the Secretariats and the Military Staffs. NATO civil and military representatives would be invited to meetings of EU bodies, especially concerning matters 'where the capabilities and expertise of the Alliance are concerned'. It was considered a huge step towards institutionalising EU–NATO cooperation.[61] However, the Conclusions stated that for the formal category of meeting, the 'organisational arrangements' remained to be agreed between the two organisations.

An exchange of letters which took place between the Swedish EU Presidency and the NATO-SG on 24 January 2001 is the main document regulating in a formal way the format of meetings between NATO and the EU.[62] It provides that

> ... meetings between the NAC and PSC will be held not less than three times, and EU/ NATO ministerials not less than once, per EU Presidency. Either organisation may request additional meetings as necessary.

As a meetings schedule, these sentences are unspectacular. What could be more interesting from the point of view of legal scholarship is the legal nature of this instrument.

When subjects of international law perceive a shared future benefit in regulating any aspect of their relations in a binding and predictable manner, they usually wish to leave little room for uncertainty as to what precisely their respective rights and obligations as parties to an agreement consist of. From a sociological point of view, it

---

may lead to the application of a particular legal rule to that situation. *Cf.* H.G. Schermers / N.M. Blokker, *International Institutional Law* (1995), p. 770 at §1245.

60   European Council, Nice, Annex VII to Annex VI, at II, CP 47, pp. 204.

61   M. Kremer / U. Schmalz, *Nach Nizza – Perspektiven der GESVP* (2001), p. 168.

62   Permanent arrangements for consultation and cooperation between the EU and NATO. Exchange of letters between George Robertson, Secretary-General of NATO, and Anna Lindh, Swedish FM and Chairman of the Council of the European Union, 24 Jan. 2001 (released by the Council on a request by the author on 10 May 2004) [Hereinafter: EU–NATO exchange of letters, 24 Jan. 2001]. The exchange of letters is reproduced in full in the Annex. The operative provisions are also contained in Council Doc. 5251/1/01 of 16 Jan. 2001 (with the same title).

lies in the very nature of a contract to condense agreement existing between different minds as to a certain state of affairs – consisting in rights and obligations – at a single point in time. A contract perpetuates that state of affairs beyond such point, even though the parties' interests initially underlying the contract may change.[63] Thus, any party may subsequently use the contract's terms as a benchmark for the other's compliance, and especially for seeking redress in case the other party departs from them. The law of treaties generally regulates questions of agreements between subjects of international law considered by the parties as binding,[64] but, in stating the formal minimum requirements for a treaty, it also provides the conditions for its own applicability.

Even at first glance, the form as well as circumstances of conclusion of the exchange of letters of 24 January 2001 leave much to be desired in the way of certainty. Before entering into an analysis of its content, then, the first question to be asked is whether the law of treaties is applicable.

The general law of treaties applies between States.[65] The special law of treaties between international organisations adapts this general set of rules as necessary for this more particular group of subjects of international law.[66] It has been the object of a long-standing project of codification by the ILC, resulting in the Vienna Convention on the Law of Treaties between States and International Organisations of 1986 (hereinafter VCLTIO).[67] This convention, however, is far yet from entering into force.[68] Some EU and NATO member States have signed and ratified it – and it is conceivable that those could be bound to adhere to its content via estoppel[69] – but

---

63   Except in cases where these interests change abruptly and substantially, *cf.* Art. 62 VCLT.

64   *Cf.* Art. 2 VCLTIO; R. Bernhardt, *Treaties*: in: EPIL IV, p. 927; M.N. Shaw, *International Law* (4th ed. 1997), p. 73–4; A. Cassese, *International Law* (2001), p. 126; A. Verdross / B. Simma, *Universelles Völkerrecht* (1984), § 534, p. 337; G. Schwarzenberger, *A Manual of International Law* (6th ed. 1976), p. 24–5.

65   Art. 1 and 6 VCLT.

66   R. Jennings / A. Watts, *Oppenheim's International Law* (9th ed. 1992), p. 1220.

67   25 ILM 543, opened for signature on 21 March 1986. On the VCLTIO in general, see only K. Zemanek (ed.), *Agreements of International Organizations and the Vienna Convention on the Law of Treaties* (1971); E. Klein / M. Pechstein, *Das Vertragsrecht internationaler Organisationen* (1985); H. Isak / G. Loibl, *United Nations Conference on the Law of Treaties between States and International Organizations or between International Organizations*, 38 ÖsterrZÖR (1987); P.K. Menon, *The law of treaties between states and international organizations* (1992).

68   Even though the VCLTIO applies to States and international organisations in the same manner, only ratifications by States are counted towards the total number required for entry into force (Art. 85 VCLTIO). To date, it is ten ratifications short of the thirty-five needed (United Nations Treaty Collection, status as of 31 March 2003).

69   *Cf.* Art. 18 VCLT.

neither of the two organisations has in itself done so.[70] Nevertheless, its content is held, to a large degree, to reflect existing customary international law.[71]

A treaty under international law requires the following characteristics: subjects (who in the case of the exchange of letters of 24 January 2001 must also be international organisations), a minimum form, a meeting of the minds, consent to be bound by its contents, and treaty-making power.[72]

These characteristics shall be tried against the exchange of letters of 24 January 2001, one by one, below. The international law applied must be that of the time of conclusion. This is of particular importance for the internal European law, which must therefore be applied in the version of the Treaty of Amsterdam, then still in force.[73]

International organisations

Although the exact canon of defining characteristics for an international organisation is still not entirely clear,[74] these characteristics would certainly include permanent membership, a constituent instrument[75] which establishes the organisation under

---

70   *Cf.* Art. 34 VCLTIO. The EU and NATO member States not having ratified are: Iceland, Norway, Portugal, France, Ireland, Luxembourg, Finland, the United States, Canada, Turkey and Poland (status as of 31 March 2003).

71   See only R. Bernhardt, *Treaties – Addendum 1999*, in EPIL IV, pp. 931–2; in more cautious terms, but lastly reaching the same conclusion: I. Brownlie, *Principles of Public International Law* (5th edn, 1998), p. 608. See also the comments by States in the UNGA 6th Ctte: e.g. 'The articles successfully reflected treaty law as currently practised', GAOR (37th Sess.), 6th Ctte., Summary Records of Meetings, UN-Doc. A/C.6/37/SR. 46, p. 13 at para. 53 (Federal Republic of Germany); Convention on the Law of Treaties between States and International Organizations or between International Organizations: Report of the Secretary-General, Addendum, UNGA (38th Sess.), UN-Doc. A/38/145/Add.1, p. 3, at para. 1 (Bulgaria); *ibid.*, p. 5, para. 1 (Vietnam).

72   *Cf.* K. Doehring, *Völkerrecht* (1999), § 334, pp. 143–4; US Department of State, Coordination and Reporting of International Agreements, § 181.2 Criteria, 27 April 1981, 22 Code of Federal Regulations, Part 181, see 46 Federal Register 35917 of 13 July 1981.

73   The Treaty of Nice (amending the TEU) only entered into force on 1 February 2003. Where other versions than Amsterdam used, this will be specifically indicated, e.g. TEU(MT) for the Treaty on European Union, Maastricht version or TEU(NT) for the Treaty on European Union, Nice version.

74   On the varying definitions, *cf.* (among others) I. Brownlie, *Principles of Public International Law* (1998), pp. 677 (esp. at n.2, with many further references); M.N. Shaw, *International Law* (1997), pp. 908; A. Cassese, *International Law* (2001), pp. 70; H.G. Schermers / N.M. Blokker, *International Institutional Law* (1995), pp. 20–31, §§ 29–45; V. Epping, *Internationale Organisationen*, in: K. Ipsen, Völkerrecht (4th edn 1999), pp. 390; R. Bindschedler, *International Organizations, General Aspects*, in: EPIL II, pp. 1289; P. Fischer / H.F. Köck, *Allgemeines Völkerrecht* (5th edn 2000), pp. 201–2.

75   R. Bindschedler, *ibid.*, p. 1289.

international law,[76] a place of headquarters with a secretariat,[77] at least one organ fulfilling particular functions within the organisation,[78] and a defined scope of activity which serves the common aims of its members.[79] Summarily speaking, it seems fair to assume that for both the EU and NATO, all of these characteristics apply today.[80] For completeness, however, they shall be briefly described below.

For the EU, membership is defined by its founding treaty, the TEU of Maastricht (TEU), and later versions. The TEU serves as its charter, establishing the organisation's status versus its member states, and the respective rights and obligations. Its main permanent seat is Brussels, where most of its organs are located, with the exception of the European Court of Justice in Luxembourg, and part of the European Parliament's activities in Strasbourg. The scope of activity of the EU is defined in the TEU's Art. 1, taking the European Communities' scope of activity as a basis, plus the areas added to it by the TEU (Title V, Common Foreign and Security Policy and Title VI, Justice and Home Affairs). These additional areas are intergovernmental – not supranational like the subject matter of the EC. As a result, they would fall under the same rules as any subject matter governed by an international treaty.

NATO, in the same manner, has a permanent membership which – similarly to the EU – is established by its founding treaty, the North Atlantic Treaty of 1949 (NAT),[81] together with its accession protocols for later members (the last accessions, in 2004, were Estonia, Latvia, Lithuania, Slovakia, Slovenia, Bulgaria and Romania). As an organisational charter, the NAT does not contain much detail. The only organ expressly mentioned is the North Atlantic Council; all other of its many organs derive their competence indirectly from the NAT.[82] Their existence is, however, crucial for the exercise of the organisation's functions and the organisation could not operate for a single day without them. Thus, additionally, the doctrine of implied powers[83]

---

76   H.G. Schermers / N.M. Blokker, *International Institutional Law* (1995), p. 31, at § 45.

77   *Ibid.*

78   R. Wolfrum, *International Organizations, Headquarters*, in: EPIL II, p. 1309–1310.

79   R. Bindschedler, EPIL II.

80   G. Hafner, *The Amsterdam Treaty and the treaty-making power of the European Union*, in: Liber Amicorum for Professor I. Seidl-Hohenveldern, in honour of his 80th birthday (1998), pp. 263–5, however, still expresses doubts as to according full status as an international organisation to the EU.

81   34 UNTS 243.

82   See above, Chapter 3 (NATO Today).

83   *Reparation for Injuries Suffered in the Service of the United Nations*, Adv. Op., 1949 ICJ Rep., p. 174, 182: 'Under international law the organization must be deemed to have those powers, which, though not expressly provided in the Charter, are conferred upon it by necessary implication as being necessary to the performance of its duties.' See also H.F. Köck, *Die 'implied powers' der Europäischen Gemeinschaften als Anwendungsfall der 'implied powers' internationaler Organisationen überhaupt*, in: K. Böckstiegel et al., *Völkerrecht, Recht der internationalen Organisationen, Weltwirtschaftsrecht*, Festschrift für I. Seidl-Hohenveldern (1988); M. Zuleeg, *International Organizaions, Implied* Powers, in: EPIL II, fn. 74, p. 1313; *cf.* also R. Jennings / A. Watts, *Oppenheim's* (1992), p. 1219–20.

can be applied to bring them within the scope of the NAT.[84] This system of agencies far exceeds what could be regarded as the minimum requirement for an international organisation's secretariat – many international organisations need to make do with much smaller infrastructure. NATO's main headquarters is in Brussels. The organisation's traditional scope of activity has been collective defence, as provided in Art. 5 NAT.[85] Starting with the Strategic Concept of 1991,[86] and building on this with the new Strategic Concept of 1999[87] and the Prague Declaration of 2002,[88] this has been expanded to international crisis management operations 'out of area',[89] to maintain international peace and security.[90]

Subjects of international law

Common legal terminology defines a subject of international law as 'an entity capable of possessing international rights and duties and having the capacity to maintain its rights by bringing international claims'.[91]

The EU's status as a subject of international law is a contentious question today. The TEU is silent on the topic, in contrast to the TEC which establishes such a quality for the EC beyond doubt.[92] This absence alone weighs heavily against according the EU such a status on the basis of the text of the Amsterdam Treaty. Such a conclusion, still drawn by many scholars,[93] is supported by the history of

---

84   *Cf.* G. Nolte, *Die 'neuen' Aufgaben von NATO und WEU*, 54 HJIL (1994), pp. 102–110, who uses the doctrine to extend NATO's original treaty functions even in matters as far-reaching as the external security of the organisation.

85   In some cases, preparatory action to guard against possible future Art. 5 contingencies fell under Art. 4 NAT, as happened in the case of NATO AWACS support for Turkey in the run-up to the Iraq war in spring 2003, see NATO Press Release (2003)40 of 16 April 2003.

86   The Alliance's Strategic Concept, Agreed by the Heads of State and Government participating in the meeting of the North Atlantic Council in Rome on 7–8 November 1991, paras. 14,15 and especially 20, reprinted in: *NATO Handbook*, (October 1995), p. 235.

87   The Alliance's Strategic Concept, Approved by the Heads of State and Government participating in the meeting of the North Atlantic Council in Washington D.C. on 23–24 April 1999, para. 31, CP 47, p. 30.

88   NATO Prague Summit Declaration by Heads of State and Government, 21 November 2002, paras. 11 and 12, NATO Press Release (2000) 127, 21 Nov. 2002 (= 42 ILM 244).

89   'Out of area': outside the geographical limits foreseen in Art. 5 NAT ('Europe or North America') or the preamble of the NAT ('the Euro-Atlantic area').

90   These new tasks of NATO are partly to be effected by those members able and willing to do so (possibly in a WEU framework), utilising the concept of Combined Joint Task Forces (CJTF). They have been argued to be covered by the Art. 4 NAT. See above Chapter 3 (NATO Today).

91   I. Brownlie, *Principles of Public International Law* (5th edn, 1998), p. 57.

92   Art. 281 TEC.

93   E.g. Generally J.W. de Zwaan, *The Legal personality of the European Communities and the European Union*, 30 NYIL (1999) w.f.r.; K. Lanearts / E. de Smijter, *The European*

negotiations on this question during the 1996 Amsterdam Conference, where a draft containing a provision establishing international legal personality for the EU did not find unanimous support among the Member States.[94] Contrastingly, an increasing part of legal opinion seems to point to the evolution of the institutional structure and procedures of the Union as contained in the TEU (for example the mere existence of the European Council)[95] and to the competencies the Union has gained since Maastricht, chiefly regarding external representation and treaty-making powers.[96] These factors lead many to conclude that the Union indeed has international legal personality today, as many other international organisations do.[97] The international legal principle of implied powers, established by the ICJ in its 1949 Reparations Case[98] is often cited as an argument in this regard.[99] In addition, great importance is laid on the evolving practice of the EU regarding the interpretation and use of its external competencies.[100] The accession treaties of Austria, Finland and Sweden of 1995, for example, were addressed to the Council of the EU not to the individual member States.[101] Evidence of further relevant practice has become increasingly available during recent years, as the Union has started to enter into legal relations

Union as an Actor under International Law, 19 YBEL (1999/2000), p. 130.

94   G. Hafner, *The Amsterdam Treaty*, in: Lib. Am. Seidl-Hohenveldern (1998), p. 266; W. Schroeder, *Verfassungsrechtliche Beziehungen zwischen Europäischer Union und Europäischen Gemeinschaften*, in: A. von Bogdandy (ed.), *Europäisches Verfassungsrecht* (2003), p. 376.

95   H.-J. Cremer, Commentary to Art. 24 TEU, in: C. Caliess / H.J. Blanke (eds.), *Kommentar zu EU-Vertrag und EG-Vertrag* (2nd edn 2002), p. 212; W. Schroeder, *Verfassungsrechtliche Beziehungen zwischen EU und EG*, in: A. von Bogdandy (2003), pp. 386–390; P. Craig / G. de Búrca, *EU Law* (3rd edn 2003), p. 36.

96   G. Hafner, *The Amsterdam Treaty*, in: Lib. Am. Seidl-Hohenveldern (1998), p. 276; M. Hilf / E. Pache, *Der Vertrag von Amsterdam*, 11 NJW (1998), p. 710.

97   G. Hafner, *The Amsterdam Treaty*, in: Lib. Am. Seidl-Hohenveldern (1998), p. 283; *cf.* W. Schroeder, *Verfassungsrechtliche Beziehungen zwischen EU und EG*, in: A. von Bogdandy (2003), pp. 386; Editorial comments, *The European Union – A new international actor*, 38 CMLR (2001), p. 825, 827; R.A. Wessel, *The Constitutional Relationship between the European Union and the European Community: Consequences for the Relationship with the Member States*, pp. 10–13, in: A. von Bogdandy / J.H.H. Weiler (eds.), *European Integration – The New German Scholarship*; Jean Monnet Working Paper 9/03.9 (2003); *cf.* already A. von Bogdandy / M. Nettesheim, *Die Verschmelzung der Europäischen Gemeinschaften in der Europäischen Union*, 36 NJW (1995), p. 2327.

98   Reparation for Injuries Suffered in the Service of the United Nations, Adv. Op., ICJ Rep. 1949, p. 182.

99   E.g. I. Seidl-Hohenveldern / G. Loibl, *Das Recht der Internationalen Organisationen einschließlich der supranationalen Gemeinschaften* (1996), p. 11; *cf.* G. Hafner, *The Amsterdam Treaty*, in: Lib. Am. Seidl-Hohenveldern (1998), p. 283.

100   H. Krück, *Gemeinsame Außen- und Sicherheitspolitik*, in: J. Schwarze (ed.), *EU-Kommentar* (2000), pp. 108–9.

101   Decision of the Council of the EU of 1 Jan. 1995 95/1/EC, Euratom, ECSC, OJ L 001/1–219 of 1 Jan. 1995.

with third parties. A great number of these agreements concern its new peacekeeping activities (both military and civilian) in the Balkans.[102] They are for example troop stationing agreements with the host States[103] or agreements regulating participation of third countries (mostly EU accession candidates) in EU peacekeeping operations.[104] The recent Agreement on the Security of Information concluded with NATO in March 2003 should also be mentioned,[105] as should EU treaty-making practice with Iceland and Norway in the area of the Schengen *aquis*, integrated into the EU system by the Amsterdam Treaty.[106] All these recent international agreements simply refer to 'the European Union' as the contracting party, language which thus also reflects the opinion of an increasing number of contracting countries.[107]

At the time of writing, the entire EU's legal architecture is undergoing fast and fundamental change which looks likely to be eventually incorporated into the new European Constitution. The current Treaty Establishing a Constitution for Europe[108] provides in its Art. I-7 that 'the Union shall have legal personality'. In conclusion, legal personality in the specific case of the Berlin Plus can therefore be implied from the Union's powers enshrined in the relevant provisions on external representation in Title V of the TEU, mainly Art. 18 and Art. 24. This is a case of the general principle of implied powers.

NATO's quality as a subject of international law is today undisputed.[109] Even though it has until recently not endeavoured to conclude treaties on the international

---

102   But see also, for example, the EU-Lebanon Agreement on Co-operation in the Fight against Terrorism, 17 April 2002, Council Doc. 7494/02.

103   See for example the Status-of-Forces agreements with Albania (OJ L 93/50 of 10/4/2003), Bosnia (OJ L 293/2 of 29/10/2002), Federal Republic of Yugoslavia (OJ L 125/2 of 5/5/2001) and Macedonia (OJ L 241//1 of 11/09/2001 and OJ L 82/45 of 29/3/2003).

104   See for example the Agreements of the European Union with third states on the participation of those states in the European Union Police Mission (EUPM) in Bosnia and Herzegovina, OJ L 64/38 of 7/3/2003 (Poland), OJ L 197/38 of 5/8/2003 (Russia) and OJ L 239/1–46 of 25/09/2003 (all others); Agreement between the EU and Cyprus on the latter's participation in the EU's peacekeeping operation in the Democratic Republic of Congo, OJ L 253/22 of 7/10/2003; Agreement between the European Union and the Swiss Confederation on the participation of the Swiss Confederation in the European Union military crisis management operation in Bosnia and Herzegovina (Operation *Althea*), Council Doc. 15653, 13 Dec. 2004.

105   Agreement between the European Union and the North Atlantic Treaty Organisation on the Security of Information of 14 March 2003, OJ EU L 80/36 of 27/3/2003.

106   K. Famira, *Der freie Personenverkehr in Europa – Schengen nach Amsterdam* (2004), p. 256; Treaty of Amsterdam, OJ C 340, 10 Nov. 1997, Protocol integrating the Schengen *aquis* into the framework of the European Union, Art. 6.

107   *Cf.* G. Hafner, *The Amsterdam Treaty*, in: Lib. Am. Seidl-Hohenveldern (1998), pp. 281–2.

108   Treaty Establishing a Constitution for Europe, Brussels, 6 Aug. 2004, CIG 87/04.

109   See only J.S. Ignarski, *North Atlantic Treaty Organization*, in EPIL III, p. 649.

level,[110] it has for a long time had agreements with its member States on its status in their respective internal legal systems.[111]

Form

Exchange of notes is today a very popular form of concluding a treaty by States and international organisations.[112] The basic characteristic setting it apart from treaties is that the signatures do not appear in one, but in two separate documents.[113] Exchanges of notes are mostly used for regulating smaller aspects falling within a larger framework between the parties.[114] Notes exchanged in order to conclude an international treaty commonly relate to one another, and the second note repeats the same operative text as the first note, in effect answering it.[115] They use treaty terminology (for example 'shall', not 'will').[116] Further important formal characteristics are a clause specifying the date of entry into force (often the first offering note leaves this open to the replying party), and, in some cases, a denunciation clause. Mostly, the notes carry the heading *note verbale* (or similar) and refer to the proposal to conclude an 'Agreement'. As with all international treaties, the form of an exchange of notes can be indicative, yet is not decisive, for its legal nature.[117] The content and the language in which it is expressed are more important. This is also the view taken by the legal services of various international organisations, such as NATO's.[118]

In the present case, the parties exchanged two letters, clearly relating to each other several times, which restated basic provisions on the frequency of regular meetings between the EU and NATO. However, the text uses 'will' and 'may' to denote the parties' rights and obligations. This is untypical language for a binding exchange of notes. There is no clause specifying 'entry into force', 'taking effect', or any such similar formulation, and no denunciation procedure is provided. Neither the proposing letter by Robertson nor the reply of the same day by Swedish Foreign Minister Lindh carry any heading. Instead, they simply start by 'Dear...'. In circumscribing the operative provisions the parties speak of 'arrangements' which

---

110   See below at p. 136.

111   See only: Agreement on the Status of the North Atlantic Treaty Organisation, national representatives and international staff, 12 Dec. 1951, 200 UNTS 4.

112   I. Sinclair, *The Vienna Convention on the Law of Treaties* (1984), p. 39; A. Aust, *Modern Treaty Law and Practice* (2000), p. 21.

113   P. Reuter, *Introduction to the Law of Treaties* (1995), p. 62.

114   *Ibid.* See e.g. France-WEU (1967), 1306 UNTS 173; United Kingdom-WEU (1974), 1400 UNTS 3; United Nations-EC (1980), 1159 UNTS 423.

115   P. Reuter, *Introduction to the Law of Treaties* (1995), p. 62.

116   A. Aust, *The Theory and Practice of Informal International Instruments*, 35 ICLQ (1986), p. 787 at 800.

117   Common Art. 2 (1) (a) *in fine* VCLT and VCLTIO; A. Aust, *Modern Treaty Law and Practice* (2000), p. 20–21.

118   Personal telephone interview with the NATO Legal Service, 3 June 2004.

bespeaks a rather informal kind of understanding, rather than of an 'agreement'. In conclusion, very few of the formal characteristics for a binding exchange of notes are assembled.

Meeting of the minds

In the proposing letter by Robertson, NATO welcomes 'the intention of the European Union that this dialogue should be pursued through a regular pattern of meetings at Ministerial, NAC-PSC, MC and expert level as well as through contacts with secretariats'. Following this, the replying letter by the EU Presidency notes 'with satisfaction the identity of views between the EU and NATO'.

However, there may be a problem with the identity of the actors who are involved. The first letter from the NATO-SG starts with 'Dear Javier' (in Robertson's own hand) and is thus clearly addressed to the 'Secretary General/High Representative', with only a 'cc:' to the 'EU Presidency'. In the replying letter, however, the EU Presidency and the High Representative have switched roles: that letter comes from the EU Presidency itself, with only a 'cc:' to the High Representative! All this seems odd from a procedural point of view. It may even simply be a formal mistake on the part of the Presidency. However, under the international law of treaties, only the EU as a whole possesses international legal personality (if indeed it does[119]). None of the Union's organs do so in their own capacity.[120] Hence, both the High Representative (as 'offeree') and the EU Presidency (as 'accepting party') could in reality only represent *the European Union* vis-à-vis NATO. As a consequence, the international person to whom the offer was made and the one who replied were in truth identical.

NATO shares this view. Indeed, it was quite happy to receive a reply from the EU Presidency (which it deemed to be the 'higher' organ) rather than from the High Representative to whom it had originally sent its proposal.[121] Although such factual considerations should not easily impact on the legal conclusions drawn on the basis of the law (that is, the provisions of the VCLTIO as reflecting international customary law), for practical purposes they should not be disregarded.

The meeting of the minds of the two parties as to the content of the 'arrangements' thus seems evident.

---

119   On the question of the EU's legal personality, which was still contentious in January 2001, see above at pp. 128.

120   *Cf.* K. Famira, *Der freie Personenverkehr in Europa – Schengen nach Amsterdam* (2004), p. 255.

121   Personal telephone interview with the NATO Legal Service, 3 June 2004. The example given by the NATO Legal Service to illustrate this position was the following: In any private commercial contract between two companies, any offeror, having sent a commercial offer to the procurement officer of a prospective client firm, would of course be delighted to receive a reply by that company's president himself!

Consent to be bound

The consent of the parties to be bound by an exchange of notes is sometimes directly expressed in their text.[122] This is, however, not always the case. In absence of expressly provided consent to be bound, language, general context, and the title offer indication, not only as to form (see above), but in addition as to consent to be bound.

The proposing letter by Robertson could contain such a consent to be bound for NATO. In the last paragraph it is stated

> I propose that the relevant Nice documents and the results of the NATO Ministerial meeting constitute the elements for the permanent arrangements on consultation and cooperation between NATO and the EU.[123]

This could be read as consent to be bound to the 'relevant Nice documents', meaning Annex VII to Annex VI (II. Arrangements for consultation outside times of crisis) of the EU's Nice Presidency Conclusions of December 2000 before.[124] It is certainly language normally found in binding exchanges of letters.

Lindh's reply accepts the meeting schedule proposed in Robertson's letter,[125] but in restating the operative provisions it leaves out any reference to those 'relevant Nice documents'. Lindh merely looks forward, at the end of her letter, to 'implementing these arrangements'.[126] It goes without saying that any understanding, whether

---

122   See e.g.
  – the three Exchanges of letters constituting agreements between NATO and Austria, concerning the transit for the purpose of the multinational peace operation in Bosnia (IFOR), on privileges and immunities, and on protection of information, 14, 15 and 20 Dec. 1995, 1912 UNTS 261, 271 and 287: 'which(,) in the event of your agreement, will become binding upon [the parties]' (common phrase) followed by 'I propose that this letter and [the affirmative reply] constitute an agreement, which will enter into force...' (in agreements of 15 and 20 Dec.);
  – the Exchange of letters constituting an agreement between the NATO and Ireland in relation to Ireland's responsibilities for participation in KFOR, 25 and 27 Aug. 1999, 2141 UNTS 244: 'I have the honour to propose that this letter and your reply confirming the agreement ... shall constitute an Agreement which shall enter into force on the date of your reply'.

123   See above, EU–NATO exchange of letters, 24 Jan. 2001. Letter from NATO, last paragraph.

124   CP 47, pp. 204–5.

125   See above, EU–NATO exchange of letters, 24 Jan. 2001. Letter from the Swedish Presidency, para. 1.

126   See above, EU–NATO exchange of letters, 24 Jan. 2001. Z. Lachowski, *The military dimension of the European Union* (2002), p. 164 notes in this regard that Sweden as a non-NATO EU member 'may have been more constrained in attempting to develop EU–NATO cooperation than the succeeding Belgian presidency'.

binding or not, must be implemented. The EU's consent to be bound to 'relevant Nice documents' is not recognisable in this formulation.

Treaty-making power

International organisations, unlike States, do not enjoy treaty-making power by virtue of their mere existence.[127] Rather, the VCLTIO, which is largely customary international law,[128] states in its Art. 6 that 'the capacity of an international organisation to conclude treaties is governed by the rules of that organisation'. This rule is widely accepted.[129] The 'rules of the organisation' include 'in particular, the constituent instruments, relevant decisions and resolutions, and established practice of the organisation' (Art. 2/1/j VCLTIO). A closer look at the drafting history of this provision shows that the term 'established practice' as such 'is not intended to freeze practice at a particular moment in an organization's history'[130] but allows an international organisation to adjust its internal rules to changing circumstances also after the entry into force of its constituent treaty.[131] It makes sense to regard the

---

127   E.g. I. Brownlie, *Principles of Public International Law* (1998), pp. 681–2; W. Heintschel von Heinegg, *Die völkerrechtlichen Verträge als Hauptrechtsquelle des Völkerrechts*, in: K. Ipsen, *Völkerrecht* (4th edn 1999), p. 97; K. Zemanek, *International Organizations, Treaty-Making Power*, in: EPIL III, p. 1343. The contrary view is taken by e.g. F. Seyersted, *Objective International Personality of Intergovernmental Organizations*, 34 Nordisk Tidsskrift for International Ret (1964), p. 99; K. Zemanek, *ibid. – Addendum 1991*, p. 1346 (adjusting his earlier position, above). The ILC, in drafting Art. 6 VCLTIO, tried to harmonise those two views, *cf.* e.g. YBILC 1974, Vol. I, p. 235, para. 58 (Kearney); YBILC 1981, Vol. II, Part 2, p. 127, Commentary to Art. 6. See also Preambular para. 11 of the VCLTIO.

128   See above at fn. 71.

129   Resolution adopted by the Institute of International Law at its Centenary Session, Rome, 5–15 Sept. 1973, AnnIDI, Vol.55 (1973), p. 797, at II.; A. Verdross / B. Simma, *Universelles Völkerrecht* (1984), pp. 437–8; W. Heintschel von Heinegg, *Die völkerrechtlichen Verträge*, in: K. Ipsen, *Völkerrecht* (1999), p. 97. The present text of Art. 6 represented a compromise between two camps of States, regarding the question whether international organisations had inherent or only derived treaty-making capacity. See e.g. YBILC 1974, Vol. II, Part 1, p. 148, fn. 75 (listing comments by States); H. Isak / G. Loibl, *UN Conference on the Law of Treaties*, 38 ÖsterrZÖR (1987), pp. 64–65; P.K. Menon, *The law of treaties* (1992), pp. 20–25 (with further references).

130   Convention on the Law of Treaties between States and International Organizations or between International Organizations: Report of the Secretary-General, Addendum, UNGA (38th Sess.), UN-Doc. A/38/145/Add.1, p. 40, at para. 10 (Comment by the EEC); *cf.* also Commentaries to Art. 2: YBILC 1981, Vol. II, Part 2, p. 124 at para. 24; YBILC 1981, Vol. II, Part 2, p. 21 at para. 25. But see also H. Isak / G. Loibl, *UN Conference on the Law of Treaties*, 38 ÖsterrZÖR (1987), pp. 64–66.

131   *Ibid.*; Commentary to Art. 6, YBILC 1974, Vol. II, Part 1, p. 152, at para. 28 (Third Report, Special Rapporteur Reuter); comments and observations of governments and international organisations: YBILC 1981, Vol. II, Part 2, p. 183, at para. 6 (Canada); *ibid.*, p.

practice of an organisation in its treaty-making as sufficient legal basis to conclude a treaty, if one takes into account that most international organisations lack express references in their constituent instruments concerning treaty-making capacity.[132] This approach also seems in line with the general rule of Art. 31/3/b VCLT. Art. 7/3/b VCLTIO, stating the conditions for full powers, allows for representation of an international organisation where 'it appears from the circumstances that it was the intention ... to consider that person as representing the organisation for such purposes'.[133]

For the EU, internal rules on concluding treaties with third parties in the area of the CFSP are provided expressly in Art. 24 TEU.[134] According to this provision, the Presidency, *acting upon authorisation of the Council*, is entitled to negotiate such agreements,[135] which are then concluded by the Council acting unanimously on a

---

198, at para. 10 (United Nations); *ibid.*, p. 199, at para. 6, under Article 6 etc. (ILO); YBILC 1982, Vol. II, Part 2, p. 140, under Article 2, at para. 2 (Council of Europe); Observations of delegations, GAOR (36th Sess.), 6th Ctte., Summary Records of Meetings, UN-Doc. A/C.6/36/SR. 42, p. 11 at para. 50 *in fine.* (Italy); *ibid.* GAOR (37th Sess.), 6th Ctte., Summary Records of Meetings, UN-Doc. A/C.6/37/SR. 51, p. 20 at para. 91 (Austria). – sceptical: Díaz González (YBILC 1981, Vol. I, p. 10–11, at para. 29); – arguing against this interpretation: YBILC 1981, Vol. II, Part 2, p. 189, IV. at para. 2 (Romania); Observations of delegations, GAOR (36th Sess.), 6th Ctte., Summary Records of Meetings, UN-Doc. A/C.6/36/SR. 40, p. 18 at para. 64 (GDR); *ibid.* SR. 43, p. 3, at para. 6 (Romania); *ibid.* (37th Sess.), UN-Doc. A/C.6/37/SR. 48, p. 13 at para. 50, and Convention on the Law of Treaties between States and International Organizations or between International Organizations: Report of the Secretary-General, Addendum, UNGA (38th Sess.), UN-Doc. A/38/145/Add.1, p. 4, at para. 5 (Comments by Bulgaria). This approach follows the concept of implied powers as expressed by the ICJ (fn. 83) in its 1949 Reparation for Injuries advisory opinion (K. Zemanek, *International Organizations, Treaty-Making Power*, in: EPIL III, p. 1345).

132   H. Isak / G. Loibl, *UN Conference on the Law of Treaties*, 38 ÖsterrZÖR (1987), p. 54.

133   As opposed to the latest draft by the ILC of 1982 (YBILC 1982, Vol. I, p. 251), that provision as it was finally adopted by the Vienna Convention in 1986 left out the phase '[it appears from] the *practice* of the competent organs' [emphasis added]. This may be an indication that States deemed that particular flexibility was necessary in this regard, to cover the existing variety of international organisations which differ widely in their internal structures.

134   See generally S. Marquardt, *Article 24 EU*, in: V. Kronenberger, *The EU and the international legal order* (2001), pp. 333; G. Hafner, *The Amsterdam Treaty*, in: Lib. Am. Seidl-Hohenveldern (1998); M. Hilf / E. Pache, *Der Vertrag von Amsterdam*, 11 NJW (1998), p. 709; W. Heintschel von Heinegg, *Rechtliche Aspekte bei der Neufassung der GASP durch den Vertrag von Amsterdam*, Die Friedenswarte 73 (1998) 2, p. 157 at 160–1; C. Thun-Hohenstein, *Der Vertrag von Amsterdam* (1997), p. 74; S. Langrish, *The Treaty of Amsterdam: Selected Highlights*, 23 ELR (1998), pp. 13–14.

135   The Council, in turn, derives its treaty-making capacity directly from the member States as parties to the TEU.

recommendation from the Presidency, when this is necessary for the implementation of the CFSP.[136]

Since the member States were initially averse to transferring treaty-making competence to the Union as a whole,[137] such international agreements are considered to be concluded by the Union only in their representation.[138] In light of the changing opinion concerning the international legal personality of the Union, this may also now be changing.[139]

An obstacle to the treaty-making power of the EU inherent in Art. 24 TEU might be the opt-out possibility open to any member State with regard to any international treaty for constitutional reasons, contained in the latter part of the article. However, this has apparently not hindered the Union from concluding a number of treaties in the area of its ESDP,[140] particularly on crisis management,[141] all of which were duly authorised by Council Decisions under Art. 24 TEU.

---

136   This follows the general provision of Art. 13, para. 3, first sentence TEU, according to which the Council 'shall take the decisions necessary for the implementation' of the CFSP 'on the basis of the general guidelines defined by the European Council'.

137   *Cf.* R. Geiger, *External Competences of the European Union and the Treaty-Making Power of its Member States*, 14 Ariz. J. Int'l & Comp. L. (1997), p. 320).

138   See Declaration on Draft Article J.14 [now Art. 24] TEU, annexed to the Final Act of the Treaty of Amsterdam, http://europa.eu.int/eur-lex/en/treaties/dat/amsterdam. html#0131010021 (visited 28/12/03); P. Craig / G. de Burca, *EU Law* (2nd edn, 1998), p. 40; M. Cremona, *External Relations and External Competence*, in: P. Craig / G. de Burca, *The Evolution of EU Law* (1999), p. 168; W. Heintschel von Heinegg, *Rechtliche Aspekte - GASP - Amsterdam*, (1998), p. 160–1. Krück argues, however, that the question of who the final contracting partner under Art. 24 is – the Union or the member States – may be subject to change in light of developing practice by later European Summits (H. Krück, *Gemeinsame Außen- und Sicherheitspolitik*, in: J. Schwarze (ed.), *EU-Kommentar* (2000), pp. 108–9). S. Marquardt, *Article 24 EU*, in: V. Kronenberger, *The EU and the international legal order* (2001), at p. 349, concludes on the basis of the wording of the TEU that the European Union is committed to such agreements itself, holding that recourse to the *travaux préparatoires* of Art. 24 under Art. 31 VCLT is not even necessary, as the provisions of the TEU are sufficiently clear (*ibid.*, p. 344). Other authors deny Art. 24 such clarity: see e.g. S. Langrish, *The Treaty of Amsterdam*, ELR (1998), p. 13–14; C. Thun-Hohenstein, *Der Vertrag von Amsterdam* (1997), p. 24–5; Hilf/c, fn. 135, p. 709.

139   See above pp. 128. *Cf.* P. Craig / G. de Búrca, *EU Law* (2003), p. 37; compare the change, in relevant part, from their 2nd edn of 1998, p. 40.

140   See e.g. the Agreement between the European Union and the North Atlantic Treaty Organisation on the Security of Information of 14 March 2003, OJ EU L 80/36 of 27/3/2003.

141   See e.g. the agreements of the EU with various countries on the stationing of Monitoring Missions (EUMM) and Police Missions (EUPM): Albania (EUMM agreement of 28 March 2003, OJ EU L 93/50 of 10/4/2003; Council Decision 2003/252/CFSP of 24 Feb. 2003); Bosnia (EUPM agreement of 4 Oct. 2002, OJ EU L 293/2 of 29/10/2002; Council Decision 2002/845/CFSP of 30 Sept. 2002), Poland (Agreement of 24/2/2003 on participation in EUPM Bosnia, OJ EU L 64/38 of 7/3/2003; Council Decision 2003/157/CFSP of 19 Dec. 2002); FYROM (EUMM agreement of 31 Aug. 2001, OJ EC L 241/2 of 11/9/2001; Council Decision 2001/682/CFSP of 30 Aug. 2001); Federal Republic of Yugoslavia (EUMM

The EU generally maintains a liberal stance on the interpretation of 'established practice' regarding treaty-making provisions of international organisations according to Art.2/1/j VCLTIO.[142] Thus, in applying its own respective constitutional provisions in practice, it could have easily departed from the strict wording of Art. 24 TEU, for example by also allowing organs *other* than the President authorised by the Council to conclude treaties for it. This would have allowed it to soften the requirements of that article, in line with Art. 31/3/b VCLT. Contrastingly, however, it accords great importance to the terms of Art. 24 TEU,[143] fulfilment of which also obligates to publish agreements under Art. 24 in the Official Journal.[144] To date, the Union has concluded a number of treaties in the area of ESDP, particularly in crisis management, all of which were duly authorised by Council Decisions under Art. 24 TEU.[145] A closer look at this treaty-concluding history moreover reveals that the procedure required by Art. 24 TEU was painstakingly followed every single time the EU concluded a treaty with an outside party under international law.[146] There are, in addition, no incidents of practice or interpreting statements of EU member States or organs (namely, 'circumstances' according to Art. 7/3/b VCLTIO) which would provide grounds for any interpretation deviating from the wording of Art. 24 TEU. The conclusion must be that, even though the EU was at all times free to depart from the strict wording of Art. 24 TEU, it has never done so in its treaty-making practice, and still considers the Council represented by the Presidency as the only organ competent to conclude treaties under Title V TEU in its name. The traditional strong reservations of member States against giving the Union any more competence than absolutely necessary which were evident from the drafting stages of Art. 24 seem to have persisted.

NATO's constituent treaty is the NAT. Like in many other international organisations,[147] it does not contain any provisions on treaty-making power. Thus recourse must be had to NATO's practice relevant to the conclusion of treaties.

---

agreement of 9 April 2001, OJ EC L 125/2 of 5/5/2001; Council Decision 2001/352/CFSP of 9 April 2001).

142   See above at fn. 131 (Comment by the EEC).

143   See only: Council of the European Union, Agreements Office Website, Introduction, http://ue.eu.int/accords/pres.asp?lang=en (visited 25/08/03).

144   Art. 13 (f), Regulation (EC) 1049/2001 of the European Parliament and of the Council 30 May 2001 regarding public access to European Parliament, Council and Commission Documents, OJ EU L 145/43 of 31/5/2001. The tradition to publish international treaties goes back to W. Wilson's 'Open Covenants ... openly arrived at', contained in Point I of his Fourteen Points, speech before Congress, 8 Jan. 1918, A.S. Link et al. (eds.), *The Papers of Woodrow Wilson*, 45 (1984), p. 536.

145   See the agreements above at fns. 103 to 106.

146   See the respective Council decisions accompanying the above agreements, *ibid.*

147   E.g. the UNC.

In NATO, procedural rules often simply develop by custom.[148] Such practice may also serve as interpretation of the NAT by way of 'subsequent conduct'.[149] Past practice shows that many agreements, both with member States[150] and with third parties,[151] were concluded for NATO by its SG. Today international agreements concluded by NATO are always concluded by its SG.[152] Written rules on the procedure of authorisation of the SG for concluding various agreements with third parties also probably exist in some form. All of those documents would, however, be classified. Agreements of NATO with other international organisations are rare: in 1996, NATO concluded an international agreement on the security of information (SIA) with the WEU.[153] Its contents were not published, so inferences as to the practice prevailing

---

148   Custom forms a much greater share of NATO's internal law than the EU's. See below Chapter 8 (Berlin Plus Agreement).

149   J.S. Ignarski, *North Atlantic Treaty Organization*, in EPIL III, p. 650–1; *cf.* Art. 31/3/b VCLT.

150   E.g. United States: agreement concerning the application of Part VI of the Agreement on NATO national representatives and international staff, 3 March 1981, 1307 UNTS 423 (*cf.* above fn. 112); Supplemental Arrangement concerning the employment by NATO bodies of United States nationals, 3 June 1983, 2005 UNTS 189; Interim Tax Reimbursement Agreement between the US government and NATO, 29 Feb. 1984, 2005 UNTS 653 – United Kingdom: Exchange of notes constituting an agreement regarding the application in the UK of article 10 of the NATO-SOFA, 29 May 1974, 1017 UNTS 345 – Netherlands: Exchange of letters constituting an agreement concerning the work of the NATO airborne early warning and control programme management agency (NAPMA) in the Netherlands, 11 Sept. 1979, 1183 UNTS 21 – Belgium: Convention Additionnelle à la Convention conclue le 16 Sept. 1971 entre le Royaume de Belgique et l'OTAN relative à la Concession à l'OTAN d'un Terrain situe à Bruxelles en vue de la réalisation du Siège Permanent de cette Organisation, 22 June 1988, *Moniteur Belge* 1994, p. 1898 of 29/01/1994; Protocole amenant la Convention Additionnelle ...; *ibid.*, 10 July 1996, *Moniteur Belge* 1998, p. 25640 of 11/8/1998 – Italy: Scambio di lettere Italia-NATO per un emendamento integrativo all'articolo 4 dell'Accordo del 5 febbraio 1968, sui privilegi en immunità del personale del Collegio di Difesa della NATO a Roma, *Gazzetta Ufficiale Della Repubblica Italiana*, No.94, p. 4 of 23/4/2001.

151   E.g. Russia: Founding Act on Mutual Relations, Cooperation and Security between NATO and the Russian Federation, 27 May 1997, 36 ILM 1006 (1997) (not legally binding) – Austria: The three exchanges of letters constituting agreements, concerning the transit for the purpose of the multinational peace operation in Bosnia (IFOR), on privileges and immunities, and on protection of information of 14, 15 and 20 Dec. 1995, 1912 UNTS 261, 271 and 287 – Bosnia: General Framework Agreement for Peace in Bosnia and Herzegovina (Dayton, 21 Nov. 1995), Appendix B to Annex 1A; Agreement Between the Republic of Bosnia and Herzegovina and the North Atlantic Treaty Organisation (NATO) Concerning the Status of NATO and its Personnel, http://www.nato.int/ifor/gfa/gfa-ap1a.htm (visited 13/07/03); – Ireland: Exchange of letters constituting an agreement between the NATO and Ireland in relation to Ireland's responsibilities for participation in KFOR, 25 and 27 Aug. 1999, 2141 UNTS 244.

152   Personal telephone interview with the NATO Legal Service, 3 June 2004.

153   See NATO Press Release (96)66, of 2 May, 1996. The agreement was not published in full but is mentioned in the Declaration issued by the Western European Union Council

on NATO's treaty-making capacity in that case are hard to draw. In July 2000 an *interim* SIA was concluded with the EU, and signed by the SG.[154] This was followed by the permanent EU–NATO SIA in March of 2003,[155] similarly signed by the SG.[156] It is hard to imagine that NATO should have departed from its continued practice in concluding agreements – in particular with the EU – in the single instance of the exchange of letters of 24 January 2001. Rather, it is very reasonable to assume that the practice would have simply remained unchanged.

The unpublished 1996 SIA with the WEU aside, it is hard to find precedents of the SG representing NATO for the purposes of a legally binding treaty with another international organisation. The interim EU–NATO SIA of 2000 cannot serve as such a precedent as it was not binding.[157] However, this agreement may still qualify as preceding 'circumstances' in the sense of Art. 7/3/b VCLTIO. As such, it would further support the prevailing NATO practice of concluding agreements through its SG.

In the present case, the proposing letter by George Robertson was answered by Anna Lindh, acting as 'Chairman of the Council of the European Union', which is the usual procedure according to Art. 24 TEU. However, none of the other acts usually attending at the conclusion of an agreement by the EU can be found in the present case from the public records available: first, there was no express recommendation by the Presidency to the Council and second, there was no authorisation from the Council to the Presidency to conclude the treaty as recommended.

Furthermore, the whole exchange of letters was not published in the Official Journal, and was held classified by both organisations for more than three years after its conclusion.[158]

---

of Ministers, Birmingham, 7 May 1996, V., (http://www.weu.int/documents/960507en.pdf, visited 13/07/03), and in the Final Communiqué of the NATO Ministerial Meeting in Berlin, 3 June 1996, NATO Press Release M-NAC-1(96)63, para. 20.

154   See below Chapter 9 (Security of Information).

155   See above fn. 141.

156   To draw a retro-active analogy here might seem problematic at first sight. Circumstances make it very likely, however, that this agreement would have been concluded in the same formal manner at a point in time before the Berlin Plus. It is very likely that the practice in question would be unchanged in either case.

157   See below Chapter 9 (Security of Information).

158   See above EU–NATO exchange of letters, 24 Jan. 2001. Its existence was first made public in the Final Communiqué of the North Atlantic Council meeting in Budapest on 29–30 May 2001, para. 42 (CP 51, p. 8). During those three years, it was mentioned in writings on European security only in passing (e.g. Z. Lachowski (2002), p. 164; H. Boguslawska, *Le lien transatlantique* (2003), p. 22; R.A. Wessel, JCSL (2003), p. 278). *Cf.* NATO Handbook (2001), p. 103.

Whether these omissions concern 'a rule of fundamental importance' (Art. 46, para. 2 VCLTIO) for the EU, which would allow the EU to invoke their violation in order to void the agreement cannot be answered for certain.[159]

The issue of the correct legal base in EU law for the exchange of letters of 24 January 2001 was in fact discussed among EU member States at the time. The conclusion from this discussion was that there was no need for a legally binding agreement in accordance with Art. 24 TEU.[160] The Council's Legal Service likewise does not consider it as a binding 'international agreement' but rather as an 'administrative arrangement'[161] between the dependent organs of two international organisations, regulating minor procedural aspects.[162]

Drawing together the results of this short inquiry, it would seem that the exchange of letters of 24 January 2001 features little of the evidence normally found in a binding exchange of notes. As a result of this scarcity of characteristics, it cannot be described as binding. This conclusion is furthermore supported by all the actors who were involved: NATO, the Council and the then Swedish Presidency of the EU.

The EU and NATO have proceeded to hold joint meetings in regular format since the beginning of 2001, at various levels. PSC-NAC meetings, held monthly, are always announced to the public in advance.[163] The NATO SG is also regularly invited to attend the Informal Meetings of EU Defence Ministers.[164] More elaborate formats have also been developed for meetings at MC and MS level.[165]

As the exchange of letters of 24 January 2001 is based on the Nice Council Conclusions, its provisions will likely have to be rewritten when the European Constitution enters into force.

---

159   The violation of the rule, even if it concerned internal EU procedure, could have been 'objectively evident' to NATO according to normal practice of international organisations and to good faith, owing to its overlapping membership with the EU. *Cf.* the parallel argument with regard to the Berlin Plus agreement, below Chapter 8 (Berlin Plus Agreement).

160   Written information to the author from the Swedish Ministry of Foreign Affairs, Security Policy Department, 21 July 2004.

161   Such 'administrative arrangements' should be distinguished from binding 'administrative agreements' which are also common in international relations between States. E.g. in Austria the latter are known as *Verwaltungsübereinkommen* (the lowest category of international treaties in the constitutional legal order, *cf.* Austrian Fed.Law.Gaz. No. 49/1921). *Cf.* F. Cede / H. Brand, *Der völkerrechtliche Vertrag – Ein Leitfaden für die österreichische Praxis*, Diplomatic Academy Vienna, Occasional Papers 2/1997, p. 9.

162   Personal telephone interview with the Legal Service of the Council of the European Union, 25 May 2004.

163   See e.g. NATO Press Release (2004)165, 26 Nov. 2004.

164   See e.g. NATO Press Release (2004)125, 16 Sept. 2004.

165   See e.g. Modalities for meetings between the Military Committees of NATO and the EU, 27 March 2003, Council Doc. 7870/03.

LEFT OUT BEFORE 2002: EU–NATO COOPERATION IN TIMES OF CRISIS

The Nice Presidency Conclusions had also contained detailed provisions on 'EU–NATO relations in times of crisis', that is, in the preparatory phase prior to a peacekeeping operation. It was stated that

> In the emergency phase of a crisis, contacts and meetings will be stepped up, including those at ministerial level if appropriate, so that, in the interests of transparency, consultation and cooperation, the two organisations can discuss their assessments of the crisis and how it may develop, together with any related security problems.[166]

NATO-SG G. Robertson, in his proposing letter to the High Representative of 24 January 2001,[167] made brief reference to the EU's Nice proposals:

> We endorsed the view of the EU that in the emergency phase of a crisis contacts and meetings will be stepped up.

This same passage was, however, missing in the ensuing reply from the Swedish Presidency.[168] Hence, from a formal point of view, the matter of EU–NATO consultation from the time leading up to a crisis cannot be said to have been included in the subject matter regulated by the exchange of letters of 24 January 2001. It should be pointed out that EU–NATO consultation in times of crisis did concern part of the Berlin Plus agreement which, despite the EU's detailed Nice proposals, was still being negotiated in January 2001. In light of NATO's comment on the Berlin Plus negotiations in mid-December 2000 that 'nothing will be agreed until everything is agreed',[169] the phrase above in NATO-SG G. Robertson's letter cannot be read as substantive proposal to extend to subject matter of the exchange of letters, in addition to the matter of EU–NATO consultation *outside* of crises, also to the area of EU–NATO consultation *in* crisis. Regulation of that second question would have to await the conclusion of the 'Berlin Plus' package deal in December 2002.[170]

Today, PSC-NAC meetings are part of the in-crisis consultation format under the Berlin Plus agreement.[171]

---

166   European Council, Nice, 7–9 Dec. 2000, Presidency Conclusions, IV. Common European Security and Defence Policy, Annex VII to Annex VI, III., CP 47, pp. 205.

167   See above, EU–NATO exchange of letters, 24 Jan. 2001.

168   *Ibid.*

169   Ministerial Meeting of the North Atlantic Council held at NATO headquarters, Brussels on 14 and 15 December 2000, Final Communiqué, NATO Press Release M-NAC 2(2000)124, para. 33. *Cf.* below Chapter 8 (Berlin Plus Agreement).

170   See below, Chapter 8 (Berlin Plus Agreement).

171   For a practical example, see e.g. Council Joint Action 2003/92/CFSP of 27 January 2003 on the European Union military operation in the Former Yugoslav Republic of Macedonia, Art. 10, OJ L 34/26 of 11.02.2003.

Chapter 5

Is there a 'NATO Primacy' in the EU–NATO Relationship?

INTRODUCTION

> The key is ... avoiding what I would call the Three Ds: *decoupling*, *duplication*, and *discrimination*. ...
>
> First, we want to avoid *decoupling*: Nato is the expression of the indispensable transatlantic link. It should remain an organisation of sovereign allies, where European decision-making is not unhooked from broader Alliance decision-making.
>
> Second, we want to avoid *duplication*: defence resources are too scarce for allies to conduct force planning, operate command structures, and make procurement decisions twice – once at Nato and once more at the EU. And third, we want to avoid any *discrimination* against Nato members who are not EU members.[1]
>
> On matters of trans-Atlantic concern the European Union should make clear that it would undertake an autonomous mission through its European Security and Defense Identity only *after* the North Atlantic Treaty Organization had been offered the opportunity to undertake that mission but had referred it to the European Union for action; ... [2]

NATO's primacy as an institution has been a constant in the transatlantic relationship throughout the Cold War, and continued undisputed during the longest part of the 1990s. In legal terms, it is enshrined both in the NAT and the TEU. It is in the political sphere, however, where its importance has been greatest. The two statements above, made by US policy-makers in 1998 and 1999, make a strong claim for maintaining this primacy versus the EU. They also neatly encapsulate what it is about: no decoupling, duplication and discrimination (the '3Ds'), and a 'right of first refusal' for NATO regarding crisis management operations. Albright's statement was made in reaction to the Franco-British St-Malo Summit in December 1998 which had issued a statement on the need for EU 'autonomy' in defence; the US Senate's resolution came in the wake of the 1999 Cologne European Council which adopted this goal.

---

1   M. Albright (US Secretary of State), *The Right Balance Will Secure NATO's Future*, Financial Times, 7 Dec. 1998, p. 22 [emphases added].

2   US Senate, Resolution 208, 28 Oct. 1999, para. (1), 106th Cong., 1st Sess., 145 Cong. Rec. S 13430 [emphasis added].

This chapter will describe NATO primacy as a political and legal claim and will determine its content, as well as its existence in fact, as exactly as possible. A general section shall trace its evidence from the late 1990s until today. Particular parts will then deal with each of its four elements. The last one – NATO's 'right of first refusal' – is probably most important. The result should be a more comprehensive understanding of NATO primacy as claimed by the US policy-makers and more 'Atlanticist' European countries. This result should then be able to be tested against some of the evidence presented in the subsequent chapters.

NATO PRIMACY IN LEGAL TERMS

The texts of both founding treaties of the EU and NATO, read in conjunction, contain a clear preference for NATO's role in European security in general.

Art. 8 NAT contains a general conflict clause regarding past, present and future third engagements in favour of obligations of the parties arising from the NAT. It is a very strong conflict clause, comparable to Art. 103 UN Charter (to which it is, however, subjected[3]). The historical origins of this clause should be seen in the fact that, in 1949, both Britain and France were still parties to war-time military alliances with the Soviet Union dating from the Second World War.[4] Art. 8 not only binds the parties to refrain from conflicting legal commitments with third parties, but also between themselves.[5] The reach of this article goes beyond the obligations contained in the NAT, that is, mutual self-defence.[6] This last point – that Art. 8 NAT extends to activities outside mutual defence – has, however, been rejected by recent scholarship.[7]

In conformity with that legal restriction on NATO members, Art. J.4 [later: Art. 17] TEU was drafted and subsequently interpreted as preventing any diminution of the role of NATO, a point of particular importance to the then John Major government of the UK.[8] It is still today read as an expression of NATO's legal primacy in the TEU.[9] In addition, it establishes a 'close vinculation' of the defence policies of the EU and NATO.[10] The requirement of compatibility with NATO is seen to set clear

---

3   See above, Chapter 3 (NATO Today).

4   K. Ipsen, *Rechtsgrundlagen* (1967), p. 23; *cf.* R. Heindel et al., *The North Atlantic Treaty in the United States Senate*, 43 AJIL (1949), p. 633 at 658–9.

5   *Ibid.*, p. 24.

6   *Ibid.*

7   E.g. C. von Buttlar, *The EU's new relations with NATO shuttling between reliance and autonomy*, 6 ZEuS 3 (2003), p. 399 at 405.

8   See speech by J. Major (British PM) moving the bill on the Maastricht Treaty in the British Parliament, partly reprinted in: WEU Assembly Doc. 1333, para. 182.

9   A.G. Harryvan / J. van der Harst, *A threat of Rivalry?* (2000), p. 409; G. Burghardt / G. Tebbe, *Artikel J.4.*, in: Groeben / Thiesing / Ehlermann (eds.), *Kommentar zum EU-/EG-Vertrag* (Vol. 5, 5th edn 1997), p. 946 at § 18. *Contra* V. Epping, *Rechtliche Rahmenbedingungen der GASP* (2002), p. 106.

10   M. Álvarez Verdugo, *Consulta y Cooperación entre UE y OTAN* (2002), pp. 475–6.

legal limits for ESDP.[11] On the other hand, according to Art. 17, para. 4 TEU, the *CFSP*, in turn, sets limits to closer military cooperation of member States in the framework of the WEU or NATO, although it is less clear how the EU would control this.[12] The treaty-based primacy of NATO in the EU has been maintained in the new European Constitution,[13] to NATO's satisfaction.

THE POLITICAL DIMENSION

Historical background

NATO's primacy was inherent in the Western European security architecture during the Cold War, as it was based on the absence of any other security organisation in Western Europe with its own assigned forces.[14] In the uncertain atmosphere that prevailed in 1990, the need for continuing the existing arrangement which guaranteed American military presence in Europe was perceived by all European leaders, even in France.[15] With regard to the EC, which had since the 1986 SEA embarked on a path to acquire a political dimension, the general tenor at the time seemed to be that the Community should not 'usurp or overtake the alliance military role' by adopting an independent military approach.[16] The planned project of the Maastricht Treaty should thus, in the view of many, such as the British and the Italians, retain the overall primacy of NATO.[17] Regarding political consultation of the allies relating to security and defence, such as the recognition question of the new ex-Yugoslav republics, NATO should also remain the main forum.

This basic position was maintained by the allies while a new European Security and Defence Identity (ESDI) was introduced in the Summits of the North Atlantic Council in January 1994[18] and June 1996.[19] The ESDI and CJTF concepts,[20] both purely NATO-internal processes, were seen, particularly by the United States, as formulas to accommodate growing European calls for independence in security

---

11   *Ibid.*, p. 485.

12   G. Burghardt / G. Tebbe, *Artikel J.4.*, in: Groeben / Thiesing / Ehlermann (1997), p. 957 § 20.

13   Art. I-41, paras. 2 and 7 European Constitution.

14   *Cf.* W. Link, *Die NATO im Geflecht internationaler Organisationen* (1999), p. 11.

15   *Ibid.*, p. 13.

16   NATO-SG M. Wörner, cited in: W. Bradford, *The WEU ... the new sick man of Europe* (2000), p. 21

17   A. Menon, *Defence policy and integration in Western Europe*, CSP (1996), p. 264 at 268.

18   Ministerial Meeting of the North Atlantic Council/ North Atlantic Cooperation Council, NATO Headquarters, Brussels, 10–11 Jan. 1994, Declaration of the Heads of State and Government, para. 3.

19   Ministerial Meeting of the North Atlantic Council, Berlin, 3 June 1996, Final Communiqué, NATO Press Communiqué M-NAC-1(96)63, para. 7.

20   See above, Chapter 3 (NATO Today).

affairs, while ensuring overall NATO primacy.[21] The new provisions in the Maastricht Treaty relating to an independent European Common Foreign and Security Policy (CFSP) raised many fears among those arguing for maintaining the status quo in face of uncertain future political developments in Eastern Europe. Critics warning of the 'potentially dangerous illusion'[22] of Maastricht cited the 'gradual dissociation of the United States'[23] from NATO as a possible outcome of all measures taken within the framework of the WEU. The general long-term fear of 'abandonment'[24] led to a conservative attitude among political commentators in Europe, lest the tried and trusted transatlantic Alliance should in any way be endangered. In this sense, NATO was still seen as a 'vital organization for European security'.[25] The provisions of the Maastricht Treaty reflected this conservatism, and the CFSP was set firmly in the context of the preservation of the primacy of NATO.[26] When the EU made the WEU its 'defence arm' in the 1996 Amsterdam Treaty, it also took on board the latter's institutional and legal dependence on NATO in crisis management. In effect, the EU thereby also subordinated part of its activities to the Alliance.[27]

Evolution after the Helsinki European Council

Preserving NATO's political primacy in the field of security and defence had been one of the main motivations, at least from the British point of view, for the St-Malo Declaration.[28] When the St-Malo initiative for EU military 'autonomy' bore first fruit in the Helsinki Headline Goal at the end of 1999, that document still acknowledged NATO's primacy,[29] but not anymore in such absolute terms as previous EU documents. While NATO remained 'the foundation of the collective defence of its members' it would only 'continue to have *an important role* in crisis management'.[30] Compared with earlier descriptions of NATO's role in European documents as 'vital', 'central' or 'fundamental' from the time before the St-Malo Summit, this marked an important tendency towards relativising the position of NATO which had hitherto

---

21   P. Cornish, *Partnership in Crisis* (1997), p. 66; T.C. Salmon / A.J.K. Shepherd, *Toward a European Army* (2003), p. 170.

22   C. Gray, cited in: A. Kintis, *NATO-WEU: An Enduring Relationship*, 3 EFAR (1998), p. 560.

23   J. Schwarz, cited in: *ibid.*, p. 561.

24   *Cf.* above, Chapter 1 (Transatlantic Relations).

25   H.G. Krenzler / A. Schomaker, *A new Transatlantic Agenda*, 1 EFAR (1996), p. 11.

26   A. Deighton, *The European Security and Defence Policy*, 40 JCMS (2002), p. 724.

27   *Cf.* W. Lang, *Sind WEU und NATO noch Allianzen?*, 13 ÖJIP (1996), p. 5.

28   S. Biscop, *In Search for a Strategic Concept for the ESDP*, 7 EFAR (2002), p. 475.

29   A. Treacher, *The EU's Resistable Transformation*, 9 EFAR (2004), p. 64.

30   European Council, Helsinki, 10–11 Dec. 1999, Presidency Conclusions, II. Annex IV, CP 47, p. 84 [emphasis added]. This formulation became standard for the EU's definition of its role *vis-à-vis* NATO, *cf.* Reply given by the Council Working Party on General Affairs to a Written Question (E-0007/01), Council Doc. 7472/01, 2 April 2001.

been completely unchallenged. At Helsinki, the EU decided on the creation of military bodies for the EU's future crisis management functions.[31] Most importantly, it created the Headline Goal of a pool of crisis management forces of 60 000 to be put at the Union's disposal according to its own security policy priorities.[32] The description of the Headline Goal and its functions lacked any direct reference to NATO primacy (and thus differed markedly from the spirit of the Maastricht Treaty). In this regard, the Helsinki document only repeated the St-Malo formula of 'where NATO as a whole is not engaged'[33] without further specification.[34]

The 'NATO first' principle continued to be part of European security language throughout 2000.[35] As late as 2002, when the option of EU-autonomous crisis management operations had fully entered the debate, most European policy-makers still bowed to the old reflex (arguably still caused by fear of US abandonment[36]) of giving NATO preference over more Euro-independent options, for example when it came to deciding whether the EU's first peacekeeping mission should be conducted with recourse to NATO assets or not.[37] But the pieces had started to move. Questions of a different nature began being asked. Militarily, the EU and NATO faced each other in a very vertical relationship. In terms of political space and ambition, however, they were equals. How was this dichotomy reconcilable in the long term? 'We cannot expect a subordinate relationship for long'[38] would seem to summarise the search for a new balance in European security that was starting around the turn of the millennium.

NATO reacted to this new mood early on, by adding to Albright's 'Three Ds', SG Robertson's 'Three Is': '*improvement* of European defence capabilities; *inclusiveness* and transparency for all Allies; and the *indivisibility* of Trans-Atlantic security, based on our shared values'.[39] The US accepted this formula,[40] and subsequently translated

---

31   Helsinki, *ibid.*, CP 47, p. 87. These military bodies were first set out in the Presidency Conclusions of the European Council, Cologne, 3–4 June 1999, CP 47, p. 44.

32   Helsinki, *ibid.*, CP 47, p. 83.

33   Helsinki, *ibid.*, CP 47, p. 84.

34   On this point, see below, p. 156.

35   See e.g. G. Gustenau, *GASP – eine Herausforderung für die 'Post-Neutralen'?* (2000), p. 16.

36   See above p. 24.

37   *Cf.* H. Boguslawska, *Le lien transatlantique* (2003), p. 23. This was a political question too, as well as a military-technical matter. Even in discussions limited to the procedure of Berlin Plus, the issue of decision-making autonomy for *both* organisations was hard to avoid (*cf.* H. Ojanen, *Theories at a loss? EU–NATO fusion* (2002), p. 13), and lastly became part of the eventual Berlin Plus agreement.

38   A. Moens, *Developing a European intervention force*, Int. Jour. (2000), p. 269.

39   Speech by G. Robertson at the Annual Session of the NATO Parliamentary Assembly, Amsterdam, 15 Nov. 1999, NATO Speeches, https://www.nato.int/docu/speech/1999/s991115a.htm (visited 16/04/04) [emphases added].

40   Speech by S. Talbott (US Dep. Sec. of State) before the NAC, NATO HQ, *The State of the Alliance: An American Perspective*, 15 Dec. 1999, http://www.nato.int/docu/speech/1999 /s991215c.htm (visited 07/05/04).

the third of these principles into 'indivisibility of security structures'.[41] Now that the EU was starting to build its own military decision-making bodies, this meant that the US would call for a concrete EU-NATO relationship, so that organisational decisions about future military operations would not be taken in isolation by either organisation.[42] For the United States, coupling European crisis management to NATO decision-making procedures was vital for maintaining the transatlantic 'transmission belt' for US political influence[43] by which it could ensure that European politics did not develop away from US interests.[44] The 'zero hour' of ESDP institutionalisation was thus perceived by NATO as a window of opportunity to regain ground lost since St-Malo and re-establish NATO's monopoly in security, defence and crisis management formally and in practice.[45]

By 2002, however, even political scientists specialising in NATO could not dispense with at least some fleeting reference to ESDP when describing the general evolution of the Alliance:

> as the emergence of the CESDP project has illustrated, European members of NATO have not always pursued their security and defence efforts within the NATO context.[46]

'NATO first', once a principle, was now viewed as one option among several when talking about possible methods to stabilise the European continent.[47] Duplication, decoupling and autonomy began to sound less like slogans and more like real potential outcomes.[48] Perhaps ESDP was still presented to American audiences essentially as a means to fill NATO's 'European pillar' with real life.[49] Its definition in 2002 by the European Convention, however, struck a different chord: 'The European defence policy cannot be defined without making *reference* to NATO'.[50] RELEX Commissioner C. Patten, himself hailing from the British Eurosceptic Conservatives, wrote of the need to 'take fully into *consideration* the concerns of [NATO allies]'.[51]

---

41   M. Albright / W. Cohen, *Getting ESDI Right: Europe Should Beef up its Military Capabilities*, Wall Street Journal Europe, 24 March 2000.

42   C. von Buttlar, *The EU's new relations with NATO*, 6 ZEuS 3 (2003), p. 413.

43   See above, Chapter 1 (Transatlantic Relations).

44   *Cf.* A. Pradetto, *Funktionen militärischer Konfliktregelung durch die NATO*, in: Timmermann / Pradetto (2002), p. 204.

45   R. Seidelmann, *EU-Krisenreaktionskräfte*, 25 Integration 2 (2002), p. 120.

46   J. Medcalf, *NATO and the Extra-European Challenge* (2002), p. 9.

47   C.-R. Ancuța, *EU CFSP and the Transatlantic Relationship*, 9 Rom.J.Int.Aff. 2-3 (2003), p. 165.

48   J. Howorth, *ESDP and NATO - Wedlock or Deadlock?*, 38 Coop. & Confl. 3 (2003), p. 252.

49   J. Fischer, *Europa und die Zukunft der transatlantischen Beziehungen*, Speech at Princeton University, 19 Nov. 2003, http://www.auswaertiges-amt.de/www/de /ausgabe_ archiv?archiv_id=5116 (visited 11/12/03).

50   Barnier Report, para. 25, CP 57, p. 253 [emphasis added].

51   C. Patten, *Europäische Sicherheits- und Verteidigungspolitik*, Integration 1 (2000), p. 15 [translation from German by the author, emphasis added].

Such words, weighed carefully against the original spirit of NATO primacy as spelt out in the Maastricht Treaty of 1992, were already far removed from such a spirit, and reflected the new trend of rising EU defence autonomy which prevailed in 2002. This trend was more evident from EU documents than from most statements made by European leaders[52] or single MEPs.[53]

A US commentator of ESDP at the beginning of 2004 already felt free to ascertain that 'the principle has been established that the EU can develop a stronger defence identity independent of NATO'.[54]

THE THREE DS

Discrimination

The discrimination issue concerns the position of non-EU NATO allies in EU crisis management operations. It has two aspects: the position of this group of countries in EU operations with recourse to NATO assets[55] and their position in EU-autonomous operations[56]. Before St-Malo, only the first variant existed. Under the 1996 Berlin Accords,[57] the NAC had to decide on the release of its assets to the WEU or EU by consensus, so possibilities for discrimination against non-EU NATO States were imaginably small.[58] After the possibility of EU-autonomous operations became real, however, so did that of discrimination. As a result, virtually all non-EU NATO members (at the time Poland, Hungary, the Czech Republic, Norway, Iceland, Turkey, Canada and the United States) made clear their concerns about being sidelined.[59] Even though the NAT arguably does not forbid discrimination between its parties (in a form of 'flexibility'), discrimination does clearly contradict NATO's basic tenet of the 'indivisibility of security' in a fundamental way. This principle symbolises the abiding sense within NATO of a sharing of experience, risks and a

---

52   *Cf.* A. Martino (Italian MoD), cited in: *La coopération atlantique 'base' de l'Europe de la Défense, selon l'Italie*, AFP, 3 Oct. 2003.

53   *Cf.* Mr. Gollinsch, Mr. van Orden, cited in: Note d'information sur les travaux du Parlement Européen, Council Doc. 7421/03, 13 March 2003, p. 3.

54   F.S. Larrabee, *ESDP and NATO: Assuring Complementarity* (2004), p. 52.

55   Option 2 under the 2003 NATO/EU Consultation document (See Chapter 2 (ESDP today) above).

56   Options 3 and 4, *ibid.*.

57   See above, Chapter 3 (NATO Today).

58   *Cf.* C. von Buttlar, *The EU's new relations with NATO*, 6 ZEuS 3 (2003), p. 405. In spite of this, British government sources had warned as early as 1991 that 'European defence co-operation should not marginalise other allies, that is, the United States' (D. Hurd, UK Defence Sec., speaking at the presentation of the text of the Maastricht Treaty in the House of Commons, 20 Nov. 1991, cited in: WEU Assembly Doc. 1333, para. 172 *in fine*).

59   C. von Buttlar, *ibid.*, p. 406. For an overview of the discrimination issue, with emphasis on Turkey and Norway, see S. Tofte, *Non-EU NATO Members and the Issue of Discrimination*, in: J. Howorth / J. Keeler (eds.), *Defending Europe* (2003), pp. 135–156.

political-strategic perspective.[60] As a response particularly to Turkey's concerns in this regard,[61] NATO's Strategic Concept adopted in April 1999 underlined that, if and when NATO put its military assets at the disposal of the WEU or the EU, this could only happen 'taking into account the *full participation* of *all* European Allies if they were so to choose'.[62] The EU's reaction to NATO's Strategic Concept at its Cologne Summit in June 1999 was that

> We want to develop an effective EU-led crisis management in which NATO members, as well as neutral and non-allied members, of the EU can participate *fully and on an equal footing* in the EU operations.
>
> We will put in place arrangements that allow non-European allies and partners to take part *to the fullest possible extent* in this endeavour.[63]

A textual analysis of these provisions quickly reveals that EU members and non-EU members are neatly separated into two different paragraphs. The meaning of 'NATO members' in the first paragraph is restricted to those NATO members who are also 'of the EU' by the comma before the latter expression.[64] In other words, according to the Cologne provisions, only full EU members would enjoy participation 'fully and on an equal footing' whereas other NATO members would be relegated to participate 'to the fullest extent possible', a determination to be made in a concrete case by none other than the EU itself.[65]

The EU's Cologne text startled NATO, most of all the US government, who let it be known in October that

> We and our Canadian neighbours will be watching closely to see how the EU defines its security relationship with the other six Allies who do not happen to be EU members: Iceland ... , Norway, Hungary, Poland, the Czech Republic, and, of course, Turkey.[66]

This stance was fully supported by both parts of Congress in separate resolutions passed shortly thereafter.[67] The EU's Helsinki Summit in December 1999, however, while promising to define 'appropriate arrangements' that would allow non-

---

60   C. von Buttlar, *ibid.*

61   C. von Buttlar, *ibid.*

62   1999 NSC, para. 30 *in fine* [emphasis added].

63   European Council, Cologne, 3–4 June 1999, CP 47, para. 3, CP 47, p. 42 [emphases added].

64   Contrariwise, if 'of the EU' would only refer to the 'neutral and non-allied members', then the comma would have been put *after* 'of the EU' instead.

65   *Contra* C. von Buttlar, *The EU's new relations with NATO*, 6 ZEuS 3 (2003), p. 406–7, who reads the Cologne provision as 'right in the sense' of the aforegone passage in NATO's 1999 Strategic Concept (fn. 62).

66   S. Talbott, speech, London, 7 Oct. 1999, CP 47, p. 56.

67   Senate Res. 208 (see above fn. 2), para. (5); House Res. 59, 2 Nov. 1999, para. (9), 106th Cong., 1st Sess., 145 Cong.Rec. H 11212.

EU European NATO members to contribute to EU military crisis management,[68] stressed the Union's 'decision-making autonomy' and the 'single institutional framework' in this regard.[69] Clearly, a certain degree of discrimination was being regarded as inevitable, also because of the quasi-constitutional nature of European integration.[70] This political line was continued and elaborated half a year later at the Feira Summit in June 2000. Two formats of discussion for the 'participation issue' were created. 'EU + 6' for consultations with non-EU European NATO allies, and 'EU + 15' for consultations in addition with all other EU accession candidates who were not NATO members (with at least two meetings per EU Presidency for each group).[71] Only the first format is of interest here. In case of an operation requiring NATO assets, participation by non-EU European NATO allies would be, if they so wished, automatic. In case of an EU-autonomous operation, however, it would be conditional on the invitation to participate by the Council.[72] In deciding which option to choose, 'particular attention' would be given to consultation with the six non-EU European allies,[73] presumably in the 'EU + 6' format. Once taking part in an operation, however, all participants would be represented on an equal basis in a 'committee of contributors'.[74] The entire procedure was developed and consolidated in the EU's Nice Summit,[75] including the 'Committee of Contributors'.[76] However, even with those detailed provisions, non-EU European NATO members did not enjoy the same rights as EU members. Firstly, the views of the Committee only had to be 'taken into account' by the PSC which exercised political control and strategic direction of the entire operation.[77] Secondly, only those third countries deploying 'significant' military forces would have the same rights and obligations as EU members in the day-to-day management of the operation.[78] 'The Six' were not satisfied with this arrangement. Poland maintained that the Nice arrangements could not substitute a real cooperation with third countries under ESDP, and Turkey deemed that the 'Committee of Contributors' only related to 'decision making', while the

---

68   Helsinki, *ibid.*, para. 28 (4th bullet), CP 47, p. 82.

69   *Ibid.* and p. 88.

70   F. Heisbourg, *European defence takes a leap forward*, NATO Review, Spring/ Summer 2000, p. 8 at 10.

71   European Council, Santa Marta da Feira, 19–20 June 2000, Annex I, Appendix I, paras. 9 and 10, CP 47, p. 128.

72   *Ibid.*, para. 19, CP 47, p. 129.

73   *Ibid.*, para. 18.

74   *Ibid.*, para. 21, CP 47, p. 130. The 'Committee of Contributors' for peacekeeping operations stems from UN practice.

75   European Council, Nice, 7–9 Dec. 2000, Presidency Conclusions, CP 47, pp. 168, Annex VI to Annex VI, CP 47, pp. 199–208.

76   *Ibid.*, pp. 202–3.

77   *Ibid.*, p. 203.

78   *Ibid.*

more important 'decision shaping' was left to the EU alone.[79] In the secret 'Ankara document' of December 2001[80] which finally secured Turkey's support,[81] various of these concerns were addressed in detail: ESDP would never be used against a NATO member.[82] In addition, even in case of EU-autonomous operations, if an Ally would raise concerns because of an operation being conducted in its geographic proximity, the Council would consult with it and decide on the participation of that Ally. This was read by some as a guarantee of non-intervention in Turkey's near-abroad, particularly the Aegean.[83] In addition, detailed and well-prepared consultations, already at peace-time, should enable 'the Six' to contribute meaningfully to ESDP and associate themselves with EU decisions, actions and declarations on ESDP.[84] It was to take another year, and some adaptations, until both Greece and Turkey accepted the 'Ankara document'.[85] The question was finally regulated in the Berlin Plus agreement of December 2002 which, by direct reference, included the 'relevant Nice arrangements' on participation of non-EU European NATO allies, as well as the material contents of the 'Ankara document', which are reproduced in the Brussels European Council Presidency Conclusions of 24-24 October 2002.[86]

The Berlin Plus agreement has addressed most of the concerns covered by the principle of non-discrimination against non-EU European NATO allies. But it is not binding under international law.[87] Of course, it could be argued that neither are the European Council's numerous Presidency Conclusions setting up autonomous ESDP

---

79   H. Boguslawska, *Le lien transatlantique*, (2003), p. 25. This mirrors complaints regularly made by NATO PfP partner States concerning inclusion in decision-making procedures for NATO-led crisis management operations.

80   The text of this document was never officially released, but its contents were leaked to the Greek press, see I Kathimerini, 11 Dec. 2001, p. 5 (English translation on file with the author). Its contents are known today, however, as they were included *verbatim* into the Presidency Conclusions of the European Council, Brussels, 24–25 Oct. 2002, Annex II, CP 57, pp. 136. See also Chapter 8 (Berlin Plus Agreement).

81   *Turkey largely satisfied over European defence project: Ecevit*, AFP, 2 Dec. 2001; *Türkei gibt Widerstand gegen EU-Eingreiftruppe auf*, Frankfurter Allgemeine Zeitung, 4 Dec. 2001, p. 1.

82   European Council, Brussels, 24–25 Oct. 2002, Annex II, para. 2, CP 57, p. 136. This satisfied a Turkish demand to see the old corresponding WEU restriction not to use that organisation against a NATO member, transferred into the new ESDP context. *Cf.* Western European Union Council of Ministers, Petersberg Declaration, Bonn, 19 June 1992, III. para. A; P. van Ham, *The EU and WEU: From Cooperation to Common Defence?*, in: G. Edwards / A. Pijpers, *The Politics of European Treaty Reform* (1996), pp. 313–4.

83   L. Zeccini, *Les Quinze tentent de réduire leurs divergences à Laeken...*, Le Monde, 15 Dec. 2001. *Cf.* G. Müller-Brandeck-Bocquet, *The New CFSP and ESDP Decision-Making System of the European Union*, 7 EFAR (2002), p. 257 at 280.

84   European Council, Brussels, fn.80, paras. 3 and 4, CP 57, p. 137.

85   *Auf dem Weg nach Kopenhagen*, Frankfurter Allgemeine Zeitung, 5 Aug. 2004, p. 8.

86   See below Chapter 8 (Berlin Plus Agreement).

87   See below Chapter 8 (Berlin Plus Agreement).

structures which provide for just such a discrimination.[88] But these Conclusions have, by creating institutions and procedures containing EU decision-making autonomy, already created facts on the ground which are in practice irreversible. It is impossible for the representative of a country of 'the Six'[89] to check on every step in strategic policy formulation which is taken at the level of the PSC, the EUMC or the EUMS. It should be mentioned that the EU's rules on classified information (which cover most military information) still do not allow third-country NATO members the same degree of access as an EU member State would have.[90] Turkey regularly complains during EUMC-NATO MC meetings that the Nice provisions of the Berlin Plus agreement are not applied to the extent provided; for example that the 'Committee of Contributors' for EU Operation *Althea* does not convene often enough. As a result of the examination above, it must be concluded that the non-discrimination principle as enunciated by M. Albright in 1998 has, if not disappeared, been at least somewhat eroded in the years thereafter.

In autumn 2004, however, Iceland, Norway and Romania concluded framework agreements for their participation in EU crisis management operations which refer to the October 2002 Brussels Presidency Conclusions (that is, the 'Ankara document').[91] These agreements should give those countries some participation rights in EU crisis management as a matter of hard treaty law.

Decoupling

The fear of Europe's security being decoupled from that of the United States can be expected to be voiced every time either side of the Atlantic sets out to alter one of its existing security parameters.[92] With regard to European defence, the decoupling issue goes back to intra-NATO debates in the 1990s on ESDI.[93] Nevertheless, it is

---

88   *Cf.* e.g. the NATO/EU Consultation Document (initial version of Dec. 2003 and final version of Nov. 2004). See above Chapter 2 (ESDP Today).

89   After the EU and NATO enlargements in spring 2004, this group contained five countries: Turkey, Norway, Iceland, Bulgaria and Romania.

90   All of these countries are ranked as 'Level 1' of cooperation concerning release of EU classified information, under the Council's Security Regulations, Part II, Sec. XII, para. 5 and Appendix 4, OJ L 101/1 of 11.4.2001. *Cf.* Release of EU classified information to third states and international organisations – Levels of security co-operation, Council Doc. 7592/03 (classified).

91   See Council Decision concerning the conclusion of agreements between the European Union and the Republic of Iceland, the Kingdom of Norway and Romania establishing a framework for the participation of the Republic of Iceland, the Kingdom of Norway and Romania in the European Union crisis management operations, 5 Oct. 2004, Council Doc. 12435/04.

92   See e.g. on the implication on NATO of the US withdrawal from the ABM Treaty, R. Müllerson, *The ABM Treaty: Changed Circumstances, Extraordinary Events, Supreme Interests and International Law*, 50 ICLQ 3 (2001), p. 509 at 535–6.

93   *Cf.* T. Marauhn, *Building ESDI* (1996), p. 68.

the one among the 'Three Ds' which has been the least talked-about. The US Senate Resolution 208 of October 1999 meekly asserted in 1999 that

> … the European Union's implementation of the Cologne Summit decisions should not promote a strategic perspective on transatlantic security issues that conflicts with that promoted by the North Atlantic Treaty Organization; …[94]

In line with this statement, decoupling is mostly regarded as a concern of political character today, linked with the old claim that ESDI should help make Europeans improve their military capabilities, that is, burden-sharing.[95] In spite of this, decoupling does have an aspect relating to the legal dimension of collective self-defence in NATO and the EU: There is no Art. 5-type mutual defence commitment in the EU (so far). If the EU nevertheless engages in military activity abroad which might lead to Art. 5 contingencies, the United States in particular fears that, cautiously expressed, 'a great deal of confusion would be sown':[96] the problem consists of so-called 'security commitments through the back door' which will be addressed in a later chapter.[97]

The existence of ESDP institutions making their own decisions on European security today, outside of NATO, means that some decoupling has indeed happened. However, the close cooperation structures between the EU and NATO which have been put in place would seem to minimise its negative effects. In addition, the 'transatlantic link' which is at the heart of the decoupling issue has been shown to be much more vulnerable to outside events like the Iraq crisis in 2003.

Duplication

Duplication of their work was something which Europe's security institutions attempted to avoid from an early point, even before the issue of NATO primacy as such arose.[98] Under the old NATO–WEU–EU triangle, Art. 17, para. 2 of the Amsterdam Treaty provided the EU with the WEU's limited operational capability. The WEU's Modified Brussels Treaty (MBT) itself,[99] in its Art. IV, para. 2, explicitly recognises NATO's primacy in military matters:

---

94   US Senate Res. 208 (see above fn. 2), para. (6).

95   C. von Buttlar, *The EU's new relations with NATO*, 6 ZEuS 3 (2003), p. 405; J.-Y. Haine, *ESDP and NATO*, in: N. Gnesotto (ed.), *EU Security and Defence Policy – The first five years* (2004), EU-ISS, p. 131 at 134.

96   T.C. Salmon / A.J.K. Shepherd, *Toward a European Army* (2003), p. 166.

97   See below Chapter 6 (Collective Self-Defence).

98   M. d'Oléon, *The way ahead for European defence integration*, in: L. Martin / J. Roper (eds.) *Towards a common defence policy*, WEU-ISS (1995), p. 100.

99   19 UNTS 51 and 211 UNTS 342.

Recognising the undesirability of duplicating the military staffs of NATO, the Council and its Agency will rely on the appropriate military authorities of NATO for information and advice on military matters.[100]

This provision should not, however, be read as a legal constraint, but rather as a political command (*arg.* 'will').[101] As such, it applied also to the EU whenever the Union was to call on the WEU for crisis management purposes. For the EU, the situation has not changed after the Nice Treaty, even if most references to the WEU were deleted in the TEU.

Early in 1991, then US ambassador to NATO W. Taft warned that the European pillar of NATO should not duplicate current cooperation in NATO.[102] When arguing against duplication, the United States was in the main concerned that once military structures would be duplicated in the EU, this is not only divert precious financial resources, but also lead to a direct degradation of NATO's own capabilities.[103] It was probably for this reason also that it pushed so hard for establishing an EU–NATO institutional relationship at the earliest possible point in the spring of 2000.[104]

The TEU contained the general requirement for *compatibility* with the security and defence policy established within the framework of NATO (Art. 17, para. 2 TEU). From the earliest days of ESDP, therefore, even before the formulation of the 'Three Ds', *compatibility* with NATO (echoing the text of Art. 17 TEU) was the most common answer to fears about duplication.[105] Suggesting that ESDP would do nothing more than simply add to NATO's capacity, not create something similar, this term resounded well with the US Congress[106] and has been used by European actors throughout the years.[107] Painting ESDP as a subsidiary addition to NATO would, of course, implicitly presuppose NATO primacy.[108]

---

100 Art. IV, para. 2 WEU Modified Brussels Treaty (1954).

101 *Cf.* C. von Buttlar, *The EU's new relations with NATO*, 6 ZEuS 3 (2003), p. 407. On the value of language in determining the binding character of provisions in international documents, in particular the distinction between the words 'will' and 'shall', see above Chapter 4 (EU–NATO Institutional Aspects).

102 S.R. Sloan, *The United States and European defence*, CP 39 (2000), p. 6.

103 J.P.H. Cazeau, *ESDP under the gun*, 10 U.Miami Int'l & Comp.L.Rev. (Fall 2002), p. 51 at 59.

104 See above Chapter 4 (EU–NATO Institutional Aspects). *Cf.* A. Baggett, *The Development of the European Union Common Defense and its Implications for the United States and NATO*, 31 Ga. J. Int'l & Comp.L. (Winter 2003), p. 355 at 382–3.

105 *Cf.* Informal European summit, Pörtschach, 24–25 October 1998, Press Conferences by British Prime Minister Tony Blair (Extracts), CP 47, p. 2.

106 US House of Representatives, Res. 59 (fn. 67), para. (9).

107 Answer given by Mr Patten on behalf of the Commission to a Written Question (E-0008/01), 21 Feb. 2001, para. 3, OJ 187 E/154 of 5.7.2001; M. Alliot-Marie (French Defence Min.), *Ergänzung, keine Konkurrenz,* interview in Die Welt, 4 Sept. 2003, http://www.welt. de/data/2003/09/04/163765.html (visited 05/09/03); G. Hoon (British Defence Sec.), *The Transatlantic Alliance – Opportunities and Chances*, NATO's Nations 4/2003, p. 51 at 53.

108 J.-Y. Haine, *ESDP and NATO*, in: N. Gnesotto (ed.), *EU Security and Defence Policy – The first five years* (2004), EU-ISS, p. 131 at 135.

However, also from the beginning of ESDP at St-Malo,[109] the EU had emphasised continuously that it wanted to avoid only 'unnecessary' duplication of military resources.[110] Even though it was of course open to interpretation what was 'necessary', NATO accepted, at its Summit in April 1999,[111] this alteration of the original claim by Albright.[112] It has stuck to this formula until today[113] and so, apparently, has the US.[114]

The necessity for some duplication, first implied at the bilateral St-Malo meeting was inextricably linked to the possibility for future autonomous EU peacekeeping operations, and a military capacity independent of external support.[115] 'Unnecessary duplication' thus came to be commonly used in European security parlance whenever referring to the third of the 'Three Ds'.[116] It was the same term employed by the EU in describing its cooperation also with other international organisations in other fields, such as the OSCE or the UN.[117] From there, the search went on as to what constituted 'useful',[118] 'rational'[119] or 'constructive'[120] duplication. Military capabilities of European States, particularly C^4I, air- and sealift, air-to-air refuelling and military R & D were obvious candidates,[121] as their improvement was congruent with NATO's needs. The political difficulties started, however, with the EU's initiatives to duplicate NATO's planning role.[122]

---

109   St-Malo Declaration, para. 3, CP 47, p. 8.

110   See e.g. European Council, Laeken, 14–15 Dec. 2001, Presidency Report on ESDP, para. 29 at (C) subpara. 3, CP 51, p. 128.

111   North Atlantic Council summit, Washington, DC, 24 April 1999, Final Communiqué, para. 9 c., CP 47, p. 22.

112   See above p. 147.

113   E.g. NATO-SG G. Robertson, Joint Press Meeting with EU HR J. Solana after the NAC/PSC meeting, Brussels, 21 Oct. 2003, Council Doc. S0218/03, *in fine*.

114   T.C. Salmon / A.J.K. Shepherd, *Toward a European Army* (2003), p. 165.

115   F. Heisbourg, *European defence takes a leap forward*, NATO Review (Spring/ Summer 2000), p. 8 at 10; E. Barbé / A. Bondia, *La política europea de seguridad y defensa*, Arbor No. 678 (June 2002), p. 357 at 370.

116   E.g. A.D. Rotfeld, *Europe: an emerging power* (2001), p. 175 at 193; A. Missiroli, *Der türkische Verdruss über die ESVP*, 24 Integration 4 (2001), p. 352. *Cf.* A. Nicoll, *Turkey offered role in planning EU force*, Financial Times, 14 Nov. 2000, p. 9: 'the two organisations are intended to be meshed together with a minimum of duplication'.

117   E.g. European Council, Göteborg, 15–16 June 2001, Presidency Conclusions, Annex III to the ANNEX, para. 18, CP 51, p. 47.

118   P. Quiles (President of the French defence commission), cited in: J. Vinocur, *EU Defense Autonomy Lacks Unifying Voice*, International Herald Tribune, 9 April 2001, p. 1.

119   Z. Lachowski, *The military dimension of the European Union*, SIPRI Yearbook 2002, p. 172.

120   K. Shake, *Constructive Duplication: Reducing EU reliance on US military assets*, CER working paper (2002).

121   Shake, *ibid.*, pp. 19–24.

122   *Ibid.*, p. 25.

Duplication in strategic planning capacity had, implicitly, been part of the idea of military bodies for ESDP since their earliest inception,[123] and the US had warned since that time that such initiatives could weaken the alliance's ability to deal with major crises.[124] The Tervuren initiative in April 2003[125] rekindled NATO's concerns about the EU duplicating its structures and role, and it highlighted the differing visions of EU members over ESDP.[126] Many saw Tervuren as a direct break of the Berlin Plus agreement which had been finalised only the month before. This opinion was, however, only possible by wrongly interpreting the fact that the EU *could* now draw on NATO's military resources to mean that it *should* do so in all cases.[127] In this sense, Berlin Plus would really mean full complementarity in the fullest sense, and this is why the Tervuren initiative was perceived by many NATO supporters as crossing a red line.[128] However, as shown above,[129] towards the end of 2003 the need for an independent EU military planning unit seemed to be accepted throughout the EU as whole, and was still compatible with the tenet of avoiding 'unnecessary duplication'.[130] The gradual limitation of the principle of non-duplication also became evident from the tone of statements of European leaders around that time. F. Frattini, Italian foreign minister and then EU President, for example, only applied it to NATO's *role* (without mentioning its structures)[131] and the Finnish foreign minister E. Tuomioja wrote that it was 'not a theological question but a practical and economic one'.[132]

By 2004, it was possible to say that the principle non-duplication of Alliance resources as claimed by M. Albright in 1998, had never been applied too strictly, and had quickly given way to the more elastic 'unnecessary duplication'. Furthermore, since the end of 2003, military planning structures do not seem to be covered by it any more. However, the planning facilities developed by the EU so far are

---

123   *Cf.* e.g. for the EUMS, Meeting of European Union defence ministers, Sintra, 28 Feb. 2000, para. 10, CP 47, p. 94 at 96.

124   S. Taylor, *US ambassador delivers stark warning on defence planning*, European Voice (online edition), Vol. 6, No. 41, 9 Nov. 2000.

125   See above Chapter 2 (ESDP Today).

126   A. Monaco, *EU and NATO: Competition or Cooperation?*, in: A. Weidemann / A. Simon (eds.), *The Future of ESDP* (2003), p. 40 at 45.

127   U. Schürr, *Der Aufbau einer ESVI* (2003), p. 270; DSACEUR Adm. R. Feist, *When You Come to SHAPE*, NATO's Nations 4/2003, p. 179 at 181: 'Berlin Plus is the right arrangement for EU operations. If this arrangement between the EU and NATO is working, then at least from our perspective, we don't need a double structure in the EU. That is our message.'

128   M. Dembinski / W. Wagner, *Europäische Kollateralschäden*, Aus Politik und Zeitgeschichte B 31–32 (2003), p. 31 at 35.

129   See above Chapter 2 (ESDP Today).

130   GAERC, Brussels, 17 Nov. 2003, Conclusions on ESDP, para. 3, CP 67, p. 257.

131   Cited in: T. Barber / Q. Peel, *Italy holds fast to text of Giscard proposals*, Financial Times, 3 Sept. 2003, p. 8.

132   E. Toumioja, *Europe needs to work as a whole on defence*, Financial Times, 28 Oct. 2003, p. 23.

minimal, and cannot in any substantial way duplicate those at SHAPE. The question of whether the EU can or should duplicate NATO's role is more difficult. With regard to crisis management, the EU has certainly done so for the lower-intensity peacekeeping tasks in Europe. Thus, a certain division of labour with NATO already seems to be emerging.[133] Concerning collective self-defence, until the entry into force of the European Constitution (if this happens), NATO still rules supreme, and no duplication has occurred.

'... WHERE THE ALLIANCE AS A WHOLE IS NOT ENGAGED' – NATO'S RIGHT OF FIRST REFUSAL?

Introduction

The formula that the EU could take military action 'where the Alliance as a whole is not engaged' stems from the French–British St-Malo Summit of December 1998.[134] The EU adopted the goal of St-Malo for autonomous EU military action at its Cologne Summit,[135] but it was only half a year later at Helsinki that the formula entered official EU vocabulary.[136] NATO adopted it at its Washington Summit in April 1999.[137] Both have used it ever since.[138] Most importantly, it was included in the Berlin Plus agreement between the two organisations of 2002[139] as well as in the NATO/EU Consultation Document of 2003 (for which NATO informally voiced its support).[140]

---

133   On this question in detail, see below, Chapter 7 (Military Crisis Management).

134   St-Malo Declaration, para. 3, CP 47, p. 8.

135   European Council, Cologne, 3–4 June 1999, CP 47, para. 1, CP 47, p. 41.

136   Helsinki, *ibid.*, para. 27, CP 47, p. 82: 'where NATO as a whole is not engaged'. The Cologne Summit had only contained a general clause about responding to international crises 'without prejudice to actions by NATO', *ibid.*, CP 47, p. 41.

137   North Atlantic Council summit, Washington, DC, 24 April 1999, Final Communiqué, para. 9 a., CP 47, p. 22.

138   *Cf.* Meeting of European Union defence ministers, Sintra, 28 Feb. 2000, para. 2, CP 47, p. 94; Capabilities Commitment Conference, Brussels, 20–21 Nov. 2000, para. 1, CP 47, p. 157; European Council, Nice, 7–9 Dec. 2000, Presidency Conclusions, Annex VI, para. 2, CP 47, p. 168; J. Solana, *Destined to cooperate*, Financial Times, 14 June 2001, p. 15; European Council, Göteborg, 15–16 June 2001, Presidency Conclusions, Annex, II, para. 7, CP 51, p. 33; European Convention, Barnier Report (2002), para. 10, CP 57, p. 251. *Cf.* North Atlantic Council, Brussels, 14–15 Dec. 2000, Final Communiqué, para. 30, CP 47, p. 223; North Atlantic Council meeting, Budapest, 29–30 May, 2001, Final Communiqué, para. 45, CP 51, p. 8.

139   EU–NATO Declaration on ESDP, Brussels, 16 Dec. 2002, para. 3, 42 ILM 242 (2003). *cf.* Statement by NATO's Secretary General – Berlin Plus, Brussels, 17 March 2003, CP 67, p. 48.

140   See above, Chapter 2 (ESDP Today).

However, the polemics which have arisen over the meaning of this formula since its creation[141] attest that the overall agreement by all sides over it is not as great as might at first glance appear.

First of all, the question must be separated from the '*droit de regard*' which the US enjoys over EU missions using NATO assets, by virtue of the consensus principle at the NAC.[142] 'Where NATO as a whole is not engaged' concerns a point in decision making which systematically lies before that question: whether the EU is going to engage in a mission at all. In constructive ambiguity, the 'where NATO as a whole is not engaged' formula allows several different readings.

Different readings

A first reading, sticking closely to the wording, is that the EU cannot engage in areas where NATO *is* presently not engaged. This reading lays emphasis on fact, rather than on volition. In essence, it means that the EU cannot go into areas where NATO already *happens to be* engaged,[143] that is, a geographical division of labour with in-built preference for NATO. Such a literal reading has not been disputed by any of the actors involved, and also, it is submitted, accords with common sense. The EU's take-over of NATO's peacekeeping mission in Macedonia in spring 2003 would be a good example of its application.

However, US policy-makers soon gave the 'where the Alliance as a whole is not engaged' formula another reading: that the EU should only engage in areas where NATO *chooses* not to be engaged. This reading, laying emphasis on NATO's will rather than on mere facts on the ground, would amount to what has commonly been called NATO's 'right of first refusal' vis-à-vis the EU in crisis management. The question had moved to the centre of the debate on the emerging EU–NATO relationship by the end of 2000.[144] Therefore the examination below shall focus on this second reading. Before doing so, however, a quick clarification of the term 'right of first refusal' seems in order.

---

141   E. Barbé / A. Bondia, *La PESD* (2002), p. 370.

142   M. Jopp, *GESVP* (2000), p. 248; M. Muschwig, *ESDP: Crisis of Transatlantic Relations* (2002), p. 45. As C. von Buttlar points out, 'The effective veto wielded by non-EU NATO member states, due to the EU's reliance on NATO assets, would clearly not apply if the EU were conducting an operation that did not rely on NATO assets.' (*Id.*, *The EU's new relations with NATO*, 6 ZEuS 3 (2003), p. 429).

143   *Cf.* P.H. Gordon, *Their Own Army? Making European Defense Work*, Foreign Affairs (July/Aug. 2000), p. 12 at 16.

144   *Cf.* D. Vernet, *Commentaire OTAN-UE: Clarifier les relations*, Le Monde (online edition), 22 Nov. 2000.

Concept of 'right of first refusal' in international law

'Right of first refusal' is a concept originating from the private law of contracts. It entitles the holder of such a right (which he usually derives from an earlier contract) to be the first person to be offered a given good for purchase, should it be put for sale by its owner.[145] Rights of first refusal are very common, for example, in real estate law. Two important elements emerge from this definition. Firstly, a right of first refusal implies not only the right of its holder to meet the terms of a contract before it is executed, but also the obligation of the seller to offer it to the holder. Implied consent seems to be ruled out in this regard. Secondly, a right of first refusal does not constitute an absolute veto of the holder over the sale. If he does not accept the terms of the sale (usually outside his influence), he cannot prevent the eventual sale from going ahead.

In the area of real estate law, rights of first refusal are often installed by government legislation in favour of public or private entities acting in a public interest.[146] They are often also used to regulate the land rights of indigenous minorities whose protection is also in the general public interest.[147] The international law concerning cultural objects also knows many examples of rights of first refusal for State authorities over objects of historical and artistic interest.[148] Public interest in the sense of the stronger local interest also seems to be controlling in resolving jurisdiction conflicts with rights of first refusal in US federal law[149] or in international criminal law.[150] In the international law of the sea, the 1994 Implementation Agreement to the 1982 Convention on the Law of the Sea grants a right of first refusal to a contractor who

---

145   *Black's Law Dictionary* (H.C. Black / J.R. Nolan, 6th edn, 1990), p. 1325.

146   M. Foscarinis, *Symposium: Homelessness and Human Rights: Towards an Integrated Strategy*, 19 St. Louis U. Publ. L. Rev. (2000), p. 327 at 331, n. 16.

147   P.P. Frickey, *A Common Law for Our Age of Colonialism: The Judicial Divestiture of Indian Tribal Authority over Nonmembers*, 109 Yale Law Journal (Oct. 1999), p. 1 at 83; B.A. Kahn, *The Legal Framework Surrounding Maori Claims to Water Resources in New Zealand: In Contrast to the American Indian Experience*, 35 Stan.J. Int'l L. (Winter 1999), p. 49 at 59.

148   See e.g. P.K. Tompa, *Ancient Coins as Cultural Property: A Cause for Concern?*, 4 J. Int'l Legal Stud. (Winter 1998), p. 69 at 76; I.M. Goldrich, *Balancing the Need for Repatriation of illegally removed cultural property with the interests of bona fide purchasers: applying the UNIDROIT Convention to the Case of the Gold Phiale*, 23 Fordham Int'l L.J. (Nov. 1999), p. 118 at 152, n. 206.

149   B.E. Hawk / L.L. Laudati, *Antitrust Federalism in the United State and Decentralisation of Competition Law Enforcement in the European Union: A Comparison*, 20 Fordham Int'l L.J. (Nov. 1996), p. 18 at 41.

150   O. Ben-Naftali / K.R. Michaeli, *Justice-Ability: A Critique of the Alleged Non-Justiciability of Israel's Policy of Targeted Killings*, 1.2 J'l of Int. Crim. Just. (2003), p. 368 at 371; B. Mark, *Acknowledging our International Criminals: Henry Kissinger and East Timor*, 32 Denv.J.Int'l L. & Pol'y (Winter 2003), p. 1 at 28.

enters into a joint venture with the Enterprise for exploration and exploitation of resources on the deep seabed.[151]

To recapitulate, in the public domain, a right of first refusal is often associated with a 'higher' interest which serves the common good, which is more long term, or perhaps even transcendental. It does not seem too far to speculate that many US Congressmen viewed NATO as possessing such a quality in relation to all other European security institutions, by virtue of its past achievements in the Cold War and in the Balkan Wars. Another, more realist, underlying reason for giving preference to NATO was that the Alliance was the United States' most effective political power hold in Europe.[152]

Historical background

In the Europe of the mid-1990s, a case of 'where NATO as a whole is not engaged' was still hard to imagine. US officials asserted that 'In the real world, when real threats develop, the United States will be there.'[153] This position was in part argued by SHAPE, which reasoned that what started out as non-Art. 5 activities of the Alliance (engaged under the CJTF concept) might escalate into large-scale operations requiring NATO to have complete command and control. This argument 'left some Europeans feeling that SHAPE, and its American SACEUR, was insisting on a veto over any European operation not involving the US'.[154] Even though an alternative European institution with any independent military capability did not exist at the time, such a de facto US right of veto on European capacity to act was seen by some commentators as something undesirable.[155]

As regards the WEU, the principle that this organisation was a gap-filler for threats of particular European interest 'in case NATO decided not to act' was identified by the British Secretary of Defence M. Rifkind as early as 1992.[156] It

---

151   Agreement relating to the implementation of Part XI of the United Nations Convention on the Law of the Sea of 10 Decemeber 1982, 17 Aug. 1994, Annex, Sec. 2, para. 5, UN-Doc. A/RES/48/263. *Cf.* B.H. Oxman, *Law of the Sea Forum: The 1994 Agreement on Implementation of the Seabed Provisions on the Convention on the Law of the Sea: The 1994 Agreement and the Convention,* 88 AJIL (1994), p. 687 at 693; J.A. Duff, *UNCLOS and the new Deep Seabed Mining Regime: The Risks of Refuting the Treaty,* 19 Suffolk Transnat'l L. Rev. (Winter 1995), p. 1 at 25.

152   See above, Chapter 1 (Transatlantic Relations).

153   R. Atkinson, *NATO Gives Members Response Flexibility,* Washington Post, 4 June 1996, p. A14; *cf.* P. Cornish, *Partnership in Crisis* (1997), p. 85.

154   S. Kay, *NATO and the Future of European Security* (1998), p. 135.

155   L. Stainier, *Common interests, values and criteria for action,* in: L. Martin / J. Roper (eds.), *Towards a common defence policy* (1995), p. 24; M. d'Oléon, in: *ibid.,* p. 110.

156   P.J. Teunissen, *Strengthening the defence dimension of the EU,* 4 EFAR (1999), p. 348.

was apparently not disputed,[157] even if it did not render a clear basis for planning or decision-making.[158]

Variety of opinion

Arguments for a NATO right of first refusal

Since the Clinton Administration, the US had argued that

> We would look to NATO as the preferred institution to act 'wherever possible.' At the same time, we recognized that the Alliance might not act. And in *those* circumstances, we agreed to make NATO assets and capabilities available to the European Union.[159]

It was a stance made necessary by Congressional demands for a NATO 'right of first refusal' in autumn 1999,[160] demands which also went on to interpret the 'where NATO as a whole is not engaged' formula, coming from the EU, in the same way.[161] This NATO-friendly reading in the United States was given wide credence by the meeting of British Prime Minister Tony Blair with US President G.W. Bush at Camp David on 23 February 2001. In the joint press conference following the meeting, both Bush and Blair emphatically supported the 'chooses to' interpretation of 'where NATO as a whole is not engaged'.[162] On such terms, Bush commented, the planned EU Rapid Reaction Force might indeed 'make a lot of sense to our country'.[163] Blair maintained this interpretation well into 2005,[164] when the issue of an independent

---

157   G. Bonvicini et al., *Security links in the making* (1996), p. 318; S. Fröhlich, *Der Ausbau der europäischen Verteidigungsidentität zwischen WEU und NATO*, ZEI Discussion Paper C 19 (1998), p. 17.

158   P. Schmidt, *Zum Verhältnis von GASP; NATO und WEU*, 25 ÖZP 4 (1996), p. 406.

159   Speech by S. Talbott (US Dep. Sec. of State) before the NAC, NATO HQ, *The State of the Alliance: An American Perspective*, 15 Dec. 1999, http://www.nato.int/docu/speech/1999 /s991215c.htm (visited 07/05/04) [emphasis added]. *cf.* W. Drozdiak, *US Tepid on European Defense Plan; American Stance Vexes EU leaders*, Washington Post, 7 March 2000, p. A01.

160   See above p. 147.

161   *Cf.* 106th Cong., 2nd Sess., 146 Cong. Rec. S 4037 at S 4079 (Sen. J. Biden): 'To date, the outline of the European Security and Defense Policy, or ESDP as it is called, has conformed to our wishes. It would only go into action if the alliance as a whole *chose* not to be involved' [emphasis added].

162   Joint Statement by President George W. Bush and Prime Minister Tony Blair, 23 Feb. 2001, White House Press Releases, https://www.whitehouse.gov/news/releases/2001/02/20010226.html (visited 22/08/2004); *cf.* K. Shake, *Constructive Duplication* (2002), pp. 5–7.

163   Cited in: M. Gómez Garrido, *ESDP: The Recent Debate in the United States*, OBS Working Paper No.18 (2002), p. 4.

164   T. Blair, cited in: *US-EU row on NATO, European defence has 'evolved': US official*, AFP, 27 Oct. 2003: '... there will be certain situations ... when the US doesn't *want to*

EU planning cell (which would also be able to make independent decisions) was already widely discussed.[165] So did the US.[166] The 'chooses to' interpretation has always found strong support in European security literature.[167]

There were complex political reasons prompting politicians and scholars towards this interpretation: the question of where the decision of whether NATO or the EU should intervene should be taken (the 'locus of planning'[168]) had a direct bearing on the issue of discrimination against non-EU NATO allies. If the EU could decide this question by itself, including the planning of strategic options, then these allies would in practice be unable to influence those plans, which were the basis for their later decisions in this regard: whether to consent to the release of NATO assets to the EU (via their veto in the NAC), or whether and to what degree to participate in the planned EU operation.[169] The fast creation of ESDP bodies within the EU meant that, if a crisis loomed, 'ESDP mechanisms would probably be well into play before NATO's'.[170] As demonstrated above, not all of these problems were solved in the Berlin Plus agreement.[171]

Arguments against a NATO right of first refusal

The opinion that the United States should not veto the use of NATO assets enabling European-only missions goes back to a study by the Centre on European Reform in 1998[172] which served as direct background for the British turn-around in European defence policy lastly leading to the St-Malo Declaration in December that year.[173] After St-Malo had let the genie of 'autonomy' out of the bottle, the question of whether the EU wanted to conduct an operation with or without NATO/US assets – which was directly linked to the question of whether it had to ask NATO first

---

undertake military operation. ... The EU in *those* circumstances has got to have the capability to do so.'; *Id.*, speech to the European Parliament, 23 June 2005, http://www.numberten. gov.uk /output/Page7714.asp (visited 23/06/05): 'We should be ... prepared to take on more missions of peacekeeping and peace enforcement ... with NATO or where NATO does not *want to* be engaged ...' [emphases added].

165   See above Chapter 2 (ESDP Today).

166   *NATO's job is security, US asserts*, International Herald Tribune (online edition), 26 May 2005.

167   E.g. G. Gustenau, *GASP – eine Herausforderung für die 'Post-Neutralen'?* (2000), p. 29; M. Vasiu, *The role of the ESDI*, 6 Rom.J.Int.Aff. 3/4 (2000), pp. 128, 129 and 138; H. Boguslawska, *Le lien transatlantique* (2003), p. 27; F. Faria, *Crisis management in sub-Saharan Africa – The role of the European Union*, EU-ISS Occasional Paper No. 51 (2004), p. 48.

168   C. von Buttlar, *The EU's new relations with NATO*, 6 ZEuS 3 (2003), p. 414.

169   *Ibid.*, p. 415.

170   *Ibid.*, p. 416.

171   See above p. 151.

172   C. Grant, *Can Britain lead in Europe?*, CER (1998), p. 48.

173   U. Schürr, *Der Aufbau einer ESVI* (2003), p. 225.

– began to be presented as a *political choice*: 'Does the EU wish to address this crisis alone or in alliance with the United States? This is a perfectly valid question.'[174]

Early supporters of EU military autonomy such as the European Parliament[175] and the WEU Assembly[176] soon began to negate NATO's right of first refusal outright. In 2001, French official opinion seemed to oscillate between the government which carefully derogated from it[177] and military circles who openly denied it.[178] Even NATO's Deputy SG A.M. Rizzo wrote that 'It is entirely legitimate for Europe to equip itself with crisis management instruments and want to take *firsthand* responsibility.'[179]

Evidence from EU and NATO statements

The different camps of opinion presented above may help to understand the content of the 'where NATO as a whole is not engaged' problem. However, none of them officially speak for NATO or the EU. Only official statements attributable to these organisations do so. It is these statements, therefore, that must be consulted to ascertain which of the interpretations holds.

NATO had closely stuck to the formula throughout, and never varied or interpreted its wording in any direction.[180] The EU had done so as well,[181] and had not recognised the view of the US Senate of October 1999[182] (which claimed a right

---

174   J. Howorth, *The ultimate challenge* (2000), p. 55.

175   Resolution on the European Council Report to the European Parliament on the progress achieved by the Union in 1997, 21 Oct. 1998, para. 20, 4th indent, OJ C 341/85 of 9.11.98.

176   Implementation of the Nice Summit decisions in the operational area on the European Security and Defence Policy (ESDP), WEU Assembly Doc. A/1734, 19 June 2001, para. 45.

177   Speech of A. Richard (French MoD), Munich Security Conference, 3 Feb. 2001: 'The decision to act is for the members of the European Union and them alone. ... Theoretical controversy over the right of first refusal has no foundation in reality.', http://www.securityconference.de (visited 22/08/04); *contra* J. Fitchett, *US and EU Ponder Defense Trade-Off*, International Herald Tribune, 8 Feb. 2001, p. 1.

178   'There is no question of a right of first refusal'. (Gen. J.-P. Kelche, cited in: C. Schofield / M. Smith, *EU force will not need Nato, says French military chief*, Daily Telegraph, 28 March 2001, p. 1).

179   A.M. Rizzo, *Towards a European Defence Policy*, 36 The International Spectator 3 (2001), p. 47 at 51–52 [emphasis added].

180   See the NATO statements above at fn. 138.

181   See the EU statements above at fn. 137.

182   See above at fn. 2.

of first refusal for NATO) at its next Summit in Helsinki.[183] Instead, the EU simply kept on repeating the exact same formula.[184]

Even though the EU never issued a formal interpretation of the 'where NATO as a whole is not engaged' formula, it did something else: from the Nice Summit onwards, whenever it referred in general terms to its relationship with NATO, it stressed its own 'decision-making autonomy'.[185] At the Seville Summit in June 2002, it even did so with reference to the question of 'Consultation and cooperation between EU and NATO ... in order to make possible the most appropriate military response to a given crisis'[186] which is the very situation in which NATO's right of first refusal, if it existed, would come to bear. In its NATO/EU Consultation document of December 2003, 'decision-making autonomy' and 'where NATO as a whole is not engaged' are even placed within a few words of each other.[187] NATO accepted the principle of the EU's 'decision-making autonomy' in the Berlin Plus agreement[188] and in later statements on EU–NATO cooperation.[189]

Conclusion

The question of NATO's right of first refusal cannot be answered directly from the founding treaties or other related acts of the EU or NATO. What does transpire, however, is that NATO has never in fact claimed it, and that the EU has never assented to it, be it as a matter of law or only one of policy.[190] Instead, the EU has claimed for itself the principle of the Union's 'decision-making autonomy' in its relationship

---

183   A. Pliakos, *The CESDP* (2000), p. 275 at 284; *cf.* J. Fitchett, *EU Completes Plan for Own Forces*, International Herald Tribune, 10 Dec. 1999, p. 4; *contra* W. Bradford, *The WEU ... the new sick man of Europe* (2000), p. 83.

184   US commentators of the Helsinki Summit were already starting to worry at this fact, *cf.* E.S. Duquette, *The EU's CFSP: Emerging from the US Shadow?*, 7 U.C. Davis J. Int'l L. & Pol'y (Spring 2001), p. 169 at 195: 'With each assertion of unbridled independence, the caveat of "where NATO as a whole is not engaged" grows less and less assuring to the United States.'

185   European Council, Nice, 7–9 Dec. 2000, Presidency Conclusions, CP 47, p. 169; *Ibid.*, p. 172; European Council, Göteborg, Annex: Presidency Report on ESDP, para. 31, CP 51, p. 37; *Ibid.*, Annex IV to the Annex, para. 12, CP 51, p. 54; European Council, Laeken, 14–15 Dec. 2001, Presidency Report on ESDP, para. 18; *Ibid.*, Annex I, para. 1, CP 51, p. 131; European Council, Copenhagen, 12–13 Dec. 2002, ESDP Presidency Report, para. 20, subpara. 3, CP 57, p. 176.

186   European Council, Seville, 21–22 June, 2002, Presidency Report on ESDP, para. 25, CP 67, p. 79.

187   NATO/EU Consultation Document, paras. 2 and 3, CP 67, p. 322.

188   See above fn. 140.

189   E.g. Statement by NATO's Secretary General – Berlin Plus, Brussels, 17 March 2003, CP 67, p. 49.

190   In this sense also J.-Y. Haine, *ESDP and NATO*, in: N. Gnesotto (ed.), *EU Security and Defence Policy – The first five years* (2004), EU-ISS, p. 131 at 138.

with NATO[191] which the latter has undoubtedly accepted. In conclusion, NATO does not seem to have a right of first refusal vis-à-vis the EU in crisis management, even if this runs counter to the majority of media opinion on the subject.[192] Whether this conclusion is sustained by the practice of the two organisations is another matter, which will be dealt with in a subsequent chapter.[193]

---

191 NATO's decision-making autonomy was never disputed, and often mentioned alongside the EU's.

192 E.g. *The alliance tries to strike back,* The Economist, 14 June 2003, p. 28 at 29: 'The EU force will act when NATO chooses not to'.

193 See below Chapter 7 (Military Crisis Management).

Chapter 6

Collective Self-Defence

This chapter will deal with collective self-defence in the EU and NATO, and with the interaction between these two regimes.

SELF-DEFENCE IN INTERNATIONAL LAW

A full description of the law of self-defence in international law is beyond the scope of this book. It is moreover unnecessary as the subject has been widely treated in scholarship throughout the world ever since the entry into force of the UN Charter, ranging from numerous commentaries[1] to treatises on special aspects and problems of self-defence. Moreover, after the United States, currently the most powerful actor in the international system, has subscribed to a new doctrine of pre-emptive self-defence in autumn 2002,[2] the future development of the law of self-defence seems more uncertain. Therefore, only a brief overview over self-defence in international law, including collective self-defence, is given below. Guarantees in international law, which are unidirectional in nature, will also not be treated.[3]

National law operates under a system of centralised law enforcement,[4] leaving only marginal room for self-defence. In the decentralised international system of States which lacks such a central enforcement agency, self-defence traditionally played a much broader role. However, since the gradual outlawing of the use of force in the twentieth century, and the introduction of a system of collective security under the UN Charter, it has assumed an exceptional character also internationally and is only allowed as a remedy of last resort in Art. 51 UN Charter.[5]

---

1   See only H. Kelsen, *The Law of the United Nations* (1950), pp. 791–805; J.-P. Cot (ed.), *La Charte des Nations Unies* (1991); A. Randelzhofer, *Article 51*, in: B. Simma (ed.), *Charter of the United Nations* (2002).

2   See above Chapter 1 (Transatlantic Relations).

3   On guarantees in international law, see only Y. Dinstein, *War, Aggression and Self-Defence* (2001), pp. 233–6; R. Jennings / A. Watts, *Oppenheim's* (1992), § 668, pp. 1322; H.G. Ress, *Guarantee,* in: EPIL II (1995), pp. 626–634 w.f.r.; *Ibid., Guarantee Treaties*, pp. 634–637 w.f.r.

4   B.-O. Bryde, *Self-Defence*, in: EPIL IV (2000), p. 361.

5   The only other exception to the ban on the use of force are measures by the Security Council under Arts 39–42 UN Charter. They were not widely applied until 1990, due to the paralysis of the Security Council in many areas touching the interests of the great powers during the Cold War.

Self-defence and its limits in customary international law

Compared to today, self-defence only played a minor role in international law before 1945, the year when the use of force as a legal means of policy (under the *jus ad bellum*) was banned completely by the UN Charter. However, the concept of self-defence was used as a measure for determining wrongful action by States in incidents like the *Caroline Case* of 1837.[6] In this incident, a British troop contingent entered an American harbour in pursuit of a vessel supporting hostile rebels, took possession of the ship, set it afire and then sent it across the Niagara Falls. Daniel Webster (US Secretary of State) contended in his ensuing correspondence with the British side, that an act of self-defence, in order to be justified under international law, had to fulfil several strict criteria: 'a necessity of self-defence, instant and overwhelming, leaving no choice of means, and no moment for deliberation ...'.[7] The action taken must not be '... unreasonable or excessive, since the act, justified by the necessity of self defence, must be limited by that necessity, and kept clearly within it'.[8] Since that time, the requirements of *immediacy*, *proportionality* and *necessity* have prevailed as limits for self-defence in customary international law.[9] Self-defence may not be used to achieve anything beyond the *status quo ante*.[10] There must be no practicable alternative open but defensive action.[11] These criteria are still part of the international law on self-defence today, even though they are not explicitly mentioned in Art. 51 UN Charter. Under the present system, the ultimate decision on whether they are met in a given case should not be left to the discretion of the State concerned, but should be determined by an independent judicial authority or political body (that is, the UN Security Council).[12] Unilateral assessment of the term *necessity* in a given case should thus be ruled out in theory. The forceful remedy chosen must be commensurate with the gravity of the incursion.[13]

---

6   Destruction of the 'Caroline', partly reprinted in: J.B. Moore, *A digest of international law* (1906), § 217, pp. 409–414; Correspondence between Great Britain and the United States, respecting the Destruction of the Caroline, B.F.S.P., Vol. 26 (1837–8), pp. 1372–1377; Vol. 29 (1840–1), pp. 1126–1142; Vol. 30 (1841–2), pp. 193–202.

7   B.F.S.P., Vol. 29 (1840–1), p. 1138.

8   *Ibid.*

9   R. Ago, YBILC 1980, Vol. II, Part. I, pp. 69–70; K.C. Kenny, *Self-Defence*, in: R. Wolfrum (ed.), Handbook United Nations (1995), pp. 1167–8; MN 18–24; A. Randelzhofer, *Article 51*, in: B. Simma (ed.), *Charter of the United Nations* (2002), pp. 804–5, MN 41–42; B.-O. Bryde, *Self-Defence*, in: EPIL IV (2000), pp. 362–3. A close elaboration of each of these concepts is outside the scope of this inquiry, but can be found in the above cited works.

10   B.-O. Bryde, *ibid.*, pp. 361–2.

11   *Cf.* R. Jennings / A. Watts, *Oppenheim's* (1992), p. 422.

12   *Ibid.*

13   Although it need not be symmetrical – in theory this leaves the possibility for even a first use of nuclear weapons, if all other requirements are adhered to. *Cf. Legality of the Threat or Use of Nuclear Weapons*, Adv. Op., ICJ Rep. 1996, diss.op. Higgins, pp. 583–4, para. 5. A. Randelzhofer, *Article 51*, in: B. Simma (ed.), Charter of the United Nations (2002), 805, MN 42.

Self-defence under Article 51 UN Charter

Notion of armed attack and the 'security gap' with Article 2, para. 4 UN Charter

Art. 51 UN Charter did not completely abolish the legal use of force, but it limited it to more narrowly defined cases than before: self-defence according to Art. 51 requires, in addition to the criteria of the *Caroline Case*, that 'an armed attack occurs' on the State exercising it. An official definition of this terminology is lacking until today. One of many competing definitions would be 'an armed violation of the territorial integrity and political independence of a [State], or of its ships and aircraft on the high seas'.[14] The attack should be of sufficient gravity and scale to warrant an armed counter-measure. Small frontier incidents,[15] moral, financial or logistic support for irregular forces operating inside another State fall outside this narrow definition,[16] as does mere economic pressure. However, the requirement is fulfilled where armed bands imputable to a certain State invade another State on a large scale and to substantial effect, comparable in scale and effects to that of regular forces.[17] Art. 3 of the 1974 General Assembly Resolution on the Definition of Aggression,[18] although it defines a broader situation,[19] offers useful indications for what constitutes such an 'armed attack':[20] a) invasion, bombardment, and cross-border shooting; b) blockade; c) attack on State positions abroad; d) breach of stationing agreements; e) placing territory at another State's disposal; f) participation in the use of force by militarily organised unofficial groups.

The threshold to triggering a lawful act of self-defence is thus set high by the UN Charter, in line with the spirit of the prohibition of all use of force in Art. 2, para. 4. This prohibition covers also many uses of force of smaller scale that would not reach the threshold of an 'armed attack' in Art. 51, which is understood more narrowly.[21] The resulting 'security gap' seems to be a shortcoming of the UN Charter which, in this respect, seems to give preference to security before justice.[22]

---

14   B.-O. Bryde, *Self-Defence*, in: EPIL IV (2000), p. 362

15   *Nicaragua Case*, 1986 ICJ Rep., p. 103, para. 195; A. Randelzhofer, *Article 51*, in: B. Simma (ed.), *Charter of the United Nations* (2002), p. 795 MN 20; K.C. Kenny, *Self-Defence*, in: R. Wolfrum (ed.), Handbook United Nations (1995), p. 1166, MN 14.

16   *Nicaragua Case*, 1986 ICJ Rep., p. 104, para. 195.

17   *Ibid.*, p. 103, para. 195.

18   G.A. Resolution 3314 (XXIX) on the Definition of Aggression, 14 Dec. 1974, GAOR 29th Sess., Supp. 31, p. 142.

19   Despite the French wording of Art. 51, *agression armée*, 'aggression' is a wider notion than an 'armed attack' (A. Randelzhofer, *Article 51*, in: B. Simma (ed.), *Charter of the United Nations* (2002), p. 790 MN 4).

20   *Ibid.*, p. 796 MN 21; K.C. Kenny, *Self-Defence*, in: R. Wolfrum (ed.), Handbook United Nations (1995), p. 1164, MN 10.

21   *Cf.* H. Kelsen, *The Law of the United Nations* (1950), p. 797; K.C. Kenny, *Self-Defence*, in: R. Wolfrum (ed.), Handbook United Nations (1995), p. 1162, MN 4.

22   A. Randelzhofer, *Article 51*, in: B. Simma (ed.), *Charter of the United Nations* (2002), p. 792, MN 8.

Another requirement under Art. 51 is the duty to report without delay any action by the defending State to the Security Council which may then 'take action as it deems necessary' for international peace and security. Failure to comply with this reporting duty constitutes prima facie evidence of unlawful action.[23] This underlines the character of self-defence under Art. 51 as in character a provisional measure, preliminary and subsidiary to Security Council action.[24]

Self-defence 'inherent' in Article 51

The text of Art. 51 names self-defence as an 'inherent right' (*droit naturel*). This has been taken to mean that the right exists independently of the explicit provision in the Charter.[25] As part of general international law, it preceded the Charter in time.[26] This reading, although arguably supported by the early negotiating history of the Charter[27] would in practice lead to a return of the regime on the use of force which existed before 1945. Hence, it is very controversial today.[28] Many authors argue that Art. 51 has today completely superseded and replaced the formed customary law of self-defence.[29] Other authors, followed by the ICJ, have argued that the customary right of self-defence and self-defence under Art. 51 UN Charter are identical.[30] State practice is too inconsistent to support either view.[31]

Anticipatory self-defence

The strict interpretation of Art. 51 requires the self-defending State to wait for the point in time until the attacker's violation is manifest, that is, if, 'and only if',[32] enemy troops begin to cross the frontier or drop bombs on its territory. A large part of the

---

23   *Nicaragua Case*, 1986 ICJ Rep., p. 105, para. 200 *in fine* and pp. 121–2, para. 235.

24   H. Kelsen, *The Law of the United Nations* (1950), pp. 800–1; S.A. Alexandrov, *Self-Defence Against the Use of Force in International Law* (1996), p. 104.

25   D. Bowett, *Self-Defence in International Law* (1958), p. 187.

26   R. Ago, YBILC 1980, Vol. II, Part. I, p. 61; *cf.* H. Kelsen, *The Law of the United Nations* (1950), p. 791.

27   *Cf.* S.A. Alexandrov, *Self-Defence Against the Use of Force in International Law* (1996), p. 77–78.

28   B.-O. Bryde, *Self-Defence*, in: EPIL IV (2000), p. 363; A. Randelzhofer, *Article 51*, in: B. Simma (ed.), *Charter of the United Nations* (2002), pp. 792–3, MN 11–12.

29   E.g. A. Randelzhofer, *Article 51*, in: B. Simma (ed.), *Charter of the United Nations* (2002), p. 806, MN 45.

30   R. Ago, YBILC 1980, Vol. II, Part. I, p. 67; Brownlie, *International Law and the Use of Force by States* (1963), pp. 270–5; *Nicaragua Case*, 1986 ICJ Rep., pp. 105, 121, paras. 200, 235. *cf.* B.-O. Bryde, *Self-Defence*, in: EPIL IV (2000), p. 363.

31   K.C. Kenny, *Self-Defence*, in: R. Wolfrum (ed.), Handbook United Nations (1995), p. 1163, MN 7.

32   P. Malanczuk, *Akehurst's International Law* (1997), p. 312

controversy over self-defence, in fact, hovers over *when* it may first be exercised.[33] For small States without a second-strike capacity (be it nuclear or conventional), 'being a sitting duck'[34] in face of an imminent attack might well have lethal consequences. Advances in military technology, which make it increasingly difficult to predict and prepare for a surprise attack, exacerbate the problem. This is especially so since auxiliary action by the Security Council (as provided for in the latter part of Art. 51) is far from certain to arrive in time, if at all.[35] Anticipatory self-defence is supported by those authors who argue for the existence of a traditional customary-law notion of self-defence preceding Art. 51.[36] According to them, abuse should still be prevented by the general strict requirements for self-defence, in particular the element of immediacy (see the *Caroline Case*, above).[37] As anticipatory self-defence is often invoked by States,[38] the problem is a hotly disputed one in international law, particularly since the United States has claimed it as valid law in its National Security Strategy in 2002.[39] The prevailing view seems to deny the lawfulness of anticipated self-defence,[40] except in the most exceptional of cases, much depending on the facts of the individual case.[41]

---

33   *Ibid.*, p. 311.

34   *Ibid.*, p. 314.

35   Historically, Art. 43–47 UN Charter, stipulating a standing 'UN army' under the command of the Security Council, implied an automatic response, including military measures, also for such cases.

36   E.g. A.D. Sofaer, *On the Necessity of Pre-emption*, 14 EJIL 2 (2003), pp. 209–226; *cf.* A. Randelzhofer, *Article 51*, in: B. Simma (ed.), *Charter of the United Nations* (2002), p. 803, MN 39.

37   A. Randelzhofer, *ibid.*

38   K.C. Kenny, *Self-Defence*, in: R. Wolfrum (ed.), Handbook United Nations (1995), p. 1165, MN 11.

39   See above Chapter 1 (Transatlantic Relations). *Cf.* e.g. D. Rezac, *President Bush's Security Strategy and its 'pre-emptive strikes doctrine' – a legal basis for the war against Iraq?*, 7 ARIEL (2002), pp. 223–241; M.N. Schmitt, *Preemptive Strategies in International Law*, 24 Mich.J.Int'l L. (Winter 2003), pp. 513–548; R. Kolb, *Self-Defence and Preventive War at the Beginning of the Millennium*, 59 ÖsterrZÖR (2004), pp. 111–134.

40   A. Randelzhofer, *Article 51*, in: B. Simma (ed.), *Charter of the United Nations* (2002), pp. 803–4, MN 39–40; Brownlie, *International Law and the Use of Force by States* (1963), p. 278.

41   *Cf.* B.-O. Bryde, *Self-Defence*, in: EPIL IV (2000), p. 362; H. Neuhold, *Law and Force in International Relations – European and American Positions*, 64 HJIL (2004), p. 263 at 273.

COLLECTIVE SELF-DEFENCE IN INTERNATIONAL LAW[42]

Collective self-defence was unknown to traditional international law,[43] despite the long-standing existence of treaty-based defensive alliances before the Second World War.[44] The notion first entered the negotiations on the UN Charter at the United Nations Conference in 1945 in conjunction with concerns by the Latin American countries who had recently concluded the Act of Chaltapultepec[45] containing a pledge to meet threats or acts of aggression against a Western Hemisphere country.[46] In the words of the Chairman of the drafting Committee (acting on behalf of the Colombian delegation):

> In the case of the American states, an aggression against one American state constitutes an aggression against all the American states, and all of them exercise their right of legitimate defense by giving support to the state attacked, in order to repel such aggression. This is what is meant by the right of *collective self-defence.*[47]

Many Latin American countries wanted to see such regional arrangements for collective defence included in the United Nations framework.[48] Although initially the idea of regional security sub-systems autonomous from the global organisation was rejected by many States,[49] eventually a British proposal which omitted all reference

---

42   For a good list of literature on collective self-defence in international law, see only R. Ago, YBILC 1980, Vol. II, Part. I, p. 68, n. 268.

43   N. Quoc Dinh, *La légitime défense d'après la Charte des Nations Unies*, 52 RGDIP (1948), p. 223 at 244–251; K.C. Kenny, *Self-Defence*, in: R. Wolfrum (ed.), Handbook United Nations (1995), p. 1168, MN 25; J. Delbrück, *Collective Self-Defence*, in: EPIL I (1992), p. 657. *Contra* J.L. Kunz, *Individual and Collective Self-Defence in Article 51 of the Charter of the UN*, 41 AJIL (1947), p. 879 at 874; *cf.* Y. Dinstein, *War, Aggression and Self-Defence* (2001), p. 226; *Nicaragua Case*, 1986 ICJ Rep., diss.op. Oda, pp. 256–8.

44   E.g. Nyon Agreement and Supplementary Agreement, Great Britain-France, e.i.f. 14 and 17 Sept. 1937, 181 LNTS 137; *cf.* N.J. Padelford, *International Law and Diplomacy in the Spanish Civil Strife* (1939), p. 49; Panama Declaration, 3 Oct. 1939, repr. in: Treaties and other international agreements of the United States of America (C.I. Bevans, compil.), Vol. 3, pp. 608–610; *cf.* G.K. Walker, *Anticipatory Self-Defense in the Charter Era: What the Treaties Have Said*, 31 Cornell Int'l L. J. (1998), pp. 321, w.f.r.

45   Inter-American Reciprocal Assistance and Solidarity (Act of Chapultepec), 6 March 1945, http://www.yale.edu/lawweb/avalon/intdip/interam/chapul.htm (visited 21/04/04).

46   G.K. Walker, *Anticipatory Self-Defense in the Charter Era*, 31 Corn.J.I.L. (1998), p. 321 at 351, w.f.r.

47   UNCIO, III/4/9, p. 687 [emphasis in the original].

48   UNCIO, III/4/9, p. 680–1; *cf.* L. Goodrich / E. Hambro, *Charter of the United Nations* (3rd edn, 1969), pp. 342–3; C. Kahgan, *Jus Cogens and the Inherent right to self-defence*, 3 ILSA J Int'l & Comp. L. (1997), p. 803; G.K. Walker, *Anticipatory Self-Defense in the Charter Era*, 31 Corn.J.I.L. (1998), p. 321 at 351–2, w.f.r.

49   E.g. UNCIO, III/4/9, p. 682 (N.Z.); T. M. Franck, *Recourse to force* (2002), p. 29 (U.K.).

to regional organisations, but allowed 'collective self-defence' was accepted in Article 51.[50]

Collective self-defence under Art. 51 UN Charter is subject to the same requirements and limits as individual self-defence, that is, there must be an armed attack, and the response must conform to the general limits of immediacy, necessity and proportionality.[51] It is more than simply the law of self-defence applied to several States in sum against one aggressor,[52] but rather 'defence of another State'.[53] Because of its long-term deterrent effect on potential aggressors,[54] collective self-defence is not only based on self-interest, but also on a general interest in peace and security.[55] It thus represents a true addition to the global system of collective security,[56] particularly in cases where great-power interests are involved,[57] although only as a temporary and subsidiary measure to the collective security system.[58] Mutual defence assistance effected by a regional alliance, including a regional organisation under Chapter VIII of the UN Charter, is not ruled out[59] and in fact Art.

---

50   L. Goodrich / E. Hambro, *Charter of the United Nations* (3ʳᵈ edn, 1969), p. 343.

51   Y. Dinstein, *War, Aggression and Self-Defence* (2001), pp. 237–240; see above p. 166.

52   D. Bowett, *Self-Defence in International Law* (1958), p. 216; R. Higgins, *The Legal Limits to the Use of Force by Sovereign States: United Nations Practice*, 37 BYIL (1961), p. 269 at 307; L.-A. Sicilianos, *Les réactions décentralisés à l'illicite* (1990), p. 121.

53   K. Skubiszewski, *Use of Force by States, Collective Security, Law of War and Neutrality*, in: M. Sørensen (ed.), *Manual of Public International Law* (1968), p. 769; M. Márquez Carrasco, *Problemas Actuales sobre la Prohibición del Recurso a la Fuerza en Derecho Internacional* (1998), p. 161. *Cf.* R. Ago, YBILC 1980, Vol. II, Part. I, p. 68. *Cf.* the differentiation of different cases in: Y. Dinstein, *War, Aggression and Self-Defence* (2001), pp. 222–6.

54   J. Delbrück, *Collective Self-Defence*, in: EPIL I (1992), p. 656.

55   S.A. Alexandrov, *Self-Defence Against the Use of Force in International Law* (1996), p. 102; M. Márquez Carrasco, *Problemas Actuales sobre la Prohibición del Recurso al la Fuerza en Derecho Internacional* (1998), pp. 161–2.

56   C. de Visscher, *Théories et réalités en droit international public* (4ᵗʰ edn, 1970), p. 146; U. Schürr, *Der Aufbau einer ESVI* (2003), p. 19. It is also argued, however, that collective defence pacts are systematically detrimental for the functioning of the collective security system. K.C. Kenny, *Self-Defence*, in: R. Wolfrum (ed.), Handbook United Nations (1995), p. 1169, MN 26; J. Delbrück, *Collective Self-Defence*, in: EPIL I (1992), p. 658. *Cf.* H. Kelsen, *Collective Security and Collective Self-Defense under the Charter und the United Nations*, 42 AJIL (1948), p. 783 at pp. 793–4, who points out the historical parallel to Art. 16 of the League of Nations Charter.

57   J.L. Hargrove, *Force, a Culture of Law, and American Interests*, 36 Col. J. Transnat'l L. (1998), p. 444.

58   Delbrück, *Collective Self-Defence*, in: EPIL I (1992), p. 657.

59   H. Kelsen, *The Law of the United Nations* (1950), p. 793; K. Ipsen, *Rechtsgrundlagen* (1967), p. 28; R. Jennings / A. Watts, *Oppenheim's* (1992), p. 1320; S. Verosta, *Alliance*, in: EPIL I (1992), p. 122. On the difficult theoretical separation between these two types of international organisations (which may sometimes coincide in one), see C. Walter, *Vereinte Nationen und Regionalorganisationen* (1996), pp. 47. *Cf.* Y. Dinstein, *War, Aggression and*

51 has its historical roots within those provisions.[60] However, collective self-defence may also arise spontaneously, without prior organisation.[61]

State A which comes to State B's aid against an armed attack by State C does not necessarily have to have been also subjected to the same armed attack.[62] If the latter is not the case, however, State A is even more strictly bound in its self-defence actions than State B: first, it must wait until State B actually considers itself the victim of an attack and consents to the assistance[63] (normally in express terms[64]); second, the reporting duty to the UN Security Council under Art. 51[65] is incumbent separately on each State which comes to the aid of State B.[66] The report to the Security Council does not, however, have to be made by a State before taking action, which is a major difference to measures taken under Art. 52.[67] The existence of the right of collective self-defence under customary international law is widely acknowledged today.[68]

COLLECTIVE SELF-DEFENCE TREATIES AND ALLIANCES

In the years that followed the entry into force of the UN Charter, a great number of treaties on collective self-defence, with sometimes varying degree of obligation,

---

Self-Defence (2001), p. 227, who calls collective self-defence one of the most important purposes of Art. 52, para. 1 UN Charter.

60   See above fn. 45; U.N.C.I.O., III/4/9, pp. 679–688; N. Krisch, *Selbstverteidigung und kollektive Sicherheit* (2001), p. 48–53.

61   H. Kelsen, *The Law of the United Nations* (1950), p. 796; J. Žourek, *La notion de légitime défense en droit international*, 56 AnnIDI (1975), p. 1 at 48; R. Ago, YBILC 1980, Vol. II, Part. I, p. 68; Y. Dinstein, *War, Aggression and Self-Defence* (2001), pp. 225–6; A. Randelzhofer, *Article 51*, in: B. Simma (ed.), *Charter of the United Nations* (2002), p. 802, MN 37; *cf.* S.A. Alexandrov, *Self-Defence Against the Use of Force in International Law* (1996), pp. 101–2.

62   *Nicaragua Case*, 1986 ICJ Rep., p. 110, para. 211; A. Cassese, *Article 51*, in: J.-P. Cot / A. Pellet (eds), *La Charte des Nations Unies* (2ⁿᵈ edn, 1991), p. 787; S.A. Alexandrov, *ibid.*, p. 103.

63   J. Mrazek, *Prohibition of the Use and Threat of Force: Self-Defence and Self-Help in International Law*, 29 Can.YIL (1989), p. 93; M. Márquez Carrasco, *Problemas Actuales sobre la Prohibición del Recurso a la Fuerza en Derecho Internacional* (1998), pp. 165–7 w.f.r.; A. Randelzhofer, *Article 51*, in: B. Simma (ed.), *Charter of the United Nations* (2002), p. 803, MN 38 w.f.r.; *Nicaragua Case*, 1986 ICJ Rep., p. 104, para. 195. *Contra* diss.op. Jennings, *ibid.*, pp. 544–5.

64   *Nicaragua Case*, *ibid.*, p. 120, para. 232.

65   See above p. 167.

66   Y. Dinstein, *War, Aggression and Self-Defence* (2001), p. 240.

67   S.A. Alexandrov, *Self-Defence Against the Use of Force in International Law* (1996), p. 232, w.f.r.

68   See only *Nicaragua Case*, 1986 ICJ Rep., p. 102, para. 193.

were concluded by States, bilateral[69] and multilateral,[70] and continue to be so today.[71]As the UN Charter now outlaws the offensive use of force, all alliances (at least according to their text) are defensive in nature.

As said above, a treaty is not necessary for using the right of collective self-defence under international law, but it adds to this right a certain duty of collective self-defence. The *casus foederis*, that is, the definition of the event in which the obligation to come to each other's assistance is activated, is of great importance in collective self-defence treaties;[72] so is the description of the degree of obligation owed in that case, particularly the question whether aid must include armed force or not. In past alliances, this decision was sometimes taken by an international organ of the parties, sometimes even by majority vote.[73] Beyond the legal value of a mutual defence treaty, it is often pointed out that 'The main benefit derived from such a treaty lies in the political sphere, for publication of the text serves notice to friends and foes alike as to the cords of affiliation uniting the contracting parties'.[74]

Often parties wish to go beyond the textual obligations contained in a mutual defence treaty, and create a full international organisation to serve its purpose, that is, an Alliance.[75] This would aptly describe, for example, NATO's evolution between 1949 and 1954.[76] Alliances, in addition to the formal legal obligations in the treaty,

---

69   E.g. US bilateral mutual defence treaties with the Philippines (30 Aug. 1951, 177 UNTS 133), Korea (1 Oct. 1953, 238 UNTS 199), and Japan (8 Sept. 1951, 136 UNTS 211).

70   NAT (1949), 34 UNTS 243; WEU Modified Brussels Treaty (1954), 19 UNTS 51 and 211 UNTS 342; Warsaw Pact, 14 May 1955 [hereinafter: Warsaw Pact], 219 UNTS 3; The European Defence Community Treaty (with Protocols) (not entered into force), British Command Paper, Cmd. 9127 (1954); Inter-American Treaty of Reciprocal Assistance [hereinafter: Rio Treaty], 2 Sept. 1947, 21 UNTS 77; SEATO (Manila Treaty), 8 Sept. 1954, 209 UNTS 23; CENTO (Baghdad Pact), 4 Feb. 1955, 233 UNTS 199; Balkan Pact (4 agreements, 1953/1954), 167 UNTS 21, 4 AVR (1953/1954) p. 478, 211 UNTS 237, 225 UNTS 233; ANZUS Pact, 1 Sept. 1951, 131 UNTS 83; Pact of the League of Arab States, 22 March 1945, 70 UNTS 237.

71   E.g. ECOWAS Protocol Relating to Mutual Assistance and Defence, 29 May 1981, 4 Nigeria's Treaties in Force (1990), p. 898; CIS Treaty on Collective Security, 15 May 1992, 1894 UNTS 309; AU draft African Non-Aggression Pact, 29 June 2004, AU Doc. EXP/GVT/PACT/2 Rev. 2, http://www.iss.co.za/AF/RegOrg /unity_to_union/pdfs/au/jun04/ nonaggression.pdf (visited 27/08/2004).

72   S. Verosta, *Alliance*, in: EPIL I (1992), p. 120; S. Verosta, *Casus foederis*, *ibid.*, p. 543; *cf.* R. Jennings / A. Watts, *Oppenheim's* (1992), p. 1322; Y. Dinstein, *War, Aggression and Self-Defence* (2001), p. 232.

73   S. Verosta, *Casus foederis*, in: EPIL I (1992), p. 544.

74   Y. Dinstein, *War, Aggression and Self-Defence* (2001), p. 228; *cf.* H.L. Ismay, *NATO – the first five years* (1954), p. 13.

75   Sometimes the difference between a treaty of mutual assistance and the constituent instrument of a military alliance can be hard to draw. *Cf.* Y. Dinstein, *War, Aggression and Self-Defence* (2001), p. 231.

76   See above Chapter 3 (NATO Today)

are often characterised by an integrated military command,[77] accompanied by a wide organisational structure which also serves to enhance a sense of solidarity among the members. Mixing the forces of the member States (including in joint exercises) can deliberately make it impossible for one member State to disentangle once the *casus foederis* arrives.[78] For example, American 'tripwire forces' along the inner-German border in the Cold War ensured that, in case of a Soviet attack, US troops would be engaged in the fighting from the first day, despite the 'loose' wording of Art. 5 NAT.[79]

In most alliances, the obligation to assist is reciprocal for all parties,[80] and the decision on the *casus foederis* is taken by unanimity. Because of the above-mentioned socialisation effects of an alliance, member States' individual assessments on the existence of a *casus foederis* can in practice be expected to diverge less in a formalised alliance than in a pure mutual defence treaty.

COLLECTIVE SELF-DEFENCE IN NATO

The central provision of the NAT is its mutual defence clause contained in Article 5. It is a collective defence commitment that was historically only arrived at after long negotiation, remained the *raison d'être* of the Alliance throughout the Cold War, and has seen new ways of application after the end of that period, particularly after its invocation after September 11.

History of Article 5[81]

In the years immediately after the end of the Second World War, the States of Western Europe found themselves in a vulnerable situation in face of massive Soviet military presence in Eastern Europe. The fear of a Soviet attack was sometimes even openly expressed, for example by P.-H. Spaak, then Belgian PM, at UN General Assembly in 1948.[82] This European problem was also in part grounded in national economies devastated by the war, and dispirited populations increasingly susceptible to the influence of national Communist parties, particularly in Italy and France. Governments in Western Europe were soon calling for a military assistance

---

77   Y. Dinstein, *War, Aggression and Self-Defence* (2001), p. 230.

78   *Ibid.*

79   See below at pp. 175.

80   *Ibid.*, p. 233. The only mutual defence pact in history which could arguably have intended such a kind of asymmetry of rights and obligations (with regard to East Germany) was the Warsaw Pact (219 UNTS 3). *Cf.* T. Schweisfurth, *Warsaw Treaty Organisation*, in: EPIL IV (2000), p. 1409 at 1412.

81   This section is partly based on: S. Kay, *NATO and the Future of European Security* (1998), pp. 13–34.

82   P.-H. Spaak, *Combats Inachevés*, Vol. 1, *De l'Indépendance à l'Alliance* (1969), pp. 216–7.

guarantee from the United States to provide the necessary protection for political and economic recovery. Britain in addition placed emphasis on the long-standing cultural ties reaching across the Atlantic, reinforced by the war-time coalition. These calls found sympathy within the foreign policy establishment in Washington. However, the latter had to proceed carefully if it wanted to attain a two-thirds majority for such an entangling alliance in the US Congress, known for strong isolationist positions. Accordingly, US Secretary of State G. Marshall advised that Europeans should 'come together for their own protection, see what they could do, and then turn to the United States ... to make up the difference'.[83] This American political condition was transformed into reality by Britain, France and the Benelux countries by the founding of the Western Union in 1948, a mutual defence pact which stated that

> If any of the High Contracting Parties should be the object of an armed attack in Europe, the other High Contracting Parties will, in accordance with the provisions of Article 51 of the Charter of the United Nations, *afford the party so attacked all the military and other aid and assistance in their power.*[84]

It was a strong mutual defence commitment, but politically it was only 'designed to establish a framework for a broader, transatlantic institution involving an American security guarantee'.[85] The creation of the Western Union provided the US Truman Administration with a strong argument to convince Congress of the need to help and support the efforts at common defence already in place in Western Europe. In the 'Vandenberg Resolution' approved by the US Senate on 11 June 1948, the US government was encouraged to progressively develop 'regional and other collective arrangements for individual and collective self-defense in accordance with the purposes, principles and provisions of the UN Charter'.[86]

Negotiations on the future NAT had already started in March 1948. The delegations had to consider two main pre-existing models for a collective defence guarantee.[87] The first was the strong formulation cited above, contained in the Brussels Treaty of the Western Union. The second alternative was the Rio Treaty concluded by the United States the year before which read in its Art. 3:

> The High Contracting Parties agree that an armed attack by any State against an American State shall be considered as an attack against all the American States and, consequently, each one of the said Contracting Parties *undertakes* to assist in meeting the attack in the exercise of the inherent right of individual or collective self-defense recognized by Article 51 of the Charter of the United Nations.

---

83   Cited in: S. Kay, *NATO and the Future of European Security* (1998), p. 16.

84   Art. 4, Treaty on Economic, Social and Cultural Collaboration and Collective Self-Defence, Brussels, 17 March 1948, 19 UNTS 51. [emphasis added].

85   S. Kay, *NATO and the Future of European Security* (1998), p. 17.

86   Res. of the US Senate Foreign Relations Ctte. No. 239, 11 June 1948, 80th Cong., 2nd Sess., 94 Cong. Rec., 4:7791.

87   D. Cook, *Forging the Alliance* (1989), p. 205.

... each one of the Contracting Parties may determine the immediate measures which it may individually take in the fulfilment of the obligation contained in the preceding paragraph ...[88]

This was a weaker formulation of mutual defence than in the Brussels Treaty. Parties were only obliged to *undertake* to assist (not to actually assist), and each party was free to choose the form of assistance, with military aid only mentioned as the last option.[89] Discussions soon centred on which of the two treaties should serve as the model for the future NAT. Not since the days of the Constitution of the United States 'have so many men spent so much time drafting and debating so few words'.[90] France in particular wanted as direct a military assistance as possible, its goal being that any future Third World War should be fought east of the Rhine. The British also insisted on an explicit military commitment.[91] American negotiators were careful not to overstep the already generous mandate given to them by Congress, and not to trespass on the latter's constitutional powers, lest the Treaty should fail congressional approval later (as had happened with the League of Nations Covenant in 1919). They thus wanted to steer clear of a strong commitment like in the Brussels Treaty.[92] At the same time, it was well recognised that the desired strategic deterrent effect of the treaty would not be achieved in the case of Western Europe with a provision as weak as the one in the Rio Treaty. In sum, the Brussels Treaty model went too far, and the Rio Treaty model did not go far enough.[93] The compromise eventually reached, secretly proposed by US President Truman,[94] maintained the freedom of choice of means from the Rio Treaty ('such action as it deems necessary'), but added the possibility to consider military means as one of them (rephrased as 'including the use of armed force'). The two elements were separated by a comma, a change in punctuation to make their connection seem less automatic (particularly to Congressional ears):[95]

The Parties agree that an armed attack against one or more of them in Europe or North America shall be considered an attack against them all, and consequently they agree that, if such armed attack occurs, each of them, in exercise of the right of individual or collective self-defence recognised by Article 51 of the Charter of the United Nations, will assist the Party or Parties so attacked by taking forthwith, individually, and in concert with the other Parties, *such action as it deems necessary, including the use of armed force,* to restore and maintain the security in the North Atlantic area.[96]

---

88   Rio Treaty, see above[emphasis added].
89   Rio Treaty, Art. 8 *in fine.*
90   D. Cook, fn. 87, p. 204.
91   *Ibid.*, pp. 212–3.
92   R. Heindel et al., *The North Atlantic Treaty in the United States Senate*, 43 AJIL (1949), p. 633 at 648.
93   D. Cook, fn. 87, pp. 205–6.
94   *Ibid.*, pp. 213–4.
95   *Ibid.*
96   Art. 5 NAT [emphasis added].

It was the most the United States was willing to commit at the time.[97] The NAT was signed by the representatives of the participating States on 4 April 1949.

It is important to see the mutual defence commitment as negotiated in 1948 and 1949 in its historico-political context. The American security guarantee was only conceived as a subsidiary underpinning to an already existing (and legally stronger) intra-European mutual defence commitment. Both regimes were intended to provide a backbone framework of security for Western European governments, amid which they could launch the economic (and, many argued, also cultural and spiritual) relaunch of their countries in face of internal Communist-inspired instability. The Pacts were the security-legal addition to the Marshall plan.[98] In conventional military terms (that is, not counting American nuclear capability and air power), they did not add much to the existing European capacity to withstand a Soviet attack. Nevertheless, transatlantic solidarity was very much enhanced by the strong symbolism that an attack against one was to be considered as an attack against all. In later practice the weakness of Art. 5, compared to the WEU commitment, came to be neglected by commonly repeated concepts such as the 'indivisibility of security', and by the integration of the member States' military commands.[99]

Content of the mutual defence obligation in Article 5

As has been pointed out many times in the past, Article 5 does not contain an automatic obligation for the State parties to come to the assistance of an attacked party, or to do so with military means.[100] This choice is left to each individual member State.[101] In theory each of the parties enjoys the same rights and obligations from the outset, although in practice the fact that most of the military means employed in assistance would come from the US[102] gave that country a preeminent position in any such decision. The 'free choice of means' interpretation of Art. 5 is widely supported by state practice.[103]

---

97 W. Lang, *Sind WEU und NATO noch Allianzen?*, 13 ÖJIP (1996), p. 8.

98 *Cf.* G.J. Ikenberry, *Atlantic Political Order* (2000), p. 64.

99 *Cf.* H.L. Ismay, *NATO: the first five years* (1954), p. 13: 'a promise to stand together in the event of an armed attack is no real deterrent to an aggressor unless it is backed up by armed strength'; A.F. Fernández Tomás, *El recurso al artículo quinto del Tratado de Washington tras los acontecimientos del 11 de septiembre: mucho ruido y pocas nueces*, 53 REDI 1/2 (2001), pp. 212–3.

100 W.E. Beckett, *The North Atlantic Treaty, the Brussels Treaty and the Charter of the United Nations* (1950), p. 28; S.A. Alexandrov, *Self-Defence Against the Use of Force in International Law* (1996), p. 235; A.F. Fernández Tomás, *El Recurso al Artículo Quinto*, 53 REDI 1/2 (2001), pp. 211–2.

101 H.L. Ismay, *NATO: the first five years* (1954), p. 13; K. Ipsen, *Rechtsgrundlagen* (1967), p. 42; S.A. Alexandrov, *ibid.*

102 *Cf.* K. Ipsen, *ibid.*, p. 50.

103 E.g. United States: 81st Cong., 1st Sess., 6 July 1949, 95 Cong. Rec., 7:8895: 'A commitment to take notice and to do something about it is automatic. A commitment to war is not.' (Sen. A. Vandenberg); *cf.* S.M. Walt, *The Ties That Fray* (1998/99): 'even if it is

However, it is submitted that Art. 5 contains a duty to *seriously consider* to assist another State party under armed attack with military means. The word 'deem' thus arguably carries a notion of impartial and objective judgement in good faith, far from a subjective 'feels like'.[104] Complete inaction in such a situation would be squarely against the obvious wording and spirit of Art. 5, and mere diplomatic protest would also likely be too little in most imaginable cases.

Judged by its wording, Art. 5 falls short of the full mutual defence clause contained in Art. V of the WEU's Modified Brussels Treaty of 1954.[105] 'In reality, however, the WEU clause stands back since the WEU does not have either a military structure or the political and strategic engagement of the US.'[106] As has also been pointed out,[107] NATO's practice after the conclusion of the NAT, particularly in the Cold War, shows signs of overcoming the gap towards a full mutual defence clause including military means. For example, a Ministerial Communiqué in 1962 stated that:

> The purpose of NATO is defence, and it must be clear that in case of attack it will defend its members by all *necessary* means.[108]

Absent in this sentence is the word 'deem', which lends further support for the above proposition that what is necessary in face of an attack should not be judged solely as a matter of national expediency by each State party.

---

a guarantee that we don't really want to honor' [sic]; United Kingdom: British Command Paper Cmd. 7692, cited in: R. Heindel et al., *The North Atlantic Treaty in the United States Senate*, 43 AJIL (1949), pp. 646–7 w.f.r.; Spain: A.F. Fernández Tomás, *El Recurso al Artículo Quinto*, 53 REDI 1/2 (2001), p. 212; *cf.* A. Mangas Martín, *Cuestiones judídicas relativas a la adhesión de España a la OTAN*, in: *Cursos de Derecho Internacional de Vitoria-Gasteiz* (1983), pp. 21–67.

104   *Cf.* W.E. Beckett, *The North Atlantic Treaty* (1950), p. 29; U. Schürr, *Der Aufbau einer ESVI* (2003), pp. 101–2. The words 'as it deems necessary' seem to have suggested by Sen. Vandenberg in the course of negotiations on Art. 5. D. Cook interprets them as giving 'specific consideration of particular action instead of any automatic commitment' (*Id.*, fn. 87, p. 212).

105   M. Weller, *The Promise of and Obstacles to Effective Peace-Keeping by the CIS, NATO, OSCE, WEU and UN*, remarks at a panel chaired by R. Wedgwood, ASIL/NVIR Proceedings 1997, p. 59; A.F. Fernández Tomás, *El Recurso al Artículo Quinto*, 53 REDI 1/2 (2001), p. 212; M. Warnken, *Der Handlungsrahmen der Europäischen Union im Bereich der Sicherheits- und Verteidigungspolitik* (2002), p. 97; K. Gerteiser, *Die Sicherheits- und Verteidigungspolitik der Europäischen Union* (2002), pp. 183 and 205.

106   C. von Buttlar, *ESDP – A Regional Effort within the Atlantic Alliance*, in: A. Bodnar et al. (eds), *The Emerging Constitutional Law of the European Union* (2003), p. 391. *Cf.* M. d'Oléon, *The way ahead for European defence cooperation*, in: L. Martin / J. Roper (eds), *Towards a common defence policy* (1995), p. 111: 'At present, WEU provides all its members with an 'all for one' assurance in the event of aggression, as does the Alliance in a more credible but less contractual way'.

107   E.g. K. Ipsen, *Rechtsgrundlagen* (1967), p. 174

108   NATO Ministerial Communiqué, Athens 4–6 May 1962, http://www.nato.int/docu/comm/49–95/c620504a.htm (visited 06/05/04) [emphasis added].

Despite the various changes that the nature of the obligation of Art. 5 has undergone since the end of the Cold War,[109] it is still undoubtedly the political backbone of the Alliance, without which it would collapse instantly,[110] as is seen, for example, in the attitudes prevailing among the new NATO members in Central and Eastern Europe.[111]

Content of Art. 5 in light of other related provisions

Scope of NATO's collective self-defence (Art. 6 NAT)

Traditional collective self-defence as formulated in Art. 51 UN Charter centred on the situation of an attack on the territory of a State. However, Art. 6, para. 2 NAT, in addition to the territory of the member States defined in Art. 6, para. 1, widened the mutual defence obligation for NATO members, to include

> the forces, vessels, or aircraft of any of the Parties, when in or over these territories or any area in Europe in which occupation forces of any of the Parties were stationed on the date when the Treaty entered into force or the Mediterranean Sea or the North Atlantic area north of the Tropic of Cancer.

This took into account the military situation prevailing at the time. The Warsaw Treaty Organisation, being the only other mutual defence pact with comparable capacity at the time, accepted this wide definition in its own practice. Therefore, Art. 6, para. 2 NAT may have contributed to a widening of the customary right of collective self-defence by extending the notion of 'armed attack' to the cases mentioned above.[112] This extension was reflected, by analogy, in Art. 3, para. (d) of the GA Definition of Aggression in 1974.[113]

Alliance structures (Art. 9 NAT)
Art. 5 only contains the basic duty of collective self-defence on a treaty basis. It does not provide for the establishment of a fully-fledged Alliance with an integrated military command.[114] However, Art. 9 NAT makes this possible,[115] without, however, obliging the parties to do so.[116]

---

109   *Cf.* M. d'Oléon, *The way ahead for European defence cooperation*, in: L. Martin / J. Roper (eds), *Towards a common defence policy* (1995), p. 111.

110   P. Cornish, *Partnership in Crisis* (1997), p. 78.

111   See above Chapter 3 (NATO Today). *Cf.* WEU Assembly Doc. 1439, para. 30 *in fine*.

112   *Cf.* A.F. Fernández Tomás, *El Recurso al Artículo Quinto*, 53 REDI 1/2 (2001), pp. 207–8.

113   See above fn. 18.

114   Compare, in contrast, Art. 5 of the Warsaw Pact (219 UNTS 3).

115   See above, Chapter 3 (NATO Today).

116   M. Albright (US Secretary of State), *The Right Balance Will Secure NATO's Future*, Financial Times, 7 Dec. 1998, p. 22: 'the founders of the alliance ... distinguished between

Collective self-defence against a NATO member – the NAT as a 'regional arrangement'?

The difficulty of separating mutual defence pacts from regional arrangements in practice[117] has already been mentioned. It has been argued that nothing in the wording of Art. 5 NAT forbids action against a NATO member, should that member attack another member, by the rest of the members.[118] Such a reading would, however, ignore the systematic position of Article 51 outside Chapter VIII of the UN Charter (notwithstanding its drafting history), and thereby completely blur the fundamental distinction between collective defence and collective security. In addition, ten of NATO's member States are bound by the WEU's Petersberg declaration of 1992 which stated that

> the security guarantees and defence commitments in the Treaties which bind the member States within Western European Union and which bind them within the Atlantic Alliance are mutually reinforcing and will not be invoked [...] in disputes between member States of either of the two organizations.[119]

Considering the difficulty sometimes involved in determining who is the aggressor and who the attacked, such a situation, which is very unlikely today,[120] could throw NATO into great confusion.

Invocation of Article 5 after September 11

Art. 5 was invoked for the first time in its history after the terrorist attacks on the United States on 11 September 2001. This situation was, however, very different from the one which the founding fathers of the Alliance had had in mind.[121] Nevertheless, considering the inherent flexibility of the NAT to provide for future developments,[122] it could perhaps be argued that the difference was not as great as commonly portrayed.

---

what the treaty commits us to and what it permits us to do'.

117   See fn. 59 above. In theory the separation is crystal clear: a mutual defence pact offers protection against an external aggressor (*Außenrichtung*), a regional arrangement for collective security normally does so against an aggressor from within its midst (*Binnenrichtung*).

118   H. Kelsen, *Is the North Atlantic Treaty a Regional Arrangement?*, 45 AJIL (1951), p. 165.

119   Western European Union Council of Ministers, Petersberg Declaration, Bonn, 19 June 1992, III. para. A *in fine*. *Cf*. F. Dehousse / B. Galer, *De Saint-Malo à Feira: Les Enjeux de la Renaissance du Projet de Défense Européenne*, 52 Studia diplomatica (1999), p. 40.

120   The North Atlantic area, including the territories of all NATO member States, has long been argued to constitute a 'Security Community' among which war has become unthinkable. See above Chapter 3 (NATO Today).

121   *Cf*. Statement by the North Atlantic Council, 12 Sept. 2001, NATO Press Release (2001)124.

122   See above Chapter 3 (NATO Today).

Before 11 September 2001, few people had imagined a situation in which the US itself would be at the receiving end of the mutual security pact.[123] Yet, the possibility was also never excluded, due to the reciprocal nature of the commitment.[124] Moreover, the Strategic Concept of 1999 had already acknowledged international terrorism as one of the 'risks of a wider nature' which could elicit responses under Art. 4 NAT.[125] Systematically, action taken by the parties under Art. 4 is designed to precede an invocation of Art. 5 in face of an escalating crisis, and thus directly linked to it.

Invoking Art. 5 was on the minds of political leaders of NATO member States from the very first hours after the attacks. The initiative, however, seems to have come from the United Kingdom, rather than the US itself. On the evening of 11 September 2001, PM Tony Blair telephoned NATO-SG George Robertson (who was his former defence minister) and suggested an invocation of Art. 5.[126] The option was also discussed in an ad hoc meeting in the French foreign ministry that same evening.[127] On 12 September, the NAC issued a statement saying that in the event that it should be established that the terrorist attacks against the US had been directed from abroad, this would be covered by Art. 5.[128] This put the ball in the court of the US to furnish enough evidence in this regard, a task in which the UK again seems to have given some assistance.[129] On 2 October 2001, the US delegation at NATO presented the other allies, in a classified briefing, with evidence that the source of the attacks was the terrorist network Al-Qaida, operating under the protection of the Taliban regime in Afghanistan. The full invocation of Art. 5 was subsequently announced by NATO-SG Robertson.[130] Many official organs of NATO and the member States highlighted the historic symbolism of this decision.[131] Despite this, the concrete measures taken in its implementation seemed very limited, almost token, compared with the massive

---

123   G. Robertson, *An Attack on Us All: NATO's Response to Terrorism*, remarks at the Atlantic Council of the United States, National Press Club, Washington, 10 Oct. 2001, http://www.nato.int/docu/speech/2001/s011010b.htm (visited 30/08/04).

124   *Cf.* Y. Dinstein, *War, Aggression and Self-Defence* (2001), p. 233; *cf.* G. Robertson, speech at the 38th Munich Conference on Security Policy, 3 Feb. 2002, http://www.securityconference.de (visited 24/08/04).

125   NATO Strategic Concept 1999, para. 24. *Cf.* M.A. Goldberg, *Mirage of Defense: Reexamining Article Five of the North Atlantic Treaty after the Terrorist Attacks on the United States*, 26 B.C.Int'l & Comp. L. Rev. (Winter 2003), pp. 80–1; see above Chapter 3 (NATO Today).

126   J. Medcalf, *NATO and the Extra-European Challenge* (2002), p. 209; S. Duke, *CESDP and the response to 11 September: Identifying the Weakest Link*, 7 EFAR 2 (2002), p. 162.

127   J. Medcalf, *ibid.*, p. 213.

128   Statement by the North Atlantic Council, 12 Sept. 2001, NATO Press Release (2001)124.

129   A.F. Fernández Tomás, *El Recurso al Artículo Quinto*, 53 REDI 1/2 (2001), p. 214.

130   NATO Update, *Invocation of Article 5 confirmed*, 2 Oct. 2001, http://www.nato.int/docu/update/2001/1001/ e1002a.htm (visited 30/08/04).

131   E.g. Robertson, fn. 124 above.

military capacity at the Alliance's disposal.[132] They consisted in eight measures by the allies:[133]

- enhancing intelligence sharing and cooperation;
- increased mutual assistance in preparing for terrorist counter-attacks to allied support;
- increased security for facilities on US and other allied territory;
- backfill of Allied assets specifically for anti-terrorist operations;
- blanket overflight rights;
- access to ports and airfields, including refuelling, for operations against terrorism;
- deployment of NATO's Standing Naval Force Mediterranean (STANAVFORMED) to the Eastern Mediterranean;
- deployment of five NATO AWACS to the US East Coast, to relieve US aircraft to be deployed in other operations.[134]

As will quickly be recognised, only the last two of those measures are of the kind of response classically understood under collective self-defence.[135] This was very much in line, however, with the US global strategy in its counter-response to the terrorist attacks. After September 11, virtually every collective defence treaty which the US was a party to – not only NATO – was invoked, for example the Rio Treaty and the ANZUS Treaty.[136] Action taken by US allies under those treaties was also mostly non-military or supportive.[137]

---

132   A.F. Fernández Tomás, *El Recurso al Artículo Quinto*, 53 REDI 1/2 (2001), pp. 216 and 218 ('NATO's frustrated protagonism').

133   Statement by NATO-SG G. Robertson, Brussels, 4 Oct. 2001, http://www.nato.int/docu/speech/2001/s011004b.htm (visited 30/08/04), reprinted in: CP 51, p. 155.

134   This deployment was announced in detail four days later, *cf.* Statement by NATO-SG G. Robertson, 8 Oct. 2001, NATO Press Release (2001)138; *cf.* P.D. Wolfowitz, speech at the 38th Munich Conference on Security Policy, 2 Feb. 2002, http://www.securityconference.de (visited 24/08/04).

135   NATO Issues, *Deployment of Forces*, 9 Oct. 2001, http://www.nato.int/terrorism/deployment.htm (visited 30/08/04) w.f.r.

136   J. Medcalf, *NATO and the Extra-European Challenge* (2002), p. 209, n. 48; M.N. Schmitt, *Preemptive Strategies in International Law*, 24 Mich.J.Int'l L. (Winter 2003), pp. 537–8 w.f.r; e.g. ANZUS *Government Invokes ANZUS Treaty – Prime Minister's Press Conference*, 14 Sept. 2001, http://australianpolitics.com/foreign/anzus/01-09-14anzus-invoked.shtml (visited 20/04/04); Rio Treaty: Meeting of Consultation of Ministers of Foreign Affairs, 21 Sept. 2001, OAS Doc. OEA/Ser.F/II.24, RC 24/RES.1/01, http://www.oas.org/OASpage/crisis/RC.24e.htm (visited 20.04.04).

137   E.g. Rio Treaty, *ibid. Cf.* A.D. Botticelli, *The Premier of the North Atlantic Treaty's Article V*, 26 Suffolk Transnat'l L. Rev. (Winter 2002), pp. 71–72.

From a legal standpoint, the invocation of Art. 5 after the terrorist attacks per se met little criticism and was endorsed by most of the scholarship.[138] It was rather the more fundamental question (on which the invocation was legally contingent) whether the attacks really constituted a case justifying self-defence under international law that provoked much debate,[139] particularly, if the question was answered in the affirmative, whether the action taken by the United States and the United Kingdom in Operation *Enduring Freedom* in Afghanistan autumn 2001 conformed with the legal limits of immediacy, proportionality and necessity. As to the first and the third requirement, the fact that no Al-Qaida plans for further attacks could be ascertained, does raise doubts as to the legality of the operation,[140] even if it is certainly more difficult to predict terrorist attacks than conventional ones. A full debate of the legitimacy of anticipatory self-defence against Al-Qaida was avoided by NATO, because of its potential divisiveness for the allies.[141]

However, even NATO's act of the invocation has been questioned occasionally. Firstly, the United States was, from a military point of view, not really in need of any help. Nor, did it want such help as badly as some allies wanted to offer it.[142] Thus, the attacks on the United States are said to be an 'untypical' case of Art. 5 and collective self-defence in general, not offering a good case study for judging whether the

---

138   E.g. U. Schürr, *Der Aufbau einer ESVI* (2003), p. 102. But see a critical appraisal in: C. Stahn, *'Nicaragua is dead, long live Nicaragua' – the Right to Self-defence Under Art. 51 UN Charter and International Terrorism*, in: C. Walter et al. (eds), *Terrorism as a Challenge for National and International Law: Security versus Liberty?* (2003), p. 827 at 849.

139   A.F. Fernández Tomás, *El Recurso al Artículo Quinto*, 53 REDI 1/2 (2001), pp. 209–211; M.E. O'Connell, *Lawful Self-Defense to Terrorism*, 63 U.Pitt.L.Rev. (2001–2), pp. 889–908; M. Byers, *Terrorism, The Use of Force and International Law after 11 September*, 51 ICLQ (2002), pp. 401–414; Y. Arai-Takahashi, *Shifting Boundaries of th Right of Self-Defence – Appraising the Impact of the September 11 Attacks on Jus Ad Bellum*, 36 The International Lawyer (Winter 2002), pp. 1081–1102; A. Randelzhofer, *Article 51*, in: B. Simma (ed.), Charter of the United Nations (2002), p. 802, MN 34–35; C. Stahn, *International Law at a Crossroads? – The Impact of September 11*, 62 HJIL (2002), pp. 211–238 w.f.r.; J. Quigley, *The Afghanistan War and Self-Defense*, Valp. U. L. Rev. (Spring 2003), pp. 541–562; G.K. Walker, *The lawfulness of Operation Enduring Freedom's Self-Defense Responses*, Valp. U. L. Rev. (Spring 2003), pp. 489–540; U. Schürr, *ibid.*, pp. 103–6; H. Neuhold, *Law and Force in International Relations – European and American Positions*, 64 HJIL (2004), p. 263 at 271 w.f.r.

140   A.D. Botticelli, *The Premier of the North Atlantic Treaty's Article V*, 26 Suffolk Transnat'l L. Rev. (Winter 2002), pp. 74–5; *cf.* A. González Bondia, *La OTAN y la crisis del once de septiembre*, OBS Working Papers, Breves 13/2001, http://selene.uab.es/_cs_iuee_/catala/obs/Working%20Papers/breveSito.htm (visited 16/01/2003).

141   A NATO official commented that a debate on pre-emptive strikes 'would destroy us because it would divide us beyond repair' (cited in: J. Dempsey, *America's Security Strategy: NATO challenged to make radical shift in principles and practices*, Financial Times, 21 Sept. 2002, p. 9).

142   On this point, see immediately below.

obligation really worked.[143] Secondly, according to Art. 5, the obligation of mutual assistance operates automatically. There is no need for it to be formally 'invoked'.[144] Thirdly, NATO did not attribute responsibility for the attacks of Al-Qaida to the Taliban, which would have included addressing the question of the degree of a government's involvement in attacks by militarily active groups.[145] The meeting on 2 October 2001 which produced the evidence remained classified. And fourthly, NATO's 'war against terrorism' in general went very far and was not checked at every instance against the strict requirements of self-defence in international law.[146]

Politically, it has likewise been remarked repeatedly that, for all the fanfare and symbolism of the first-time invocation of Art. 5, the United States did not need any of the help, and in truth also did not want it.[147] From an operational point of view, NATO played no role at all in the main military reaction to the attacks on the United States, which consisted in Operation *Enduring Freedom*. Only the United Kingdom, and to a very limited degree France, played any role in the fighting there.[148] Other limited supportive military contributions (such as repairing airfields and contributing to supply lines in bases in and around Afghanistan, as well as naval-based military support from the Indian Ocean and the Persian Gulf) were made by Belgium, Italy, the Netherlands, Norway, Poland and Spain.[149] They could still reasonably be counted as action under Art. 5.[150] The bulk of the allies' activity in Afghanistan, however, consisted in post-conflict peacekeeping and humanitarian aid.[151] Such activity does not fall under the collective self-defence of Art. 5. The result of this gap between the formal invocation of Art. 5 and its relatively meagre implementation in fact has been an impression

---

143   M.A. Goldberg, *Mirage of Defense* (2003), p. 92.

144   A. Siedschlag, *Für das Realitätsprinzip: Eine Kritik von Bündnisfall-Politik und Kreuzzugs-Doktrin als Reaktion auf die Terrorangriffe des 11. September*, 32 WeltTrends (2001) (cited in: O. Theiler, *Die NATO im Umbruch* (2003), p. 10, n.7).

145   A. González Bondia, *La OTAN y la crisis del once de septiembre*, OBS Working Papers, Breves 13/2001.

146   *Ibid.*

147   H. Neuhold, *Transatlantic Turbulences: Rift or Ripples?*, 8 EFAR (2003), p. 464; *cf.* J. Medcalf, *NATO and the Extra-European Challenge* (2002), pp. 210–1 and 221–2; M.A. Goldberg, *Mirage of Defense* (2003), p. 90; H. Neuhold, *Law and Force in International Relations – European and American Positions*, 64 HJIL (2004), p. 263 at 271.

148   US Mission to NATO, *NATO and other Allied Contributions to the War Against Terrorism*, http://nato.usmission.gov/allies.htm (visited 02/04/04) w.f.r.

149   *Ibid.* Some allies were not even asked for any help (J. Medcalf, *NATO and the Extra-European Challenge* (2002), p. 217). Hence, the claim on the NATO homepage that 'most of the 19 NATO Allies have had forces directly involved in operation '*Enduring Freedom*' seems somewhat overstated (NATO Issues, *NATO's contribution to the fight against terrorism*, http://www.nato.int/terrorism/index.htm (visited 30/08/04).

150   It should be remarked, however, that the most important contributions in this respect, e.g. local airbases, came from non-NATO countries in the geographical proximity of Afghanistan such as Pakistan and countries from Central Asia.

151   The remaining skirmishes with dispersed Taliban units were conducted by US forces separately from Alliance structures.

that, in the long run, the collective self-defence function of Art. 5 was not politically strengthened by Operation *Enduring Freedom*, rather the opposite. Its deterrent effect on Al-Qaida was limited (compared to the effect it would have had on a conventional foe) because terrorists are not dissuaded by the prospect of death.[152]

Nevertheless, at least in the short term, the invocation did improve the public's perception of NATO, it arguably reinvigorated the alliance's solidarity,[153] and it widened the scope of its collective defence tasks beyond Europe.[154] It is also rightly pointed out that, despite NATO's limited role in Afghanistan, Art. 5 contains nothing else than the duty to *offer* aid and assistance, not the duty to *accept* it.[155] There was also criticism that the flexible obligation in Art. 5 ('such action as it deems necessary') was a legal loophole which could come to haunt the US more than forty years after it had been included at its insistence.[156] The wide qualitative spectrum of allied support given to the US reflects just this flexibility, but in a positive way. The relative lack of NATO action in the Afghanistan campaign may also be explained by the fact that the military machine of NATO, which had worked well in conflicts in its geographical vicinity,[157] was not so well adapted for quick[158] and large-scale deployment in a far-away theatre.[159]

All these different considerations cannot, however, detract from the fundamental fact that Art. 5, in the only instance it was ever used, did not make much of a difference.

COLLECTIVE SELF-DEFENCE IN THE EUROPEAN UNION

This part describes collective self-defence in the context of the EU, traced from its historical origins until the current mutual defence clause in Art. I-41, para. 7 of the Treaty establishing a Constitution for Europe (6 August 2004, CIG 87/04). In terms of terminology it must be noted that, in the TEU, collective self-defence is called 'common defence'. Inofficially, 'mutual defence' is more often employed. In the view of this author, the three terms are synonymous, at least for the purpose of the discussion of collective self-defence in the EU framework.[160]

---

152 A.D. Botticelli, *The Premier of the North Atlantic Treaty's Article V*, 26 Suffolk Transnat'l L. Rev. (Winter 2002), p. 74.

153 *Cf. Ibid.*, p. 53.

154 J. Medcalf, *NATO and the Extra-European Challenge* (2002), p. 241

155 *Cf. ibid.*, p. 220.

156 M.A. Goldberg, *Mirage of Defense* (2003), p. 90–91; A.F. Fernández Tomás, *El Recurso al Artículo Quinto,* 53 REDI 1/2 (2001), p. 212.

157 Many of the airstrikes in Bosnia were flown out of airbases in Germany or Italy.

158 NATO did contribute military planning for the Gulf War of 1991, but the preparation phase in that case was significantly longer than in Operation *Enduring Freedom.*

159 *Cf.* A.F. Fernández Tomás, *El Recurso al Artículo Quinto,* 53 REDI 1/2 (2001), pp. 221 and 225. This deficiency had been pointed out already after the Washington Summit of April 1999, *cf.* F. Boland, *NATO's Defence Capabilities Initiative – Preparing for future challenges*, NATO Review (Summer 1999), p. 26 at 27.

160 *Cf.* M. Reichard, *The Madrid terrorist attacks*, 7 ZEuS 2 (2004), p. 318, n.15; *contra* am. N. Pereira (Rapp.), *Security policy in an enlarged Europe – a Contribution to the*

History

> What I am advocating is a Western European military alliance, with appropriate machinery
> attached to it. ... it would be an alliance within an alliance, preserving the wider structure
> of Nato. There might ultimately be a Western European alliance without Nato, ... but this
> is a matter that we do not have to judge now.[161]

Proposals like Bull's in 1983 – seldom and utopian as they were – were not completely
unknown in Western Europe in the 1980s. They were mostly eschewed, for fear of
putting the vital transatlantic security link at risk. However, they have been at the
back of many a European politician's mind. This became apparent after the Cold
War ended, when the new situation removed the previous lid on such opinions.
During the negotiations leading up the Maastricht Conference in 1991, France and
Germany, in a letter to the EC Presidency in October 1991, insisted on creating a
common foreign and security policy, which 'in the long run would include a *common
defence*'.[162] Realised in Art. J.4 TEU, this introduced a completely new dimension
into the Community framework, a military aspect. This turn was certainly not lost
on the debates which took place before ratification of the Maastricht Treaty in the
national parliaments of member States.[163]

The general idea that the CFSP could include joint defence against potential
threats to the Union had by 1993 taken root in European thinking to such a degree
that the Brussels European Council on 29 October 1993 concluded that:

> European security will, in particular, be directed at reducing risks and uncertainties which
> might endanger the territorial integrity and political independence of the Union and its
> member States.[164]

Even though this statement does not provide for meeting an 'armed attack' or an 'armed
aggression', the reference to the 'territorial integrity and political independence' of
member States is language taken directly from Art. 2, para. 4 UN Charter. The logical
link to self-defence under Art. 51 UN Charter, which is one of the two exceptions
to the rule in Art. 2, para. 4, is thus very close. It was starting to be pointed out
by commentators that a common defence to a certain degree constituted a strategic

---

Convention (WEU Assembly), CONV 661/03, 15 May 2003, paras. 7–8.

    161   H. Bull, *Civilian Power Europe; A Contradiction in Terms?*, in: L. Tsoukalis (ed.),
The European Community – past, present and future (1983), p. 164.

    162   Cited in: A. Menon, *Defence policy and integration in Western Europe*, 17 CSP
(1996), p. 264 at 269 [emphasis added].

    163   WEU Assembly Doc. 1333, *Parliamentary debates on security policy under the
Maastricht Treaty*, Report by Mr. Nuñez (Rapp.), 30 Oct. 1992, e.g. paras. 86, 95 and 99
(Italy), para. 109 (Luxembourg), paras. 129–136 and 145 (Spain), paras. 157–183 (United
Kingdom), paras. 201–2 (Denmark), paras. 210–2 and 214–5 (Ireland).

    164   Extraordinary European Council, Brussels, 28 Oct. 1993, Presidency Conclusions,
2. CFSP, at para. 2, Bull. E.C. 12–1993, at p. 8.

necessity.[165] EU member States had essential and vital interests in common which, the argument continued, should be defended.[166] As a result, it was concluded that 'the EU cannot avoid studying the future of its own collective defence'.[167] If one accepted the realist premise that collective defence is a function of the cohesiveness of state interests, the EU held greater potential than NATO in this regard.[168] Thus, the EC–NATO–EU debate seemed, in the long term, already to tilt 'towards an independent EC defence position'.[169] Nevertheless, it was obvious that Europe's military capacity to sustain such an independent defence capability was still insufficient.[170] The broad consensus was still that the role of territorial defence was one which would be best carried out outside the EU framework.[171]

Nevertheless, as the IGC 1996 drew near, there were calls for some improvement in the Common Defence Policy, indicating that a Common Defence had not been postponed *sine die*.[172] A group of countries led by Germany and France advocated a full integration of the WEU into the EU, with the EU becoming responsible for all aspects of a common security and defence.[173] According to a German proposal, the collective self-defence commitment in Art. V MBT should be included into the EU treaty framework by an amendment of Art. J.4. or by an additional protocol to the TEU.[174] The security function which the EU was to take over from the WEU was subject to NATO's absolute primacy in collective self-defence.[175] To accommodate member States which did not wish to enter into such a strong commitment, it

---

165   A. Collet, *Le Traité de Maastricht de la Défense*, 29 Rev.T.Dr.Eur. (1993), p. 225 at 232.

166   M. d'Oléon / M. Jopp, *The way ahead for European defence cooperation*, in: L. Martin / J. Roper (eds), *Towards a common defence policy* (1995), p. 103.

167   U. Nerlich, *The relationship between a European common defence and NATO, the OSCE and the United Nations*, in: L. Martin / J. Roper (eds) *Towards a common defence policy*, WEU-ISS (1995), p. 82.

168   *Ibid.*, p. 86.

169   D. Desmond, *Ever closer union? an introduction to the European community* (1994), p. 496.

170   G. Bonvicini et al., *Security links in the making* (1996), p. 329.

171   A. Menon, *Defence policy and integration in Western Europe*, 17 CSP (1996), p. 264 at 273.

172   M. d'Oléon / M. Jopp, *The way ahead for European defence cooperation*, in: L. Martin / J. Roper (eds), *Towards a common defence policy* (1995), p. 113.

173   WEU Assembly Doc. 1564, p. 62, at para. 32.

174   Proposed amendments to Article J.4 of the TEU, Letter from Mr Kinkel, Federal Minster for Foreign Affairs of Germany, to Mr van Mierlo, Minister for Foreign Affairs of the Kingdom of the Netherlands [and EU President], reprinted in: WEU Assembly Doc. 1564, p. 83 at 88; *cf.* S. Douglas-Scott, *The Common Foreign and Security Policy of the EU: Reinforcing the European Identity?*, in: *Ibid.*, *Europe's other* (1998), p. 131 at 146.

175   *cf.* A.G. Harryvan / J. van der Harst, *A threat of Rivalry? Dutch Views on European Security Today*, in: M. Dumoulin, *La Communauté européenne de défense, leçons pour demain?* (2000), p. 401 at 417.

was argued that the EU's collective self-defence should best be introduced by a 'flexibility' option.[176] This idea was very contentious.[177]

None of the above proposals were realised in the Amsterdam Treaty of 1997. In the years after Amsterdam most statements by European officials and national politicians made it clear that a common defence in Europe could only continue to be realised under NATO's Art. 5.[178] Defence commitments were not anymore a priority for the EU. Building a crisis management capacity to answer to Balkan-type scenarios was considered more urgent,[179] and this was duly reflected in the Helsinki Headline Goal of December 1999.[180] Nevertheless, the idea of including Art. V MBT into the EU treaty framework – either directly or by a protocol – survived.[181] In the same year of 1999 Teunissen remarked that 'the idea of progress towards a *European defence community* has much support among EU officials, in the European Parliament and among politicians in most of the founder States of the EU.'[182] Such a conclusion,

---

176   The model by the six members who were also full members of the WEU was presented in a proposal to the IGC (CONF/3855/97, 21 March 1997); *cf.* K. Möttölä, *Collective and co-operative security arrangements* (1998), p. 87 at 96, n. 13; WEU Assembly, Draft Recommendation on Maastricht II: the WEU Assembly's proposals for European cooperation on security and defence – reply to the annual report of the Council, reprinted in: WEU Assembly Doc. 1564, p. 52 at 55; *cf.* P. Schmidt, *Zum Verhältnis von GASP, NATO und WEU*, 25 ÖZP 4 (1996), p. 410: Table: 'Kerneuropa' + 'Kollektive Verteidigung' = '*Kern+* oder NATO' [emphasis added].

177   WEU Assembly Doc. 1564, Expl. Memo. (Antretter/Squarcialupi, Rapps.), para. 82, but see also para. 153: 'Your Rapporteurs hope that those EU member states still reluctant to enter into all the obligations a common defence requires will gradually overcome their misgivings.'

178   British-French summit, St-Malo, 3–4 Dec. 1998, Joint Declaration, para. 2; *cf.* already Commissioner H. van den Broek, *Why Europe Needs a Common Foreign and Security Policy*, 1 EFAR (1996), p. 4.

179   German Presidency Paper, Bonn, 24 Feb. 1999, Informal Reflection at WEU on Europe's Security and Defence, II.1., para. 2. *Cf.* generally Chapter 2 (ESDP today).

180   European Council, Helsinki, 10–11 December 1999, Presidency Conclusions, Annex IV, para. 7, CP 47, p. 84; *cf.* A. Deighton, *The Military Security Pool* (2000), p. 47; E. Yesson, *NATO, EU and Russia: Reforming Europe's Security Institutions*, 6 EFAR (2001), pp. 205–6; *cf.* F. Dehousse / B. Galer, *De Saint-Malo à Feira* (1999), p. 1 at 112: 'Sur le plan conceptuel, il est curieux de constater que les États membres semblent mieux s'entendre pour protéger la sécurité d'autres peuples que celle des leurs.'

181   *Cf.* P. Cornish, *Partnership in Crisis* (1997), p. 103; C. Grant, *Can Britain lead in Europe?*, CER (1998), p. 47; Heisbourg, *L'Europe de la défense dans l'Alliance atlantique*, 64 Politique étrangère (1999), p. 219 at 228; P.J. Teunissen, *Strengthening the defence dimension of the EU*, 4 EFAR (1999), p. 335; F. Dehousse / B. Galer, *De Saint-Malo à Feira* (1999), p. 102; G. Gustenau, *GASP – eine Herausforderung für die 'Post-Neutralen'?* (2000), p. 16.

182   P.J. Teunissen, *ibid.*, p. 338 [emphasis added]. It is unknown to this author whether Teunissen's choice of words was deliberate, resuscitating the old historical parallel of the failed European Defence Community in the 1950s. If it was, then that comment must be taken to mean, implicitly, that the cited support of European officials extended also to the creation of a European army (which was part of the EDC treaty).

although appearing prophetic, was in fact not very far off the mark. In 1998, the European Parliament had already passed a resolution pointing out that

> under the terms of Article 51 ... of the United Nations Charter, an organization such as the European Union has a right of individual and collective self-defence and on that basis is entitled to establish a common defence policy.[183]

Further evidence of the state of opinion among EU officials was made public when, on 10 February 2000, Commission President R. Prodi remarked during a visit in Latvia that

> Any attack or aggression against an EU member state would be an attack or aggression against the whole EU: this is the highest guarantee.[184]

The Commission downplayed the importance of Prodi's words, interpreting them to worried MEPs as a 'sense of belonging'.[185] However, as had been pointed out already in 1994,[186] and as the NATO example also shows,[187] it is exactly such a sense of solidarity which underpins a legal commitment to collective self-defence. It is the same goal the Union seeks to achieve in Art. 1 TEU.[188] Prodi's remark was not made accidentally but out of a strongly held belief. It became part of the institutional memory of the EU. This could be seen in the reaction of his spokesman to the Spanish-Moroccan maritime dispute over the Perejil islands in summer 2002 two years later: the President's spokesman deemed the Moroccan incident a threat to EU territory,[189] and thus as a case of European collective self-defence. Council

---

183   Resolution of the European Parliament on the gradual establishment of a common defence policy for the European Union, A4–0171/98, 14 May 1998, para. 5, OJ C 167/190 of 1/6/1998.

184   Reprinted *verbatim* in: *Prodi reassures EU hopefuls on security, cultures*, AFP, 10 Feb. 2000; *President jumps the gun on defence*, European Voice (online edition), Vol. 6, No. 9., 2 March 2000; *Ireland may already be committed to European military strategy*, The Irish Times, 4 March 2000, p. 10.

185   Answer given by Mr Patten on behalf of the Commission to a Written Question (E-3263/00), 30 Nov. 2000, OJ C 174 E/30 of 19.6.2001.

186   Mr. Heathcoat-Amory, Secretary of State for the Foreign Office, *The next step for the Western European Union: a British view*, The World Today, July 1994, p. 133 at 135: 'We have to recognise that common defence is deadly serious. It must be a matter of deeds, not words, of *deep-reaching solidarity*, not simply the highest common denominator – especially at a time when Europe faces new risks and new responsibilities' [emphasis added].

187   See above Chapter 3 (NATO Today).

188   Art. 1 TEU reads: '[The Union's] task shall be to organise, in a manner demonstrating consistency and *solidarity*, relations between the Member States and between their peoples' [emphasis added]. *Cf.* R.A. Wessel, *The State of Affairs in EU Security and Defence Policy: The breakthrough in the Treaty of Nice*, 8 JCSL 2 (2003), p. 265 at 287. On the European solidarity and collective self-defence, see also below at p. 187.

189   J. Monar, *The CFSP and the Leila/Perejil Island* Incident, 7 EFAR (2002), p. 251 at 253; *cf.* P. Koutrakos, *Constitutional Idiosynchrasies and Political Realities: the Emerging*

Secretariat officials also, while touching on European defence in other contexts such as the debate on classified information,[190] were beginning to use illustrative mutual defence scenarios.[191] A similar reaction was seen after September 11 in the (unsuccessful) proposal of the Belgian Presidency, which wanted the EU's statement of support to the US to sound like a commitment to collective defence which would have come close to Art. V MBT.[192]

However, the Nice European Council in December 2000, while incorporating most of the crisis management functions of the WEU into the EU, made 'absolutely no progress on defence'[193] and the Union's priority remained on crisis management during 2001.[194] Despite this, German officials still privately argued that the eventual goal of common defence, as stated in Art. 17 TEU, should not be abandoned in the long term,[195] an opinion which found support in academia.[196]

As far as the new EU candidate States in Central and Eastern Europe were concerned, most of them rejected a common defence for the EU, opting for NATO first in this regard.[197]

Political developments until the European Convention

The goal of creating a collective self-defence obligation, 'common defence' in the terms of Art. 17 TEU, has not been realised to this day,[198] as the European Council

---

Security and Defense Policy of the European Union, 10 Col. J. Eur. L. (2003), p. 86; J. Dempsey, *Assault on islet exposes EU rifts*, Financial Times, 19 July 2002, p. 19.

190   See Chapter 9 (Security of Information).

191   'Just imagine we were putting together a strategy for an EU defense against an attack by Libya.' Council Secretariat official, cited in: *Political Uproar Expected Over New EU Secrecy Code*, International Herald Tribune, 30 Aug. 2000, p. 7.

192   *Cf.* A. Middel / M. Mönninger, *Kein Blanko-Scheck für die USA*, Die Welt (online edition), 24 Nov. 2001.

193   S. Duke, *CESDP: Nice's overtrumped success?*, 6 EFAR (2001), p. 157; *cf.* R. de Wijk, *The Reform of ESDP and EU–NATO Cooperation*, 39 The International Spectator 1 (2004), p. 72.

194   M. Rizzo, *Towards a European Defence Policy*, 36 The International Spectator 3 (2001), p. 50.

195   E.g. M. Kremer / U. Schmalz, *Nach Nizza – Perspektiven der GESVP* (2001), p. 175.

196   E.g. D.M. Groves, *The European Union's Common Foreign, Security and Defense Policy*, BITS Research Report 00.3 (Nov. 2000), p. 29.

197   P.J. Teunissen, *Strengthening the defence dimension of the EU*, EFAR (1999), p. 337.

198   WEU Assembly Doc. 1333, *Parliamentary debates on security policy under the Maastricht Treaty*, Report by Mr. Nuñez (Rapp.), 30 Oct. 1992, para. 215 (debates in Ireland); A. Remiro Brotons, *Construction of European security*, 51 Review of international affairs 1089/90 (2000), p. 2 at 6; S. Bartelt, *Der rechtliche Rahmen für die neue operative Kapazität*

in Seville in June 2002 correctly stated,[199] and as has often been repeated by political and legal scholars alike. In contrast to a European defence *policy*, 'common defence' cannot be framed progressively, that is, on an evolutionary path, but requires an active unanimous decision by the European Council, and a formal treaty amendment including ratification by the national parliaments. Despite this formal barrier, the logic reasoning that without a common defence, the process of European integration would remain unfinished, never stayed far from the surface.[200]

Occasional remarks such as Commission President R. Prodi's in February 2000 raised discussions on how far the sense of European solidarity actually already extended. The old question of *'Mourir pour Dantzig?'*[201] was still mostly answered in the negative,[202] but some were already starting to speak of a de facto collective defence clause.[203] Since French President Mitterrand's suggestion in 1992,[204] there had even been occasional suggestions in French military circles to extend a nuclear deterrent umbrella over the whole of the EU – at a much reduced level, suitable for post-Cold War scenarios.[205] In mid-2002, statements from the EU were very varied

---

der Europäischen Union (2003), pp. 28–9; M. Reichard, *The Madrid terrorist attacks*, 7 ZEuS 2 (2004), p. 320.

199   European Council, Seville, 21–22 June 2002, Presidency Conclusions, Annex IV: Declaration of the European Council, para. 4: 'the Treaty on European Union does not impose any binding mutual defence commitments' (CP 57, p. 75).

200   See above Chapter 2 (ESDP Today). *Cf.* H.H. Mey, *Europäische Sicherheitsinteressen aus der Sicht Deutschlands*, in: M. Meimeth (ed.), *Die Europäische Union auf dem Weg zu einer Gemeinsamen Sicherheits- und Verteidigungspolitik* (1997), at p. 22; S. Blockmans, *A New Crisis Manager at the Horizon – The Case of the European Union*, 13 LJIL (2000), p. 257; C. Layne, *Death Knell for NATO? The Bush Administration Confronts ESDP*, Executive Summary, Cato Institute – Policy Analysis, No. 394 (2001), p. 4; *cf.* U. Schürr, *Der Aufbau einer ESVI* (2003), p. 281; R. Cooper, *The breaking of nations* (2003), p. 171.

201   *Cf.* M. Déat, *Faut-il mourir pour Dantzig?*, L'Oeuvre, 4 May 1939.

202   P. Mallard, *Défense Nationale et Défense Européenne: Deux Notions Compatibles?*, in: S. Vinçon et al., *Défense: quels projets après 2002?*, 57 Défense nationale (2001), p. 82 at 94.

203   P. van Ham, *Politics as Usual: NATO and the EU after 9–11*, in: P. van Ham et al., *Terrorism and Counterterrorism – Insights and Perspectives after September 11*, The Hague, Clingendael Institute, December 2001, p. 52; C. Hill, *The EU's capacity for conflict prevention*, 6 EFAR (2001), p. 321; *cf.* generally M. Reichard, *The Madrid terrorist attacks*, 7 ZEuS 2 (2004), p. 321.

204   J. Klein, *Europäische Sicherheitsinteressen aus der Sicht Frankreichs*, in: M. Meimeth (ed.), *Die Europäische Union auf dem Weg zu einer Gemeinsamen Sicherheits- und Verteidigungspolitik* (1997), p. 37 at 42.

205   F. Mitterrand, 'To imagine European security without a nuclear force is illusory', joint press conference with J. Major and E. Balladur following the France-British summit at Chartres, 18 Nov. 1994 (source: *Franco-British Air Support; London Delays Role in Transport Plane*, Associated Press Worldstream, 18 Nov. 1994); *cf.* G. de Nooy, *Capabilities*, in: L. Martin / J. Roper (eds), *Towards a common defence policy* (1995), pp. 37–50; P. Mallard, *Défense Nationale et Défense Européenne: Deux Notions Compatibles?*, in: S. Vinçon et al.,

on the subject. While the CFSP-HR Javier Solana had regularly issued statements of denial on the topic of collective self-defence since 1999,[206] the European Parliament and individual European leaders such as Belgium's Guy Verhofstadt were by now openly in favour of including a mutual defence clause in the Union's framework.[207] As the general opinion was slowly becoming less hostile to the idea of EU mutual defence, the old idea of including the WEU's existing Art. V mutual defence commitment into the EU re-entered the debate.[208]

'Barnier Report' on defence in the European Convention

The Laeken European Council in 2001 established the European Convention, to draft a European Constitution; part of the Convention was Working Group (WG) VIII on 'Defence'.[209] The mandate of WG VIII was, inter alia, described thus: 'Apart from the Petersberg tasks, what defence remit could be envisaged for the Union?'.[210] In a note to the members of the working group, detailing this mandate to facilitate discussions, Chairman M. Barnier summarised the state of play regarding collective

---

Défense: quels projets après 2002?, 57 Défense nationale (2001), p. 82 at 95; *cf.* T. Marauhn, *Building ESDI* (1996), pp. 76–80. It should not be forgotten that in NATO, the purpose of nuclear weapons are above all political, in prevention, coercion and war, *cf.* F. Dehousse / B. Galer, *De Saint-Malo à Feira* (1999), p. 20.

206   E.g. Speech on 17 Dec. 1999, *The Development of a Common European Security and Defence Policy – The Integration Project of the Next Decade*, reprinted in: A.A. Levasseur / R.E. Scott, *The Law of the European Union: Materials and Cases* (2001), p. 1029; *Id., 'Where does the EU Stand on Common Foreign and Security Policy?'*, Speech at the Forschungsinstitut der Deutschen Gesellschaft für Auswärtige Politik, Berlin, 14 November 2000, CP 47, p. 154; *Id., Defence & Aerospace special report: European defence: the task ahead*, European Voice (online edition), Vol. 7, No. 38, 18 Oct. 2001; *Id., CFSP: The State of the Union*, speech at the Annual Conference of the EU Institute for Security Studies, Paris, 1 July 2002, IV., CP 57, p. 105.

207   European Parliament Report, 'Adoption of the Report on the Progress Achieved in the Implementation of the CFSP', Strasbourg, 26 September 2002, under 'Tendencies of the CFSP in the period 2001–2002 and future initiatives', para. 28, CP 57, p. 124; letter from Guy Verhofstadt, PM of Belgium, to Tony Blair and Jacques Chirac, Brussels, 18 July 2002, CP 57, p. 114.

208   WEU Assembly, Resolution 112 on a European defence policy: a contribution to the Convention, Expl. Memo. (Schloten, Chair & Rapp.), para. 20; WEU Assembly Doc. 1798, 10 Oct. 2002; K. Gerteiser, *Die Sicherheits- und Verteidigungspolitik der Europäischen Union* (2002), Ch. 3 and 4; U. Schürr, *Der Aufbau einer ESVI* (2003), p. 282; J. Herbst, *Peacekeeping by the European Union*, in: A. Bodnar et al. (eds), *The Emerging Constitutional Law of the European Union – German and Polish Perspectives* (2003), p. 438.

209   The state of development of ESDP in mid-2002, centring exclusively on crisis management, would have arguably made it more apt to name the WG 'Security' or perhaps 'Security and Defence'. The fact that 'Defence' was chosen instead thus bears some significance for the subsequent discussions within the WG VIII.

210   See the mandate of WG VIII 'Defence' in CONV 206/02, 19 July 2002, p. 4.

self-defence in Europe: the goal of Art. 17 TEU had not yet been realised, and several EU member States were bound by collective self-defence commitments under Art. 5 and Art. V MBT respectively.[211] In addition, the note suggested that

> The Group should consider the question of whether an undertaking of collective self-defence should be enshrined in the Treaty or in a Protocol annexed thereto, possibly with an 'opting-in' clause for States which might not wish to subscribe to such an undertaking as of now or which might not yet have the capabilities.[212]

As the history above has shown, none of these ideas were entirely new. But they had never gained many followers. It may well be that the first-time absence of an Atlantic framework for the mutual defence debate in the European Convention allowed that debate to seriously consider breaking new ground in this field.[213] Such moves were vociferously rejected by some WG members from some non-aligned countries, and the United Kingdom[214] as well as from Portugal.[215] Members from other countries, particularly some from the Mediterranean and Austria,[216] were in favour of a direct introduction of Art. V MBT or an optional protocol to the same effect, in order to make possible a mutual defence clause in the EU treaty framework. It has been mooted that the support for a mutual defence clause, coming from a traditionally neutral country like Austria, did much to encourage the Chairman to include such an

---

211   CONV 246/02, 10 Sept. 2002.

212   *Ibid.* [italics in the original]. The fact that this paragraph was set in italics is indicative of the highly controversial nature of the suggestion at the time.

213   P. de Schoutheete, *La cohérence par la défense – Une autre lecture de la PESD*, CP 71 (2004), p. 24.

214   E.g. Report of the Select Ctte. on the European Union of the House of Lords (Ld. Tomlinson/ Ld. Maclellan), CONV 710/03, 2 May 2003, pp. 24–5; E. Tuomioja (FM Finland), *Europe needs to work as a whole on defence*, Financial Times, 28 October 2003, p. 23; *Id.. / L.* Freivalds (FM Sweden), *We want a stronger EU security policy*, Dagens Nyheter, 11 November 2003, English translation in: CP 67, p. 429 at 431. Ireland's position in the context of the Convention was made public in two early Contributions by J. Bruton, CONV 27/02, 10 April 2002, p. 61 and CONV 135/02, 20 June 2002, p. 4. For the wider EU context, see only European Council, Seville, 21–22 June 2002, Presidency Conclusions on ESDP, Annex III: National Declaration by Ireland, CP 57, pp. 74–5; *cf.* T.C. Salmon / A.J.K. Shepherd, *Toward a European Army* (2003), p. 80; for background of Ireland's neutrality and ESDP, see R. Doherty, *Ireland, Neutrality and European Security Integration* (2003).

215   *WEU Chairman: to avert divisions EU should not take charge of collective defence*, WEU Assembly Press Release 5/2002, 2 Dec. 2002.

216   E.g. Contr. by L. Dini, CONV 180/02, 9 July 2002, p. 7; *Id.*, CONV 301/02, 26 Sept. 2002, p. 4 at b); Contr. by P. Iaokimidis, CONV 389/02, 7 Nov. 2002, p. 4 at f.; Contr. by M. Giannakou, CONV 463/02, 16 Dec. 2002, CONV 462/02, p. 10; Contr. by H. Farnleitner and R.E. Bösch, CONV 437/02, 28 Nov. 2002, p. 4.

option in his Final Report.[217] Some members of the WG were openly undecided.[218] The most prominent intervention was made by the French and German Foreign Ministers D. de Villepin and J. Fischer (as members of the Convention) on 22 November 2002:

> France and Germany propose that the Member States wishing to do so transfer their current obligations in the framework of the WEU to the EU, using *enhanced co-operation.*[219]

There was nothing different in this proposal from others in the form of a mutual defence clause, except for usage of the concept of 'enhanced cooperation' (known from the TEU[220]). The Final Report of WG VIII, officially dated 16 December 2002, noted the wide divergence of views on mutual defence, but took this idea on board:

> The new Treaty *could* therefore establish a closer type of cooperation on defence, open to all Member States wishing to enter into such a commitment ... [221]

The wording was still cautious (it did after all not say that the future Treaty necessarily *should* include such a commitment), but the intention of the Chairman to steer the general consensus of the WG in this direction was clear enough. In an interview after the release of the Report, Barnier remarked that

> it is important that we have not only economic but also political solidarity. The EU is not a supermarket, and we must be able to protect each other. ...
>
> Defence used to be a taboo area in Europe, for reasons linked to the existence of NATO or of neutral countries. The first task of this working group has been to break the taboos. We succeeded in doing that.[222]

The first reactions from European institutions to the proposals made in the Barnier Report varied, but were mostly positive. The Chairman of the European Parliament's Foreign Affairs Committee welcomed it.[223] The President of the WEU Assembly,

---

217   *Cf.* also P. de Schoutheete, *La cohérence par la défense – Une autre lecture de la PESD*, CP 71 (2004), p. 29.

218   E.g. Contribution by J. Borrel et al., CONV 455/02, 11 Dec. 2002, p. 17 at 20). Spain only came out clearly in favour of EU mutual self-defence in spring 2003, *cf.* Contribution by A. Palacio, CONV 706/03, 29 April 2003, pp. 3–4 (last bullet).

219   CONV 422/02, 22 Nov. 2002, p. 4 [emphasis added; translation by the author].

220   Arts 27a–e TEU (for CFSP), 40a–40b TEU (JHA) and 43–45 TEU (general provisions). On 'enhanced cooperation' under the Convention, see above Chapter 2 (ESDP Today).

221   Final Report of the Working Group VIII – Defence, CONV 461/02, 16 December 2002, para. 63 (CP 57, p. 262) [emphasis added].

222   Cited in: D. Spinant, *Solidarity is strength for defence of member states – but NATO will still call the shots*, European Voice, 12–18 Dec. 2002, p. 8.

223   Letter from the President (No 1), WEU Assembly Press Release 5/2003, 28 Feb. 2003.

traditionally supportive of mutual defence within the EU, found it 'disappointing' because in his opinion it did not go far enough.[224] M. Barnier made clear subsequently that his proposal meant a kind of 'Eurozone for Defence'.[225] He was supported by French military circles[226] and by studies of previous years which had advocated using the concept of enhanced cooperation in defence, as had successfully been done with EMU before.[227] Official reactions from candidate countries in Central and Eastern Europe were more split.[228]

Drafting of Article I-41, para. 7 European Constitution

When the first draft articles on external action in the Constitutional Treaty were issued by the Convention Pracsidium on 23 April 2003,[229] they contained in draft Art. 30(7) a mutual defence clause based in wording on Art. V MBT,[230] as an option to be realised by interested member States under enhanced cooperation, as long as the European Council had not taken the decision to establish a 'common defence'.[231]

---

224   *President of the Assembly 'disappointed' by outcome of Defence working group of the Convention on the Future of Europe*, WEU Assembly Press Release 49/2002, 2 Dec. 2002. The WEU Assembly on the same day called for full collective self-defence clause in the EU in its Res. 111 (2002), and rejected the Franco-German proposal for a flexibility solution (CONV 422/02, see above fn. 221) as 'good intentions' (WEU Assembly, Res. 111 on the role of Europe in a new world order for peace and security – a contribution to the Convention, 2 Dec. 2002).

225   *Michel Barnier: «Eurozone for Defence»*, WEU Assembly Press Release 3/2003, 12 Feb. 2003. The term was used simultaneously for cooperation by some EU member States in both collective self-defence as well as in crisis management (see the 'battle group' concept for EU crisis operations). The areas it was applied to were different, but the conceptual origin (EMU) was the same.

226   P. Morillon, cited in: D. Spinant, *French general calls for EU to develop 'eurozone for defence'*, European Voice (online edition), Vol. 9, No. 12, 27 March 2003. Gen. Morillon had been the commander of the French UNPROFOR regiment deployed in the Bosnian conflict some years before.

227   F. Heisbourg, *New Nato, New Europe, New Division of Labour*, 34 The International Spectator 2 (1999), p. 63 at 70.

228   E.g. negative: Slovakia: Contr. by I. Korčok (Rep. of the Slovak Republic), Brussels, 20 Dec. 2002, http://www.european-convention.eu.int/docs/speeches/6433.pdf (visited 6/9/04); e.g. positive (referring to the Union's general objectives): Bulgaria: Contr. by N. Kutzkova (Rep. of the Bulgarian government), Brussels, 27–28 Feb. 2003, http://www.european-convention.eu.int/docs/speeches/9237.pdf (visited 6/9/04).

229   Draft Articles on external action in the Constitutional Treaty, CONV 685/03, 23 April 2003.

230   See Table 6.1 below.

231   Draft Articles, CONV 685/02, Art. I-30(2). The wording of Art. I-30(2) suggested that the goal of a 'common defence' had moved closer to reality than was the case in Art. 17 TEU. See above Chapter 2 (ESDP Today). It remained essentially unchanged until the final version in CIG 87/04 of 6 Aug. 2004.

The proposed amendments which followed on this draft showed a very wide spectrum – from enthusiastic WG members who wanted to go further and include a full mutual defence clause (binding on all member States), to die-hard Eurosceptics who opposed ESDP as a whole.[232] The Praesidium was accused of including the clause based on a minority opinion in the WG.[233] In a first summary on 4 June 2003 the Convention Secretariat had to admit that there was a preference for deleting the entire paragraph.[234] However, in the next draft of 26 May 2003,[235] all these suggestions (particularly those for deletion), were ignored. The only suggestion taken up concerned possible duplication of the commitment already existing in NATO.[236] This was addressed by inserting a sentence specifying a duty to cooperate with NATO in the execution of mutual defence.[237] The article remained unchanged in the version of the Constitution handed from the Convention to the European Council at Thessaloniki in June 2003.[238]

The resulting draft article of July 2003 was thus a direct realisation of the Franco-German proposal of 22 Nov. 2002,[239] and the agenda of the WG's Chairman. The Praesidium's *dirigiste* manner of riding roughshod over the majority of the opinion in the Working Group and presenting them with *faits accomplis* was certainly not

---

232   Proposed Amendments to draft Art. 40, http://european-convention.eu.int/ amendments.asp? content=30&lang=EN (visited 28/12/03)

–   *for a full mutual defence clause*: J. Voggenhuber and R. Wagener; W. Abitol; C. Muscardini; *cf.* C. Einem.

–   *no changes required*: D. de Villepin; V. Spini; M. Giannakou; G. Fini and F. Speroni; A. Duff et al.; H. Farnleitner; E. Brok et al. (on behalf of the EPP Convention Group); P.S. Inglott; *cf.* Santer et al. (except for territorial limitation).

–   *change 'shall be established' to 'may be established'*: J. Kohout; H. Thorning-Schmidt; L. Queiró.

–   *delete paragraph 7*: E. Lopes et al.; L. Hjelm-Wallén et al.; Mr. Hain (thrice); O. Demiralp; E. Lopes and M. Lobo Antunes; G.M. de Vries and T.J.A.M. de Brujn (twice); H. Hololei; T. Tiilikainen et al.; I. Svensson; T. Tiilikainen et al.; S. Yvonne-Kaufmann; D. Roche; J. Gormley; Mr. Kiljunen; Mr. Kvist; D. Hübner (*and continue using Art. V MBT instead*).

–   *delete whole Article*: S. Kalniete et al.; J.-P. Bonde and E. Seppänen; *Id.* and J. Zahradil; T. Kirkhope MEP; The Earl of Stockton MEP; D. Heathcoat-Amory.

233   Prop. Amend. by Mr. Kiljunen; Mr. Kvist (see above *ibid.*).

234   CONV 779/03, 4 June 2003, p. 20, 'Paragraph 7', 3rd indent.

235   CONV 724/03, 26 May 2003, p. 101 (see Table 6.1 below).

236   Prop. Amend. by E. Lopes et al.; L. Hjelm-Wallén et al.; Mr. Hain (twice); O. Demiralp; E. Lopes and M. Lobo Antunes; G.M. de Vries and T.J.A.M. de Brujn, (see above fn. 234).

237   CONV 724/03, 26 May 2003, pp. 101–2 (see Table 6.1 below)

238   2003/C OJ 169/1, 18 July 2003 (see Table 6.1 below).

239   See above fn. 221.

the most democratic way of achieving it.[240] It did, however, save the Constitution's mutual defence clause from being sunk altogether.

The riposte from the Atlanticist camp of EU governments, who were opposed to anything which might weaken the transatlantic security link, was not long in coming. In September 2003, one month before the opening of the IGC in Rome, the UK foreign minister J. Straw issued a report to Parliament stating

> We will not ... support all the proposals as currently set out in the Convention text. ... We will not agree to anything which is contradictory to, or would replace, the security guarantee established through NATO.[241]

This was a clear rejection of the mutual defence clause in draft Art. 40(7) of the Convention's July text.[242] The British position found broad support among EU candidate countries in Central and Eastern Europe which were to join the Union in the following year.[243] In other member States such as Germany the mutual defence clause already found a large following.[244] The European Parliament stepped up its calls for a full mutual defence clause as provided in Art. V MBT.[245] When the High Representative J. Solana listed the defence-related aspects under discussion in the IGC which were 'no longer controversial' on 5 November 2003, unsurprisingly, the mutual defence clause was not yet among them.[246]

---

240 Such complaints against the Praesidium under V. Giscard d'Estaing were heard from many sides during the European Convention, throughout the entire drafting stage of the Constitution.

241 A Constitutional Treaty for the EU – The British Approach to the European Environmental Conference 2003, Cm5934 (September 2003), p. 38, para. 95.

242 *Cf.* J. Dempsey, *Britain to set out its limits on EU defence*, Financial Times, 3 Sept. 2003, p. 8; C. Yarnoz, *Londres veta una Europa de la Defensa al margen de la Otan*, El País, 6 Sept. 2003, p. 6; J. Blitz, *EU's mutual defence pact to face flak from government*, Financial Times, 9 Sept. 2003, p. 1; M. Woolf / S. Castle, *EU Referendum: Straw tells doubters that EU Constitution is in UK's interests*, The Independent, 10 Sept. 2003; J. Blitz / J. Eaglesham, *UK set to stand firm over Nato link in EU treaty talks*, Financial Times, 10 Sept. 2003; P. Gaupp, *Britische Vorbehalte zur EU-Verfassung*, Neue Zürcher Zeitung, 11 Sept. 2003, p. 11.

243 *Cf. Lithuania's Govt sees EU draft Constitutional Treaty 'acceptable per se'*, Baltic News Service, 25 Sept. 2003; A. Kwasniewski, cited in: P.E., *'No se debe enfrentar la seguridad Europea a la política de la OTAN'*, El País, 1 Oct. 2003, p. 15.

244 E.g. F. Algieri / T. Bauer, *Defining and securing the EU's strategic defence interests – Executive summary*, p. 3, in: C. Giering (ed.), *Der EU-Reformkonvent – Analyse und Dokumentation*, CD-ROM (2003).

245 European Parliament Resolution on the Annual Report from the Council to the European Parliament on the Main Aspects and Basic Choices for CSFP, including the Financial Implications for the General Budget of the European Union, Strasbourg, 23 Oct. 2003, para. 16, CP 67, p. 235 at 240.

246 Summary of interventions by Javier Solana, EU High Representative for the CFSP, on military implications of the European Security Strategy and the Intergovernmental Conference, Brussels, 5 Nov. 2003, Council Doc. S0223/03, pp. 2–3 (CP 67, pp. 251–2).

At the meeting of the EU Foreign Ministers Conclave of the IGC on 27–28 November 2003 in Naples, the Italian Presidency tabled a wholly new draft for the mutual defence clause. Apart from dropping the complicated procedure in old Art. III-214,[247] it contained a 'full' mutual defence clause for the first time without flexibility.[248] This may have been due to a procedural mistake.[249] In any case the proposal was overtaken by events: the grand deal of the 'Big Three' over the European crisis management headquarters[250] demanded a 'watering down'[251] of the language describing the obligation of the member States to come to each other's aid. This meant dispensing with the direct reference to military means,[252] an important departure from the model of Art. V MBT, the provision from which draft Article I-40(7) had originally been inspired. Yet, if the Italian Presidency was 'convinced' that this result from Naples would hold,[253] it had not reckoned with the neutral and non-aligned member States.

Under the previous 'flexibility' version, the neutral and non-aligned member States could, even if they were opposed to mutual defence in principle, still maintain their international security status, by not participating.[254] Sweden and Finland had been against the mutual defence clause all along, and their opposition, together with Ireland's,[255] reached new heights after the Naples conclave.[256] Austria, the only neutral country which had so far supported the clause, came under internal pressure

---

247   The consultation process prior to providing assistance in Art. III-214 had shortly before been criticised as causing delays in an emergency, and thus effectively watering down the mutual defence commitment. *Cf.* WEU Assembly, Res. 117, 22 Oct. 2003, para. 2 at *(v)*, WEU Assembly Doc. A/1837.

248   CIG 52/03 ADD 1, 28 Nov. 2003 (see Table 6.1 below).

249   A.J.K. Bailes, *European defence: What are the arguments about?* (article published in Estonian in the journal 'Diplomaatia', Feb. 2004, English translation on file with the author).

250   See above Chapter 2 (ESDP Today). *Cf.* L. Zecchini, *Paris, Londres et Berlin sont parvenus a un compromis sur la défense européenne*, Le Monde, 29 Nov. 2003, p. 6.

251   C. Grant, *Europe can sell its defence plan to Washington*, Financial Times, 2 Dec. 2003, p. 23.

252   CIG 57/03, 2 Dec. 2003 (CP 67, p. 433).

253   *Cf. Italian Presidency convinced Naples initiative will allow adoption of mutual defence clause*, WEU Assembly Press Release 56/2003, 2 Dec. 2003.

254   Even in this case, however, it is submitted that a neat separation of those institutional structures and activities of ESDP which were related to implementation of the mutual defence clause and those which were not, would have been very difficult in practice, leading the States not opting into it to support it indirectly in the long term.

255   *Irish Minister says Europe does not need mutual defence pact*, WEU Assembly Press Release 59/2003, 3 Dec. 2003.

256   *Prime Minister and President downplay debate on EU defence*, Helsingin Sanomat (International online edition), 25 Sept. 2003; L.H. Pihl, *Sweden and Finland support EU security policy*, EUObserver, 17 Nov. 2003; *Finland's Foreign Ministers: EU should not create new military alliance*, WEU Assembly Press Release 57/2003, 2 Dec. 2003; L. Kirk, *Finland to stay neutral, says minister*, EUObserver, 3 Dec. 2003.

from its parliament[257] and the prospect of a presidential election looming in the next year. As a result, it also joined the neutral bandwagon.[258] On 5 December those four governments tabled an amendment to the Italian Presidency proposal from the Naples conclave, with weakened language,[259] backing up their point with hints that the draft article as contained in that proposal would be impossible to approve by their national legislations.[260]

This proposal from the neutrals was not accepted, but on 9 December the Italian Presidency tabled a new proposal of the Article, adding that the mutual defence clause 'shall not prejudice the specific character of the security and defence policy of certain Member States',[261] agreed language from the old 'Irish formula' contained in Art. 17 TEU. This last draft brought the debate over the mutual defence clause to a successful close. The defence package was never reopened again in the last half year of negotiations over the Constitution, and the text's substance remained the same until the final version in CIG 87/04 of 6 August 2004.[262]

The final agreement by the IGC on the EU mutual defence clause in December 2003 did much to clarify where the EU was heading, and had an immediate impact on the strategic perceptions of actors in the European security debate of every shade and

---

257 *Cf.* L. Kirk, *Austrian Parliament on stand-by during EU summit*, EUObserver, 10 Dec. 2003.

258 *Österreich doch für abgeschwächte EU-Beistandspflicht*, ORF Online News, http://www.orf.at/ticker/132096.html?tmp=19209 (visited 5/12/03). Neutral Austria's position in international security had been subject to some change since joining the EU. An 'Options Report' of the ruling coalition in 1998 had failed to agree on an application for full NATO membership, but had still come out in favour of integrating the WEU into the EU 'including with all rights and obligations in this context'. Since a new coalition took power in February 2000, an EU mutual defence clause had become an official government objective. The Austrian Security and Defence Doctrine of 2001 already stated that 'Austria's status in international law corresponds to that of a non-allied state rather than a neutral state.' These changes in Austrian security policy also began to be noticed at the European level as the mutual defence debate in the European Convention picked up speed. *Cf.* Österreichs Sicherheit – Optionenbericht, GASP, e.g. http://www.oeies.or.at/doku/9802sich8.html (visited 24/08/04); G. Hauser, *Österreich – dauernd neutral?* (2002), pp. 88–90; WEU Assembly Press Release 5/2003, 28 Feb. 2003. Under the present-day 'Schüssel formula' (after W. Schüssel, Austrian PM since 2000), Austria will practise solidarity within the EU, but neutrality in any conflict outside the Union. *Cf.* H. Neuhold, *Außenpolitik und Demokratie: 'Immerwährende' Neutralität durch juristische Mutation?*, in: S. Hammer et al. (eds), *Demokratie und sozialer Rechtsstaat in Europa – Festschrift für Theo Öhlinger* (2004), p. 68 at 88.

259 Letter from Erkki Tuomioja (FM Finland), Brian Cowen (FM Ireland), Benita Ferrero-Waldner (FM Austria) and Laila Freivalds (FM Sweden) to F. Frattini (EU Council President) – IGC 2003 – European Security and Defence Policy, CIG 62/03, 5 Dec. 2003 (CP 67, p. 437); see Table 6.1 below.

260 *Cf.* J. Dempsey, *Challenge to EU plans for defence*, Financial Times, 8 Dec. 2003, p. 7; L. Kirk, *Neutrals protest against mutual defence clause*, EUObserver, 8 Dec. 2003.

261 CIG 60/03 ADD 1, 9 Dec. 2003 (CP 67, p. 449).

262 See Table 6.1 below.

Table 6.1   Drafting history of the mutual defence clause in Article I-41(7) European Constitution

Document	Date	Article No.	Wording (with changes from last version1)
CONV 685/03	23 April 2003	I-30(7)	Until such time as the European Council has acted in accordance with paragraph 2 of this Article, closer cooperation shall be established, in the Union framework, as regards mutual defence. Under this cooperation, if one of the Member States participating in such cooperation is the victim of armed aggression on its territory, the other participating States shall give it aid and assistance by all the means in their power, military or other, in accordance with Article 51 of the United Nations Charter.
CONV 724/03	26 May 2003	I-40(7)	Until such time as the European Council has acted in accordance with paragraph 2 of this Article, closer cooperation shall be established, in the Union framework, as regards mutual defence. Under this cooperation, if one of the Member States participating in such cooperation is the victim of armed aggression on its territory, the other participating States shall give it aid and assistance by all the means in their power, military or other, in accordance with Article 51 of the United Nations Charter. In the execution of closer cooperation on mutual defence, the participating Member States shall work in close cooperation with the North Atlantic Treaty Organisation.
2003/C OJ 169/1	18 July 2003	I-40(7)	[unchanged]
CIG 52/03 ADD 1 (new wording proposed by Italian Presidency)	28 Nov. 2003	I-40(7)	If a Member State is the victim of armed aggression on its territory, the other Member States shall give it aid and assistance by all the means in their power, military or other, in accordance with Article 51 of the United Nations Charter.\n\nCommitments and cooperation in this area shall be consistent with commitments under NATO, which, for those States which are members of it, remains the foundation of their collective defence.

CIG 57/1/03 REV 1	5 Dec. 2003	I-40(7)	If a Member State is the victim of armed aggression on its territory, the other Member States shall give it have towards it an obligation of aid and assistance by all the means in their power, military or other, in accordance with Article 51 of the United Nations Charter. Commitments and cooperation in this area shall be consistent with commitments under NATO, which, for those States which are members of it, remains the foundation of their collective defence and the forum for its implementation.
CIG 62/03 (Proposal by Finland, Ireland, Austria and Sweden) 3	5 Dec. 2003	I-40(7)	If a Member State is the victim of armed aggression on its territory, it may request that the other Member States shall give it aid and assistance by all the means in their power, military or other, in accordance with Article 51 of the United Nations Charter. [2nd para. not cited in this proposal]
CIG 60/03 ADD 1	9 Dec. 2003	I-40(7)	If a Member State is the victim of armed aggression on its territory, the other Member States shall have towards it an obligation of aid and assistance by all the means in their power, in accordance with Article 51 of the United Nations Charter. This shall not prejudice the specific character of the security and defence policy of certain Member States. Commitments and cooperation in this area shall be consistent with commitments under NATO, which, for those States which are members of it, remains the foundation of their collective defence and the forum for its implementation.
CIG 86/04	25 June 2004	I-40(7)	[unchanged]
CIG 87/04	6 Aug. 2004	I-41(7)	[substance unchanged]

colour. For example, the outgoing head of the EU Military Committee suggested, to the alarm of NATO circles,[263] taking the defence clause outside the treaty framework, should the draft Constitution fail.[264] The change in tone from the British defence minister in February 2004 was also noticeable.[265] Some countries in Central and Eastern Europe, having stayed undecided, now started to veer towards support of the mutual defence clause.[266] So did general public opinion in the EU, although this may have had much to do with the Iraq war.[267] Nevertheless, EU mutual defence still has many opponents at the time of writing.

Legal content of EU collective self-defence

Before the European Constitution

Under the TEU, collective self-defence does not exist in the EU.[268] It is a distant future possibility mentioned in Art. 17(1) TEU, cleanly separated from legal reality by the condition of a unanimous decision by the European Council, and subsequent ratification in the member States. In the unlikely case that such a treaty amendment would happen, the European Council would presumably do more than simply declare that a 'common defence' has been established, or that the WEU has been incorporated into the EU,[269] but it would also specify its content in more detail. The current mandate to create a future 'common defence' does not contain any strict conditions in this regard. The only thing which can be said in advance is that Denmark would not participate in such a 'common defence', because it does not participate in ESDP at all, by virtue of Art. 6 of the Protocol on the position of Denmark attached to the Amsterdam Treaty.[270] Hence, judging from the current legal situation under the TEU, the EU's 'common defence' would be realised by 24 member States.

Despite the absence of a mutual defence clause under the TEU in legal terms, it is noticeable that the sense of solidarity among EU member States, and hence

---

263   E.g. D. Bereuter (President of the NATO Parliamentary Assembly), *Division of Labour: NATO, EU Can Separate Missions, Protect Unity*, Defense News, 8 March 2004, available at http://www.nato-pa.int/default.asp?shortcut=478 (visited 23/03/04).

264   L. Kirk, *EU military chief impatient after summit breakdown*, EU Observer, 17 Dec. 2003.

265   G. Hoon (UK Defence Minister), speech at the 40th Munich Security Conference, 7 Feb. 2004: 'European allies in NATO, *and through ESDP*, have a key part to play in our *collective defence* and security' [emphases added].

266   J. Dempsey, *We used to be sandwiched between the big powers*, Financial Times, 29 April 2004, p. 17.

267   P. de Schoutheete, *La cohérence par la défense – Une autre lecture de la PESD*, CP 71 (2004), p. 32.

268   See above p. 196.

269   *Cf.* F. Dehousse/B. Galer, *De Saint-Malo à Feira* (1999), p. 80.

270   Treaty of Amsterdam, Final Act, Protocol on the position of Denmark, OJ C 340, 10. 11. 1997, p. 355.

the political preparedness to assist each other in the hypothetical case of an armed attack[271] has grown further as a result of the debates in the European Convention,[272] confusing as these debates may have been.[273] A Swedish government proposal introducing a defence legislation bill in the Swedish Parliament in mid-December 2004 read in its relevant part:

> It is hardly imaginable that Sweden could remain neutral in case of an armed attack on another EU country. It is likewise hardly imaginable that the other EU members would not act in the same way.[274]

After the European Constitution

After entry into force of the European Constitution as set out in CIG 87/04 of 6 August 2004, the legal content of collective self-defence in the EU would be determined by Art. I-41, para. 7 of the Constitution. Far short of a 'political gesture',[275] this provision can easily be called 'the most important innovation' of the defence package introduced by the European Constitution.[276] The following part shall therefore look at the provision's legal scope, importance and implications.

The main obligation of assistance   The fundamental condition for member State assistance to each other is the existence of an 'armed aggression'. It is a much wider term than the 'armed attack' in Art. 51 UN Charter, Art. 5 NAT or Art. V MBT. In interpreting the meaning of this term, reference may duly be had to the Definition of Aggression by the UN General Assembly of 1974.[277] It has been accepted that this Definition contains useful indications for the term 'armed attack' in Art. 51.[278] Logically, this must be all the more true for the more closely related term of 'armed aggression' which would apply to those cases of aggression where armed force is involved. The difference between an 'armed attack' and an 'armed aggression' is not in the means employed (both involve armed force). It is rather in its intensity, its 'gravity' in the language of the GA's Definition of Aggression, language which was later interpreted by the ICJ Nicaragua Case (1986) as relating also to the 'scale and

---

271   See above p. 173.

272   P. de Schoutheete, *La cohérence par la défense – Une autre lecture de la PESD*, CP 71 (2004), p. 48.

273   *Cf.* J. Howorth, *The European Draft Constitutional Treaty and the Future of the European Defence Initiative: A Question of Flexibility*, 9 EFAR (2004), p. 483 at 495.

274   Austrian Press Agency (APA), *Schwedische Armeereform bringt neue Auslegung der Bündnisfreiheit*, 17 Dec. 2004 [Citation in German translation; translation into English by the author].

275   *Cf.* F. Cameron / G. Qille, *The Future of ESDP*, EPC Working Paper (2004), p. 10.

276   L.F.M. Besselink, *Defence: Old Problems in a New Guise?*, 1 European Constitutional Law Review (2005), p. 21 at 23.

277   See above fn. 18.

278   See above fn. 20.

effects' of the attack in question.[279] If the obligation of EU member States to come to each other's aid is widened to include 'armed aggression' below the threshold of an 'armed attack', then this arguably does much to close the oft-mentioned 'security gap' between Art. 2, para. 4 and Art. 51 UN Charter.[280] But it would do so at the price of running counter to the absolute prohibition of the use of force of Art. 2, para. 4 UN Charter. Given the legal primacy of the UN Charter over all other international instruments provided in its Art. 103 (which also binds all EU member States), this cannot legally happen. The solution must be that, even though Art. I-41, para. 7 as internal European law could oblige EU member States to come to each other's aid in cases of aggression not reaching the threshold of an armed attack, international law effectively prevents it from doing so.

Another important question is whether the assistance given by member States necessarily includes military means. As such wording was included in earlier drafts of Art. I-41, para. 7 but later dropped, the *travaux préparatoires* would arguably lead to an answer in the negative. However, according to the general rules of treaty interpretation (Arts 31 and 32 VCLT) applicable also to the European Constitution, *travaux préparatoires* are only a supplementary means of interpretation to determine the meaning of a provision after examination of its wording and object and purpose have failed to do so. The wording 'shall have towards it an obligation of aid and assistance by all the means in their power' is, however, clear enough: 'obligation' amounts to the same effect as a 'shall' (otherwise it would not be an obligation, but some 'softer' sort of commitment); 'aid and assistance' includes *any* kind of assistance, including military, the choice of which is only limited by what member States happen to have 'in their power'. The existence of such means at a given point in time (including military ones) is something that can be objectively ascertained, although it may perhaps prove difficult in practice. It is not something that may or may not be 'deemed necessary' by their governments according to the priorities of the day.[281] Hence, the obligation to assist in Art. I-41, para. 7 would seem to include also military means wherever they are available to States, despite the lack of an express reference.[282] It seems appropriate to call this wording 'quite robust and virtually constraining'.[283]

The obligation in the first sentence, standing by itself, would include all member States, save for Denmark which, by virtue of a Protocol to the Constitution, does not participate in any actions of the Union which have defence implications.[284]

279   See above fn. 17.

280   See above p. 167.

281   Compare the wording of Art. 5 NAT, *cf.* at p. 175 above.

282   In this sense also A. Marchetti, *Die ESVP nach dem Verfassungsvertrag*, presentation at ZEI Europadialog, Bonn, September 2004 (speaking notes on file with the author).

283   A. Missiroli, *Flexibility for ESDP: What is feasible, What acceptable, What desirable?*, EU-ISS, Institute Note, 26 Jan. 2004.

284   Protocols annexed to the Treaty establishing a Constitution for Europe, Protocol No. 20 on the position of Denmark, Art. 5, CIG 87/04 ADD 1, p. 298 at 302. The Protocol

The Caveat (the old 'Irish formula') – a contradiction? The second sentence of Art. I-41, para. 7 contains a no-prejudice caveat clause qualifying the mutual assistance obligation in favour of 'the specific character of the security and defence policy of certain Member States'.

These words would arguably imply a situation of certain permanence and durability (not changing rapidly according to temporal opinion polls), even if the said 'specific character' can only be determined by internal political processes of a member State. However, it does not elucidate from the ordinary meaning of these words what the 'specific character' exactly refers to, nor is there any hint as to who the 'certain member States' are. The ordinary meaning of the first two sentences of Art. I-41, para. 7 taken together thus cannot be ascertained either from the object and purpose of the article, which is purely collective self-defence, nor from their context (the phrase is found once more in Art.41, para. 2), its systematic place of origin,[285] but without any further hint as to its meaning). The only solution would be to arrive at different levels of commitment for each member State, depending on the 'specific character' (not further defined) of its respective security policy. This solution, while acceptable for crisis management, would seem absurd[286] with regard to mutual defence, because it would lead to a gross asymmetry of military obligations.[287] This solution would directly contradict the very purpose of mutual defence: the 'Three Musketeers' principle that an attack on one State is an attack on all.[288] There is, in the author's view, no room for 'variable geometry' in mutual self-defence. Hence the wording of Art. I-41, para. 7 can well be said to lead 'to a result which is manifestly absurd or unreasonable' (Art. 32 VCLT). As a consequence, one may look to the negotiating history and the circumstances of conclusion of the Article in search of enlightenment. The fact that historically the second sentence was included in order to appease the concerns of the four neutral and non-aligned member States not wanting to be bound by a mutual defence commitment[289] leads to the result that *they* are the 'certain member States' referred to.

Cyprus and Malta are also not members of any other military alliance. They could likewise possibly fall under the exception of the second sentence, but their case is more difficult, because of the dearth of *travaux préparatoires* in their case. These two States were not among the protesters against the mutual defence clause during its drafting process, and hardly participated in the formative debate which lastly led to Art. I-41, para. 7 European Constitution in its current form. Furthermore, at the

---

essentially repeats the content of the Protocol attached to the Amsterdam Treaty (see above fn. 275).

285   That is, the 'Irish formula' of Art. 17 TEU. See the negotiating history of the second sentence of Art. I-41(7) above at p. 194.

286   *Cf.* also P. de Schoutheete, *La cohérence par la défense – Une autre lecture de la PESD*, CP 71 (2004), p. 48.

287   The only alliance in which this was arguably not the case was the Warsaw Pact (see above, p. 172).

288   *Cf.* for NATO, Chapter 3 (NATO Today).

289   Austria, Finland, Ireland and Sweden. See above p. 193.

decisive session of the IGC by foreign ministers on 8 December 2003, neither country appears to have issued any statement concerning the mutual defence clause.[290] The earlier 'Barnier Report' of 16 December 2002, however, indicated that both 'remain non-aligned'.[291]

Malta's status may be possible to be established by looking at the political circumstances prevailing at the time of drafting of the European Constitution. Malta has traditionally been a neutral and non-aligned country,[292] a status which was again reasserted in Declaration No. 35 to the Final Act of the Treaty of Accession to the EU of April 2003.[293] Hence, even though Malta did not participate in the debate on the mutual defence clause, did not protest against it, and did not issue any relevant statement at the IGC, its neutral status can nevertheless be regarded as being sufficiently clear from the outset of the IGC; a conclusion which is supported by the above-mentioned side reference in the Barnier Report. Malta is thus also covered by the neutrals' caveat in the second sentence of Art. I-41, para. 7 European Constitution.

Lastly, the status of Cyprus is the most difficult. Neutrality never seems to have become an issue in the relations of that country with the EU before its accession, nor thereafter. The *avis consultatif* of the European Commission relation to Cyprus' membership application in 1993 did not pronounce itself on this point.[294] Neither does the more recent Protocol on Cyprus of the Final Act of the 2003 Treaty of Accession of the ten new member States.[295] The status of Cyprus is also affected by the existing Treaties of Establishment, of Guarantee and of Alliance of 1960,[296] none of which, however, contains any hint at neutral status for Cyprus. In 1977, a High Level Agreement between the two Presidents of the Northern and Southern Parts, setting guidelines for negotiations, did state the aim of, inter alia, a 'non-

---

290   Written information from the Austrian EU Mission to the author, 7 Sept. 2004.

291   Barnier Report, para. 38 *in fine*, CP 67 p. 255. The language is the same in the French, Spanish and Italian versions; but see the German version which reads 'will continue to have neutrality status' ('*werden weiterhin Neutralitätsstatus haben*').

292   Constitution of Malta, Ch. I, Sec. 1, para. (3): 'Malta is a neutral state'. http://www.oefre.unibe.ch/law/icl/mt00000_.html (visited 29/03/05). But see a critical assessment of Malta's neutrality in: S. Dagron, *La neutralité permanente des Etats européens*, doctoral thesis (Univ. des Saarlandes / Univ. Poitiers, 2003).

293   Final Act to the Treaty of Accession to the European Union 2003, 35. Declaration by the Republic of Malta on neutrality, OJ L 236 of 23/9/2003, p. 982.

294   Commission Opinion on the Application by the Republic of Cyprus for Membership – Extracts, doc/93/5 – 30 June 1993, http://europa.eu.int/comm/enlargement/cyprus/op_06_93/index.htm (visited 14/12/04). *Cf.* S. Dagron, *La neutralité permanente des Etats européens*, doctoral thesis (Univ. des Saarlandes / Univ. Poitiers, 2003), p. 42, n. 153.

295   Protocol No. 10 to Treaty of Accession to the European Union 2003, OJ L 236 of 23/9/2003, p. 955. The Protocol only addresses the question of partition and application of the EU *acquis* on Cyprus.

296   Treaty of Establishment of the Republic of Cyprus (UK, GR, TK, CY), Treaty of Guarantee (UK, GR, TK, CY), Treaty of Alliance (GR, TK, CY), all 16 Aug. 1960, http://www.cypnet.com/.ncyprus/history/republic/ (visited 09/09/04).

aligned federal republic',[297] but this refers to the Non-Aligned Movement and is hardly sufficient evidence of neutrality. As a result of these considerations, Cyprus should not be considered a neutral country. As a consequence, the neutrals' caveat does not apply, and Cyprus is covered by the mutual defence commitment of Art. I-41, para. 7.

As a result, the second sentence offsets and completely neutralises the obligation of the first sentence for five of those six States.[298] The extent of the aid given or received by them, depending on the case, will thus be judged anew from case to case.[299] They are not bound by the mutual defence clause, and cannot as of right call for help from other member States in case of an attack on them.

It will be quickly seen that, the legal result of Art. I-41, para. 7 is in its effects pretty identical to what a 'flexibility version' (contained in earlier drafts[300]) would have achieved. Hence, much of the academic research taken into this option in times before the European Convention,[301] is still useful (as long as the parameters it took for its basis are not different from those in Art. I-41, para. 7). For example, even while a legal obligation to assist an attacked State not participating in the mutual defence clause does not exist, such assistance is politically very likely to be given, because of the strong sense of solidarity existing between EU member States today.[302] The important deterrent function of collective self-defence[303] is thus little diminished.[304]

Moreover, judging from its wording, the term 'certain member States' is arguably apt to include more than the four neutral member States, but also those who see their specific security and defence policy, including mutual defence, realised in NATO.[305] This is quite apart from the consistency clause already contained in the second part of Art. I-41, para. 7. The second sentence is thus a fit-for-all, covering a very broad range of special interests and positions by member States with regard to the mutual

---

297   Regular Report from the Commission on Cyprus' Progress Towards Accession, November 1998, p. 13, http://europa.eu.int/comm/enlargement/report_11_98/pdf/en/cyprus_en.pdf (visited 14/12/04).

298   *Cf.* also A. Missiroli, *Mind the steps: the Constitutional Treaty and beyond*, in: N. Gnesotto (ed.), *EU Security and Defence Policy – The first five years* (2004), EU-ISS, p. 145 at 148; H. Neuhold, *Terminological Ambiguity* (2005), p. 1 at 12; L.F.M. Besselink, *Defence: Old Problems in a New Guise?*, 1 European Constitutional Law Review (2005), p. 21 at 23. *Contra*, more critical, W. Hummer, *Die neue EU als «Militärpakt» - Solidarität – Neutralität - «Irische Klausel»*, 1 EuZ (2005), p. 2 at pp. 4–5.

299   I am indebted to the Austrian EU Mission for this insight.

300   See Table 6.1 above.

301   See e.g. K. Gerteiser, *Die Sicherheits- und Verteidigungspolitik der Europäischen Union* (2002), Ch. 3 and 4; U. Schürr, *Der Aufbau einer ESVI* (2003), p. 282.

302   K. Gerteiser, *Die Sicherheits- und Verteidigungspolitik der Europäischen Union* (2002), p. 243–44; *cf.* above at fn. 205.

303   See above fn. 74.

304   K. Gerteiser, *Die Sicherheits- und Verteidigungspolitik der Europäischen Union* (2002), p. 244.

305   *Cf.* Art. 17(2) *in fine* TEU; Art. I-41(2) *in fine* European Constitution.

defence clause. Its effect on the EU mutual defence clause is therefore that 'explicit caveats or implicit waivers ... now apply to both NATO and non-allied members'.[306] Be this as it may, the question of applying the mutual defence clause is a yes-or-no issue: either it applies (then it applies mutually), or it does not. As with a pregnancy, there is no half-way truth.

Geographical scope   Art. I-41, para. 7 defines the geographical scope of the mutual defence clause as the sum of the territories of the member States. This contrasts to the situation in NATO (Arts 5 and 6 NAT),[307] and is also in opposition to many calls during the drafting process to delimit the scope more narrowly,[308] perhaps similar to the WEU's MBT (Art. V 'in Europe').[309] In light of Art. IV-440(2) European Constitution,[310] an attack on Réunion (a French overseas territory) would necessitate a response by the Netherlands. As the text of the Constitution has already been adopted, the only way to remedy this situation would be a subsequent agreement among the member States (Art. 31(3)(a) VCLT) interpreting the words 'on its territory', lest the interpretation be left to the vagaries of subsequent practice (Art. 31(3)(b) VCLT).

Possible threats and the casus foederis   Where might the 'armed aggression' which Art. I-41, para. 7 envisages come from? In 1995, the answer to this question would have been that, although such a contingency appeared highly improbable,[311] the Russian armed forces were still the standard against which the defence efforts of EU member States needed to be measured.[312] After September 11, the invocation of NATO's Art. 5 raised questions on the meaning of an 'armed attack' in the WEU.[313] These questions would also have a direct bearing on the meaning of Art. I-41, para. 7's

---

306   A. Missiroli, *After the Brussels fiasco – an ESDP without a Constitution, a CFSP without a Foreign Minister?*, EU-ISS Analysis, 15 Jan. 2004, http:/www.iss-eu.org/new/analysis/analy073.html (visited 10/03/04).

307   See above p. 180.

308   E.g. N. Pereira (Rapp.), *Security policy in an enlarged Europe – a Contribution to the Convention* (WEU Assembly), CONV 661/03, 15 May 2003, Expl. Memo., para. 18 at *(iv)*; WEU Assembly, Res. 111 on the role of Europe in a new world order for peace and security – a contribution to the Convention, 2 Dec. 2002, at II. 5; *cf.* U. Schürr, *Der Aufbau einer ESVI* (2003), p. 173; *cf.* already K. Kaiser, *Challenges and contingencies for European defence policy*, in: L. Martin / J. Roper (eds), *Towards a common defence policy* (1995), p. 29 at 30–1; U. Nerlich, *The relationship between a European common defence and NATO, the OSCE and the United* Nations, in: *ibid.*, p. 85.

309   *Cf.* Prop. Amend. to Art. I-40 by J. Santer et al. *in fine* (see above fn. 234).

310   The draft Constitution also applies to some overseas territories of the member States.

311   K. Kaiser, *Challenges and contingencies for European defence policy*, in: L. Martin / J. Roper (eds), *Towards a common defence policy* (1995), p. 29 at 30–1.

312   L. Stainier, *Common interests, values and criteria for action*, in: *ibid.*, p. 13 at 16.

313   *NATO's declaration concerning Article 5 may affect interpretation of Article V of the modified Brussels Treaty*, WEU Assembly Press Release 24/2001, 3 Oct. 2001.

'armed aggression',[314] bringing terrorist attacks conducted or directed from outside the territories of the member States within the scope of this term. However, as was already clear in the drafting process of the Constitution, incidents of such nature are already covered by Art. I-43 (Solidarity clause).[315] Hence, Art. I-41, para. 7 seems to be rather a classical mutual defence provision against conventional military attacks from third States.

When NATO invoked its Art. 5 and thus determined its *casus foederis* for the first time,[316] it did so in a decision of the NAC. Hence, it has been argued that the same role would fall, *mutatis mutandis*, to the European Council in case of Art. I-41, para. 7 European Constitution.[317] However, the same criticisms of an 'invocation' in NATO[318] apply here as well: making the execution of a mutual defence commitment contingent on a decision issued at a formal meeting – as the old Art. III-214 of the Constitution's July 2003 draft still provided[319] – goes entirely against the logic of mutual defence assistance which requires fast action. The fact that the old Art. III-214 was deleted during the drafting process of the Constitution[320] further confirms this view (*cf.* Art. 32 VCLT).

Other points   Whether the EU, as a result of Art. I-41, para. 7 will assume some of the characteristics of a traditional alliance,[321] thus coming close to what the planned but failed European Defence Community of the 1950s wanted to achieve will, if NATO's history is any guide,[322] depend less on the legal provisions of the European Constitution itself, but on external developments. At any rate, the fact that the EU started out as an economic organisation, does not seem to pose any legal barriers for such a future development.[323]

---

314   *Cf.* WEU Assembly, Res. 111 on the role of Europe in a new world order for peace and security – a contribution to the Convention, 2 Dec. 2002, at II.4; but see also N. Pereira (Rapp.), *Security policy in an enlarged Europe – a Contribution to the Convention* (WEU Assembly), CONV 661/03, 15 May 2003, para. 18 *(iii)*.

315   See generally M. Reichard, *The Madrid terrorist attacks*, 7 ZEuS 2 (2004), pp. 324–7; but see also: Letter from the President (No 1), WEU Assembly Press Release 5/2003, 28 Feb. 2003: 'it is *more* than the "solidarity clause" discussed in the European Convention' [emphasis added].

316   See above p. 179.

317   K. Gerteiser, *Die Sicherheits- und Verteidigungspolitik der Europäischen Union* (2002), p. 241.

318   See above fn. 145.

319   Art. III-214 (2), Draft Treaty Establishing a Constitution for Europe, 18 July 2003, OJ C 169/70.

320   See above p. 204.

321   *Cf.* already J. Roper, *Defining a common defence policy and common defence*, in: L. Martin / J. Roper (eds), *Towards a common defence policy* (1995), p. 8.

322   See above Chapter 3 (NATO Today).

323   *Cf.* K. Gerteiser, *Die Sicherheits- und Verteidigungspolitik der Europäischen Union* (2002), p. 243.

An implicit derogation of Art. V of the WEU Brussels Treaty?   The WEU Assembly, traditionally a forum of much debate on European security questions, had maintained throughout the early negotiations over the EU's mutual defence clause that this clause should not turn out weaker than the commitment provided under Art. V MBT.[324] Later, when the first draft came out, the WEU Assembly complained that draft Art. I-40, para. 7 'fell short' of Art. V MBT, and that, as a consequence, it could not replace or derogate from the latter, which would remain in force.[325] Its position remained the same throughout,[326] even though draft Art. I-40, para. 7 underwent significant changes until its final version.[327] The question of whether Art. I-41, para. 7 can indeed replace Art. V MBT relates to the international law of treaties (Art. 59(1)(a) VCLT) and deserves closer attention.[328] In this context it was soon noticed that, in contrast to Art. 17 TEU, the entire draft Art. I-40 did not refer to the WEU,[329] whereby the Constitution would have implicitly recognised the continuation of the existence of that organisation.

Comparison of the contents of both provisions   The WEU Assembly's arguments are evidently based on the premise that as long as there remains any aspect in Art. V MBT which is not regulated in Art. I-41, para. 7 European Constitution, that aspect, however tiny, allows the framework of the MBT as a whole to continue to stand from a legal point of view. It would therefore seem appropriate, at this point, to compare the content of the two provisions. For Art. I-41, para. 7 the results of the content analysis above will be utilised.

The first point of divergence is obviously that while Art. V MBT only speaks of an 'armed attack', Art. I-41, para. 7 European Constitution provides for reaction to an 'armed aggression'. However, even if this did constitute a difference in reach (and it is submitted above that it does not[330]), this would leave the entire scope of Art. V MBT covered by Art. I-41, para. 7 European Constitution, because the latter is actually wider.

---

324   WEU Assembly, Res. 111 on the role of Europe in a new world order for peace and security – a contribution to the Convention, 2 Dec. 2002, II.3.; N. Pereira (Rapp.), *Security policy in an enlarged Europe – a Contribution to the Convention* (WEU Assembly), CONV 661/03, 15 May 2003, para. 18 at *(ii)*.

325   E.g. N. Pereira, *ibid.*, para. 14; WEU Assembly, Res. 117, 22 Oct. 2003, para. 2, WEU Assembly Doc. A/1837; *Joint meeting with WEU Permanent Council:* ..., WEU Assembly Press Release 44/2003, 23 Oct. 2003.

326   E.g. *Assembly urges EU Constitution changes on parliaments, mutual changes, NATO*, WEU Assembly Press Release 20/2004, 4 June 2004.

327   See Table 6.1 above.

328   *Cf.* U. Schürr, *Der Aufbau einer ESVI* (2003), p. 66.

329   M. Cremona, *The Draft Constitutional Treaty: External Relations and External Action*, 40 CMLR (2003), p. 1347 at 1361.

330   For the full argument, see p. 198 above.

A second important point may be seen in the fact that Art. I-41, para. 7 European Constitution does not mention 'military means' like Art. V MBT.[331] However, neither does it exclude them, and in addition it states that member States must do all they *can* to help an attacked fellow member State. This will in virtually all cases involve armed force. The difference between the two provisions is thus negligible.

A third sticking point may be seen in the unusual verb that Art. I-41, para. 7 European Constitution uses to describe the obligation itself: 'have an obligation to', as compared to 'will' in Art. V MBT.[332] The drafting history of Art. I-41, para. 7 European Constitution furthermore suggests that some weakening effect was intended: an earlier draft read 'shall'.[333] However, the term 'obligation', even if unusual treaty language, is still unmistakable: it is a binding commitment. There is thus no difference in its legal effect to Art. V's 'will'.

The fourth point arises out of a comparison of the geographical reach of the two articles. While action under Art. V MBT shall only be taken in response to attacks 'in Europe', Art. I-41, para. 7 European Constitution uses 'on [a member State's] territory' without further specification. There are evidently some EU member States which have national territory outside Europe, particularly former colonial powers such as Britain, France and Spain. Taken literally (and considering Art. IV-440, para. 2 European Constitution there is no reason to do otherwise), the mutual defence obligation of Art. I-41, para. 7 European Constitution extends to those overseas territories as well. This is a real difference in scope between Art. V MBT and Art. I-41, para. 7 European Constitution. However, as was the case above, Art. I-41, para. 7 European Constitution actually goes *beyond* Art. V in this respect, thus legally 'eclipsing' the latter's geographical reach. The only way in which this conclusion could be evaded is by interpreting the term 'in Europe' in Art. V MBT to mean more than the parties' *national territory* in Europe, that is, extending perhaps to a case in which a British ship was attacked in the EEZ of any WEU member State (including in its own).[334] In this case there would be a margin of cases covered by Art. V MBT which Art. I-41, para. 7 European Constitution would not cover. But taking a side look at Art. 6, para. 2 NAT,[335] it is to be expected that such an important specification would have been made in the MBT itself, rather than being left to uncertain interpretation of the words 'in Europe'. Hence, 'in Europe' in Art. V MBT means nothing more than the national territories of the WEU member States in Europe (including the territorial sea), and the above conclusion holds.

---

331 It will be remembered from the negotiation history of Art. 5 NAT (see above pp. 172) that this aspect is significant for delimiting the scope of an obligation in any mutual assistance clause.

332 Art. 5 NAT also uses 'will'. In mutual defence clauses the difference between 'will' and 'shall' thus does not seem to be as great as in general international treaty language. *Cf.* Chapter 4 (EU–NATO Institutional Aspects).

333 See Table 6.1 above.

334 *Cf.* Art. 3 (d), Definition of Aggression, see above fn. 18.

335 See above p. 177. The NAT was already in existence when the Brussels Treaty was modified in 1954.

In conclusion, the content of Art. I-41, para. 7 European Constitution seems to be the same as Art. V MBT in some respects, more in others, but falling short in none. The argument of the WEU Assembly above can thus be refuted. However, it remains to be seen whether a derogation has truly taken place according to the law of treaties.

Termination of the WEU Brussels Treaty by conclusion of the European Constitution (Art. 59 VCLT)?   According to Art. 59 VCLT,

> A treaty shall be considered as terminated if all the parties to it conclude a later treaty relating to the same subject-matter and:
>
> (a) it appears from the later treaty or is otherwise established that the parties intended that the matter should be governed by that treaty; ...

Before entering on the problem proper, it would seem advisable to ascertain if 'the subject-matter' and 'the matter' in Art. 59 VCLT mean the same thing. A quick look at the French[336] and Spanish[337] versions of Art. 59 VCLT (*cf.* Art. 33(3) VCLT) reveals that this is indeed the case, as both these versions use the same term respectively, in both instances.

The European Constitution, if it enters into force, will have done so after the MBT. Hence it is possible to consider applying Art. 59 VCLT. The WEU currently has ten States parties, all of whom would also be parties to the Treaty establishing a Constitution for Europe.[338] The subject-matter, collective self-defence, is the same in both. It appears from the European Constitution that the ten WEU countries wanted to regulate the matter of collective self-defence on a clean slate in a new treaty: the words 'Western European Union' or 'WEU' are nowhere mentioned in the entire main text of the European Constitution including Declarations and Annexes, only once in a Protocol on the implementation of Art.I-41, para. 2.[339] Conversely, neither is there any provision in which the ten WEU members would expressly denounce their obligations in the MBT. The question thus seems to hinge on the standard of proof which the word 'appears' in Art. 59 VCLT demands for establishing the intention of the parties to terminate the earlier treaty. P. Reuter rephrases subpara. (a) thus:

> Such an intention may be apparent either from that treaty itself ... or from any other piece of evidence.[340]

---

336   'matière', repr. in: S. Rosenne, *The Law of Treaties – A guide to the legislative history of the Vienna Convention* (1970), p. 311.

337   'materia', *ibid.*

338   The fact that the circle of parties of the later treaty is wider than in the first does not matter as long as all the parties of the first treaty are also present in the later one. *Cf.* T.O. Elias, *The Modern Law of Treaties* (1974), p. 111; P. Reuter, *Introduction to the Law of Treaties* (1995), p. 139; A. Aust, *Modern Treaty Law and Practice* (2000), p. 236.

339   See above Chapter 2 (ESDP Today).

340   P. Reuter, *Introduction to the Law of Treaties* (1995), p. 139.

Going back further in history, this condition seems to have arisen in the Separate Opinion of J. Anzilotti in the 1939 *Electricity Company of Sofia and Bulgaria Case*:

> it is generally agreed that, beside express abrogation, there is also tacit abrogation resulting from the fact that ... the whole matter which formed the subject of [the earlier provisions] is henceforward governed by the new provisions.[341]

A. McNair, writing eight years before the adoption of the VCLT, seemed to assume a higher standard of proof concerning evidence from the later treaty:

> Termination, is, however, most frequently implied simply from the fact that the parties have entered into a later treaty the terms of which are such that one *can only assume* upon comparing the two treaties that they intended to terminate the earlier one.[342]

The drafting history of Art. 59 VCLT shows that the intention of the parties mentioned therein was central to the ILC.[343] An earlier draft even read

> (a) The parties in question have indicated their intention that the matter should thereafter be governed by the later treaty;[344]

The term 'appears' – together with a reference to the preparatory work and the circumstances of conclusion[345] – was introduced by the Special Rapporteur who deemed it desirable to '*amplify* the expression "the parties in question have indicated their intention" by specifying how this intention is to be ascertained'.[346] In other words, 'appears' was introduced to broaden the scope of possible evidence to include the preparatory work of the treaty besides direct interpretations of the parties (which are often absent). This history, then, suggests that the standard of proof demanded by 'appear' in Art. 59 VCLT is not as high as suggested by A. McNair, nor something like 'beyond the shadow of doubt', but closer to something like 'beyond reasonable doubt'. This would still include a careful examination of the statements of the parties and the preparatory work to the later treaty. Logical inferences from some pieces of the preparatory work, such as, *a contrario*, *a maiore ad minus* and so on would seem permissible provided they are employed with care and not out of context.

There are few 'pieces of evidence' available whether the WEU member States wanted to terminate the MBT in concluding the European Constitution. The 'Barnier Report' of 16 Dec. 2002, however, reasonably hints that the option of including a mutual defence clause was chosen in order to allow those member States in favour

---

341   77 PCIJ (1939), Ser. A/B, p. 92; *cf.* 15 YBILC (1963), Vol. II, p. 72.

342   A. McNair, *The Law of Treaties* (1961), p. 508 [emphasis added].

343   E.g. 18 YBILC (1966), Vol. I, Part I, p. 55, para. 55 (Ago); *ibid.*, Vol. II, p. 31 (Comment by Israel).

344   *Ibid.*, Vol. I, Part I, p. 54.

345   This element was later redrafted as 'otherwise established'.

346   *Ibid.*,Vol. II, p. 33, para. 6 [emphasis added].

of such a clause 'to take over the commitments of the WEU Treaty ... within the framework of the Union rather than outside the Union'.[347] In other words, what the drafters evidently wanted to avoid was continuing the unsatisfactory situation of having some member States bound by a European-only mutual defence clause in a framework different from the EU, in effect splitting mutual defence in Europe into three parts.[348] From this it may be inferred that they did not merely want to create a new mutual defence obligation (on top of the two already existing in NATO and the WEU), but to completely replace Art. V MBT by the new provision in the European Constitution. Moreover, the fact that the WEU is never mentioned in the entire European Constitution (save for Protocol No. 24 which is of dubious nature[349]) cannot be by accident, and represents additional evidence that the European Constitution indeed did intend to finally relegate the WEU to history.

In conclusion, should the European Constitution enter into force, its Art. I-41, para. 7 would derogate Art. V MBT. As Art. V is the only provision of the MBT still operable, this would arguably also have the effect of terminating the WEU as a whole. The WEU would have 'completed its purpose',[350] not only for crisis management, but also for the one 'residual function' left to it under the Marseille Declaration of November 2000,[351] that is, mutual defence. Should the European Constitution as a whole fail, EU collective self-defence will only remain a political notion,[352] and Art. V MBT will legally continue to stand.

RELATIONSHIP OF THE EU'S AND NATO'S MUTUAL DEFENCE OBLIGATIONS

Before the European Constitution

Before the entry into force of the European Constitution, collective self-defence does not exist in the EU.[353] In the unlikely case that the European Council takes the unanimous decision to establish a 'common defence' according to Art. 17 TEU, it is hard to ascertain what the relationship of this obligation would be to Art. 5 NAT, as the scope of the 'common defence' thus established would first have to be decided

---

347   Barnier Report, para. 63.
348   *Cf.* N. Pereira (Rapp.), *Security policy in an enlarged Europe – a Contribution to the Convention* (WEU Assembly), CONV 661/03, 15 May 2003, para. 15.
349   See above Chapter 2 (ESDP Today).
350   The term was originally used by the Cologne European Council to denote the future termination of the WEU's functions in crisis management, *cf.* European Council, Cologne, 3–4 June 1999, Declaration of the European Council on Strengthening the Common European Policy on Security and Defence, para. 5, CP 47, p. 42.
351   *Cf.* WEU Ministerial Council, Marseille, 13 Nov. 2000, Marseille Declaration, para. 1, CP 47, p. 147.
352   See above Chapter 2 (ESDP Today).
353   See above p. 197.

in the European Council's decision. In case that the rules on the EU's relationship to NATO concerning the common defence *policy* (that is, in crisis management) are applied *mutatis mutandis* to collective self-defence, Art. 17(1) para. 2 already today contains a clear primacy for mutual defence obligations arising for NATO members out of the NAT.[354] This has often been confirmed by the European Council and other EU meetings stating that 'NATO remains the foundation of the collective defence of its members',[355] a sentence which is even held to be a direct authentic interpretation of Art. 17(1) para. 2 TEU[356] and is also included in the EU–NATO Berlin Plus agreement of December 2002.[357] This primacy of NATO in collective self-defence is in line with Art. 8 NAT which contains a strong conflict clause in favour of NATO,[358] possibly even reaching beyond the area of collective self-defence.[359]

The mutual defence obligation of the EU (whatever form it takes) would thus only exist to the extent that it would not impinge on the overriding NAT. In case of doubt, the spirit of Art. 17 also calls for a preference for the NAT. In effect, only in cases where the NAT is *clearly* not affected would the EU's mutual defence obligation under TEU come into play. This would limit the latter's application to attacks on non-NATO EU member States which, in addition, must not affect the security of any NATO member State (*cf.* Art. 4 NAT). Such cases are in practice hard to conceive.

The problem of 'backdoor security guarantees' would exist before as well as after the entry into force of the European Constitution, therefore its treatment shall be reserved for the following section.

After the European Constitution

As was already clear from its early drafting stages,[360] the mutual defence clause of Art. I-41, para. 7 European Constitution contains a clear preference for collective self-defence to be executed under the NAT wherever that other commitment might be affected. This is

354 C. Hill calls it 'the Treaty's continued genuflections before NATO', *cf. Id.*, *The EU's Capacity for Conflict Prevention*, 6 EFAR (2001), p. 320.

355 E.g. Informal meeting of EU foreign ministers, Eltville, 13–14 March 1999, German proposal, para. 2, CP 47, p. 17 at 18; European Council, Helsinki, 10–11 December 1999, Presidency Conclusions, Annex IV, para. 6, CP 47, p. 84; European Council, Nice, 7–9 Dec. 2000, Presidency Conclusions, Annex VI, Introduction, CP 47, p. 169; *cf.* European Council, Cologne, 3–4 June 1999, Declaration of the European Council on Strengthening the Common European Policy on Security and Defence, para. 5, CP 47, p. 42.

356 M. Álvarez Verdugo, *Consulta y Cooperación entre UE y OTAN* (2002), p. 474.

357 EU–NATO Declaration on ESDP, 16 Dec. 2002, first part, para. 2, 42 ILM 242 (2003).

358 *Cf.* M. Fleuß, *Die operationelle Rolle der WEU in den neunziger Jahren* (1996), p. 95.

359 See above Chapter 5 (NATO Primacy).

360 *Cf.* M. Cremona, *The Draft Constitutional Treaty*, 40 CMLR (2003), p. 1347 at 1361.

clear from the second sentence of the first paragraph (the 'Irish formula' in a new context) and from the second paragraph which states that any action taken under Art. I-41, para. 7 European Constitution must be consistent with NATO and thus codifies the sentence often repeated before by the European Council that 'NATO remains the foundation of the collective defence of its members'.[361] In this primary aspect the situation is little different under the new European Constitution from the situation, described above, which would prevail under the old TEU if the European Council decided to establish a 'common defence'.[362] Art. 8 NAT would in any case remain unchanged and its legal effects on EU mutual defence would also remain the same.

However, even though Art. I-41, para. 7 European Constitution replaces the old mutual defence commitment of Art. V MBT for the former WEU members,[363] it starts on a clean slate, devoid of any of the legal constraints to which that older provision was subjected. This concerns in particular two issues. Firstly, Art. IV MBT required WEU members to work in close cooperation with NATO in the execution of the MBT (including Art. V), and it expressly forbade duplicating NATO's military staffs.[364] Secondly, the Art. V MBT could never be used against a NATO member.[365] The WEU Assembly's calls to include these two restrictions in the new EU mutual defence clause[366] were apparently not heeded. The second problem would seem to be mitigated by virtue of the EU–NATO Berlin Plus agreement of 16 Dec. 2002. This agreement, by incorporating a letter from the EU's High Representative 13 Dec. 2002,[367] also includes the principle that ESDP (and thus the EU's mutual defence clause) will never be used against a NATO member.[368] However, as will be shown below, Berlin Plus is a non-binding agreement.[369] In effect, the EU's mutual defence clause is legally free from both constraints.

Another problem would be founded in the fact that some EU member States protected by the EU mutual defence clause would not be NATO members. If those States would be attacked, other EU member States, who *are* NATO members, would have come to their aid, implicating themselves in the conflict and thus drawing in also the rest of NATO, through Art. 5 NAT. The non-NATO EU members would thus benefit from Art. 5 NAT 'through the back door'. The problem has been known

---

361   See above fn. 360.

362   See above p. 193

363   See above p. 184.

364   It could be argued, however, that even this prohibition was not absolute and did not extend to all aspects the WEU's mutual defence. *Cf.* K. Gerteiser, *Die Sicherheits- und Verteidigungspolitik der Europäischen Union* (2002), p. 206.

365   WEU Petersberg Declaration (1992), see above.

366   E.g. WEU Assembly, Res. 117, 22 Oct. 2003, para. 2 at *(iii)* and *(iv)*, WEU Assembly Doc. A/1837.

367   See below Chapter 8 (Berlin Plus Agreement).

368   See also above Chapter 5 (NATO Primacy). *Cf.* already K. Gerteiser, *Die Sicherheits- und Verteidigungspolitik der Europäischen Union* (2002), p. 224.

369   See below Chapter 8 (Berlin Plus Agreement).

throughout the history of mutual defence guarantees.[370] In the context of discussions over a future EU mutual defence commitment in the mid-1990s it was recognised early on,[371] becoming more acute as ESDP began to take shape.[372] It was argued that any future EU mutual defence clause would need to be concerted with NATO in order to avoid 'backdoor security guarantees'.[373] One solution, suggested by the US in view of the coming EU eastward enlargement[374] and supported occasionally in literature,[375] was that simply no EU member State could participate in a future EU mutual defence clause unless it was also a NATO member. The problem continued to be raised after the IGC had agreed to the final version of the old Art. I-40, para. 7 draft Constitution in Dec. 2003.[376] The text of the final Art. I-41, para. 7 European Constitution evidently offers no solution for it.

The problem may in reality not be as serious in the case of the EU's and NATO's mutual defence clauses. The legal loophole consists of EU member States which are not also NATO members. At the time of writing only Austria, Cyprus, Finland, Ireland, Malta and Sweden fall into this category. Austria,[377] Finland, Ireland, Malta and Sweden do not benefit from the mutual defence guarantee in Art. I-41, para. 7 European Constitution, and hence cannot enter NATO's security guarantee through the back door either. The only country which benefits from NATO's 'backdoor security guarantee' is Cyprus.[378]

---

370 *Cf.* Y. Dinstein, *War, Aggression and Self-Defence* (2001), pp. 231–2.

371 E.g. WEU Assembly Doc. 1439, 10 Nov. 1994, Expl. Memo. (Mr. Soell, Rapp.), para. 108; WEU Assembly Doc. 1564, 9 May 1997, Expl. Memo. (Antretter/Squarcialupi, Rapps.), para. 31, 6th indent.

372 *Cf.* M. Kremer / U. Schmalz, *Nach Nizza – Perspektiven der GESVP* (2001), p. 167 at 169; V. Epping, *Rechtliche Rahmenbedingungen der GASP* (2002), p. 108.

373 K. Möttölä, *Collective and co-operative security arrangements* (1998), p. 87 at 96.

374 C. von Buttlar, *The European Union's Security and Defence Policy – A Regional Effort within the Atlantic Alliance*, in: A. Bodnar et al. (eds), *The Emerging Constitutional Law of the European Union* (2003), p. 387 at 391 w.f.r.

375 E.g. K. Gerteiser, *Die Sicherheits- und Verteidigungspolitik der Europäischen Union* (2002), pp. 208–9.

376 F.S. Larrabee, *ESDP and NATO: Assuring Complementarity* (2004), p. 51 at 62.

377 For the current status of Austria's neutrality under the 'Schüssel formula' see above at fn. 260.

378 See Figure 6.1 below.

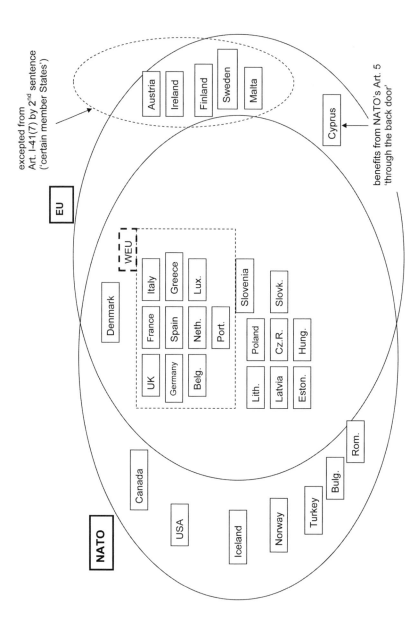

Figure 6.1   EU and NATO states in Europe and North America as covered by Art.5 NAT and Art.I-41(7) European Constitution

Chapter 7

Military Crisis Management

EU RAPID REACTION FORCE AND THE NATO RESPONSE FORCE

EU Rapid Reaction Force (ERRF)

History

As the Balkan experiences showed, the post-Cold War environment required armies markedly different from those used for defence of the national territory; armies capable of reacting fast to humanitarian crises which might erupt far away from that territory were needed. During the 1990s, efforts to address this need had been discussed within the WEU[1] or under NATO's CJTF concept.[2] One effort which came close to realisation was the UN Rapid Reaction Force, planned in 1995 as a heavily-armed standby force to protect vulnerable regular UN peacekeeping personnel suffering damage (including hostage-taking) by the warring parties in the Bosnian civil war.[3] The European Rapid Reaction Force (ERRF) was directly inspired from this force.

Helsinki Headline Goal[4]

The Helsinki European Council on 10–11 December 1999[5] defined five benchmarks for a future ERRF:

1. deployable within 60 days;
2. sustainable for 1 year;

---

1   A. Menon, *Defence policy and integration in Western Europe*, 17 CSP (1996), p. 264 at 269.

2   P. Cornish, *Partnership in Crisis* (1997), pp. 75–6.

3   Letter dated 9 June 1995 from the Secretary-General addressed to the President of the Security Council, UN-Doc. S/1995/470, Annex, pp. 4–5; *cf.* SC-Res. 998, 16 June 1995, para. 9. *Cf.* D.A. Leurdijk, *The Rapid Reaction Force*, International Peacekeeping (Oct.–Nov. 1995), pp. 132–5; *Id.*, *The United Nations and NATO in Former Yugoslavia, 1991–1996* (1996), pp. 67–73.

4   For the wider ESDP background of the Helsinki Headline Goal, see above Chapter 2 (ESDP Today).

5   European Council, Helsinki, 10–11 December 1999, Presidency Conclusions, II. Common European Policy on Security and Defence, para. 28, CP 47, p. 82.

3. forces of up to 60 000 troops;
4. operable by 2003;
5. for the full range of the Petersberg tasks.

These benchmarks were the result of an intense consultation process between the four large member States France, Germany, the UK and Italy.[6] They became known as the 'Helsinki Headline Goal' (HHG).[7] The Headline Goal was not a legal obligation but a 'political commitment' by the member States.[8] The ERRF is also not a standing European army,[9] but a pool of military modules from which an intervention force can be assembled to respond to a humanitarian crisis of the kind foreseen by the Petersberg tasks.[10] The ERRF was conceived as a force for crisis management action abroad, but it was not clear at the beginning how far away from Europe it would reach.[11] Neither the TEU nor the European Council conclusions place any geographical limit on the Union's action.[12] Informally, an operational radius of 4000 km from Brussels was assumed as a planning guideline.[13]

Military capabilities

Most military analysts pointed out already in 2000 that most of the capabilities which the Headline Goal required were unrealistic to realise by 2003, particularly for a

---

6   M. Muschwig, *ESDP: Crisis of Transatlantic Relations* (2002), p. 30; *cf.* Anglo-French summit, London, 25 Nov. 1999, CP 47, p. 77.

7   Some of the benchmarks above, for example the time-frame of 60 days, bear some similarity to the 'Brahimi Report' on the reform of UN peacekeeping (30/90 days). *Cf.* Report of the Panel on Peace Operations, 21 Aug. 2000, UN-Doc. A/55/305-S/2000/809, p. 15, at para. 88.

8   Meeting of European Union defence ministers, Sintra, 28 Feb. 2000, Annex: Elaboration of the Headline Goal – 'Food for Thought' Paper, CP 47, p. 103; European Council, Nice, 7–9 Dec. 2000, Presidency Conclusions, Annex I to Annex VI, CP 47, p. 179; *cf.* G. Quille, *'Battle groups' to strengthen EU military crisis management?*, ESR No. 22 (April 2003).

9   Helsinki European Council, fn. 5 above, para. 27; J. Solana, *Europe handelt dann alleine*, interview in Der Spiegel, 19 June 2000, p. 203; *contra* J. Howorth, *European defence and the changing politics of the EU*, 39 JCMS (2001), p. 768.

10   *Cf.* generally A. Deighton, *The Military Security Pool* (2000); A. Moens, *Developing a European intervention force*, 55 International Journal (1999/2000), p. 263.

11   Meeting of European Union defence ministers, Sintra, 28 Feb. 2000, Annex: Elaboration of the Headline Goal – 'Food for Thought' Paper, CP 47, p. 104; *cf.* A.D. Rotfeld, *Europe: an emerging power* (2001), p. 194.

12   Barnier Report, para. 10, CP 67, p. 251.

13   IISS, The Military Balance 2001/02, International Institute for Security Studies (London), p. 286; *cf. Die EU plant eine Super-Armee*, Die Welt (online edition), 17 Nov. 2000. The 4000 km-limit was taken over from the WEU's illustrative mission profiles for Petersberg Missions and associated scenarios (WEU Doc. C(96)267 of 24 Sept. 1996, classified). *Cf.* M. Kremer / U. Schmalz, *Nach Nizza – Perspektiven der GESVP* (2001), p. 178, n. 55.

campaign on the scale of Kosovo.[14] Consequently, 'capability goals' came to the fore of the subsequent elaboration process for the Headline Goal.[15] The capability needs of the Headline Goal for the various scenarios of the Petersberg tasks were listed in a preliminary catalogue on 22 September 2000 which already identified some 'slots' to be filled for the achievement of the Headline Goal in 2003.[16] On 20–21 November 2000 a first Capabilities Commitment Conference took place where States pledged to commit a total of 100 000 troops, approximately 400 combat aircraft and 100 vessels,[17] at this stage representing still little more than virtual figures.[18] The capability generation process[19] developed into a Capabilities Development Mechanism (CDM), and later into a detailed European Capabilities Action Plan (ECAP)[20] with more than 15 expert panels identifying and reviewing each of the military capability shortfalls (for example airlift) individually.[21]

Political purposes behind the ERRF

A national army serves the political objective to preserve its nation-state. The ERRF was built with a different objective in mind. When strategic goals for the ERRF were formulated,[22] it was clear that the Balkan wars of the 1990s were the relevant yardstick: Europe should in the future be able to do on its own what it could not to in Bosnia.[23] Some said that the EU was committing a mistake by 'preparing for the

---

14   For details see IISS, The Military Balance, *ibid.*, pp. 283–291.

15   E.g. Meeting of European Union defence ministers, Sintra, 28 Feb. 2000, Annex: Elaboration of the Headline Goal – 'Food for Thought' Paper, CP 47, pp. 103–7.

16   Informal meeting of EU defence ministers, Ecouen, 22 Sept. 2000, Presidency Conclusions, CP 47, pp. 143–6.

17   Capabilities Commitment Conference, Brussels, 20–21 Nov. 2000, CP 47, p. 160. The individual national contributions are listed in: Implementation of the Nice Summit decisions in the operational area on the European Security and Defence Policy (ESDP), WEU Assembly Doc. A/1734, 19 June 2001, Appendix I; see also the table in: T. Sköld, *States Pledge Resources for Crisis Management*, ESR, No. 3 (2000), pp. 2–3.

18   L. Zecchini, *Le corps militaire européen de réaction rapide devrait compter 100 000 soldats*, Le Monde (online edition), 22 Nov. 2000.

19   See e.g. European Council, Nice, 7–9 Dec. 2000, Presidency Conclusions, Annex I to Annex VI: Military Capabilities Commitment Declaration, CP 47, pp. 176–185.

20   Conference on EU Capability Improvement, Brussels, 19 Nov. 2001, Statement on European Military Capabilities, paras. 9–12, CP 51, pp. 98–9.

21   See e.g. Meeting of defence ministers, GAERC, Brussels, 19 Nov. 2002, Summary of the intervention by J. Solana, CP 57, p. 147.

22   Such as the Meeting of European Union defence ministers, Sintra, 28 Feb. 2000, Annex: Elaboration of the Headline Goal – 'Food for Thought' Paper, Step 1. Strategic Context, CP 47, pp. 103–4.

23   T.A. Chafos, *The European Union's Rapid Reaction Force...* (2003), p. 44; F.S. Larrabee, *ESDP and NATO: Assuring Complementarity* (2004), p. 51 at 63.

last war'.[24] But such a narrow view is not supported by the larger context in which the ERRF was created. The post-Cold War security environment did contain the phenomenon of 'new wars': not state-to-state conflict over national territory, but internal conflicts fought over ethnicity, religion and identity. Such internal conflicts could affect the security of EU member States, for example through refugee flows. The ERRF was one of the first Western military forces designed exclusively to deal with these 'new wars'.[25] These conflicts are not resolved purely by UN-style classical peacekeeping, but by a much broader and long-term preventive policy which includes also economic and diplomatic means.[26] Among these policy tools, deployment of military forces is only one 'tool in the box', even if it is most likely one of last resort.[27] Another new feature of the post-Cold War security environment, shown for example in the Kosovo war, is that today the gravity of a given humanitarian situation plays a huge role in forming the opinions of national élites to intervene in a given crisis.[28] The primary reason is that public opinion is much more susceptible through the modern media – one of the effects of globalisation. Geographical distance does not matter in this respect. Hence, the hypothetical 4000 km perimeter assumed by the Helsinki Headline Goal may not make much sense, as the EU's mission to the DRC in summer 2003 showed.[29] Although the creation of the ERRF was clearly conditioned by the desire to redeem EU's absence of action in ex-Yugoslavia, it was in addition imbued with the values of a post-modern, European society conscious of living in a globalising world.

However, not all rationales for the ERRF were altruistic ones. There were also reasons inherent in European politics and European integration. As shown in a chapter above, part of the rationale for ESDP was that, during the Kosovo campaign, European governments had found they lacked the capabilities to play 'the part' they wanted to play in the security game on their own continent.[30] An important aim of the ERRF was therefore to develop the capabilities needed to play this part.[31] Another desired effect of improved military capabilities was that, once in existence, they would strengthen the factual basis for 'EU decision-making autonomy' versus

---

24   J. Bolton, *The Threat to NATO's Future*, Financial Times, 11 Feb. 2000, p. 19; M.V. Rasmussen, *Turbulent Neighbourhoods: How to Deploy the EU's Rapid Reaction Force*, 23 CSP 2 (2002), pp. 41 and 48.

25   M.V. Rasmussen, *ibid.*, p. 49

26   'Second-generation' peacekeeping, see above Introduction – On terminology in international security.

27   M.V. Rasmussen, *ibid.*, p. 57

28   *Ibid.*, p. 52

29   See below, p. 249.

30   See above Chapter 2 (ESDP Today).

31   M.V. Rasmussen, *Turbulent Neighbourhoods: How to Deploy the EU's Rapid Reaction Force*, 23 CSP 2 (2002), p. 42

NATO and the United States,[32] and thus help to 'redress the balance in transatlantic relations'.[33]

Past experiences, and direct input from NATO

The ERRF was not built in a vacuum. Practical experience which the UK and France had gained from cooperation on the ground in Bosnia[34] was augmented by institutional knowledge from the CJTF concept.[35] In addition, a WEU audit of assets and capabilities dating from 1996 was fed into the first Headline Goal Force Catalogue in 2000.[36]

NATO was also directly involved in the drawing up of capability goals, utilising experience from its own 'force generation'. A joint EU–NATO 'Ad hoc working group' on collective capabilities began work on 28 July 2000.[37] From that time, NATO experts began contributing military and technical advice to the work of EU experts on the establishment of a catalogue of forces and capabilities for the EU 'Headline Goal Task Force' (HTF), in the format of the 'HTF Plus'.[38]

New Headline Goal 2010

At the Laeken European Council on 14–15 December 2001 the ERRF was declared partly operational, for the less demanding options under the Petersberg tasks.[39]

---

32   European Council, Nice, 7–9 Dec. 2000, Presidency Conclusions, Annex I to Annex VI, CP 47, p. 179; Implementation of the Nice Summit decisions in the operational area on the European Security and Defence Policy (ESDP), WEU Assembly Doc. A/1734, 19 June 2001, paras. 78 and 88.

33   WEU Assembly, Rec. 723 on the EU headline goal and NATO Response Force (NRF), 3 June 2003, Explanatory Memorandum (Rivolta, Rapp.), para. 79, WEU Assembly Doc. A/1825.

34   W. Wallace, *Europe's armies are already quietly integrating*, Financial Times, 16 Feb. 2004, p. 17.

35   O. Theiler, *Gleichberechtigte Partnerschaft*, IFDT (online edition), Vol. 2 (2001), http://www.ifdt.de/0102/Artikel/Theiler.htm (visited 16 March 2004).

36   Meeting of European Union defence ministers, Sintra, 28 Feb. 2000, Annex: Elaboration of the Headline Goal – 'Food for Thought' Paper, CP 47, p. 102. *Cf.* WEU Doc. C(96)267 of 24 Sept. 1996 (classified). The idea of such an audit was already suggested by M. d'Oléon, *The way ahead for European defence integration*, in: L. Martin / J. Roper (eds.) *Towards a common defence policy*, WEU-ISS (1995), p. 108.

37   J. Howorth, *The ultimate challenge* (2000), p. 39.

38   European Council, Nice, 7–9 Dec. 2000, Presidency Conclusions, Annex I to Annex VI, CP 47, p. 183; Implementation of the Nice Summit decisions in the operational area on the European Security and Defence Policy (ESDP), WEU Assembly Doc. A/1734, 19 June 2001, para. 77. IISS, The Military Balance 2001–2002, The International Institute for Strategic Studies (London), p. 284; Opening statement by NATO-SG G. Robertson at the NATO-EU Ministerial Meeting, 30 May 2001, Budapest, NATO Speeches, http://www.nato.int/docu/speech/2001/s010530a.htm (visited 14/12/04).

39   European Council, Laeken, 14–15 Dec. 2001, Presidency Conclusions, Annex II at (A), CP 51, p. 120.

However, as predicted in previous years, the high benchmarks of the Helsinki Headline Goal of December 1999 were not attained by the end of 2003, a recognition which became more and more widespread throughout 2003.[40] The ERRF was thus never declared 'fully' operational as such[41] – this would have implied that it would be able to conduct peace enforcement on the scale of the Kosovo campaign. As a result, a new Headline Goal was developed, reflecting these shortfalls, but also the first practical and institutional experiences which the Union had made in the field of crisis management. Its first elements, particularly the new deadline of 2010, started to crystallise in diverse public statements by national and EU officials in the second half of 2003.[42] The new 'Headline Goal 2010' was approved by the Council on 17 May 2004[43] and adopted by the European Council on 15 June 2004.[44]

Like its predecessor, the Headline Goal 2010 seems to be cast after the experience of European crisis management failures of the Balkan wars in the 1990s.[45] Added to this is the new integrated conceptual approach towards crisis management to which the EU has subscribed in its European Security Strategy (ESS) of December 2003. The Headline Goal 2010 contains key concepts of the ESS such as prevention, the 'mixed toolbox' approach (combining civil and military means as adequate, in a long-term strategy), and close cooperation with the United Nations.[46] Also welded into it are the 'lessons learned' from the first EU-led peacekeeping operations in 2003.[47]

---

40   E.g. Franco-British summit, Le Touquet, 4 February 2003, Declaration on Strengthening European Cooperation in Security and Defence, 3) a), CP 67, p. 36 at 38.

41   Even though, paradoxically, the 1999 Helsinki Headline Goal was declared met in 2003, *cf.* Intervention by J. Solana, Brussels, 5 Nov. 2003, CP 67, p. 250; GAERC meeting with EU defence ministers, Intervention by J. Solana, Brussels, 17 Nov. 2003, CP 67, p. 273.

42   E.g. Informal meeting of EU defence ministers, Rome, 3–4 Oct. 2003, Remarks by J. Solana, CFSP-HR, para. 3, CP 67, p. 231; European Parliament Resolution on the Annual Report from the Council to the European Parliament on the Main Aspects and Basic Choices for CFSP, including the Financial Implications for the General Budget of the European Union, Strasbourg, 23 Oct. 2003, para. 37, CP 67, p. 243; GAERC, Brussels, 17 Nov. 2003, ESDP Conclusions, para. 19, CP 67, p. 260; Franco-British Declaration Strengthening European Cooperation in Security and Defence, London, 24 Nov. 2003, at (a), CP 67, p. 282; European Council, Brussels, 12 Dec. 2003, ESDP Presidency Report, paras. 7 and 25 b., CP 67, pp. 301 and 308.

43   *Cf.* Draft Council Conclusions on ESDP, 14 May 2004, paras. 4–7, Council Doc. 9485/04.

44   European Council, Brussels, 14 June 2004, Presidency Report on ESDP, para. 10 and Annex I, Council Doc. 10547/04 [hereinafter: Headline Goal 2010]. On the Headline Goal 2010 in general, see G. Quille, *Implementing the defence aspects of the European Security Strategy: the Headline Goal 2010*, ESR, No. 23 (2003), pp. 5–7.

45   E.g. 'The availability of effective instruments including military assets will often play a crucial role at the beginning of a crisis,' Headline Goal 2010, para. 1.

46   See also the Joint Declaration on EU–UN cooperation in Crisis Management, New York, 24 Sept. 2003, CP 67, p. 217.

47   Headline Goal 2010, para. 2. When it came to the first military operations in 2003, member States seem to have side-stepped the Helsinki catalogue process in their ad hoc force

Already in its format, the Headline Goal 2010 varies greatly from its predecessor in 1999. Whereas the original Helsinki Headline Goal was encapsulated in a paragraph with five key benchmarks, the Headline Goal 2010 stretches over eight pages. The commitment of member States – still voluntary in nature[48] – is simply a repetition of the original one of 1999: to be able to implement (now until the new deadline of 2010) 'the *whole* spectrum of crisis management operations covered by the Treaty on European Union'.[49] Implied in this repetition is the admission that the original Headline Goal was not achieved as planned.[50] The entire document focuses more on capability creation than on substantive benchmarks, in line with the original stated goal in October 2003 'to shift emphasis *from quantity to quality*'.[51] Part of this shift is a new focus on 'interoperability', 'deployability' and 'sustainability'.[52] Surprisingly, most of the main substantive benchmarks for the ERRF from the Helsinki Headline Goal of 1999 – 50–60 000 troops, within 60 days, sustainable for at least 1 year – are nowhere to be found. It is hard to say whether this constitutes a silent dropping of that previous goal, because the document chooses to focus on the new 'battle group concept': minimum force packages (which can fight alone or as part of a larger operation) of elite troops at high readiness, able to deploy within 10 days of a decision by the EU.[53] This new element of the ERRF is to be attained by 2007.[54] Other benchmarks are only found in the particulars, with regard to individual programmes focusing on special capabilities (for example airlift), called 'milestones'.[55]

The shift away from overall benchmarks is also due to an increased focus on process.[56] This gives the impression that perhaps the process *is* part of the 'Goal' which the document seeks to achieve. However, this does not mean that the document mostly contains empty language. With regard to the armed forces of the member States, for instance, the Headline Goal 2010 has this to say:

> This approach requires Member States to voluntarily transform their forces by progressively developing a high degree of interoperability, both at technical, procedural and conceptual levels. Without prejudice to the prerogatives of Member States over defence matters, a coordinated and coherent development of equipment compatibility, procedures, concepts,

---

generation, *cf.* G. Quille, *The Headline Goal 2010*, ESR, No. 23 (2003), p. 5.

48   *Cf.* Headline Goal 2010, para. 14, 2nd indent.
49   Headline Goal 2010, para. 2 [emphasis added]. This said spectrum refers to the three old Petersberg tasks in Art. 17 TEU, even though an extended list is already contained in the European Constitution. The drafting of the European Constitution and that of the Headline Goal 2010 thus seem to have been entirely separate processes, with one exception: the inclusion of the 'battle groups' in the Headline Goal 2010.
50   *Cf.* also Headline Goal 2010, para. 16.
51   Remarks by J. Solana, fn. 42, para. 2, 2nd indent [emphasis in the original].
52   Headline Goal 2010, para. 3.
53   *Ibid.*, para. 4.
54   *Ibid.*, paras. 5 e) and 16, 5th indent.
55   *Ibid.*, para. 5.
56   *Ibid.*, see e.g. the heading to para. 6.

command arrangements and defence planning is a primary objective. In this regard, commonality of security culture should also be promoted.[57]

This goal of defence integration, carefully calibrated against national sovereignty of the member States, replicates some of NATO's existing efforts. However, if realised, it would arguably even go beyond them. In such a case, a European army, not explicitly rejected by the Headline Goal 2010 in contrast to its predecessor, would seem to move closer to reality. With in-built flexibility for developments further in the future, the Headline Goal 2010 lastly specifies that 'a longer term vision beyond 2010 will be formulated with the objective of identifying trends in future capability developments and requirements and increasing convergence and coherence', a closing sentence which would seem to support the above impression.

In sum, the Headline Goal 2010 of June 2004, while very detailed on the subject of development of military capabilities, has not made it clearer what the ERRF is or what it should be, nor what the record is on achieving its original aims stated in Helsinki five years earlier.[58]

NATO Response Force (NRF)

At the informal meeting of NATO defence ministers in Warsaw on 25 September 2002, US Secretary of Defense D. Rumsfeld proposed to his colleagues the creation of a NATO Response Force, 21 000 troops strong, of all three services (land, sea, air) at a high readiness level, able to deploy within five days without any geographical limitation,[59] for operations around the world lasting 7–30 days.[60] In the wake of September 11, Rumsfeld saw it necessary 'that NATO have a capability that can be deployed in a matter of hours and days; a warfighting capability'.[61] The purpose of the force was above all to be an agile military weapon against asymmetric threats like international terrorism. It would act in high-intensity interventions, either in isolated operations or as a spearhead force for a larger operation involving also other allied troops. Before becoming US official policy, the idea of a NATO 'Spearhead Response Force' had already been discussed among US defence academics.[62]

---

57   Headline Goal 2010, para. 8.

58   *Cf.* also the assessment in F. Cameron / G. Qille, *The Future of ESDP*, EPC Working Paper (2004), pp. 11–13.

59   The proposal thus also went some way towards finally overcoming NATO's 'out of area'/'out of Europe' debate. *Cf.* J. Medcalf, *NATO and the Extra-European Challenge* (2002), p. 267.

60   *Cf.* Press Conference by US Secretary of Defense, D. Rumsfeld, Warsaw, 25 Sept. 2002, http://www.nato.int/docu/speech/2002/s020925c.htm (visited 30/05/03).

61   *Ibid.*

62   E.g. H. Binnendijk / R. Kugler, *Transforming Europe's Forces*, 44 Survival 3 (2002), pp. 117–132.

The project was officially endorsed at NATO's Ministerial Summit in Prague on 21–22 November 2002,[63] but only as a commitment of political character,[64] mirroring the experience of the ERRF.[65] To maintain the high level of readiness required, the 21 000 troop body should be subject to rotation every six months.[66] The Declaration by Heads of State and Government declared that the force should attain an initial operating capability (about 5000) not later than October 2004, reaching full capability two years later, that is, in October 2006.[67] Although formally only a political measure, the NRF was introduced in the Declaration under a general heading of collective self-defence:

> We are determined to deter, disrupt, defend and protect against any attacks on us, in accordance with the Washington Treaty and the Charter of the United Nations. ... We have therefore decided to:
>
> a. Create a NATO Response Force ...[68]

Hence, some of its subsequent activity should be able to be subsumed under Art. 5 NAT.[69]

A centrepiece of the NRF project is to serve as a 'catalyst' (in the words of the Prague Declaration) for military transformation in the armed forces of the allies towards more technologically-capable, smaller, and more mobile forces.[70] The focus on capability development is even more central than in the ERRF. It may be seen as a continuation of the efforts of NATO's earlier Defence Capabilities Initiative (DCI), initiated under SG G. Robertson.[71]

---

63   NATO Summit, Prague, 21–22 Nov. 2002, Declaration by the Heads of State and Government, para. 4.a., CP 57, p. 157.

64   U. Schürr, *Der Aufbau einer ESVI* (2003), p. 250; *cf.* Franco-British Declaration Strengthening European Cooperation in Security and Defence, London, 24 Nov. 2003, CP 67, p. 281.

65   G. Quille, *The Headline Goal 2010*, ESR, No. 23 (2003), p. 5.

66   R. Feist (DSACEUR), *When you come to SHAPE*, NATO's Nations 3/2003, p. 179 at 180; J. Howorth, *ESDP and NAT: Wedlock or Deadlock?*, 38 Coop. & Confl. 3 (2003), p. 235 at 238–9; *cf.* U. Schürr, *Der Aufbau einer ESVI* (2003), p. 249.

67   NATO Summit, Prague, 21–22 Nov. 2002, Declaration by the Heads of State and Government, para. 4.a., CP 57, p. 157.

68   *Ibid.*, para. 4.

69   *Cf.* WEU Assembly, Rec. 723 on the EU headline goal and NATO Response Force (NRF), 3 June 2003, Explanatory Memorandum (Rivolta, Rapp.), para. 49, WEU Assembly Doc. A/1825.

70   NATO Secretary General J. de Hoop Scheffer, First Press Statement, reprinted in: NATO's Nations 4/2003, p. 17; H. Binnendijk / R. Kugler, *Europeans should say 'yes' to Rumsfeld*, International Herald Tribune, 24 Oct. 2002, p. 4; R. de Wijk, *The Reform of ESDP and EU–NATO Cooperation*, 39 The International Spectator 1 (2004), p. 75; *The alliance tries to strike back,* The Economist, 14 June 2003, pp. 28–9.

71   See NATO Summit, 25 April 1999, NATO Press Release NAC-S(99)69.

From its conception, the NRF is designed to serve operations mainly according to US strategic global interests.[72] The United States prefers 'coalitions of the willing' for such operations, a preference which is reflected in the structure of the NRF.[73] This lack of will by the United States to share decision-making control may have initially dampened the incentive for European allies to contribute to the force.[74] Moreover, the general political purpose of the NRF is designed in the logic of the new US concept of security which has been described as 'non-mandated, pre-emptive, frequent',[75] even if the decision on deployment is still taken by the North Atlantic Council as a whole.[76] This logic also seems to clash with some allies' traditions of parliamentary approval before sending troops abroad on any mission.[77]

The direct military use which the United States will derive from the NRF for its future military interventions is likely to be marginal.[78] However, political importance accrues to the project as it gives NATO continued relevance to the United States,[79] a role which the NATO staff probably takes an active part in fostering.[80] SACEUR Gen. J. Jones cast it in positive terms in a statement before the US Senate Armed Services Committee: 'The NRF is truly the transformational vehicle for NATO's military capability in the twenty-first century, and is worthy of our most focused support.'[81] However, if the NRF project failed, NATO would be sidelined by the

---

72   *What is Nato for? Not to be a universal soldier, that's for sure*, The Guardian, 19 Nov. 2002, p. 21; T.A. Chafos, *The European Union's Rapid Reaction Force...* (2003), p. 36.

73   H. Boguslawska, *Le lien transatlantique* (2003), p. 37.

74   *Cf.* P.H. Gordon, *Bridging the Atlantic Divide*, Foreign Affairs (Jan./Feb. 2003), p. 70 at 83.

75   J. Howorth, *ESDP and NATO: Wedlock or Deadlock?*, 38 Coop. & Confl. 3 (2003), p. 235 at 241.

76   *Cf.* H. Binnendijk / R. Kugler, *Europeans should say 'yes' to Rumsfeld*, International Herald Tribune, 24 Oct. 2002, p. 4.

77   *Cf.* J. Dempsey, *Nato launches rapid reaction force*, Financial Times, 16 Oct. 2003, p. 8; *Entsendegesetz – Fraktionen können sich nicht einigen*, Frankfurter Rundschau, 12 Feb. 2004, p. 1.

78   T.A. Chafos, *The European Union's Rapid Reaction Force...* (2003), p. 52; *contra* J. Howorth, *ESDP and NATO: Wedlock or Deadlock?*, 38 Coop. & Confl. 3 (2003), p. 235 at 241, who opines that for 'an overstretched US, there is some potential mileage in the arrangement'.

79   *Cf.* H. Binnendijk / R. Kugler, *Europeans should say 'yes' to Rumsfeld*, International Herald Tribune, 24 Oct. 2002, p. 4; H. Bacia, *Washington schlägt Nato-Eingreiftruppe vor*, Frankfurter Allgemeine Zeitung, 25 Sept. 2002, p. 6; C. Stelzenmüller, *Spitze, aber wofür?*, Die Zeit, 9 Oct. 2003, p. 8.

80   For the phenomenon of a self-preservation instinct of international organisations in international relations theory ('internalism'), see above Chapter 3 (NATO Today).

81   Statement of Gen. J.L. Jones, USMC, Commander, US European Command, before the Senate Armed Services Committee, 4 March 2004, p. 20, http://armed-services.senate. gov/statement /2004/March/Jones.pdf (visited 15/09/04).

United States, and the Alliance would be reduced to a political forum and a pool of forces.[82]

As had already become apparent in mid-2003,[83] the NRF attained its initial operating capability, one year ahead of schedule, officially on 15 October 2003.[84] Allied troops contributions came to 9000, also exceeding the original quantitative objective.[85] Only the low level of participation of US forces was lamented.[86] Shortly before, the allies had conducted a war game in Colorado Springs, which shed somewhat more light on the mission profile for which the NRF was created: an intervention in 2007 in a fictitious Middle Eastern country being threatened by a terrorist insurgency.[87]

In sum, the overall purpose and direction of the NRF thus shows marked differences to the ERRF. The compatibility of the two, in light also of this aspect, will be studied next.

Relationship between the ERRF and the NRF

Both the ERRF and the NRF are based on political commitments made by the member States of the EU and NATO. A legal obligation to commit troops, material and other support does not exist in either case. Where no norms or legal obligations exist, a legal conflict cannot arise. The question of compatibility of the two forces thus seems entirely removed from the legal sphere. It is therefore only open to political and factual inquiry, and it is from this premise that the following analysis departs.

---

82   WEU Assembly, Rec. 723 on the EU headline goal and NATO Response Force (NRF), 3 June 2003, Explanatory Memorandum (Rivolta, Rapp.), para. 72 (*cf.* also paras. 58 and 64), WEU Assembly Doc. A/1825.

83   *NATO plans 5,000-strong strike force*, Reuters UK, 30 May 2003.

84   SHAPE News, *NATO launches Response Force*, 15 Oct. 2003, http://www.nato. int/shape/news /2003/10/i031015.htm (visited 27/10/03).

85   For a list of individual national contributions to the first 2003 tranche of 9000 troops, e.g. NATO's Nations 3/2003, p. 108. The national percentages of these contributions are, however, likely to change until full capacity is reached in 2006. For example, the German contribution, currently at app. 12 %, is likely to rise to app. 23 % in 2006. The French contribution is also expected to rise from currently app. 18 % to app. 25 % in 2006. *Cf. Bundeswehr stellt Großteil der Nato-Eingreiftruppe*, Frankfurter Rundschau, 18 Aug. 2003, p. 5; *Germany ready to offer more than 5,000 troops to new NATO force*, AFP, 18 Aug. 2003; M. Alliot-Marie (French defence minister), speech at the 40th Munich Security Conference, 7 Feb. 2004.

86   *Cf.* WEU Assembly, Rec. 723 on the EU headline goal and NATO Response Force (NRF), 3 June 2003, Preambular para. vi. and para. 4, WEU Assembly Doc. A/1825.

87   P. Spiegel, *War game at Nato talks highlights the need for quick deployment*, Financial Times, 10 Oct. 2003, p. 8.

The NRF's relationship with the ERRF was the key question raised from its beginning,[88] a question the answer to which is not clear.[89]

The most evident problem is that both the ERRF and the NRF draw on the same set of national forces of the member States, forces which are thus in many cases 'double-hatted'.[90] The question of the implications of this double assignment in practice went unanswered for a long time.[91] What would happen if, for example, NATO wanted to engage in an international military operation against terrorism, using the NATO Response Force (NRF) while the EU at the same time planned to engage in a peace-enforcement action in its near abroad, using the Rapid Reaction Force (ERRF)? The two organisations would then find themselves in political competition for the same military resources,[92] rendering their operations mutually exclusive. Solutions varied. A well-designed rotation system between the two forces might be a way around this problem.[93] Similar discussions have already been held in the EU–NATO Capability Group, about the coherence of respective capability criteria of the EU Battle Groups to the NRF.[94] But then the question could easily be put, from a technical point of view, why the capabilities of the two forces should not

---

88   J. Howorth, *ESDP and NATO: Wedlock or Deadlock?*, 38 Coop. & Confl. 3 (2003), p. 240; ; F.S. Larrabee, *ESDP and NATO: Assuring Complementarity* (2004), p. 51 at 64; R. de Wijk, *The Reform of ESDP and EU–NATO Cooperation*, 39 The International Spectator 1 (2004), p. 71 at 75.

89   T.C. Salmon / A.J.K. Shepherd, *Toward a European Army* (2003), p. 173; A. Monaco, *EU and NATO: Competition or Cooperation?*, in: A. Weidemann/ A. Simon (2003), p. 40 at 44.

90   Contr. from S.-Y. Kaufmann to the European Convention, CONV. 681/03, 11 April 2003; p. 9; *The alliance tries to strike back,* The Economist, 14 June 2003, p. 28 at 29; D. Hamilton, *Three Strategic Challenges for a Global Transatlantic Partnership*, 8 EFAR (2003), p. 543 at 549; M. Walker, *The UK Armed Forces and NATO*, NATO's Nations 4/2003, p. 40; Informal meeting of EU defence ministers, Rome, 3–4 Oct. 2003, Remarks by J. Solana, CFSP-HR, para. 10, CP 67, p. 232; *cf.* Preliminary Draft Reply to Written Question E-0334/03 put by C. Muscarini, p. 3, Council Doc. 7881/03, 31 March 2003; K. Feldmayer, *Kein Gestaltungsspielraum für Struck*, Frankfurter Allgemeine Zeitung, 19 Sept. 2003, p. 5; J.-Y. Haine, *ESDP and NATO*, in: N. Gnesotto (ed.), *EU Security and Defence Policy – The first five years* (2004), EU-ISS, p. 131 at 142; S. Biscop, *Able and Willing? Assessing the EU's Capacity for Military Action*, 9 EFAR (2004), p. 509 at 524.

91   *Cf.* A. Monaco, *NATO Response Force: More than a 'paper army'?*, ISIS NATO Notes, Vol. 5, No. 7 (Oct. 2003).

92   M. Gómez Garrido, *ESDP: The Recent Debate in the United States*; OBS Working Paper No.18 (2002), p. 4; A. Monaco, *ibid.*; *cf.* H. Bacia, *Keine Konkurrenz*, Frankfurter Allgemeine Zeitung, 5 Nov. 2002, p. 12.

93   WEU Assembly, Rec. 723 on the EU headline goal and NATO Response Force (NRF), 3 June 2003, Explanatory Memorandum (Rivolta, Rapp.), para. 76 (*cf.* also paras. 58 and 64), WEU Assembly Doc. A/1825.

94   GAERC, Brussels, 22 Nov. 2004, Military Capability Commitment Conference, Draft Declaration on European Military Capabilities, para. 16, CP 75, p. 298; European Council, Brussels, 16–17 Dec. 2004, ESDP Presidency Report, para. 29, CP 75, p. 354;

be entirely joined together.[95] Another solution, often advanced by NATO, argues for a functional division of labour between the ERRF and the NRF. The ERRF would take on the 'low-end' tasks of crisis management, such as humanitarian and rescue operations and peacekeeping, while the NRF would deal with 'high-end' intense combat situations, including forced entry.[96] The NRF's task description and general outlook would conform with such a view: its tasks could be described as a catalogue of 'reinforced Petersberg missions'[97] on a global scale.[98] But from the ERRF's point of view, such a division of labour ignores that the ambition of the Petersberg tasks has, in addition to humanitarian and rescue tasks and peacekeeping, always in theory included tasks of combat forces in crisis management, including 'peacemaking' (that is, peace enforcement).[99] The Helsinki Headline Goal refers to the 'full scope' of these tasks, 'including the most demanding among these'.[100] A manifestation of this ambition for more demanding missions is the EU's new 'battle groups' project, now also found in the Headline Goal 2010, and which is also covered by the European Constitution.[101] The Battle Groups would, militarily speaking, be doing more or less exactly what the NRF does. This problem, although recognised in early 2004,[102] was apparently still unaddressed at that time. The idea of an ERRF/NRF division

---

Outcome of Proceedings EUMC 24 November 2004, Council Doc. 15255/04 EXT 2, 11 May 2005, para. 5.

95   *Cf.* F. Algieri / T. Bauer, *Defining and securing the EU's strategic defence interests – Executive summary*, p. 4, in: C. Giering (ed.), *Der EU-Reformkonvent* (2003).

96   *Cf.* G. Robertson, speech at the EU [European Parliament] Ctte. on Foreign Affairs, Human Rights, Defence Policy and Common Security, 8 Oct. 2002, NATO Speeches, http://www.nato.int/docu/speech/2002/s021008a.htm (visited 10/06/03); R. Pszcel, (NATO Spokesman's Office), *Geteilte Rollen von EU und NATO*, EU-Nachrichten, No. 42, 28 Nov. 2002, p. 3; A.J.K. Bailes, *Reaktionsstreitmacht der NATO*, Internationale Politik 1/2003, p. 49 at 51; A. Monaco, *EU and NATO: Competition or Cooperation?*, in: A. Weidemann / A. Simon (2003), p. 40 at 44; T.A. Chafos, *The European Union's Rapid Reaction Force...* (2003), p. 20, 53; J. Howorth, *ESDP and NATO: Wedlock or Deadlock?*, 38 Coop. & Confl. 3 (2003), p. 240; *cf.* already H. Binnendijk / R. Kugler, *Europeans should say 'yes' to Rumsfeld*, International Herald Tribune, 24 Oct. 2002, p. 4.

97   WEU Assembly, Rec. 723 on the EU headline goal and NATO Response Force (NRF), 3 June 2003, Explanatory Memorandum (Rivolta, Rapp.), para. 26, WEU Assembly Doc. A/1825.

98   *Ibid.*, Appendix, para. 12.

99   *Cf.* R. de Wijk, *The Reform of ESDP and EU–NATO Cooperation*, 39 The International Spectator 1 (2004), p. 76.

100 Nice, 7–9 Dec. 2000, Presidency Conclusions, Annex I to Annex VI – Military Capabilities Commitment Declaration, Annex I to Annex VI, para. 2, CP 47, p. 176.

101 Arts I-41(6), III-312 and Protocol No. 23 of the European Constitution. See above Chapter 2 (ESDP today).

102 E.g. K. Pries / M. Winter, *Berlin für EU-Elitetruppen*, Frankfurter Rundschau, 11 Feb. 2004, p. 6; H. Bacia, *Kampfbereit in 15 Tagen*, Frankfurter Allgemeine Zeitung, 12 Feb. 2004, p. 6; *NATO commander: EU force weakens alliance*, The Washington Times (online edition), 5 March 2004.

of labour touches on the relationship between the EU and NATO as a whole and is discussed in broader terms in the following section.

The common parlance found in EU and NATO public documents – including in NATO's Prague Declaration as well as in the EU–NATO Berlin Plus agreement – was that the ERRF and the NRF should be 'compatible' and their military capability development 'mutually reinforcing', 'respecting the autonomy of both organisations'.[103] These terms had already been used to describe the relationship between the capability programmes in the EU and NATO, before the time of the NRF.[104] However, as was also recognised early, the two capability-building processes are not per se mutually reinforcing,[105] but rather require careful coordination in order to become so.[106] Frequent exchange of information between the EU and NATO in this domain was thus increasingly recognised as critical by 2004.[107]

The political aspect of the ERRF/NRF dichotomy was more far-reaching. Even before the NRF had been officially decided at the Prague Summit in November 2002,

---

103   NATO Summit, Prague, 21–22 Nov. 2002, Declaration by the Heads of State and Government, para. 4.a., CP 57, p. 157; GAERC, Brussels, 19–20 May 2003, Conclusions, European Security and Defence Policy, para. 17, CP 67, p. 88; *cf.* NATO Parliamentary Assembly, Res. 317 on NATO Structural Reform and ESDP (2002), para. 15.g.; European Parliament Resolution on the Annual Report from the Council to the European Parliament on the Main Aspects and Basic Choices for CFSP, including the Financial Implications for the General Budget of the European Union, Strasbourg, 23 Oct. 2003, para. 42, CP 67, p. 235 at 243; Draft Council Conclusions on ESDP, 14 May 2004, paras. 4–7, Council Doc. 9485/04; *cf.* Franco-British summit, Le Touquet, 4 February 2003, Declaration on Strengthening European Cooperation in Security and Defence, 3) (c), CP 67, p. 36 at 39; European defence meeting – 'Tervuren', Meeting of the Heads of State and Government of Germany, France, Luxembourg and Belgium on European Defence, Brussels, 29 April 2003, para. 1, CP 67, p. 78 ('interoperable'); UK-Italy summit, Rome, 21 Feb. 2003, Declaration: Defence and Security, para. 6, CP 67, p. 41 ('harmonious development').

104   E.g. Ministerial Meeting of the North Atlantic Council held at NATO Headquarters, Brussels, 15 Dec. 1999, Final Communiqué, NATO Press Release M-NAC2(99)166, para. 20.a.; Meeting of European Union defence ministers, Sintra, 28 Feb. 2000, Annex: Elaboration of the Headline Goal – 'Food for Thought' Paper, CP 47, p. 104; European Council, Nice, 7–9 Dec. 2000, Presidency Conclusions, Annex I to Annex VI – Military Capabilities Commitment Declaration, paras. 6 (f) and 9, CP 47, pp. 180 and 184; Implementation of the Nice Summit decisions in the operational area on the European Security and Defence Policy (ESDP), WEU Assembly Doc. A/1734, 19 June 2001, para. 82.

105   Informal meeting of EU defence ministers, Rethymnon (Greece), 4–5 Oct. 2002, Summary of the Intervention of J. Solana, EU High Representative for the CFSP, CP 57, p. 133.

106   E.g. Meeting of European Union defence ministers, Sintra, 28 Feb. 2000, Annex: Elaboration of the Headline Goal – 'Food for Thought' Paper, CP 47, p. 106; *cf.* D. Hamilton, *Three Strategic Challenges for a Global Transatlantic Partnership*, 8 EFAR (2003), p. 543 at 549.

107   GAERC, Brussels, 17 Nov. 2003, Conclusions, European Security and Defence Policy, para. 17, CP 67, p. 259; EU Council Secretariat, Progress Report on the Battle Group Concept, Council Doc. 10282/04, 9 June 2004, para. 6; European Council, Brussels, 14 June 2004, Presidency Report on ESDP, para. 12, Council Doc. 10547/04.

some European States feared that the initiative could undermine the ERRF,[108] and hence attached to their support for the new US initiative the condition that the NRF should not prejudice the Helsinki Headline Goal.[109] The EU CFSP-HR J. Solana was overheard saying that the two forces were 'not necessarily compatible'.[110] Other sides pointed out more explicitly that the *raison d'être* of the ERRF and the NRF was not the same,[111] and that this conceptual chasm invited political competition,[112] or at least led to the question which of the two had political primacy.[113] As a result, the much-sought complementarity between the ERRF and the NRF is only able to be achieved through close political cooperation.[114] The process of mutual information exchange which started in 2004[115] would seem like a step in the right direction to overcome the divisions, real or imagined. Political awareness at the top level notwithstanding, it is to be expected that, in the event of competing NATO and EU demand for a capability, this matter would be resolved in consultation between the cognisant NATO and EU commanders at the lowest practical level.

DIVISION OF LABOUR IN MILITARY CRISIS MANAGEMENT BETWEEN THE EU AND NATO?

Introduction

The idea of a division of labour between the EU and NATO is a political issue, not just a military-technical one.[116] The debate seems to have been sparked off

---

108   J. Medcalf, *NATO and the Extra-European Challenge* (2002), p. 267.

109   E.g. Chronique des faits internationaux – Organisation du Traité de l'Atlantique Nord, Sommet de Prague 21–22 Nov. 2002, 57 RGDIP (2003), p. 154; *Grüne Bedenken gegen 'Enduring Freedom'*, Frankfurter Allgemeine Zeitung, 15 Nov. 2002, p. 2. French defence minister M. Alliot-Marie even proposed that the NRF should be at the service equally to NATO and the EU. *Cf. Id.*, speech at the 39th Munich Security Conference, 8 Feb. 2003. In this sense also J.-Y. Haine, *ESDP and NATO*, in: N. Gnesotto (ed.), *EU Security and Defence Policy – The first five years* (2004), EU-ISS, p. 131 at 142.

110   H. Bacia, *Keine Konkurrenz*, Frankfurter Allgemeine Zeitung, 5 Nov. 2002, p. 12.

111   R. Kempin, *The new NATO Response Force: Challenges for and Reactions from Europe*, Copenhagen Peace Research Institute Working Paper 29/2002, p. 17; WEU Assembly, Rec. 723 on the EU headline goal and NATO Response Force (NRF), 3 June 2003, Explanatory Memorandum (Rivolta, Rapp.), para. 38, WEU Assembly Doc. A/1825; T.A. Chafos, *The European Union's Rapid Reaction Force...* (2003), p. 57.

112   See also above fn. 92.

113   WEU Assembly, Rec. 723 on the EU headline goal and NATO Response Force (NRF), 3 June 2003, Explanatory Memorandum (Rivolta, Rapp.), para. 5, WEU Assembly Doc. A/1825.

114   *Cf. ibid.*, para. 78.

115   See above fn. 107.

116   WEU Assembly, Rec. 723 on the EU headline goal and NATO Response Force (NRF), 3 June 2003, Explanatory Memorandum (Rivolta, Rapp.), para. 45, WEU Assembly

by the new incoming US Administration in 2000,[117] a move which represented a change in position the United States had until that point, always arguing against a functional division of labour between NATO and EU crisis management.[118] One could perhaps say that the American stance was precipitated. It was not clear in 2000 whether the EU could ever attain the capabilities to engage in any operation beyond mere humanitarian aid, disaster relief or evacuation tasks.[119] Notwithstanding the EU's Helsinki mandate, there was also some ambiguity as to whether it *wanted* to conduct operations across the *full* spectrum of the Petersberg tasks, including peace enforcement.[120] In spite of these uncertainties, by 2000 it had already become clear that role specialisation between NATO and the EU was a serious issue which would require attention in the future.[121]

Before entering into the question proper, the question of a division of labour between the EU and NATO must be separated from another, very similar, debate about a division of labour in security efforts of Europe and the United States. That other debate is set in the context of the wider *transatlantic* relationship which is not exactly the same as the EU–NATO relationship.[122] The transatlantic division of labour issue is also older than the year 2000. The difference between the two can be quickly spotted: arguments relating to the *transatlantic* division-of-labour debate always refer to a division of labour *within* NATO, that is, between the allies. A division of labour between European allies and the United States is mostly seen as undesirable, because it undermines the basic tenet of the indivisibility of allied security.[123] Regarding a division of labour between the EU and NATO, however, opinions are different.

Doc. A/1825.

117   E.g. C. Rice (US National Security Advisor), cited in: M.R. Gordon, *Bush would stop U.S. peacekeeping in Balkan fights*, New York Times, 21 Oct. 2000, p. 1; *cf.* K. Donfried, *European Security and Defense Policy: The View from the United States*, in: W. Hoyer / G.F. Kaldrack (eds.), *ESVP* (2002), p. 200.

118   E.g. A. Vershbow (US amb. to NATO), cited in: W. Drozdiak, *U.S. Tepid on European Defense Plan*, Washington Post, 7 March 2000, p. A01; *cf.* F. Heisbourg, *New Nato, New Europe, New Division of Labour*, 34 The International Spectator 2 (1999), p. 63 at 67.

119   S. Duke, *CESDP: Nice's overtrumped success?*, 6 EFAR (2001), p. 159.

120   S. Blockmans, *A New Crisis Manager at the Horizon – The Case of the European Union*, 13 LJIL (2000), p. 259; *cf.* M. Vasiu, *The role of the ESDI*, 6 Rom.J.Int.Aff. 3/4 (2000), p. 125 at 145, n. 27.

121   A. Deighton, *The Military Security Pool* (2000), p. 52;

122   See above Chapter 1 (Transatlantic Relations).

123   G. Robertson, *Die NATO und die EU*, in: W. Hoyer / G.F. Kaldrack (eds.), *ESVP* (2002), pp. 188–9; J. Medcalf, *NATO and the Extra-European Challenge* (2002), p. 258; F. Heisbourg, *L'Europe de la défense dans l'Alliance atlantique*, 64 Politique étrangère 2 (1999), p. 219 at 220–1; P.H. Gordon, *Bridging the Atlantic Divide*, 82 Foreign Affairs 1 (2003), p. 70 at 82; O. Theiler, *Die NATO im Umbruch* (2003), p. 276; T.C. Salmon / A.J.K. Shepherd, *Toward a European Army* (2003), p. 4; F.S. Larrabee, *ESDP and NATO: Assuring Complementarity* (2004), p. 51 at 68; *contra* C.-R. Ancuţa, *EU CFSP and the Transatlantic Relationship*, 9 Rom. J. Int. Aff. 2/3 (2003), pp. 168–9.

History

The idea that crisis management should know a division of labour among the involved international institutions, based on a distinction between military and humanitarian tasks, is as old as the Dayton agreement.[124] The role of the EU in European crisis management was in many ways pre-determined by the WEU, particularly after the Amsterdam Treaty. When the WEU started, in the 1990s, to acquire a minor role in European crisis management, its dependency on the capabilities of NATO relegated it to limited and supportive tasks such as embargo control, peace-keeping and enforcement on a limited scale.[125] This limitation was expressed not only by the WEU's tasks defined in the Petersberg Declaration of 1992,[126] but also by the restrictive reading which was apparently given to a third of these tasks ('tasks of combat forces in crisis management, including peacemaking').[127] Thus, after the Amsterdam IGC, the resulting division of labour between the WEU and NATO in which 'humanitarian actions[128] and peacekeeping' fell to the WEU, and the rest, that is, 'defence' broadly understood,[129] was left for NATO. In some quarters this was already then resented.[130] The WEU's role in this division of labour was automatically applied to the EU, once the latter donned the WEU's crisis management boots. Additionally, the EU was seen as the ideal source of economic and political means (for example sanctions) which could contribute to the spectrum of security measures applied to cope with future humanitarian crises.[131]

Functional division of labour

'High-end' and 'low-end' tasks

Crisis management, in the sense the term was coined in the post-Cold War world, denotes all measures intended to prevent or defuse a humanitarian crisis or a conflict, mitigate its effects on human populations once it has broken out, stabilise the region after a ceasefire has been reached, and prevent its recurrence in the long term. As the recent experience since the first wars of independence of Slovenia and Croatia has shown, the spectrum of possible measures is very wide. It ranges from good offices

---

124   *Cf.* E. Greco, *UN-NATO Interaction: Lessons from the Yugoslav Experience*, 32 The International Spectator 3/4 (1997), p. 121 at 136.

125   G. Bonvicini et al., *Security links in the making* (1996), p. 317.

126   See above Chapter 2 (ESDP Today).

127   *Cf.* P. Cornish, *Partnership in Crisis* (1997), p. 100.

128   Not meaning 'humanitarian intervention'.

129   *Cf.* F. Dehousse, *After Amsterdam: A Report on the Common Foreign and Security Policy of the European Union*, 9 EJIL (1998), p. 536.

130   P. Schmidt, *Zum Verhältnis von GASP; NATO und WEU*, 25 ÖZP 4 (1996), p. 406.

131   G. Bonvicini et al., *Security links in the making* (1996), p. 317; W. Lang, *Sind WEU und NATO noch Allianzen?*, 13 ÖJIP (1996), p. 14.

or economic and diplomatic pressure to a full military campaign which, in means and effects, may well equal a full war. Measures in between include humanitarian aid, rescue operations, classical peacekeeping, and more robust forms of peacekeeping up to peace enforcement (called 'peacemaking' in the TEU[132]). These categories are relatively well established by the time of writing of this book.[133] Most of them, including in the Petersberg catalogue, are classified according to how much armed force is involved. Measures more peaceful in character are placed at the 'low end' of the spectrum (meaning low combat intensity), whereas harder measures are at the 'high end' (meaning high combat intensity). The terms 'high' and 'low' carry no normative content, they are simply two opposite directions on a scale.

As NATO's Kosovo campaign showed, high-end tasks require special military capabilities such as the ability to quickly deploy troops into a given region, the ability to maintain an operation there, to suppress enemy air defences, intelligence (including from satellites), and other military technology, which, broadly speaking, only the United States possesses to a large degree today. Low-end tasks require special skills as well, sometimes summarised as 'soft power' or 'civil power': the experience and ability to push the warring parties towards a peaceful resolution of the conflict. No measure is applied in isolation. However, the wrong mix can have disastrous consequences, as the international community learned in Bosnia.[134]

The division-of-labour debate between the EU and NATO is about which of the organisations should take over what part of the above-mentioned spectrum. The natural answer, coming from the days of the WEU, would be that NATO is better suited to engage in high-end tasks, whereas the EU, with its wealth of experience as an economic and political organisation, should take on the low-end tasks, also because it lacks significant military capabilities. As the discussion below will show, the idea of this basic division of labour, although supported by most sides, is not entirely undisputed.

Arguments for a functional division of labour

A division of labour between the EU and NATO along high-end/low-end lines is supported not only by the Bush Administration of the United States,[135] but also by the two countries most influential in ESDP, Britain and France.[136] The same is true, broadly speaking, for the European Parliament, the NATO Parliamentary

---

132   For the difference in terminology between the EU and the United Nations, see above Introduction – on terminology in international security.

133   A typical crisis management operation would be outfitted with a very clear mandate of its tasks and the measures it is entitled to take (including rules of engagement).

134   See above Chapter 2 (ESDP Today).

135   See above p. 239.

136   E.g. Informal meeting of EU defence ministers, Rome, 29 Aug. 2003, British Non-Paper 'Food for Thought', at d), CP 67, p. 206; M. Alliot-Marie (French defence minister), speech at the 40th Munich Security Conference, 7 Feb. 2004, at 2.2.

Assembly,[137] as well as many defence analysts.[138] Most arguments advanced in favour of such a division of labour point to the fact that the EU and NATO are organisations with very distinct qualities and strengths: whereas NATO is much better capable of threatening and projecting force,[139] 'the European Union, because of its DNA, because of its origin, is more into the humanitarian, civil-economic, crisis prevention and post-conflict rehabilitation side of things',[140] sometimes summarily called 'soft security'.[141] In Macedonia, division of labour was at the heart of EU–NATO cooperation until the EU's complete takeover in April 2003. It was successful,[142] and was lastly broadened and formalised in the 'EU–NATO Concerted approach to the Western Balkans' in July 2003.[143] Developments on the ground in Kosovo and even in Afghanistan also seem to go in the same direction[144] (in Afghanistan without direct EU involvement).

Concerning military capability, it is a fact today that the EU still does not have the capability to engage in the upper end of the Petersberg tasks on its own.[145] There

---

137   E.g. European Parliament Resolution on the Annual Report from the Council to the European Parliament on the Main Aspects and Basic Choices for CFSP, including the Financial Implications for the General Budget of the European Union, Strasbourg, 23 Oct. 2003, para. 33, CP 67, p. 235 at 242 ('complementary'); D. Bereuter (President of the NATO Parliamentary Assembly), *Division of Labour: NATO, EU Can Separate Missions, Protect Unity*, Defense News, 8 March 2004, available at http://www.nato-pa.int/default. asp?shortcut=478 (visited 23/03/04).

138   E.g. N. Neuwahl, *The Atlantic Alliance: For Better or Wars...*, 8 EFAR (2003), p. 427 at 432; H. Borchert, *The Future of Europe's Security and Defense Policy (ESDP) and the Limits of Intergovernmentalism*, in: A. Weidemann / A. Simon (2003), p. 59; *cf.* H. Neuhold, *Transatlantic Turbulences: Rift or Ripples?*, 8 EFAR (2003), p. 457 at 462 (who discusses this outcome as one of several options); *cf.* P. Cornish / G. Edwards, *Beyond the EU/NATO dichotomy: the beginnings of a European strategic culture*, 77 International Affairs (2001), p. 587 at 603.

139   T.A. Chafos, *The European Union's Rapid Reaction Force...* (2003), p. 45.

140   G. Lenzi, *The WEU between NATO and EU*, 51 Studia Diplomatica (1998), p. 167 at 172; *cf.* T.A. Chafos, *ibid.*, p. 55; E.J. Kirchner, *Final Report on a Study of the Relationship between ESDP Objectives and Capabilities*, NATO-EAPC Fellowship papers 2001–2003, http://www.nato.int/acad/fellow/01–03/kirchner.pdf (visited 12/12/04), p. 24.

141   C. Hill, *The EU's capacity for conflict prevention*, 6 EFAR (2001), p. 322; A. Menon, *Enhancing the Effectiveness of the EU's Foreign Defence Policies*, CEPS Policy Brief No. 29 (Dec. 2002), p. 4.

142   T.C. Salmon / A.J.K. Shepherd, *Toward a European Army* (2003), p. 78.

143   EU–NATO concerted approach to the Western Balkans, Brussels, 29 July 2003, para. 5, CP 67, p. 201.

144   S. Duke, *CESDP and the EU response to 11 September*, 7 EFAR (2002), pp. 165–6.

145   J. Howorth, *The ultimate challenge* (2000), p. 73; G. Gustenau, *GASP – eine Herausforderung für die 'Post-Neutralen'?* (2000), p. 20; M. Kremer / U. Schmalz, *Nach Nizza – Perspektiven der GESVP* (2001), p. 170; T.A. Chafos, *The European Union's Rapid Reaction Force...* (2003), p. 54; N. Eitelhuber, *Europäische Streitkräfte unter dem Zwang der Beschneidung – Partner der USA nur bei friedenssichernden* Einsätzen, SWP-Studie No. 8,

may also not be enough political consensus to build the military-technical apparatus which would be necessary to achieve this.[146]

A closer look at the respective strategic planning scenarios of the EU and NATO furthermore substantiates that a functional division of labour is already taking place: whereas the EU seems to concentrate its planning on peacekeeping, humanitarian relief and post-conflict stabilisation, NATO has followed the impetus of the United States, shifting its attention to operations involving quick deployment, high-intensity combat, with the threats envisaged generally being international terrorism and WMD.[147] A certain consensus for the EU to tackle the low end of crisis management had thus developed by 2003.[148]

Arguments against a functional division of labour

There is, however, also opposition to a functional division of labour in crisis management between the EU and NATO. Negative arguments come foremost from the neutral and non-aligned EU member States, not members of NATO, which take the view that the EU should have the capacity to tackle all types of crisis management operations, including the most complex and demanding ones.[149] This view is also increasingly echoed in some parts of defence academia.[150] The rationale for a functional division of labour is criticised as unhealthy for the EU's long-term global role, because of its limiting assumptions.

Firstly, there is the question of where the dividing line between 'high-end' and 'low-end' lies (and thus between the EU's and NATO's respective fields of activity) or how it is going to be defined. If the separation is drawn according to the psychological 'intervention threshold' for Europe held by US policy-makers, as is

---

March 2003; *cf.* already F. Dehousse / B. Galer, *De Saint-Malo à Feira: Les Enjeux de la Renaissance du Projet de Défense Européenne*, 52 Studia diplomatica (1999), p. 93.

146   H. Boguslawska, *Le lien transatlantique* (2003), p. 32; J. Herbst, *Peacekeeping by the European Union*, in: A. Bodnar et al. (eds.), *The Emerging Constitutional Law of the European Union – German and Polish Perspectives* (2003), p. 422; *cf.* P. Mallard, *Défense Nationale et Défense Européenne: Deux Notions Compatibles?*, in: S. Vinçon et al., *Défense: quels projets après 2002?*, 57 Défense nationale (2001), p. 82 at 94.

147   A. Monaco, *'A crisis in Atlantia' puts Berlin Plus to the Test*, ISIS NATO Notes, Vol. 5, No. 8 (2003); Assembly of the WEU, *The United States national security strategy and its consequences for European defence* (Report by Rapp. Mr. Gubert), para. 38, WEU Assembly Doc. A/1824, 13 May 2003; K. Shake, *Constructive Duplication* (2002), p. 14.

148   A. Monaco, *EU and NATO: Competition or Cooperation?*, in: A. Weidemann / A. Simon (2003), p. 40 at 43.

149   E. Tuomioja (FM Finland), L. Freivalds (FM Sweden), *We want a stronger EU security policy*, Dagens Nyheter, 11 November 2003, English translation in: CP 67, p. 429 at 430.

150   E.g. H. Ojanen, *Theories at a loss? EU–NATO fusion* (2002), p. 14; D. Hamilton, *Three Strategic Challenges for a Global Transatlantic Partnership*, 8 EFAR (2003), p. 543 at 545.

sometimes argued,[151] then the division of labour between the EU and NATO would be left entirely for the United States to define. It would be a 'right of first refusal' revisited.[152] Not only would this solution belie the essence of a real equal partnership between the EU and NATO,[153] it also cannot answer what would happen to ESDP if the United States one day decided that NATO should also go into low-end tasks.[154]

Secondly, arguments which point to Balkans operations as a positive example of EU–NATO functional division of labour also acknowledge that in those operations NATO went in to do the hard fighting (which it was best suited for), leaving the post-conflict mopping-up to others: long-term stabilisation and nation-building, all costly in terms of humanitarian assistance and economic aid.[155] The problem is that such a pattern leaves the initiative to the United States, with the EU, ever the junior partner, trailing behind to pick up the greater part of the bill for policies made elsewhere[156] (and probably being thanked less for it by the media and by local populations). Defence analysts are starting to argue that such a division of labour 'would encourage the United States to behave irresponsibly: they could conduct wars without having to deal with the long-term consequences'.[157]

Thirdly, and this has become evident already in the comparison of the ERRF with the NRF,[158] the Petersberg tasks could include even a high-intensity operation on the scale of the Korean War.[159] The ambition which ESDP represents does not contain an inherent limitation such as a functional division of labour would necessitate.[160]

Fourthly, as favourable as such a functional division of labour may seem to NATO, it may in the long term contribute to eroding political coherence amongst the Alliance's members.[161]

---

151   *Cf.* A. Treacher, *The EU's Resistable Transformation*, 9 EFAR (2004), p. 61.

152   *Cf.* above Chapter 5 (NATO Primacy).

153   A. Monaco, *EU and NATO: Competition or Cooperation?*, in: A. Weidemann / A. Simon (2003), p. 40 at 44.

154   Such a development was, for example, advocated in 2004 by H. Binnendijk, one of the original intellectual architects of the NATO Response Force, *cf. Id.*, *A new, but necessary, job for NATO; Postwar planning*, International Herald Tribune, 9 April 2004, p. 6.

155   *Cf.* T.A. Chafos, *The European Union's Rapid Reaction Force...* (2003), pp. 35, 37 and 47.

156   T.C. Salmon / A.J.K. Shepherd, *Toward a European Army* (2003), p. 174; A.K.J. Bailes, cited in: A. Beatty, *EU-US plot a joint strategy to tackle failed states and conflicts*, European Voice, Vol. 11, No. 23, 16 June 2005, p. 2.

157   J. Springford, *A European way of war?*, Report on a seminar held at the CER, 19 Dec. 2003, http://www.cer.org.uk/pdf/report_wayofwar_dec03.pdf (visited 22/08/04).

158   See above p. 236.

159   F. Heisbourg, *Europe's Strategic Ambitions: The Limits of Ambiguity*, 42 Survival 2 (2000), p. 1 at 6.

160   *Cf.* S. Biscop, *Able and Willing? Assessing the EU's Capacity for Military Action*, 9 EFAR (2004), p. 509 at 510.

161   *Cf.* R. Freckmann, *Die NATO im 21. Jahrhundert*, IFIR Themenschwerpunkt, No. 01/2005, p. 8.

In summary, even though a functional division of labour in crisis management between the EU and NATO is supported by the majority of official and academic opinion, as well as by most facts on the ground, it contains some theoretical contradictions if one agrees that the EU should one day become a global security actor.

Geographical division of labour

The global security interests of the United States are moving away from Europe, particularly since September 11.[162] In a congruent development, Europe is focusing crisis management efforts on its near vicinity, in particular the Balkans.[163] This near-abroad focus accords with the EU's current limited power projection capabilities.[164] This development is broadly welcomed by US defence planners.[165] But the EU also has security interests in other regions of the world, for example Africa,[166] as was shown by its second military operation in the DRC.[167] Should there be a division of labour between the EU and NATO in geographical terms, leaving some areas of the world to the EU, and others to the Alliance? While NATO or the United States have so far not pronounced themselves on this question, it is definitely answered in the negative by EU officialdom[168] and by European academics.[169]

EU–NATO INTERACTION IN CRISIS MANAGEMENT – CONFIRMATION OF NATO PRIMACY?

The general concept of NATO primacy, in its various sub-aspects, has been presented in Chapter 5. The subsequent section looks at the relevant practice. This practice consists in peacekeeping operations in which the EU and NATO were or are involved

---

162   See Chapter 1(The Wider Perspective).

163   N. Neuwahl, *The Atlantic Alliance: For Better or Wars...*, 8 EFAR (2003), p. 427 at 428.

164   E.g. in taking over SFOR from NATO in December 2004, the EU faced none of the transport and logistic problems NATO has to overcome for ISAF. *Cf.* S. Taylor, *If NATO cannot deliver as a credible force, how can the EU?*, European Voice (online edition), Vol. 10, No. 21, 10 June 2004.

165   N. Winn, *Towards a Common European Security and Defence Policy? The Debate on NATO, the European Army and Transatlantic Security*, 8 Geopolitics 2 (2003), p. 47 at 60.

166   Franco-British Declaration Strengthening European Cooperation in Security and Defence, London, 24 Nov. 2003, CP 67, p. 281.

167   See below p. 249.

168   E.g. Summary of remarks made by J. Solana EU CFSP-HR at the informal meeting of EU defence ministers, Noordwijk, 17 Sept. 2004 (Council Doc. S0340/04), 4th bullet: 'As a global actor, we should be able to project our force whenever needed.' *Cf.* A. Monaco, *NATO and the EU – In 'Harmony' over* Macedonia, ISIS NATO Notes, Vol. 5, No. 2 (2003), p. 2 at 3; *cf.* also the question of the ERRF's geographical remit, above p. 214.

169   E.g. A. Deighton, *The European Security and Defence Policy*, 40 JCMS (2002), p. 719 at p. 734; *cf.* M. Kremer / U. Schmalz, *Nach Nizza – Perspektiven der GESVP* (2001), p. 175.

jointly in some way. Follow-up reports on these missions already are increasingly available at the time of writing, particularly for EU Operation *Concordia,*[170] hence this section shall concentrate on elements of EU–NATO interaction.

EU operations with recourse to NATO assets ('option 2')

EU Operation Concordia *(Macedonia) in 2003*[171]

From 1 April to 15 December 2003 the EU led its first small peacekeeping operation in Macedonia involving some 350 lightly armed military personnel. The operation was a continuation of NATO's earlier *Allied Harmony* mission, in place since the Ohrid Framework Agreement of August 2001 between the Slav and Albanian populations.[172] The EU's mission was requested by the Macedonian government and covered by the mandate of the United Nations in Security Council Resolution 1371 from 26 September 2001.[173] Its main task was to ensure the implementation of the Ohrid Agreement, including by patrolling the ethnic Albanian-populated regions of Macedonia that border Albania and Serbia-Montenegro, including Kosovo. The mission saw wide participation by 13 member States and by 14 third States (most of them EU candidates). It was originally launched for a period of six months,[174] but later extended until 15 December 2003.[175] France acted as framework nation for the first period. In this mission, the EU drew on planning facilities and other logistical support from NATO under the Berlin Plus agreement.[176]

After the conclusion of the Ohrid agreement, EU Special Representative François Léotard had already suggested in October 2001 that the EU should take

---

170   For general descriptions of Operation *Concordia*, see e.g. A. Missiroli, *The European Union: Just a Regional Peacekeeper?*, 8 EFAR (2003), pp. 498–9; *Id.* / D. Lynch, *ESDP Operations*, EU-ISS, http://www.iss-eu.org/esdp/09-dvl-am.pdf (visited 12/12/04), pp. 3–4; A. Monaco, *NATO and the EU – In 'Harmony' over Macedonia*, ISIS NATO Notes, Vol. 5, No. 2 (2003), pp. 2–3; *Id.*, *Operation Concordia and Berlin Plus: NATO and the EU take stock*, ISIS NATO Notes, Vol. 5, No. 8 (2003). For an overview of documents relating to the mission, see: Operation *Concordia* – Lessons Learned Process, Council Doc. 15484/04, 28 Nov. 2003. For finance aspects, see e.g. Council Doc. 5561/1/03 REV 1, 10 Feb. 2003.

171   For a good overview of EU Operation *Concordia*, see only G. Lindstrom, *On the ground: ESDP operations*, in: N. Gnesotto (ed.), *EU Security and Defence Policy – The first five years* (2004), EU-ISS, p. 111 at 116–8.

172   Ohrid Framework Agreement, 13 Aug. 2001, http://www.coe.int/T/E/Legal_affairs/ Legal_co-operation/Police_and_internal_security/Police_cooperation/OHRID%20Agreeme nt%2013august2001.asp (visited 11/08/2004).

173   *Cf.* the broadly worded mandate in para. 5.

174   Council Dec. 2003/202/CFSP, 18 March 2003, OJ L 76/43 of 22/3/2003.

175   Council Dec. 2003/563/CFSP, 29 July 2003, OJ L 190/20 of 30/7/2003.

176   *Cf.* only G. Robertson, *Nato Evolving - Time to Deliver*, The World Today (Royal Institute of International Affairs, London), June 2003, p. 12.

over *Allied Harmony* from NATO. This was judged premature at the time.[177] As long as the Berlin Plus agreement on the borrowing of NATO military assets was not concluded, a takeover was permanently postponed.[178] Once Berlin Plus was concluded, Operation *Concordia* was seen as the first test of the EU–NATO strategic partnership established therein.[179] This was also in view of a possible later takeover by the EU of NATO's SFOR mission in Bosnia.[180] Implementation of the procedure provided by Berlin Plus was meticulous and detailed,[181] due partly to US insistence that the agreement be implemented to the letter before NATO handed over control in Macedonia.[182] Preparations included, inter alia, a 'Specific Agreement on the use of NATO assets for the EU-led military operation in FYROM', following a standing 'model contract' on the release, monitoring and recall of NATO assets.[183] Its main contents were set out in a letter from the NATO-SG of 17 March 2003.[184]

In terms of troop composition, Operation *Concordia* was largely a continuation of NATO's *Amber Fox* mission under a different name.[185] Continuity was expressly desired by the EU.[186] The vast majority of soldiers who had participated in the former NATO mission had already come from EU countries. Even before the takeover, the force command had been held successively by the United Kingdom, Germany, and then the Netherlands,[187] while the United States had only contributed a handful of

---

177   S. Duke, *CESDP and the EU response to 11 September*, 7 EFAR (2002), p. 165; Shake, *Constructive Duplication: Reducing EU reliance on US military assets*, CER Working Paper (2002), p. 6.

178   The original takeover date had been 27 Oct. 2002. *Cf.* T. Franks, *Nato 'may prolong' Macedonia mission*, BBC News World Edition (online), 18 Sept. 2002.

179   H. Vincze, *Beyond symbolism: the EU's first military operation seen in its context* (2003), p. 5; *cf.* H. Bacia, *EU löst NATO ab*, Frankfurter Allgemeine Zeitung, 13 March 2003, p. 5.

180   D. Cronin, *Testing times ahead as EU prepares for historic peacekeeping debut in Macedonia*, European Voice (online edition), Vol. 9, No. 10, 13 March 2003; *Die EU übernimmt militärische Mission in Mazedonien*, Frankfurter Allgemeine Zeitung, 1 April 2003, p. 6; *Going military*, The Economist (online edition), 3 April 2003.

181   See generally Council Dec. 2003/92/CFSP, 27 Jan. 2003, Art. 10 (Relations with NATO), OJ L 34/26 of 11/2/2003; Operation *Concordia* – Lessons Learned Process, Council Doc. 15484/04, 28 Nov. 2003.

182   J. Dempsey, *Macedonia calls on EU take over NATO role*, Financial Times (online edition), 20 Jan. 2003; D. Cronin, *Testing times ahead as EU prepares for historic peacekeeping debut in Macedonia*, European Voice (online edition), Vol. 9, No. 10, 13 March 2003.

183   *Cf.* A. Monaco, *NATO and the EU – In 'Harmony' over* Macedonia, ISIS NATO Notes, Vol. 5, No. 2 (2003), p. 3

184   *Cf.* Council Doc. 15484/04, 28 Nov. 2003, p. 15.

185   *Cf.* T.A. Chafos, *The European Union's Rapid Reaction Force...* (2003), p. 47.

186   Council Doc. 6916/1/03 REV 1, 6 March 2003, p. 2, 1st bullet.

187   *Ibid.*

support staff.[188] March 2003 did not mean 'EU in and NATO out'.[189] NATO stayed involved with the mission in numerous ways. Firstly, the EU of course relied on its assets and planning capabilities (including the DSACEUR as Operation Commander) under the Berlin Plus agreement, and as agreed specifically before the start of the mission. Operative command structures were provided by NATO's AFSOUTH Command in Naples, although formally under an EU chain of command.[190] In addition, the EU was able to call for NATO reinforcement or evacuation in any time of need. A reserve for such a contingency was held ready at KFOR, operating under AFSOUTH.[191] Some logistical and reconnaissance support was also provided to Operation *Concordia* directly by KFOR.[192] Lastly, NATO retained a small number of its own troops in Macedonia.[193]

Because Operation *Concordia* was the first test case for the Berlin Plus cooperation framework hammered out in years of negotiation, both the EU and NATO eagerly awaited comparing notes in a follow-up 'lessons learned' process.[194] Overall, the mission was judged a success of ESDP,[195] and of Berlin Plus in particular.[196] However, some practical problems arose in the daily conduct of the operation: there were problems with the security clearances of the officials from Sweden, Finland and Austria who were working at the EU cell at SHAPE.[197] The United States was reportedly concerned about the sharing of information.[198] The most structural problem, however, concerned the EU Command Element in AFSOUTH. Many

---

188   H. Vincze, *Beyond symbolism: the EU's first military operation seen in its context* (2003), p. 4; C. Schwegmann, *EU-Friedensmissionen* (2002).

189   J. Solana, CFSP-HR, Remarks on the launch of the EU-led military operation in the former Yugoslav Republic of Macedonia (*Concordia*), Brussels, 31 March 2003, para. 4, CP 67, p. 71.

190   *Cf.* H. Vincze, *Beyond symbolism: the EU's first military operation seen in its context* (2003), p. 4; H. Bacia, *EU löst NATO ab*, Frankfurter Allgemeine Zeitung, 13 March 2003, p. 5.

191   IISS, *The Military Balance 2003/04*, p. 31; C. Mace, *Putting 'Berlin Plus' into Practice: Taking Over from NATO in FYROM*, ESR, No. 16 (2003), p. 3.

192   H. Boguslawska, *Le lien transatlantique* (2003), p. 23.

193   E. Jannson, *EU 'army' takes over duties in Macedonia*, Financial Times, 2 April 2003, p. 10.

194   EU–NATO Ministerial meeting, Brussels, 4 December 2003, Joint Press Statement by the NATO Secretary General and the EU Presidency, para. 1, CP 67, p. 285; *cf.* already European Council, Thessaloniki, 20 June 2003, Presidency Report on ESDP, para. 28 f).

195   F. Algieri / T. Bauer, *Europa – die gespaltene Macht. Die Konventsvorschläge zur Sicherheits- und Verteidigungspolitik*, in: C. Giering (ed.), *Der EU-Reformkonvent* (2003), p. 103 at 110.

196   A. Monaco, *Operation Concordia and Berlin Plus: NATO and the EU take stock*, ISIS NATO Notes, Vol. 5, No. 8 (2003).

197   *Ibid.* Continuous contact between EU and NATO officials during an EU operation calling on NATO assets is provided by the Berlin Plus agreement. *Cf.* below Chapter 8 (Berlin Plus Agreement).

198   *Ibid.*

countries felt that this element was in practice not really under EU control, but under NATO's.[199] This would raise questions about the autonomy of EU decision-making and action in Operation *Concordia*.[200]

After its termination, the mission was followed by an EU police mission, involving some 200 officers, which should help train the Macedonian police forces to international standards.[201] This mission contained no NATO elements or support.

Operation *Concordia* was a good showpiece for EU–NATO cooperation at work, most of all the Berlin Plus agreement. However, perhaps precisely because the transfer from *Amber Fox* was so well planned and predictable, it does not make very good evidence for answering some open questions of the EU–NATO relationship, such as that of NATO primacy.[202] When the EU harmoniously takes over an existing peacekeeping operation from NATO, this is different from a situation in which both would like to *start* an operation. Only the latter case, however, could really help to answer questions such as the 'right of first refusal'.

EU Operation Althea *(Bosnia) from 2004*

At the time of writing, the EU Operation *Althea* in Bosnia-Herzegovina had only recently started, on 2 December 2004. It is too early at the time of writing to assess the conduct of this operation in light of the EU–NATO relationship. However, its preparatory process stretched over a long time, starting with the EU's official offer at the 2002 Copenhagen Summit to take over SFOR from NATO. On the basis of this preparatory phase, some preliminary conclusions can already be drawn.

History   After the conclusion of the Dayton Framework Agreement in 1995, various international actors, such as the EU and the UN, were engaged in the long and arduous process of nation-building in Bosnia. The military side of its implementation in Bosnia-Herzegovina fell to NATO, the only international organisation then capable of doing so, and also the only one who enjoyed enough credibility from all sides. US involvement in Bosnia had only come with great hesitancy, as the scale of the humanitarian catastrophe and European incapacity to prevent it had found ears even in Congressional corridors. Fundamentally, however, Bosnia was never an essential US foreign policy interest. The only remaining US interest in Bosnia, apart from generally preserving stability and security in Europe as a whole, was seen in the danger of Iranian influence in Bosnia.[203] This gap between actual commitment and lack of underlying political interest began to be felt soon after the end of the Bosnian war. Already in 1997, the 'Bosnia Force

---

199   *Ibid.*; K. Kastner, *Quelle culture de sécurité et de défense pour l'Union européenne?*, ENA thesis, Promotion Romain Gary «2003–2005» (2005) (on file with the author), p. 55.

200   *Cf.* already T.C. Salmon / A.J.K. Shepherd, *Toward a European Army* (2003), p. 128.

201   *Cf.* Council Joint Action on the European Union Police Mission in the Former Yugoslav Republic of Macedonia (EUPOL 'Proxima'), 29 Sept. 2003, CP 67, pp. 222–230. That mission was extended until the end of 2005 (Council Doc. 13169/04, classified).

202   See above Chapter 5 (NATO Primacy).

203   *Ibid.*

Options Project' identified various potential scenarios of downsizing the peacekeeping mission with a view to reducing US participation, and turning it over to an international organisation other than NATO.[204] The UN was not seen as being up to such a task, but 'a rapid reaction force ... with a European or other security component on the ground' was.[205] Indeed, EU RELEX Commissioner H. van den Broek had already in 1996 suggested a major European role in the follow-up mission to SFOR. ESDP did not exist yet, so the only format imaginable for this was a CJTF.[206]

Political developments from the 2002 EU Copenhagen Summit until the 2004 NATO Istanbul Summit The hand-over of NATO's SFOR mission to the EU was controversial for a long time.[207] The EU for the first time officially proposed it at its Copenhagen Summit in December 2002,[208] apparently on the basis of a Franco-British proposal.[209] A joint plan by France and Britain followed in February 2003.[210] France and Britain had a central interest in Bosnia. They had been the principal European UNPROFOR contributing States, a common experience which had also contributed to the rise of ESDP.[211] In a way, one could therefore see the EU's takeover of the Bosnian mission as the French-British UNPROFOR experience from the early 1990s having come full circle. These proposals from the EU did not, at first, resonate positively with NATO. At its Summit in Madrid on 3 June 2003 the Alliance confirmed, while referring to the ongoing development of EU–NATO relations, 'our continued presence in the Balkans'.[212] NATO evidently judged the idea of an EU takeover by 2004 premature.[213] However, in September 2003 Germany

---

204 The 'Bosnia Force Options Project' was conducted at George Mason University together with the UN. Its contributors were security experts and academics and military personnel from NATO and the UN. *Cf.* D.F. Davis / B.C. DeGrasse, *What Follows the Current NATO Involvements in Bosnia? – Options for a Policy Debate*, 4 International Peacekeeping 3/4 (1998), pp. 76–81.

205 *Ibid.*, p. 78.

206 B. Clark, *EU could take lead in Bosnia next year*, Financial Times, 4 May 1996, p. 2.

207 *Cf.* A. Missiroli / D. Lynch, *ESDP Operations*, EU-ISS, http://www.iss-eu.org/esdp/09-dvl-am.pdf (visited 12/12/04), p. 6.

208 European Council, Copenhagen, 12–13 Dec. 2002, Presidency Conclusions, para. 29, CP 57, p. 170.

209 WEU Assembly, Rec. 723 on the EU headline goal and NATO Response Force (NRF), 3 June 2003, Explanatory Memorandum (Rivolta, Rapp.), para. 14, WEU Assembly Doc. A/1825.

210 A. Monaco, *NATO and the EU – In 'Harmony' over* Macedonia, ISIS NATO Notes, Vol. 5, No. 2 (2003), p. 2 at 3; J. Howorth, *ESDP and NATO: Wedlock or Deadlock?*, 38 Coop. & Confl. 3 (2003), p. 235 at 249; *cf.* Franco-British summit, Le Touquet, 4 February 2003, Declaration on Strengthening European Cooperation in Security and Defence, 1), CP 67, p. 36 at 37.

211 See above Chapter 1 (The Wider Perspective)

212 Ministerial Meeting of the North Atlantic Council, Madrid, 3 June 2003, Final Communiqué, NATO Press Release (2003)059, paras. 8 and 9.

213 *Cf.* S. Castle, *EU troops not ready to take on Bosnian role, says Nato chief*, The Independent (online edition), 5 Aug. 2003.

officially joined the French-British proposal,[214] and on 4 October 2003 an informal meeting of EU defence ministers ended with the EU declaring readiness to take over SFOR, in line with the Copenhagen proposal. Britain offered to be the 'managing state' of a future EU force.[215] Now NATO began to move as well. At the informal NATO defence ministers meeting in Colorado Springs in mid-October, NATO Secretary General G. Robertson indicated general agreement of the allies that the takeover could take place, but damped rumours that this might happen as soon as the end of the year or mid-2004.[216] Robertson mentioned a timeframe of 12 to 18 months.[217] The EU mission would be conducted in reliance on NATO assets under the Berlin Plus agreement.[218] On 4 December, NATO officially agreed to look into the option of concluding SFOR and hand it over to the EU under Berlin Plus by the end of 2004, but also stated that it would retain a headquarters there after the transfer.[219] 'Exploratory contacts' between the EU and NATO on the issue started in January 2004.[220] As Berlin Plus would be the format for the mission, the 'lessons learned' from Operation *Concordia* in the previous year were already fed into these discussions, in particular, the question of the chain of command, which had been somewhat controversial in *Concordia*.[221]

By May 2004, although no official step had yet been taken, the EU was already busy preparing for the transfer at the end of the year.[222] At its Istanbul Summit on 28 June 2004, NATO formally decided to terminate SFOR, and noted the readiness of the EU to take it over under the Berlin Plus format. A NATO HQ would however

---

214   *Paris und Berlin prüfen EU-Truppe für Bosnien*, DPA – Europadienst, 18 Sept. 2003.

215   Remarks by J. Solana, EU HR-CFSP, at the Informal Meeting of Defence Ministers, Rome, 3–4 Oct. 2003, Council Doc. S0193/03, p. 2; *cf. EU says it is ready to take over from NATO in Bosnia*, AFP, 4 Oct. 2003; P. Ames, *EU willing to take on Bosnian peacekeeping mission by mid-2004*, AP, 4 Oct. 2004; *EU defence ministers agree on British command of Bosnia force: diplomats*, AFP, 4 Oct. 2003; *Britain ready to head EU force for Bosnia: source*, AFP, 4 Oct. 2003.

216   *Cf. And for my next task*, The Economist, 4 Jan. 2003, p. 24; *EU takeover of SFOR command in Bosnia mid-2004*, NATO's Nations 3/2003, p. 164.

217   P. Spiegel, *EU closer to taking over Bosnia pace role*, Financial Times, 10 Oct. 2003, p. 7.

218   *Ibid.*

219   Ministerial Meeting of the North Atlantic Council, Brussels, 4 Dec. 2003, para. 8, NATO Press Release (2003)152; EU–NATO Ministerial Meeting, Brussels, 4 Dec. 2003, Joint Press Statement by the NATO Secretary General and the EU Presidency, CP 67, p. 285.

220   A. Beatty, *EU peacemakers to take over Bosnia*, EUObserver, 22 Jan. 2004; *cf.* J. de Hoop Scheffer (NATO Secretary General), speech at the 40th Munich Security Conference, 7 Feb. 2004; *cf.* already European Council, Brussels, 12 Dec. 2003, Presidency Conclusions, para. 88, CP 67, p. 296.

221   *La OTAN tendrá un papel 'residual' en Bosnia cuando se traspase el poder a la UE en diciembre*, El Mundo (online edition), 10 March 2004; A. Beatty, *Deal with NATO moves closer*, EUObserver, 11 March 2003.

222   Council Conclusions on ESDP, 14 May 2004, para. 3, Council Doc. 9485/04; *cf.* H. Bacia, *EU-Rüstungsagentur im Juni*, Frankfurter Allgemeine Zeitung, 7 April 2004, p. 2.

remain in Sarajevo, as well as some residual tasks of NATO in the country (such as hunting war criminals sought by the ICTY).[223]

Role of the United States   The US position on the transfer determined the political developments above at virtually all times. Despite its fundamentally ambiguous military commitment to the Balkans, the United States was the principal architect of peace in Bosnia. Thus, US diplomats were aware of the fragility of this peace and its continuing dependence on a strong international military presence. US Senators were also skeptical about the EU's fundamental ability to do NATO's job in Bosnia over a long time.[224] The EU's proposal at the Copenhagen Summit in 2002 therefore came as a surprise for the United States.[225] Its first reaction was that the EU was not ready to take on such a complex and demanding operation without any US involvement.[226] A premature takeover could endanger past US and NATO achievements in Bosnia, for example if the EU mismanaged a renewed flaring-up of local hostilities. In addition, there were many interlinks of SFOR with KFOR which would be lost if one of the two operations was given up.[227] But there were also more general political reasons relating to the US military presence in the Balkans. A ceding of SFOR meant giving up an important piece in the European security playing field,[228] and thus a loss of power in an important area of European politics.[229] The United States has no direct voice in ESDP, in contrast to NATO. The EU's choice of Berlin Plus as the format for the mission, apart from military-technical necessity, was

---

223   Istanbul Summit Communiqué issued by the Head of State and Government participating in the meeting of the North Atlantic Council, 28 June 2004, para. 8, NATO Press Release (2004)096.

224   See e.g. the remarks by Sen. J. Biden in the US Senate, 23 May 2001, 107th Cong., 1st Sess., 147 Cong. Rec. S 5529 at 5531: 'If my fears prove correct, and we withdraw our troops, I predict that renewed fighting in Bosnia is just a matter of time.'

225   D. Triantaphyllou, *Balkans: The Transition from a Reduced Commitment*, Institute Note, 14 March 2003, Institute of Security Studies – Task Forces 2003, p. 2, http://www.iss-eu.org/activ/content/rep9.pdf (visited 31/04/2003).

226   K. Carstens, *EU not ready for Bosnia, says US*, European Voice (online edition), Vol. 9, No. 21, 5 June 2003; *US blocks takeover of SFOR*, ESR No. 18 (2003), p. 9; *cf.* H. Vincze, *Beyond symbolism: the EU's first military operation seen in its context* (2003), p. 10; T.A. Chafos, *The European Union's Rapid Reaction Force...* (2003), p. 45.

227   *Cf.* C. Schwegmann, *EU-Friedensmissionen auf dem Balkan – eine Alternative zur NATO?*, Studien und Berichte zur Sicherheitspolitik 5/2002, Austrian Federal Ministy for Defence, p. 10, http://www.bmlv.gv.at/pdf_pool/publikationen/09_euf_01_schweg.pdf (visited 12/08/2004).

228   *Cf.* Vincze, *ibid.*, p. 10; R. de Wijk, *The Reform of ESDP and EU–NATO Cooperation*, 39 The International Spectator 1 (2004), p. 73; J. Dempsey, *US and EU in dispute on control of Bosnia force*, Financial Times, 9 March 2004, p. 2.

229   *Cf.* P. Ashdown's remarks in this respect: 'It is not in the nature of superpowers to give up areas in which they have major influence' (cited in: I. Black, *Ashdown backs creation of EU Bosnia force*, The Guardian (online edition), 8 Oct. 2003). The problem alluded to by Ashdown is well treated in e.g. C. Kupchan, *The End of the American Era* (2002).

made also to address those US fears by keeping NATO involved in Bosnia.[230] So was the choice of Britain as the first lead nation for the mission, the EU country which the United States trusts most to ensure that ESDP does not develop against US interests. In autumn 2003 signals increased that the US position on the takeover had begun to shift.[231] This change in US policy perception was caused by the need to ease the strain on extended US military commitments such as Iraq and Afghanistan, by freeing up troops tied down in SFOR.[232] In the background, the long-standing fact that US military commitments in Bosnia had always exceeded its long-term political interest there,[233] may have helped the shift in Washington come about.

After NATO's decision in principle to hand over SFOR to the EU in December 2003, the attention of the United States turned, in spring 2004, to saving as many competencies as possible into the new mission. Of particular importance were the tasks of hunting down war criminals and counter-terrorism issues.[234] 'Technical' questions were also contested, such as the military rank of NATO and EU officers in the mission – of high symbolic value.[235] The general US hesitancy to cede powers in Bosnia at the time could be discerned, for instance, in the way SACEUR Gen. J. Jones deliberately downplayed the importance of the future EU mission in front of the US Senate in March 2004, calling it a 'policing mission'.[236] In the preparatory process to *Althea* in spring 2004, the EU also sent direct messages to the United States addressing this problem. In February, for example, the EU stated that

---

230   P. Spiegel, *France seeks to ease US fears over Nato role in any EU-led Bosnia force*, Financial Times, 29 Oct. 2003, p. 10.

231   M. Zapf / J. Zepelin, *EU übernimmt Friedensmission in Bosnien doch*, Financial Times Deutschland (online edition), 5 Sept. 2003; B. Esturielas, *La UE asumira el Mando en Bosnia si EE UU se retira*, El País, 18 Sept. 2003, p. 4; R. Burns, *U.S. ambassador says 'we can see an end' to NATO peacekeeping in Bosnia*, AP Worldstream, 9 Oct. 2003; T.E. Ricks, *Troops May Leave Bosnia In '04, Commander Says*, Washington Post (online edition), 11 Oct. 2003.

232   D. Thuburn, *NATO Chief in Bosnia Calls Stability 'Very Fragile'*, World Markets Analysis, 19 Sept. 2003; A. Monaco, *NATO Response Force: More than a 'paper army'?*, ISIS NATO Notes, Vol. 5, No. 7 (Oct. 2003); *In a move that could free up US troops for other hot spots, the European Union has offered to take over peacekeeping in Bosnia*, Broadcast News, 4 Oct. 2003; P. Ames, *EU willing to take on Bosnian peacekeeping mission by mid-2004*, AP, 4 Oct. 2003; I. Black, *Ashdown backs creation of EU Bosnia force*, The Guardian (online edition), 8 Oct. 2003. A similar problem was being faced by Canada at the time. *Cf.* S. Alberts, *McCallum plans to pull NATO troops from Bosnia*, The Ottawa Citizen, 9 Oct. 2003.

233   *Cf.* above Chapter 1 (The Wider Perspective).

234   J. Dempsey, *General to lead EU's military planners*, Financial Times, 5 April 2004, p. 5.

235   A. Schnauder, *Verteidigungspolitik: Nato will Bosnien-Mandat nicht aufgeben*, Die Presse (online edition), 6 April 2004.

236   Statement of Gen. J.L. Jones, USMC, Commander, US European Command, before the Senate Armed Services Committee, 4 March 2004, p. 20, http://armed-services.senate. gov/statemnt/2004 /March /Jones.pdf (visited 15/09/04).

The EU and the US are in full agreement on the need for a cooperative and concerted approach towards BiH. That is for us essential. Our experience in BiH shows that we are most effective when we are united.[237]

Concerning the more technical military details of implementation of the Berlin Plus agreement in the preparation of the mission, the United States seemed not to worry about every single detail anymore,[238] as it had done one year previously before the start of Operation *Concordia*. This is indicative of the increased mutual trust which characterised the EU–NATO relationship in 2004, gained already from practical day-to-day cooperation. Problems in the preparatory phase of Operation *Althea* rather seemed to concern issues such as the operation's budget portions for participating non-EU NATO allies.[239]

Position of the local population in Bosnia The degree to which the United States would remain to be involved in Bosnia was regarded as important not least by the local population. Among the Bosnian populace, the EU does not today enjoy the same local prestige as the United States has since 1995. In the words of the High Representative P. Ashdown, the Bosnians

> regard Europeans as the people who sat there and did nothing for four years while they were slaughtered. The Americans are the people who came in and saved them. That's unfair ... But we do have a credibility problem.[240]

The Bosnian wish to have NATO stay as long as possible[241] seems understandable from recent historical experience. This is in spite of many mitigating factors which could be listed in the EU's favour in Bosnia: economically and politically, through nation-building, the EU has in fact committed much more resources to the country than the United States; the EU is generally expected to improve the human rights sensitivity of the Bosnia mission;[242] and lastly, for geographical reasons, also has a stronger long-term interest. R. Cooper flatly remarks in this regard that 'it is power that makes countries feel secure, not goodwill'.[243]

---

237 Council Doc. 6574/04, 20 Feb. 2004, p. 3, para. 11.

238 J. Dempsey, *EU Bosnia plan gets green light*, Financial Times (online edition), 26 April 2004.

239 D. Cronin, *EU facing battle over costs of peacekeeping in Bosnia*, European Voice (online edition), Vol. 10, No. 32, 23 Sept. 2004.

240 Cited in: I. Black, *Ashdown backs creation of EU Bosnia force*, The Guardian (online edition), 8 Oct. 2003. *Cf.* also, R. Keane, *EUFOR Mission for Bosnia by the end of 2004*, ESR No. 23 (2004), p. 1 at 2.

241 *Cf. Bosnia wants NATO to remain as peacekeeping force until it has become its member*, BBC International Monitoring Reports, 4 Oct. 2003.

242 This point was raised by Amnesty International, which commented unfavourably on SFOR's past dealing with human rights abuses. *Question of the week*, European Voice (online edition), Vol. 10, No. 26, 15 July 2005.

243 R. Cooper, *The breaking of nations* (2003), p. 162.

The open preference of Bosnian authorities for working with the United States rather than with the EU was identified as a problem which could hamper a future EU mission in practice, in particular if the future role of NATO and the United States in Bosnia were not clearly defined.[244] As a result, the EU started to involve local authorities in the preparation for the mission to the highest degree possible.[245] A public joint visit by high officials from the EU Council Secretariat and NATO-IS to Bosnian authorities took place in autumn 2004. Formal agreement of the Bosnian government for the transfer of authority from NATO to the EU was carefully secured,[246] an act which the additional experience of the EU Special Representative was instrumental in triggering. According to first reports, the efforts made by the EU, to give Bosnians some sense of political ownership in the transfer process, seems to have paid off in terms of increased local acceptance of the new EU mission.

The mission   The EU military mission *Althea* in Bosnia-Herzegovina, the sixth ESDP operation in total,[247] started officially on 2 December 2004.[248] On that day, NATO's SFOR mission, a continuation of the IFOR mission implementing the Dayton Peace Accords from 1995, came to an end. The operation is now carried out with recourse to NATO assets according to the Berlin Plus agreement.[249] Its key objectives are to provide deterrence and to contribute to a safe and secure environment in Bosnia.[250] Before the handover, the troop strength of the NATO mission, originally at 60 000 after the Bosnian war, had already been reduced to 7000 by the end of 2004, as the security situation gradually improved. *Althea* started out with about this number of troops (coming from more than 30 countries).[251] This is a commitment much larger than *Concordia*, and it arguably stretches EU military capabilities to the limit.[252] Britain is the lead nation with overall command in the mission, and was

---

244   *Cf.* M. Winter, *EU übernimmt Bosnien-Mission*, Frankfurter Rundschau, 27 April 2004, p. 1.

245   See e.g. Press Statement by CFSP-HR J. Solana and N. Radovanovic (Bosnian defence minister), 12 May 2004, Council Doc. S0132/04.

246   See Letter dated 19 November 2004 from the Permanent Representative of Bosnia and Herzegovina to the United Nations addressed to the President of the Security Council, UN Doc. S/2004/917.

247   *Cf.* J. Solana, speech at the Annual Conference of the EU-ISS, Paris, 10 Sept. 2004, Council Doc. S0232/04.

248   J. Solana, Launch of EU '*Althea*' operation in Bosnia and Herzegovina, Sarajevo, 2 Dec. 2004, Council Doc. S0337/04; D. Dombey / E. Jansson, *Changing of the guard: the EU seeks to show the US it is serious about defence*, Financial Times. 2 Dec. 2004, p. 11.

249   EU Council Secretariat Factsheet, EU military operation in Bosnia and Herzegovina (Operation EUFOR – *Althea*), ATH/03 (update 3), 29 Nov. 2004, p. 2.

250   *Ibid.*, p. 1.

251   *Cf.* EU Council Press Briefing announcement, Launch of EU Operation *Althea* in Bosnia and Herzegovina, Brussels, 29 Nov. 2004.

252   *Cf.* already A. Missiroli, *The European Union: Just a Regional Peacekeeper?*, 8 EFAR (2003), p. 501; *cf.* J. Dempsey, *EU rules out Haiti mission*, Financial Times, 19 Feb. 2004, p. 3.

followed by Italy in 2006.[253] The UN Security Council's peacekeeping mandate for Bosnia has been renewed in UNSC Resolution 1551 of 9 July 2004. It is a robust mandate ('all necessary measures').[254] This had been expressly insisted upon by the EU.[255] According to UNSC Resolution 1575 of 22 November 2004, which further elaborated this mandate, the EU now has the 'main peace stabilization role under the military aspects' of the Dayton Peace agreement,[256] specified in its Annexes 1A and 2. The resolution's para. 10 refers to an earlier exchange of letters delineating the tasks between the EU and NATO in Bosnia after 2 December, sent to the Security Council on 19 November.[257]

The overall context of the mission is different from *Concordia* in Macedonia because the EU already had a vast number of programmes and structures in place in Bosnia before the end of 2004, notably the Stabilisation and Association Process (SAP) by the Commission. This is in line with the EU's general 'mixed measures' approach to security,[258] as was also spelt out by the EU in February 2004:

> In Bosnia and Herzegovina, the EU would simultaneously deploy military, police and other civilian instruments in pursuit of a single objective – the continued stabilisation and transformation of a post conflict society into one which in due course could become part of European integration.[259]

Harmonising inter-pillar objectives, especially between Council and Commission competencies, was thus regarded as crucial early on in the preparation process.[260] The overall task of ensuring coherency between EU institutions in Bosnia falls to the EU Special Representative, as a *primus inter pares*.[261]

Delineation of tasks between the EU and NATO   As it did already with Operation *Concordia* in 2003, the EU stressed that a high degree of continuity with the previous

---

253   *Cf. Lenkungsausschuss*, Süddeutsche Zeitung, 15 July 2004, p. 7.

254   UN Security Council Resolution No. 1551, 9 July 2004, paras. 10, 11 and 13.

255   E.g. GAERC, Brussels, 24 Feb. 2003, Conclusions, European Security and Defence Policy, para. 1, CP 67, p. 46; Council Doc. 6574/04, 20 Feb. 2004, p. 3, para. 7.

256   UNSCR 1575, 22 Nov. 2004, para. 11.

257   EU–NATO exchange of letters of 17 and 18 Nov. 2004 on delineation of tasks, UN Doc. S/2004/915 and S/2004/916, 19 Nov. 2004. *Cf.* also Operation *Althea* – Military Advice on Delineation of Tasks, Council Doc. 14770/04, 16 Nov. 2004 (classified).

258   This approach was formally adopted by the EU in the European Security Strategy of 12 Dec. 2003, p. 11, para. 2.

259   Council Doc. 6574/04, 20 Feb. 2004, p. 5, para. 9.

260   A. Monaco, *Operation Concordia and Berlin Plus: NATO and the EU take stock*, ISIS NATO Notes, Vol. 5, No. 8 (2003).

261   Council Joint Action on the European Union military operation in Bosnia and Herzegovina, 12 July 2003, Preambular para. (3) and Art. 7, Council Doc. 11226/2/04 REV 2 (en); *cf.* already R. Keane, *EUFOR Mission for Bosnia by the end of 2004*, ESR No. 23 (2004), pp. 1–2.

NATO mission was intended. As 80 per cent of SFOR troops were already European, this is in fact the case.[262]

Initial EU planning for Operation *Althea* started after the European Council in December 2003. Only some months later did it become clear that NATO would remain present in Bosnia after the hand-over, and wanted to maintain a headquarters there as well as operational tasks. With regard to these remaining NATO responsibilities, the EU repeatedly stressed the importance of a clear definition of competencies in the preparatory process.[263] The EU's planning pressures must have been compounded by the fact that the political delineation of tasks with NATO, which only became fixed in late autumn of 2004, is a logical prerequisite for any more detailed technical operational planning.[264] The tug-of-war with NATO seems to have been a tough one,[265] but in the end NATO kept its Headquarters in Sarajevo as demanded in December 2003,[266] tasked with defence reform of the Bosnian army, and preparation of Bosnia for the PfP. The remaining NATO HQ Sarajevo is of high symbolic value particularly for the local population. This became evident in a joint newspaper article by EU CFSP-HR J. Solana and NATO-SG J. de Hoop Scheffer, which sent clear reassuring messages to the Bosnian public in this regard.[267] NATO continues to have the main responsibility for hunting war criminals and terrorists, although the EU can also 'contribute' in this and would retain the overall command responsibility.[268] The EU Council's Factsheet of 29 November 2004, however, gives a different impression: NATO is nowhere mentioned in the context of cooperation of the EU mission with the ICTY.[269]

The division of labour in Bosnia after 2 December 2004 is set out in formal terms in an exchange of letters between the two Secretaries-General of the EU and NATO which leaves the 'full authorities under Annex 1A and 2' of the Dayton Peace agreement with both the EU and NATO, but states that EUFOR will have the

---

262   *Cf.* Council Doc. 6574/04, 20 Feb. 2004, p. 3, para. 5 and p. 5, para. 5.

263   E.g. Council, 2563rd meeting, External Relations, Brussels, 23 Feb. 2004, Council Doc. 6294/04, p. 10.

264   This conditionality would also affect, for instance, the missions's Public Information policy in the run-up to the transfer of authority.

265   *Cf.* M. Winter, *In der Logik*, Frankfurter Rundschau, 27 April 2004, p. 3.

266   Meeting of the North Atlantic Council in Defence Ministers Session, Brussels, 1 Dec. 2003, Final Communiqué, para. 6, NATO Press Release (2003)148.

267   J. Solana (EU CFSP-HR) / J. de Hoop Scheffer (NATO Secretary General), *Guiding Bosnia along the road to Brussels*, International Herald Tribune, 15 July 2004, p. 6: ' ...the authorities of Bosnia are being consulted and remain fully engaged. ... NATO's long-term political commitment will ... remain unchanged. The establishment of a NATO headquarters will be proof of this.'

268   *Cf.* M. Winter, *EU übernimmt Bosnien-Mission*, Frankfurter Rundschau, 27 April 2004, p. 1.

269   EU Council Secretariat Factsheet, EU military operation in Bosnia and Herzegovina (Operation EUFOR – *Althea*), ATH/03 (update 3), 29 Nov. 2004, p. 2, 9th bullet.

'main stabilization role'.[270] Implementation of these arrangements is to be ensured by the DSACEUR, who is also the Force Commander. Apart from these general parameters, much of the delineation of daily tasks between the EU and NATO which had not been solved in detail at the political level remained to be worked out on the operational level.

EU–NATO cooperation in the Balkans also extends beyond Bosnia today, as EUFOR and KFOR have mutual support arrangements for transfer of tactical reserves from one operation to the other, should the need ever arise.[271]

Formal preparatory procedure in 2004   Administrative preparation for *Althea* was even more detailed than for *Concordia* the previous year. Its sequence shows many parallels, both following the procedure under the Berlin Plus agreement.

The EU Council approved the General Concept for Operation *Althea* on 26 April 2004, allowing for the start of detailed military planning.[272] This General Concept sets the planned overall troop level at 7000,[273] and apparently made a first delineation of competencies between the EU and NATO in *Althea*.[274]

In an exchange of letters of 30 June and 8 July 2004 between the EU-SG/HR and the NATO-SG, the EU and NATO agreed, pursuant to the Berlin Plus agreement, that NATO would again make its DSACEUR available as EU Operation Commander, and that the EU Operational Headquarters would be located at SHAPE.[275]

After NATO had agreed to terminate SFOR at the end of the year, the EU issued a Joint Action (JA) on the EU military operation in Bosnia and Herzegovina on 12 July 2004.[276] The Joint Action establishing Operation *Concordia* in Macedonia of 27 January 2003[277] clearly served as a model (although the *Althea* JA is somewhat more detailed). There are, moreover, some important differences. For example, while the

270   EU–NATO exchange of letters of 17 and 18 Nov. 2004 on delineation of tasks, UN Doc. S/2004/915, para. 3 and S/2004/916, para. 2, 19 Nov. 2004.

271   *Cf.* GAERC, 18 March 2005, Informal Meeting of Defence Ministers, Summary of Work, http://www.eu2005.lu/en/actualites/documents_travail/2005/03/18defresume/ (visited 25/06/05).

272   *Cf.* European Council, Brussels, 15 June 2004, Presidency Conclusions, Presidency Report on ESDP, para. 3, Council Doc. 10547/04.

273   This number apparently originated from a suggestion by DSACEUR Adm. Rainer Feist. *Cf. Admiral: Für Bosnien 7000 EU-Soldaten nötig*, Süddeutsche Zeitung, 14 Feb. 2004.

274   *Cf.* J. Dempsey, *EU Bosnia plan gets green light*, Financial Times (online edition), 26 April 2004.

275   *Cf.* Council Joint Action on the European Union military operation in Bosnia and Herzegovina, 12 July 2003, Preambular para. (13), Council Doc. 11226/2/04 REV 2 (en). The exchange of letters is classified. Only its first part (the letter from the EU Secretary-General/ High Representative to the NATO Secretary General of 30 June 2004) was released by the Council on 31 Aug. 2004 on a request by the author.

276   Council Joint Action on the European Union military operation in Bosnia and Herzegovina, 12 July 2003, Council Doc. 11226/2/04 REV 2 (en).

277   Council Dec. 2003/92/CFSP, 27 Jan. 2003, OJ L 34/26 of 11/2/2003.

Concordia JA made the launching of the operation contingent on a specific decision by the Council (Art. 1), the *Althea* JA leaves this future act more open ('once all relevant decisions have been made', Art. 1). Where the *Concordia* JA referred to a SOFA to be concluded with Macedonia (Art. 12), the operation *Althea* directly takes over the SOFA already in place as part of the Dayton peace agreement (Preamb. para. 8), with no specific substantive provision to regulate the matter. The ad hoc financing mechanism established by the *Concordia* JA (Art. 9) seems to have served as model for the permanent mechanism for financing ESDP operations (Athena) established in February 2004.[278] The *Althea* JA already uses this mechanism (Art. 12).

In autumn, administrative preparatory steps followed quickly. The Concept of Operations for *Althea* was approved by the Council on 13 Sept. 2004.[279] A Force Generations Conference took place two days later.[280] Before the month was out, third (that is, non-EU) States' contributions to the future military operation had been accepted[281] and a Committee of Contributors set up.[282] In an exchange of letters on 28 September and 8 October between the two SGs, NATO Command Elements at AFSOUTH Naples were put at the disposal of the EU.[283]

The Operation Plan (OPLAN), was agreed on 11 October, after NAC-PSC consultations;[284] the Council Decision to launch the Operation on 2 December 2004 finally came on 25 November 2004.[285]

Most documents relating to EU–NATO cooperation in the preparation process for Operation *Althea* are classified,[286] but, as this preparatory process can be assumed to draw on the lessons learned from Operation *Concordia*,[287] existence may nevertheless be inferred for some of them. Such documents would include:

---

278   Council Doc. 5770/04 of 17 Feb. 2004; *cf.* A. Missiroli, *€uros for ESDP: financing of EU operations*, EU-ISS, Occasional Paper 45 (June 2003).

279   GAERC, 13 Sept. 2004, Council Conclusions on ESDP, Council Doc. 12067/04, p. 10. Concept for the European Union (EU) Military Operation in Bosnia and Herzegovina (BiH) – Operation *Althea*, 29 Sept. 2004, Council Doc. 12576/04.

280   *Cf.* Summary of remarks made by J. Solana EU CFSP-HR at the informal meeting of EU defence ministers, Noordwijk, 17 Sept. 2004 (Council Doc. S0340/04), p. 3, 3rd bullet. 'Force Generation' is a term also used by NATO in its regular five-yearly force plans.

281   PSC Decision BiH/1/2004 on the acceptance of third States' contributions to the European Union military operation in Bosnia and Herzegovina, 21 Sept. 2004, OJ L 324/20 of 27/10/2004, amended by OJ L 357/39 of 2/12/2004.

282   PSC Decision BiH/3/2004 on the setting-up of the Committee of Contributors for the European Union military operation in Bosnia and Herzegovina, 29 Sept. 2004, OJ L 325/64 of 28/10/2004, amended by OJ L 357/39 of 2/12/2004.

283   *Cf.* PSC Decision BiH/4/2004, OJ L 357/38 of 2/12/2004, Preambular para. 1. The said exchange of letters is classified.

284   GAERC Conclusions, 11 Oct. 2004, Council Doc. 12767/04, p. 18.

285   Council Dec. 2004/803/CFSP of 25 Nov. 2004 on the launching of the European Union military operation in Bosnia and Herzegovina, OJ L 353/21 of 27/11/2004.

286   E.g. PSC Report on the way ahead following the lessons identified from the planning phase of operation *Althea*, Council Doc. 9764/05, 7 June 2005 (classified).

287   Operation *Concordia* – Lessons Learned Process, Council Doc. 15484/04, 28 Nov. 2003.

- the request by the EU to NATO for release of assets and capabilities (letter by CFSP-HR);
- NATO's reply to the EU request for NATO assets and capabilities (letter by NATO-SG);
- the EU–NATO exchange of letters on the release, monitoring, return or recall of NATO common assets and capabilities (known as the 'Model Contract'[288]);
- the Specific Agreement on the use of NATO assets and capabilities for the EU-led military operation in BiH.

Overall, the EU organs seemed satisfied with the implementation of the *Althea* transfer in June 2005.[289]

Importance of Operation Althea *for the shifting EU–NATO relationship*   Operation *Althea* represents a challenge to the EU in different ways.[290] First of all, the nation-building process in Bosnia-Herzegovina remains a formidable task, an end of which is not in sight for the moment.[291] Furthermore, *Althea* is another crucial test for the European Security Strategy[292] and the Berlin Plus agreement.[293] In contrast to Operation *Concordia* in Macedonia, in Bosnia EU and NATO troops are working side by side in the field (for example hunting war criminals[294]), not only at headquarters in SHAPE or Naples. The lessons identified from the EU–NATO transfer in *Concordia* were worked into the *Althea* transfer, but their value seems to have been limited, as the management and planning challenge in *Althea* was certainly of a different scale and nature.

At the time of Operation *Concordia*, a general framework defining the long-term EU–NATO relationship was still missing.[295] The grand deal on ESDP reached in December 2003[296] has also ushered in a new phase and brought the 'strategic partnership' begun by the Berlin Plus agreement[297] closer to reality. Echoing this,

288   F. Cameron / G. Qille, *The Future of ESDP*, EPC Working Paper (2004), p. 27.

289   European Council, Brussels, 16–17 June 2005, Presidency Conclusions, para. 85, Council Doc. 10255/05

290   *Cf.* A. Beatty, *EU prepares for Bosnia mission*, EUObserver, 30 Nov. 2004.

291   *Cf.* e.g. W. Graf Vitzthum / I. Winkelmann (eds.), *Bosnien-Herzegovina im Horizont Europas* (2003); M. Ducasse-Rogier, *Recovering from Dayton: From 'peace-building' to 'state-building' in Bosnia and Herzegovina*, Helsinki Monitor 2004, No. 2, pp. 76–90.

292   H. Mahony, *Irish asked to implement EU security strategy*, EUObserver, 8 Jan. 2004.

293   J. de Hoop Scheffer (NATO Secretary General), speech at the 40th Munich Security Conference, 7 Feb. 2004; *cf.* already G. Lindstrom, *2003 Transatlantic Conference: The EU and the U.S.: Partners in Stability?*, EU-ISS Institute Note, 22–23 April 2003, p. 4, 3rd bullet.

294   *Cf.* J. Solana (EU CFSP-HR) / J. de Hoop Scheffer (NATO Secretary General), *Guiding Bosnia along the road to Brussels*, International Herald Tribune, 15 July 2004, p. 6.

295   A. Missiroli, *The European Union: Just a Regional Peacekeeper?*, 8 EFAR (2003), p. 501.

296   See above Chapter 2 (ESDP Today).

297   See Berlin Plus Sgreement.

NATO also spoke of a 'milestone' in December 2004.[298] Operation *Althea* falls into this new phase, and this can be seen reflected in the language of its preparatory documents.[299] In more general terms, the *Althea* transfer represents the most visible signal for the gradually shifting balance in EU–NATO relations, towards more responsibility of Europeans for their own security.[300]

However, for much the same reasons as with Operation *Concordia* in 2003,[301] no further evidence has yet emerged from Operation *Althea* concerning the question of NATO primacy or the problem of a NATO 'right of first refusal'. Consultation between the EU and NATO before the takeover seems to have been close at all levels.[302] Behind the scenes, the EU had already been busy preparing for the Bosnia takeover since at least April 2004. Yet, it is noticeable that the EU took no official step in this direction before NATO had officially declared it would terminate SFOR at the end of the year. Only after the Istanbul Summit in June 2004 did the EU quickly issue the *Althea* JA on 12 July. It can be imagined that this held up progress in the EU's operational planning, starting by the appointment of the Operation Commander, a detriment which added to time pressures in the subsequent preparatory phase. The fact that the EU nevertheless did respect, against operational time pressures, the politically important Istanbul Summit before proceeding with more detailed planning would perhaps seem to confirm the first reading of the 'where NATO as a whole is not engaged' formula ('where NATO *already happens* not to be engaged').[303] However, this reading is in any case already undisputed.

NATO Operation KFOR (Kosovo): possibilities for a future EU takeover

After Bosnia, should the EU also take over KFOR, being NATO's last remaining peacekeeping operation in the Balkans?[304] KFOR is currently twice as large as SFOR was (about 17 500 troops). Europeans already gained some experience in its operational command when the Eurocorps lead the KFOR headquarters for six months starting in spring 2000.[305] However, NATO has no intention of leaving

---

298   Ministerial Meeting of the North Atlantic Council, 9 Dec. 2004, Final Communiqué, NATO Press Release (2004)170, para. 5.

299   E.g. Council Doc. 6574/04, 20 Feb. 2004, p. 4, para. 4.

300   M. Leonard, *Why Europe will run the 21st century* (2005), p. 130.

301   See above p. 235.

302   *Cf.* Draft ESDP Presidency Report, 13 Dec. 2004, Council Doc. 15547/04, para. 28.

303   See above Chapter 5 (NATO Primacy).

304   *Cf.* D. Leonard, *What the Union should do for Kosovo*, European Voice (online edition), Vol. 11, No. 1, 13 Jan. 2005.

305   S. Blockmans, *A New Crisis Manager at the Horizon – The Case of the European Union*, 13 LJIL (2000), p. 255, n.1; M. Kremer / U. Schmalz, *Nach Nizza – Perspektiven der GESVP* (2001), p. 171.

Kosovo for the time being,[306] a position which was reaffirmed in December 2003.[307] Nevertheless, the fact that the EU has taken over an operation as large as SFOR from NATO has invariably raised similar questions about KFOR as well.[308] The EU is keeping its options open on this question.[309] It must be pointed out that the security situation on the ground in Kosovo is even more volatile than in Bosnia.[310] As events in spring of 2004 demonstrated, any peacekeeping operation in Kosovo must be able to check an unexpected renewed outbreak of civil strife there.[311] The civil unrest in Kosovo in spring 2004 also prompted some calls (not further elaborated), such as by German defence minister P. Struck, for more EU responsibility in the province.[312] However, the present EU–NATO consensus seems to regard maintenance of the NATO command as desirable at least until the status issue of Kosovo has been resolved.[313] In addition, the United States is as popular in Kosovo, for the same reasons as in Bosnia,[314] while the EU is not trusted by the local population to have military capacity to provide order on its own, without American leadership.[315] After the resolution of the status issue, however, the EU will probably take over KFOR

306 D. Triantaphyllou, *Balkans: The Transition from a Reduced Commitment*, Institute Note, 14 March 2003, EU-ISS – Task Forces 2003, p. 3, http://www.iss-eu.org/activ/content/rep9.pdf (visited 31/04/2003).

307 Meeting of the North Atlantic Council in Defence Ministers Session, Brussels, 1 Dec. 2003, Final Communiqué, para. 7, NATO Press Release (2003)148.

308 *Cf.* already C. Schwegmann, *EU-Friedensmissionen auf dem Balkan – eine Alternative zur NATO?*, Studien und Berichte zur Sicherheitspolitik 5/2002, Austrian Federal Ministry for Defence, p. 10, http://www.bmlv.gv.at/pdf_pool/publikationen/09_euf_01_schweg.pdf (visited 12/08/2004); B.S. Posen, *ESDP and the Structure of World Power*, 39 The International Spectator 1 (2004), p. 5 at 16.

309 *Cf.* J. Solana, EU CFSP-HR, comments on resignation of H. Holkeri, UN Special Representative to Kosovo, 25 May 2004, Council Doc. S0144/04: 'The European Union will remain strongly engaged in Kosovo, with a view to bringing peace, stability and prosperity to its people and to the region. According to plan, I intend to visit Kosovo ... to look at recent and *future* developments.' [emphasis added]; European Council, Brussels, 16–17 June 2005, Presidency Conclusions, Annex III (Declaration on Kosovo), para. 10, Council Doc. 10255/05.

310 C. Schwegmann, *EU-Friedensmissionen auf dem Balkan – eine Alternative zur NATO?*, Studien und Berichte zur Sicherheitspolitik 5/2002, Austrian Federal Ministy for Defence, p. 23, http://www.bmlv.gv.at/pdf_pool/publikationen/09_euf_01_schweg.pdf (visited 12/08/2004); F.S. Larrabee, *ESDP and NATO: Assuring Complementarity* (2004), p. 51 at 65.

311 D. Manca, *From global to local: Ethnic violence in Kosovo reminds NATO about security in its backyard*, ISIS NATO Notes, Vol. 6, No. 2 (2004).

312 *Struck für mehr Verantwortung der EU im Kosovo*, Frankfurter Allgemeine Zeitung, 6 April 2004, p. 1.

313 F.S. Larrabee, *ESDP and NATO: Assuring Complementarity* (2004), p. 51 at 65.

314 See above p. 253.

315 M. Mertens, *'Die Amerikaner müssen bleiben'*, Frankfurter Allgemeine Zeitung, 4 Feb. 2004, p. 5.

as well. The Union may eventually take over all peacekeeping from NATO in the Balkans.[316] For any such future endeavours, the lessons learned from the *Althea* transfer will be important for both NATO and the EU.

EU operations without recourse to NATO assets ('option 3')

Operation Artemis *(Democratic Republic of Congo)*

The EU got its first opportunity to launch an independent crisis management operation in June 2003.[317] Throughout the spring of that year, inter-ethnic violence had broken out in the town of Bunia in the east of in the DRC, between the Hema and Lendu tribal factions, creating some 300 000 refugees.[318] The spreading humanitarian catastrophe was beyond the means of the local MONUC peacekeeping mission to control. The UN Secretary General requested, in a letter to the Security Council, the international community to take urgent action.[319] It was not the classical scenario the planners of the ERRF had envisaged. Nevertheless a Union peacekeeping role outside Europe, particularly in Africa, had been considered before.[320] The worsening humanitarian situation caused a meeting of EU defence ministers to task the High Representative with drafting a positive response to the UN from the EU. France had made an early decision to intervene,[321] and it offered to lead such a mission as framework nation under the 'framework nation concept'.[322] On 30 May 2003 the UN Security Council passed a resolution authorising States to use 'all necessary means' (a robust mandate) to restore order in Bunia.[323] The EU Council took a Joint

---

316   *Cf.* W. Drozdiak, *The North Atlantic Drift*, 84 Foreign Affairs (Jan./Feb. 2005), pp. 88–98.

317   On *Operation Artemis* in general, see C. Mace, *Operation Artemis: Mission improbable?*, ESR, No. 18 (2003), pp. 5–6.

318   See in general, Second special report of the Secretary-General on the UN Mission in the Democratic Republic of Congo, 27 May 2003, UN-Doc. S/2003/566.

319   Letter dated 15 May 2003 from the Secretary-General addressed to the President of the Security Council, 28 May 2003, UN-Doc. S/2003/574.

320   C. Hill, *The EU's capacity for conflict prevention*, 6 EFAR (2001), pp. 318–9; Yesson, *NATO, EU and Russia: Reforming Europe's Security Institutions*, 6 EFAR (2001), p. 220; A. Krause, *The European Union's Africa Policy: The Commission as Policy Entrepreneur in the CFSP*, 8 EFAR (2003), p. 221 at 230–1; Franco-British summit, Le Touquet, 4 February 2003, Declaration on Strengthening European Cooperation in Security and Defence, 1), CP 67, p. 36 at 37.

321   A French operation code-named *Operation Mamba* was already under preparation. *Cf.* F. Faria, *Crisis management in sub-Saharan Africa* (2004), p. 40.

322   L. Kirk / A. Beatty, *European forces for Congo peace mission*, EUObserver, 19 May 2003; L. Kirk, *France ready to lead UN Congo force*, *ibid.*, 30 May 2003.

323   SC Res. 1484 (2003), 30 May 2003, para. 4.

Action to intervene under the mandate given by the Security Council on 5 June,[324] and the first French advance troops arrived in Bunia two days later.[325] After securing the airport, an airlift support bridge was built to Entebbe in Uganda, and the EU mission gradually took control over the entire town.[326] General security conditions quickly improved.[327] Overall, 1800 troops, more than half of them from France, were involved in the operation which was limited in time until 1 September 2003. Some third countries also sent troop contingents.[328] The decision of the EU to intervene was accompanied by euphoria in Brussels and many national capitals,[329] and much was made of the fact that Operation *Artemis* did not rely on NATO military support.[330]

The EU–NATO relationship generally seemed to take a back seat in the preparatory stage of Operation *Artemis*.[331] This is interesting because it was exactly for such independent EU missions (option 3 under the later NATO/EU Consultation document of December 2003[332]) that a NATO 'right of first refusal' had for years been claimed by a variety of actors, in and outside NATO, according to the oft-

---

324 Council Joint Action 2003/423/CFSP of 5 June 2003 on the European Union military operation in the Democratic Republic of Congo, OJ L 143/50 of 11/6/2003. *Cf.* also Council Decision 2003/432/CFSP of 12 June 2003 on the launching of the European Union military operation in the Democratic Republic of Congo, OJ L 147/42 of 14/6/2003.

325 S. Sengupta, *First French troops arrive in Congo*, International Herald Tribune (online edition), 7 June 2003.

326 *Cf.* C. Link, *UN-Truppe übernimmt Kongo-Einsatz*, Frankfurter Rundschau (online edition), 2 Sept. 2003.

327 *Cf.* GAERC, Brussels, 21 July 2003, Conclusions on Africa – Democratic Republic of Congo and the Great Lakes Region, CP 67, p. 196.

328 *Cf.* PSC Decisions of 1 July 2003 on the acceptance of third States' contributions, 2003/500/CFSP, OJ L 179/19 of 9/7/2003; PSC Decision of 31 July 2003 amending *ibid.*, 2003/605/CFSP, OJ L 206/32 of 15/8/2003; PSC Decision of 11 July 2003 on the setting up of a Committee of Contributors, 2003/529/CFSP, OJ L 184/13 of 23/7/2003.

329 J. Dempsey, *EU set to back peacekeeping force for Congo*, Financial Times (online edition), 3 June 2003; *EU to Send Peacekeepers To Congo*, Washington Post, 4 June 2003, p. A20; M. Winter / R. Meng, *EU schickt Soldaten nach Kongo*, Frankfurter Rundschau (online edition), 4 June 2003; S. Castle, *Military mission to Africa is first for the EU*, The Independent (online edition), 5 June 2003.

330 J. Dempsey, *Congo mission to test EU defence policy*, Financial Times (online edition), 6 June 2003; J.-P. Tuquoi / L. Zecchini, *L'Union européenne dépêche une force d'intervention au Congo, sans l'aide de l'OTAN*, Le Monde, 5 June 2003; M. Wiegel / N. Busse, *Ohne Rückgriff auf die Nato*, Frankfurter Allgemeine Zeitung, 12 June 2003, p. 2. Only days before, the Economist had written that the EU 'would probably not be able, for instance, to intervene on its own to stop war in the Congo'. (*Europe's not-so-rapid-reaction force*, The Economist (online edition), 22 May 2003).

331 From the EU's announcement of the decision to intervene (Council Doc. 9957/03, 5 June 2003) to the closing press releases (e.g. Council Doc. S0168/03, 1 Sept. 2003), NATO was not mentioned in any EU document relation to the mission.

332 See above Chapter 2 (ESDP Today).

repeated formula that the EU could engage in such missions only 'where NATO as a whole is not engaged'.[333]

It has been argued above that the existence of such a 'right of first refusal' in favour of NATO has never existed on the basis of public statements made by NATO or the EU.[334] However, practice by these two organisations, coupled with respective *opinio juris*, can change such a state of affairs, establishing a rule of special custom, particularly when occasions for practice are few.[335]

Subjects of international law become bound via custom when they indicate, over successive times, that they regard themselves as being so bound in a certain manner and act accordingly henceforth. As regards the legal assessment of relevant practice, it is submitted that actions are most telling when they are taken in *contrast* to evident political interests, out of a perceived sense of obligation.[336] The existence of a customary norm is thus best evidenced by the *difference* in behaviour it induces in a subject, compared to a situation where that norm did not exist. Put otherwise, if a subject evidently stood to gain something by acting contrary to the norm, yet nonetheless stuck to it, this is clear evidence of *opinio juris*.

Bearing these considerations in mind, it is instructive to look at the EU's and NATO's behaviour before the decision that the EU should conduct an independent crisis management operation without the use of any NATO assets, that is, outside the Berlin Plus format which had previously been used for Operation *Concordia* in Macedonia.

In May 2003, the EU quickly had to decide whether to use a NATO-supported operation format (option 2) or an independent one under its 'Framework Nation Concept' (option 3). It seemed, for the first time, the latter was a real possibility, so the EU was, for practical purposes, unhampered by whatever NATO would say on the matter. Nevertheless, if there had existed a general NATO 'right of first refusal' between NATO and the EU as a matter of international law, the EU would have been obliged to first ask NATO whether the Alliance had any interest in such a mission, before the EU proceeded on its own.

The mission, initially planned as a purely French operation, was planned within a very short time frame, reacting to quick events on the ground in Bunia. From such records as are publicly available, an EU 'consultation' or a 'request' with NATO does not seem to have been made, even after the decision to conduct the mission under an EU banner in principle had been taken by EU member States in mid-May 2003 (and to start planning it, as every day counted).

At the NATO Summit on 3 June 2003 in Madrid, the EU CFSP-HR J. Solana outlined the EU's plans for the mission to the NAC. In the ensuing Press Conference,

---

333   See above Chapter 5 (NATO Primacy).

334   See above Chapter 5 (NATO Primacy).

335   *Cf.* F.R. Kirgis Jr., *NATO Consultations as a Component of National Decision-Making*, 73 AJIL (1979), p. 403.

336   *Cf. ibid.*, citing examples of US practice in NATO, at pp. 378 and 385.

NATO-SG G. Roberton stated that 'that NATO would not want to be engaged'[337] because NATO's strategic interests were elsewhere. He was, however, putting a good face to a situation which had already been decided by the EU before. The NAC meeting on 3 June 2003 was more a briefing of the EU's plans by the High Representative than genuine consultation prior to the EU's taking a decision. The opinion that the EU had 'side-stepped'[338] the 'right of first refusal' which NATO believed to be part of the Berlin Plus agreement was clear from the remarks of one of Robertson's staff:

> Obviously, we could not be hostile to a humanitarian operation, but we are most disturbed by the methodology: at first, France said that it would be an international force on the basis of a 'coalition of the willing', then it planted the European flag over it. How not to consider it as a deliberate plan to shortcut the 'permanent arrangements' agreed between NATO and the European Union?[339]

However, NATO apparently decided to swallow such misgivings, did not officially protest at the EU's behaviour, and instead wished the EU success in the mission.[340] The EU insisted afterwards that 'NATO was regularly and timely informed of the EU's intentions, in full respect of the spirit and of the letter of the crisis consultation arrangements'.[341]

What is the legal import from those actions? The EU, spoke of existing 'crisis consultation arrangements' with NATO; this formulation likely refers to the Nice Presidency Conclusions on EU/NATO consultation in times of crisis of December 2000, being part of the 2002 Berlin Plus agreement.[342] For EU operations conducted without NATO assets such as *Artemis*, those Nice Conclusions, however, only provided for the EU to keep NATO informed on the general progress of the operation,[343] not for any previous consultation. Be that as it may, the EU does not seem to have acted as if it felt in any way bound by a hypothetical 'right of first refusal' norm to consult NATO

---

337   Press Conference by NATO Secretary General, Lord Robertson with Greek Foreign Minister G. Papandreou, EU Presidency and J. Solana, EU High Representative, following the NATO-EU Meeting, Madrid, 3 June 2003, NATO Speeches, http://www.nato.int/docu/speech/2003 /s030603i.htm (visited 4/6/03).

338   *Cf. EU sending troops to Congo, sidestepping NATO*, Toronto Star (online edition), 4 June 2003.

339   L. Zecchini, *Les nouveax habits de l'OTAN*, Le Monde, 19 June 2003 [English translation from: H. Vincze, *Beyond symbolism: the EU's first military operation seen in its context* (2003), p. 5, http://www.weltpolitik.net/texte/policy/concordia/beyond_symbolism. pdf (visited 15/08/2004). *Cf.* H. Vincze, *ibid.*

340   *Cf.* L. Zecchini, *ibid.*

341   Council of the European Union, EU–NATO Co-operation, Background – the Framework for Permanent Relations and Berlin Plus, para. 11, http://ue.eu.int/uedocs/cmsUpload/03-11-11 %20Berlin%20Plus%20press%20note%20BL.pdf (visited 11/12/04).

342   See below Chapter 8 (Berlin Plus Agreement).

343   European Council, Nice, Presidency Conclusions, Annex VII to Annex VI, III. (C), CP 47, p. 206.

before Operation *Artemis*. If such a right ever existed, one could argue that the Union placed political interests above it and ignored it. It has been reported that 'some inside NATO considered that the principle of consultation had not really been implemented, and that Operation *Artemis* was more a fait accompli than the result of a due process of consultation'.[344] Publicly, however, NATO does not seem to have pressed the point.

Of course, it is possible that NATO was taken by surprise, finding out that, while it thought it had consented to a purely French mission in a traditional French interest area in Africa,[345] that mission had turned overnight into a fully-fledged EU project, well advanced in its planning. Perhaps it judged that, at the Madrid Summit, the decisive point when a claim under a 'right of first refusal' could validly have been made, had passed. The political context of the ongoing conflict in Iraq, and more particularly, the aftershocks of the transatlantic rift NATO had experienced in the spring (especially the perceived loss of trust among some key allies), may indeed have made it difficult for NATO to discern what was going on in Brussels with respect to Africa in late May and early June. After the EU mission went ahead, NATO acquiesced in the situation. In sum, before the launching of the Congo mission, neither the EU nor NATO had given evidence of a 'right of first refusal' existing between them.

When, one year later in June 2004, the possibility surfaced that the EU might send a second peacekeeping mission to the DRC, the question seems not to have been raised anymore.[346]

EU operation in Moldova?

In July and September of 2003, discussions arose within the EU about a possible EU military peacekeeping operation in Moldova, part of which had broken away as the 'Transnistrian Republic' in 1990.[347] The Moldovan scenario would have been very different from EU peacekeeping activity in the Balkans, as no bloodshed was so far involved. The importance of the situation to the EU was mainly that the breakaway Transnistrian Republic presented a source of regional instability and crime, above

---

344   J.-Y. Haine, *ESDP and NATO*, in: N. Gnesotto (ed.), *EU Security and Defence Policy – The first five years* (2004), EU-ISS, p. 131 at 141.

345   *Cf.* WEU Assembly Doc. 1439, para. 11.

346   *Cf.* W. Wallis, *Brussels considers sending troops to help UN in Congo peacekeeping*, Financial Times, 8 June 2004, p. 10; A. Beatty, *EU poised for another Congo mission*, EUObserver, 8 June 2004; *EU erwägt Militäreinsatz*, Frankfurter Rundschau, 8 June 2004, p. 7.

347   *UE-Moldavia: La UE deja para septiembre debate sobre posible envio de fuerza*, Efe Spanish Newswire Services, 22 July 2003; V. Socor, *The EU can Secure Its Own Neighborhood*, Wall Street Journal Europe, 27 July 2003; *'FAS': EU diskutiert ueber Militaereinsatz in Moldawien*, DPA, 6 Sept. 2003; *EU discussing peacekeeping mission to Moldova: report*, AFP, 7 Sept. 2003; D. Brössler, *Ein Test für Europa: Die Niederlande wollen, dass sich die EU am Dnjestr als Sicherheitsmacht beweist*, Süddeutsche Zeitung, 10 Sept. 2003, p. 11. *Cf.* A. Monaco, *EU and NATO: Competition or Cooperation?*, in: A. Weidemann / A. Simon (2003), p. 40 at 41, 43.

all smuggling and human trafficking.[348] At the origin of the discussions seems to have been a proposal from the Dutch OSCE Chairmanship-in-Office,[349] although this was later categorically denied by Dutch FM Jaap de Hoop Scheffer.[350] The PSC apparently studied all options for action under ESDP in Moldova, a police mission, and also a military mission under the various formats.[351] Option 2 (Berlin Plus, using NATO assets) appeared the most apparent, but option 3 (EU autonomously) was also not ruled out. Discussions were also held on all options with NATO in the PSC-NAC format. The United States favoured a mission with NATO involvement. In the case of the EU's independent Congo mission in Africa, the Americans might have accepted a fait accompli by the EU, but in Europe the possibility of such a mission quickly turned into an important question of power. US ambassador to NATO N. Burns vehemently rejected the idea during an NAC meeting on 15 July 2003.[352] After the summer, the matter cooled down.[353] EU action on Moldova has since been restricted to diplomatic activity.[354] It was not before June 2005 that the EU again began elaborating plans to send a border-monitoring mission to Moldova, following a joint request by the Moldovan and Ukrainian governments.[355]

---

348   *Cf.* generally D. Lynch, *Russia faces Europe*, EU-ISS Chaillot Paper No. 60 (2003), pp. 87 and pp. 96.

349   S. Castle, *Chaos in Moldova prompts call for peacekeeping force*, The Independent (online edition), 15 July 2003; J. Dempsey, *Congo the test for EU's peacekeeping skills*, Financial Times, 15 July 2003; A. Benkö / M. Malek, *Akteure des Konflikts um Transnistrien (Moldau) – Unter besonderer Berücksichtigung der Möglichkeiten und Grenzen eines EU-Engagements*, 53 Südosteuropa 1 (2005), pp. 56 at 74–6.

350   OSCE Press Release SEC.PR/412/03 of 17 July 2003.

351   D. Spinant / D. Cronin, *EU diplomats 'not sure' about sending troops to Moldova*, European Voice (online edition), Vol. 9, No. 28, 24 July 2003.

352   M. Winter, *Von weißen Elefanten und bitteren Pillen*, Frankfurter Rundschau, 2 Sept. 2003, p. 3.

353   But see the European Parliament Resolution on the Annual Report from the Council to the European Parliament on the Main Aspects and Basic Choices for CFSP, including the Financial Implications for the General Budget of the European Union, Strasbourg, 23 Oct. 2003, para. 65, CP 67, p. 235 at 246–7, welcoming the proposals for an ESDP mission in Moldova.

354   See e.g. Sixth Meeting of the Co-operation Council between the European Union and the Republic of Moldova, Council Doc. 6295/04, 24 Feb. 2004; Declaration of the Presidency on behalf of the European Union on the closure of Moldovan schools in Transnistria, Council Doc. 11771/04, 28 July 2004; *Javier Solana, EU Representative for the CFSP, writes to Russian Foreign Minister Sergey Lavrov on deteriorating situation in Transnistria*, Council Press Release S0208/04, 31 July 2004; *Javier Solana, EU Representative for the CFSP, sends diplomatic mission to Moldova*, Council Press Release S0210/04, 9 Aug. 2004. The possibility of an EU military peacekeeping operation in Moldova is still occasionally referred to in the press, *cf.* A. Beatty, *Russia may be offered bigger say in European security*, EUObserver, 26 Feb. 2004.

355   A. Beatty, *EU mission en route for Transniester frontier*, European Voice, Vol. 11, No. 22, 9 June 2005, p. 4; *Id.*, *EU 'set to give OK' to monitors in Transniester*, European

As meeting records of both the NAC and the PSC are classified, it is hard to tell whether NATO invoked a 'right of first refusal' in the case of Moldova.[356] However, judging from the actions of the EU and NATO in this case, it is interesting to note that neither proceeded with any plans for Moldova.[357] If a 'right of first refusal' was ever claimed or rejected, it was not backed up by any action. A 'right of first refusal' can only be exercised by its holder by 'meeting the contract' himself[358] and would have entailed taking action. Hence, the evidence in case of Moldova is much more inconclusive than in the case above of the Congo mission. As a result, the conclusions drawn from the analysis of the actions relating to the Congo mission above continue to stand. The Moldovan case has also not shown NATO to have a 'right of first refusal' over EU crisis management.

EU–NATO interaction regarding support to the AU in Darfur

Calls for a clearer coordination between the EU and NATO in addressing rising crises on the globe had never ceased.[359] This need became evident once more as each of the two organisations made ready to support the African Union (AU) in its crisis management mission in Darfur (Sudan) in June 2005, at first independently of each other.

The humanitarian catastrophe in Darfur, although already raging for years, had come to number at least 180 000 dead and 2.5 million in danger of starvation as a result of the conflict in that region. The UN Security Council addressed the issue more urgently than ever before in the first half of 2005,[360] inter alia referring the matter to the ICC. Impressions of a genocide were almost universally shared by the international community. The AU decided on 28 April 2005 to increase the troop presence of its AMIS mission in Sudan from 2200 at the time to about 6200 by September[361] (a figure which was to rise later). The AU's claims for 'ownership' of the problem were generally accepted by Western countries, probably also because of

---

Voice, Vol. 11, No. 24, 23 June 2005, p. 4.

356   After an EU–NATO meeting on 16 July 2003, an unnamed diplomat was reported as saying that the meeting had shown that 'the Alliance is not likely to undertake the operation itself, as ... Washington is not interested, but would let the Europeans do it' (cited in: D. Spinant, *EU eyes controversial peace mission to strife-torn Moldova*, European Voice (online edition), Vol. 9, No. 27, 17 July 2003).

357   A joint NATO-Moldovan project to destroy antipersonnel and landmine stocks had, however, been successfully implemented in 2003. *Cf.* IISS, *The Military Balance 2003/04*, p. 31.

358   See above Chapter 5 (NATO Primacy).

359   *Cf.* remarks of NATO-SG J. de Hoop Scheffer, cited in: A. Föderl-Schmid, *Nato respektiert Österreichs Position*, Der Standard (online edition), 23 May 2005.

360   UNSCR 1590 (24 March 2005), 1591 (29 March 2005) and 1593 (31 March 2005).

361   Communiqué of the 28th meeting of the AU Peace and Security Council, 28 April 2005, Addis Ababa, PSC/PR/Comm.(XXVIII), para. 9.

political sensibilities which would have been involved with sending white soldiers to Africa. However, as AU members lacked the military capabilities, particularly to transport troops from other parts of Africa to the region, external help was needed to fill the gap.

Although discussions within the EU about sending a crisis management mission (police or military) to Darfur had never gained much support,[362] the EU already had a legal framework in place for giving military training and crisis management support to the AU.[363] It focused on capacity building, planning support, disarmament, demobilisation and reintegration of combatants and security sector reform and EU internal and external coordination.[364] Some human, technical and logistic assistance in terms of military and police planners and observers, besides financial assistance for AMIS, had already been provided to the AU for Darfur in 2004,[365] without this assistance taking the form of a proper ESDP operation. By April 2005, the EU received a list of priority needs from the AU.[366] On 26 May, an offer including all possible support to military, police and civilian efforts was made on a pledging conference in Addis Ababa. Coordination with other international organisations such as NATO was recognised by that time.[367]

Concerning NATO, this was just about time. On 26 April 2005 NATO too had received a letter from the AU, asking for logistical support to AMIS. This assistance request was detailed by a high-ranking visit from the AU at NATO HQ on 17 May. By 24 May, NATO had agreed that the elements to be provided to the AU would include strategic airlift, training (command and control, operational planning), and use of intelligence by AMIS.[368] The final decision was announced at the NATO defence

---

362 *Cf.* J. Dempsey, *EU-led forces 'could intervene' in Sudanese conflict*, Financial Times, 13 April 2004, p. 6; A. Beatty, *Offer of police mission to Sudan*, EUObserver, 6 Sept. 2004.

363 Declaration by the Presidency on behalf of the European Union on the occasion of the launching of the Peace and Security Council of the African Union, Addis Ababa, 25 May 2004, Council Doc. 9813/04; Common Position 2004/85/CFSP of 26 Jan. 2004 concerning conflict prevention, management and resolution in Africa, OJ L 21/25 of 28/1/2004; Action Plan for ESDP support to Peace and Security in Africa, Council Doc. 10538/4/04 REV 4, 16 Nov. 2004; Guidelines for implementing ESDP support to Peace and Security in Africa, Council Doc. 15542/1/04 REV 1, 9 Dec. 2004.

364 GAERC, Brussels, 22 Nov. 2004, European Security and Defence Policy, CP 75, p. 284.

365 European Council, Brussels, 16–17 Dec. 2004, ESDP Presidency Report, para. 40, CP 75, p. 356.

366 EU-Africa Ministerial Meeting, Luxembourg, 11 April 2005, Council Doc. 7995/05, p. 3.

367 GAERC, Conclusions on Sudan, Council Doc. 9243/05, 23 May 2005, para. 8; European Council, Brussels, 16–17 June 2005, Presidency Conclusions, para. 72, Council Doc. 10255/05.

368 NATO's assistance to the African Union for Darfur, NATO Topics, http://www.nato.int/issues/darfur/index.html (visited 18/06/05).

ministers meeting on 9 June,[369] and NATO airlifts for troops from AU countries started on from 1 July.[370]

A few days before NATO's decision on 9 June, an open split broke out between members of the EU and NATO on the question which organisation should coordinate measures in support of AMIS, particularly airlift.[371] The United States and Canada preferred NATO (through SHAPE) as coordination institution, while France favoured the EU. Other countries like Germany or the UK were undecided or wanted to use both organisations.[372] The pressure of the situation on the ground in Darfur, however, contributed to a quick solution of this renewed competition issue by 9 June.[373] In the event, both organisations agreed to provide support staff to the AU-led military cell in Addis Ababa,[374] with the choice of organisation being left to individual member States.[375]

The open relief evidenced by defence ministers after the NATO meeting on 9 June testifies to the fact that everyone wanted to avoid a repetition of the EU–NATO competition issue which had caused great rifts in 2003 during the Iraq crisis and the European Convention. Rather, the general impression was that consultation by all sides in the EU and NATO on the Darfur support issue was very close in those days. There was coordination at the military level. In addition, in an effort of mutual transparency, NATO kept the EU informed on the general aspects of its support to AMIS. Nowhere was there heard, from public sources at least, any talk of a NATO primacy, a NATO right of first refusal, or a geographical division of labour leaving Africa to the EU for historical reasons. Even if a general NATO right of first refusal had existed, it could arguably not have been applied in this case. For the EU's help to the AU had been running already since 2004. At that time NATO had not appeared particularly interested in Africa. In effect, the brief Darfur split between the EU and NATO was another example showing that these theoretical precepts could quickly be sidelined by the priorities of the day, given political will and pragmatism. A few weeks after the incident, Darfur was already being presented as a positive example of EU–NATO cooperation.[376]

---

369   Meeting of the North Atlantic Council in Defence Ministers Session, Brussels, 9 June 2005, Final Communiqué, para. 9, NATO Press Release (2005)076.

370   *NATO starts airlifting African Union troops to Darfur*, NATO Update, 1 July 2005.

371   D. Dombey, *Nato-EU spat hits airlift to Darfur*, Financial Times, 8 June 2005, p. 4.

372   *Nato's Darfur mission on as partners deny split*, The East Standard (Kenya) (online edition), 11 June 2005.

373   *Cf. Nato and EU Must End Squabble Over Darfur Airlift*, Human Rights Watch, Press Release, 9 June 2005.

374   *Green light for NATO support to African Union for Darfur*, NATO Update, 9 June 2005; D. Dombey, *Nato defends deal on Darfur airlift*, Financial Times, 10 June 2005, p. 3.

375   *NATO agrees on Darfur aid, sets aside strains with EU*, AFP, 9 June 2005.

376   E.g. J. de Hoop Scheffer, *A Changing Alliance in a Changing World*, speech in Bratislava, 30 June 2005, http://www.nato.int/docu/speech/2005/s050630a.htm (visited 01/07/05).

Chapter 8

Berlin Plus Agreement[1]

INTRODUCTION

On 16 December 2002, the EU and NATO announced the conclusion of an agreement on cooperation on international security, the Berlin Plus agreement (BP).[2] It was instantly hailed by the press as a breakthrough in EU–NATO relations.[3] Combined with the NATO-EU agreement on the Security of Information, concluded in March 2003,[4] this agreement opened the long-awaited possibility for the EU to engage in limited crisis management in its 'near abroad'. The EU peacekeeping operations undertaken in Macedonia and Bosnia in 2003 and 2004 under this agreement give ample evidence of its importance.

The question of legally binding force will become important in the future whenever competing needs from the EU for NATO or US equipment, or for the 'double-hatted' forces,[5] arise.[6] In such a case, both actors could soon find themselves reverting to legal arguments, as part of their strategies for achieving certain political goals.[7]

The essentials of this agreement had been prepared for a long time before, and it had been generally expected to be finalised in an international treaty between the two

---

1   Parts of this chapter appeared already in a shortened version in: M. Reichard, *Some Legal Issues Concerning the EU–NATO Berlin Plus Agreement*, 73 NJIL (2004), pp. 37–67.

2   EU–NATO Declaration on ESDP, 16 Dec. 2002, NATO Press Release (2002)142 and 42 ILM 242 (2003).

3   *NATO agrees to help new EU force*, International Herald Tribune (online edition), 16 December 2002; *EU to deploy troops after deal with Nato*, Financial Times, 16 December 2002, p. 6; *EU and NATO Sign Military Cooperation Deal*, Deutsche Welle (online edition), 17 December 2002; *NATO, EU in peacekeeping* pact, The Washington Times (online edition), 17 December 2002; *Clearing the Way for EU–NATO Cooperation*, The Washington Post, December 18 2002, p. A24.

4   OJ L 80/36 of 27/7/2003.

5   The concept of double-hatted forces, governing the command status answerable to both the WEU and NATO, is part of the 'Petersberg tasks'. See Western European Union Council of Ministers, Petersberg, Bonn, 19 June 1992, Declaration, II. para. 6., http://www.weu.int/documents/920619peten.pdf (visited 23/07/03). These tasks were incorporated into the EU system by the Amsterdam Treaty, Art. 17/2 TEU.

6   See above Chapter 7 (Military Crisis Management).

7   Compare I. Johnstone, *Security Council Deliberations: The Power of the Better Argument*, 14 EJIL 3 (2003), pp. 437–480.

organisations, possibly outside the treaty system of the EU. This section will address the question of its legal nature, which is far from clear.

CONTENT OF THE AGREEMENT

The exact wording of the agreement is unfortunately not available to the public as it is a formal decision of the North Atlantic Council (NAC), and thus classified. The NAC decision is based on a classified exchange of letters between the EU's High Representative for the Common and Security Policy Javier Solana and NATO's Secretary General George Robertson. The following content was released in a NATO statement to the press:

> EU–NATO Declaration on ESDP[8]
>
> THE EUROPEAN UNION AND THE NORTH ATLANTIC TREATY ORGANISATION,
>
> Welcome the strategic partnership established between the European Union and NATO in crisis management, founded on our shared values, the indivisibility of our security and our determination to tackle the challenges of the new Century;
>
> Welcome the continued important role of NATO in crisis management and conflict prevention, and reaffirm that NATO remains the foundation of the collective defence of its members;
>
> Welcome the European Security and Defence Policy (ESDP), whose purpose is to add to the range of instruments already at the European Union's disposal for crisis management and conflict prevention in support of the Common Foreign and Security Policy, the capacity to conduct EU-led crisis management operations, including military operations where NATO as a whole is not engaged;
>
> Reaffirm that a stronger European role will help contribute to the vitality of the alliance, specifically in the field of crisis management;
>
> Reaffirm their determination to strengthen their capabilities;
>
> Declare that the relationship between the European Union and NATO will be founded on the following principles:
>
> Partnership: ensuring that the crisis management activities of the two organisations are mutually reinforcing, while recognising that the European Union and NATO are organisations of a different nature;
>
> Effective mutual consultation, dialogue, cooperation and transparency;

---

8   NATO Press Release (2002)142, 16 Dec. 2002.

Equality and due regard for the decision-making autonomy and interests of the European Union and NATO;

Respect for the interests of the Member States of the European Union and NATO;

Respect for the principles of the Charter of the United Nations, which underlie the Treaty on European Union and the Washington Treaty, in order to provide one of the indispensable foundations for a stable Euro-Atlantic security environment, based on the commitment to the peaceful resolution of disputes, in which no country would be able to intimidate or coerce any other through the threat or use of force, and also based on respect for treaty rights and obligations as well as refraining from unilateral actions;

Coherent, transparent and mutually reinforcing development of the military capability requirements common to the two organisations;

To this end:

The European Union is ensuring the fullest possible involvement of non-EU European members of NATO within ESDP, implementing the relevant Nice arrangements, as set out in the letter from the EU High Representative on 13 December 2002;

NATO is supporting ESDP in accordance with the relevant Washington Summit decisions, and is giving the European Union, inter alia and in particular, assured access to NATO's planning capabilities, as set out in the NAC decisions on 13 December 2002;

Both organisations have recognised the need for arrangements to ensure the coherent, transparent and mutually reinforcing development of the capability requirements common to the two organisations, with a spirit of openness.

From 16 December 2002, therefore, the EU can count – on an 'assured' basis – on borrowing the planning capabilities necessary for the conduct of crisis management operations. What is further meant by 'inter alia, and in particular' only becomes clear after a thorough scanning of the negotiating history: in short, it means that alliance assets *other* than mere planning facilities, above all 'pre-identified' *physical* military hardware such as mobile headquarters, airborne early-warning stations and US satellite imaging, remains 'presumed' to be available from NATO, but only on a case-by-case basis.

BACKGROUND AND NEGOTIATING HISTORY

At its Berlin Ministerial Meeting of 1996, NATO decided to 'build a European Security and Defence Identity within the Alliance',[9] in order to 'enable all European Allies to make a more coherent and effective contribution to the missions and activities of the Alliance'[10] under the political control and strategic direction of the

---

9   Ministerial Meeting of the North Atlantic Council, Berlin, 3 June 1996, Final Communiqué, NATO Press Communiqué M-NAC-1(96)63, para. 2.
10   *Ibid.*, para. 5.

WEU.[11] The WEU was revived in this new context. It would now become NATO's 'European pillar'. In addition, the WEU would act as the EU's defence arm. The WEU thus, already then, acted as the link between the EU and NATO.[12] These two interlaced functions, were welcomed by the Alliance at the time.[13]

The Treaty of Maastricht, which founded the EU in 1992, referred to the WEU as an 'integral part of the development of the European Union'[14] which would be developed as its defence component. That treaty also echoed NATO's interpretation that the WEU would at the same time, strengthen the 'European pillar' within NATO.[15]

In a next step, Art. 17 TEU, as amended by the Treaty of Amsterdam in 1997, formally introduced the possibility of the EU to draw on WEU resources for its own budding defence efforts.[16] Through this provision, the indirect possibility was opened to also draw on NATO resources. The complex double-link security arrangements between the EU, the WEU and NATO throughout the 1990s have, however, been analysed before[17] and are not of central interest here.

European Security and Defence Policy takes shape – staking out of positions

In December 1998, the United Kingdom and France suggested that the EU should have the capacity for autonomous military action.[18] The US government attached three political conditions for this: no decoupling from the Alliance, no duplication of already scarce defence resources, and no discrimination against NATO members who were not EU members.[19] At its Summit in Washington in April 1999, NATO acknowledged the French-British statement of St-Malo and saw itself ready to provide the EU with 'ready access' to NATO planning capabilities for EU-led operations in which the Alliance as a whole was not engaged.[20] It distinguished for the first time, however, between *planning capabilities*, access to which by the EU should

---

11   The WEU had asked for the option of drawing on NATO's collective assets as early as 1993. See Declaration, WEU Council of Ministers, Luxembourg, 22 November 1993, I., para. 3, http://www.weu.int/documents/931122en.pdf (visited 23/07/03).

12   See above (Introduction).

13   North Atlantic Council, Brussels, 19 Dec. 1991, Final Communiqué, para. 12

14   Treaty on European Union made at Maastricht (1992), Final Act, Declaration (No 30) on Western European Union, paras. 1 and 2.

15   *Ibid.*, paras. 2 and 4.

16   M. Warnken, *Der Handlungsrahmen der EU* (2002), pp. 159, argues that a series of international treaties were, by implication, concluded by the EU and the WEU to this effect.

17   See above (Introduction).

18   See above Chapter 2 (ESDP Today).

19   Albright, Madeleine K., *The Right Balance Will Secure NATO's Future*, Financial Times, 7 December 1998, p. 22. For a fuller treatment of these events see above Chapter 5 (NATO primacy).

20   North Atlantic Council Summit, Washington, DC, 24 April 1999, Final Communiqué, para. 10, CP 47, p. 22.

be 'assured', and *other* capabilities and common assets.[21] In the view of NATO, the latter ones should be 'pre-identified' under a 'presumption of availability', but not 'assured'.[22] The distinction became a regular part of NATO documents referring to the EU assets-borrowing issue.[23]

Germany, which held the rotating EU Presidency chair in early 1999, addressed NATO's interests as voiced in the Washington Summit, and proposed that any future European defence effort would include 'arrangements to ensure EU/NATO transparency and consultation'.[24] If the EU seriously wanted to engage in crisis management, the WEU's functions in this respect (the 'Petersberg tasks') would have to be incorporated in the EU treaty system in the narrower sense, a transformation which was envisioned to be completed by the end of 2000.[25]

The EU also began at this time to distinguish two types of military operations: those which would require making use of NATO assets and capabilities, and other operations (of lower scale and intensity) which would not.[26] This differentiation was carried through successive Summits thereafter.[27]

At the European Council in Cologne, the EU repeated the differentiation between future operations led autonomously which could make use of 'national command

---

21   *Ibid.*

22   *Ibid.*

23   See e.g. North Atlantic Council meeting, Budapest, 29–30 May 2001, Final Communiqué, para. 49, NATO Press Release M-NAC 1(2001)77.

24   Informal meeting of EU foreign ministers Eltville, 13–14 March 1999, German proposal, para. 3, CP 47, p. 18.

25   *Cf.* Art. 17/3 TEU; European Council, Cologne, 3–4 June, 1999, CP 47, pp. 41, Declaration of the European Council on Strengthening the Common European Policy of Security and Defence, para. 5. The WEU began to prepare its legacy in its Ministerial Council at Luxembourg, on Nov. 22–23, 1999, see: WEU Ministerial Council, Luxembourg, 22–23 November 1999, Luxembourg Declaration, para. 10, CP 47, p. 69; WEU Ministerial Council, Porto, 15–16 May, paras. 4 and 5, CP 47, p. 113.

26   This distinction appeared first in a German Presidency Paper of 1999, Bonn, 24 February 1999, called 'Informal Reflection at WEU on Europe's Security and Defence', at II., para. 2, CP 47, p. 15. It was since carried through successive EU Summits: see e.g. European Council, Cologne, Annex III: Presidency Report on Strengthening the Common European Policy on Security and Defence, para. 3., CP 47, p. 44; Meeting of European Union defence ministers, Sintra, 28 February, 2000, paras. 18 and 19, CP 47, p. 99–100; European Council, Göteborg, 15–16 June 2001, CP 51, pp. 30, Annex IV to the ANNEX, III., para. 16, CP 51, p. 55 and was part of the discussions on the future of European defence in the Convention (e.g. L. Dini, Contribution on 'European Defence', Brussels, 26 September 2002, para. 1, CP 57, p. 203.

27   E.g. European Council, Cologne, Annex III: Presidency Report on Strengthening the Common European Policy on Security and Defence, para. 3., CP 47, p. 44; Sintra EU Defence Ministers meeting, 28 February 2000, paras. 18 and 19, CP 47, p. 95; European Council, Göteborg, 15–16 June 2001, CP 51, pp. 30, Presidency Conclusions, Annex IV to the ANNEX, III., para. 16, CP 51, p. 55 and was part of the discussions on the future of European defence in the Convention (e.g. L. Dini, Contribution on 'European Defence', Brussels, 26 September 2002, para. 1, CP 57, p. 203).

structures providing multinational representation in headquarters',[28] and those led with help of NATO assets. As to the issue of asset-borrowing, it accepted NATO's distinction made at the Washington Summit between planning capabilities and other assets, by referring to the cornerstones of future EU-led operations with NATO support in similar terms: The EU would require 'assured access to NATO planning capabilities';[29] availability of 'pre-identified' NATO capabilities and common assets for use in EU-led operations would have to be 'presumed'.[30]

Helsinki Headline Goal of December 1999

The European Council Summit in Helsinki in December 1999[31] opened the possibility for participation of non-EU countries (NATO members or otherwise) in any such operation,[32] but only 'in the event of an operation requiring recourse to NATO assets and capabilities'. This left open the question of those States' participation in operations where such recourse would *not* be required by the EU.[33] Even in the first case, participation would only be open 'upon a decision by the Council to launch an operation'.[34]

Until 1999, all EU efforts at future military operations in the remit of its European Security and Defence Policy (ESDP) had been dependent on its institutional link with the WEU. Where these operations also required substantial technological hardware such as support from GPS satellites, ready operational command and control structures, and long-range air transport capacity, the WEU was in turn dependent on

---

28   *Ibid.*, Annex III, Presidency Report on Strengthening of the Common European Policy on Security and Defence, under 4. 'Implementation', CP 47, pp. 44–5.

29   *Ibid.* In subsequent EU documents, the word 'assured' was used synonymously with 'guaranteed', see e.g. European Council, Nice, 7–9 Dec. 2000, Presidency Conclusions, CP 47, pp. 168, Appendix to Annex VII to Annex VI, at (1), CP 47, p. 207.

30   European Council, Cologne, Annex III: Presidency Report on Strengthening of the Common European Policy on Security and Defence, under 4. 'Implementation', CP 47, p. 44–5. The distinction between the two groups of Alliance assets became firmly established in EU documents referring to the subject matter from that time onwards. See e.g. Sintra EU Defence Ministers meeting, 28 February 2000, para. 18, CP 47, p. 99; European Council, Göteborg, 15–16 June 2001, CP 51, pp. 30, Presidency Conclusions, Göteborg European Council Presidency Report on the European Security and Defence Policy, Annex IV to the Annex: Exercise Policy of the European Union, paras. 3, 12, 26, CP 51, pp. 53, 54, 58; European Council, Laeken, 14–15 Dec. 2001, CP 57, pp. 110, Presidency Conclusions, Annex II: Declaration on the Operational Capability of the Common European Security and Defence Policy, at (B), under 'Finalisation of the Arrangements with NATO', CP 51, p. 121.

31   See above Chapter 5 (NATO Primacy).

32   European Council, Helsinki, Presidency Conclusions, II., Annex 1 to Annex IV, CP 47, p. 88.

33   *Ibid.*

34   *Ibid. Cf.* above Chapter 5(NATO Primacy).

NATO which decided on the borrowing of these assets on a case-by-case basis.[35] The decision to release these assets was taken by the NAC, deciding by consensus,[36] and was fully revocable at any time.[37] From the Helsinki Summit onwards, however, the WEU's cooperation system with NATO started to be taken over by the EU itself,[38] which thus entered into a direct relationship with the Alliance.[39]

At a Ministerial Meeting of the NAC held only four days after the European Helsinki Summit, NATO pronounced itself to be in general agreement with the EU plans laid out there.[40]

However, NATO also began to stake out more detailed conditions. At the NAC's Ministerial Meeting held in Florence in 24 May 2000, it stressed the need to ensure 'effective mutual consultation, cooperation and transparency'[41] and underlined 'the importance of ... involvement of non-EU European Allies in the structures which the EU is setting up'.[42] Arrangements for EU access to NATO planning capabilities should be 'assured', whereas access to Alliance's 'collective assets and capabilities' would only be of a 'ready' nature.[43] This essentially repeated the distinction first drawn at the Washington Summit.[44]

35   *Cf.* NATO Ministerial Council, 3 June, 1996, Berlin, Final Communiqué, para. 7, NATO Press Communiqué M-NAC-1 (96)63.

36   J.S. Ignarski, *North Atlantic Treaty Organization*, in EPIL III, p. 648.

37   '[The Alliance] will ... assist the European Allies to act by themselves as required through the readiness of the Alliance, on a case-by-case basis and by consensus, to make its assets and capabilities available for operations in which the Alliance is not engaged militarily under the political control and strategic direction of the WEU or as otherwise agreed, taking into account the full participation of all European Allies if they were so to choose.' – The Alliance's Strategic Concept, Approved by the Heads of State and Government participating in the meeting of the North Atlantic Council in Washington D.C. on 23–24 April 1999, para. 30, CP 47, pp. 29–30.

38   See Ministerial Meeting of the North Atlantic Council, Florence, 24 May 2000, Final Communiqué, para. 27 (NATO Press Release M-NAC-1(2000)52.

39   *Cf.* K. Gerteiser, *Die Sicherheits- und Verteidigungspolitik der Europäischen Union* (2002), p. 203.

40   Ministerial Meeting of the North Atlantic Council held at NATO headquarters, Brussels, on 15 December 1999, Final Communiqué, NATO Press Release M-NAC2(99)166, para. 20.

41   NATO Florence Ministerial, 24 May 2000, para. 27.

42   *Ibid.*, para. 29.

43   *Ibid.*, para. 27.

44   See above Chapter 7 (Military Crisis Management).

Feira: first procedural proposals from the EU

At its next Summit in Feira, on 19–20 June 2000, the European Council proposed basic procedures for cases in which the EU wished to draw on Alliance assets.[45] The EU's proposals were laid out in greater detail in two Appendices to Annex I of the Feira Presidency Conclusions. Appendix 1 on the 'participation' issue[46] envisaged a regime that should adequately address NATO's 'no discrimination' demand.[47] It included regularly timed meetings between the EU 15 with the six non-EU European NATO members (EU+6 format), and with the fifteen EU candidates and other interested countries (EU+15 format), distinguishing between different stages in the build-up to a crisis leading to an EU-led military intervention.[48] Appendix 2 listed principles on which the future EU–NATO relationship in joint crisis management should, in the view of the EU, develop: full respect of the autonomy of EU decision-making; a basis of shared values, equality and a spirit of partnership; recognition of equal footing; the different nature of the two organisations (hence the need to adapt WEU–NATO relations to an EU–NATO framework); and the avoidance of discrimination against any of their members.[49] EU access to NATO assets and capabilities should be regulated in an 'agreement'.[50] A draft had apparently already been circulated.[51]

This draft agreement was named the 'Berlin Plus' agreement by the European Council.[52] 'Plus' demonstrated in wording that the issue in this new relationship was not simply the transfer of the NATO–WEU relations (Berlin Accords of June 1996[53]) to the EU. Rather, in order be able to decide more independently, in particular in times of crises, the EU sought 'assured' access to the operational facilities from NATO, once that organisation had decided not to engage in an operation itself. These issues were subsequently further elaborated on.

---

45   European Council, Santa Marta da Feira, 19–20 June 2000, Annex I: Presidency Report on Strengthening the Common European Security and Defence Policy, II.D., CP 47, p. 125.

46   See above Chapter 5 (NATO Primacy).

47   *Cf.* S. Rynning, *Why not NATO? Military Planning in the European Union*, The Journal of Strategic Studies, Vol.26, No.1 (March 2003), p. 64.

48   European Council, Feira, CP 47, pp. 127

49   *Ibid.*, pp. 130. These points henceforth constituted working principles in areas where EU–NATO co-operation took place. See e.g. for the 'equal footing' element: NATO International Military Staff Press Release after the First Meeting of EU and NATO Military Committees, 12 June 2001, CP 51, p. 19; European Council, Göteborg, 15–16 June 2001, CP 51, pp. 30, Presidency Conclusions, Annex IV to the ANNEX, II., para. 12., CP 51, p. 54. All of them became constitutive elements of the eventual Berlin Plus agreement text.

50   European Council, Feira, *ibid.*, Appendix 2, A.3, CP 47, p. 132.

51   *Ibid.*, Appendix 2, B.2.(c), CP 47, p. 132.

52   The name had been used for the first time in the Sintra EU Defence Ministers meeting, 28 February 2000, CP 47, p. 95, para. 4.

53   Ministerial Meeting of the North Atlantic Council, Berlin, 3 June 1996, Final Communiqué, NATO Press Communiqué M-NAC-1(96)63. See also above Chapter 3.

The growing difference between the Concepts of ESDI and ESDP[54] began to weigh in also on the issue of asset-borrowing under negotiation. Both sides repeatedly stated that they saw the two projects – which shared the purpose of raising the level of military capabilities in Europe[55] – as mutually reinforcing.[56] In asset-borrowing, however, the difference of ESDP as compared to ESDI was that under the former the EU would work side by side with NATO, on a level playing field.

Nice: participation of non-EU Allies and 'permanent arrangements'

At the European Summit of Nice in December 2000, the EU elaborated its proposals on asset-borrowing to NATO, building on the fundamentals from Helsinki and Feira, also concerning 'participation' of non-EU NATO members and EU accession candidates: in the pre-operational phase to a crisis 'dialogue and consultation will be intensified at all levels ... to ensure that the countries potentially contributing to such an operation are informed of the EU's intentions', particularly with regard to military implications.[57] Even more consideration would be given in planning operations which would require the use of NATO assets and capabilities, before the Council took a decision.[58] In the operational phase of *autonomous* EU-led operations, the views of potential non-EU NATO participants would be heard once the Council *had* chosen the strategic military options. After approval of the operation concept, they would formally be invited to participate. In case of other (that is, non-NATO) countries which were EU accession candidates, such an invitation was optional for the Council.[59] This differentiation between NATO members (*'will* ... be

---

54   See above Chapter 2 (ESDP Today).

55   In NATO, this effort was called the Defence Capabilities Initiative (DCI). In the EU, it was the single most important point in the 'Headline Goal Task Force' project started at the Helsinki Summit, leading to subsequent 'Capability Commitment Conferences' in November 2000 and 2001, and eventually a detailed 'European Capabilities Action Plan'(ECAP). The role of European military capabilities is a problem beyond the scope of this book.

56   For NATO statements on this point, see e.g. speech by Strobe Talbott, US Deputy Secretary of State *America's Stake in a Strong Europe*, Remarks at a Royal Institute of International Affairs Conference on the Future of NATO, London, 7 October 1999, CP 47, p. 58–9.; Meeting of the North Atlantic Council in Defence Ministers Session, Brussels, Dec. 2, 1999, Final Communiqué, para. 17 (NATO Press Release D(99)156); Meeting of the North Atlantic Council in Defence Ministers Session, Brussels, Dec. 5, 2000, Final Communiqué, para. 16 (NATO Press Release M-NAC-D-2(2000)114). For the EU, see e.g. Anglo-French summit, London, 25 Nov. 1999, Joint Declaration on European Defence, para. 6, CP 47, p. 78; Sintra EU Defence Ministers meeting, 28 February 2000, Annex, under 'Food for Thought Paper', CP 47, p. 102; European Council, Feira, Annex I, Appendix 2, under 'Issues and Modalities for the Interim Period', A. 2., CP 47, p. 131.

57   European Council, Nice, Presidency Conclusions, Annex VI to Annex VI, III. (A), CP 47, p. 201.

58   *Ibid.*

59   *Ibid.*, (B), CP 47, pp. 201–2.

invited') and non-NATO members ('*may* ... be invited') went back to the Helsinki Summit.[60] The distinction between the two kinds of operations was also drawn at the level of operations planning: Alliance planning bodies in the case of operations requiring NATO assets, and 'European strategic level headquarters' in autonomous operations.

Provisions on the envisaged standing arrangements for EU–NATO consultation and cooperation repeated the guiding principles on cooperation between the two organisations from the previous Feira Summit.[61] But they also went further: the EU envisioned 'permanent arrangements for EU–NATO consultation and cooperation' and it hoped 'for a favourable reaction from NATO'.[62] It stressed the 'importance which it attaches to being able, when necessary, to make use of the assured access to NATO's assets and capabilities' and it would 'call on NATO for operational planning' in this regard. In Annexes, detailed procedures on regular as well as time-flexible additional joint EU–NATO meetings were suggested, at different organisational levels.[63] Cooperation of EU and NATO bodies had already taken place in some previous instances, as in the build-up of military capabilities being part of the 'Headline Goal Task Force'.[64] In times of crisis, contacts and meetings would be 'stepped up'.[65] A procedure for calling on Alliance assets was laid out, first identifying whether and which particular assets were to be used, then forwarding a formal request, and lastly the hand-over of the assets at a PSC/NAC meeting.[66] NATO bodies were to be included at each step.[67] Throughout the operation, NATO would be kept informed of the use of its assets.[68] Even in the case of autonomous crisis management operations of the EU or NATO, each would keep the other informed about the general progress of the operation. Lastly, in an additional Appendix to the last Annex,[69] details were spelt out for the envisioned 'Permanent arrangements of EU/NATO consultation and cooperation on the Implementation of Paragraph 10 of the Washington Communiqué'.[70] These were summarised under three headings:

---

60   European Council, Helsinki, Presidency Conclusions, II., Annex 1 to Annex IV, under 'Consultation and cooperation with non-EU countries and with NATO', CP 47, p. 88.

61   European Council, Nice, Presidency Conclusions, Annex VII to Annex VI, CP 47, pp. 203–4.

62   *Ibid.*, Annex VI., IV., CP 47, pp. 203–4.

63   These included the PSC, the NAC, the NATO and EU Military Committees, and NATO's Policy Coordination Group and Politico-Military Group.

64   See above Chapter 6 (Collective Self-Defence).

65   European Council, Nice, Presidency Conclusions, Annex VII to Annex VI, III. (A), CP 47, p. 205.

66   *Ibid.*, Annex VII to Annex VI, III. (A) and (B), CP 47, p. 205–6.

67   *Ibid.*, Annex VII to Annex VI, III. (B), CP 47, p. 206.

68   *Ibid.*, p. 206.

69   European Council, Nice, Presidency Conclusions, Appendix to Annex VII to Annex VI, CP 47, pp. 206–8.

70   For background to the three sub-headings below, see only Council of the European Union, EU–NATO Co-operation, Background – the Framework for Permanent Relations and

(1) *Guaranteed permanent access to NATO's planning capabilities (Without case-by-case NATO authorisation)*:
The highest contact point on the NATO side would be the DSACEUR (traditionally a European), who could, after negotiations had taken place, lastly refuse an EU request when it conflicted with NATO assets needed for an Article 5 operation. The EU would in this case have access to 'those NATO planning capabilities which remain available'. Contrariwise, this meant that, barring the unlikely event of an attack against an Alliance member, NATO would have no legal obstacles to refusing an EU request outright. This was a significant concession. As Art. 4 NAT was not mentioned, the Alliance would not even retain the last word on the use of its own resources when one of its members felt threatened by such an attack.

(2) *Presumption of availability of pre-identified assets and capabilities (where NATO retained the last decision on their release)*:
A detailed procedure was suggested in which experts from both organisations would jointly pre-identify potential assets. Availability would be formally confirmed at a subsequent PSC/NAC meeting. Procedurally, this would be the last barrier at which NATO could refuse a request for assets. After that point in time, they could not be recalled by NATO until the end of the operation, except in cases of Article 5, and those assets which NATO had previously reserved for its own non-Article 5 operations.

(3) *Identification of a series of command options made available to the EU*:
Once the request had been granted, the chain of command for those NATO assets concerned would shift to an EU-appointed commander. The EU would (via the Council, acting through its three sub-bodies established at the Summit) retain political control and strategic direction of the operation, although it would regularly report to NATO on its development.

Towards agreement at Copenhagen

One week later, the NAC commented on these proposals, and found itself broadly in agreement, as the year before.[71] It envisioned a genuine strategic partnership in crisis management between NATO and the EU.[72] It also welcomed and endorsed many of the single points spelt out in detail in the EU Nice document, laying particular importance on the issue of participation and non-discrimination against non-EU

Berlin Plus, para. 11, http://ue.eu.int/uedocs/cmsUpload/03–11–11%20Berlin%20Plus%20press%20note%20BL.pdf (visited 11/09/04).

71   Ministerial Meeting of the North Atlantic Council held at NATO headquarters, Brussels on 14 and 15 December 2000, Final Communiqué, NATO Press Release M-NAC 2(2000)124.

72   *Ibid.*, para. 28.

NATO members.[73] In particular, it agreed to the need for 'permanent arrangements' between NATO and the EU. Although it was not mentioned at this instance, this also implied the distinction between planning capabilities and other assets. However, NATO also made clear that the EU proposals would only be realised as a package deal, referring in this regard specifically to the participation issue: 'Nothing will be agreed until everything is agreed',[74] a sentence which would often be repeated in the months to come.[75] On this remaining point, it was evident that some NATO members were still not satisfied with the EU's proposals on permanent agreements which would involve the transfer of Alliance assets. Turkey, in particular, feared that once an autonomous EU force came into being (not any more under US control, but with automatic access to NATO's strategic resources), the very existence of this force might prejudice Turkey's security interests close to its borders, notably with regard to Cyprus.[76] In addition, Turkey's veto in the NAC was seen as potential leverage in the question of its accession to the EU.[77]

From late 1999, NATO had begun to recognise publicly that the changing division of labour in European security, although it was to its advantage, would require adaptation of its internal defence planning system.[78] This aspect was added as a fourth point to the three cornerstones of a future Berlin Plus agreement identified by the EU at Nice.[79]

At the Göteborg European Council on 15–16 June 2001, NATO's emphasis on the 'participation issue' was duly addressed.[80]

---

73   *Ibid.*, paras. 28–32.

74   *Ibid.*, para. 33.

75   E.g. NATO Budapest Ministerial, 29–30 May 2001, Final Communiqué, para. 49; *NATO in the 21st Century*, Address by the Chairman of the Military Committee, Admiral Guido Venturoni to the NATO Defense College Senior Course 100, NATO Defense College, Rome, Italy, Feb.28 2002, http://www.nato.int/docu/speech/2002/s020228a.htm (visited 23/07/03).

76   H.T. Oğuzlu, *Turkey and the European Union: The Security Dimension*, 23 CSP 3 (2002), p. 78. See also above Chapter 5 (NATO Primacy, Discrimination).

77   H.T. Oğuzlu, *ibid.*, p. 74 w.f.r.

78   An Alliance for the 21st Century – Washington Summit Communiqué issued at the meeting of the North Atlantic Council in Washington, D.C. on 24 April 1999, para. 10 at d.; Ministerial Meeting of the Defence Planning Committee and the Nuclear Planning Group, Final Communiqué, para. 5, NATO Press Release M-DPC/NPG-2(99)157, Dec. 2, 1999; NATO Florence Ministerial, 24 May 2000, para. 30; Ministerial Meeting of the Defence Planning Committee and the Nuclear Planning Group, Final Communiqué, para. 4, NATO Press Release M-DPC/NPG-1(2000)59, Dec. 8, 2000. After the 2002 Prague Summit, NATO commands are being reduced and consolidated See above Chapter 3 (NATO Today).

79   NATO Budapest Ministerial, 29–30 May 2001, Final Communiqué, para. 49 at d., NATO Press Release M-NAC 1(2001)77; NATO Handbook 2001, p. 98; NATO Fact Sheets, Strengthening European Security and Defence Capabilities, under 'EU–NATO relations develop' at d., 15 Dec., 2000.

80   European Council, Göteborg, 15–16 June 2001, CP 51, pp. 30, Annex, V., para. 41, CP 51, p. 39.

At Barcelona, on 15–16 March 2002, the European Council offered an enticement to NATO, to help it finally agree on the Berlin Plus arrangements on asset-borrowing. It demonstrated its willingness to relieve NATO of its peacekeeping duty in Macedonia, 'on the understanding that the permanent arrangements on EU–NATO cooperation ("Berlin Plus") would be in place by then'.[81] The offer was repeated at the Seville Summit on 21–22 June 2002.[82]

By that time, the European Council had kept stressing the need to conclude permanent arrangements with NATO for drawing on its assets and capabilities for two years, with growing urgency.[83] Berlin Plus, once concluded, would substantially increase the Union's available capabilities for crisis management.[84] The call was often echoed in statements made by other European institutions[85] which sometimes even openly took issue with the Turkish position which was the reason for the deadlock.[86] But repeated negotiating efforts failed to find a solution acceptable to all sides.[87] As frustration grew with the lack of progress,[88] some EU member States

---

81   European Council, Barcelona, 15–16 March 2002, CP 57, pp. 48, Presidency Conclusions, Part II, para. 61 (= *ibid.*).

82   European Council, Seville, 21–22 June 2002, Presidency Conclusions, para. 14., CP 57, p. 73, and *ibid.*, Presidency Report on ESDP, II., para. 4, CP 57, p. 76.

83   European Council, Göteborg, 15–16 June 2001, CP 51, pp. 30, Presidency Conclusions, V., Annex, VII., para. 48 at a., 2nd indent, CP 51, p. 40; European Council, Seville, Presidency Report on ESDP, VI., para. 26, CP 57, p. 80 and *ibid.*, XII., para. 36, *ibid.*, p. 81; European Council, Laeken, Presidency Conclusions, Annex II, (B) under 'Finalisation of the Arrangements with NATO', CP 51, p. 121; *ibid.*, Presidency Report on European Security and Defence Policy, para. 30, CP 51, p. 129.

84   European Council, Laeken, Presidency Conclusions, Annex II, under 'Finalisation of the Arrangements with NATO', CP 51, p. 121.

85   See e.g. Informal meeting of EU defence ministers, Saragossa, 22–23 March 2002, Summary of Interventions by Javier Solana, EU High Representative for the CFSP, under 'EU–NATO cooperation', CP 57, p. 51; *cf.* European Parliament Report, 'Adoption of the Report on 'the Progress Achieved in the Implementation of the CFSP'', Strasbourg, 26 September 2002, at F., CP 57, p. 119; G. Stuart, Contribution to the Defence Working Group of the European Convention, para. 3, London, 22 November 2002, CP 57, p. 218; The European Convention, Final Report of the Working Group VIII – Defence ('Barnier Report'), WG VIII 22, CONV 461/02, 16 December 2002, para. 26.

86   See e.g. European Parliament Report, 'Adoption of the Report on "the Progress Achieved in the Implementation of the CFSP"', Strasbourg, 26 September 2002, para. 21, CP 57, p. 123; *Spain exerts pressure for finalisation of the agreement between NATO and the EU*, WEU Parliamentary Assembly, Press Releases 2002, http://www.assembly-weu.org/en/presse/cp/2002/16.html (visited 23/07/03).

87   E.g. the British attempt at the EU–NATO Ministerial meeting in Reykjavik, 14–15 May 2002, CP 57, p. 60; Ministerial Meeting of the North Atlantic Council Held in Reykjavik, 14 May 2002, Final Communqué, para. 16, NATO Press Release 1(2002)59.

88   See e.g. Conference on EU Capability Improvement, Brussels, 19 November 2001, Statement on Improving European Military Capabilities, IV., under 'EU/NATO relations', first bullet, CP 51, p. 101; *Lack of NATO assets 'highly regrettable' says EU military chief*, European Voice (online edition), Vol.7, No.42, 15 November 2001.

– such as France and Belgium – even considered an EU operation in Macedonia without resolving the problem, that is, without drawing on NATO assets.[89]

NATO, for its part, repeatedly kept stressing that final conclusion of Berlin Plus depended on a satisfying resolution of the 'participation issue'.[90] Nevertheless, it was convinced of the necessity to 'lock in' the existing cooperation arrangements with EU which were so far operating on an improvised basis.[91]

At the Brussels Summit, on 24–25 October 2002, the EU concluded that the future Berlin Plus agreement should contain a clause on 'implementing the [relevant] Nice provisions',[92] and contain a reference to the Charter of the United Nations, whose principles both the TEU and the NAT were built on.[93] There was a gradual rapprochement between the EU and NATO at that meeting,[94] which was the result of a softening of the EU's and Turkey's respective positions.[95] Renewed efforts were made to accommodate Turkish fears over the Cyprus question: '... under no circumstances, nor in any crisis, will ESDP be used against an Ally', on the understanding of reciprocity.[96] The 'participation issue' was dealt with at this Summit again at great length, setting out in detail proposals on the involvement of non-EU European allies in future EU-led crisis management operations. These procedures included: respect by certain EU member States of their NATO obligations;[97] participation of the non-EU European Allies in peace-time ESDP consultations; relations with the EUMS and national HQs involved in EU-led operations; involvement in EU-led exercises; modalities for participation in EU-led operations; and lastly involvement in preparation, planning and management of an EU-led operation.[98]

---

89   Letter from Guy Verhofstadt, PM of Belgium, to Tony Blair and Jacques Chirac, Brussels, 18 July 2002, CP 57, pp. 112–3; Financial Times, 11 January 2003, p. 6.

90   E.g. Ministerial Meeting of the North Atlantic Council Held in Reykjavik on 14 May 2002, Final Communiqué, para. 16, NATO Press Release M-NAC-1(2002)59.

91   Speech by NATO Secretary General, Lord Robertson, at the EU Committee on Foreign Affairs, Human Rights, Defence Policy and Common Security, Brussels, 8 October 2002, at para. 21, http://www.nato.int/docu/speech/2002/s021008a.htm (visited 28/12/03).

92   European Council, Brussels, 24–25 October 2002, Presidency Conclusions, III., para. 18., CP 57. p. 135. This part of the Presidency Conclusions was based on the 'Ankara document' which had been drafted already in December 2001, but had failed to get agreement by all sides then. See above Chapter 5 (NATO Primacy).

93   *Ibid.*, para. 20.

94   J.-Y. Haine, in: CP 57, p. 135 (introductory text to the Brussels European Council Presidency Conclusions).

95   H.T. Oğuzlu, *Turkey and the European Union*, 23 CSP 3 (2002), p. 77.

96   European Council, Brussels, 24–25 October 2002, Presidency Conclusions, Annex II, para. 2, CP 57, p. 136–7. On the political background for this phase, *cf.* S. Rynning, *Why not NATO? Military Planning in the European Union*, The Journal of Strategic Studies, Vol.26, No.1 (March 2003), p. 65.

97   *Cf.* Art. 17 TEU.

98   European Council, Brussels, 24–25 October 2002, Presidency Conclusions, Annex II, CP 57, p. 136–140. Those provisions were repeated in their entirety in the letter by the CFSP-HR of 13 December (see below at fn. 105).

At its Summit in Prague on 21–22 November 2002, NATO remained 'committed to making the progress needed on all various aspects of our relationship' and also noted 'the need to find solutions satisfactory to all Allies on the issue of participation by non-EU European Allies, in order to achieve a genuine strategic partnership'.[99] Since the document required also Turkish agreement, this call for a final conclusion of Berlin Plus naturally came out less urgent and more balanced.

One month later, after three years of difficult negotiations, the Copenhagen Summit of the European Council delivered the long-sought-for breakthrough. Following intense efforts of the High Representative Javier Solana,[100] Greece had softened its categorical opposition to Turkish EU membership. In addition, the EU issued, on condition of fulfilment of its political criteria for membership decided in that same city nine years earlier (the 'Copenhagen criteria'),[101] the concrete date of December 2004 for the decision on beginning accession negotiations with Turkey.[102] As a consequence, Turkey finally allowed a comprehensive agreement to be concluded between the EU and NATO on all outstanding permanent arrangements.[103] In an additional Declaration, the European Council stated that Berlin Plus would 'apply only to those EU Member States which are also either NATO members or parties to the "Partnership for Peace", and which have consequently concluded bilateral security agreements with NATO'. In order to further assuage Turkish security concerns, Cyprus would not take part in EU military operations conducted using NATO assets once it had become a member of the EU.[104] The EU's High Representative Javier Solana informed the NATO-SG George Robertson that the European Council had agreed on modalities to implement the Nice provisions on participation of non-EU NATO Allies in EU-led operations using NATO assets.[105]

---

99   NATO Prague Summit Declaration by Heads of State and Government, 21 November 2002, para. 3–4, NATO Press Release (2000) 127 and 42 ILM 244.

100   'The future of Europe is intrinsically linked to that of its defense. If Turkey wishes to take its place in Europe, then it must also play its part in the European defense project. If Turkey understands and accepts this, it will wish to contribute toward the definition of permanent military arrangements between NATO and the EU', J. Solana, *Europe's path for Turkey*, International Herald Tribune, 7 December 2002, p. 6.

101   European Council, Copenhagen, 21–22 June 1993, Presidency Conclusions, para. I.13., fifth and sixth para., Bull. E.C., 6–1993, p. 13.

102   European Council, Copenhagen, 12–13 December 2002, Presidency Conclusions, para. 19, CP 57, p. 169.

103   *Ibid.*, para. 27, CP 57, p. 170. E. Lenski, *Turkey and the EU: On the Road to Nowhere?* 63 HJIL (2003), p. 102 at n.180, argues that Turkey's long-time intransigence on this point did more harm that good in advancing its interests for eventual EU accession.

104   *Ibid.*, Annex II: Declaration of the European Council Meeting in Copenhagen, para. 3, CP 57, p. 171. This restriction applied likewise to Malta, for other reasons.

105   Statement by the NATO Secretary-General, 13 December 2002, NATO Press Release (2002)140; Letter of the High Representative for the Common and Security Policy, Javier Solana, to the Rt.Hon. Lord Robertson of Port Ellen, Secretary-General of the North Atlantic Treaty Organization, 13 December 2002, Council of the European Union documents, EN (original).

On 16 December 2002, Solana and Robertson announced their signature of Berlin Plus at a joint Press Conference.[106] The detailed arrangements for implementing each of the technical elements of the agreement were in place in March 2003,[107] in time for the EU's take-over of NATO's mission in Macedonia. In subsequent statements, NATO and the EU made clear that this was the key to deepening their cooperation in matters of international security.[108]

LEGAL NATURE

Is Berlin Plus an international treaty?

A treaty under international law requires the following characteristics: subjects (who in the case of Berlin Plus must also be international organisations), an adequate form (under the VCLT), a meeting of the minds, consent to be bound by its contents, and treaty-making power.[109]

These characteristics shall be tried against the Berlin Plus agreement, one by one, below.

The law applied must be that at the time of conclusion. This is of particular importance for the European law internal to the EU, which must therefore be applied in the version of the Treaty of Amsterdam, still in force in December 2002.[110]

The general considerations relating to the law of treaties made above with regard to the EU–NATO exchange of letters of 24 January 2001[111] apply as well to the Berlin Plus agreement.

---

106   NATO Press Releases (2002)141 and (2002)142.

107   See the remarks by NATO-SG G. Robertson at a Press Point with CFSP-HR J.Solana at NATO HQ, 11 March 2003, first para., http://www.nato.int/docu/speech/2003/s030311a. htm (visited 28/12/03). Those additional arrangements, tying together the entire 'Berlin Plus Package' under a 'Framework Agreement', consisted of an exchange of letters between the NATO-SG and the EU CFSP-HR dated 17 March 2003. *Cf.* F. Cameron / G. Quille, *The Future of ESDP*, EPC Working Paper (2004), p. 28.

108   See e.g. Speech by NATO-SG, Lord Robertson at the City Forum, London, 24 January, 2003, http://www.nato.int/docu/speech/2003/s030124a.htm (visited 28/12/03); remarks by CFSP-HR J.Solana at a Press Point with NATO-SG G.Robertson at NATO HQ, following the NAC/PSC 18th meeting, 11 March 2003, third para., http://www.nato.int/docu/ speech/2003/s030311a.htm (visited 28/12/03); European Council, Thessaloniki, June 19–20 2003, Presidency Conclusions, VIII: External Relations, CFSP and ESDP, para. 60; Joint Press Statement by NATO-SG G. Robertson and the EU Presidency at the NATO Ministerial Meeting, Madrid, 3 June 2003, NATO Press Release (2003)056, paras. 2 and 3.

109   See above Chapter 4 (The Institutional Framework).

110   The Treaty of Nice (amending the TEU) only entered into force on 1 February, 2003, more than two months after the conclusion of the Berlin Plus. Where other versions than Amsterdam used, this will be specifically indicated, e.g. TEU(MT) for the Treaty on European Union, Maastricht version or TEU(NT) for the Treaty on European Union, Nice version.

111   See above Chapter 4 (The Institutional Framework).

The documents considered as primary sources are the text of the press statement,[112] and the three additional documents it refers to, and thereby incorporates:[113] the 'relevant Nice arrangements'[114] and the 'letter from the EU High Representative on 13 December 2002'[115] (both regarding the participation issue) and the 'NAC decisions on 13 December 2002'[116] (regarding the asset-borrowing aspect). As the text of the press statement is very vague, recourse will be had to the negotiating history of the agreement, as described above, in addition to the 'relevant Nice arrangements',[117] following the rules of interpretation contained in Art. 31 and 32 of the Vienna Convention on the Law of Treaties.[118] Naturally, these provisions cannot apply directly (whether as treaty obligations or via custom) until such time as when the quality of the Berlin Plus agreement as a treaty has been established. Recourse to the negotiating history would seem, however, suitable in *analogy* to Art. 32 VCLT and VCLTIO throughout the analysis below for three reasons:

- The main primary source is in parts extremely terse and worded in very general terms. The supplementary primary sources are only partly available to the public.
- Some of the proposals made by NATO and the EU prior to conclusion, as contained in their respective statements (especially provisions contained in European Summit Conclusions, see above in the historical part), are on the other hand sufficiently concrete and apt to constitute parts of a treaty. They may well be seen as self-executing.[119] The Berlin Plus agreement itself only incorporates certain provisions of the Nice European Summit Presidency Conclusions (Annex VI to Annex VI[120]). These, however, must be interpreted in their proper context, that is, further declarations by the EU and NATO surrounding those Nice provisions.
- Whatever the outcome of the inquiry as to the legal nature of Berlin Plus, interpretation of non-binding agreements according to the law of treaties is considered admissible.[121] It should pose even less of a problem if it turns out to be a treaty.

---

112   See above at p. 274.
113   *Cf.* Art. 31, para. 2 VCLT and VCLTIO.
114   Annex VI to Annex VI, of the Nice Presidency Conclusions.
115   See fn. 105.
116   Records of the NAC are classified. These decisions therefore are unfortunately not available for this inquiry.
117   *Cf.* Art. 31, 32 VCLT and VCLTIO.
118   1155 UNTS 331 [hereinafter: VCLT].
119   See below at p. 296.
120   See above Chapter 7 (Military Crisis Management).
121   See below at fn. 201.

As has been demonstrated above, the negotiations of Berlin Plus were atypical in that it did not take place in a single conference, but was a long process of one statement following upon the next, stretching over roughly three years.[122]

We shall proceed by testing the general requirements for a treaty under international law, already used for the exchange of letters of 24 January 2001.[123] Out of those six requirements, with regard to the first two – 'international organisations' and 'subjects of international law' – the Berlin Plus agreement faces a situation very much identical to that governing the EU–NATO exchange of letters of 24 January 2001.

Furthermore, concerning in particular the requirement of 'subjects of international law', by the time the EU and NATO were finalising Berlin Plus, the debate on the international legal personality for the EU was entering into its crucial phase. The European Convention's Working Group III (Legal Personality) had already then issued its Final Report in which it had recommended 'by a broad consensus' to confer explicit legal personality on the Union.[124] The parties must thus have been aware of the changes lying ahead.

Concerning the particular subject matter of Berlin Plus, it is moreover difficult to see how, in the process of building a common security and defence policy,[125] the EU should exercise its functions, given its present lack of technological, logistic and infrastructure resources in the military sphere, without being able to rely on external help, such as from NATO. This factual deficiency arguably makes international legal personality for the EU *a priori* indispensable, at least on a functional basis, and limited to the subject matter of cooperation with NATO.[126] Indeed, in the time preceding the conclusion of the Berlin Plus agreement, such military support from NATO to the EU was expected to be eventually realised through conclusion of a binding international agreement.[127]

---

122   EU statements are available to a very satisfying extent. Many documents issued by NATO and reports of meetings of defence ministers, however, are classified and thus less readily available for research. Nevertheless, as the negotiating process was increasingly very transparent between the two organisations, the EU documents give a good indication of the respective positions likely held by NATO at a given time (*cf.* e.g. at p. 278). This in part compensates for the shortfall in the NATO documents.

123   See above Chapter 4 (Institutional Framework).

124   European Convention, Final report of Working Group III on Legal Personality, 1 Oct. 2002, CONV 305/02, para. 8.

125   See Art. 11/1/3rd indent, Art. 17 TEU.

126   *Cf.* G. Hafner, *The Amsterdam Treaty*, in: Lib. Am. Seidl-Hohenveldern (1998), p. 272.

127   *Cf.* S. Marquardt, *The Conclusion of International Agreements under Article 24 of the Treaty on European Union*, in: V. Kronenberger (ed.), *The EU and the international legal order* (2001), p. 347; M. Warnken, *Der Handlungsrahmen der EU* (2002), pp. 210 and 212; W. Schroeder, *Verfassungsrechtliche Beziehungen zwischen EU und EG*, in: A. von Bogdandy (2003), p. 391.

The first two requirements do not require any more elaboration. Neither does any of the theories already laid out above in the analysis of the exchange of letters of 24 January 2001. It is only the next four requirements – form, meeting of the minds, consent to be bound and treaty-making power – that we examine with regard to the Berlin Plus agreement.

Form

Treaties as such do not necessarily require written form.[128] Following the general law of contracts, the absolute minimum requirements are an express offer by one party, followed by an express acceptance of that same offer by the other party. Under the treaty-based law of treaties, it is sufficient to exchange instruments referring to one another.[129] Under the customary international law of treaties, even oral commitments or the exchange of signals can constitute a binding treaty.[130] Hence, instruments titled 'Declarations' or 'Gentlemen's Agreements' normally do not qualify as international treaties.[131]

The formal structure of Berlin Plus bears some resemblance to the structure of international resolutions and treaties, with a basic separation between preambular and operative parts. Berlin Plus has three main parts: the first part is worded like a preamble; the second part, describing the principles on which the future EU–NATO relationship will be based, establishes a framework for cooperation which, owing to its lack of precision and its broad subject matters, would seem to be of similar nature, ideally suited for purposes of additional interpretation of a treaty text;[132] and the last part entitled 'To This End' would seem to contain the operative provisions, spelling out the concrete duties and obligations of the parties.

The EU, at least as late as the Nice Summit, voiced clear plans to NATO publicly on the exact procedure any future cooperation in the area of international security should, in its view, take.[133] The relevant parts of this Summit's Conclusions – their material content aside – may be read as an offer without great difficulty.[134] NATO,

---

128 I. Brownlie, *Principles of Public International Law* (1998), p. 610; R. Bernhardt, *Treaties*: in: EPIL IV, p. 927; K. Doehring, *Völkerrecht* (1999), p. 144; W. Wengler, *Die Wirkungen nichtrechtlicher Verträge zwischen Staaten*, 22 AVR (1984), p. 324; US Department of State, Coordination and Reporting of International Agreements, § 181.2 Criteria, 27 April 1981, 22 Code of Federal Regulations, Part 181, see 46 Federal Register 35917 of 13 July 1981, § 181.2 (5).

129 Art. 13 VCLTIO and VCLT; I. Brownlie, *Principles of Public International Law* (1998), p. 612 w.f.r.

130 R. Bernhardt, *Treaties*: in: EPIL IV, p. 927; critical, but lastly affirmative P. Guggenheim / K. Marek, *Verträge, völkerrechtliche*, in: K. Strupp / H.-J. Schlochauer, *Wörterbuch des Völkerrechts*, Vol.3 (1962); A. Verdross / B. Simma, *Universelles Völkerrecht* (1984), pp. 440–1.

131 On this characteristic of the BP, see below at p. 304.

132 This follows modern international treaty practice (as well as much internal EU legislation) in placing a 'Definitions' section before the operative provisions.

133 European Council, Nice, Presidency Conclusions, Annex VI., IV., CP 47, p. 172.

134 See below at p. 278.

for its part, indicated that it would agree to these terms at its Washington Summit in April 1999 and subsequent ministerial meetings, without however pronouncing itself at what date and in what form it would do so. The successive statements made by the EU and NATO since St-Malo unmistakably referred to one another, helping the two sides to narrow the gaps between their positions over time. However, this 'exchange' stretches over a significant period. It cannot be pinned down to any specific date. This is so even if one accepts that the main cornerstones of NATO-to-EU asset borrowing were in fact undisputed since the EU's detailed proposals of the Nice Summit.[135] The form of Berlin Plus did not become any clearer in the subsequent negotiating history: it was only revealed at the time of conclusion, when agreement between the two sides had certainly been reached. In conclusion, the Berlin Plus agreement would seem to broadly fulfil the formal requirements for an international treaty.[136]

Meeting of the minds

As with a contract between private persons, the parties to an international treaty need to agree to a clearly circumscribed content. Before this content is established, the treaty cannot enter into force. The meeting of the minds occurs when an offer is matched by an acceptance, if both are intended to establish legally binding force.

Since the St-Malo Declaration, and building on the aim expounded therein in subsequent successive Conclusions of European Summits, the EU had voiced its intent to acquire an autonomous capacity to engage in military crisis management in its near abroad,[137] should NATO choose not to become engaged as a whole.[138] Unnecessary duplication of existing infrastructure should be avoided in this process.[139] That same intent is also evident from the step-by-step integration of

---

135   The important character of the provisions of the Nice Summit is further evidenced by the fact that the 'participation' provisions of the Berlin Plus make exclusive reference to it, dispensing with references to any other European Council Summits before and after.

136   On the Title as a 'Declaration', see below: Is the Berlin Plus a Non-Binding Agreement?, at p. 288.

137   European Council, Cologne, Annex III, Presidency Report on Strengthening the Common European Policy on Security and Defence, para. 4.

138   European Council, Helsinki, Presidency Conclusions, II., para. 27.

139   St-Malo Declaration, para. 3, CP 47, p. 8; Helsinki European Council, *ibid.*; European Council, Nice, Presidency Conclusions, Annex I to Annex VI, para. 1, CP 47, p. 176; European Council, Göteborg, 15–16 June 2001, CP 51, pp. 30, Presidency Conclusions, Annex IV to the ANNEX, II., CP 51, p. 55; European Council, Laeken, Presidency Report on European Security and Defence Policy, para. 29 (C), CP 51, p. 128; General Affairs Council, Brussels, 13 May 2002, European Security and Defence Policy, under 'Orientations by the Presidency on the re-inforcement of co-operation in the field of armaments', CP 57, p. 58; European Convention, L. Dini, Contribution on 'European Defence', Brussels, 26 Sept. 2002, para. 1, reprinted in: CP 57, p. 203; *ibid.*, G. Stuart, Contribution to the Defence Working Group, London, 22 Nov. 2002, para. 3, reprinted in: CP 57, p. 218; *ibid.*, Final Report of the External Action Working Group (Dehaene Report), Brussels 16 Dec. 2002, paras. 36, 59 and 64 (reprinted in: CP 57, pp. 226).

the WEU into the EU begun under the Amsterdam Treaty,[140] an integration which included all existing arrangements on military cooperation which the WEU already had with NATO. Any military operation, such as the 'Petersberg tasks', would require drawing on the existing array of resources at the disposal of the Atlantic Alliance. By including the WEU in its treaty system, the EU can be said to have also recognised this particular need at least by the Amsterdam Treaty in 1996. Subsequently, the intention became clear at the Summit of Helsinki to do away with the WEU intermediary in matters of security, and engage in relations with NATO directly, as an equal partner with autonomous decision-making authority.[141] Access to the Alliance planning capabilities would have to be 'assured', other assets and logistical resources would be 'pre-identified' and 'presumed available'.[142] In the last sub-Appendix to the Nice Presidency Conclusions, the EU outlined in great detail what it meant by this.[143] The detailed proposal for an agreement with NATO may be seen as the EU's 'offer' or 'negotiating position' at the time of the Nice Summit, in which significant concessions to NATO's demands, as spelled out principally in Secretary of State Albright's '3 D's'[144] and the Washington Summit Communiqué,[145] may be discerned. In reply, NATO soon saw itself ready to provide for the necessary arrangements, but brought its own demands to the negotiating table: no decoupling of Europe from the Alliance as a whole; full participation of those of its members who were not (yet) members of the EU, most importantly Turkey; and the aforesaid distinction between planning capabilities and other assets.[146] The last condition essentially meant that, even if the 'permanent arrangements' with the EU should lead to an international treaty, only access to planning capabilities would be binding in the strict sense of the word. Those two elements, participation of non-EU Allies and asset-borrowing, each of which is given in consideration for the other, form the core of Berlin Plus. The compromise was the result of a long process of multilateral negotiation which took place not at one forum but several, and involved a number of countries, a few of them, however – the United States, Britain and France – giving the key impulses.

At the time of the EU's Nice Summit, the parameters around which an eventual agreement would boil down to had become concrete enough to allow for the creation of four distinct negotiating groups involving representatives of NATO and the EU:[147]

---

140 See fn. 25; *cf.* generally R.A. Wessel, *The EU as a Black Widow: Devouring the WEU to Give Birth to a European Security and Defence Policy*, in: V. Kronenberger (ed.), *The EU and the international legal order* (2001).

141 See above Chapter 7 (Military Crisis Management).

142 See above Chapter 7.

143 See above Chapter 7.

144 See above Chapter 7.

145 See above Chapter 7.

146 See above Chapter 7.

147 Also, the EU at this time gave itself the necessary institutional structures to be able to bargain such an agreement with sufficient backing of expert personnel. For ESDP institutions, see above Chapter 2 (ESDP Today).

the two organisations were 'getting down to the details'. This is also indicative of a general agreement. Since that time, the meeting of the minds as to the objective material content of Berlin Plus can be said to have been clear. This does not, however, prejudice in any way the most important questions, namely *whether*, *when*, and *how* they actually wanted to be bound.

Consent to be bound

In order for an agreement to be binding, its parties need to spell out clearly their intention to be bound henceforth by its contents.[148] To satisfy this requirement, it is not enough just to define those contents, however precisely this may be done. Consent may be expressed by an act of formal confirmation, by signature, by ratification, by exchange of instruments, or by accession, depending on the respective provisions in the treaty.[149]

There are no official statements by the parties available at the time of writing whether in concluding the Berlin Plus agreement they intended to bind themselves under international law or not.[150]

Even at first glance, however, the title 'Declaration'[151] suggests that an intention for binding force seems to have been far from the drafters' minds, as treaties are rarely called 'Declarations'. The fact of non-publication (and non-registration with the UN, Art. 102 UN Charter) rather hints at an intention of the parties to keep the agreement outside the sphere of international scrutiny (including scholarly research), thus making it difficult for either party to claim legal rights from it in front of an international court. In case of dispute, the other party to the agreement would thus be the only authority to whom such a claim could be effectively communicated.

---

148   W. Heintschel von Heinegg, *Die völkerrechtlichen Verträge als Hauptrechtsquelle des Völkerrechts*, in: K. Ipsen, *Völkerrecht* (4th edn 1999), p. 97; O. Schachter, *The Twilight Existence of Nonbinding International Agreements*, 71 AJIL (1977), p. 296; M. Virally, *La distinction entre textes internationaux de portée juridique et textes internationaux dépourvus de portée juridique*, 60 (I) AnnIDI (1983), p. 357; A. Aust, *The Theory and Practice*, 35 ICLQ (1986), p. 794; US Department of State Criteria, fn. 128, § 181.2 (1) and (3).

149   Art. 11, 12, 13 and 15 VCLTIO; *cf.* generally M.N. Shaw, *International Law* (1997), pp. 637.

150   News reports on the parties' intentions before the conclusion of the Berlin Plus agreement are purely speculative, see e.g. *European Rapid Reaction Force Seen As 'Phantom'*, BBC Monitoring International Reports, 4 April 2003. Statements and speeches by their representatives are equally inconclusive, see e.g. the speech by NATO-SG G. Robertson at the EU Committee on Foreign Affairs, Human Rights, Defence Policy and Common Security, Brussels, 8 Oct. 2002, NATO Speeches, http://www.nato.int/docu/speech/2002/s021008a.htm (visited 23/07/03).

151   Most of the press commentators (see fn. 3) glossed over this fact, reporting on the conclusion of the Berlin Plus as an 'Agreement' or 'Pact', terms commonly reserved in international law for instruments of legally binding force. On the Title of the Berlin Plus agreement as a 'Declaration', see below: Is the Berlin Plus a Non-Binding Agreement?, at p. 288

Although it is hard to speculate on the real intentions of the parties at the time of conclusion, they may well have wanted to keep Berlin Plus outside the formal possibility of international litigation altogether. Such litigation is usually excluded for non-binding agreements.[152] In drawing up Berlin Plus, the parties would have needed to pay particular heed to the dispute settlement provisions of Art. 66 VCLTIO. Naturally, that Convention is neither yet in force, nor is the EU or NATO a party to it.[153] Nevertheless, to a large part it reflects already existing customary law[154] which could also be true specifically for the provisions specific to international organisations in its Art. 66.[155] Should this be the case – a possibility the parties could not safely ignore – then Berlin Plus would normally fall under the dispute settlement regime provided in Art. 66(4) and the Annex to the VCLTIO, including an ad hoc Arbitral Tribunal or a Conciliation Commission.[156] The only way in which the parties could escape this was by *not* concluding it as an international treaty.

152　See below at p. 304.

153　See above at fn. 70.

154　See above at fn. 71.

155　The article's draft dated from the United Nations Conference on the Law of Treaties (YBILC 1982, Vol. II, Part 2, p. 64, Commentary to Art. 66, at para. 1–2). It also incorporated the experience with dispute settlement provisions of UNCLOS (see e.g. GAOR (35th Sess.), 6th Ctte., Summary Records of Meetings, UN-Doc. A/C.6/35/SR. 54, p. 10 at para. 39 (India); *ibid.* (37th Sess.), A/C.6/37/SR. 40, p. 7 at para. 26 (Jamaica); *ibid.*, A/C.6/37/SR. 43, p. 11 at para. 48 (Egypt); *ibid.* SR. 49, p. 4, at para. 8 (Romania); *cf. ibid.*, A/C.6/37/SR. 44, p. 11 at para. 46 (China)). Its procedure can thus be said to have been already well known in the international community at large, certainly by the end of 2002.

The question whether the material provisions of Art. 66 reflect international practice, especially the question whether international organisations should be granted a status equal to States in this regard, does not seem settled yet:

　－ arguing for this: e.g. United States in the UNGA 6th Ctte. '... binding settlement did not represent a leap in the dark, but was based on existing practice' (GAOR (35th Sess.), 6th Ctte., Summary Records of Meetings, UN-Doc. A/C.6/35/SR. 43, p. 17 at para. 71); *cf. ibid.* (37th Sess.), UN-Doc. A/C.6/37/SR. 48, p. 21 at para. 92 *in fine* (Spain);

　－ arguing against: 'Draft article 66 ... did not adequately reflect international practice' (GAOR (37th Sess.), 6th Ctte., Summary Records of Meetings, UN-Doc. A/C.6/37/SR. 46, p. 15 at para. 62 (Mongolia)); *ibid.*, SR. 49, p. 10, at para. 30 (Afghanistan); *ibid.*, SR. 51, p. 8, at para. 36 (Hungary); *ibid.*(38th Sess.), UN-Doc. A/C.6/38/SR. 35, p. 2 at para. 3 (USSR); Convention on the Law of Treaties between States and International Organizations or between International Organizations: Report of the Secretary-General, UNGA (38th Sess.), UN-Doc. A/38/145, p. 4, at para. 4 (Byelorussia); *ibid.*, p. 5, para. 1 (Czech.); *ibid.*, p. 8, para. 12 (GDR); *ibid.*, Add.1, p. 5, para. 3 (Vietnam); *cf. ibid.*, Add.1, p. 15, para. 16 (Venez.). It was also widely maintained that Art. 66 would only be established within a treaty framework (YBILC 1982, Vol. I, p. 156, at para. 3 (Special Rapporteur Reuter)).

On the general question of equality of international organisations to States, *cf.* also H. Isak / G. Loibl, *UN Conference on the Law of Treaties*, 38 ÖsterrZÖR (1987), pp. 64–66.

156　Excepting breaches of peremptory norms, in which case Art. 66, para. 1 provides makes possible adjudication by the ICJ.

The two material (and complementary) obligations contained in the agreement which shall be examined are: *a)* the question whether the EU wished to bind itself to the 'participation' of non-EU NATO members as stipulated in the text, and *b)* whether NATO wished to bind itself to guaranteeing the EU recourse to its various military assets.

a)   For the EU, the right to draw on different NATO assets was essential to enable it to engage in crisis management operations. Although that right is one of the main contents of the agreement, its analysis would not be fruitful in this context because, considered in isolation from the other parts, it entails only benefits for the EU. The willingness of the EU to enjoy this right may thus safely be assumed.[157] The same may be said about the intention of the EU to specifically bind NATO to such an obligation, as a reliable framework for military cooperation was clearly within the same interest. These assumptions are supported by all the EU's previous statements at European Summits, as well as from the accompanying political developments.

The EU's obligation to 'ensure the fullest possible involvement' of non-European allies in its operation planning is worded too inconclusively to make it possible to pin the organisation down to engaging in any specific action on the basis of that text alone. However, reference is made to 'the relevant Nice arrangements'. This means Annex VI to Annex VI, of the Nice Presidency Conclusions.[158] Those provisions, stretching over several pages, contain detailed procedural provisions which in principle do not require any more refinement in order to be put into effect. They are of self-executing quality and thus certainly capable of binding the EU. The same can be said about the High Representative's letter of 13 December.[159]

Consequently, in agreeing to be bound by the text of Berlin Plus, the EU also agreed to effect 'participation' of non-EU NATO members in the decision-making procedures relating to its crisis management operations, according to the relevant provisions of the Nice Presidency Conclusions.

b)   NATO's obligations to provide planning capabilities are worded in more concrete terms: planning capabilities – meaning mainly the facilities located at the SHAPE – are 'assured' to the EU. However, the ordinary meaning, in particular the sentence structure of this provision, limits the term 'assured' to the planning capabilities, thus excluding all other assets. It follows necessarily that these other assets are 'given' by NATO to the EU, but not on an assured basis, like the planning capabilities. This distinction is highly indicative of NATO's consent to be bound: from the text, it may be construed for the planning capabilities, but not for the other assets.[160]

---

157   See p. 270; *cf.* M. Warnken, *Der Handlungsrahmen der EU* (2002), at p. 151, who draws a similar conclusion with regard to the EU's drawing on WEU assets a few years before.

158   See the historical part above, at p. 267.

159   See at fn. 105. That letter repeats in wording the provisions of the European Council, Brussels, 24–25 October 2002, Presidency Conclusions, Annex II., CP 57. p. 135.

160   Art. 31 VCLTIO.

The nature of the second obligation, to provide those other assets, can only be determined by properly interpreting the term 'inter alia, and in particular'. As, standing alone, that term's meaning would be obscure, regard may duly be had to the agreement's preparatory work[161] which consists of its negotiating history, in particular the list of assets first found in the Washington Summit Communiqué[162] and elaborated at the EU's Nice Summit.[163] By negative inference, that term can only mean the assets *remaining* after deducting planning capabilities: physical military hardware such as transport aircraft, satellite imaging and C^3I.[164] Those assets will be given to the EU on a case-by-case basis only.[165] Owing to the officially classified nature of the exchange of letters between Solana and Robertson and the NAC decisions of 13 December 2002, however, the content of neither obligation – not even of the duty to provide planning capabilities – is possible to be ascertained exactly.

It should be borne in mind, of course, that a propensity for spelling out legal obligations in very general terms, leaving enough political manoeuvring room for later contingencies, is traditionally part of NATO's legal culture.[166] This can be ascribed to its nature as a military organisation, but also arguably to Anglo-American common law tradition in a wider sense. A large part of NATO's internal organisational law, such as, for example, the duty of member States to consult each other on certain issues,[167] exists only in the form of custom, although this makes it no less binding. In contrast to this, the EU approach to intra-organisation rules is more influenced by continental legal traditions of positivistic regulation to the finest detail.[168] Differences in the internal legal cultures of the EU and NATO[169] may serve to explain *why* NATO's obligations are so vaguely worded. However, this does not dispense from the general requirement under international law for consent to a treaty

---

161   Art. 32 VCLTIO.

162   See the historical part above, at p. 276.

163   See the historical part above, at p. 280.

164   C^3I = Command & Control, Communications and Intelligence. *Cf.* IISS, *The Military Balance 2003/2004*, List of Military Abbreviations (inside back).

165   The EU confirmed this limitation of 'assured access' to NATO's planning capabilities as early as the European Council, Nice, Presidency Conclusions, CP 47, p. 207–8.

166   *Cf.* E. Stein / D. Carreau, *Law and Peaceful Change in a Subsystem: 'Withdrawal' of France from the North Atlantic Treaty Organization'*, 62 AJIL (1968), p. 578 and p. 606. A good example of this difference is the difference in wording between Art. 5 NAT and Art. V WEUT. The former (in contrast to the latter) does not literally oblige a party to military aid in case of an armed attack on an Alliance member. Nevertheless, the provision has been interpreted to mean just that from the founding days of the Alliance.

167   *Cf.* F.R. Kirgis Jr., *NATO Consultations as a Component of National Decision-Making*, 73 AJIL (1979), p. 372.

168   I am indebted to Prof. Hanspeter Neuhold for this insight.

169   *Cf.* on this aspect of the EU–NATO relationship J.-Y. Haine, *ESDP and NATO*, in: N. Gnesotto (ed.), *EU Security and Defence Policy – The first five years* (2004), EU-ISS, p. 131.

to be expressed in unambiguous terms. Hence, it must be accepted that NATO did not intend to be legally bound by any part of the Berlin Plus agreement.

Treaty-making power

According to Art. 6 VCLTIO, the treaty-making power of international organisations follows the internal rules of organisations where such rules exist.[170] Art. 46 VCLTIO in particular provides that when a treaty is concluded for an organisation in 'manifest' breach of a fundamental rule of that organisation regarding the competence to conclude treaties, it may be voided.[171] A violation is manifest where it is 'objectively evident' to any international organisation acting in accordance with the normal practice, and in good faith (Art. 46, para. 3).[172]

As both the EU and NATO are international organisations, they may conclude treaties with other subjects of international law, subject to the limitations on treaty-making capacity set in their own respective statutes.

The EU always concludes international treaties with third parties in strict adherence to the procedure provided in Art. 24 TEU.[173] This procedure requires the EU Presidency to make a recommendation to the Council, following upon which the Presidency is, in turn, empowered in a Council Decision to conclude the respective agreement.[174] Both the respective Decision and the treaty are then published in the Official Journal of the EU.

The EU has in the past adhered strictly to this rule in its relevant practice. Of particular importance, this includes the as yet only existing case of a published treaty with NATO, the Security of Information (SIA) Agreement of mid-March 2003.[175] It is difficult to see why this practice, underpinned by positive law, should have been different two months before, at the time of the conclusion of Berlin Plus.[176]

---

170   See also Chapter 4 (EU–NATO Institutional Aspects).

171   *Cf.* J.A. Frowein, *Nullity in International Law*, in: EPIL III, p. 744; P.K. Menon, *The law of treaties between states and international organizations* (1992), p. 97.

172   *Cf.* E. Klein / M. Pechstein, *Das Vertragsrecht internationaler Organisationen* (1985), pp. 27–31. Additionally, an earlier draft added (in an additional para. 4 to Art. 46) a subjective criterion in defining that a violation was manifest if 'it is or ought to be within the cognizance of any ... other contracting organization.' (YBILC 1982, Vol. I, p. 133, at para. 36, emphasis added).

173   For the full discussion, see above Chapter 4 (Institutional Framework).

174   See e.g. Council Decision 2003/211/CFSP of 24 Feb. 2003 (OJ L 80/35 of 27.3.2003) authorising the Greek Presidency to conclude the 2003 Agreement on the Security of Information with NATO.

175   Agreement between the European Union and the North Atlantic Treaty Organisation on the Security of Information of 14 March 2003, OJ EU L 80/36 of 27/3/2003. S. Marquardt, *Article 24 EU*, in: V. Kronenberger, *The EU and the international legal order* (2001) expected the Art. 24-procedure to be used for a future SIA agreement as well as other future EU–NATO agreements.

176   At that time, the TEU already applied in its Nice version, but there are no changes there to the Amsterdam version of the relevant provision of Art. 24 TEU.

The High Representative for the CFSP[177] assists the Council in formulating policy, and in conducting political dialogue with third parties. He is provided with a secretariat and other special staff (for example the Policy Planning and Early Warning Unit[178]). This eminently important position within the CFSP[179] – and particularly within its emerging ESDP – does not, however, include the capacity to conclude an international treaty with binding force for the EU or its member States.

Extending Art. 24 to include treaty-making power for the High Representative would be contrary to its wording, and would fundamentally break with the established relevant practice of the EU. Furthermore, its drafting history makes it highly unlikely that the member States would have wanted the provision to be interpreted in any direction further restricting their competence.[180]

Berlin Plus was concluded by the High Representative – not the President of the EU or the Council itself – and he was not authorised to do so by either of those two organs. As a result of this clear deviation from the wording of Art. 24 and relevant practice thereto, he did not have treaty-making capacity as an EU organ.

This conclusion appears realistic in the political context. The conclusion of Berlin Plus presented uncharted territory for both parties. It was the first time NATO gave away any of its military resources to another international actor in a systematic way (not case by case, as previously with the WEU). It may have wanted to 'test' how the EU used its assets before engaging in a legal commitment for doing so. The EU, for its part, had never before had military dealings with an outside party.[181] Also, it may have shunned a legal commitment to NATO for symbolic reasons of its perceived need for autonomy in the military sphere.[182] For both, it was a situation of some uncertainty.[183] In order to safeguard maximum flexibility in this new area, a form would have had to be chosen for Berlin Plus which was strikingly different from the conclusion of a binding agreement. Having the *High Representative* conclude it – and *not* the statutory organ empowered to do so according to Art. 24 – might have

---

177   His functions and powers are circumscribed in Arts 18(3) and 26 TEU and Art.207(2) TEC.

178   The Policy Planning and Early Warning Unit (PPEWU), reporting to the CFSP-HR, was established pursuant to Declaration No. 6 annexed to the final act of the Treaty of Amsterdam, http://europa.eu.int/eur-lex/en/treaties/selected/livre468.html (visited 23/07/03).

179   S. Marquardt, *Article 24 EU*, in: V. Kronenberger, *The EU and the international legal order* (2001), p. 336.

180   See above Chapter 4 (Institutional Framework).

181   The European Union Police Mission in Bosnia and Herzegovina (which took over since Jan 1, 2003 from the UN International Police Task Force (IPTF)) is not a military operation, although it also falls under ESDP.

182   *Cf.* also the EU's consistent affirmation over the years of its 'decision-making autonomy' versus NATO, see above Chapter 5 (NATO Primacy).

183   W. Wengler mentions that it is exactly this kind of situation which may motivate parties to opt for a non-binding agreement (*Id.*, *Die Wirkungen nichtrechtlicher Verträge*, 22 AVR (1984), p. 314).

seemed the best way to demonstrate in public terms that the Berlin Plus agreement was no more than a 'Declaration'.

On the other hand, had the EU and NATO concluded the Berlin Plus agreement as an 'International Treaty' with its present material content and wording, it could, under the customary international law as reflected by Art. 46 VCLTIO, subsequently have been voided by the EU at any time, for a breach of its internal treaty-making competence provisions (that is, Art. 24 TEU). Such a breach could be said to be 'manifest' also to NATO, as knowledge of the exact content of that article could be imputed to it, owing to the largely overlapping membership of the two organisations.

NATO normally concludes international treaties and other agreements through its SG.[184] This was the case here as well. Thus, NATO's treaty-making power can be affirmed in this case.

Drawing together these considerations, NATO-SG George Robertson was, in theory, empowered to bind NATO to Berlin Plus by signing the agreement. However, as *both* parties to an agreement need to be fully empowered, failure to be empowered even for one party – the EU – ultimately denies it the quality of an international treaty.

Conclusions on binding force

In the years prior to the conclusion of the Berlin Plus agreement, hopes were high, particularly by the EU, that the agreement would take the form of an international treaty,[185] particularly as a legally binding framework was so far largely absent for ESDP[186]. After closely examining the characteristics of Berlin Plus, however, it must be concluded that the eventual document does not meet enough requirements to qualify as one. The strongest evidence supporting such a conclusion are the title as 'Declaration', lack of specific treaty-making capacity of the EU, and its half-secret nature, hinting at NATO's lack of consent to be bound. As a consequence, none of NATO's assets, including planning capabilities, are 'assured' to the EU in a legal sense. The question now turns to what else Berlin Plus might be.

---

184   For the full argument, see above Chapter 4 (Institutional Framework).

185   *Cf.* S. Marquardt, *Article 24 EU*, in: V. Kronenberger, *The EU and the international legal order* (2001), p. 347; M. Warnken, *Der Handlungsrahmen der EU* (2002), pp. 210 and 212; K. Ridderbusch, *Das Phantom der EU-Eingreiftruppe*, Die Welt (online edition), 4 April 2002, at para. 7.

186   *Cf.* L. Pnevmaticou, *Aspects Juridiques de la Politique Européenne de Sécurité et de Défense*, OP 31 (2001).

Is Berlin Plus a non-binding agreement?[187]

Non-binding agreements have become popular with subjects of international law, including international organisations,[188] to regulate their relations in many different fields,[189] ranging from transport, defence[190] and arms control[191] to development aid and human rights[192]. A very prominent example is the Helsinki Final Act of 1975.[193] A non-binding agreement does 'not engage the legal responsibility' of its parties; non-compliance by any of them 'would not be a ground for a claim for reparation or for judicial remedies'.[194] In wartime military planning between allies, they are frequent.[195] There are many possible reasons why subjects of international law choose non-binding agreements over binding treaties:[196] lack of formality (avoiding lengthy ratification procedures),[197] no obligation to publish them,[198] the higher degree of confidentiality that results from this,[199] and the relative ease and speed with which amendments can be effected[200]. This may be one of the reasons why non-binding agreements are often found in the field of *peacetime* military-technical

---

187   Many of the legal arguments used in this part are logical complements to the arguments discussed under D.1.b., Consent to be bound, at p. 279 above. Nevertheless, as will become clear below (see p. 287), a negative answer to the question whether an instrument is legally binding must not in all cases lead one to conclude that that instrument is a non-binding agreement.

188   A. Aust, *The Theory and Practice*, 35 ICLQ (1986), p. 795.

189   W. Wengler, *Die Wirkungen nichtrechtlicher Verträge*, 22 AVR (1984), pp. 312, 313.

190   A. Aust, *The Theory and Practice*, 35 ICLQ (1986), pp. 787, 811.

191   C. Lipson, *Why are Some International Agreements Informal?* (1991), p. 496.

192   C. Lipson, *ibid.*, p. 533; P.M. Eisemann, *Le Gentlemen's agreement comme source du droit international*, 106 Journal du droit international (1979), p. 337.

193   C. Lipson, *ibid.*, pp. 533–4.

194   Schachter, *The Twilight Existence of NBAs*, 71 AJIL (1977), p. 300; *cf.* R.B. Bilder, *Managing the Risks of International Agreement* (1981), pp. 24–34; W. Wengler, *Die Wirkungen nichtrechtlicher Verträge*, 22 AVR (1984), pp. 307–327; A. Aust, *The Theory and Practice of Informal International Instruments*, 35 ICLQ (1986), pp. 787–812; C. Lipson, *Why are Some International Agreements Informal?*, 45 International Organization 4 (1991), pp. 495–538; R.R. Baxter, *International Law in 'Her Infinite Variety'*, 29 ICLQ (1980), pp. 549–566.

195   *Cf.* W. Wengler, *Die Wirkungen nichtrechtlicher Verträge*, 22 AVR (1984), pp. 315–6.

196   A. Aust, *The Theory and Practice*, 35 ICLQ (1986), p. 789; C. Lipson, *Why are Some International Agreements Informal?* (1991), p. 501.

197   C. Lipson, *ibid.*, p. 514.

198   In contrast to treaties, see Art. 102 UNC. *Cf.* C. Lipson, *ibid.*, p. 537.

199   Hidden treaties, on the other hand – such as the secret 1939 protocols between Germany and the Soviet Union which declared the Baltic States as part of the Soviet sphere – have become very seldom after the end of the First World War. *Cf.* C. Lipson, *Why are Some International Agreements Informal?* (1991), pp. 525 and 535–6.

200   H. Neuhold, *The Inadequacy of Law-Making by International Treaties: 'Soft Law' as an Alternative?*, in: R. Wolfrum / V. Röben (eds.), *Developments of International Law in Treaty Making* (2005), p. 39 at 51.

cooperation, where changes in the modern weapons systems are frequent, and with them the need to adjust the agreement flexibly. For example, in the areas of non-proliferation as well as in disarmament (for example, many aspects of the SALT process implementation in the Cold War), non-binding agreements are a common form of international instrument.[201] The advantages of simplicity, speed, flexibility and confidentiality are sometimes seen to outweigh the benefit of legally binding force, because each party assumes the other has more incentives to stick to the agreement than to break it.[202] In other words, formally ratified treaties 'raise the political cost of non-compliance'.[203] However, this may be equally true for a non-binding agreement in some situations.[204] Additionally, a non-binding agreement makes it possible for the parties to regulate a subject matter in isolation from any larger, more contentious, issues.[205] For example, it often enables regular commercial exchange between China and Taiwan, without touching on the bigger question of the claim by both to the sole legitimate government of China.[206] There are few areas in which their use today would be considered impossible.[207] For interpretation of non-binding agreements, the relevant rules of the law of treaties may be used.[208]

Although they are formally 'below' the level of treaties, it would be simplistic to identify non-binding agreements simply as the remaining quantity from the whole of international agreements, minus treaties. They constitute a category in their own right, set apart from instruments such as oral agreements or memoranda of understanding (MoUs),[209] which are even less concrete and ascertainable.[210] Often, even though parties may not want to legally bind themselves, they will still want to avoid vague and ambitious language which might lead to dangerous misunderstandings. As a result, NBAs are often written and drafted in detailed, restrictive language

---

201   H.K. Ress, *Non-Binding Agreements – Addendum 1995*, in: EPIL III, p. 611; *cf.* C. Lipson, *ibid.*, p. 520.

202   C. Lipson *ibid.*, pp. 508–518; W. Wengler, *Die Wirkungen nichtrechtlicher Verträge*, 22 AVR (1984), p. 308 deems such 'sociological' questions outside the sphere of legal inquiry.

203   C. Lipson, *ibid.*, pp. 508–514.

204   H. Neuhold, *The Inadequacy of Law-Making by International Treaties* (2005), p. 39 at 50–51 speaks of 'soft countermeasures' in this context.

205   C. Lipson, *ibid.*, p. 526.

206   *Ibid.*

207   One such area are agreements on alterations of territorial sovereignty (W. Wengler, *Die Wirkungen nichtrechtlicher Verträge*, 22 AVR (1984), p. 313).

208   A. Aust, *The Theory and Practice*, 35 ICLQ (1986), p. 793; W. Wengler, *ibid.*, p. 318.

209   MoUs are sometimes used where the international legal personality of at least one party is lacking, as for example in the case of the Global Environmental Facility (GEF). *Cf.* M. Ehrmann, *Die Globale Umweltfazilität (GEF)*, 57 HJIL (1997), p. 606.

210   H. Neuhold, *The Inadequacy of Law-Making by International Treaties* (2005), p. 39 at 48.

very similar to treaties.[211] P.M. Eisemann calls them *accords informels normatifs*, according them all the characteristics of international treaties, save for the consent of the parties to be bound.[212]

The difference between a binding treaty and a non-binding commitment depends on the intentions of the parties.[213] These intentions can be elucidated by reference to the text and the circumstances of the agreement concerned.[214] The language used in a document is a good yardstick in order to positively ascertain its quality as a non-binding agreement. In British practice, for example

> use of terms such as 'shall', 'agree' and 'enter into force' denote an intention to conclude a treaty. Using 'will' rather than 'shall', avoiding terms such as 'agree' or 'undertake' ... denote[s] an intention to create something less than a treaty.[215]

Calling an agreement a 'Declaration' is often indicative of intent by the parties to avoid binding effect.[216] Although the law of treaties does not contain a canon of typical expressions for binding instruments, 'Declaration' is commonly associated with lack of binding force at law.[217] Furthermore, this is the case where the language is phrased as a description of a *policy*, *purpose* or *intent*:[218] 'lack of precision in itself seems to be a reason for ascribing non-binding character to a text'[219]. In contrast, legal obligations are usually formulated as descriptions of the future *conduct* of the parties.[220] Such descriptions then do acquire binding force, owing also to their precision.

Breach of a non-binding agreement cannot be responded to by international litigation[221] because it does not create a 'dispute' under international law.[222] Neither

---

211   C. Lipson, *Why are Some International Agreements Informal?* (1991), pp. 532, 534.

212   P.M. Eisemann, *Le Gentlemen's agreement* (1979), p. 336; *cf.* A. Aust, *The Theory and Practice*, 35 ICLQ (1986), pp. 795–6

213   See above at fn. 148.

214   R. Bernhardt, *Treaties*, in: EPIL IV, p. 928; H. Neuhold, *The Inadequacy of Law-Making by International Treaties* (2005), p. 39 at 48.

215   A. Aust, *The Theory and Practice*, 35 ICLQ (1986), p. 800.

216   F. Münch, *Non-Binding Agreements*, in: EPIL III, p. 607; but see also M. Virally, *La distinction*, 60 (I) AnnIDI (1983), p. 198; *id.*, *Comments on the 1968 Draft Convention on the Law of Treaties – Non-binding Agreements*, 29 HJIL (1969), p. 3.

217   F. Münch, *ibid.*, p. 609.

218   *Ibid.*

219   *Ibid.*; against this view: R. Bernhardt, *Treaties*, in: EPIL IV, p. 928.

220   *Id.*, EPIL III, p. 610.

221   W. Wengler, *Die Wirkungen nichtrechtlicher Verträge*, 22 AVR (1984), p. 315; H. Neuhold, *The Inadequacy of Law-Making by International Treaties* (2005), p. 39 at 50.

222   *Ibid.*, p. 321. The will of the parties to exclude judicial dispute settlement does not have to be expressly stated in the document, but may also be implied from their relevant statements (*ibid.*, p. 316).

does it justify taking sanctions contravening international law countermeasures.[223] However, as non-binding agreements legally leave them their freedom of action under international law – called *Resthandlungsfreiheit* by W. Wengler[224] – they can still find enough ways to effectively react to a 'breach' of the NBA by another party. The principle of reciprocity also accounts for the effective implementation of 'soft law' agreements.

Let us now look at the particular circumstances and characteristics of Berlin Plus:

- Concerning document language, the EU's obligation to NATO contained in the 'relevant Nice arrangements'[225] for limited inclusion of some non-EU NATO members in any future decision-making on military operations which include the use of NATO *matériel* is arguably worded in precise enough terms to create an obligation.[226] However, NATO's obligation to allow for EU access (assured or not) to its planning and logistic infrastructure is only precise enough to engender a legal duty if one knows the details of the NAC decisions of 13 December 2002 – evidence which is not publicly available.[227] In the main text (that is, the Press Release), expressions such as 'shall', 'undertake' or 'agree' are not used a single time, not even 'will'. Rather, the parties' obligations are phrased as 'is ensuring' and 'is giving'. This differs sharply from language used in documents intended to be binding. Lastly, the document is presented as a 'Declaration'.

- The subject matter of Berlin Plus clearly lies in the general field of defence and the military. Secret documents are the rule in this area.[228] The Berlin Plus agreement is a typical example. The particular subject matter of the Berlin Plus agreement consists of crisis management and peacekeeping. This field combines characteristics and situations from two of the traditional types of military agreements, in peacetime and in wartime: crisis management requires a relatively high level of alert readiness, to be prepared for cases where hostilities escalate or are resumed unexpectedly. This is typical of alliances in wartime. At the same time, concrete combat intensity in crisis management is fairly low, compared with an all-out war campaign. Non-binding agreements are common in both these fields. Other situations in the area of defence, on the other hand, have been regulated by treaties. A prominent example is arms control.[229] In arms control, however, the relationship between the parties is of adversarial nature, making detailed verification procedures also

---

223   F. Münch, *Non-Binding Agreements*, in: EPIL III, p. 611.
224   W. Wengler, *Die Wirkungen nichtrechtlicher Verträge*, 22 AVR (1984), p. 309, 322.
225   See above at p. 275.
226   See above at p. 296.
227   See above at p. 296.
228   Even if today this casts a shallow light on their quality as legally binding treaties.
229   C. Lipson, *Why are Some International Agreements Informal?* (1991), p. 520.

necessary. Crisis management such as regulated in Berlin Plus differs from such situations, because it is cooperative, not adversarial, in nature, and the two organisations in question share today a high, and growing, degree of mutual trust.[230] Thus, for regulating matters of crisis management between two international organisations such as NATO and the EU, a non-binding agreement would have seemed a very logical choice.

- A look at surrounding political events support this. In December of 2002, the transatlantic dispute on use of force in Iraq – although it had yet to reach its peak in the following spring – had already significantly strained relations within NATO.[231] Luckily, this appeared to have no impact on the matter of evolving technical cooperation between the EU and NATO, in building European capabilities for near-abroad crisis management. Moreover, the parties of Berlin Plus had just overcome the long-time 'Turkish deadlock'.[232] They thus had a clear interest to isolate the matter of the nearly concluded EU–NATO arrangements, by avoiding any link to the larger ongoing dispute on the international use of force against Iraq.
- Lastly, considering the high degree of legal and political interdependence existing today between the EU and NATO, it is hard to imagine any party (especially the EU) using their freedom of action under international law to react to a breach of the Berlin Plus agreement in any way other than political (for example by international litigation or reprisals which are precluded for lack of a breach of an international obligation). Any disagreement played out in this way would do much more damage to the overall shared cause than retribution could ever bring.

It is the author's view, therefore, that Berlin Plus is a non-binding agreement. But as the EU and NATO proceed to cooperate in crisis management, utilising Berlin Plus, legal obligation might arise from other sources.

Other sources of binding force

Regional customary law

Customary international law, it is sometimes maintained, may be formed instantly if its prerequisites are sufficiently established from the first moment.[233] For customary

---

230 See also the Second Part (Principles), para. 2, of the Berlin Plus agreement.

231 A full account of these events is outside the scope of this book. But see above Chapter 1 (Transatlantic Relations).

232 See above p. 285.

233 R. Jennings / A. Watts, *Oppenheim's* (1992), p. 30; M.N. Shaw, *International Law* (1997), p. 62; B. Cheng, *United Nations Resolutions on Outer Space: 'Instant' International Customary Law?*, 5 Indian Journal of International Law (1965), pp. 45–6; H. Lauterpacht, *Sovereignty over Submarine Areas*, 27 BYIL (1950), p. 393; *North Sea Continental Shelf*

international law of regional[234] or even bilateral[235] character, the circle of actors which need to fulfil state practice and *opinio juris* is naturally smaller. However, in that case the standard of proof for uniformity of practice is higher than in universal customary international law, and the element of obligation between the actors concerned must be more clearly stated.[236]

The EU had never claimed a *right* to engage in limited near-abroad peacekeeping with the help of NATO assets – it had merely expressed its *wish* to do so.[237] A general duty of NATO in this regard was also, it seems, never debated. Moreover, the EU would have needed to do so in face of the only other subject of international law which was affected in this regard[238] – NATO.[239] In the year-long and intense dialogue it conducted with NATO, intentions of this kind do not seem to ever have surfaced.

NATO, for its part, would have needed to act in a way to show it felt obliged to support the EU in its plans to build an autonomous crisis management capacity, using its planning capabilities and other assets. It would have needed to back this opinion up with concrete practice. NATO did exactly the opposite: it reserved the final word on permanent agreements on the use of its assets until the 'participation issue' had been solved to the satisfaction of all its members.[240] Even when it finally agreed on such an arrangement, it did so only in non-binding form.[241] This must be interpreted as an unwillingness generally to bind itself in any way on this question, whatever the legal source. Moreover, as the EU kept calling for a duty to be created for NATO

Cases, 1969 ICJ Rep., p. 43; Against this view: R. Bernhardt, *Customary International Law*, in: EPIL I, p. 902; A. Verdross / B. Simma, fn. 130, p. 361–2; N.Q. Dinh / P. Dailler / A. Pellet, *Droit International Public* (6th edn, 1999), p. 325.

234   *Asylum Case*, 1950 ICJ Rep., p. 276; *Case Concerning Rights of Nationals of the United States of America in Morocco*, 1952 ICJ Rep., p. 200 ; *cf.* A. Verdross / B. Simma, fn. 130, p. 359 (giving examples for the Latin American region).

235   *Case concerning the Right of Passage over Indian Territory*, 1960 ICJ Rep., p. 39.

236   R. Jennings / A. Watts, *Oppenheim's* (1992), p. 30 w.f.r; M.N. Shaw, *International Law* (1997), pp. 72–3; I. Brownlie, *Principles of Public International Law* (1998), p. 10; G. Fitzmaurice, *The Law and Procedure of the International Court of Justice, 1951–54: General Principles and Sources of Law*, 30 BYIL (1953), pp. 68–9; Case *Concerning Military and Paramilitary Activities in and against Nicaragua*, 1986 ICJ Rep., pp. 97–8.

237   See above at pp. 273.

238   *Cf.* F.R. Kirgis Jr., *NATO Consultations*, 73 AJIL (1979), p. 374, who – writing on NATO's internal customary law – argues that obligations under customary international law need to be tested in a situation where the party concerned stood to gain something by not abiding, yet still abided by it as a matter of perceived obligation.

239   Or alternatively, the United States, which owns the largest part of the military resources at the disposal of the Alliance.

240   See at p. 269 above.

241   See at p. 285 and p. 290 above.

to provide those assets,[242] therefore those calls attested to a clear recognition that no such duty on the part of NATO had yet been established.[243]

In conclusion, there is no duty on either party arising out of regional customary international law which would oblige them to adhere to the contents of the Berlin Plus agreement.

Estoppel

Estoppel, a principle generally recognised in international law which is founded of the principle of good faith,[244] bars a party from adopting successively different positions – by word or action – on a given issue, and thereby causing prejudice to another party.[245] It applies whenever the other party has made substantial investments, of whatever nature, relying on the other's position. Obligations arising by estoppel have the same binding force on a party as treaties.[246]

Normally, benefits exchanged pursuing a non-binding agreement cannot be retrieved if the other party fails to deliver, because a non-binding agreement does not create any legal obligation, and the general principle of unjust enrichment[247] – even though it applies to frustrated treaties[248] – does not seem to apply to non-binding agreements.[249] Nevertheless, a non-binding agreement may give rise to legal consequences where one party relies on its performance by the other party, and plans or makes investments accordingly. In such a case, the aggrieved party may seek redress under the title of estoppel.[250]

---

242 See at p. 270 above.

243 *Cf.* M. Warnken, *Der Handlungsrahmen der EU* (2002), at p. 209, commenting on the status of EU–NATO legal relations in 2001.

244 J.P. Müller / T. Cottier, *Estoppel*, in: EPIL II, p. 118.

245 *Temple of Preah Vihear Case*; 1962 ICJ Rep., pp. 143–4; J.P. Müller / T. Cottier, *ibid.*, p. 116.

246 *North Sea Continental Shelf Case*, 1969 ICJ Rep., p. 26; J.P. Müller / T. Cottier, *ibid.*, p. 117–8.

247 C. Schreuer, *Unjust Enrichment*, in: EPIL IV, pp. 1243; *Lena Goldfields Arbitration*, 5 Annual Digest (1930), pp. 3; W. Friedmann, *Some impacts of Social Organization on International Law*, 50 AJIL (1956), p. 505; G.C. Rodríguez-Iglesias, *El enriquecimiento sin causa como fundamento de responsabilidad internacional*, 34 REDI (1982), p. 387; *Shannon & Wilson, Inc.* v. *AEOI*, 9 Iran-USCTR (1985-II), p. 402; *Schlegel Corp.* v. *NICIC*, 14 Iran-USCTR (1987-I), p. 180; A. McNair, *The Seizure of Property and Enterprises*, 6 NILR (1959), p. 240.

248 See Art. 69 VCLT and VCLTIO.

249 W. Wengler, *Die Wirkungen nichtrechtlicher Verträge*, 22 AVR (1984), pp. 323–4.

250 A. Aust, *The Theory and Practice*, 35 ICLQ (1986), pp. 807–812. To a less predictable extent, Aust also considers that such rights could be claimed alternatively due to a Unilateral Act, especially in a case of a bilateral instrument. *Ibid.*, pp. 808–9. *Cf.* also H. Neuhold, *The Inadequacy of Law-Making by International Treaties* (2005), p. 39 at 52, who argues that consistent application of 'soft law' may over time lead to *opinio juris*, one of the prerequisites for the eventual formation of customary international law.

Binding force through estoppel for the EU?   As long as EU activity on its ESDP was limited to mere statements at European Summits, the amount of real damage which could be incurred by any other subject of international law by relying on them was conceivably small. On 1 April 2003, however, the EU took over NATO's small peacekeeping mission in Macedonia, based on UN Security Council Resolution 1371, since renamed 'Operation *Concordia*'.[251] For this mission, it used planning facilities and other logistical support from NATO.[252] Had the EU subsequently decided to abandon this mission all of a sudden, NATO would have had to quickly step in again to prevent a renewed destabilisation of Macedonia and thus a failure of its past nation-building achievements there. This act would have caused clear detriment to NATO, as it would have bound its resources anew for a mission in Europe. Part of the damage to NATO in that case would have been strategic: this action by the EU would have occurred at a time when NATO was increasingly looking for a more global role in the long term. In Afghanistan, NATO had begun to engage in its first 'out of area' peacekeeping mission (with Canada as lead nation[253]) from 11 August 2003.[254] More missions of this kind were considered an option at the time.[255] During that time also, NATO decided to provide support for the Polish occupation sector in post-war Iraq,[256] and there were discussions (never realised) to station troops there in its own name.[257] Moreover, it plans to convert itself into an organisation better equipped to counter asymmetric threats such as international terrorism.[258] The EU, by starting Operation *Concordia*, for the first time demonstrated its real capacity and willingness for managing security in its near abroad. This sent a clear signal to NATO, giving it more flexibility to engage in serious planning for operations beyond Europe.[259] It also entailed allocating less military resources to its activities

---

251   *EU 'army' takes over duties in Macedonia*, Financial Times, 2 April 2003, p. 10; *Die EU übernimmt militärische Mission in Mazedonien*, Frankfurter Allgemeine Zeitung, 1 April 2003, p. 6.

252   See above Chapter 7 (Military Crisis Management).

253   *Kanada übernimmt Führung der Isaf-Truppe*, Frankfurter Rundschau, 27 May 2003.

254   Ministerial Meeting of the North Atlantic Council held in Madrid, 3 June 2003, Final Communiqué, para. 3; *cf. NATO to stay in Afghanistan as long as needed: ISAF*, AFP, 3 Aug. 2003; *Nato eyes extended peacekeeping role across Afghanistan*, Financial Times, 5 Aug. 2003, p. 7.

255   *Cf.* The Economist, June 7th 2003, p. 26 (Lord Robertson's remarks at the Evian Summit of the G8).

256   *NATO Council makes decision on Polish request*, NATO update (online edition), 21 May 2003; see also: NATO Ministerial Meeting, Madrid, 3 June 2003, Final Communiqué, para. 5; *NATO steht Polen im Irak bei*, Süddeutsche Zeitung, 22 May 2003.

257   *U.S. considers putting NATO in charge of Iraq*, Seattle Times, 9 July 2003, p. A1; *U.S. Lawmakers Press Rumsfeld to Seek NATO, UN Forces for Iraq*, Bloomberg.com Online News, 9 July 2003.

258   For a fuller treatment of this development of the Alliance, see the Chapter 'NATO today' above.

259   See Financial Times, 11 January 2003, p. 6.

in Europe as a matter of long-term strategic planning, a course of action which, once started, was reversible only at great cost. Any reversal of policy in the opposite direction by the EU would have likely entailed immediate financial consequences for NATO. Thus these considerations may lead to the conclusion that the EU, from the moment it raised its flag in Macedonia, was bound under international law by way of estoppel to continue at least its Operation *Concordia* for the time being. In other words, notwithstanding the legal nature of the Berlin Plus agreement, such a duty could arise out of the EU's specific actions in implementing the agreement.

Binding force through estoppel for NATO? NATO, for its part, had also in the years which preceded the Berlin Plus agreement, given more and more concrete political assurances that it wanted a more prominent crisis management role for the EU in Europe.[260] The EU had, as yet, no reason to believe it could rely on those assurances. Neither did it legally have cause for doing so, as no EU military operation which would need NATO's strategic support had yet come into being. With the takeover of the mission in Macedonia, this also changed. The logistical support provided by NATO was now the lifeline of the EU's Operation *Concordia* in that country. Should NATO suddenly withdraw this support, the EU operation would very likely have to be immediately aborted – given the lack of military planning capabilities at the disposal of single EU members, outside the NATO infrastructure.[261] This situation would have put EU troops there at great risk. If the fragile situation in Macedonia escalated again into a crisis (as it had come close to in the past), those troops might be unable to extract themselves safely. Having relied on NATO's assurance, the EU would suffer high detriment in terms political and diplomatic, financial costs, and maybe loss of human lives of its citizens stationed there. Thus, for the same reason as the EU, NATO was precluded from acting in such a way for the entire duration of Operation *Concordia*.[262]

Position of Berlin Plus in European law

For the time being, Berlin Plus*per se* does not form part of the TEU. The institutional arrangements created at successive European Summits in preparation for its

---

260 See e.g. the Alliance's Strategic Concept, Agreed by the Heads of State and Government participating in the meeting of the North Atlantic Council in Rome on 7–8 November 1991, para. 22, reprinted in: NATO Handbook, (October 1995), p. 239.

261 *Cf.* A. Baggett, *The Development of the European Union Common Defense and Its Implications for the United States and NATO*, 31 Ga.J.Int'l & Comp. L. (2003), p. 369, who mentions this case *in abstracto*, without, however, pronouncing herself on the legal implications such an action might have.

262 The scenario painted here is an extreme case. In fact, on 16 July 2003, NATO decided to extend its support to the EU's Operation *Concordia* (*NATO support to EU operation extended*, NATO Update, 16 July 2003, http://www.nato.int/docu/update/2003/07-july/e0716f.htm (visited 23/07/03). This support lasted until the end of the mission on 15 Dec. 2003.

implementation, including its conclusion with NATO, are not binding on the Union.[263] In the discussions within the European Convention, however, suggestions were made to include a reference to Berlin Plus in the future European Constitution.[264] This could arguably have made its contents binding on the EU. None of these ideas, however, seems to have found their way into the European Constitution.[265]

---

263   See above, at p. 300.

264   See e.g. European Convention, Reactions to the draft articles of the revised text of Part One (Volume I) – Analysis, 4 June 2003 (CONV 779/03), Art. I-39, para. 3, remark by associate member P. Hain, at 1st indent.

265   Treaty Establishing a Constitution for Europe, 6 Aug. 2004, CIG 87/04.

Chapter 9

Security of Information

INTRODUCTION

Like any State, an international organisation has certain documents circulating through its bureaucracy which it wants to keep outside the purview of the general public, because their premature disclosure might damage the organisation's interests. Those interests are, in turn, determined by the main goals the organisation was created to achieve and safeguard. Some rules on the security of information probably do exist in every international organisation. The organisation's internal culture, however, influences the exact form these public-access rules take, ranging from very liberal to very restrictive. That internal culture is also often characterised by the organisation's ultimate purpose. Human rights and environmental organisations, for example, would certainly want that the information they have collected in their activities should be distributed as fast and as widely as possible, and many such organisations take an active role in furthering this. Military alliances, in contrast, continuously draw up contingency plans for all diverse kind of security threats which, logically, they will take great care not to let fall into irresponsible or even dangerous hands. An organisation's internal security culture is also influenced by the traditions in its member States on handling access to public documents.

Both NATO and the EU today have firm security of information (SI) rules in place for handling sensitive information within their own bureaucracies. They also have, since March 2003, a permanent agreement on the exchange of such information between them. Yet, while NATO has had detailed internal SI regulations for more than fifty years, the subject is something very new to the EU and can only be understood as a result of its recently acquired Security and Defence Policy. For the EU, going into defence brought the need to classify certain documents so as to not prejudice the effectiveness of its military operations. That need was realised as soon as ESDP began to take serious form. In building its own SI framework, the EU relied heavily on the experiences some of its member States already had gained for many years as NATO members. In addition, SI rules already created within the WEU (which bore a significant NATO imprint) served as precedents. A one-way influence from NATO to the EU can be perceived in EU–NATO relations concerning SI from the very beginning of ESDP. The EU never had many SI regulations before it began venturing into the realm of defence. What it did have since a long time ago, however, was a strong internal organisational culture. Even as ESDP made its first stirrings, the new principle of transparency, including a general right of access of EU citizens to documents of the Union, became embedded in the EU treaty framework. It took no long time for those two movements – one for greater restriction of documents in the areas touching on ESDP and one for public transparency – to clash across the EU system. The result of this debate flowed into the now existing regime of classified documents reigning today between the EU and NATO. The present regime thus cannot be properly understood without having recourse to its various origins. This chapter will describe each of them in detail, and finish with a summary of the current state of the law under the EU–NATO Security of Information Agreement of 2003.

SECURITY OF INFORMATION IN NATO

General description

NATO's rules on security of information – drawn up in the mid-1950s, at the onset of the Cold War[1] – are enshrined in a document called C-M(55)15(Final),[2] a current version of which is still not publicly available today.[3] A revised security policy referred to as C-M(2002)49 was adopted in 2002 but it also remains out of reach for the public.[4]

The policy consists of four parts ('Enclosures'). Enclosure A is the 'Security Agreement by the Parties to the North Atlantic Treaty' from 6 January 1950.[5] It has now been superseded by the 'Agreement between the Parties to the North Atlantic Treaty for the security of information' of 6 March 1997[6]. The Agreement (which is open to all members of the Alliance) obliges the parties to 'protect and safeguard' classified information originating from NATO or from a member State, to 'maintain the security classification', not to use the information for purposes other than those flowing from the NAT, and not to disclose any such information without consent of the originator.[7] Furthermore, it summarises the above obligations for State parties, detailed under Enclosures B, C and D, for example to have all personnel dealing with classified information 'appropriately cleared' before they take up their duties, and to conduct a screening fit to determine the 'loyalty and trustworthiness' of such persons.

---

1   A. Roberts, *Entangling Alliances: NATO's Security of Information Policy and the Entrenchment of State Secrecy*, 36 Cornell Int'l L.J. 2 (2003), pp. 329–360. http://faculty.maxwell.syr.edu/asroberts /documents/journal/roberts_cilj_2003.pdf (visited 03/10/03), p. 4.

2   Security within the North Atlantic Treaty Organization, Note by the Secretary General, Chairman of the Council, NATO Document No. C-M(55)15(Final), last available issue of 31 July 1964, http://faculty.maxwell.syr.edu/asroberts/foi/library/gsoia/NATO_CM_55_15_final_1964.pdf (visited 03/10/03).

3   A. Roberts, *Entangling Alliances* (2003), p. 332.

4   *Ibid.*, p. 334–5.

5   NATO C-M(55)15(Final), p. 3.

6   Canada Treaty Series 1998/56 [hereinafter: 1997 NATO Security of Information Agreement]. The agreement is also available at http://nettax.interia.pl/serwis/Publikatory/du/2000/nr%2064 /poz.740ang.htm (visited 03/10/03).

7   *Ibid.*, Art. 1.

NATO's Security Agreement has strongly influenced the internal SI regimes created by third parties wanting to exchange information with NATO on a permanent basis (such as the PfP countries, as well as the SI regulations of the WEU and the EU.[8]

Enclosures B, C and D contain detailed guidelines on handling of classified information in NATO.[9]

On the basis of the information available about this document, A. Roberts describes the main features of the policy under five headings – breadth, depth, centralisation, controlled distribution and personnel controls:[10]

*   *Breadth:* NATO's security policy applies to all parts of government of a member State (not just the military)[11].
*   *Depth:* The security policy defines four classification markings for documents: 'Top Secret',[12] 'Secret',[13] 'Confidential'[14] and 'Restricted'[15]. The marking 'Cosmic' (only applied to 'Top Secret' documents) further denotes that the document may not be passed outside the organisation without the consent of the originator. A 'Cosmic Top Secret' Document could, for example, contain highly sensitive information such as historical plans by NATO to invade in a neutral country should that country be attacked by Warsaw Pact forces. A 'NATO' marking establishes NATO's ownership over the document. 'Confidential' documents contain information the unauthorised disclosure of which would be 'prejudicial to the interests of NATO'. Documents falling even below this threshold are still, however, classified by the 'Restricted' category. Thus, NATO's classification requirements reach down to a very broad range of information.
*   *Centralisation:* Member States are required to keep national registries of all

---

8   See below at p. 320 (WEU), and p. 323 (EU).

9   Some of NATO's subsidiary bodies have their own set of rules for handling classified information which, however, seldom differ greatly from the main standard of C-M(55)15(Final). See e.g. NATO Research and Technical Organisation (RTO) Technical Publication Policy, 4th Issue – March 2001, Section VINATO/PfP UNCLASSIFIED, AC/323-D/22, http://faculty.maxwell.syr.edu/asroberts/foi /library/nato_rto_pubrules.pdf (visited 04/10/03).

10   A. Roberts, *Entangling Alliances* (2003), pp. 336–9.

11   NATO C-M(55)15(Final), p. 5, para. 1 only refers to 'the secrets in which all have a common interest'.

12   'Information ... the unauthorised disclosure of which would result in exceptionally grave damage to [NATO]', *Ibid.*

13   'Information ... the unauthorised disclosure of which would result in serious damage to NATO', *Ibid.*

14   'Information ... the unauthorised disclosure of which would be prejudicial to the interests of NATO', *Ibid.*

15   'Information ... which requires security protection but less than that required for CONFIDENTIAL', NATO C-M(55)15(Final), p. 16. *Cf.* the respective description in the RTO publication policy, fn. 9: 'undesirable to the interest of NATO'.

persons allowed to hold NATO-classified documents, those that currently hold them, and a list of all such documents in circulation. Copies are to be made only when necessary, and all copies must also be duly recorded and their fate traced to the point where a 'destruction certificate' is issued.[16] In addition, a 'national security organization' is responsible for the screening of personnel and for collecting intelligence on espionage, sabotage and subversion.[17] Coordination of the national security policies of member States is effected by the 'Standing Group Security Committee' (made up of a representative from France, the United Kingdom and the United States).[18] This centralised control is found again at the organisation level, where a Security Bureau is responsible for the 'overall coordination' of security in NATO. The Standing Group has conducted regular inspections on the national security offices (NSO) from the beginning of the 1950s,[19] who must also report any breaches of security in their areas of responsibility.[20] Furthermore, 'it is expected that disciplinary action will be taken against any individual who is responsible for the compromise of NATO classified information'.[21] There is no explicit duty on member States, however, to establish criminal penalties, as is common in many States for the release of state secrets.

- *Controlled distribution:* NATO's security policy contains two fundamental rules on the day-to-day handling of classified documents. According to the *need to know* principle, 'Information must be confined to those whose duties make such access essential. No person is entitled solely by virtue of rank or appointment.'[22] The principle of *originator control*[23] makes it impossible to distribute or declassify information without the consent of the government from which the information originated.[24] Where information is passed outside NATO, this principle even applies to unclassified documents.[25]

- *Personnel controls:* The procedure to be used by member States for screening individuals for access to classified documents includes 'positive vetting', that is, an active investigation into the individual's private background[26] (normally

---

16   NATO C-M(55)15(Final), p. 29. paras.27–28.

17   *Ibid.*, p. 5, para. 3 (a) (1) and p. 15, para. 15.

18   *Ibid.*, p. 14.

19   *Cf.* A. Roberts, *Entangling Alliances* (2003), p. 341.

20   NATO C-M(55)15(Final), pp. 39–40.

21   Ibid, p. 39, para. 10.

22   Ibid, p. 19.

23   The term 'originator control' is synonymous with the term 'authorship rule' as it is often found in literature describing the principle of transparency within the European Union, *Cf.* P. Craig / G. de Búrca, *EU Law* (2003), p. 394.

24   NATO C-M(55)15(Final), pp. 22–23; A. Roberts, *Entangling Alliances* (2003), p. 348.

25   NATO C-M(55)15(Final), p. 11, para. 3.

26   *Ibid.*, p. 7, para. 9 'the fullest practicable use should be made of the technique of background investigation'.

going back at least ten years, or from the date of their eighteenth birthday[27]), including past nationality, education, employment, credit standing, political affiliation, social conduct, foreign connections and travel and sexual orientation, all of which is interpreted broadly.[28] The investigation regularly includes a similar procedure for the vetted person's spouse.[29] Informing of the vetted person, or a possibility to be heard on the matter of their own investigation is not provided in the policy. As a result of the vetting procedure, the individual concerned should be shown to have 'unquestioned loyalty [and] such character, habits, associates and discretion as to cast no doubt upon their trustworthiness'.[30] To some degree, such personnel screening practices are quite common in the administrative hiring practice for the civil services of Western countries, but the NATO rules compromise individual rights to a far higher degree. They are stricter even than screening rules for individuals in the US classification policy.[31]

As classification of too many documents can quickly lead to a clogging of the bureaucracy and generally hinders the smooth running of the organisation in times of crisis, it was soon recognised that the practice of classifying must be exercised with discretion.[32] This includes limiting the classification to the part of a document to which it is relevant, and only based on its own content (so that the remaining parts may be handled with greater ease).[33] Where a group of documents with different classification degree are held together, the covering letter or memorandum must carry the highest security marking[34] (a rule which could be called *collective classification*).

NATO's security policy encompasses all aspects and areas which may touch on classified documents. Apart from the sensitive personnel aspect, this includes 'Basic

---

27   Security within the North Atlantic Organization, Supplemental Security Principles and Practices, NATO Confidential Supplement to Document C-M(55)15(Final), 1 January 1961,   http://faculty.maxwell.syr.edu/asroberts/foi/library/gsoia/NATO_CM_55_15_Supp. pdf (visited 03/10/03)), p. 3, para. 1 (a).

28   *Ibid.*, p. 3.

29   *Ibid.*, pp. 5–6.

30   NATO C-M(55)15(Final), p. 7

31   *Cf.* A. Roberts, *Entangling Alliances* (2003), p. 348. For a summary overview on the law of public access to military information in the United States, see K.A. Buck, *National Security and the First Amendment: Access to Classified Information: Constitutional and Statutory Dimensions: The First Amendment – an absolute right?*, 26 William & Mary Law Review 1985, pp. 851–861.

32   NATO C-M(55)15(Final), p. 8, para. 16 'Matter which is to be protected by classification should be subject to regular review, and care should be taken to avoid over-classification'; *Ibid.*, p. 23, para. 10 '[Member States] should downgrade [the classification] wherever possible so that the security system is not overloaded'.

33   NATO C-M(55)15(Final), p. 22, para. 22.

34   *Ibid.*, p. 23, para. 8.

Principles',[35] handling by commercial enterprises, for example the defence industry (thus termed 'Industrial Security'[36]), physical security including storage,[37] transport[38] and the security of buildings[39] which house such documents, procedures in case of breach of security,[40] and rules for handling classified documents at international conferences[41]. All of these rules are fairly detailed.

Documents of 'historical significance' are normally opened to the public when they are thirty years old and older, or earlier when the NAC has responded favourably to a declassification request.[42]

This stringent security policy must be seen against the time background of the Cold War[43] and the McCarthy era in the United States in which it originated.[44] Its strict standards, developed mostly in the 1950s, were only achieved against much opposition from other allied governments who often found them in conflict with their national legislation.[45]

The policy continues to be the general framework of reference for national security policies of NATO member States (and for many PfP countries). Sometimes, when faced with a claim for public disclosure of government documents which contain a reference to information classified by NATO, such a government is not even able to name as the real reason for their denying the disclosure the NATO security policy, as this entire policy is by itself of classified nature.[46]

NATO'S SI policy has been criticised by advocates of open government for being outdated; according to them, it errs on the side of caution in favour of an overly secretive military culture which, in the case of an international organisation, is also immune to democratic control. Some NATO member States concede in internal communications that the 'existing policy does not reflect the working realities of today, particularly nations' reliance on information technology'.[47]

---

35   *Ibid.*, p. 5.

36   *Ibid.*, p. 45.

37   *Ibid.*, p. 28.

38   *Ibid.*, p. 25.

39   *Ibid.*, pp. 20–21.

40   *Ibid.*, pp. 38–39.

41   *Ibid.*, pp. 40–43.

42   NATO Archives, Policy Statement (Extracts), http://www.nato.int/archives/policy.htm (visited 03/10/03).

43   *Cf.* A. Roberts, *Entangling Alliances* (2003), p. 332; *Cf.* NATO C-M(55)15(Final), p. 7 (on Personnel Security): 'Particularly close scrutiny in the screening process should be given to: ... (b) Persons who are of Russian or Satellite origin or connection' [emphasis added].

44   At least some of the passages seems to have been taken verbatim from US national security of information rules then in force, as appears from remaining traces of references to 'the security of the nation' (e.g. in NATO C-M(55)15(Final), p. 7, para. 11) throughout the text.

45   A. Roberts, *Entangling Alliances* (2003), p. 340.

46   *Ibid.*, pp. 353–5.

47   E.g. Briefing Note describing rationale for adoption of new NATO Security Policy. Released in response to an Access to Information Act request to the Canadian Department

Legal nature of the NATO security policy

Qualification of the 1997 Security Agreement between NATO members as an international treaty does not seem overly problematic, as all the respective necessary requirements[48] are fulfilled. Its parties are States, and thus primary subjects of international law. It is titled as an 'Agreement', separated in Preambular and Operative Parts. It contains clear and precise language fit to engender direct obligations such as is commonly used in binding international instruments.[49] It has a provision on entry into force.[50] The formulations 'Have agreed as follows' and the usage of the word 'shall' before the main obligations clearly establish a meeting of the minds as well as consent to be bound. It is not known, however, how many NATO countries have become parties to it yet.[51] Those which have not are only bound by the older version of 1950 in Enclosure A of document C-M(55)15(Final)[52].

In contrast, Enclosures B, C and D of C-M(55)15(Final) lack many if not all of the constitutive characteristics. For example, throughout the text, the parts which should theoretically be the operative provisions are preceded by formulations such as 'it may be necessary', 'will', 'should' or 'it is a useful procedure to ...'. The headings of the single chapters read 'Principles', 'Standards' and 'Procedures'. There is no explicit reference in either version of the Security Agreement (old or new) incorporating them. The fact that they were at one point included in a single document (C-M(55)15(Final)) together with a binding treaty does not, by itself, seem sufficient to establish the intention of the drafters to make them binding: it appears more as a circumstance from the point of view of intra-organisational practice. In conclusion, the legal nature of these guidelines remains doubtful and they should – owing to the fact that they are otherwise quite precise and detailed – probably be conceived of as intra-organisational soft law.

Influence of the NATO security policy on third parties

NATO has been the first and primary security organisation in Europe for decades. As a result, the NATO Security of Information policy became the standard for almost any piece of regulation in this area in Europe.[53] In the European region, it has greatly influenced the development of similar policies within the WEU and, recently,

---

of Foreign Affairs and International Trade, File A-2002–00184, October 2002; http://faculty. maxwell.syr.edu/asroberts /foi/library/DFAIT_A_2002_00184.pdf (visited 03/10/03).

48   *Cf.* above Chapter 4 (Institutional Framework).

49   *Cf.* above Chapter 4 (Institutional Framework).

50   1997 NATO Security of Information Agreement, Art. 7.

51   At the time of writing, it has not been registered with the United Nations Treaty Series.

52   See Chapter 8 (Berlin Plus Agreement).

53   Indeed, were NATO a country, the concept of 'extra-territoriality' would spring to mind.

also within the EU. These policies will be treated below in separate parts.[54] The most direct exemplary power of the NATO SI policy can be perceived as NATO's security-of-information agreements (SIA) with accession candidate countries and other PfP countries. These countries, lacking much political leverage, had to adopt NATO security-of-information standards more or less unchanged. An interesting example is the SIA of NATO with Austria of 1995.[55] The operative provisions of this agreement replicate, with some formal adaptations, the exact text of the 1997 NATO SIA, down to the article numbers.

NATO also made clear to accession candidates for its second round of enlargement in Central and Eastern Europe in March 2004 that the adoption of NATO-compatible SI standards was a necessary prerequisite for eventual membership in the Alliance.[56] Thus, in order to be able to conclude SIAs with NATO,[57] those candidate countries rushed to enact respective legislation,[58] often reversing the more liberal laws on government transparency which they had recently enacted as part of their accession process to the EU.[59] Romania in particular was very public about such moves.[60] Two more cases in Central and Eastern Europe serve to illustrate this development.

Bulgaria's Law on the Protection of Classified Information (2002)[61] includes typical NATO SI features such as breadth,[62] need to know,[63] classification markings and definitions near-identical to NATO's,[64] physical security[65] and industrial

---

54   See below at p. 320 (WEU), and p. 323 (EU).

55   Exchange of letters constituting an Agreement between Austria and the North Atlantic Treaty Organization on the Protection of Information, 1912 UNTS 288–293.

56   NATO Membership Action Plan, 24 April 1999, NATO Press Release NAC-S(99)66; Speech by NATO Secretary General George Robertson at the Romanian Parliament, 3 March 2003, para. 20, http://www.nato.int/docu/speech/2003/s030303a.htm (visited 04/10/03).

57   *Cf.* Chairman's Summary of the NATO Aspirant Countries Defense Ministerial Meeting, Sofia 12–13 October 2000, para. 4, http://www.expandnato.org/sofia.html (visited 04/10/03).

58   A. Roberts, *NATO, Secrecy, and the Right to Information*, East European Constitutional Review (Fall 2002/Winter 2003), pp. 86–87, http://www.isn.ethz.ch/php/news/Declassification /declassification_Roberts.pdf (visited 19/12/2003).

59   A. Roberts, *Entangling Alliances* (2003), pp. 329–330.

60   *NATO officials discuss Statute of Romania's National Security Agency*, BBC Monitoring International Reports, 12 June 2002; A. Pop, *Romania's Challenge*, NATO Review, Spring 2003, para. 4 http://www.nato.int/docu/review/2003/issue1/english/analysis. html (visited 04/10/03).

61   [Hereinafter: Bulgarian SI law]. The full text is available at http://faculty.maxwell. syr.edu /asroberts/foi/library/secrecylaws/BG_class_info_law.pdf (visited 04/10/03).

62   Motives to the draft law on the Protection of Classified Information, http://www. aip-bg.org /documents/zzki_mot_eng.htm (visited 04/10/03) [Hereinafter: Bulgarian SI law, Motives].

63   Bulgarian SI law, Art. 83, para. 2; *Cf.* Bulgarian SI law, Motives.

64   Bulgarian SI law, Art. 28.

65   *Ibid.*, Ch. Six, Sec. I.

security[66]. State secrets are seemingly protected for up to 50 years, which widely exceeds even NATO's absolute limit of 30 years. The Bulgarian SI Law did not, of course, go without due criticism in the country.[67]

Slovenia's Classified Information Act (2001)[68] includes industrial security,[69] collective classification,[70] and the same classification markings as NATO (although the definition of the lowest 'Restricted' category differs)[71]. Personnel screening criteria replicate the NATO guidelines in detail.[72] Even the question *whether* a certain piece of secret information exists may itself be a secret and thus a Slovenian government agency receiving a request 'shall not be obliged to either confirm or deny the existence of the requested information'.[73] This form of information clouding is exactly what C-M(55)15(Final) asks NATO governments to do.[74] However, the Slovenian law is confined to public security, defence, foreign affairs and intelligence[75] and thus does not incorporate NATO's breadth. In addition, in contrast to NATO SI guidelines, Slovenia provides for certain exemptions to the need-to-know rule (for the highest State officials).[76] Bulgaria provides the same exemptions concerning the area of personnel screening.[77] Both countries also provide for some procedural rights for the individual in personnel screening.[78] None of these particularities are found in the NATO policy.

NATO is likely to have concluded SIAs with all of its accession candidates and other PfP partners,[79], and has also been looking into concluding SIAs as a condition for establishing closed security links with Mediterranean countries[80].

---

66   *Ibid.*, Ch. Six, Sec. VI.

67   E.g. O. Stefanov, *For whom are secret services?*, World News Connection, 28 Aug. 2003.

68   [Hereinafter: Slovenian SI law]. The full text is available at http://nato.gov.si/eng /documents/classified-info-act/ (visited 04/10/03).

69   *Ibid.*, Art. 1, para. 3.

70   *Ibid.*, Art. 14.

71   *Ibid.*, Art. 13.

72   *Ibid.*, Art. 25.

73   *Ibid.*, Art. 19.

74   See above at Chapter 8 (Berlin Plus Agreement).

75   Slovenian SI law, Art. 4.

76   *Ibid.*, Art. 3.

77   *Cf.* Bulgarian SI law, Art. 39(1).

78   *Cf.* Slovenian SI law, Art. 25; Bulgarian SI law, Art. 42 and 43.

79   See. e.g. for Estonia: *Estonia, Britain to sign Agreement on Protection of Classified Data*, Baltic News Service, 10 Dec. 2003.

80   See e.g. NAC Meeting of Foreign Ministers, Budapest, 29–30 May 2001, Communiqué M-NAC-1(2001)77, para. 66, cited in: List of NATO's Communiqués since 1990 Referring to the Mediterranean Region and/or NATO's Mediterranean Dialogue, http:// www.nato.int/med-dial/comm.htm (visited 04/10/03).

SECURITY OF INFORMATION IN THE WESTERN EUROPEAN UNION

The WEU had become a dormant organisation before it was reactivated as NATO's European pillar in the 1990s,[81] and its SI rules only came into being at that time. They bear a strong NATO imprint. The WEU's SI rules are even less accessible than NATO's, but their basic structure seems to be the same: a Security Agreement between the Parties of the main treaty (the MBT), complemented by detailed Security Regulations on handling classified documents.

The WEU Security Agreement is not accessible to the public,[82] but an SIA which the WEU concluded with Sweden in 1997[83] allows some inferences to be drawn about the former's content. This is because the operative provisions repeat the basic obligations of NATO's Security Agreement of 1997.[84] Hence, the WEU Security Agreement should probably closely resemble the NATO counterpart.

The WEU Security Regulations – contained in WEU document RS 100 – are accessible in parts.[85] Their structure – and some entire parts in wording – are clearly based on NATO's C-M(55)15(Final) and repeat most of the latter's rules and principles, plus some new parts accounting for advances in information technology,[86] terrorist threats,[87] and release of classified information to third parties (for example NATO countries not being members of the WEU)[88].

The five basic features of the NATO security policy[89] are found again in WEU's RS 100: breadth;[90] depth;[91] centralisation, that is, the duty to assign national security agencies for keeping track of all classified documents in circulation and all persons cleared to handle them;[92] controlled distribution, including the need-to-know

---

81   *Cf.* above Chapter 1(The Wider Agreement).

82   Letter from the WEU Secretariat to the author, 29 Aug. 2003.

83   The agreement is available at http://faculty.maxwell.syr.edu/asroberts/foi/library /sweden_weu_agr.pdf (visited 04/10/2003).

84   See the 1997 NATO Security of Information Agreement above. In fact, the NATO Security Agreement was concluded only days before the said SIA between the WEU and Sweden.

85   WEU Security Regulations, RS 100 (January 1996), http://faculty.maxwell.syr.edu/ asroberts/foi /library/weo_sec_reg.pdf (visited 04/10/03).

86   *Ibid.*, Sec. X., p. 42.

87   *Ibid.*, Sec. XI., p. 62.

88   *Ibid.*, Sec. XII, p. 64; *Cf.* also *Ibid.*, p. 6, para. 24.

89   See above at p. 298.

90   WEU Security Regulations (1996), p. 3, para. 8.

91   *Ibid.*, p. 3, para. 8; except for the NATO equivalent for 'Restricted' which is defined as information the disclosure of which would be 'disadvantageous' to the interests of the WEU.

92   *Ibid.*, p. 8, para. 12.

principle[93] and the principle of originator control;[94] and personnel controls including 'positive vetting'[95]. There is a provision on 'collective classification',[96] and a duty for WEU officials to avoid over-classification.[97] Separate sections exist on industrial security,[98] physical security (security of buildings),[99] action to be taken in cases of breaches of security,[100] and rules for use of classified documents on international conferences[101]. Among the innovations of RS 100 are a provision requiring personnel screening at least every five years,[102] and a chapter containing a whole new regime (including Annexes) on the release of WEU classified information to 'states that are not signatories to the Modified Brussels Treaty or other international organisations'.[103] Information is released to these third parties depending on the nature and content of such information, and depending on the measure of perceived advantages to the organisation. Decisions to release information are taken on a case-by-case basis, depending on the desired degree of cooperation with the third party and on the confidence able to be placed in it. Depending on these criteria, there are three levels of cooperation: States whose security policy is 'very close' to the WEU's (Level 1),[104] States whose position is 'markedly different' (Level 2),[105] and those whose policy 'cannot be assessed' (Level 3)[106]. The WEU Council may also decide that there is a long-term need for the exchange of classified information, and may draw up 'agreements on security procedures for the exchange of classified information'.[107] The WEU seems to have concluded a number of such agreements on the exchange of classified documents[108] with neutral countries and its other associate

---

93   *Ibid.*, p. 3, para. 7/d). The need-to-know principle is emphasised as 'fundamental to all aspects of security'. Interestingly, it is only cited, not explained. The assumption seems reasonable that its understanding among WEU members could be taken for granted by the time the WEU Security Regulations were drafted.

94   WEU Security Regulations (1996), p. 12, para. 2.

95   *Ibid.*, p. 4, para. 10.

96   *Ibid.*, p. 12, para. 8.

97   *Ibid.*, p. 5, para. 17 and p. 12, para. 6.

98   *Ibid.*, Sec. XIII, p. 66.

99   *Ibid.*, Sec. IV, p. 14 (classified).

100   *Ibid.*, Sec. IX, p. 40 (classified).

101   *Ibid.*, Sec. VIII, p. 36 (classified).

102   *Ibid.*, p. 20, para. 2.

103   See above at fn. 88.

104   WEU Security Regulations (1996), p. 65, para. 5; Annex 5, *Ibid.*, pp. 99.

105   *Ibid.*; Annex 6, *Ibid.*, p. 102.

106   *Ibid.*; Annex 7, *Ibid.*, p. 107.

107   *Ibid.*, p. 65, para. 7.

108   P. Rater, *Greece maintains block on cooperation between NATO and WEU*, AFP, 28 March 1997.

members in Central and Eastern Europe, for example with Sweden[109] and Slovakia[110] in 1997, and later probably with Ireland[111].

All the provisions on third-party release are important technical prerequisites for the WEU's cooperation with NATO and those of its member States not members of the WEU (mainly the US). A. Roberts mentions a NATO-WEU SIA, concluded 1992.[112] The WEU concluded another SIA with NATO in 1996[113] (the same year it adopted document RS 100), but that document also is not open to the public[114].

In 1999, the WEU concluded 'arrangements for enhanced cooperation'[115] with the EU.[116] These arrangements included, in annexes, two separate exchanges of letters with the Council and the Commission on the exchange of classified information. In terms of Union politics, this already shows a significant degree of institutional independence of the Council and the Commission from one another, and the Union's whole. Legally, however, there is no doubt today that the institutions of the EU do not possess international legal personality nor treaty-making power of their own.[117] Thus agreements entered into by them can only bind the Union itself, subject to the normal conditions of international treaty law,[118] otherwise they are non-binding. The two 'arrangements' above, seem to be binding treaties, as both 'arrangements' feature sufficient characteristics to qualify as binding exchange of instruments under international law. Their material content is worded in almost exactly the same terms as the WEU-Sweden SIA of 1997, and is thus presumably drawn from the main WEU SIA which follows the NATO model.

The rules contained in document RS 100 were important precedents for later SI regulations in the EU, especially for the 'Lindh decision' of March 2001.[119] Indeed,

---

109   See above at fn. 83.

110   *Security agreement with Western European Union signed*, BBC Summary of World Broadcasts, 24 April 1997.

111   S. Denham, *Now we know why Ireland doesn't want you to know its big secrets*, The Sunday Times (London), 26 Sept. 1999.

112   A. Roberts, *Entangling Alliances* (2003), p. 335.

113   NATO Press Release (96)66 of 2 May 1996; *Cf.* Declaration issued by the Western European Union Council of Ministers, Birmingham, 7 May 1996, V., (http://www.weu.int/ documents /960507en.pdf, visited 13/07/03); *Cf.* Final Communiqué of the NATO Ministerial Meeting in Berlin, 3 June 1996, NATO Press Release M-NAC-1(96)63, para. 20; J.R. Schmertz / M. Meier, *WEU and NATO enter into agreement to increase role of Europeans*, International Law Update, Vol. 2, No. 6, June 1996; *NATO, WEU sign 'security pact'*, United Press International 6 May 1996; *Nato and WEU agree to swap secrets*, The Independent (London), 7 May 1996, p. 10.

114   Letter to the author, fn. 82.

115   Not 'enhanced cooperation' in the meaning of the TEU (e.g. Arts 27 *et seq.* TEU).

116   Council Decision of 10 May 1999 concerning the arrangements for enhanced cooperation between the European Union and the Western European Union (1999/404/CFSP), OJ L 153/22 of 19/6/1999.

117   ECJ, *Dinecke Algera v Common Assembly of the ECSC* [1957] ECR 39.

118   *Cf.* above Chapter 4 (Institutional Framework).

119   See below at p. 334.

later European SI legislation (which is mostly public) follows the wording and structure of the WEU Security Regulations so closely that retroactive inferences can be drawn concerning the WEU Security Regulations' unpublished parts.

SECURITY OF INFORMATION IN THE EUROPEAN UNION

Early period (until mid-2000)

Before 1993, the institutions of the EC were generally reluctant to share any of their internal documents with the wider public, a habit likely stemming from diplomatic traditions.[120] In 1993, a non-binding Code of Conduct was signed by the Commission and the Council which formalised the public's right to access information originating from within their bureaucracies.[121] In the Amsterdam Treaty the right to information was for the first time enshrined in binding form. Article 255 TEC in its revised version states that 'any citizen of the Union ... shall have a right of access to European Parliament, Council and Commission documents', subject to principles to be elaborated in later secondary legislation.[122] Arts 28 and 41 TEU respectively extend this principle to the 2nd and 3rd pillars. This establishes the so-called 'transparency principle' – founded in member States' traditions of open government – in each of the different regimes elaborated by the different EU institutions on access to their documents. The introduction of the transparency principle was meant to increase confidence of the EU citizen in the Union's institutions, by making those institutions behave in accordance with the precepts of *good administration.*[123] This development should be seen in the context of increasing calls among international lawyers and international relations theorists for accountability of international organisations.[124] However, at the Amsterdam conference, member States reserved, in Declaration No. 35 to the Treaty, the explicit right 'to request the Commission or the Council not to communicate to third parties a document from that State without its prior agreement'.[125] This is an active or 'soft' form of originator control, which is conceived as an exception from the general rule of transparency enshrined in Art. 255 TEC (as it has to be expressly requested). It stands in contrast to the passive or 'hard' form of originator control found in NATO and the WEU. Hard originator

---

120   *Cf.* A. Frost, *Restoring Faith in Government: Transparency Reform in the United States and the European Union*, 9 European Public Law (2003), pp. 93–95.

121   Code of Conduct concerning public access to Council and Commission documents, 93/730/EC, OJ L 340/41 of 31/12/1993.

122   See below at p. 340 (REG 1049/2001).

123   D.M. Curtin, *Citizens' Fundamental Right of Access to EU Information: An Evolving Digital Passepartout?*, 37 CMLR (2000), p. 7 at 11 [emphasis in the original].

124   *Cf.* A. Reinisch, *Governance without Accountability?*, 44 GYIL (2001), p. 270 at 275.

125   Declaration (No 35) on Article 255 (ex Article 191a(1)) of the Treaty establishing the European Community, http://europa.eu.int/eur-lex/en/treaties/dat/amsterdam.html#0137050052 (visited 17/12/2003) [hereinafter: Amsterdam Declaration No. 35].

control places the onus on the requesting party to obtain consent from the originator before being able to receive any document. After the entry into force of the European Constitution, Art. 255 TEC will be replaced by Art. II-102 European Constitution, with due restrictions similar to those existing for Art. 255 TEC.[126]

To this day there is no Union-wide uniform procedure on access to documents. Rather, rules differ from institution to institution. Despite the existence of different access regimes, documents are widely exchanged between the European Parliament, the Council and the Commission. This makes a certain degree of common standards necessary, particularly concerning classified documents. The jurisprudence of the ECJ and its Court of First Instance has over time developed 'a significant and substantial body of law relating to the right of access to documents'.[127]

Council

The Council's early rules on public access to its documents gave paramount importance to the 'principle of allowing the public wide access to Council documents'.[128] There were a few exceptions, such as for the protection of public interest, including public security and international relations.[129] Before the birth of the Union's CFSP, there was little need to further specify terms such as 'public security'. But from the moment the Union ventured into foreign policy and defence, more detailed restrictions in this regard soon became necessary. The Staff Note introducing the Council Decision No 24/95 on Measures for the Protection of Classified Information to Council personnel stated that 'the new areas of competence we have acquired ... particularly in the spheres of common foreign and security policy and cooperation on justice and home affairs, clearly require the introduction of rules and procedures designed to guarantee the protection and security of certain documents',[130] even though the then SG of the Council Jürgen Trumpf pointed out that the new rules should 'not in any way prejudice' the Council's existing rules on transparency[131]. Decision No 24/95 introduced three classification categories: 'Secret', 'Confidentiel' and 'Restreint' (the French denomination applying equally to all language versions).[132] Its Art. 3

---

126   Art. I-50(3) and III-399 European Constitution.

127   P. Craig / G. de Búrca, *EU Law* (2003), p. 394.

128   Council Decision of 20 December 1993 on public access to Council documents (93/731/EC), OJ L 340/43 of 31/12/1993.

129   *Ibid.* Art. 4, para. 1.

130   Council of the European Union, Staff Note: Decision on measures to protect classified information, 30/1/1995, contained in Council Document 9151/95, p. 1, para. 1.

131   *Ibid.*, p. 4, para. 3.

132   Decision No 24/95 on Measures for the Protection of Classified Information applicable to the General Secretariat of the Council, annexed to the Staff Note, fn. 130, Art. 2/1.

contained a provision on 'collective classification'[133] in this regard. The highest two categories were conceived as only 'for occasional, even exceptional use'.[134]

In 1998, enhanced cooperation of the EU with the WEU made necessary an upgrade of the rules on handling classified information in the Council. This was effected in Council Decision 98/319/EC of 27 April 1998.[135] In this decision, the need-to-know principle was introduced,[136] as were arrangements for the security clearance of the personnel of the General Secretariat. Personnel screening was left to member States,[137] subject to some common guidelines. Authorisations were to be valid for five years,[138] as in the WEU. The personnel screening procedure did not, however, include NATO's principle of 'positive vetting'.[139] Rather, it was provided that 'security screening shall be carried out with the assistance of the person concerned', which included the possibility for the person concerned to appeal against a negative decision by the national screening authority.[140] The Decision's preamble contained a positive conflict clause in favour of the transparency principle.[141]

The general policy of the Council on classified documents until mid-2000 remained one of openness in principle,[142] with some restrictions concerning public security,[143] on the basis of the above documents.[144] By 2000, an SI policy had been successfully introduced to account for new needs arising out of the CFSP, while avoiding the all-encompassing breadth used by in NATO and the WEU. Transparency and the rights of the individual had been preserved to the utmost degree possible, following the general democratic traditions of EU member States.

Commission

The Commission's regime on access to its documents and handling classified information were enshrined in Commission Decision C(94)3282 of 30 November

---

133   *Cf.* at fn. 34 above (NATO Security Policy).

134   Staff Note, fn. 130, p. 3.

135   Council Decision of 27 April 1998 relating to the procedures whereby officials and employees of the General Secretariat of the Council may be allowed access to classified information held by the Council (98/319/EC), OJ L 140/12 of 12/5/1998, Preambular Paragraph 3.

136   *Ibid.*, Art. 1/1.

137   *Ibid.*, Art. 1/3.

138   *Ibid.*, Art. 2/2.

139   *Cf.* at fn. 26 above (NATO Security Policy).

140   Council Dec. 98/319/EC, Arts 3 and 4.

141   *Ibid.*, last Preambular Paragraph.

142   See e.g. Council Dec. of 6 December 1999 on the improvement of information on the Council's legislative activities and the public register of Council documents (2000/23/EC), OJ L 9/22 of 13/1/2000, Preambular Paragraph 1.

143   *Ibid.*, Art. 2.

144   See e.g. Council Dec. of 5 June 2000 adopting the Council's Rules of Procedure (2000/396/EC, ECSC, Euratom), OJ L 149/21 of 23/6/2000, Art. 10, note (¹).

1994.[145] The rules provided by this Decision in parts already bear striking resemblance to NATO's Policy as contained in C-M(55)15(Final). It thus seems likely that NATO experiences of some EU member States somehow found their way into the document's draft. Whether NATO officials were directly involved in the drafting is very hard to guess as, in 1994, the EU was still far from entering into any kind of cooperation with NATO. Yet, the Commission's 1994 SI policy already did provide expressly for the handling of classified information from WEU and NATO.[146] Classification markings were the same as in NATO and the WEU. This included the highest 'Top Secret' category (introduced in the Council only in 2000[147]), and a provision on 'collective classification'.[148] The definitions of classification markings covered, in addition to the interests of the EU or the member States, also the interests of 'another organization'.[149] Originator control[150] and need-to-know[151] were included. The screening procedure for personnel was entirely left to member States, but should in any case 'be carried out with the agreement of the person concerned',[152] thus preventing 'positive vetting'.[153] Authorisations for access to classified documents were to be reviewed every five years.[154] The policy also contained a centralised registry role for the Commission's Security Office,[155] parts on industrial security,[156] physical security,[157] and detailed provisions on safeguards to be used in producing, transporting (including through electronic means) and destroying classified documents[158]. Breaches of security were covered in a similar manner to NATO and the WEU,[159] the decision on criminal prosecution being left to the member State of the person concerned.[160]

The Commission's rules on classified documents were partly replaced in 1999 by Commission Decision 1999/218/EC of 25 February 1999.[161] In that Decision, the need-

---

145   Commission Decision of 30 November 1994 on the security measures applicable to classified information produced or transmitted in connection with the activities of the European Union (C(94)3282), European Commission Security Office, Brussels, 1 March 1995.

146   *Ibid.*, Art. 6a.

147   By the 'Solana decision', see below at p. 312.

148   Commission Dec. C(94)3282, Art. 4.

149   *Ibid.*, Art. 5.

150   *Ibid.*, Art. 8.

151   *Ibid.*, Art. 10.

152   *Ibid.*, Art. 12/2.

153   *Cf.* at fn. 26 above (NATO Security Policy).

154   Commission Dec. C(94)3282, Art. 11/3.

155   *Ibid.*, Art. 14 and 16/3.

156   *Ibid.*, Art. 9.

157   *Ibid.*, Arts 28–32.

158   *Ibid.*, Arts 18–27.

159   *Ibid.*, Art. 33.

160   *Ibid.*, Art. 33/6.

161   Commission Decision of 25 February 1999 relating to the procedures whereby officials and employees of the European Commission may be allowed access to classified

to-know principle was further elaborated.[162] The relevant personnel screening processes of the member States were subjected to general minimum guidelines,[163] including also the possibility to appeal against a negative decision[164]. Temporary authorisations of up to three months (unknown in NATO or the WEU) were made possible.

In sum, the Commission had, by 2000, taken significant steps to safeguard its classified information – in some aspects even 'overtaking' the Council. The principle of transparency was weaker. Yet employees of the Commission enjoyed roughly the same rights in the personnel screening procedure as their colleagues in the Council.

European Parliament

The European Parliament has traditionally been the most unequivocal supporter of openness in the Union, including the right for EU citizens and residents to access EU documents. From the practical side, however, EP involvement in the Union's foreign policy and defence, where classified documents are commonly used, is marginal.

The most authoritative statement of the European Parliament on handling classified documents in the EU may be seen in the Resolution on openness within the EU of 12 January 1999.[165] The Resolution calls, inter alia, for:

- the establishment of a single code on public access to EU documents;[166]
- inclusion of all classified documents in public registers, with an indication that they are confidential;[167]
- a simplification and clearer definition of classification markings;[168]
- a tighter definition of the exceptions of 'protection of the public interest' and its subheadings;[169]
- all not-replied-to requests to count as approved, rather than vice versa;[170]
- release of those parts of sensitive documents which, considered in isolation, are not sensitive (preventing 'collective classification').[171]

This Resolution is, however, not binding on the actual practice of the Council or the Commission.

---

information held by the Commission (1999/218/EC), OJ L 80/22 of 25/3/1999.

162 *Ibid.*, Art. 1.

163 *Ibid.*, Art. 1/3 and Art. 3.

164 *Ibid.*, Arts 4 and 5. These provisions were taken directly from Council Decision 98/319/EC (see fn. 135 above).

165 Resolution on openness within the European Union, A4–0476/98, OJ C 140/20 of 14/4/1999.

166 *Ibid.*, para. 1.

167 *Ibid.*, para. 4 (iii).

168 *Ibid.*, para. 4 (iv).

169 *Ibid.*, para. 4 (v).

170 *Ibid.*, para. 4 (vii).

171 *Ibid.*, para. 4 (ix) *cf.* the *Hautala* Case (ECJ), fn. 270.

'Solana decision' (Council) 26 July and 14 August 2000

At the Helsinki European Council of December 1999, a hitherto-existing taboo within the EU, defence and military matters, was finally broken. The new 'defence dimension of the European Union' was manifested by the Headline Goal Task Force. In the process, it was recognised among the Union's new security and defence establishment that one of the requirements for an ESDP able to react fast to an erupting crisis was better intelligence, including a workable system to exchange classified documents.[172] Javier Solana had taken over the GSC in October 1999 after concluding his term as NATO-SG (1995–1999). He had often been reported as complaining about the lack of security for a future military infrastructure in the Secretariat's buildings in Brussels ('as many holes as Swiss cheese').[173] These security gaps had to be closed if the EU wanted to enter into a closer cooperation with NATO,[174] a development which started with Solana.[175] The EU knew that the Alliance would not release any of its classified documents without adequate safety standards put in place at the receiving end.[176] Solana's plans were laid out in a secret 'Note for the Committee of Permanent Representatives regarding the Security Plan for the Council' of 30 June 2000, stating that the 'higher level of security required to protect information under the ESDP makes it necessary to amend existing legislation or to adopt new texts'.[177] Breaches of security should, according to the note, be penalised by member States in the same manner as provided for by Art. 194 Euratom Treaty (which dated from 1957, at the height of the Cold War, and was designed to protect interests then of geostrategic importance).[178] The British Foreign Office at the time commented that 'the Council Secretariat is keen to push through amendments

---

172   *Cf. Europe 'Needs Special Forces and Better Spies'*, The Independent (London), 24 Nov. 1999, p. 19.

173   E.g. *Nato secrecy spooks EU suits: The push for open government has come up against closed doors*, Financial Times, 18 Nov. 2000, p. 11; *Military men make a splash in Brussels*, The Guardian, 30 March 2001.

174   See S. Ilsemann et al., *Argwohn bestätigt*, Der Spiegel, No. 23, 5 June 2000, p. 172.

175   From the end of 1999, the new 'Solana-Roberson connection' ushered in the first institutional contacts between the EU and NATO.

176   Council letter to Jelle van Burren, dated 26 June (agreed at the General Affairs Council on 10 July 2000) in response to a request for access to the Outcome of Proceedings of the Interim Military Working Group (IMWG), cited in: Statewatch, House of Lords – European Union – Eighth Report; *Cf.* M.E. de Leeuw, *The regulation on public access to European Parliament, Council and Commission documents in the European Union*, 28 ELR (2003), pp. 328–9.

177   Council Doc. SN 3328/1/00 REV 1, at 4., reprinted in: Statewatch, *Council Security Plan: background to the 'Solana Decision'*, http://www.statewatch.org/secret/solana1.htm (visited 02/09/03).

178   This project got as far as the drafting stages (See Council Doc. SN 3328/1/00), but discussions on the subject stopped in 2001 and it has since then been in abeyance (written information from the Council's General Secretariat to the author, 7 October 2003).

to the texts as quickly as possible', that is, using a fast-track procedure.[179] Solana's note also mentioned the intention of concluding security agreements with NATO 'as soon as possible. This could be done through an exchange of letters, following the precedent of the GSC/WEU agreement of 15 April 1999'.[180]

Solana set about closing the perceived security gaps in the GSC in two steps. First, he amended, in a 'Decision on measures for the protection of classified information applicable to the General Secretariat of the Council' the older more liberal rules contained in Decision 24/95.[181] The new Decision added a new 'Top Secret' classification marking to the three markings already existing, thus making the GSC's classification system comparable to and compatible with NATO's.[182] The possibility for officials to change a document's specific classification marking (with the consent of the SG)[183] was abolished. The principle of 'hard' originator control was introduced.[184] It extended also to documents originating from third parties, for example NATO or the United States. Less than a month later, on 14 August 2000, the Council issued a Decision on public access to Council documents[185] amending earlier legislation[186]. This second Decision exempted wholesale all documents down to 'Confidentiel' classification level; in addition, those documents 'on matters concerning the security and defence of the Union, or one of its Member States or on military *or non-military* crisis management [meaning also pure police missions]' were exempted.[187] The exception was further extended to documents which enabled 'conclusions to be drawn regarding the content of classified information' (unless written consent of the document's author could be obtained).[188] This clause – in combination with the 'collective classification' rule (which remained unchanged from Decision 24/95) – created a spillover effect[189] for the strict security rules prevailing for military documents, into documents of all other areas which merely mentioned

---

179 House of Lords, Select Committee on European Union Eighth Report, APPENDIX 2, Explanatory Memorandum submitted by the Foreign and Commonwealth Office on proposals for amendments to the 1993 Council Decision (93/731/E2) on public access to Council documents and the 1999 Decision on the public register of Council documents (2000/23/E2), http://www.parliament.the-stationery-office.co.uk/pa/ld200001/ldselect/ldeucom/31/3104.htm (visited 30/08/03).

180 Council Doc. SN 3328/1/00 REV 1. For the abovementioned 1999 GSC/WEU agreement, see above at fn. 116.

181 Decision of the Secretary-General of the Council/High Representative for the Common and Security Policy of 27 July 2000, 2000/C 239/01, OJ C 239/1 of 23/8/2000 [hereinafter: Decision of the Council SG, 27 July 2000].

182 *Ibid.*, Art. 2.

183 See Art. 3/3 of Dec.24/95.

184 Decision of the Council SG, 27 July 2000, Art. 4.

185 Council Decision 2000/527/EC, OJ L 212/9 of 23/8/2000.

186 Decision 93/731/EC and 2000/23/EC were amended.

187 Emphasis added.

188 Art. 1/2, Council Decision 2000/527/EC, OJ L 212/9 of 23/8/2000.

189 Statewatch, Analysis of the Decision of 14 August 2000 to amend the 1993 code of access to EU documents, http://www.statewatch.org/newcode3.htm (visited 29/08/2003).

them. It would give external parties like NATO or the US an effective veto over release of a considerable range of EU documents.[190] This clearly went far beyond the widest interpretation of the previous regulation, which had only known exceptions for 'public security' and 'international relations'.[191] Furthermore, according to the 14 August 2000 Decision, none of the documents covered by the exception should appear in the public register of Council documents, meaning that their very existence would be secluded from the public.[192] This move towards secrecy of public documents was taken up by the Commission, at that time itself in the process of preparing a Regulation to implement Art. 255 TEC[193]. The Commission commented on the Council's Decision, that it would 'undertake ... to ensure that the same level of protection is afforded to documents concerning the ESDP'.[194] The measures taken by the Council and Commission in summer 2000 exemplify a general tendency of the EU to import NATO organisational culture into ESDP.[195]

The two Decisions of summer 2000 met with fierce criticisms from Denmark, the Netherlands, Finland and Sweden.[196] In their Statement accompanying the Decision of 14 August 2000 (which they had voted against), they considered that the confidentiality of ESDP documents could be guaranteed 'without the a priori exclusion' from public access and the public register. They upheld the importance of finalising a Regulation on public access according to Article 255 TEC.[197] Finland in particular had pushed for *all* documents to be included in the public register in its Presidency of the Council the previous year,[198] no matter what their chances (for example due to their military content) of ever being released. A Council decision passed at the end of the Finnish Presidency opened with the words that

---

190   *Cf.* Statewatch, House of Lords – European Union – Eighth Report, http://www. statewatch.org /news/2001/mar/3105.htm (visited 30/08/03)

191   See above at p. 309.

192   Art. 2/1, Council Decision 2000/527/EC, OJ L 212/9 of 23/8/2000.

193   That Regulation was at the time already advanced in the legislative process. See Commission Proposal regarding public access to European Parliament, Council and Commission Documents, COM(2000) 30 final/2, 2000/0032 (COD) [hereinafter: Commission's draft of February 2000].

194   Council Decision amending Decision 93/731/EC on public access to Council documents and Decision 2000/23/EC on the improvement of information on the Council's legislative activities and on the public register of Council documents, Statement by the European Commission, Council Doc. 10782/00.

195   *Cf.* K. Kastner, *Quelle culture de sécurité et de défense pour l'Union européenne?*, ENA thesis, Promotion Romain Gary «2003–2005» (2005) (on file with the author), p. 53.

196   All of these countries have fairly liberal public-access regulations in their domestic sphere.

197   Council Decision 2000/527/EC, OJ L 212/9 of 23/8/2000, Statement by the Danish, Netherlands, Finnish and Swedish delegations (fn. 194).

198   Council Decision 2000/23/EC, see above at fn. 142.

Openness vital for democracy and accountability within the European Union and information to the public is one of the instruments to enhance such openness.[199]

Open-government NGOs criticised in particular the 'enables conclusions to be drawn' provision in the Decision of 14 August 2000 which in their view would lead to 'contamination' of the general right of access to EU documents (through the spill-over effect into areas unrelated to defence described above); they further charged that there was no explanation from the Council why in particular 'non-military crisis management' should also be covered by the wide exemption.[200]

Criticism was also directed at the speed and haste in which the Decision was 'rushed through' the 'written procedure' in the COREPER in the middle of summer, prompting charges of a 'military coup in the middle of summertime'. Some of the surprised delegations simply walked out of the preparatory meetings.[201] The Green Party in the EP accused Solana of 'introducing NATO's secretive measures through the back door'.[202] The European Federation of Journalists (EFJ) described the Council's action as 'riding roughshod over rhetoric promising public involvement in the debate about the future of Europe'.[203] Furthermore, prior to the issuing of the second Decision in August, as COREPER was considering different options on the table, copies of the drafts had been denied by the Council to NGOs because this 'could fuel public discussion on the subject and raise questions among the Council's partners [that is, NATO] as to the latter's reliability as regards the respect of its obligations under the security arrangements'.[204] In particular, the timing was seen as deliberate in order to influence the Union-wide public-access Regulation then in the making, and to 'circumvent any parliamentary consultation' or consultation with civil society.[205] Reactions in the general press were also far from supportive.[206]

---

199   *Ibid.*, Preambular paragraph (1). On the question on accountability of international organisations in general, see above at fn. 124.

200   Statewatch News online, *Solana, secrecy: analysis*, http://www.statewatch.org/newcode3.htm (visited 29/08/03).

201   T. Bunyan, *Secrecy and Openness in the European Union* (2002), http://www.freedominfo.org/case/eustudy.htm (visited 30/08/2003), Ch. 6.

202   Statewatch News Online: Green Party press release, 26 July 2000, http://www.statewatch.org/news/jul00/05solana4.htm (visited 29/08/2003).

203   KnowEurope Bulletin: In Focus article, *EP seminar discusses new limits on access to documents, as EU bends to NATO on security and defence*, 24 Sept. 2000, http://www.knoweurope.net/html/ticker/3400_1.htm (visited 28/08/2003).

204   Council letter to Tony Bunyan, 14 Aug. 2000 in response to a request for access to the document setting out the options for changing the 1993 Decision put before the COREPER meeting on 26 July, cited in: Statewatch, House of Lords – European Union – Eighth Report, http://www.statewatch.org/news/2001/mar/3105.htm (visited 30/08/03).

205   *Cf. Ibid.*

206   E.g. *Political Uproar Expected Over New EU Secrecy Code*, International Herald Tribune, 30 Aug. 2000, p. 7; *EU members OK blanket security rules*, The Guardian, 31 Aug. 2000, International News; *Nato secrecy spooks EU suits: The push for open government has come up against closed doors*, Financial Times, 18 Nov. 2000, p. 11.

As a consequence of these events, the Netherlands, on 9 October 2000, filed action under Art. 230 TEC against the legality of the Council's Decision of 14 August, arguing that such legislation could only have been based on Art. 255 TEC, not on Art. 207 TEC (as in fact it had), and that the Council had, by forestalling the implementation of Art. 255 in a future public-access Regulation, infringed the prerogatives of the Commission and the EP.[207] Furthermore, the substantive provisions of the new legislation were held by the Netherlands to be in opposition to the spirit of Art. 255 and Art. 28 TEC.[208] The case was withdrawn from the register of the Court on 6 June 2002, probably because political agreement on the future Interinstitutional Agreement between the Council and the EP of November 2002[209] was by then already becoming apparent.

Consultation and exchanges of views subsequently took place between the EP, the Commission, the Council and the European Ombudsman, but the camps remained entrenched on security of information: the EP wanted open access to EU documents, whilst the Council and the Commission argued for the necessity of 'space to think', that is, some restrictions.[210]

The EP proper – after some weeks of deliberations in its Legal Affairs and Internal Market Committee (the Decisions had only been published in the OJ on 23 August)[211] – on 23 October 2000 also brought action against the Council under Art. 230 TEC.[212] It pleaded breach of an essential procedural requirement, as the correct legal basis for the decisions taken was Art. 255, para. 2, necessitating the co-decision procedure according to Art. 251 (which would have involved consultation of the EP). In addition, it pleaded breach of the general duty incumbent on EU organs to cooperate in good faith (Art. 10 TEC), and breach of the principle of institutional equilibrium. The case was also withdrawn from the register of the Court on 3 March 2002.

NATO declined an invitation to a working seminar within the EP's Committee on Citizen's Freedoms and Rights on 18 September 2000. In its letter replying to the Committee's invitation to attend, NATO argued that 'an organisation ... has to have

---

207   Case C-369/00, OJ C 319/19 of 4/11/2000, Netherlands v. Council.

208   *Ibid., Cf. Council of Ministers: Dutch go to Court over Classified Documents*, European Report, No. 2530, 27 September 2000.

209   See below at p. 343.

210   *Institutional Reform: Parliament, Council and Commission Discuss together Access to Documents*, European Report, 20 Sept. 2000.

211   See e.g. Statewatch News online, *Greens/EFA challenge Solana's 'military coup'*, http://www.statewatch.org/news/sept00/04greenprl.htm (visited 30/08/2003); Letter from Ana Palacio, Chair of the Legal Affairs Committee, to Nicole Fontaine, President of the European Parliament, reprinted in; *Ibid.*, http://www.statewatch.org/news/sept00/palacio1. htm (visited 30/08/2003).; *Ibid., Solana/NATO Decision on access to documents – European Parliament to decide whether to take the Council to court*, http://www.statewatch.org/news/ sept00/05epaction.htm (visited 29/08/2003); *Ibid., European Parliament votes in favour of legal action over the 'Solana Decision'*, http://www.statewatch.org/news/sept00/09eplegal. htm (visited 29/08/2003).

212   Case C-387/00, OJ 355/15 of 9/12/2000, Parliament v. Council.

a security infrastructure in place which satisfies NATO's security requirements'.[213] NATO's Security Office also referred to the recently concluded interim Security Agreement with the Council. NATO at the time evidently did not trust all institutions of the EU regarding the handling of classified information to the same degree. At a time when it was already exchanging such information with the Council,[214] it declined to even discuss the subject with the EP on a formal level.

Solana, defending the new measures, maintained that 'our ability to run ESDP effectively would be impossibly compromised if we were not able to give these guarantees [to NATO]' and that 'in general, a spirit of openness will continue to prevail'.[215]

The importance of the new public-access regulations for the development of ESDP was immediately visible: on 26 July 2000 the GSC concluded an interim Agreement on the Security of Information with NATO, by exchange of letters.[216] This Agreement – which will be described in detail below[217] – had evidently been prepared in detail before. Curiously, Solana's reply to NATO-SG George Robertson's letter of 26 July was sent out even *before* NATO's letter was officially received by the Council's Secretariat (by date stamp), prompting questions by NGOs how the High Representative could already 'reply to a letter he had not received'.[218]

After the conclusion of this interim Agreement however, neither NATO nor the EU, lost sight of their eventual goal of a permanent and comprehensive successor agreement with the Union as a whole. In order for this to happen, further adaptations were soon considered necessary in the EU's overall security regulations.

'Lindh decision' (Council) of 19 March 2001

On 19 March 2001 the Council issued a Decision adopting its new Security Regulations.[219] The Decision was adopted by the Council as an 'A' point, that is,

---

213 Letter from B. Austin, Acting Director, NATO Office of Security, to G. Watson, Chair of the Committee of Citizen's Freedoms and Rights, 23 Aug. 2000, NOS/2(2000)102, http://www.statewatch.org/news/sept00/NATO.PDF (visited 29/08/2003).

214 NATO had been exchanging classified information with the Council since the 'Interim Security Agreements' of 26 July 2000. See below at p. 330.

215 Speech by Javier Solana, November 2000, Stockholm, cited in: *Defence: 'No loyalty clash for EU troops'*, European Report, No. 2542, 8 November 2000.

216 Interim EU–NATO Security of Information Agreement with NATO, consisting in an exchange of letters between the CFSP-HR and the NATO-SG, 26 July 2000, http://faculty.maxwell.syr.edu/asroberts/foi/library/eu_nato_interim.pdf (visited 28/08/03) [hereinafter: EU–NATO interim SIA (2000)].

217 See below at p. 345.

218 Statewatch News online: *The Solana/Robertson exchange of letters, 26 July 2000*, 29 June 2002, http://www.statewatch.org/news/2002/mar/16solana.htm (visited 30/08/2003).

219 Council Decision 2001/264/EC of 19 March 2001 adopting the Council's security regulations, OJ L 101/1 of 11/4/2001 [hereinafter: Council Security Regulations (2001)].

without a vote.[220] These Regulations (covering over 60 pages) concern not only classified documents, but also 'physical security', security-related personnel aspects, the handling of sensitive information originating from the Council by member States (including national security agencies), and relations of the Council with third States or international organisations regarding sensitive information. The Security Regulations were adopted as part of the Council's Rules of Procedure,[221] and centred expressly on documents with military and defence implications. As the Decision was taken during the Swedish Presidency of the Council, its byname soon became the 'Lindh decision', after then Swedish foreign minister Anna Lindh. These Security Regulations of March 2001 are still in force today.

The 'Solana decision' of summer 2000[222] had contented itself with taking over general fundamental principles of NATO's C-M(55)15(Final) document, such as the need-to-know or originator control. The new EU Security Regulations from 2001, however, copy almost in wording, and certainly in spirit, the 1996 WEU Security Regulations.[223] This already becomes clear from a quick comparison of the content structure. Most of the differences are only formal, adapting the legal terminology of the WEU to the EU context, plus new terminology accounting for advances in information technology since 1996.[224] As the WEU Security Regulations were themselves closely modelled on NATO's, this was the most direct importation of NATO's security standards that the EU had yet experienced. An Explanatory Memorandum of the UK Foreign and Commonwealth Office to Parliament of 21 December 2000 seems to confirm this view.[225]

Yet, there were still a few differences compared to the WEU Security Regulations: there was a possibility for Council servants to appeal against a negative decision concerning personnel security clearance;[226] concerning IT security, the need-to-know was somewhat softened;[227] lastly, there was no 'informing duty' for national authorities if they became aware of a compromise to the organisation's security through one of their own officials[228].

The 2001 EU Security Regulations further include rules known from the NATO and WEU counterparts, for example 'collective classification'.[229] Provisions on the

---

220   *Cf.* Statewatch, *European Parliament takes Council to court for failure to consult over new (NATO) classification code – the 'Solana Two Decision'*, http://www.statewatch. org/news/2001/oct /11Aepsecreg.htm (visited 28/08/2003).

221   OJ L 149/21 of 23/6/2000; Preamble of the Decision.

222   See the 'Solana decision' above at p. 328.

223   See above at p. 320.

224   E.g. Council Security Regulations (2001), Part II, Sec. XI.

225   Cited in: Statewatch, *European Parliament takes Council to court* (2001).

226   Council Security Regulations (2001), Part II, Sec. VI, paras.5–7.

227   *Ibid.*, Part II, Sec. XI, paras. 15 and 16.

228   *Ibid.*, Part II, Sec. V.; compare the WEU Security Regulations (1996), Part II, Sec. V 1.e).

229   *Ibid.*, Part II, Sec. III, para. 7.

need-to-know are more detailed than the WEU's,[230] preventing an overly broad reading of this principle. Temporary security clearances can be issued for six months[231] (compared with three in the Commission[232]). The Regulations evidence the need (typical for military organisations) for safety against foreign intelligence intrusion: in their pertinent part, it is stated that 'EU classified information may be compromised ... by the activities of services which target the EU ... or by subversive organisations'.[233] This wording makes clear that terrorist organisations are also considered among possible threats to the Union, to be dealt with under ESDP. Information transmitted electronically must be encrypted where necessary.[234] Recognising, however, that electronic encryption may backfire by preventing expedient decision making in times of crisis, the Security Regulations provide exceptions from encryption in circumstances of 'impending or actual crisis, conflict, or war situations; and ... when speed of delivery is of paramount importance, and means of encryption are not available'.[235] The hard lessons learnt by NATO in the 1950s with an overly restrictive classification system[236] seem to have flowed into this provision. However, it is not clear who will decide in case of doubt whether such a situation of crisis exists.

Of particular interest is the classification structure: it maintains the four categories existing in the Council since the 'Solana decision': Très Secret UE, Secret UE, Confidentiel UE and Restreint UE.[237] A comparison of these categories with national security classifications of individual EU member States is provided in Appendix 2 of the 'Lindh decision'. This list also includes rubrics for WEU and NATO classified documents, with empty spaces in the case of NATO. This is explained in a footnote: 'correspondence with NATO classification levels will be established when the Security Agreement between the EU and NATO is negotiated'.[238] For an official piece of legislation published in the Official Journal this is rather unusual. It attests to the strong intention by the Council in 2001 to conclude the said Agreement with NATO, an intention which is thus even given some legal significance.

A definition of the classification markings, with usage examples, are provided in Appendix 3 of the 'Lindh decision'. This part of the Security Regulations reads more like an internal instruction manual ('Practical classification guide') than a legal text (as indeed also does most of NATO's C-M(55)15(Final)). The highest category (Très Secret UE) is to be used for information the compromise of which could cause 'exceptionally grave prejudice to the essential interests of the European Union or

---

230   *Ibid.*, Part II, Sec. VI.
231   *Ibid.*, Part II, Sec. VI, paras.15.
232   See above at p. 327.
233   Council Security Regulations (2001), Part II, Sec. X, para. 3.
234   Council Security Regulations (2001), Part II, Sec. XI, Ch.V.
235   *Ibid.*, Part II, Sec. XI, para. 68.
236   See above at p. 315.
237   The French versions of the classification markings are also used in the English-language version of the Security Regulation's text.
238   Council Security Regulations (2001), Appendix 2, at n.1.

one of its member States'.[239] Such information is defined as 'information which, if released, would be likely to threaten directly the internal stability of a member State, cause exceptionally grave damage to international relations, lead to widespread loss of life, cause equally grave damage to the operational effectiveness or security of member States or other contributors' forces, or cause severe long-term damage to the EU or Member States economy'. The other categories contain similar definitions on the same interests of the Union and its member States, with decreasing importance. The definition of the lowest category (Restreint), however, was completely redefined and broadened: compared with the 'Solana decision' in which information falling under this category was defined as information the disclosure of which would be 'inappropriate or immature',[240] the new definition was 'disadvantageous to the interests of"[241]. It includes, *inter alia*, all cases where disclosure could:

- cause substantial distress to individuals, ...
- cause financial loss or facilitate improper gain or advantage, ...
- prejudice the investigation or facilitate the commission of crime, ...
- disadvantage EU or Member States in commercial policy negotiations with others, ...
- impede the effective development or operation of EU policies [or]
- undermine the proper management of the EU and its operations.[242]

The scope of protection afforded by these Security Regulation is extremely broad in more than one respect. Firstly, it applies to areas reaching beyond ESDP, mostly JHA (even outside those JHA documents relating to 'non-military crisis management'[243]). Other Community policy areas such as commerce, competition, and the criminal jurisdictions of the very member States are also affected. This effect was intended, as was confirmed for example by the UK government.[244] A Cold-War-era element of 'breadth' may be discerned here. If member States consider there is a problem with over-classification, they can, acting through their representatives in the Security Committee, refer the matter to the SG as a matter of management.[245] This possibility, however, is only open to member States' executive branches, not national

---

239   *Ibid.*, Appendix 3, at p. 54; compare to the NATO Security Policy's equivalent at fn. 12.

240   Art. 2/1 (d), Decision of the Council SG, 27 July 2000.

241   http://www.statewatch.org/news/2001/oct/11Aepsecreg.htm (visited 28/08/2003).

242   Council Security Regulations (2001), Appendix 3, at p. 57.

243   See the 'Solana decision' above at p. 312; *Cf.* Statewatch, *European Parliament takes Council to court* (2001).

244   Supp. Explanatory Memorandum of 18 January 2001 by Keith Vaz MP, Minister for Europe, to the House of Commons, cited in: House of Commons Select Committee on European Scrutiny, Sixth Report, Security of Documents, http://www.parliament.the-stationery-office. co.uk/pa /cm200001/cmselect/cmeuleg/28-vi/2814.htm (visited 13/12/2003).

245   Council Security Regulations (2001), Part II, Sec. I, para. 1 (b) and paras.3–4; *Cf.* Letter from Keith Vaz MP, Minister for Europe, FCO, to Lord Brabazon of Tara, Chairman of

parliaments, other EU institutions, or the public in general. In practice, even though the EU uses the same formal classification markings as NATO, over-classification (in documents of comparable content) does not seem to occur as often as in the practice of the Alliance.

Secondly, the scope of the Council's new Security Regulations extends beyond the security of the EU and its member States: it also includes the security of other international organisations (notably the WEU and NATO) and the security of third countries (for example those offering troop contributions to peacekeeping operations of the Union). The inclusion of the latter category of countries was likely dictated by the practicable consideration that many of the potential third-country contributors to Union peacekeeping operations in 2001 would be Union member States from mid-2004. For that reason, their interests should already at that point enjoy roughly the same amount of protection as those of full member States. Provisions on transmitting classified information to third parties replicated *mutatis mutandis* the three-level system employed by the WEU.[246]

These sweeping changes in the Council's public-access rules did not go down well with the EP, national parliaments, civil society groups, and academics, and the criticism of these groups was duly not long in coming. A Swedish lawyer, concerned about his country's long tradition of open government, commented that, with this Council Decision, the Swedish Presidency had 'scored an own goal'.[247] Criticism by NGOs was levelled mainly at three points. First, with the widening of classification definitions, the 'contamination' effect (the introduction of standards of military secrecy into other policy areas) was seen to become even more severe than in the 'Solana decision'.[248] Secondly, many civil society groups had difficulties with the employment of terms such as 'subversive', which form common parlance in the military and intelligence fields, but are shunned in the broader spectrum of the EU's policies, some of which the Council also serves.[249] Thirdly (in close alignment with the argument made by the Netherlands in its Case against the Council regarding the 'Solana Decision'[250]), it was pointed out that

These Decisions by the Council *undermine the discussions on the new code of access* [the later REG 1049/2001]. The Council has used the 'space' left before a new code is

---

the House of Lords Select Ctte. on European Union, 30 April 2001, http://www.parliament.the-stationery-office.co.uk/pa/ld200102/ldselect/ldeucom/12/12107.htm (visited 13/12/2003).

246 *Ibid.*, Appendices 4–6; compare the WEU Security Policy (1996).

247 U. Öberg, *Slutreplik Från Stenbrottet – Svar på Olle Abrahamssons artikel 'Obefogad ängslan för den svenska offentlighetsprincipen'*, Europarättslig Tidskrift, No. 3 (2001), Årgång 4, p. 398.

248 Statewatch, *European Parliament takes Council to court* (2001).

249 The term 'subversive' appears four times in the Council's Security Regulations, in Part I (Basic Principles and Minimum Standards), para. 5 (a) (i) and para. 21; Sec. IV, para. 3 (c) and Sec. X, para. 3; *Cf.* Statewatch, *European Parliament takes Council to court* (2001).

250 See above at fn. 207.

adopted – whenever that will be – to protect the interests of governments and NATO over the citizens' right to know.[251]

The EP took the Council to court again. Its arguments and pleas were much along the lines of its first case against the Council regarding the 'Solana decision' of the year before:[252] breach of essential procedural requirements, namely lack of consultation of the Parliament as a result of the wrong legal base. The Council, treating the Security Regulations as a mere internal operation, had based the Decision on Art. 207 TEC and Art. 24 of its Rules of Procedure, ignoring their wider import, which would have necessitated a proper legislative procedure under Art. 308 TEC (which includes the initiative of the Commission and, importantly, consultation of the EP). Once more, the EP argued, the Council had ignored its duty of sincere cooperation under Art. 10 TEC and the principle of interinstitutional balance. The EP lent legal weight to NGOs' warnings of an 'undermining' of the coming public-access Regulation by the 'Lindh decision', citing Art. 255 TEC to the effect that the Council, respecting the hierarchical order of secondary legislation provided in Art. 255 paras. 2 and 3, would have been obliged to wait for that Regulation to be issued before adopting its Security Regulations in the present form.[253] The case was withdrawn from the register of the Court on 11 December 2002.

In the British Parliament, the House of Lords' Select Committee on European Union – already before enactment of the Decision – took issue with the wide discretion left to the Council under the new definition regarding the scope of documents to be withheld.[254] There were hardly safeguards against over-classification or against 'abuse or misuse of power' and 'the public interest and legitimate interests of third parties' were not seen as sufficiently protected. The Committee also questioned the Decision's provisions on 'routine destruction' of documents,[255] as well as the Decision's relationship with Art. 255 TEC. The comments made by the British government in response to these Parliamentary queries produce valuable insights into the influence which considerations of conforming with NATO standards played in the drafting and adoption process of the 'Lindh decision'. Concerning the issue of 'contamination' through over-classification and 'collective classification' provided in the text, the UK Minister for Europe replied that this was 'entirely within accordance with established practice in the United Kingdom *and elsewhere*'.[256] One

---

251   T. Bunyan, cited in: Statewatch Press Release of 20 March 2001, http://www.fitug. de/debate /0103/msg00308.html (visited 30/08/2003).

252   See above at fn. 212.

253   Case C-260/01, OJ C 245/13 of 1/9/2001, Parliament v. Council, *Cf.* Öberg, fn. 247, p. 399.

254   Letter from Lord Tordoff to Keith Vaz MP, 21 February 2001, House of Lords Select Committee on European Union, First Report, Part 24., http://www.parliament.the-stationery-office.co.uk/pa/ld200102/ldselect/ldeucom/12/12103.htm (visited 30/08/2003).

255   See Council Security Regulations (2001), Part II, Sec. VII, paras.31–34.

256   Letter from Keith Vaz MP to Lord Tordoff, 6 March 2001, House of Lords Select Committee on European Union, First Report, Part 24., http://www.parliament.the-stationery-office.co.uk/pa /ld200102/ldselect/ldeucom/12/12104.htm (visited 13/12/2003) [emphasis added]

may see, in the use of the term 'established practice', an example of the general prohibition for NATO governments to cite the document C-M(55)15(Final) directly in communication with the public (which, for this purpose, seems to include even Parliament), making it necessary for those governments to deliberately cloud the obligation in different terms, for example by referring to political usage or common practice.[257] The Committee apparently bought the Minister's argument.[258] Concerning the manner of adoption, it has already been pointed out above that the 'Lindh decision' was adopted as an 'A' point, that is, without a vote. On 16 March 2001, the Minister wrote a second letter in reply to the Committee, concerning the imminent adoption, stating

> ... the Presidency have given us notice that they do not intend to wait any longer before putting the proposals to the ministers at the General Affairs Council on 19 March. We support the substance of the new regulations ... If we were to insist that a vote be taken, and then vote against it, *it would send a false signal about our commitment to security to others outside the EU (NATO, the United States*, and other third countries), on whose cooperation we will rely for ESDP to work. ... the United Kingdom will [therefore] lift its outstanding reserve ...[259]

At a time when the permanent SIA agreement between the EU and NATO was in the negotiating stages, clearly neither the Council nor one of the member States (and certainly not the UK) wanted to create the impression with NATO that introduction of the latter's security rules would in any way run up against problems of constitutional nature within the EU, which would in the medium term have compromised the conclusion and implementation of any such future EU–NATO SI agreement.

Regulation (EC) No. 1049/2001 on public access to documents of 30 May 2001

The Regulation (EC) No. 1049/2001 of the European Parliament and of the Council regarding public access to European Parliament, Council and Commission documents of 30 May 2001[260] has been widely commented and analysed.[261] For the

---

257 See above p. 316.

258 It may be that the discretion given by the security regulations to the originator is 'in accordance with established practice in the United Kingdom and elsewhere' but ...' (Letter from Lord Tordoff to Keith Vaz MP, 22 March 2001, House of Lords Select Committee on European Union, First Report, Part 24., http://www.parliament.the-stationery-office.co.uk/pa/ld200102/ldselect /ldeucom/12/12106.htm (visited 30/08/2003)).

259 Letter from Keith Vaz MP to Lord Tordoff, 16 March 2001, House of Lords Select Committee on European Union, First Report, Part 24., http://www.parliament.the-stationery-office.co.uk/pa /ld200102/ldselect/ldeucom/12/12105.htm (visited 13/12/2003) [emphasis added].

260 OJ L 145/43 of 31/5/2001.

261 See e.g. S. Peers, *The New Regulation on Access to Documents: A Critical Analysis*, Queen's Papers on Europeanisation No. 6/2002, http://www.qub.ac.uk/ies/onlinepapers/poe6–

present discussion, however, only its defence-related parts are of interest, mainly Arts 4 (exceptions) and Art. 9 (treatment of sensitive documents).

The drafts of REG 1049/2001 dating before the 'Solana decision' of 2000 show a fairly liberal public-access regime, oriented after the historical purpose of Art. 255.[262] Those drafts contain no notion of 'sensitive documents' (a concept alien to the EU's founding treaties). Therefore exceptions to the general principle of transparency could only be made – for example in case of 'defence and international relations'[263] – judging each case on its own merits (not by means of blank categories). There was also no originator control, except for member States in the 'soft' form,[264] mandated as a matter of primary law.[265] This was later changed in the substantial redrafting as the Commission reacted to the 'Solana decision'.[266]

REG 1049/2001 starts out in its Preamble stating that 'in principle, all documents of the institutions should be accessible to the public'.[267] However, already in the same Preamble both the category of sensitive documents (Preambular para. 9) as well as the rules of procedure of the individual EU institutions (Preambular para. 17)[268] are exempted from this rule. Furthermore, Preambular para. 7 articulates a positive duty for each EU institution to 'respect its security rules', conferring *lex specialis* character to those security rules in relation to REG 1049/2001. This effect was, however, already intended by the drafts of REG 1049/2001 which date before the 'Solana decision', as elucidated from the Explanatory Memorandum accompanying the Regulations's draft of February 2000.[269]

Art. 4 establishes two groups of exceptions to the general rule of transparency. The first (para. 1) offers *absolute* protection, the second (para. 2) offers *relative* protection, that is, 'unless there is an overriding public interest in disclosure'.

02.pdf (visited 17/12/2003); M.E. de Leeuw, *The regulation on public access*, 28 ELR (2003); Y. Bock, *Ein Sieg für die Transparenz? Die neue Verordnung über den Zugang der Öffentlichkeit zu Dokumenten der EU*, 55 DÖV (2002) pp. 556–562; C. Heitsch, *Die Verordnung über den Zugang zu Dokumenten der Gemeinschaftsorgane im Lichte des Transparenzprinzips* (2003); B. Wegener, Commentary to Art. 255 TEC, in: C. Caliess / H.J. Blanke (eds), *Kommentar zu EU-Vertrag und EG-Vertrag* (2nd edn 2002), p. 2254.

262   *Cf.* the Commission's draft of February 2000.

263   *Ibid.*, Art. 4 (a).

264   See above p. 311.

265   See Amsterdam Treaty, Declaration No. 35.

266   *Cf.* Statement by the Commission to the 'Solana decision', see above at p. 314.

267   Preambular para. 11.

268   Preambular para. 17, mentioning the institutions' rules of procedure, does not establish derogatory power of the Regulation over those rules of procedure in case of conflict with the Regulation, but only states that they 'should ... if necessary, be modified or be repealed'. This leaves discretion to the respective institutions, e.g. the Council, whether or not such a conflict exists and whether any changes are necessary. M.E. de Leeuw, *The regulation on public access*, 28 ELR (2003), p. 339, finds this 'highly objectionable', particularly in the light of the lack of legal remedies against the institution's decisions on access to their documents.

269   See the Commission's draft of February 2000, p. 4.

Both 'defence and military matters' and 'international relations' are in the absolute protection class. The scope of the defence exception is narrower than in previous Council documents, as there is no mention of 'non-military crisis management'. Para. 4 establishes some form of originator control, should the Council be in doubt about the importance of the third-party information sought for release. Para. 6 manifests a restrictive interpretation of the 'collective classification' principle: 'if only parts of the requested document are covered by any of the exceptions, the remaining parts of the document shall be released'. The right to receive at least partial access to those parts of a document not requiring protection by classification is in accordance with the case law of the ECJ.[270] However, the greater part of sensitive EU defence documents belongs to the Council, and may thus be 'collectively classified' the Council's Security Regulations. The Council's Security Regulations are as *leges speciales*, themselves immune to the provisions of REG 1049/2001. Hence Art. 6 of REG 1049/2001, intended to ease access to EU documents, would seem to be of limited value in practice. The maximum time limit for exceptions is 30 years (exactly as in NATO[271]).

Art. 9 goes into the heart of the matter of exceptions[272] by defining 'sensitive documents' as classified documents of sensitivity down to the 'Confidentiel' marking, 'in accordance with the rules of the institution concerned'. This effectively imports the scope of definitions for these documents as contained in the Council's Security Rules into the exceptions of REG 1049/2001. Para. 3 establishes a hard form of originator control which extends not only to the release, but also, importantly, to the listing of any reference to the document (even the sole document number) in the holding institution's public register. Para. 4 establishes the rule – also contained in NATO's C-M(55)15(Final)[273] – that the institution refusing access to the document should phrase its refusal in language 'which does not harm the interests protected in Article 4'. In combination with the power to withhold some documents entirely from the register, this means that an institution is able (and indeed legally compelled) to deny existence of a document, even where a requesting party may already be aware of its existence. There is no separate 'conclusions-to-be-drawn'-type provision[274] in the entire Regulation, but this element is already incorporated by reference to the institutions' own classification definitions.

The general procedural rule in Art. 8 (3) that 'failure by the institution to reply ... shall ... entitle the applicant to institute court proceedings against the institution and/or make a complaint to the Ombudsman, under the relevant provisions of the EU Treaty'

---

270   Case C-353/99P, *Council* v. *Hautala*, [6 Dec. 2001], ECR I – not yet reported, para. 31; Case C-353/01P, *Council and Commission* v. *Mattila* [22 Jan. 2004], ECR I – not yet reported, paras. 18–24. The regulation even pre-empted the Court's final judgement, which confirmed the CFI's judgement of 19 July 1999.

271   See above at p. 311.

272   Although it is not titled as such, *Cf.* M.E. de Leeuw, *The regulation on public access*, 28 ELR (2003), p. 338.

273   See above Chapter 8 (The Berlin Plus Agreement).

274   *Cf.* the 'Solana decision', at p. 328.

is a last-ditch loophole in the generally prohibitive character of these public-access rules for defence documents. Should an institution therefore omit to issue a reply within 15 working days, the applicant may possibly achieve release of the document in court proceedings before the ECJ, even concerning matters of defence.

Lastly, while respecting that the EU's institutions will handle requests for release of their documents according to their own Security Rules, REG 1049/2001 foresees the elaboration of common access standards through an interinstitutional agreement.[275]

The EP and the Netherlands withdrew their cases against the 'Solana decision' before the ECJ after the issuing of REG 1049/2001.[276] The EP's case against the 'Lindh decision', however, remained pending for the time being.

Criticism was voiced from journalist groups at the time of adoption of REG 1049/2001, that the wider public, as its main addressee, was not in any way consulted in its final drafting (which occurred though a trialogue between the Council, the Commission and the EP over five months).[277] On the face of text of REG 1049/2001, one material conflict of provisions exists between Preambular paragraph 10 affirming Declaration No. 35 to the Amsterdam Treaty which establishes only a soft form of originator control,[278] and the substantive provision of Art. 9, para.3 which establishes hard and passive originator control. One scholar, commenting on the complete exclusion of some documents from the register, argues that the underlying presumption that just the document number of a sensitive document will somehow threaten public security 'cross[es] over the line separating sensible precaution from sheer paranoia'.[279] Furthermore, the blank exclusion of documents from public scrutiny (which is exactly the point of creating a category of 'sensitive documents') is seen as incompatible with the proportionality principle in EC law.[280] Another scholar, calling Art. 9 'an amended version of the "Solana decision"',[281] objects to the delegation of the exceptions' scope to the internal rules of the institutions which, she argues, should have been included in REG 1049/2001 itself.[282]

Latest developments in the EU

Council

In implementation of the 'Lindh decision', the Council on 8 October 2002 set internal security categories and established a procedure regarding the exchange of classified

---

275 Preambular paragraph 9, Art. 9/7, Art. 15/2; *Cf.* below at p. 328.

276 See above at fns 207 and 212.

277 *Protest against new code of access to EU documents*, EUObserver, 2 May 2002.

278 *Cf.* above at p. 308.

279 S. Peers, *The New Regulation: A Critical Analysis*, Queen's Papers on Europeanisation No. 6/2002, p. 24.

280 *Ibid.*, p. 26.

281 M.E. de Leeuw, *The regulation on public access*, 28 ELR (2003), p. 340.

282 *Ibid.*, p. 339.

documents with third parties, using a three-level system.[283] The relevant note by the GSC stresses the ultimate authority of the Council over its own documents.[284] NATO and PfP members are accorded level 1 status, for the reason that they are subject to regular inspections from the NATO Office of Security under NATO document C-M(2000)49.[285] This high level of trust in NATO is arguably not only due to the Council's limited means (which would make it a quixotic task to build an own inspection system) but also an expression of the Council's regarding its interests as being perfectly identical to NATO's on SI. Responsibility for granting release within the Council falls to the PSC (in case of a matter under the CFSP) or to COREPER (in all other cases).[286]

Commission

On 29 November 2001, the Commission adopted its own Rules on Security. They are a verbatim copy of the Rules adopted by the Council in the 'Lindh decision' of 19 March 2001, after formal changes.[287]

European Parliament

One day before, on 28 November 2001, the EP issued a Bureau Decision on public access to its documents, in implementation of REG 1049/2001,[288] which regulates registration and release of documents. The Decision provides that any document received in the Parliament's public register will be entered there, subject to the limitations of Art. 9 of REG 1049/2001.[289] Hard originator control and the conclusions-to-be-drawn element, as provided in REG 1049/2001, are fully implemented.[290] Requests for release are subject to the limitations of both Art. 4 and Art. 9 of REG 1049/2001.[291] Interestingly however, with regard even to classified documents, the originator control is softened somewhat: third-party documents raising doubt as to their quality are released if the originating institution has failed to reply to a request by the Parliament to make its position known.[292]

---

283 Note from the General Secretariat of the Council to the Security Committee, *Release of EU classified information to third parties and international organisations*, 8 October 2002, Council Doc. 12869/02.

284 *Ibid.*, para. 9.

285 C-M(2000)49 is the successor to NATO C-M(55)15(Final). The note is one of the rare occurrences in which it is expressly named.

286 Council Doc. 12869/02, *Release of EU classified information to third parties* Annex II.

287 Commission Decision of 29 November 2001 amending its internal Rules of Procedure, 2001/844/EC, ECSC, Euratom, OJ L 317/1 of 3/12/2001.

288 OJ C 274/1 of 29/12/2001.

289 *Ibid.*, Art. 4/5.

290 *Ibid.*, Art. 17.

291 *Ibid.*, Art. 5/1.

292 *Ibid.*, Art. 9.

Interinstitutional Agreement (European Parliament/Council) of 20 November 2002

Also in implementation of the mandate of REG 1049/2001, the EP and the Council concluded an 'Interinstitutional Agreement concerning access by the European Parliament to sensitive information of the Council in the field of security and defence policy' on 20 November 2002.[293] The contents had been negotiated for almost two years, going back to a draft by the French Presidency in October 2000.[294] After its conclusion, the EP withdrew its last case outstanding against the Council before the ECJ.[295]

The scope of the Interinstitutional Agreement extends to classified information, 'whatever its origin ... or state of completion, held by the Council'.[296] This shows the will of the EP to obtain information on the Council's decision-making process regarding measures in ESDP at the earliest possible point in time, exercising its general function of democratic control. The Agreement cites principles such as sincere cooperation and mutual trust between the institutions. This is probably a result of the EP's past pains over the 'Solana' and 'Lindh' decisions, as also expressed in its past legal suits against the Council.[297] According to the Agreement, either the Parliament's President or the Chairman of the Committee on Foreign Affairs, Human Rights, Common Security and Defence Policy, may request information concerning ESDP, including 'sensitive' information, from the Council.[298] In case of sensitive information, a committee of four EP members 'shall be *informed* by the [Council] of the content ... *where it is required* for the exercise of the powers'[299] which the EP enjoys in the second pillar as a matter of primary law (Art. 3.3).

These powers refer to the EP's right of consultation, questioning and recommendation on the main aspects and the basic choices of the CFSP (Art. 21 TEU) and to its right of information in cases of enhanced cooperation (Arts 27c, 27d and 44a TEU). For example, in order to consider the possibility of the EU engaging in a peacekeeping operation, the EP would need to evaluate the record of the Union's peacekeeping experience from other such operations lying in the past. This would seem to be impossible without also having recourse to, inter alia, past intelligence reports containing military data. Art. 3.3. suffers from imprecision, and this could be deliberate. Firstly, there is no provision on who will judge, in case of conflict, whether it is necessary or not for the Parliament to see a certain document in order to properly fulfil its functions as provided. Even though, in case of doubt,

---

293   OJ C 298/1 of 30/11/2002 [hereinafter: Interinstitutional Agreement (2002)].

294   The French draft is reprinted in: Statewatch News online, *Council to offer deal to head off court action*, 19 October 2000, http://www.statewatch.org/news/oct00/10coun-ep. htm (visited 30/08/2003); *Cf. Nato secrecy spooks EU suits: The push for open government has come up against closed doors*, Financial Times, 18 Nov. 2000, p. 11.

295   *Cf.* above at fn. 253.

296   Interinstitutional Agreement (2002), Art. 1.1.

297   See the pleas of the EP before the ECJ above at p. 332 and p. 338.

298   Interinstitutional Agreement (2002), Art. 3.1.

299   Emphases added.

the Parliament could probably argue with the principle of implied powers, the fact of actual possession of the documents by the Council gives the latter much factual leverage in the matter. Secondly, it is very possible for the Council to 'inform' the Parliament's selected committee of the content of the information sought by the latter, without ever showing a single copy of a classified document, let alone an original. The Council could do this by 'information factsheets' or even orally, which would still respect the wording of this obligation. Documents of the highest classification (Très secret/Top Secret) are exempted from the scope of the Agreement.[300]

The EP implemented measures providing for a safe handling of classified information within its premises in a Decision of 23 October 2002.[301] These measures include personnel vetting in accordance with the need-to-know principle,[302] especially designed secure rooms (physical security),[303] and provisions on criminal prosecution of leaking by Parliament personnel[304]. The Decision was taken even before conclusion of the Interinstitutional Agreement, which attests generally to the Council's great caution in sharing its sensitive information, even with a sister institution of the EU. According to recent working experiences by MEPs, the Decision seems to have made the Parliament effectively watertight against information leakage (in contrast for example to the Commission), which has gained the Parliament more and more confidence from the Council in the process.[305]

'INTERIM SECURITY ARRANGEMENTS' BETWEEN THE GSC AND NATO OF 26 JULY 2000

On 26 July 2000 (and perhaps also on the next day 27 July[306]) the GSC and NATO concluded 'Interim Security Arrangements' concerning the exchange of classified information between them, by an exchange of letters,[307] signed by NATO-SG George Robertson and the CFSP-HR Javier Solana. This had been made possible by the previous introduction of more stringent security rules for the Council as a result of

---

300   *Ibid.*

301   OJ 298/4 of 30/11/2002.

302   *Ibid.*, Art. 8

303   *Ibid.*, Art. 4

304   Arts 10 and 11.

305   Oral comment by M. Ferber MEP, at a panel discussion of the Europa-Forum of the Hanns-Seidel-Stiftung, *Zustand und Zukunft der Europäischen Sicherheits- und Verteidigungsunion*, Munich, 1 December 2003.

306   The question is unclear from the records, see Statewatch News online, *26 July 2000 – the day of the infamous 'Solana decision' – how did Mr Solana reply to a letter he had not received?*, 29 June 2002, http://www.statewatch.org/news/2002/mar/16solana.htm (visited 23/08/2003).

307   See the EU–NATO interim SIA (2000) above.

the 'Solana decision'.[308] By November 2000, the Arrangements were described as 'fully operational' by the General Secretariat[309].

The 'Preamble' of these exchanges of letters mentioned the need for the EU and NATO to consult on military issues and to coordinate their military responses to crises; further, that this consultation, in order to be effective, required the exchange of classified information. Each party pledged to duly protect information of the other party, and to maintain its established security classification in accordance with the security rules of the originating party.[310] For NATO documents, those rules were document C-M(55)15(Final);[311] for the EU they were at the time still Decision 24/95[312]. Classified information was not to be used beyond the immediate purpose of its transfer, with strict originator control regarding release to third parties. There was a general obligation to have 'appropriately security cleared' all personnel which deal with classified information. The NATO Office of Security (NOS) was responsible for 'security interim measures' in implementation of the arrangements, but it was not clear what these measures would consist of. In its last sentence, the exchange of letters foresaw the eventual conclusion of a 'Security Agreement' between the parties in the future.

The 'arrangements' as they stood raise several questions also having a bearing on their legal nature.

Firstly, the terms 'EU' and 'Council' are used interchangeably, so it is not clear in precise terms which of the two will actually be bound.[313] However, since the Council does not have the international capacity to conclude an agreement with a third party in its own name,[314] the answer must needs be that it is the Union itself which is the party, with the Council only acting as its dependent organ. This conclusion serves to reconcile the confusion in the abovementioned use of terms.

Secondly, due to the illogical discrepancy between the Council's receipt date stamp on Robertson's letter of 26 July, and the date of Solana's letter in reply (also 26 July), the exact date of conclusion is in doubt: the date stamp says that the letter was received by the Council only on 27 July (!). In his letter of 26 July, Solana even twice expressly acknowledges having received Robertson's letter of 26 July, which, from the records, he could not have done until one day later. NGOs commenting on this circumstance called it 'quite intriguing'.[315] Presuming correctness of the records, the

---

308   See above at p. 328.

309   Council Doc. 13708/00, ESDP: Organisational and implementing measures in the General Secretariat of the Council, 22 Nov. 2000, p. 1

310 Notice the similarity of these obligations to the 1997 NATO Security of Information Agreement.

311   See above NATO C-M(55)15(Final).

312   See above at fn. 130.

313   This mix of the two terms stems already from NATO's mandate to negotiate the 'arrangements' which it received on the Ministerial Meeting of the NAC in Florence on 24 May 2000 (Final Communiqué, NATO Press Release, M-NAC-1(2000)52, para. 29).

314   See above at p. 323.

315   Statewatch, fn. 306.

only logical explanation seems to be that Solana in fact did not wait until receiving Robertson's letter, but that he replied before, knowing already what its exact content would be. This formal error gives proof of the high degree of trust which prevailed already in mid-2000 between the Council and NATO, a development in which the person of Solana as former NATO-SG certainly was the most important factor.[316] Officially, the two parties subsequently always referred to the Arrangements as having been concluded on 26 July 2000.[317]

Thirdly, there is the fact that reference is made to the Council's Decision 24/95. But that decision had provided a less stringent régime for EU classified documents than did the new successor regime.[318] It was repealed – through the 'Solana decision' – on the next day after the 'arrangements' were concluded. In other words, one day after conclusion of the GSC-NATO arrangements of 26 July 2000, Decision 24/95 was already a dead letter. If this was an omission on the part of the Council's legal service, it would be, from a formal-legal standpoint, a serious one. The fact that it was allowed to happen, however, is indicative of the underlying interests and real intentions. The reference to Decision 24/95 concerned protection of EU-classified information by NATO. Such documents would in any case benefit from the security rules prevailing inside NATO, stricter than those in Decision 24/95. What elucidates is that the majority of documents expected to be exchanged under the 'arrangements' would involve a one-way transfer from NATO to the Council, with hardly any documents going the other way. It seems a reasonable guess that, considering the tight time-frame in which the 'arrangements' were concluded simultaneously with the 'Solana decision' by the Council, this formal-legalistic error, which could do no real harm, was simply neglected.

Fourthly, in order to establish legally binding force for a document in question, recourse is often had, inter alia, to its language.[319] For its interpretation, subsequent practice of the parties in its implementation is important.[320] In this regard we find some factors hinting at legally binding force of the 'arrangements', and some militating against it. Some formulations used such as 'shall' before most obligations, provisions on 'I have the honour to propose the following', 'taking effect' and 'entry into force' in relevant part, are akin to those commonly employed in legally binding exchanges of letters between subjects of international law. On the other hand, the letter contains only 'Arrangements', which stands in contrast to an eventual future permanent 'Agreement', also mentioned. This contrast in terminology surely

---

316 For the importance of the 'Solana-Robertson connection' at the beginning of the EU–NATO relationship, *cf.* above Chapter 3 (NATO Today).

317 E.g. Council Decision 2003/211/CFSP of 24 February 2003 concerning the conclusion of the Agreement between the European Union and the North Atlantic Treaty Organisation on the Security of Information, OJ L 80/35 of 27/3/2003.

318 The 'Solana decision', see above.

319 *Cf.* above Chapter 4 (Institutional Framework).

320 Art. 31/3/b VCLT.

cannot be accidental.[321] In addition, an internal Council note of 22 November 2000 called the 'arrangements' 'fully operational',[322] language which, though indicating successful implementation, is hardly used for a legally binding text. Moreover, the exchange of letters lacks a denunciation clause, which is also a typical feature of binding exchanges of letters.[323]

Fifthly, and this ultimately decides the question, the 'arrangements' were concluded for the EU by the SG of the Council/CFSP-HR. This is in clear and manifest contradiction to the EU's internal provisions concerning the capacity to conclude treaties with third parties (Art. 24 TEU).[324] It thus constitutes an absolute barrier for legally binding force for the 'arrangements'. The 'Interim Security Arrangements' were hence a non-binding agreement.

AGREEMENT ON THE SECURITY OF INFORMATION BETWEEN THE EU AND NATO OF 14 MARCH 2003

> Arrangements for handling classified information must be robust enough, and satisfy the rightly demanding standards set by the EU and NATO Security Authorities and by allied governments.[325]

The above statement was made by the British Minister for Europe in a correspondence with the House of Lords in February 2003. It shows that, as was also stated in the Interim GSC-NATO Security Arrangement of 26 July 2000, nothing short of a permanent and fully comprehensive international agreement on exchange of classified information between the EU and NATO would be required in order for the machinery of their growing cooperation to become operable. On 14 March 2003, the EU and NATO finally concluded this Agreement.[326] It was signed in Athens by NATO-SG George Robertson for NATO and by the President of the Council Georgios Papandreou for the EU and took effect immediately,[327] replacing the 'Interim Security

---

321   The fact that US Secretary of Defense William Cohen, among other government representatives, later referred to the 'arrangements' as an 'interim security *agreement*' [emphasis added] would not seem to have any legal significance in this regard (see: Remarks at the Informal NATO Defense Ministerial Meeting, 10 October 2000, Birmingham, http://www.defenselink.mil/speeches /2000/s20001010-secdef.html (visited 29/08/2003)).

322   Council Doc. 13708/00.

323   *Cf.* above Chapter 4 (Institutional Framework).

324   *Cf.* above Chapter 4 (Institutional Framework).

325   Letter to The Lord Grenfell, Chairman, Select Committee on the European Union, House of Lords from Dr Denis MacShane MP, Minister for Europe, Foreign and Commonwealth Office, dated 5 February 2003 – Scrutiny of ESDP, http://www.parliament.uk/parliamentary_committees /lords_s_comm_c/cwm_c.cfm (visited 18/12/2003).

326   Agreement between the European Union and the North Atlantic Treaty Organisation on the Security of Information, 14 March 2003, OJ L 80/36 of 27.3.2003. The Agreement had not been registered with the United Nations Treaty Series at the time of writing.

327   *Ibid.*, Art. 16.

Arrangements' of 26 July 2000[328]. The EU Presidency had been expressly authorised by the Council to conclude it, in a Decision of 14 February 2003.[329] The conclusion was generally seen as an expression of the unprecedented degree of trust prevailing between the two organisations, in particular after the conclusion of the Berlin Plus agreement at the Copenhagen European Council the previous December.[330]

In substance, the Agreement clearly builds upon the text of the Interim Security Arrangements of 26 July 2000 (including its purpose described in the Preamble), but it is more detailed and features some additions. Most importantly, its overall structure and material content leaves no doubt as to the quality of the Agreement as a binding international treaty. The parties are now clearly named as NATO and the EU. Both signatories have been 'respectively duly authorised' by their principals. In case of the EU, the authorising Council Decision makes express reference to Art. 24 TEU. The material obligations to protect and safeguard classified information of the other party, and concerning security of personnel are the same as in the Interim Arrangements. There is again a duty of the receiving party to maintain the same classification marking given to a document by the providing party (Art. 4 (b)). As the EU is generally not as prone to over-classification of documents as NATO,[331] this duty could over time affect overall coherence in the EU's classification practice. The 'principle of originator control' and the 'need-to-know principle' are expressly spelt out.[332] For the principle of originator control, this is a debut. Correspondence of classified documents is centralised with a single organ on either side, the Council's Registry Office and the NATO-SG. The Agreement has 'framework' character, as it leaves detailed aspects to be elaborated subsequently by the parties: 'security arrangements', to be implemented by the respective Security Offices of the Council, the Commission and NATO (Art. 11)[333] and 'standards of reciprocal security protection' (Art. 12). The express naming of the Commission and the Council as separate institutions responsible for implementation in an international agreement to which, legally, only the EU as a whole is a party, should not lead to the wrong conclusion that the international legal personality of the Union was somehow split in two in this case.[334] The earlier Interim Agreement of 26 July 2000 did not know such a distinction, as it was only concluded by the GSC of the EU. One reason could

---

328   *Ibid.*, Art. 18.

329   See above Council Decision 2003/211/CFSP of 24 February 2003.

330   George Robertson, cited by Agence France Presse, *EU and NATO sign security agreement in Athens*, 14 March 2003.

331   See above p. 321.

332   Arts. 5, para. 1 and 9 (b), respectively.

333   Those three institutions are listed in paragraphs (a), (b) and (c), in that order. It is interesting to note that until the draft of 17 February 2003 (Council Doc. 5652/03), NATO was listed first. In the final version, it is listed last. This may have to do with the fact that the Agreement was published in the European Union's Official Journal (pursuant to Art. 13 (f) of REG 1049/2001). The drafters might have wanted to avoid the impression among the OJ's readers (mostly the EU constituency) that NATO was in any way the pre-eminent party.

334   *Cf.* above at fn. 117.

be seen in a political victory of the Commission, asserting some influence also in the second pillar. It will be remembered that both the Council and the Commission also concluded separate security agreements with the WEU in 1999.[335] It is submitted that the separation was also necessary because of the stronger binding force of the Agreement (in contrast to its 2000 predecessor), which binds the Union as a whole, making it wise to address both EU institutions directly under the Agreement.

Prior to the actual exchange of classified information, each Party must have ensured itself of the capacity of the other to protect its information (Art. 14), a provision which was partly carried over from the Interim Agreement, but added to by the condition of fulfilling the implementation conditions of Arts 11 and 12. Art. 15 contains a conflict clause in favour of the Agreement against all other similar agreements the parties may enter into with other third parties.

As a first act of implementation of this Agreement by the EU, level 1 cooperation status regarding classified information was accorded to NATO,[336] filling the gap in the Annex of its various Security Regulations which the 'Lindh decision' had left[337]. Permission for the CFSP-HR to release EU classified information to NATO was given by the Council on 24 March 2003.[338]

On 3 June 2003, the Council, the Commission and NATO attuned their reciprocal security standards to one another in detail, pursuant to Art. 12.[339] The format of conclusion seems to have been a classified exchange of letters.

There is no evidence from the public register of the Council at the time of writing whether the particular 'Security Arrangements' mentioned in Art. 11 have yet been implemented by the Council, the Commission or NATO. It is likely, though, that classified information has already been exchanged between the EU and NATO under this Agreement, from the simple fact that the EU has taken over already two of NATO's peacekeeping missions in the Balkans.

CONCLUSIONS

In its initial stages, the ESDP was – and still is – dependent on external help from NATO. For this reason, the EU had to import NATO's rules on security of information (dating largely from the Cold War) before cooperation with NATO could start. The EU's strict standards on the handling of classified information, however, were not solely established for the purpose of meeting NATO's demands in this regard, but

---

335　See above at p. 355.

336　Council Security Committee, Release of EU Classified Information to third States and International Organisations – Authority Release EUCI to NATO, 18 March 2003, Council Doc. 7558/03.

337　See above at p. 336.

338　Council Decision on the release of information under the EU–NATO Security Agreement, 24 March 2003, Council Doc. 7588/03.

339　*Cf.* Security Standards for the Protection of Classified Information exchanged between NATO and the EU, 3 June 2003, Council Doc. 10006/03.

also for intrinsic reasons: from a practical point of view, any kind of defence policy (whether dependent on NATO or not) would have made necessary comparable rules on the security of information.

Efforts to establish a new EU security of information regime, however, soon began to run up against fundamental constitutional principles of the Union, such as transparency and proportionality. For years, an inter-institutional battle was waged to work out the exact balance between those principles and the legislative requirements for a workable security and defence policy for the Union. As a result, the present state of EU law on security of information closely follows NATO's rules, enshrined in the NATO Security Policy. However, the EU regime does allow for some public scrutiny through the European Parliament, and also for some employee rights. In addition, the simple fact that the vast majority of EU legislation on the subject is published presents a fundamental difference to NATO's security rules. Current security of information law for the EU would therefore seem to strike the right balance for a post-Cold War security and defence policy intended primarily for peacekeeping activities in the near abroad.

Chapter 10

Conclusion: A Shifting Balance

This book started with a broad overview of transatlantic relations starting from the Cold War area. The political predominance of the United States in Western Europe which characterised the Cold War initially seemed little altered by the process of European integration, begun in earnest with the Maastricht Treaty of 1992. The consolidation of a new European whole was a piecemeal process, unnoticed and moreover humbled by the absence of European capacity to act during the wars in the former Yugoslavia. The Iraq war in spring 2003, however, showed that European political unity versus United States interests was, if far yet from reality, an idea which attracted significant attention throughout the continent. At the same time, a look back at the Iraq crisis reveals that European disunity was strongest whenever Europeans wanted to act in direct opposition to the United States' interests. As a result, the idea of an equal partnership between the two, recognising common interests and values, perhaps even on a formalised basis, has gained much ground. It is against this background that the EU–NATO relationship has been approached.

One of the processes through which the growing of a European whole seems most visible is the creation of the European Security and Defence Policy. Initially a direct response to European foreign policy failures during the Balkan wars, ESDP has today proved a flexible peacekeeping tool also in a world threatened by international terrorism. ESDP is also able to accommodate the very different security outlooks of the Union's 25 member States – those who do not want to take part altogether, those who require constant internal checks for 'neutrality compatibility' before taking every new step, and finally those member States capable of manning an entire 'EU' peacekeeping operation out of their own resources. The European Convention has moved the attention of European policy-makers to the 'high end' of the Petersberg tasks, a process duly reflected in the creation of 'battle groups' at the end of 2004. In mid-2003, around the time of the finalisation of the European Constitution by the Convention, the first, somewhat unexpected, independent EU peacekeeping operation took place in the DRC. The issue of such EU security structures entirely independent of NATO caused some ruffles within both the EU and NATO in 2003, particularly the question of independent EU headquarters. The resolution of this issue in December 2003 marked a new step of maturity in EU–NATO relations, relations which also became more formalised in the 'NATO/EU Consultation, Planning and Operations' document. This document can be read, like a cascading decision tree, as a menu for choice on European crisis management, ranging from entirely NATO to entirely EU, with various levels of cooperation in between. Clear preference falls to operations dominated or at least supported by NATO. Nevertheless, if past political developments are any guide, the future points in the opposite direction, and EU-autonomous operations are becoming more and more likely. This prediction is mirrored in the shifting balance in European security from NATO to the EU.

NATO has seen two great transformations since the end of the Cold War. The first came as a result of the changed European security environment after the collapse of the Cold War. The second was as a response to September 11. Today, even though the Alliance's legal parameters have changed little since 1949, politically it bears a radically different face. Preoccupation with collective defence has in practice today moved to the sidelines of NATO's daily activity. Many of the issues being dealt with at NATO headquarters today, such as small arms and light weapons (SALW) and post-conflict antipersonnel mines disposal, are far removed from collective defence. Moreover, on the military side, NATO today seeks to streamline itself into a pool of flexible specialist forces for combating international terrorism and other asymmetric threats around the world. At the same time, the Alliance continues to manage two major peacekeeping operations involving a significant amount of regular forces of its members, in Kosovo and in Afghanistan. All of the Alliance's panoply of functions still benefit from the existence of a well-oiled integrated military organisation. Those structures were originally designed to counter an external attack in Europe, but have many other uses.

The EU and NATO both adapted to new security challenges over the years. From the 1990s onwards, their functions thus started to converge from two different sides. Institutional contacts, however, were nil until the end of 1999. Today, EU–NATO meetings across different fields of cooperation have become quite regular. The institutional framework for this cooperation is only partly accessible to the public. One interesting example is the exchange of letters of 24 January 2001 which was only recently released to the public. A legal analysis of this document has revealed that it is not binding under international law. In EU–NATO cooperation, informally evolving practice rather seems to be the norm. It is hard to say where this aversion to enter into legal obligations stems from (to date, only one binding EU–NATO agreement has been concluded in the technical area of security of information), but it is a distinctive characteristic of the EU–NATO relationship.

The question of NATO primacy fully entered the academic debate with Madeleine Albright's famous 'Three 3Ds', which in 1998 summed up the United States' conditions for the possibility of the EU building its own security functions: no duplication of existing NATO structure, no discrimination against non-EU NATO members, and no decoupling from Alliance structures. A fourth condition was added by the US Congress: that NATO should have a 'right of first refusal' versus the EU on any peacekeeping activity. These four conditions duly reflected US interests in Europe in 1998. Opinions on these conditions in Europe diverged for a long time. Today, contrasting the political and legal essence of these claims against past practice of both the EU and NATO, it is possible to say that none of them has been systematically upheld. Neither NATO as such, nor the United States, has pressed them recently. The resolution of the contentious issue of EU military headquarters at the end of 2003 seems to have indirectly contributed to the quietening down of the 'NATO primacy' question too.

NATO used to be Europe's only working collective defence institution after the end of the Cold War. Since the introduction of a collective defence clause in the European Constitution (not yet in force) this monopoly is gone. The new EU mutual defence clause raises many questions. It is clear that it does not encompass the neutral and non-aligned EU member States, that is, Austria, Finland, Ireland and Sweden, if they so decide. Malta could also be covered by this exception. The above countries are not bound by a collective defence in legal terms. However, the high degree of political solidarity existing today between all EU member States increasingly blurs the practical line between them and the rest of the EU member States in this regard. After close examination, it has become clear that the EU mutual defence clause is stronger in content than NATO's Art. 5, even though its language seems to cloud this fact. As a consequence the EU mutual defence clause may well legally eclipse Art. V of the WEU's Modified Brussels Treaty if the European Constitution enters into force.

Further, collective defence may cause problems between the EU and NATO regarding so-called 'security guarantees through the back door': any NATO ally could, without having granted an express guarantee to a given non-Alliance member, be unwittingly dragged into a conflict in the case where the EU mutual defence clause becomes operative in favour of a non-NATO country. The caveat for neutral and non-aligned EU member States in the EU's mutual defence clause seems to alleviate this problem, save for Cyprus, which is not a NATO member, but is still covered by the EU mutual defence clause.

The European Rapid Reaction Force and the NATO Response Force are well-treated subjects in scholarship today. What is less clear is their political and legal relationship. A possible answer could lie in a division of labour between the two, but the crux lies in drawing a clear line dividing the tasks between those two forces which, being military resource pools, draw on the same troops. A division of labour along high-end/low-end lines would not spell well for the EU's long-term ambitions as a global security actor. At the same time, the Union's real military capability shortfalls place natural limits on just such ambitions.

The question of the relationship between the European Rapid Reaction Force and the NATO Response Force is another aspect of the theoretical question of NATO primacy. This question, which remains at best unclear from EU and NATO statements over time, cannot be decided in the affirmative from the EU and NATO peacekeeping practice either. Aside from theoretical discussions about EU peacekeeping involvement in Kosovo or Moldova, this practice consists of three real cases of peacekeeping operations where a NATO primacy could have been played out. Two of these cases, Operation *Concordia* (Macedonia) and Operation *Althea* (Bosnia) were too untypical to render good answers to the question and one, Operation *Artemis* (DRC) seems to answer it in the negative.

Currently, the EU is able to draw on some of NATO's planning facilities and other military assets under the Berlin Plus agreement. Careful legal analysis reveals that

Berlin Plus is a non-binding agreement. Yet, it may give rise to legal consequences for its parties, through estoppel. This would apply to all of the EU's peacekeeping operations which utilise NATO planning capabilities or military assets under the Berlin Plus format, that is, Operation *Concordia* in Macedonia (already concluded) and Operation *Althea* in Bosnia (started on 2 December 2004). The position of the Berlin Plus agreement under European law is still unclear. The further evolution of its legal import will largely depend on how it is implemented by the parties. In this sense, future political arguments traded over the issue of European defence – both within the EU and across the Atlantic – are likely to contain legal aspects, even if the parties will not go to court over them. This may cause all the actors involved, that is, NATO, the EU and their member States, to perceive their freedom of action as being subjected to the legal obligations they have incurred, and adjust their strategies accordingly. Berlin Plus is another significant example testifying to the emerging new balance in European security between NATO and the EU.

Lastly, EU–NATO cooperation in security of information, which has seen very little scholarly attention so far, highlights the importance of values in the EU–NATO relationship. NATO's internal security-of-information policy and accompanying culture dated from the Cold War. However, in contrast to practically every other part of the Alliance, this policy proved resilient against change in the 1990s. It even prevailed over the EU's policy of openness of public information, as soon as the two regimes began to interact from 2000 onwards. Today, the theoretical level of security for classified documents prevailing in the EU is essentially comparable to NATO, if one leaves aside some limited oversight rights of the European Parliament, and the role of the European Court of Justice which has also in the past been seized with cases concerning public access to classified documents.

Looking at the European security landscape in the mid-1990s, NATO was the pre-eminent, in many field the only, actor on the scene. Ten years later, the Alliance has shifted its attention more and more away from Europe, while the EU is moving centre stage. The resulting shift in political balance is a step-by-step, ongoing process between the two organisations and their member States, reflecting real political priorities and changing institutional roles. On some of those steps at least, this book hopes to have shed some light.

Selected Bibliography[1]

BOOKS AND TREATISES

Alexandrov, S.A. *Self-Defence Against the Use of Force in International Law* (1996)

Algieri, F./Bauer, T. *Europa – die gespaltene Macht. Die Konventsvorschläge zur Sicherheits- und Verteidigungspolitik*, in: C. Giering (ed.), *Der EU-Reformkonvent – Analyse und Dokumentation*, CD-ROM (2003)

Aust, A. *Modern Treaty Law and Practice* (2000)

Ball, M. *NATO and the European Union Movement* (1957)

Band, D.L. *The Military Committee of the North Atlantic Alliance* (1991)

Bartelt, S. *Der rechtliche Rahmen für die neue operative Kapazität der Europäischen Union* (2003)

Bilder, R.B. *Managing the Risks of International Agreement* (1981)

Black, H.C./Nolan, J.R. *Black's Law Dictionary* (6th edn, 1990)

Blanck, K. *Die europäische Sicherheits- und Verteidigungspolitik im Rahmen der europäischen Sicherheitsarchitektur* (2005)

Bonvicini, G. et al. (eds) *A new Partnership for Europe* (1996)

Bowett, D. *Self-Defence in International Law* (1958)

Bowett, D.W. *United Nations Forces: A Legal Study of United Nations Practice* (1964)

Brenner, M. (ed.), *NATO and Collective Security* (1998)

Brownlie, I. *Principles of Public International Law* (5th edn, 1998)

Brownlie, I. *International Law and the Use of Force by States* (1963)

Cassese, A. *International Law* (2001)

Council on Foreign Relations, *Renewing the Atlantic Partnership*, Report of an Independent Task Force sponsored by the Council on Foreign Relations under C.A. Kupchan (project director) and H.A. Kissinger and L.A. Summers (co-chairs), 2004

Cede, F./Brand, H. *Der völkerrechtliche Vertrag – Ein Leitfaden für die österreichische Praxis*, Diplomatic Academy Vienna, Occasional Papers 2 (1997)

---

1   Excluded for brevity reasons are: newspaper articles, newsletters, documents other than NATO or EU or international treaties, European Convention documents, press releases, speeches, and miscelleaneous sources such as personal interviews.

Chafos, T.A. *The European Union's Rapid Reaction Force and the North Atlantic Treaty Organization Response Force: A Rational Division of Labor for European Security* (2003)

Cirincione, J. et al., *WMD in Iraq: Evidence and Implications*, Carnegie Endowment for International Peace (2004), http://www.ceip.org/files/pdf/Iraq3FullText.pdf (visited 16/07/2004)

Cook, D. *Forging the Alliance: NATO, 1945 to 1950* (1989)

Cooper, R. *The breaking of nations: order and chaos in the twenty-first century* (2003)

Cornish, P. *Partnership in Crisis – the US, Europe and the Fall and Rise of NATO* (1997)

Cot, J.-P. (ed.) *La Charte des Nations Unies* (1991)

Craig, P./de Burca, G. *EU Law* (2nd edn, 1998)

Craig, P./de Burca, G. *EU Law* (3rd edn, 2003)

Dagron, S. *La neutralité permanente des Etats européens*, doctoral thesis (Univ. des Saarlandes/Univ. Poitiers, 2003)

Desmond, D. *Ever closer union? An introduction to the European community* (1994)

Deutsch, K. *Political community and the North Atlantic area* (1957)

Dinh, N.Q./Dailler, P./Pellet, A. *Droit International Public* (6th edn, 1999)

Dinstein, Y. *War, Aggression and Self-Defence* (3rd edn, 2001)

Doehring, K. *Völkerrecht* (1999)

Doherty, R. *Ireland, Neutrality and European Security Integration* (2003)

van Eekelen, W.F. *Debating European Security 1948–1998* (1998)

Ehrhart, H.-G./Klingenburg, K. *UN-Friedenssicherung 1985–1995* (1996)

Elias, T.O. *The Modern Law of Treaties* (1974)

Ettmayer, W. *Eine geteilte Welt – Machtpolitik und Wohlfahrtsdenken in den Internationalen Beziehungen des 21. Jahrhunderts* (2003)

European Union Institute for Security Studies (Paris), *European Defence, proposal for a White Paper* (2004)

Famira, K. *Der freie Personenverkehr in Europa – Schengen nach Amsterdam* (2004)

Fischer, P./Köck, H.F. *Allgemeines Völkerrecht* (5th edn, 2000)

Fleuß, M. *Die operationelle Rolle der WEU in den neunziger Jahren* (1996)

Franck, T.M. *Recourse to force – state action against threats and armed attacks* (2002)

Gerteiser, K. *Die Sicherheits- und Verteidigungspolitik der Europäischen Union* (2002)

Geyrhalter, D. *Friedenssicherung durch Regionalorganisationen ohne Beschluß des Sicherheitsrates* (2002)

Goodrich, L./Hambro, E. *Charter of the United Nations* (3rd edn, 1969)

Haas, R.N. *Intervention – the use of American military force in the post-Cold War world* (1999)

Haas, R.N. *The Opportunity: America's Moment to Alter History's Course* (2005)

Hauser, G. *Österreich – dauernd neutral?* (2002)

Heitsch, C. *Die Verordnung über den Zugang zu Dokumenten der Gemeinschaftsorgane im Lichte des Transparenzprinzips* (2003)

Heller, F.H./Gillingham, J. R (eds) *NATO: The founding of the Atlantic Alliance and the Integration of Europe* (1992)

Herdegen, M. *Völkerrecht* (2nd edn, 2002)

Hillen, J. *Blue Helmets – The Strategy of UN Military Operations* (2nd edn, 2000)

Hufnagel, F.-E. *UN-Friedensoperationen der zweiten Generation – Vom Puffer zur Neuen Treuhand* (1996)

International Institute for Security Studies (London), *The Military Balance 2001/02*

International Institute for Security Studies (London), *The Military Balance 2003/04*

Ipsen, K. *Rechtsgrundlagen und Institutionalisierung der Atlantisch-Westeuropäischen Verteidigung* (1967)

Ismay, H.L. *NATO – the first five years* (1954)

Jennings, R./Watts, A. *Oppenheim's International Law* (9th edn, 1992)

Jürgens, T. *Die Gemeinsame Außen- und Sicherheitspolitik* (1994)

Kastner, K. *Quelle culture de sécurité et de défense pour l'Union européenne? – Les défis d'une approche civilo-militaire globale pour la Politique européenne de Sécurité et Défense*, ENA thesis, Promotion Romain Gary «2003-2005» (2005) (on file with the author)

Kay, S. *NATO and the Future of European Security* (1998)

Kelsen, H. *The Law of the United Nations* (1950)

von Kielmansegg, S. *Die Verteidigungspolitik der Europäischen Union – eine rechtliche Analyse* (2005)

Klabbers, J. *The Concept of Treaty in International Law* (1996)

Klein, E./Pechstein, M. *Das Vertragsrecht internationaler Organisationen* (1985)

Koslowski, G. *Die NATO und der Krieg in Bosnien-Herzegowina – Deutschland, Frankreich und die USA im internationalen Krisenmanagement* (1995)

Krisch, N. *Selbstverteidigung und kollektive Sicherheit* (2001)

Kupchan, C. *The End of the American Era: U.S. Foreign Policy and the Geopolitics of the Twenty-first Century* (2002)

Leonard, M. *Why Europe will run the 21st century* (2005)

Leurdijk, D.A. *The United Nations and NATO in Former Yugoslavia, 1991–1996: Limits to Diplomacy and Force* (1996)

Lindstrom, G. (ed.), *Shift or Rift: Assessing US-EU relations after Iraq*, European Union Institute for Security Studies (2003)

Lindstrom, G./Schmitt, B. (eds), *One year on – lessons from Iraq*, CP 68 (2004)

Link, A.S. et al. (eds) *The Papers of Woodrow Wilson*, 45 (1984)

Malanczuk, P. *Akehurst's International Law* (1997)

Marauhn, T. *Building a European Security and Defence Identity* (1996)

Márquez Carrasco, M. *Problemas Actuales sobre la Prohibición del Recurso a la Fuerza en Derecho Internacional* (1998) von Martens, F. *Völkerrecht – Das Internationale Recht der Civilisierten Nationen* (1883)

Martin, L./Roper, J. (eds) *Towards a common defence policy*, WEU-ISS (1995)

Max Planck Institute for Comparative Public Law and International Law, Heidelberg, Tätigkeitsbericht 2003 (A. van Aaken, ed.)

McCoubrey, H./Morris, J. *Regional Peacekeeping in the Post-Cold War Era* (2000)

McNair, A. *The Law of Treaties* (1961)

Mearsheimer, J.J. *Conventional deterrence* (1983)

Medcalf, J. *Going Global? The North Atlantic Treaty Organisation and the Extra-European Challenge*, Ph.D. Dissertation, University of Bath, 2002 (unpublished on file with the author)

Meimeth (ed.), M. *Die Europäische Union auf dem Weg zu einer Gemeinsamen Sicherheits- und Verteidigungspolitik* (1997)

Menk, T.M. *Gewalt für den Frieden – Die Idee der kollektiven Sicherheit und die Pathognomie des Krieges im 20. Jahrhundert* (1992)

Menon, P.K. *The law of treaties between states and international organizations* (1992)

Minnerop, P. *Paria-Staaten im Völkerrecht?* (2004)

Morgenthau, H. *Politics among nations* (1993, brief ed., rev. by K.W. Thompson)

Müller, J.P. *Vertrauensschutz im Völkerrecht* (1971)

Neuhold, H. *Internationale Konflikte – erlaubte und unerlaubte Mittel ihrer Austragung* (1977)

Nye, Jr., J.S. *The paradox of American* power (2002)

Padelford, N.J. *International Law and Diplomacy in the Spanish Civil Strife* (1939)

Pernice, I. *Die Sicherung des Weltfriedens durch Regionale Organisationen und die Vereinten Nationen* (1972)

Peters et al., J.E. *European Contributions to Operation Allied Force – Implications for Transatlantic Cooperation*, MR-1391-AF, RAND Corp. (2001)

Reuter, P. *Introduction to the Law of Treaties* (1995)

Rezac, D. *Militärische Intervention als Problem des Völkerrechts* (2002)

Rosenne, S. *The Law of Treaties – A guide to the legislative history of the Vienna Convention* (1970)

Salmon, T.C./Shepherd, A.J.K. *Toward a European Army – A Military Power in the Making?* (2003)

Schaefer, M. *Die Funktionsfähigkeit des Sicherheitsmechanismus der Vereinten Nationen* (1981)

Schermers, H.G./Blokker, N.M. *International Institutional Law* (1995)

Schmidl, E.A. *Im Dienste des Friedens – Die österreichische Teilnahme an Friedensoperationen seit 1960* (2001)

Schürr, U. *Der Aufbau einer europäischen Sicherheits- und Verteidigungsidentität im Beziehungsgeflecht von EU, WEU, OSZE und NATO* (2003)

Schwarzenberger, G. *A Manual of International Law* (6th edn, 1976)

Siekmann, R.C.R. *National Contingents in United Nations Peace-Keeping Forces* (1991)

Seidl-Hohenveldern, I./Loibl, G. *Das Recht der Internationalen Organisationen einschließlich der supranationalen Gemeinschaften* (1996)

Shaw, M.N. *International Law* (1997)

Sicilianos, L.-A. *Les réactions décentralisés à l'illicite* (1990)

Sinclair, I. *The Vienna Convention on the Law of Treaties* (1984)

Sloan, S. *NATO's Future – Towards a new Transatlantic Bargain* (1987)

Spaak, P.-H. *Combats Inachevés*, Vol. 1, *De l'Indépendence à l'Alliance* (1969)

Theiler, O. *Die NATO im Umbruch* (2003)

Thompson, K.W. (ed.), *NATO and the Changing World Order: An Appraisal by Scholars and Policymakers* (1996)

Thun-Hohenstein, C. *Der Vertrag von Amsterdam* (1997)

Timmermann, H./Pradetto, A. (eds), *Die NATO auf dem Weg ins 21. Jahrhundert* (2002)

Verdross, A./Simma, B. *Universelles Völkerrecht* (1984)

de Visscher, C. *Théories et réalités en droit international public* (4th edn, 1970)

Graf Vitzthum, W./Winkelmann, I. (eds), *Bosnien-Herzegovina im Horizont Europas* (2003)

Walt, S.M. *The Origins of Alliances* (1987)

Walter, C. *Vereinte Nationen und Regionalorganisationen* (1996)

Waltz, K. *Theory of international politics* (1979)

Warg, G. *Von Verteidigung zu kollektiver Sicherheit – Der Nato-Vertrag auf Rädern* (2004)

Warnken, M. *Der Handlungsrahmen der Europäischen Union im Bereich der Sicherheits- und Verteidigungspolitik* (2002)

Williams, P. (comp.) *North Atlantic Treaty Organization*, International Organizations series (1994)

Zemanek, K. (ed.) *Agreements of International Organizations and the Vienna Convention on the Law of Treaties* (1971)

ARTICLES

Abbasi, N.M. *Security Issues between the US and EU within NATO* (2000): 83

Abbasi, N.M. *Evolving a Common European defence: Challenges to the EU*, 21 Strategic Studies 2 (2001): 77

d' Alema, M. *A New NATO for a New Europe*, 34 The International Spectator 2 (1999): 29

Álvarez Verdugo, M. *La relación de Consulta y Cooperación entre la Unión Europea y la Otan*, REDI No. 12.Year 6 (May-Aug. 2002): 471

Ancuţa, C.-R. *EU CFSP and the Transatlantic Relationship*, 9 Rom.J.Int.Aff. 2-3 (2003): 152

Arai-Takahashi, Y. *Shifting Boundaries of the Right of Self-Defence – Appraising the Impact of the September 11 Attacks on Jus Ad Bellum*, 36 The International Lawyer (Winter 2002): 1081

Asmus, R.D./Blackwill, R./Larrabee, F.S. *Can NATO Survive?*, 19 The Washington Quarterly 2 (1996): 79

Asmus, R.D. in: Lindstrom, G./Schmitt, B. (eds), *One year on – lessons from Iraq*, CP 68 (2004): 131

Asmus, R.D./Kugler, R.L./Larrabee, F.S. *Building a New NATO*, 72 Foreign Affairs (Sept./Oct. 1993): 28

Asmus, R.D. *Rebuilding the Atlantic Alliance*, Foreign Affairs (Sept./Oct. 2003): 20

Aust, A. *The Theory and Practice of Informal International Instruments*, 35 ICLQ (1986): 787

Baggett, A. *The Development of the European Union Common Defense and its Implications for the United States and NATO*, 31 Ga. J. Int'l & Comp.L. (Winter 2003): 355

Bailes, A.J.K. *EU and US Strategic Concepts: A Mirror for Partnership and Difference?*, 39 The International Spectator 1 (2004): 19

Bailes, A.J.K. *European defence: What are the arguments about?* (article published in Estonian in the journal 'Diplomaatia', Feb. 2004, English translation on file with the author)

Bailes, A.J.K. *Reaktionsstreitmacht der NATO*, Internationale Politik 1/2003: 49

Barbé, E./Bondía, A.G. *La Política Europea de Seguridad y Defensa en el Escenario Internacional Actual*, Arbor No. 678 (2002): 357

Baxter, R.R. *International Law in 'Her Infinite Variety'*, 29 ICLQ (1980): 549

Benkö, A./Malek, M. *Akteure des Konflikts um Transnistrien (Moldau) – Unter besonderer Berücksichtigung der Möglichkeiten und Grenzen eines EU-Engagements*, 53 Südosteuropa – Zeitschrift für Gegenwartsforschung 1 (2005): 56

Ben-Naftali, O./Michaeli, K.R. *Justice-Ability: A Critique of the Alleged Non-Justiciability of Israel's Policy of Targeted Killings*, 1.2 J'l of Int. Crim. Just. (2003): 368

Bereschi, Z. *The Dilemma of the Future of Transatlantic Relations: Multilateralism or Unilateralism?*, Rom. J. Int. Aff. 2-3 (2003): 177

Bernhardt, R. *Customary International Law*, in: EPIL III (1992): 898

Bernhardt, R. *Treaties*: in: EPIL III (2000): 927, *– Addendum 1999*: 931

Bertram, C. in: G. Lindstrom/B. Schmitt (eds), *One year on – lessons from Iraq*, CP 68 (2004): 13

Besselink, L.F.M. *Defence: Old Problems in a New Guise?*, 1 European Constitutional Law Review (2005): 21

Beuve-Mery, H./Grasset, P. *La défense européenne: rapports transatlantiques*, 57 Défense nationale 11 (2000): 17

Beyerlin, U./Reichard, M. *German Participation in United Nations Environmental Activities: From Stockholm to Johannesburg*, 46 GYIL (2003): 123

Biggio, F.A. *Neutralizing the threat: Reconsidering Existing Doctrines in the Emerging War on Terrorism*, 34 Case W. Res. J. Int'l L. (Fall 2002): 1

Bildt, C. in: Lindstrom, G./Schmitt, B. (eds), *One year on – lessons from Iraq*, CP 68 (2004): 21

Bindschedler, R. *International Organizations, General Aspects*, in: EPIL II: 1289

Binnendijk, H./Kugler, R. *Transforming Europe's Forces*, 44 Survival 3 (2002): 117

Biscop, S. *Able and Willing? Assessing the EU's Capacity for Military Action*, 9 EFAR (2004): 509

Biscop, S. *In Search for a Strategic Concept for the ESDP*, 7 EFAR (2002): 473

Biscop, S. *The UK's Change of Course: a New Chance for the ESDI*, 4 EFAR (1999): 253

Blanck, K. *Flexible Integration in the Common Foreign and Security Policy*, EI Working Paper No. 61 (2004)

Blockmans, S. *A New Crisis Manager at the Horizon – The Case of the European Union*, 13 LJIL (2000): 255

Bock, Y. *Ein Sieg für die Transparenz? Die neue Verordnung über den Zugang der Öffentlichkeit zu Dokumenten der EU*, 55 DÖV (2002): 556

von Bogdandy, A./Nettesheim, M. *Die Verschmelzung der Europäischen Gemeinschaften in der Europäischen Union*, 36 NJW (1995): 2324

Boguslawska, H. *Le lien transatlantique et le développement de l'identité européenne de sécurité et de défense* (2003), NATO-EAPC Fellowship papers 2001–2003, http://www.nato.int/acad/fellow/01-03/boguslowska.pdf (visited 11/08/2004)

Bonvicini, G. et al. *Security Links in the Making*, in: Bonvicini, G. et al. (eds), *A renewed partnership for Europe – tackling European security challenges by EU–NATO interaction* (1996): 307

Borchert, H. *The Future of Europe's Security and Defense Policy (ESDP) and the Limits of Intergovernmentalism*, in: A. Weidemann/A. Simon (eds), *The Future of ESDP, A Conference Report 'The (not so) Common European Security and Defence Policy'* (2003): 55

Botticelli, A.D. *The premier of the North Atlantic Treaty's Article V: Is Article V Still a Deterrent?*, 26 Suffolk Transnat. L. Rev. (2002): 51

Bradford, W. *The Western European Union, Yugoslavia, and the (dis)integration of the EU, the new sick man of Europe*, 24 B.C. Int'l & Comp. L. R. (2000): 13

Brimmer, E. in: G. Lindstrom/B. Schmitt (eds), *One year on – lessons from Iraq*, CP 68 (2004): 139

Broek, H. van den *Why Europe Needs a Common Foreign and Security Policy*, Guest Editorial, 1 EFAR (1996): 1

Bryde, B.-O. *Self-Defence*, in: EPIL IV (2000): 361

Bull, H. *Civilian Power Europe; A Contradiction in Terms?*, in: L. Tsoukalis (ed.), *The European Community – past, present and future* (1983): 149

Burghardt, G./Tebbe, G. *Artikel J.4.*, in: Groeben/Thiesing/Ehlermann (eds), *Kommentar zum EU-/EG-Vertrag* Vol. 5 (5th edn 1997): 946

von Buttlar, C. *The EU's new relations with NATO shuttling between reliance and autonomy*, 6 ZEuS 3 (2003): 399

von Buttlar, C. *The European Union's Security and Defence Policy – A Regional Effort within the Atlantic Alliance*, in: A. Bodnar et al. (eds), *The Emerging Constitutional Law of the European Union* (2003): 387

Byers, M. *Terrorism, The Use of Force and International Law after 11 September*, 51 ICLQ (2002): 401

Cameron, F./Qille, G. *The Future of ESDP*, EPC Working Paper (2004)

Cassese, A. *Article 51*, in: J.-P. Cot/A. Pellet (eds), *La Charte des Nations Unies* (2ⁿᵈ edn, 1991): 771

Cazeau, J.P.H. *European security and defense policy under the gun*, 10 U.Miami Int. Comp.L.Rev. (2002): 51

Chace, J. *Is NATO Obsolete?*, in: K.W. Thompson (ed.), *NATO and the Changing World Order: An Appraisal by Scholars and Policymakers* (1996): 61

Cheng, B. *United Nations Resolutions on Outer Space: 'Instant' International Customary Law?*, 5 Indian Journal of International Law (1965): 23

Chronique des faits internationaux – Organisation du Traité de l'Atlantique Nord, Sommet de Prague 21-22 novembre 2002, 57 RGDIP (2003): 154

Clarke, M./Cornish: *The European defence project and the Prague summit*, 78 International Affairs 4 (2002): 777

Clawson, P. *US and European priorities in the Middle East*, in: *Shift or Rift* (2003): 127

Collet, A. *Le Traité de Maastricht de la Défense*, 29 Rev.T.Dr.Eur. (1993): 225

Cornish, P./Edwards, G. *Beyond the EU–NATO dichotomy: the beginnings of a European strategic culture*, 77 International Affairs (2001): 587

Cremer, H.-J. Commentary to Art. 24 TEU, in: C. Caliess/H.J. Blanke (eds), *Kommentar zu EU-Vertrag und EG-Vertrag* (2ⁿᵈ edn 2002): 209

Cremona, M. *External Relations and External Competence*, in: P. Craig/G. de Burca, *The Evolution of EU Law* (1999): 143

Cremona, M. *The Draft Constitutional Treaty: External Relations and External Action*, 40 CMLR (2003): 1347

Cremona, M. *The Union as a Global Actor: Roles, Models and Identity*, 41 CMLR (2004): 553

Curtin, D.M. *Citizens' Fundamental Right of Access to EU Information: An Evolving Digital Passepartout?*, 37 CMLR (2000): 7

Daalder, I.H./Lindsay, J.M. *American foreign policy and transatlantic relations in the age of global politics*, in: *Shift or Rift* (2003): 91

Daalder, I.H. *NATO, the UN, and the Use of force*, 5 International Peacekeeping 1/2 (1999): 26

Dassu, M. in: G. Lindstrom/B. Schmitt (eds), *One year on – lessons from Iraq*, CP 68 (2004): 29

Davis, D.F./DeGrasse, B.C. *What Follows the Current NATO Involvements in Bosnia? – Options for a Policy Debate*, 4 International Peacekeeping 3/4 (1998): 76

Dehousse, F./Galer, B. *De Saint-Malo à Feira: Les Enjeux de la Renaissance du Projet de Défense Européenne*, 52 Studia diplomatica (1999): 1

Dehousse, F. *After Amsterdam: A Report on the Common Foreign and Security Policy of the European Union*, 9 EJIL (1998): 525

Deighton, A. *The European Security and Defence Policy*, 40 JCMS (2002): 719

Deighton, A. *The Military Security Pool: Towards a New Security Regime for Europe?*, 35 The International Spectator 4 (2000): 41

Delbrück, J. *Collective Security*, in: EPIL I (1992): 646

Delbrück, J. *Collective Self-Defence*, in: EPIL I (1992): 656

Dembinski, M./Wagner, W. *Europäische Kollateralschäden*, Aus Politik und Zeitgeschichte. B 31-32: 31

Dobbins, J. in: G. Lindstrom/B. Schmitt (eds), *One year on – lessons from Iraq*, CP 68 (2004): 147

Donfried, K. *European Security and Defense Policy: The View from the United States*, in: Hoyer/ Kaldrack, *ESVP* (2002): 190

Douglas-Scott, S. *The Common Foreign and Security Policy of the EU: Reinforcing the European Identity?*, in: *Id.*, *Europe's other* (1998): 131

Doyle, M. in: *UN Peacekeeping: An Early Reckoning of the Second Generation*, 89 ASIL Proceedings 1995: 275

Drozdiak, W. in: G. Lindstrom/B. Schmitt (eds), *One year on – lessons from Iraq*, CP 68 (2004): 153

Drozdiak, W. *The North Atlantic Drift*, 84 Foreign Affairs (Jan./Feb. 2005): 88

Ducasse-Rogier, M. *Recovering from Dayton: From 'peace-building' to 'state-building' in Bosnia and Herzegovina*, Helsinki Monitor 2004, No. 2: 76

Duff, J.A. *UNCLOS and the new Deep Seabed Mining Regime: The Risks of Refuting the Treaty*, 19 Suffolk Transnat'l L. Rev. (Winter 1995): 1

Duffield, J.S. *Why NATO persists*, in: K.W. Thompson (ed.), *NATO and the Changing World Order: An Appraisal by Scholars and Policymakers* (1996): 99

Duke, S. *CESDP and the response to 11 September: Identifying the Weakest Link*, 7 EFAR 2 (2002): 153

Duke, S. *CESDP: Nice's Overtrumped Success?*, 6 EFAR 2 (2001): 155

Duke, S. *The European Security Strategy in a Comparative Framework: Does it Make for Secure Alliances in a Better World?*, 9 EFAR (2004): 459

Duquette, E.S. *The EU's CFSP: Emerging from the U.S. Shadow?*, 7 U.C. Davis J. Int'l L. & Pol'y (Spring 2001): 169

Editorial comments, *The European Union – A new international actor*, 38 CMLR (2001): 825

Ehrmann, M. *Die Globale Umweltfazilität (GEF)*, 57 HJIL (1997): 565

Eisemann, M. *Le Gentlemen's agreement comme source du droit international*, 106 Journal du droit international (1979): 326

Eitelhuber, N. *Europäische Streitkräfte unter dem Zwang der Beschneidung – Partner der USA nur bei friedenssichernden Einsätzen*, SWP-Studie No. 8, March 2003

Eliassen, K.A. *Introduction: The New European Foreign and Security Policy Agenda*, in: *Id.* (ed.), *Foreign and Security Policy in the European Union* (1998): 1

Epping, V. *Internationale Organisationen*, in: K. Ipsen, Völkerrecht (4th edn, 1999): 390

Epping, V. *Rechtliche Rahmenbedingungen der Gemeinsamen Außen- und Sicherheitspolitik der EU*, 44 NZWR 3 (2002): 90

Faria, F. *Crisis management in sub-Saharan Africa – The role of the European Union*, OP 51 (2004)

Fernández Tomás, A.F. *El recurso al artículo quinto del Tratado de Washington tras los acontecimientos del 11 de septiembre: mucho ruido y pocas nueces*, 53 REDI 1/2 (2001): 205

Fiedler, W. *Unilateral Acts in International Law*, EPIL III (2000): 1018

Fitzmaurice, G. *The Law and Procedure of the International Court of Justice, 1951– 54: General Principles and Sources of Law*, 30 BYIL (1953): 1

Foscarinis, M. *Symposium: Homelessness and Human Rights: Towards an Integrated Strategy*, 19 St. Louis U. Publ. L. Rev. (2000): 327

Freckmann, R. *Die NATO im 21. Jahrhundert – Bedrohungen, Herausforderungen und Chancen*, IFIR Themenschwerpunkt, No. 01/2005

Frickey, P. *A Common Law for Our Age of Colonialism: The Judicial Divestiture of Indian Tribal Authority over Nonmembers*, 109 Yale Law Journal (Oct. 1999): 1

Friedmann, W. *Some impacts of Social Organization on International Law*, 50 AJIL (1956): 505

Fröhlich, S. *Der Ausbau der europäischen Verteidigungsidentität zwischen WEU und NATO*, ZEI Discussion Paper C 19 (1998)

Frost, A. *Restoring Faith in Government: Transparency Reform in the United States and the European Union*, 9 European Public Law (2003): 87

Frowein, J.A. *Nullity in International Law*, in: EPIL III (1997): 743

Gallagher, M.M. *Declaring Victory and Getting out [of Europe]: Why the North Atlantic Treaty Organization Should Disband*, 25 Houston J. Int. L. (2003): 341

Gärtner, H. *Security Concepts*, 8 Rom. J. Int'l Aff. (2002): 19

Gazzini, T. *NATO Coercive Military Activities in the Yugoslav Crisis (1992–1999)*, 12 EJIL 3 (2001): 391

Gazzini, T. *NATO's Role in the Collective Security System*, 8 JCSL 2 (2003): 231

Geiger, R. *External Competences of the European Union and the Treaty-Making Power of its Member States*, 14 Ariz. J. Int'l & Comp. L. (1997): 319

Ginsberg, R. *Together apart: ESDP, CFSP, and a New Transatlantic Security Compact*, in: A. Maurer/K.-O. Lang/E. Whitlock (eds), *New Stimulus or Integration Backlash? EU Enlargement and Transatlantic Relations* (2004), SWP Berlin: 36

Gnesotto, N. *EU, US: visions of the world, visions of the other*, in: Lindstrom, G. (ed.), *Shift or Rift: Assessing US-EU relations after Iraq*, EU-ISS (2003): 7

Gnesotto, N. in: G. Lindstrom/B. Schmitt (eds), *One year on – lessons from Iraq*, CP 68 (2004): 51

Gnesotto, N. *Introduction*, in: CP 51: vii.

Gnesotto, N. *Preface*, in: G. Lindstrom/B. Schmitt (eds), *One year on – lessons from Iraq*, CP 68 (2004): 7

Goldberg, M.A. *Mirage of Defense: Reexamining Article Five of the North Atlantic Treaty after the Terrorist Attacks on the United States*, 26 B.C.Int'l & Comp. L. Rev. (Winter 2003): 77

Goldrich, I.M. *Balancing the Need for Repatriation of illegally removed cultural property with the interests of bona fide purchasers: applying the UNIDROIT Convention to the Case of the Gold Phiale*, 23 Fordham Int'l L.J. (Nov. 1999): 118

Gómez Garrido, M. *ESDP: The Recent Debate in the United States*, OBS Working Paper No.18 (2002)

Gompert, D.C. *What does America want of Europe?*, in: Lindstrom, G. (ed.), *Shift or Rift:Assessing US-EU relations after Iraq*, EU-ISS (2003): 43

González Bondia, A. *La OTAN y la crisis del once de septiembre*, OBS Working Papers, Breves 13/2001, http://selene.uab.es/_cs_iuee_/catala/obs/Working%20Papers/breveSito.htm (visited 16/01/2003)

Gordon, P.H. *Bridging the Atlantic Divide*, 82 Foreign Affairs 1 (2003): 70

Gordon, P.H. in: G. Lindstrom/B. Schmitt (eds), *One year on – lessons from Iraq*, CP 68 (2004): 161

Gordon, P.H. *Their Own Army? Making European Defense Work*, Foreign Affairs (July/Aug. 2000): 12

Grant, C. *Can Britain lead in Europe?*, CER (1998)

Grant, C. *EU defence takes a step forward*, CER briefing note, Dec. 2003

Grant, C. *European defence post-Kosovo?*, CER (1999)

Grant, C. in: G. Lindstrom/B. Schmitt (eds), *One year on – lessons from Iraq*, CP 68 (2004): 61

Greco, E. *UN-NATO Interaction: Lessons from the Yugoslav Experience*, 32 The International Spectator 3/4 (1997): 121

Groves, D.M. *The European Union's Common Foreign, Security and Defense Policy*, BITS Research Report 00.3 (Nov. 2000)

Guggenheim, P./Marek, K. *Verträge, völkerrechtliche*, in: Strupp, K./Schlochauer, H.-J. *Wörterbuch des Völkerrechts*, Vol. 3 (1962)

Gustenau, G. *Die Europäische Gemeinsame Außen- und Sicherheitspolitik – eine Herausforderung für die 'Post-Neutralen'? – Eine Einschätzung aus österreichischer Sicht*, in: *Id.*, Sicherheitspolitischer Dialog Österreich-Slowenien (2000): 15

Gustenau, G. in: G. Lindstrom/B. Schmitt (eds), *One year on – lessons from Iraq*, CP 68 (2004): 71

Haglund, D.G. *Must NATO fail? Theories, myths, and policy dilemmas*, International Journal (1995): 651

Hafner, G. *Certain Issues of the Work of the Sixth Committee at the Fifty-Sixth General Assembly*, 97 AJIL (2003): 147

Hafner, G. *The Amsterdam Treaty and the treaty-making power of the European Union – some critical comments*, in: *Id.* (ed.), Liber Amicorum for Professor I. Seidl-Hohenveldern, in honour of his 80th birthday (1998): 257

Haine, J.-Y. *A new impetus for ESDP?*, EU-ISS Bulletin No. 11 (July 2004)

Haine, J.-Y. *ESDP and NATO*, in: N. Gnesotto (ed.), *EU Security and Defence Policy – The first five years* (2004), EU-ISS: 131

Haine, J.-Y. *Idealism and Power: The New EU Security Strategy*, Current History (March 2004): 107

Haine, J.-Y. in: CP 57: 135 (introductory text to the Brussels European Council Presidency Conclusions)

van Ham, P. *Politics as Usual: NATO and the EU after 9-11*, in: *Id.*, *Terrorism and Counterterrorism – Insights and Perspectives after September 11*, The Hague, Clingendael Institute, December 2001

van Ham, P. *The EU and WEU: From Cooperation to Common Defence?*, in: G. Edwards/A. Pijpers, *The Politics of European Treaty Reform* (1996): 306

Hamilton, D. *Three Strategic Challenges for a Global Transatlantic Partnership*, 8 EFAR (2003): 543

Hargrove, J.L. *Force, a Culture of Law, and American Interests*, 36 Col. J. Transnat'l L. (1998): 433

Harryvan, A.G./van der Harst, J. *A Threat of Rivalry? Dutch Views on European Security Today*, in: M. Dumoulin, *La Communauté européenne de défense, leçons pour demain?* (2000): 401

Hassner, P. in: G. Lindstrom/B. Schmitt (eds) *One year on – lessons from Iraq*, CP 68 (2004): 79

Hawk, B.E./Laudati, L.L. *Antitrust Federalism in the United State and Decentralisation of Competition Law Enforcement in the European Union: A Comparison*, 20 Fordham Int'l L.J. (Nov. 1996): 18

Heathcoat-Amory, D., Secretary of State for the Foreign Office *The next step for the Western European Union: a British view*, The World Today (Royal Institute of International Affairs, London), July 1994: 133

Heindel, R. et al. *The North Atlantic Treaty in the United States Senate*, 43 AJIL (1949): 633

Heintschel von Heinegg, W. *Die völkerrechtlichen Verträge als Hauptrechtsquelle des Völkerrechts*, in: K. Ipsen, *Völkerrecht* (4th edn, 1999): 97

Heintschel von Heinegg, W. *Rechtliche Aspekte bei der Neufassung der GASP durch den Vertrag von Amsterdam*, Die Friedenswarte 73 (1998) 2: 157

Heisbourg, F. *Europe's Strategic Ambitions: The Limits of Ambiguity*, 42 Survival 2 (2000): 1

Heisbourg, F. *European defence takes a leap forward*, NATO Review, Spring/Summer 2000: 8

Heisbourg, F. *L'Europe de la défense dans l'Alliance atlantique*, 64 Politique étrangère (1999): 219

Heisbourg, F. *New Nato, New Europe, New Division of Labour*, 34 The International Spectator 2 (1999): 63

Heisbourg, F. *US-European relations: from lapsed alliance to new partnership?*, 41 International Politics (2004): 119

Herbst, J. *Peacekeeping by the European Union*, in: A. Bodnar et al. (eds), *The Emerging Constitutional Law of the European Union – German and Polish Perspectives* (2003): 413

Hestermeyer, H. *Die völkerrechtliche Beurteilung des Irakkrieges im Lichte transatlantischer Rechtskulturunterschiede*, 64 HJIL (2004): 315

Higgins, R. *The Development of International Law by the Political Organs of the United Nations*, 59 ASIL Proceedings (1965): 166

Higgins, R. in: *UN Peacekeeping: An Early Reckoning of the Second Generation*, 89 ASIL Proceedings 1995: 275

Higgins, R. *The Legal Limits to the Use of Force by Sovereign States: United Nations Practice*, 37 BYIL (1961): 269

Hilf, M./Pache, E. *Der Vertrag von Amsterdam*, 11 NJW (1998): 705

Hill, C. *The EU's capacity for conflict prevention*, 6 EFAR (2001): 315

Hoffmann, S. *The crisis in transatlantic relations*, in: Lindstrom, G. (ed.), *Shift or Rift – Assessing US-EU relations after Iraq*, EU-ISS (2003): 13

Hoffmann, S. *US-European relations: past and future*, 79 International Affairs (2003): 1029

Holbrooke, R. *America, A European Power*, 74 Foreign Affairs, (March/April 1995): 38

Hopkinson, W. *New Relationships*, The World Today, July 2003: 16

Howorth, J. *Discourse, Ideas, and Epistemic Communities in European Security and Defence Policy*, 27 West European Politics (2004): 211

Howorth, J. *ESDP and NATO - Wedlock or Deadlock?*, 38 Coop. & Confl. 3 (2003): 235

Howorth, J. *European Defence and the Changing Politics of the EU*, 39 JCMS (2001): 765

Howorth, J. *European integration and defence: the ultimate challenge* (2000), WEU-ISS CP 43

Howorth, J. *The European Draft Constitutional Treaty and the Future of the European Defence Initiative: A Question of Flexibility*, 9 EFAR (2004): 483

Hulsman, J. in: G. Lindstrom/B. Schmitt (eds), *One year on – lessons from Iraq*, CP 68 (2004): 169

Hummer, W. *Die neue EU als «Militärpakt» - Solidarität – Neutralität - «Irische Klausel»*, 1 EuZ (2005): 2

Huntington, S.P. *The Lonely Superpower*, Foreign Affairs (March-April 1999): 35

Ignarski, J.S. *North Atlantic Treaty Organization*, in: EPIL III (1997): 646

Ikenberry, G.I. *Strengthening the Atlantic Political Order*, 35 The International Spectator 3 (2000): 57

Isak, H./Loibl, G. *United Nations Conference on the Law of Treaties between States and International Organizations or between International Organizations*, 38 ÖsterrZÖR (1987): 49

Jakáb, A. *The Constitutional Charter of 'Serbia and Montenegro'* (English summary), 63 HJIL (2003): 801 at 814-5

Johnstone, I. *Security Council Deliberations: The Power of the Better Argument*, 14 EJIL 3 (2003): 437-480

Jopp, M. *GASP und ESVP im Verfassungsvertrag – eine neue Angebotsvielfalt mit Chancen und Mängeln*, 26 Integration 4 (2003): 550

Jopp, M. *Gemeinsame Europäische Sicherheits- und Verteidigungspolitik*, Jahrbuch der europäischen Integration 1999/2000: 243

Kagan, R. *Power and Weakness*, Policy Review No. 113 (June and July 2002)

Kahgan, C. *Jus Cogens and the Inherent right to self-defence*, 3 ILSA J Int'l & Comp. L. (1997): 767

Kahn, B.A. *The Legal Framework Surrounding Maori Claims to Water Resources in New Zealand: In Contrast to the American Indian Experience*, 35 Stan.J. Int'l L. (Winter 1999): 49

Kaiser, K. *Challenges and contingencies for European defence policy*, in: Martin/ Roper (eds), *Towards a common defence policy* (1995)

Kelsen, H. *Collective Security and Collective Self-Defense under the Charter und the United Nations*, 42 AJIL (1948): 783

Kelsen, H. *Is the North Atlantic Treaty a Regional Arrangement?*, 45 AJIL (1951): 162

Kempin, R. *The new NATO Response Force: Challenges for and Reactions from Europe*, Copenhagen Peace Research Institute Working Paper 29/2002

Kenny, K.C. *Self-Defence*, in: R. Wolfrum (ed.), Handbook United Nations (1995): 1162

Kiani, M. *The Changing Dimensions of UN Peacekeeping*, 24 Strategic Studies 1 (2004): 177

Kinder, I. *Institucionalna struktura i pravni položaj Sjevernoatlantske organizacije*, 19 Zabornik Pravnog Fakulteta Sveucilista u Rijeci (1998): 257 at 282 (Summary in English)

Kintis, A. *NATO-WEU: An Enduring Relationship*, 3 EFAR (1998): 537

Kirchhof: *Die rechtliche Struktur der Europäischen Union als Staatenverbund*, in: A. von Bogdandy (ed.), *Europäisches Verfassungsrecht* (2003): 893

Kirchner, E.J. *Final Report on a Study of the Relationship between ESDP Objectives and Capabilities*, NATO-EAPC Fellowship papers 2001-2003, http://www.nato.int/acad/fellow/01-03/kirchner.pdf (visited 12/12/04)

Kirgis Jr., F.R. *NATO Consultations as a Component of National Decision-Making*, 73 AJIL (1979): 372

Klein, J. *Europäische Sicherheitsinteressen aus der Sicht Frankreichs*, in: M. Meimeth (ed.), *Die Europäische Union auf dem Weg zu einer Gemeinsamen Sicherheits- und Verteidigungspolitik* (1997): 37

Köck, H.F. *Die 'implied powers' der Europäischen Gemeinschaften als Anwendungsfall der 'implied powers' internationaler Organisationen überhaupt*, in: K. Böckstiegel et al., *Völkerrecht, Recht der internationalen Organisationen, Weltwirtschaftsrecht*, Festschrift für I. Seidl-Hohenveldern (1988)

Kohler-Koch, B. *Die GASP im kommenden Jahrzehnt – Gewappnet für Krisen?*: in: R. Hierzinger (ed.), *Europäische Leitbilder* (2001): 155

Kolb, R. *Self-Defence and Preventive War at the Beginning of the Millennium*, 59 ÖsterrZÖR (2004): 111

Koutrakos, P. *Constitutional Idiosyncrasies and Political Realities: the Emerging Security and Defense Policy of the European Union*, 10 Col. J. Eur. L. (2003): 69

Kovacs, C. *US-European Relations from the Twentieth to the Twenty-First Century*, 8 EFAR (2003): 435

Krause, A. *The European Union's Africa Policy: The Commission as Policy Entrepreneur in the CFSP*, 8 EFAR (2003): 221

Kremer, M./Schmalz, U. *Nach Nizza – Perspektiven der Gemeinsamen Europäischen Sicherheits- und Verteidigungspolitik*, 24 Integration (2001): 167

Krenzler, H.G./Schomaker, A. *A new Transatlantic Agenda*, 1 EFAR (1996): 9

Krisch, N. *Amerikanische Hegemonie und liberale Revolution im Völkerrecht*, 43 Der Staat (2004): 267

Krück, H. *Gemeinsame Außen- und Sicherheitspolitik*, in: J. Schwarze (ed.), *EU-Kommentar* (2000): 108

Krüger, D. *Die EVG – Ein Vorbild für eine zukünftige Europaarmee?*, in: Hoyer/Kaldrack (2002): 43

Kunz, J.L. *Individual and Collective Self-Defence in Article 51 of the Charter of the UN*, 41 AJIL (1947): 879

Kupchan, C. *The Rise of Europe, America's Changing Internationalism, and the End of U.S. Primacy*, 118 PSQ (2003): 205

Lachowski, Z. *The military dimension of the European Union*, SIPRI Yearbook 2002: 151

Lanearts, K./de Smijter, E. *The European Union as an Actor under International Law*, 19 YBEL (1999/2000): 95

Lang, W. *Sind WEU und NATO noch Allianzen?*, 13 ÖJIP (1996): 1

Langrish, S. *The Treaty of Amsterdam: Selected Highlights*, 23 ELR (1998): 3

Larrabee, S. *ESDP and NATO: Assuring Complementarity*, 39 The International Spectator 1 (2004): 51

Larsen, H. *Concepts of Security in the European Union After the Cold War*, 54 Australian J. Int'l Aff. (2000): 337

Lauterpacht, H. *Sovereignty over Submarine Areas*, 27 BYIL (1950): 376

Layne, C. *Death Knell for NATO? The Bush Administration Confronts ESDP*, Executive Summary, Cato Institute – Policy Analysis, No. 394 (2001)

Lebel, G. *Défense en Europe*, 60 Défense nationale 2 (2004): 175

de Leeuw, M.E. *The regulation on public access to European Parliament, Council and Commission documents in the European Union*, 28 ELR (2003): 324

Lejins, A. in: G. Lindstrom/B. Schmitt (eds), *One year on – lessons from Iraq*, CP 68 (2004): 87

Lenski, E. *Turkey and the EU: On the Road to Nowhere?* 63 HJIL (2003): 102

Lenzi, G. *The WEU between NATO and EU*, 51 Studia Diplomatica (1998): 167

Leurdijk, D.A. *The Rapid Reaction Force*, International Peacekeeping (Oct.-Nov. 1995): 132

Lindstrom, G. *2003 Transatlantic Conference: The EU and the US: Partners in Stability?*, EU-ISS Institute Note, 22-23 April 2003

Lindstrom, G. *On the ground: ESDP operations*, in: N. Gnesotto (ed.), *EU Security and Defence Policy – The first five years* (2004), EU-ISS: 111

Link, W. *Die NATO im Geflecht internationaler Organisationen*, Aus Politik und Zeitgeschichte (1999) B 11: 9

Lipson, C. *Why are Some International Agreements Informal?*, 45 International Organization 4 (1991): 495

Ludlow, D.L. *Preventive Peacemaking in Macedonia: An Assessment of U.N. Good Offices Diplomacy*, Brigham Young University Law Review (2003): 761

Luif, P. *EU Cohesion in the UN General Assembly*, OP 49 (2003)

Lynch, D. *Russia faces Europe*, EU-ISS CP 60 (2003)

Mackinlay, J./Chopra, J. *Second Generation Multinational Operations*, in: Diehl: F. (ed.), *The Politics of Global Governance: international organizations in an interdependent world* (1997): 175

Mallard, P. *Défense Nationale et Défense Européenne: Deux Notions Compatibles?*, in: Vinçon, S. et al., *Défense: quels projets après 2002?*, 57 Défense nationale (2001): 82

Mangas Martín, A. *Cuestiones jurídicas relativas a la adhesión de España a la OTAN*, in: *Cursos de Derecho Internacional de Vitoria-Gasteiz* (1983): 21

Mark, B. *Acknowledging our International Criminals: Henry Kissinger and East Timor*, 32 Denv.J.Int'l L. & Pol'y (Winter 2003): 1

Marquardt, S. *The Conclusion of International Agreements under Article 24 of the Treaty on European Union*, in: V. Kronenberger (ed.), *The European Union and the international legal order* (2001): 333

Martenczuk, B. *The Legal Bases of ESDP*, in: A. Weidemann/A. Simon (eds), *The Future of ESDP, A Conference Report 'The (not so) Common European Security and Defence Policy'* (2003): 29

McArdle Kelleher, C. in: G. Lindstrom/B. Schmitt (eds), *One year on – lessons from Iraq*, CP 68 (2004): 177

McCalla, R.B. *NATO's persistence after the Cold War*, 50 International Organization (1996): 445

McNair, A. *The Seizure of Property and Enterprises*, 6 NILR (1959): 218

Mendelson, M. *Book Reviews*, 10 EJIL (1999): 477

Menon, A. *Defence Policy and Integration in Western Europe*, 17 CSP (1996): 264

Menon, A. *Enhancing the Effectiveness of the EU's Foreign Defence Policies*, CEPS Policy Brief No. 29 (Dec. 2002)

Mey, H.H. *Europäische Sicherheitsinteressen aus der Sicht Deutschlands*, in: M. Meimeth (ed.), *Die Europäische Union auf dem Weg zu einer Gemeinsamen Sicherheits- und Verteidigungspolitik* (1997): 21

Missiroli, A./Lynch, D. *ESDP Operations*, EU-ISS, http://www.iss-eu.org/esdp/09-dvl-am.pdf (visited 12/12/04)

Missiroli, A. *After the Brussels fiasco – an ESDP without a Constitution, a CFSP without a Foreign Minister?*, EU-ISS Analysis, 15 Jan. 2004, http:/www.iss-eu.org/new/analysis/analy073.html (visited 10/03/04)

Missiroli, A. *Flexibility for ESDP: What is feasible, What acceptable, What desirable?*, EU-ISS, Institute Note, 26 Jan. 2004

Missiroli, A. *Mind the Gaps – across the Atlantic and the Union*, in: Lindstrom, G. (ed.), *Shift or Rift:Assessing US-EU relations after Iraq*, EU-ISS (2003): 77

Missiroli, A. *Mind the steps: the Constitutional Treaty and beyond*, in: N. Gnesotto (ed.), *EU Security and Defence Policy – The first five years* (2004), EU-ISS: 145

Missiroli, A. *Sicherheitspolitische Kooperation zwischen Europäischer Union und Nato: Der türkische Verdruss über die Europäische Sicherheits- und Verteidigungspolitik*, 24 Integration 4 (2001): 340

Missiroli, A. *The European Union: Just a Regional Peacekeeper?*, 8 EFAR (2003): 493

Missiroli, A. *€uros for ESDP: financing of EU operations*, EU-ISS, Occasional Paper 45 (June 2003).

Moens, A. *Developing a European intervention force*, 55 International Journal (1999/2000): 247

Monaco, A. *Who takes care of European Security? EU and NATO: Competition or Cooperation?*, in: A. Weidemann/A. Simon (eds), *The Future of ESDP, A Conference Report 'The (not so) Common European Security and Defence Policy'* (2003): 40

Monar, J. *The CFSP and the Leila/Perejil Island* Incident, 7 EFAR (2002): 251

Moravcsik, A. in: G. Lindstrom/B. Schmitt (eds), *One year on: lessons from Iraq,* , CP 68 (2004): 185

Möttölä, K. *Collective and cooperative security arrangements in Europe*, in: M. Koskenniemi, *International Law Aspects of the European Union* (1998): 87

Mrazek, J. *Prohibition of the Use and Threat of Force: Self-Defence and Self-Help in International Law*, 29 Can.YIL (1989): 81

Müller, H. *Das transatlantische Risiko – Deutungen des amerikanisch-europäischen Weltordnungskonflikts*, Aus Politik und Zeitgeschichte (2004), B 3-4: 7

Müller, J.P./Cottier, T. *Estoppel*, in: EPIL II (1995)

Müller-Brandeck-Bocquet, G. *The New CFSP and ESDP Decision-Making System of the European Union*, 7 EFAR (2002): 257

Müllerson, R. *The ABM Treaty: Changed Circumstances, Extraordinary Events, Supreme Interests and International Law*, 50 ICLQ 3 (2001): 509

Münch, F. *Comments on the 1968 Draft Convention on the Law of Treaties – Non-binding Agreements*, 29 HJIL (1969): 1

Münch, F. *Non-Binding Agreements*, in: EPIL III (1997): 606

Muschwig, M. *European Security and Defense Policy: European vs. Unites States: Crisis of Transatlantic Relations: Nato and the Future European Security and Defense Identity (ESDI)*, 13 Miami Int'l & Comp.L.Rev. (2002): 13

Nerlich, U. *The relationship between a European common defence and NATO, the OSCE and the United* Nations, in: Martin, L./Roper, J. (eds) *Towards a common defence policy*, WEU-ISS (1995): 69

Neuhold, H. *Außenpolitik und Demokratie: 'Immerwährende' Neutralität durch juristische Mutation?*, in: S. Hammer et al. (eds), *Demokratie und sozialer Rechtsstaat in Europa – Festschrift für Theo Öhlinger* (2004): 68

Neuhold, H. *Collective Security After 'Operation Allied Force'*, 4 Max Planck UNYB (2000): 73

Neuhold, H. *Law and Force in International Relations – European and American Positions*, 64 HJIL (2004): 263

Neuhold, H. *Terminological Ambiguity in the Field of International Security: Legal and Political Aspects*, Festschrift für Jost Delbrück (forthcoming, 2005)

Neuhold, H. *The Inadequacy of Law-Making by International Treaties: 'Soft Law' as an Alternative?*, in: Wolfrum, R./Röben, V. (eds), *Developments of International Law in Treaty Making* (2005): 39

Neuhold, H. *The Provisions of the Amsterdam Treaty on the CFSP: Cosmetic Operation or Genuine Progress?*, in: G. Hafner et al. (eds), Liber Amicorum for Professor I. Seidl-Hohenveldern, in honour of his 80th birthday (1998): 495

Neuhold, H. *Transatlantic Turbulences: Rift or Ripples?*, 8 EFAR (2003): 457

Neuwahl, N. *The Atlantic Alliance: For Better or Wars...*, 8 EFAR (2003): 427

Nolte, G. *Die 'neuen Aufgaben' von NATO und WEU: Völker- und verfassungsrechtliche Fragen*, 54 HJIL (1994): 95

de Nooy, G. *Capabilities*, in: Martin, L./Roper, J. (eds) *Towards a common defence policy*, WEU-ISS (1995): 37

Nye Jr., J.S. *U.S. Power and Strategy after Iraq*, Foreign Affairs (July/Aug. 2003): 60

O'Connell, M.E. *Lawful Self-Defense to Terrorism*, 63 U.Pitt.L.Rev. (2001–2): 889

Öberg, U. *Slutreplik Från Stenbrottet – Svar på Olle Abrahamssons artikel 'Obefogad ängslan för den svenska offentlighetsprincipen'*, Europarättslig Tidskrift, No. 3 (2001), Årgång 4: 396

Oğuzlu, H.T. *Turkey and the European Union: The Security Dimension*, 23 CSP 3 (2002): 61

Ojanen, H. *Theories at a loss? EU–NATO fusion and the 'low-politicisation' of security and defence in European integration*, Finnish Institute of International Affairs, Working Paper 35 (2002)

d' Oléon, M./Jopp, M. *The way ahead for European defence integration*, in: Martin, L./Roper, J. (eds) *Towards a common defence policy*, WEU-ISS (1995): 99

Onyszkiewicz, J. in: G. Lindstrom/B. Schmitt (eds), *One year on – lessons from Iraq*, CP 68 (2004): 95

Ortega, M. *The Achilles heel of transatlantic relations*, in: *Shift or Rift* (2003): 147

Oxman, B.H. *Law of the Sea Forum: The 1994 Agreement on Implementation of the Seabed Provisions on the Convention on the Law of the Sea: The 1994 Agreement and the Convention*, 88 AJIL (1994): 687

Pagani, F. *A New Gear in the CFSP Machinery: Integration of the Petersberg Tasks in the Treaty on European Union*, 9 EJIL (1998): 737

Patten, C. *Europäische Sicherheits- und Verteidigungspolitik*, Integration 1 (2000): 7

Peers, S. *The New Regulation on Access to Documents: A Critical Analysis*, Queen's Papers on Europeanisation No. 6/2002, http://www.qub.ac.uk/ies/onlinepapers/poe6-02.pdf (visited 17/12/2003)

Peters, A. *European Democracy after the 2003 Convention*, 41 CMLR (2004): 37

Picone, P. *Il peace-keeping nel mondo attuale; tra militarizzazione e amministrazione fiduciaria*, 79 RDI (1996): 5

Pliakos, A. *The Common European Policy of Security and Defense: Some Considerations Relating to its Constitutional Identity*, 6 Col. J.Eur. L. (Fall 2000): 275

Pnevmaticou, L. *Aspects Juridiques de la Politique Européenne de Sécurité et de Défense*, WEU-ISS OP 31 (2001)

Posen, B.R. *ESDP and the Structure of World Power*, 39 The International Spectator 1 (2004): 5

Pradetto, A. *Funktionen militärischer Konfliktregelung durch die NATO bei der Neuordnung Europas*, in: H. Timmermann/A. Pradetto (eds), *Die NATO auf dem Weg ins 21. Jahrhundert* (2002): 191

Quigley, J. *The Afghanistan War and Self-Defense*, Valp. U. L. Rev. (Spring 2003): 541

Quoc Dinh, N. *La légitime défense d'après la Charte des Nations Unies*, 52 RGDIP (1948): 223

Randelzhofer, A. *Article 51*, in: B. Simma (ed.), *Charter of the United Nations* (2002): 788

Rasmussen, M.V. *Turbulent Neighbourhoods: How to Deploy the EU's Rapid Reaction Force*, 23 CSP 2 (2002): 41

Rau, M. *NATO's Strategic Concept and the German Federal Government's Authority in the Sphere of Foreign Affairs: The Decision of the German Federal Constitutional Court of 22 November 2001*, 44 GYIL (2001): 545

Reichard, M. *Conference Report – 'The (not so) Common European Foreign and Security Policy' – Max Planck Institute for Comparative Public Law and International Law – Heidelberg, Germany, 19–20 September 2003*, 5 German Law Journal 2 (2004): 177

Reichard, M. *Some Legal Issues Concerning the EU–NATO Berlin Plus Agreement*, 73 NJIL (2004): 37

Reichard, M. *The Madrid terrorist attacks: a midwife for EU mutual defence?*, 7 ZEuS 2 (2004): 313

Reinisch, A. *Governance without Accountability?*, 44 GYIL (2001): 270

Remiro Brotons, A. *Construction of European security*, 51 Review of international affairs 1089/90 (2000): 2

Ress, H.G. *Guarantee Treaties,* in: EPIL II (1995): 634

Ress, H.G. *Guarantee,* in: EPIL II (1995): 626

Ress, H.-K. *Non-Binding Agreements – Addendum 1995*, in: EPIL III (1997): 611

Rezac, D. *President Bush's Security Strategy and its 'pre-emptive strikes doctrine' – a legal basis for the war against Iraq?*, 7 ARIEL (2002): 223

Risse, T. *Auf dem Weg zu einer gemeinsamen Außenpolitik? Der Verfassungsvertrag und die europäische Außen- und Sicherheitspolitik*, 26 Integration 4 (2003): 564

Rizzo, A.M. *Towards a European Defence Policy*, 36 The International Spectator 3 (2001): 47.

Roberts, A. *Entangling Alliances: NATO's Security of Information Policy and the Entrenchment of State Secrecy*, 36 Cornell Int'l L.J. 2 (2003): 329

Roberts, A. *NATO, Secrecy, and the Right to Information*, East European Constitutional Review (Fall 2002/Winter 2003): 86, http://www.isn.ethz.ch/php/news/Declassification/declassification_Roberts.pdf (visited 19/12/2003)

Robertson, G. *Die NATO und die EU: Partner oder Rivalen?*, in: W. Hoyer/G.F. Kaldrack (eds), *Europäische Sicherheits- und Verteidigungspolitik* (2002): 181

Robertson, G. *Nato Evolving – Time to Deliver*, The World Today (Royal Institute of International Affairs, London), June 2003: 11

Rodríguez-Iglesias, G.C. *El enriquecimiento sin causa como fundamento de responsabilidad internacional*, 34 REDI (1982): 387

Roper, J. *Defining a common defence policy and common defence*, in: Martin, L./Roper, J. (eds) *Towards a common defence policy*, WEU-ISS (1995): 7

Rotfeld, A.D. *Europe: an emerging power*, SIPRI Yearbook 2001: 175

Ruge, B. *Europäische Sicherheits- und Verteidigungspolitik*, in: A. Weidemann/A. Simon (eds), *The Future of ESDP, A Conference Report 'The (not so) Common European Security and Defence Policy'* (2003): 33

Rynning, S. *Why not NATO? Military Planning in the European Union*, The Journal of Strategic Studies, Vol.26, No.1 (March 2003): 53

Schachter, O. *The Twilight Existence of Nonbinding International Agreements*, 71 AJIL (1977): 296

Scherff, D. *Die Fähigkeit der Europäischen Union zum aktiven Krisenmanagement: Lehren aus den Vermittlungsbemühungen 1991/92 während des jugoslawischen Bürgerkriegs und der derzeitige Konflikt im Kosovo*, 47 Südosteuropa (1998): 298

Schmalz, U. *Aufbruch zu neuer Handlungsfähigkeit: Die Gemeinsame Außen-, Sicherheits- und Verteidigungspolitik unter deutscher Ratspräsidentschaft*, 22 Integration (1999): 191

Schmidt: *Zum Verhältnis von GASP, NATO und WEU*, 25 ÖZP 4 (1996): 403

Schmitt, M.N. *Preemptive Strategies in International Law*, 24 Mich..J.Int'l L. (Winter 2003): 513

de Schoutheete, P *La cohérence par la défense – Une autre lecture de la PESD*, EU-ISS CP 71 (2004)

Schreuer, C. *Unjust Enrichment*, in: EPIL III (2000): 1243

Schroeder, W. *Verfassungsrechtliche Beziehungen zwischen Europäischer Union und Europäischen Gemeinschaften*, in: A. von Bogdandy (ed.), *Europäisches Verfassungsrecht* (2003): 376

Schwegmann, C. *EU-Friedensmissionen auf dem Balkan – eine Alternative zur NATO?*, Studien und Berichte zur Sicherheitspolitik 5/2002, Austrian Federal Ministry for Defence, http://www.bmlv.gv.at/pdf_pool/publikationen/09_euf_01_schweg.pdf (visited 12/08/2004)

Sedivy, J. in: G. Lindstrom/B. Schmitt (eds), *One year on – lessons from Iraq*, CP 68 (2004): 103

Seidelmann, R. *Das ESVP-Projekt und die EU-Krisenreaktionskräfte: Konstruktionsdefizite und politische Perspektiven*, 25 Integration 2 (2002): 111

Serra, N. in: G. Lindstrom/B. Schmitt (eds), *One year on – lessons from Iraq*, CP 68 (2004): 113

Serwer, D. *The Balkans: from American to European leadership*, in: Lindstrom, G. (ed.), *Shift or Rift: Assessing US-EU relations after Iraq*, EU-ISS (2003): 169

Seyersted, F. *Objective International Personality of Intergovernmental Organizations*, 34 Nordisk Tidsskrift for International Ret (1964): 1

Shake, K. *Constructive Duplication: Reducing EU reliance on US military assets*, CER, Working Paper (2002)

Shaw, J. *Flexibility in a 'reorganized' and 'simplified' treaty*, 40 CMLR (2003): 279

Sjursen, H.E. *Coping – or not Coping – with Change: Norway in European Security*, 5 EFAR (2000): 539

Skubiszewski, K. *Use of Force by States, Collective Security, Law of War and Neutrality*, in: M. Sørensen (ed.), *Manual of Public International Law* (1968): 739

Sloan, S. *A Perspective on the Future of the Transatlantic Bargain*, Presentation to the NATO Parliamentary Assembly, Ottawa, 4 Oct. 2001, http://www.atlanticcommunity.org/NPAtext.html (visited 29/05/03).

Sloan, S.R. *The United States and European defence*, CP 39 (2000)

Smith, D. *Europe's peacebuilding hour? – Past failures, future challenges*, 55 Journal of International Affairs (Columbia University) (2002): 441

Sofaer, A.D. *On the Necessity of Pre-emption*, 14 EJIL 2 (2003): 209

Solana, J. *The Washington Summit: A New NATO for the Next Century*, 34/2 The International Spectator (1999): 37

Stahn, C. *International Law at a Crossroads? – The Impact of September 11*, 62 HJIL (2002): 211

Stahn, C. *'Nicaragua is dead, long live Nicaragua' – the Right to Self-defence Under Art. 51 UN Charter and International Terrorism*, in: C. Walter et al. (eds), *Terrorism as a Challenge for National and International Law: Security versus Liberty?* (2003): 827

Stainier, L. *Common interests, values and criteria for action*, in: Martin/Roper (eds, 1995): 13

Stavridis, S. *'Militarising' the EU: the Concept of Civilian Power Europe Revisited*, 34 The International Spectator 4 (2001): 43

Stein, E/Carreau, D. *Law and Peaceful Change in a Subsystem: 'Withdrawal' of France from the North Atlantic Treaty Organization'*, 62 AJIL (1968): 577

Terpan, F. *Premier semestre 2004*, 60 Défense nationale 8/9 (2004): 99

Teunissen, P.J. *Strengthening the defence dimension of the EU: An evaluation of Concepts, Recent Initiatives and Developments*, 4 EFAR (1999): 327

Tiilikainen, T. *To Be or Not to Be?: An Analysis of the Legal and Political Elements of Statehood in the EU's External Identity*, 6 EFAR (2001): 223

Tofte, S. *Non-EU NATO Members and the Issue of Discrimination*, in: J. Howorth/J. Keeler (eds), *Defending Europe* (2003): 135

Tompa: K. *Ancient Coins as Cultural Property: A Cause for Concern?*, 4 J. Int'l Legal Stud. (Winter 1998): 69

Treacher, A. *From Civilian Power to Military Actor; The EU's Resistable Transformation*, 9 EFAR (2004): 49

Trempont, J. *La communauté Européenne de Défense*, 1 ICLQ (1952): 519

Triantaphyllou, D. *Balkans: The Transition from a Reduced Commitment*, Institute Note, 14 March 2003, EU-ISS – Task Forces 2003, http://www.iss-eu.org/activ/content/rep9.pdf (visited 31/04/2003)

Triantaphyllou, D. *The interplay between the EU and the United States in the Balkans*, in: Lindstrom, G. (ed.), *Shift or Rift: Assessing US-EU relations after Iraq*, EU-ISS (2003): 191

Trybus, M. *The EC treaty as an instrument of European defence integration*, 39 CMLR (2002): 1347

Vasconcelos, A. in: G. Lindstrom/B. Schmitt (eds), *One year on – lessons from Iraq*, CP 68 (2004): 121

Vasiu, M. *The role of ESDP in the new security environment*, 6 Rom. J. Int. Aff. 3/4 (2000): 128

Velitchkova, G. *NATO-OSCE Interaction in Peacekeeping: Experience and Prospects in Southeast Europe*, NATO/EAPC Research Fellowship paper (2002): 17-18, http://www.nato.int/acad/fellow/99-01/Velitchkova.pdf (visited 13/03/05)

Venturoni, G. *NATO and the Challenges of European Security*, 34 The International Spectator 2 (1999): 43

Verbeke, J. *A new security concept for a new Europe*, 51 Studia diplomatica (1998): 125

Verosta, S. *Alliance*, in: EPIL I (1992): 119

Verosta, S. *Casus foederis*, in: EPIL I (1992): 543

Vinçon, S. et al. *Défense: quels projets après 2002?*, 57 Défense nationale 6 (2001): 82

Vincze, H. *Beyond symbolism: the EU's first military operation seen in its context* (2003), http://www.weltpolitik.net/texte/policy/concordia/beyond_symbolism.pdf (visited 15/08/2004)

Virally, M. *La distinction entre textes internationaux de portée juridique et textes internationaux dépourvus de portée juridique*, 60 (I) AnnIDI (1983): 328

Wallander, C.A. *Institutional Assets and Adaptability: NATO After the Cold War*, 54 International Organization 4 (2000): 705

Walker, G.K. *Anticipatory Self-Defense in the Charter Era: What the Treaties Have Said*, 31 Cornell Int'l L. J. (1998): 321

Walker, G.K. *The lawfulness of Operation Enduring Freedom's Self-Defense Responses*, Valp. U. L. Rev. (Spring 2003): 489

Walt, S.M. *The Ties That Fray*, The National Interest (1998/1999, Winter edition): 13

Wegener, B. Commentary to Art. 255 TEC, in: C. Caliess/H.J. Blanke (eds), *Kommentar zu EU-Vertrag und EG-Vertrag* (2nd edn 2002): 2254

Weller, M. *The European Union within the 'European Security Architecture'*, in: M. Koskenniemi, *International Law Aspects of the European Union* (1998): 57

Wedgwood, R. *The Promise of and Obstacles to Effective Peace-Keeping by the CIS, NATO, OSCE, WEU and UN*, ASIL/NVIR Proceedings 1997: 57

Wengler, W. *Die Wirkungen nichtrechtlicher Verträge*, 22 AVR (1984): 307

Wessel, R.A. *The Constitutional Relationship between the European Union and the European Community: Consequences for the Relationship with the Member States*, in: A. von Bogdandy/J.H.H. Weiler (eds), *European Integration – The New German Scholarship*; Jean Monnet Working Paper 9/03.9 (2003)

Wessel, R.A. *The State of Affairs in EU Security and Defence Policy: The breakthrough in the Treaty of Nice*, 8 JCSL 2 (2003): 265

Wessel, R.A. *Revisiting the International Legal Status of the EU*, 5 EFAR (2000): 507

Wessel, R.A. *The EU as a Black Widow: Devouring the WEU to Give Birth to a European Security and Defence Policy*, in: V. Kronenberger (ed.), *The European Union and the international legal order* (2001): 405

White, N.D. *Commentary on the Report of the Panel on United Nations Peace Operations (The Brahimi Report)*, 6 JCSL 1 (2001): 127

de Wijk, R. in: G. Lindstrom/B. Schmitt (eds), *One year on – lessons from Iraq*, CP 68 (2004): 41

de Wijk, R. *The Reform of ESDP and EU–NATO Cooperation*, 39 The International Spectator 1 (2004): 71

Winn, N. *Towards a Common European Security and Defence Policy? The Debate on NATO, the European Army and Transatlantic Security*, 8 Geopolitics 2 (2003): 47

Wolfrum, R. *International Organizations, Headquarters*, in: EPIL II: 1309

Wouters, J./ Naert, F. *How effective is the European Security Architecture? Lessons from Bosnia and Kosovo*, 50 ICLQ (2001): 540

Wright, J. *Trusting Flexible friends: the dangers of flexibility in NATO and the Western European Union/European Union*, 20 CSP 1 (1999): 111

Yesson, E. *NATO, EU and Russia: Reforming Europe's Security Institutions*, 6 EFAR (2001): 197

Zemanek, K. *International Organizations, Treaty-Making Power*, in: EPIL III (1997): 1343. – *Addendum 1991*: 1346

Zielonka, J. *Transatlantic Relations beyond the CFSP*, 35 The International Spectator 4 (2000): 27

Žourek, J. *La notion de légitime défense en droit international*, 56 AnnIDI (1975): 1

Zuleeg, M. *International Organizaions, Implied* Powers, in: EPIL II: 1313

de Zwaan, J.W. *The Legal personality of the European Communities and the European Union*, 30 NYIL (1999): 75

DOCUMENTS

EU

Council

A Secure European in a Better World – European Security Strategy, 8 Dec. 2003, Council Doc. 15895/03

Concept for the European Union (EU) Military Operation in Bosnia and Herzegovina (BiH) – Operation Althea, 29 Sept. 2004, Council Doc. 12576/04

Conference on EU Capability Improvement, Brussels, 19 November 2001, Statement on Improving European Military Capabilities, CP 51, p. 100

Council Conclusions on ESDP, 14 May 2004, Council Doc. 9385/04

Council Dec. 2000/23/EC, 6 December 1999, on the improvement of information on the Council's legislative activities and the public register of Council documents, OJ L 9/22 of 13/1/2000

Council Dec. 2000/396/EC, ECSC, Euratom, 5 June 2000, adopting the Council's Rules of Procedure, OJ L 149/21 of 23/6/2000

Council Dec. 2000/527/EC, 15 Aug. 2000, amending Decision 93/731/EC on public access to Council documents and Council Decision 2000/23/EC on the improvement of information on the Council's legislative activities and the public register of Council document, OJ L 212/9 of 23/8/2000

Council Dec. 2001/264/EC, 19 March 2001, adopting the Council's security regulations, OJ L 101/1 of 11/4/2001.

Council Dec. 2001/352/CFSP, 9 April 2001, concerning the conclusion of the Agreement between the European Union and the Federal Republic of Yugoslavia (FRY) on the activities of the European Union Monitoring Mission (EUMM) in the FRY, OJ EC L 125/1 of 5/5/2001

Council Dec. 2001/682/CFSP, 30 Aug. 2001, concerning the conclusion of the Agreement between the European Union and the Former Yugoslav Republic of Macedonia (FYROM) on the activities of the European Union Monitoring Mission (EUMM) in FYROM, OJ EC L 241/1 of 11/9/2001

Council Dec. 2002/845/CFSP, 30 Sept. 2002, concerning the conclusion of the Agreement between the European Union and Bosnia and Herzegovina (BiH) on the activities of the European Union Police Mission (EUPM) in BiH, OJ EU L 293/1 of 29/10/2002

Council Dec. 2003/157/CFSP, 19 Dec. 2002, concerning the conclusion of the Agreement between the European Union and the Republic of Poland on the participation of this State to the European Union Police Mission (EUPM) in Bosnia and Herzegovina, OJ EU L 64/37 of 7/3/2003

Council Dec. 2003/202/CFSP, 18 March 2003, relating to the launch of the EU military operation in the Former Yugoslav Republic of Macedonia, OJ L 76/43 of 22/3/2003

Council Dec. 2003/211/CFSP, 24 Feb. 2003, concerning the conclusion of the Agreement between the European Union and the North Atlantic Treaty Organisation on the Security of Information, OJ L 80/35 of 27/3/2003

Council Dec. 2003/252/CFSP, 24 Feb. 2003, concerning the conclusion of the Agreement between the European Union and the Republic of Albania on the activities of the European Union Monitoring Mission (EUMM) in the Republic of Albania, OJ EU L 93/49 of 10/4/2003

Council Dec. 2003/563/CFSP, 29 July 2003, on the extension of the European Union military operation in the Former Yugoslav Republic of Macedonia, OJ L 190/20 of 30/7/2003

Council Dec. 2003/92/CFSP, 27 Jan. 2003, on the European Union military operation in the Former Yugoslav Republic of Macedonia, OJ L 34/26 of 11/2/2003

Council Dec. 2004/803/CFSP, 25 Nov. 2004, on the launching of the European Union military operation in Bosnia and Herzegovina, OJ L 353/21 of 27/11/2004

Council Dec. 98/319/EC, 27 April 1998, relating to the procedures whereby officials and employees of the General Secretariat of the Council may be allowed access to classified information held by the Council, OJ L 140/12 of 12/5/1998

Council Dec. amending Decision 93/731/EC on public access to Council documents and Decision 2000/23/EC on the improvement of information on the Council's legislative activities and on the public register of Council documents, Statement by the European Commission, Council Doc. 10782/00

Council Dec. concerning the conclusion of agreements between the European Union and the Republic of Iceland, the Kingdom of Norway and Romania establishing a framework for the participation of the Republic of Iceland, the Kingdom of Norway and Romania in the European Union crisis management operations, 5 Oct. 2004, Council Doc. 12435/04

Council Dec. No 24/95 on Measures for the Protection of Classified Information applicable to the General Secretariat of the Council, annexed to Staff Note: Decision on measures to protect classified information, 30/1/1995, contained in Council Doc. 9151/95

Council Dec. of 10 May 1999 concerning the arrangements for enhanced cooperation between the European Union and the Western European Union (1999/404/CFSP), OJ L 153/1 of 19/6/1999

Council Dec. of 20 Dec. 1993 on public access to Council documents (93/731/EC), OJ L 340/43 of 31/12/1993

Council Dec. of 22 Jan. 2001 setting up the Military Committee (2001/79/CFSP), OJ EC L 27/4 of 30/1/2001

Council Dec. of 22 Jan. 2001 setting up the Military Staff (2001/80/CFSP), OJ EC L 27/7 of 30/1/2001

Council Dec. of 22 Jan. 2001 setting up the Political and Security Committee (2001/78/CFSP), OJ EC L 27/1 of 30/1/2001

Council Dec. of 27 April 1998 relating to the procedures whereby officials and employees of the General Secretariat of the Council may be allowed access

The EU–NATO Relationship: A Legal and Political Perspective

to classified information held by the Council (98/319/EC), OJ L 140/12 of
12/5/1998

Council Dec. on the release of information under the EU–NATO Security Agreement,
24 March 2003, Council Doc. 7588/03

Council Dec. of 17 Feb. 2004 establishing a mechanism to administer the financing
of the common costs of European Union operations having military or defence
implications, Council Doc. 5770/04

Council Doc. 10282/04, 9 June 2004, EU Council Secretariat, Progress Report on
the Battle Group Concept

Council Doc. 12869/02, 8 Oct. 2002, Release of EU classified information to third
states and international organisations

Council Doc. 13708/00, 22 Nov. 2000, ESDP: Organisational and implementing
measures in the General Secretariat of the Council

Council Doc. 6574/04, 20 Feb. 2004, Initial Public Master Messages on possible
ESDP mission, including a military component, in Bosnia and Herzegovina

Council Doc. 6916/1/03 REV 1, 6 March 2003, EU-led Operation in Former Yugoslav
Republic of Macedonia – Master messages

Council Doc. 7421/03, 13 March 2003, Note d'information sur les travaux du
Parlement Européen (Mr. Gollinsch, Mr. Van Orden)

Council Doc. SN 3328/1/00 REV 1, at 4., reprinted in: Statewatch, *Council Security
Plan: background to the 'Solana Decision'*, http://www.statewatch.org/secret/
solana1.htm (visited 02/09/03)

Council Joint Action 2003/423/CFSP of 5 June 2003 on the European Union military
operation in the Democratic Republic of Congo, OJ L 143/50 of 11/6/2003

Council Joint Action 2003/92/CFSP of 27 January 2003 on the European Union
military operation in the Former Yugoslav Republic of Macedonia, Art. 10, OJ L
34/26 of 11/02/2003

Council Joint Action 2004/551/CFSP on the establishment of the European Defence
Agency, 12 July 2004, OJ L 245/17 of 17/07/04

Council Joint Action establishing a European Union Institute for Security Studies of
20 July 2001, OJ L 200/1 of 25/7/2001

Council Joint Action establishing a European Union Satellite Centre of 20 July 2001,
OJ L 200/5 of 25/7/2001

Council Joint Action on the European Union military operation in Bosnia and
Herzegovina, 12 July 2003, Council Doc. 11226/2/04 REV 2 (en)

Council Joint Action on the European Union Police Mission in the Former Yugoslav
Republic of Macedonia (EUPOL 'Proxima'), 29 Sept. 2003, CP 67, pp. 222

Council letter to Jelle van Burren, dated 26 June (agreed at the General Affairs
Council on 10 July 2000) in response to a request for access to the Outcome
of Proceedings of the Interim Military Working Group (IMWG), Statewatch,
House of Lords – European Union – Eighth Report, http://www.statewatch.org/
news/2001/mar/3105.htm (visited 30/08/03)

Council letter to Tony Bunyan, 14 Aug. 2000 in response to a request for access to
the document setting out the options for changing the 1993 Decision put before

the COREPER meeting on 26 July, Statewatch, House of Lords – European Union – Eighth Report, http://www.statewatch.org/news/2001/mar/3105.htm (visited 30/08/03)

Council of the European Union, Agreements Office Website, Introduction, http://ue.eu.int/accords/pres.asp?lang=en (visited 25/08/03)

Council of the European Union, EU–NATO Cooperation, Background – the Framework for Permanent Relations and Berlin Plus, http://ue.eu.int/uedocs/cmsUpload/03-11-11%20Berlin%20Plus%20press%20note%20BL.pdf (visited 11/12/04)

Council of the European Union, Staff Note: Decision on measures to protect classified information, 30 Jan. 1995, contained in Council Doc. 9151/95

Council Security Committee, Release of EU Classified Information to third States and International Organisations – Authority Release EUCI to NATO, 18 March 2003, Council Doc. 7558/03

Council, 2563rd meeting, External Relations, Brussels, 23 Feb. 2004, Council Doc. 6294/04

Decision of the Council of the EU of 1 Jan. 1995 95/1/EC, Euratom, ECSC, OJ L 001/1-219 of 1 Jan. 1995

Decision of the Secretary-General of the Council/High Representative for the Common and Security Policy of 27 July 2000, 2000/C 239/01, OJ C 239/1 of 23/8/2000

Declaration of the Presidency on behalf of the European Union on the closure of Moldovan schools in Transnistria, Council Doc. 11771/04, 28 July 2004

Declaration on Solidarity against Terrorism, 25 March 2004, annexed to the 'Declaration on Combating Terrorism', Brussels European Council 25/26 Council Doc. 7906/04

Draft Council Conclusions on ESDP, 14 May 2004, Council Doc. 9485/04

Draft Council Conclusions on ESDP, 22 Nov. 2004, Council Doc. 14887/2/04 REV 2

Draft ESDP Presidency Report, 13 Dec. 2004, Council Doc. 15547/04

EU Council Press Briefing announcement, Launch of EU Operation Althea in Bosnia and Herzegovina, Brussels, 29 Nov. 2004

EU Council Secretariat Factsheet, EU military operation in Bosnia and Herzegovina (Operation EUFOR – Althea), ATH/03 (update 3), 29 Nov. 2004

EU Plan of Action on Combating Terrorism, 11 June 2004, Council Doc. 10010/3/04 REV 3

Note from the General Secretariat of the Council to the Security Committee, *Release of EU classified information to third parties and international organisations*, 8 October 2002, Council Doc. 12869/02

Operation *Concordia* – Lessons Learned Process, Council Doc. 15484/04, 28 Nov. 2003

Preliminary Draft Reply to Written Question E-0334/03 put by C. Muscarini, p. 3, Council Doc. 7881/03, 31 March 2003

Principles and arrangements for setting up the four working groups, Council Doc. 10025/1/00 REV 1, 5 July 2000

Progress report on the Battle Group Concept, 9 June 2004, Council Doc. 10282/04

PSC Decision BiH/1/2004 on the acceptance of third States' contributions to the European Union military operation in Bosnia and Herzegovina, 21 Sept. 2004, OJ L 324/20 of 27/10/2004, amended by OJ L 357/39 of 2/12/2004

PSC Decision BiH/3/2004 on the setting-up of the Committee of Contributors for the European Union military operation in Bosnia and Herzegovina, 29 Sept. 2004, OJ L 325/64 of 28/10/2004, amended by OJ L 357/39 of 2/12/2004

PSC Decision BiH/4/2004, OJ L 357/38 of 2/12/2004

PSC Decision of 1 July 2003 on the acceptance of third States' contributions, 2003/500/CFSP, OJ L 179/19 of 9/7/2003

PSC Decision of 11 July 2003 on the setting up of a Committee of Contributors, 2003/529/CFSP, OJ L 184/13 of 23/7/2003.

PSC Decision of 31 July 2003, amending the Political and Security Committee Decision DRC/1/2003 on the acceptance of third States' contributions to the EU military operation in the Democratic Republic of Congo, OJ L 206/32 of 15/8/2003

Reply given by the Council Working Party on General Affairs to a Written Question (E-0007/01), Council Doc. 7472/01, 2 April 2001

Security Standards for the Protection of Classified Information exchanged between NATO and the EU, 3 June 2003, Council Doc. 10006/03

Sixth Meeting of the Cooperation Council between the European Union and the Republic of Moldova, Council Doc. 6295/04, 24 Feb. 2004

Solana, J. EU CFSP-HR, comments on resignation of H. Holkeri, UN Special Representative to Kosovo, 25 May 2004, Council Doc. S0144/04

Commission

Answer given by Mr Patten on behalf of the Commission to a Written Question (E-0008/01), 21 Feb. 2001, OJ 187 E/154 of 5/7/2001

Answer given by Mr Patten on behalf of the Commission to a Written Question (E-3263/00), 30 Nov. 2000, OJ C 174 E/30 of 19/6/2001.

Answer given by Mr Patten on behalf of the Commission to a Written Question (E-1116/01), OJ C 318/208 of 13/11/2001

Commission Decision of 30 November 1994 on the security measures applicable to classified information produced or transmitted in connection with the activities of the European Union (C(94)3282), European Commission Security Office, Brussels, 1 March 1995

Commission Decision of 25 February 1999 relating to the procedures whereby officials and employees of the European Commission may be allowed access to classified information held by the Commission (1999/218/EC), OJ L 80/22 of 25/3/1999

Commission Decision of 29 November 2001 amending its internal Rules of Procedure, 2001/844/EC, ECSC, Euratom, OJ L 317/1 of 3/12/2001

Commission Opinion on the Application by the Republic of Cyprus for Membership – Extracts, doc/93/5 – 30 June 1993, http://europa.eu.int/comm/enlargement/cyprus/op_06_93 /index.htm (visited 14/12/04)

Commission Proposal regarding public access to European Parliament, Council and Commission Documents, COM(2000) 30 final/2, 2000/0032 (COD)

Parliament

European Parliament Report, 'Adoption of the Report on "the Progress Achieved in the Implementation of the CFSP"', Strasbourg, 26 September 2002, CP 57, p. 118

European Parliament Resolution on the Annual Report from the Council to the European Parliament on the Main Aspects and Basic Choices for CFSP, including the Financial Implications for the General Budget of the European Union, Strasbourg, 23 Oct. 2003, CP 67, p. 235

Letter from Ana Palacio, Chair of the Legal Affairs Committee, to Nicole Fontaine, President of the European Parliament, reprinted in: Statewatch News online, *Greens/EFA challenge Solana's 'military coup'*, http://www.statewatch.org/news/sept00/04greenprl.htm (visited 30/08/2003)

Resolution of the European Parliament on the gradual establishment of a common defence policy for the European Union, A4-0171/98, 14 May 1998, OJ C 167/190 of 1/6/1998

Resolution on openness within the European Union, A4-0476/98, OJ C 140/20 of 14/4/1999

Resolution on the European Council Report to the European Parliament on the progress achieved by the Union in 1997, 21 Oct. 1998, OJ C 341/85 of 9/11/1998

Written question E-0334/03 by Cristiana Muscardini (UEN) to the Council, 12.02.2003, reprinted in: Council Doc. 7881/03

Intergovernmental Conference (IGC)

IGC 2003 – Naples Ministerial Conclave: Presidency Proposal, CIG 52/03 ADD 1, 28 Nov. 2003

IGC 2003 – Defence, CIG 57/03, 2 Dec. 2003, reprinted in: CP 67, p. 433

IGC 2003 – European Security and Defence Policy, CIG 60/03 ADD 1, 9 Dec. 2003, reprinted in: CP 67, p. 449

Letter from Erkki Tuomioja (FM Finland), Brian Cowen (FM Ireland), Benita Ferrero-Waldner (FM Austria) and Laila Freivalds (FM Sweden) to F. Frattini (EU Council President) – IGC 2003 – European Security and Defence Policy, CIG 62/03, 5 Dec. 2003, reprinted in: CP 67, p. 437

Provisional consolidated version of the draft Treaty establishing a Constitution for Europe, CIG 86/04, 25 June 2004
Treaty Establishing a Constitution for Europe, Brussels, CIG 87/04, 6 Aug. 2004

Other

Code of Conduct concerning public access to Council and Commission documents, 93/730/EC, OJ L 340/41 of 31/12/1993
Declaration (No 35) on Article 255 (ex Article 191a(1)) of the Treaty establishing the European Community, http://europa.eu.int/eur-lex/en/treaties/dat/amsterdam. html#0137050052 (visited 17/12/2003)
Declaration No.6 annexed to the final act of the Treaty of Amsterdam, http://europa. eu.int/eur-lex/en/treaties/selected/livre468.html (visited 23/07/03)
Declaration on Draft Article J.14 [now Art. 24] TEU, annexed to the Final Act of the Treaty of Amsterdam, http://europa.eu.int/eur-lex/en/treaties/dat/amsterdam. html#0131010021 (visited 28/12/03)
Draft Treaty Establishing a Constitution for Europe, adopted by consensus by the European Convention on 13 June and 10 July 2003, 2003/C OJ 169/1 of 18 July 2003
European Council, Barcelona, 15–16 March 2002, Presidency Conclusions, CP 57, pp. 48
European Council, Brussels, 12 Dec. 2003, Presidency Conclusions, CP 67, pp. 292
European Council, Brussels, 14 June 2004, Presidency Report on ESDP, Council Doc. 10547/04
European Council, Brussels, 16–17 Dec. 2004, Presidency Conclusions, Council Doc. 16238/04
European Council, Brussels, 17–18 June 2004, Presidency Conclusions, Council Doc. 10679/04
European Council, Brussels, 24–25 Oct. 2002, Presidency Conclusions, CP 57, p. 135
European Council, Cologne, 3–4 June 1999, Presidency Conclusions, CP 47, p. 41
European Council, Copenhagen, 12–13 Dec. 2002, Presidency Conclusions, CP 57, p. 165
European Council, Copenhagen, 21–22 June 1993, Presidency Conclusions, Bull. E.C., 6-1993
European Council, Göteborg, 15–16 June 2001, CP 51, p. 30
European Council, Helsinki, 10–11 Dec. 1999, CP 47, p. 82
European Council, Laeken, 14–15 Dec. 2001, CP 57, p. 110
European Council, Nice, 7–9 Dec. 2000, Presidency Conclusions, CP 47, p. 168
European Council, Santa Marta da Feira, 19–20 June 2000, CP 47, p. 120
European Council, Seville, 21–22 June 2002, Presidency Conclusions, CP 57, p. 73
European Council, Thessaloniki, 19–20 June 2003, Presidency Conclusions, CP 67, p. 142

Extraordinary European Council, Brussels, 28 Oct. 1993, Presidency Conclusions, Bull. E.C. 12-1993

Final Act to the Treaty of Accession to the European Union 2003, 35. Declaration by the Republic of Malta on neutrality, OJ L 236 of 23/9/2003, p. 982

GAERC Conclusions, 11 Oct. 2004, Council Doc. 12767/04

GAERC meeting with EU defence ministers, Intervention by J. Solana, Brussels, 17 Nov. 2003, CP 67, p. 273

GAERC, 13 Sept. 2004, Council Conclusions on ESDP, Council Doc. 12067/04

GAERC, Brussels, 17 Nov. 2003, Conclusions on ESDP, CP 67, p. 256

GAERC, Brussels, 19-20 May 2003, Conclusions, European Security and Defence Policy, CP 67, p. 85

GAERC, Brussels, 21 July 2003, Conclusions on Africa – Democratic Republic of Congo and the Great Lakes Region, CP 67, p. 194

GAERC, Brussels, 24 Feb. 2003, Conclusions, European Security and Defence Policy, CP 67, p. 46

GAERC, Brussels, 8–9 Dec. 2003, Conclusions, European Security and Defence Policy, EU military rapid response, CP 67, p. 287

General Affairs Council, Brussels, 13 May 2002, European Security and Defence Policy, under 'Orientations by the Presidency on the re-inforcement of cooperation in the field of armaments', CP 57, p. 57

German Presidency Paper, Bonn, 24 Feb. 1999, Informal Reflection at WEU on Europe's Security and Defence, CP 47, p. 14

Informal European summit, Pörtschach, 24–25 October 1998, Press Conferences by British Prime Minister Tony Blair (Extracts), CP 47, p. 1

Informal meeting of EU defence ministers, Ecouen, 22 Sept. 2000, Presidency Conclusions, CP 47, p. 143

Informal meeting of EU defence ministers, Rethymnon (Greece), 4–5 Oct. 2002, Summary of the Intervention of J. Solana, EU High Representative for the CFSP, CP 57, p. 132

Informal meeting of EU defence ministers, Rome, 29 Aug. 2003, British Non-Paper 'Food for Thought', CP 67, p. 204

Informal meeting of EU defence ministers, Rome, 3–4 Oct. 2003, Remarks by J. Solana, CFSP-HR, CP 67, p. 231

Informal meeting of EU defence ministers, Saragossa, 22–23 March 2002, Summary of Interventions by Javier Solana, EU High Representative for the CFSP, under 'EU–NATO cooperation', CP 57, p. 49

Informal meeting of EU foreign ministers, Eltville, 13–14 March 1999, German proposal, CP 47, p. 17

Joint Declaration by the Heads of State and Government of the EU, the President of the European Parliament, the President of the European Commission and the HR-CFSP, Brussels, 14 September 2001, CP 51, p. 147

Joint Declaration on EU-UN cooperation in Crisis Management, New York, 24 Sept. 2003, CP 67, p. 217

Meeting of defence ministers, GAERC, Brussels, 19 Nov. 2002, Summary of the intervention by J. Solana, CP 57, p. 147

Meeting of European Union defence ministers, Sintra, 28 Feb. 2000, CP 47, p. 94

Meeting of European Union defence ministers, Sintra, 28 Feb. 2000, Annex: Elaboration of the Headline Goal – 'Food for Thought' Paper on headline and capability goals, CP 47, p. 102

Protocol No. 10 to Treaty of Accession to the European Union 2003, OJ L 236 of 23/9/2003, p. 955

Regular Report from the Commission on Cyprus' Progress Towards Accession, November 1998, http://europa.eu.int/comm/enlargement/report_11_98/pdf/en/cyprus_en.pdf (visited 14/12/04)

Treaty of Amsterdam, Final Act, Protocol on the position of Denmark, OJ C 340 of 10/11/1997, p. 355

NATO

Final Communiqués of Sessions of the North Atlantic Council (by date)

17 Sept. 1949, setting up the Defence Ctte., the Military Ctte., the Military Standing Group, and five Regional Planning Groups

18 Nov. 1949, establishing a Defence Financial and Economic Committee

16–18 Sept. 1950, setting up a centralised command

20–25 Feb. 1952, appointing a Secretary-General heading a unified international secretariat, and the NAC in permanent session in Paris

5–16 Dec. 1966, establishing a Nuclear Defence Affairs Ctte. and a Nuclear Planning Group

5–6 Dec. 1978, MoU for the setting up of an AWACS programme

25–26 June 1980, establishing a 'Science for Stability' programme

OTHER

An Alliance for the 21st Century – Washington Summit Communiqué issued at the meeting of the North Atlantic Council in Washington, D.C. on 24 April 1999

The Alliance's Strategic Concept, Agreed by the Heads of State and Government participating in the meeting of the North Atlantic Council in Rome on 7–8 November 1991, reprinted in: NATO Handbook (October 1995), p. 235

The Alliance's Strategic Concept, Approved by the Heads of State and Government participating in the meeting of the North Atlantic Council in Washington D.C. on 23–24 April 1999, CP 47, p. 24

NATO Office of Information and Press, *The Combined Joint Task Forces Concept*, in: The Reader's Guide to the NATO Summit in Washington, 23-25 April 1999, p. 67

Briefing Note describing rationale for adoption of new NATO Security Policy. Released in response to an Access to Information Act request to the Canadian Department of Foreign Affairs and International Trade, File A-2002-00184, October 2002

Bi-MNC Directive MC-327/1, 'NATO Doctrine for Peace Support Operations', Brussels, 16 October 1998

Chairman's Summary of the NATO Aspirant Countries Defense Ministerial Meeting, Sofia 12–13 October 2000, http://www.expandnato.org/sofia.html (visited 04/10/03)

Charter on a Distinctive Partnership between the North Atlantic Organization and Ukraine, 9 July 1997, http://www.nato.int/docu/basictxt/ukrchrt.htm (visited 28/08/03)

Declaration on a transformed North Atlantic Alliance issued by the Heads of State and Government participating in the meeting of the North Atlantic Council, London, 6 July 1990 ('The London Declaration'), http://www.nato.int/docu/basictxt/b900706a.htm (visited 11/08/2004)

Declaration on Terrorism, issued a the Meeting of the North Atlantic Council in Foreign Ministers Session, Brussels, 2 April 2004, NATO Press Release (2004)057

Final Communiqué of the NATO Ministerial Meeting in Berlin, 3 June 1996, NATO Press Release M-NAC-1(96)63

Founding Act on Mutual Relations, Cooperation and Security between NATO and the Russian Federation, 27 May 1997, 36 ILM 1006 (1997)

Istanbul Summit Communiqué issued by the Head of State and Government participating in the meeting of the North Atlantic Council, 28 June 2004, NATO Press Release (2004)096

Joint Press Statement by NATO-SG G. Robertson and the EU Presidency at the NATO Ministerial Meeting, Madrid, 3 June 2003, NATO Press Release (2003)056

Letter from B. Austin, Acting Director, NATO Office of Security, to G. Watson, Chair of the Committee of Citizen's Freedoms and Rights, 23 Aug. 2000, NOS/2(2000)102, http://www.statewatch.org/news/sept00/NATO.PDF (visited 29/08/2003)

List of NATO's Comminiqués since 1990 Referring to the Mediterranean Region and/or NATO's Mediterranean Dialogue, http://www.nato.int/med-dial/comm.htm (visited 04/10/03)

Meeting of the North Atlantic Council in Defence Ministers Session, Brussels, 1 Dec. 2003, Final Communiqué, NATO Press Release (2003)148

Meeting of the North Atlantic Council in Defence Ministers Session, Brussels, 2 Dec. 1999, Final Communiqué, NATO Press Release D(99)156

Meeting of the North Atlantic Council in Defence Ministers Session, Brussels, 5 Dec. 2000, Final Communiqué, NATO Press Release M-NAC-D-2(2000)114

Ministerial Meeting of the Defence Planning Committee and the Nuclear Planning Group, Final Communiqué, NATO Press Release M-DPC/NPG-2(99)157, Dec. 2, 1999

Ministerial Meeting of the Defence Planning Committee and the Nuclear Planning Group, Final Communiqué, NATO Press Release M-DPC/NPG-1(2000)59, Dec. 8, 2000

Ministerial Meeting of the North Atlantic Council /North Atlantic Cooperation Council, NATO Headquarters, Brussels, 10–11 January 1994, Declaration of the Heads of State and Government, (NATO Press Communiqué M-1(94)3)

Ministerial Meeting of the North Atlantic Council held at NATO Headquarters, Brussels, 15 Dec. 1999, Final Communiqué, NATO Press Release M-NAC2(99)166

Ministerial Meeting of the North Atlantic Council held at NATO headquarters, Brussels on 14–15 December 2000, Final Communiqué, NATO Press Release M-NAC 2(2000)124

Ministerial Meeting of the North Atlantic Council held in Madrid, 3 June 2003, Final Communiqué

Ministerial Meeting of the North Atlantic Council, 9 Dec. 2004, Final Communiqué, NATO Press Release (2004)170

Ministerial Meeting of the North Atlantic Council, Berlin, 3 June 1996, Final Communiqué, NATO Press Communiqué M-NAC-1(96)63

Ministerial Meeting of the North Atlantic Council, Brussels, 4 Dec. 2003, NATO Press Release (2003)152

Ministerial Meeting of the North Atlantic Council, Florence, 24 May 2000, Final Communiqué, NATO Press Release M-NAC-1(2000)52

Ministerial Meeting of the North Atlantic Council, Reykjavik, 14 May 2002, Final Communiqué, NATO Press Release 1(2002)59

Ministerial Meeting of the North Atlantic Council/North Atlantic Cooperation Council, NATO Headquarters, Brussels, 10–11 Jan. 1994, Declaration of the Heads of State and Government, NATO Press Communiqué M-1(94)3

NACC Ad Hoc Group on Cooperation in Peacekeeping (established by the Ministerial Meeting of the NAC, 10–11 June 1993, http://www.nato.int/docu/comm/49-95/c930611b.htm (visited 28/07/04)

NATO Archives, Policy Statement (Extracts), http://www.nato.int/archives/policy.htm (visited 03/10/03)

NATO Budapest Ministerial, 29–30 May 2001, Final Communiqué, NATO Press Release M-NAC 1(2001)77

NATO Fact Sheets, Strengthening European Security and Defence Capabilities, under 'EU–NATO relations develop', 15 Dec. 2000

NATO Handbook, NATO Office of Information and Press (1995)

NATO Handbook, NATO Office of Information and Press (2001)

NATO International Military Staff Press Release after the First Meeting of EU and NATO Military Committees, 12 June 2001, CP 51, p. 19

NATO Istanbul Summit Communiqué issued by the Heads of State and Government participating in the meeting of the North Atlantic Council, Istanbul, 28 June 2004, NATO Press Release (2004)096

NATO Membership Action Plan, 24 April 1999, NATO Press Release NAC-S(99)66 and http://www.nato.int/issues/map/index.html (visited 11/08/2004)

NATO Ministerial Communiqué, Athens 4–6 May 1962, http://www.nato.int/docu/comm/49-95/c620504a.htm (visited 06/05/04)

NATO Parliamentary Assembly, Res. 317 on NATO Structural Reform and ESDP (2002)

NATO Prague Summit Declaration by Heads of State and Government, 21 November 2002, NATO Press Release (2000) 127 and 42 ILM 244

NATO Press Release (2003)40, 16 April 2003, Conclusion of Operation Display Deterrence and Article 4 security consultations

NATO Press Release (2004)125, 16 Sept. 2004, NATO Secretary General invited to attend European Union Meeting

NATO Press Release (2004)165, 26 Nov. 2004, North Atlantic Council meeting with Political and Security Committee of the European Union

NATO Press Release (96)66, 2 May, 1996, Signature of Security Agreement between NATO and WEU

NATO Press Release (98)149, 7 Dec. 1998, Austrian Minister of Foreign Affairs in his capacity as President of EU Council Meets with NATO Secretary General

NATO Research and Technical Organisation (RTO) Technical Publication Policy, 4th Issue – March 2001, Section VINATO/PfP UNCLASSIFIED, AC/323-D/22, http://faculty.maxwell.syr.edu/asroberts/foi/library/nato_rto_pubrules.pdf(visited 04/10/03)

NATO/WEU Operation Sharp Guard, IFOR Final Factsheet, 2 Oct. 1996, http://www.nato.int/ifor/general/shrp-grd.htm (visited 21/12/04)

North Atlantic Cooperation Council (inauguration announced in the NATO Ministerial Communiqué from 20 Dec. 1991, http://www.nato.int/docu/comm/49-95/c911220a.htm (visited 28/07/04)

North Atlantic Council, Brussels, 14–15 Dec. 2000, Final Communiqué, CP 47, pp. 222

North Atlantic Council, 12 Sept. 2001, NATO Press Release (2001)124

North Atlantic Council, statement on Iraq Issued by the Heads of State and Government participating in the meeting of the Istanbul, 28 June 2004, NATO Press Release (2004)098

North Atlantic Council, Washington, DC, 24 April 1999, Final Communiqué, CP 47, pp. 20

Partnership for Peace Programme (launched by the Ministerial Meeting of the NAC/NACC, 10–11 Jan. 1994, http://www.nato.int/docu/comm/49-95/c940110a.htm)

Security within the North Atlantic Organization, Supplemental Security Principles and Practices, NATO Confidential Supplement to Document C-M(55)15(Final), 1st January, 1961, http://faculty.maxwell.syr.edu/asroberts/foi/library/gsoia / NATO_CM_55_15_Supp. pdf (visited 03/10/03)

Security within the North Atlantic Treaty Organization, Note by the Secretary General, Chairman of the Council, NATO Document No. C-M(55)15(Final), last available issue of 31st July, 1964, http://faculty.maxwell.syr.edu/asroberts/foi/library/gsoia /NATO_CM_55_15_final_1964.pdf (visited 03/10/03)

Study on NATO Enlargement (1995), http://www.nato.int/docu/basictxt/enl-9501.htm (visited 04/04/2004)

INTERNATIONAL TREATIES AND OTHER INSTRUMENTS

Treaties and non-binding agreements

Agreement between the EU and Cyprus on the latter's participation in the EU's peacekeeping operation in the Democratic Republic of Congo, OJ L 253/22 of 7/10/2003

Agreement between the European Union and Bosnia and Herzegovina (BiH) on the activities of the European Union Police Mission (EUPM) IN BiH, 4 Oct. 2002, OJ EU L 293/2 of 29/10/2002

Agreement between the European Union and the Federal Republic of Yugoslavia on the activities of the European Union Monitoring Mission (EUMM) in the Federal Republic of Yugoslavia, 9 April 2001, OJ EC L 125/2 of 5/5/2001

Agreement between the European Union and the Former Yugoslav Republic of Macedonia on the activities of the European Union Monitoring Mission (EUMM) in the Former Yugoslav Republic of Macedonia, 31 Aug. 2001, OJ EC L 241/2 of 11/9/2001

Agreement between the European Union and the North Atlantic Treaty Organisation on the Security of Information of 14 March 2003, OJ EU L 80/36 of 27/3/2003

Agreement between the European Union and the Swiss Confederation on the participation of the Swiss Confederation in the European Union military crisis management operation in Bosnia and Herzegovina (Operation ALTHEA), Council Doc. 15653, 13 Dec. 2004

Agreement between the Member States of the European Union concerning the status of military and civilian staff seconded to the institutions of the European Union, of the headquarters and forces which may be made available to the European Union in the context of the preparation and execution of the tasks referred to in Article 17(2) of the Treaty on European Union, including exercises, and of the military and civilian staff of the Member States put at the disposal of the European Union to act in this context (EU SOFA), 17 Nov. 2003, OJ C 321/6 of 31/12/2003

Agreement between the Republic of Bosnia and Herzegovina and the North Atlantic Treaty Organisation (NATO) Concerning the Status of NATO and its Personnel, http://www.nato.int/ifor/gfa/gfa-ap1a.htm (visited 13/07/03)

Agreement concerning the application of Part VI of the Agreement on NATO national representatives and international staff, 3 March 1981, 1307 UNTS 423

Agreement on the Status of the North Atlantic Treaty Organisation, national representatives and international staff, 12 Dec. 1951, 200 UNTS 4

Agreement relating to the implementation of Part XI of the United Nations Convention on the Law of the Sea of 10 December 1982, 17 Aug. 1994, UN-Doc. A/RES/48/263

Agreements of the European Union with third states on the participation of those states in the European Union Police Mission (EUPM) in Bosnia and Herzegovina, OJ L 64/38 of 7/3/2003 (Poland), OJ L 197/38 of 5/8/2003 (Russia) and OJ L 239/1-46 of 25/09/2003 (all others)

AU draft African Non-Aggression Pact, 29 June 2004, AU Doc. EXP/GVT/ PACT/2 Rev. 2, http://www.iss.co.za/AF/RegOrg/unity_to_union/pdfs/au/jun04/ nonaggression.pdf (visited 27/08/2004)

Balkan Pact (4 agreements, 1953/1954), 167 UNTS 21, 4 AVR (1953/1954) p. 478, 211 UNTS 237, 225 UNTS 233

Commonwealth of Independent States Treaty on Collective Security, 15 May 1992, 1894 UNTS 309

Convention Additionnelle à la Convention conclue le 16 Sept. 1971 entre le Royaume de Belgique et l'OTAN relative à la Concession à l'OTAN d'un Terrain situe à Bruxelles en vue de la réalisation du Siège Permanent de cette Organisation, 22 June 1988, *Moniteur Belge* 1994, p. 1898 of 29/01/1994. Protocole amenant la Convention Additionnelle [...], 10 July 1996, *Moniteur Belge* 1998, p. 25640 of 11/8/1998

ECOWAS Protocol Relating to Mutual Assistance and Defence, 29 May 1981, 4 Nigeria's Treaties in Force (1990), p. 898

EU Status-of-Forces agreements with Albania (OJ L 93/50 of 10/4/2003), Bosnia (OJ L 293/2 of 29/10/2002), Federal Republic of Yugoslavia (OJ L 125/2 of 5/5/2001) and Macedonia (OJ L 241//1 of 11/09/2001 and OJ L 82/45 of 29/3/2003)

EU-Lebanon Agreement on Cooperation in the Fight against Terrorism, 17 April 2002, Council Doc. 7494/02

European Defence Community Treaty (with Protocols) (not entered into force), British Command Paper, Cmd. 9127 (1954)

Exchange of letters constituting an Agreement between Austria and the North Atlantic Treaty Organization on the Protection of Information, 20 Dec. 1995, 1912 UNTS 288

Exchange of letters constituting an Agreement between Austria and the North Atlantic Treaty Organization concerning the transit for the purpose of the multinational peace operation in Bosnia (IFOR), 14 and 16 Dec. 1995, 1912 UNTS 261

Exchange of letters constituting an Agreement between Austria and the North Atlantic Treaty Organization on privileges and immunities, 15 and 16 Dec. 1995, 1912 UNTS 271

Exchange of letters constituting an agreement between the NATO and Ireland in relation to Ireland's responsibilities for participation in KFOR, 25 and 27 Aug. 1999, 2141 UNTS 244

Exchange of letters constituting an agreement concerning the work of the NATO airborne early warning and control programme management agency (NAPMA) in the Netherlands, 11 Sept. 1979, 1183 UNTS 21

Exchange of notes between the United Kingdom and the Western European Union (1974), 1400 UNTS 3

Exchange of notes between the United Nations and the European Community (1980), 1159 UNTS 423

Exchange of notes constituting an agreement regarding the application in the UK of article 10 of the NATO-SOFA, 29 May 1974, 1017 UNTS 345

General Framework Agreement for Peace in Bosnia and Herzegovina, Dayton, 21 Nov. 1995, 35 ILM 75 (1996)

Inter-American Reciprocal Assistance and Solidarity (Act of Chapultepec), 6 March 1945, http://www.yale.edu/lawweb/avalon/intdip/interam/chapul.htm (visited 21/04/04)

Inter-American Treaty of Reciprocal Assistance, 2 Sept. 1947, 21 UNTS 77

Interim Tax Reimbursement Agreement between the US government and NATO, 29 Feb. 1984, 2005 UNTS 653

NATO Security of Information Agreement, 6 March 1997, Canada Treaty Series 1998/56, available at http://nettax.interia.pl/serwis/Publikatory/du/2000/nr%2064/poz.740ang.htm (visited 03/10/03)

North Atlantic Treaty, 4 April 1949, 34 UNTS 243

Nyon Agreement and Supplementary Agreement, Great Britain-France, e.i.f. 14 and 17 Sept. 1937, 181 LNTS 137

Ohrid Framework Agreement, 13 Aug. 2001, http://www.coe.int/T/E/Legal_affairs/Legal_cooperation/Police_and_internal_security /Police_cooperation/OHRID%20Agreement%2013august2001.asp (visited 11/08/2004)

Pact of Mutual Cooperation Between the Kingdom of Iraq, the Republic of Turkey, the United Kingdom, the Dominion of Pakistan, and the Kingdom of Iran (Baghdad Pact), 4 Feb. 1955, 233 UNTS 199

Pact of the League of Arab States, 22 March 1945, 70 UNTS 237

Panama Declaration, 3 Oct. 1939, repr. in: Treaties and other international agreements of the United States of America (C. I. Bevans, compil.), Vol. 3, pp. 608

Scambio di lettere Italia-NATO per un emendamento integrativo all'articolo 4 dell'Accordo del 5 febbraio 1968, sui privilegi en immunità del personale del Collegio di Difesa della NATO a Roma, *Gazzetta Ufficiale Della Repubblica Italiana*, No. 94, p. 4 of 23/4/2001

Security Treaty between Australia, New Zealand and the United States of America (ANZUS), 1 Sept. 1951, 131 UNTS 83

Southeast Asia Collective Defence Treaty (Manila Pact), 8 Sept. 1954, 209 UNTS 23

Supplemental Arrangement concerning the employment by NATO bodies of United States nationals, 3 June 1983, 2005 UNTS 189

Treaty of Alliance (GR, TK, CY), 16 Aug. 1960, http://www.cypnet.com/.ncyprus/history/republic/ (visited 09/09/04)

Treaty of Establishment of the Republic of Cyprus (UK, GR, TK, CY), 16 Aug. 1960, http://www.cypnet.com/.ncyprus/history/republic/ (visited 09/09/04)

Treaty of Friendship, Cooperation and Mutual Assistance, 14 May 1955 (Warsaw Pact), 219 UNTS 3

Treaty of Guarantee (UK, GR, TK, CY), 16 Aug. 1960, http://www.cypnet.com/. ncyprus/history/republic/ (visited 09/09/04)

Treaty on Economic, Social and Cultural Collaboration and Collective Self-Defence, Brussels, 17 March 1948, 19 UNTS 51, as amended by the Paris Agreements, 23 October 1954, 211 UNTS 342 (WEU-MBT)

Treaty on European Union, Maastricht, OJ C 191, 29/7/1992

U.S.–Japan mutual defence treaty, 8 Sept. 1951, 136 UNTS 211

U.S.–Korea mutual defence treaty, 1 Oct. 1953, 238 UNTS 199

U.S.–Philippines bilateral mutual defence treaty, 30 Aug. 1951, 177 UNTS 133

Vienna Convention on the Law of Treaties between States and International Organisations or between International Organizations, opened for signature on 21 March 1986, 25 ILM 543

Vienna Convention on the Law of Treaties, 22 May 1968, 1155 UNTS 331

WEU Security Agreement with Sweden, available at http://faculty.maxwell.syr.edu/ asroberts/foi/library/sweden_weu_agr.pdf (visited 04/10/2003)

Instruments between the EU and NATO

EU–NATO Concerted Approach to the Western Balkans, Brussels, 29 July 2003, CP 67, p. 200

EU–NATO Declaration on ESDP, 16 Dec. 2002, NATO Press Release (2002) 142 and 42 ILM 242 (2003)

EU–NATO exchange of letters of 17 and 18 Nov. 2004 on delineation of tasks, UN Doc. S/2004/915 and S/2004/916, 19 Nov. 2004

EU–NATO Ministerial meeting in Reykjavik, 14–15 May 2002, CP 57, p. 60

EU–NATO Ministerial meeting, Brussels, 4 December 2003, Joint Press Statement by the NATO Secretary General and the EU Presidency, CP 67, p. 285

European Defence: NATO/EU Consultation, Planning and Operations, Council Press Release, 15 Dec. 2003

Interim EU–NATO Security of Information Agreement with NATO, consisting in an exchange of letters between the CFSP-HR and the NATO-SG, 26 July 2000, http://faculty.maxwell.syr.edu/asroberts/foi/library/ eu_nato_interim.pdf (visited 28/08/03)

Letter of the High Representative for the Common and Security Policy, Javier Solana, to the Rt.Hon. Lord Robertson of Port Ellen, Secretary-General of the North Atlantic Treaty Organization, 13 December 2002, Council of the European Union documents, EN (original)

Modalities for meetings between the Military Committees of NATO and the EU, 27 March 2003, Council Doc. 7870/03

Permanent arrangements for consultation and cooperation between the EU and NATO. Exchange of letters between George Robertson, Secretary-General of

NATO, and Anna Lindh, Chairman of the Council of the European Union, 24 Jan. 2001 (released by the Council on a request by the author on 10 May 2004, reproduced in full in the Annex below)

JUDGMENTS

Permanent Court of International Justice

Electricity Company of Sofia and Bulgaria Case, 77 PCIJ Rep. 1939), Ser. A/B, p. 64

International Court of Justice (including Advisory Opinions)

Temple of Preah Vihear Case, 1962 ICJ Rep.
Asylum Case, 1950 ICJ Rep.
Case Concerning Military and Paramilitary Activities in and against Nicaragua, 1986 ICJ Rep.
Case Concerning Rights of Nationals of the United States of America in Morocco, 1952 ICJ Rep.
Case concerning the Right of Passage over Indian Territory, 1960 ICJ Rep.
Certain Expenses of the United Nations, ICJ Rep. 1962
Legality of the Threat or Use of Nuclear Weapons, Adv. Op., ICJ Rep. 1996
Nicaragua Case, 1986 ICJ Rep.
North Sea Continental Shelf Case, 1969 ICJ Rep.
Reparation for Injuries Suffered in the Service of the United Nations, Adv. Op., 1949 ICJ Rep.

European Court of Justice

ECJ, *Dinecke Algera* v. *Common Assembly of the ECSC* [1957] ECR 39
Case C-369/00, OJ C 319/19 of 4/11/2000, *Netherlands* v. *Council*
Case C-387/00, OJ 355/15 of 9/12/2000, *Parliament* v. *Council*
Case C-260/01, OJ C 245/13 of 1/9/2001, *Parliament* v. *Council*
Case C-353/99P, *Council* v. *Hautala*, [6 Dec. 2001], ECR I – not yet reported
Case C-353/01P, *Council and Commission* v. *Mattila* [22 Jan. 2004], ECR I – not yet reported

Other international cases

Lena Goldfields Arbitration, 5 Annual Digest (1930), p. 3
Schlegel Corp. v. *NICIC*, 14 Iran-U.S.C.T.R. (1987-I), p. 180

Shannon & Wilson, Inc. v. *AEOI*, 9 Iran-U.S.C.T.R. (1985-II), p. 402

National courts

German Federal Constitutional Court, 'AWACS' judgement, 90 BVerfGE (1994), p. 286. English translation in 106 ILR (1997), p. 319
German Federal Constitutional Court, 104 BVerfGE (2001), p. 151, English summary on http://www.bverfg.de/entscheidungen/frames/es20011122_2bve000699en (visited 06/04/2004)

Annex

Exchange of letters between George Robertson, Secretary-General of NATO, and Anna Lindh, Swedish FM and Chairman of the Council of the European Union, 24 Jan. 2001 (released by the Council on a request by the author on 10 May 2004)

eu2001.se

Ministry for Foreign Affairs
Minister for Foreign Affairs

Stockholm, 24 January 2001

The Rt. Hon. Lord Robertson of Port Ellen
Secretary-General
North Atlantic Treaty Organisation
BRUSSELS
Belgium

Dear George,

Thank you for the letter addressed to the Secretary-General/High
Representative, Dr. Solana, where you propose that the relevant Nice
documents and the results of the NATO Ministerial meeting constitute the
elements for the permanent arrangements on consultation and co-operation
between NATO and the EU.

I am pleased to inform you that the Council on 22 January welcomed the
positive reaction of the Ministerial meeting of the North Atlantic Council of
14 and 15 December 2000 to the EU proposals on the EU-NATO permanent
arrangements for consultation and co-operation, contained in the Presidency
report approved by the European Council in Nice on the European Security
and Defence Policy.

The Council confirmed that meetings between the NAC and PSC will be held
not less than three times, and EU/NATO ministerials not less than once, per
EU Presidency. Either organisation may request additional meetings as
necessary. The Council noted with satisfaction the identity of views between
the EU and NATO.

On this basis I conclude that the EU and NATO are in agreement on the
permanent arrangements for consultation and co-operation, and I am looking
forward to our future collaboration in implementing these arrangements.

Yours sincerely,

Anna Lindh
Chairman of the Council of the European Union

cc: Secretary General/High Representative

DE L'ATLANTIQUE NORD

NORTH ATLANTIC TREATY
ORGANIZATION

LE SECRETAIRE GÉNÉRAL
SECRETARY GENERAL

BOULEVARD LEOPOLD III
B-1110 BRUXELLES

The Rt. Hon.
Lord Robertson of Port Ellen
SG(2001)0040

24 January 2001

Dear Javier,

First of all, let me congratulate you on the successful outcome of the Nice European Council meeting. The Alliance notes and welcomes the proposals made on this occasion for permanent arrangements to ensure full transparency, consultation and cooperation between our two organisations.

Alliance Foreign Ministers, at their meeting on 14/15 December, agreed inter alia that consultation and cooperation will be developed between NATO and the EU on questions of common interest relating to security, defence and crisis management, so that crises can be met with the most appropriate military response and effective crisis management ensured.

Ministers looked forward to the early establishment of such mutually satisfactory arrangements based on the principles enunciated in Washington and at subsequent Ministerial meetings, which will be taken into account in the framework agreement establishing these arrangements.

The Alliance welcomed the intention of the European Union that this dialogue should be pursued through a regular pattern of meetings at Ministerial, NAC-PSC, MC and expert level as well as through contacts with secretariats. In our view, meetings between the NAC and the PSC outside times of crisis should be held no less than three times, and Ministerial meetings once, per EU Presidency; either organisation may request additional meetings as necessary. We endorsed the view of the EU that in the emergency phase of a crisis contacts and meetings will be stepped up.

NATO also welcomed the Nice provisions on invitations for the NATO Secretary General, CMC, and DSACEUR, in accordance with his terms of reference, to EU meetings. For our part, on the basis of reciprocity, we will invite the EU Presidency, and you to NATO meetings. The CMC or his representative will similarly be invited to meetings of the NATO MC.

TEL : (32)(0)2.707.49.177707.41.11 - FAX : (32)(0)2.707.45.85

Our Foreign Ministers also agreed that these proposals constitute the basis for the permanent NATO/EU agreement, and expressed the Alliance's readiness to work to finalise this agreement without delay.

In accordance with the decisions above, I propose that the relevant Nice documents and the results of the NATO Ministerial meeting constitute the elements for the permanent arrangements on consultation and cooperation between NATO and the EU.

Yours ever,

His Excellency
Dr Javier Solana
Secretary General/High Representative
Council of the European Union
Rue de la Loi, 175
1048 Bruxelles

cc: EU Presidency

Index

A-400M transport aeroplane 78
abandonment *see* international relations
    theory
accord informel normatifs 303
Active Endeavour (NATO Operation) 115
administrative arrangements 144
Afghanistan 22, 29, 33, 40, 41, 45, 93, 105,
    116, 118, 187, 189, 190, 191, 243,
    254, 295, 308, 354
Africa 75, 76, 90, 95, 167, 246, 264, 265,
    268, 269
African Union (AU) 270
Agenda for Peace 11, 13, 14, 51
Al-Qaida 33, 40, 187, 189, 190, 191
Alba (multilateral Operation) 55
Albania 55, 134, 140, 247
Allied Command Transformation
    (ACT) 107
Allied Harmony (NATO Operation) 247, 248
Althea (EU Operation) 17, 88, 95, 118, 157,
    250, 254, 255, 256, 257, 258, 259,
    260, 261, 262, 264, 355, 356
    connection to NATO operations in
      Afghanistan and Iraq 22
    delineation of tasks between the EU and
      NATO 257
    mandate 257
    mission description 256
    position of the local population in
      Bosnia 255
    preparatory procedure 259
    role of the United States 253
AMIS (AU Operation) 270
Amsterdam Treaty 55, 60, 63, 65, 72, 121,
    123, 130, 131, 132, 133, 134, 136,
    139, 140, 150, 151, 158, 194, 208,
    211, 241, 273, 276, 288, 290, 293,
    298, 299, 323, 340, 342
Ankara document 94, 156, 157, 286
ANZUS Treaty 179, 188
Artemis (EU Operation) 17, 75, 90, 96, 264,
    265, 267, 268, 355

    mandate 265
Asia 15, 22, 28, 29, 36, 37, 190
Austria 26, 54, 77, 80, 133, 137, 139, 142,
    144, 199, 204, 205, 207, 211, 223,
    249, 318, 355
AWACS 102, 104, 113, 115, 118, 132, 188

backdoor security guarantees *see* collective
    self-defence
Balkan Wars 15, 22, 42, 92, 165
    WEU intervention plan (1991) 52
Belgium 51, 62, 75, 82, 83, 85, 108, 137,
    142, 190, 196, 198, 238, 286
Berlin blockade 109
Berlin Plus agreement 1, 6, 17, 19, 66, 69,
    81, 82, 84, 86, 88, 90, 91, 92, 93, 94,
    95, 108, 126, 127, 142, 144, 145,
    151, 156, 161, 162, 167, 169, 222,
    238, 247, 248, 249, 250, 252, 253,
    255, 256, 259, 261, 267, 280, 284,
    285, 286, 288, 289, 290, 291, 292,
    294, 300, 304, 305, 309, 349, 355
    legal nature 288
    negotiating history 275
    under European law 309
Bosnia 12, 13, 17, 19, 22, 51, 52, 54, 55,
    56, 58, 59, 74, 88, 95, 104, 114, 118,
    134, 137, 140, 142, 191, 227, 229,
    242, 248, 250, 251, 252, 253, 254,
    255, 256, 257, 258, 259, 260, 261,
    262, 273, 299, 355, 356
Bosnia Force Options Project (1997) 251
Brahimi Report 11, 12, 13, 226
Bulgaria 24, 130, 131, 139, 157, 201, 318,
    319
burden-sharing 5, 47, 113, 158
Bush doctrine 39, 119

C3I (Command & Control, Communications
    and Intelligence) 297
Canada 24, 99, 100, 101, 113, 130, 138,
    153, 254, 272, 308, 312